THE Road TO
OZ

THE Road TO OZ

The **Evolution, Creation,** and **Legacy** of a
Motion Picture Masterpiece

JAY SCARFONE AND
WILLIAM STILLMAN

Guilford, Connecticut

An imprint of The Rowman & Littlefield Publishing Group, Inc.
4501 Forbes Blvd., Ste. 200
Lanham, MD 20706
www.rowman.com
Distributed by NATIONAL BOOK NETWORK

British Library Cataloguing in Publication Information available

Library of Congress Cataloging-in-Publication Data available

ISBN 978-1-4930-3629-5 (hardcover/paperback)
ISBN 978-1-4930-3553-8 (e-book)

Contents

For Grace—
Who always manages to guide us to the Yellow Brick Road

Acknowledgments

The authors are indebted to the following individuals for their time and support of this volume: Jackie Ackerman, Victoria Appell, Del Armstrong, Dale Barker, Dorothy Barrett, Margaret Barrett (Heritage Auctions), Lee Batchler, Florence Baum, Stanton Baum, Ozma Baum Mantele, Sue Campbell Culpepper, Brian Chanes (Profiles in History), Billy Clarke, James Comisar, Barry Conrad, John Stanley Donaldson, Brian Gari, Janet Cantor Gari, Meredythe Glass, Donna Stewart Hardway, Douglas Hopkinson, Laura Kennedy, Kristine Kreuger (AMPAS/Margaret Herrick Library), Michelle Kutasi, Herbert Lahr, Sylvia Lewis, Jerry Maren, Caren Marsh-Doll, Fred M. Meyer, Cliff Miles, Kathi Miles, Kenneth Montgomery, George Morgan, Sheila Paul, Margaret Pellegrini, Meinhardt Raabe, Grace Ressler, Bob Roberts, Mickey Rooney, Ann Rutherford, Charles Schram, David Schwager, David Selditz, Jeff Selditz, Dave Smith, Bonnie Snyder, Martin Spellman, Bonnie Thiele, William Tuttle, Holly Van Leuven, Michelle Wadley, Bob Weatherwax, and Jane Withers.

Introduction

On Wednesday afternoon, May 24, 1939, Howard Dietz, Si Seadler, and Billy Ferguson—Metro-Goldwyn-Mayer's top publicity men—attended the New York Allied convention of theater exhibitors at the Astor Hotel in New York City. New York Allied was a chapter of the national Allied, and the three men represented Metro at the studio's display exhibit little more than two months before *The Wizard of Oz* premiered. The conversation piece of the MGM exhibit also proved to be a non sequitur: a voice-test machine with a placard that read, "Have your voice tested. If we like it, MGM will sign you up. If we don't, we'll send you down the street to Warners." The crack was a brassy reflection of the status Metro had achieved in its fifteen years as Hollywood's most prominent and prestigious motion picture studio—a status to which there was no comparison, be it Warner Bros., Twentieth Century Fox, Columbia, or RKO.

When production of *The Wizard of Oz* was under way in October 1938, W. R. Wilkerson, publisher of *the Hollywood Reporter* and columnist of its Tradeviews feature, summarized the epoch of entertainment that MGM had attained at the time:

> In the recent production history of Metro-Goldwyn-Mayer, they never have been in such an advantageous spot as they are at present. MGM actually has twelve pictures finished and awaiting release—a schedule that takes them through every week, with a release, until the last day of the year. A condition new to MGM and one that certainly will place them in a position of doing even greater pictures than they have in the past, because of breathing space, in their rush to meet release dates . . . It used to be that MGM missed a release date here and there, costing them a pretty penny for such a miss-out. At other times they used to ship their picture from the MGM lab

right into the theatre projection rooms, around the country, in an effort to meet that release. All this necessitated quite a rush and contributed much to upset organization for the making of better pictures. It did not give them sufficient time to advertise and publicize their production efforts. Consequently, with the organization now running smoothly, with releases far ahead, with opportunities to see pictures much in advance of release to scheme better advertising, publicity and exploitation, *and most important*, to give the producers a "breather," Metro should jump far ahead of itself in making the entertainment that won for it the reputation of "the Tiffany of production." Metro's big effort comes at a time when the industry needs it most, because nothing means anything other than good pictures, and good pictures will kill off all the obstacles MGM, and every other production organization and the entire picture industry, has been burdened with for months.

In its heyday MGM's Culver City studios were home to the most glamorous and popular movie actors in the world. To this day their identities remain recognizable in surname alone: Crawford, Gable, Garbo, Harlow, Shearer, Tracy—icons as mysterious and untouchable as gods and revered nearly as such by the pedestrian public, who were mesmerized by the spell of their idols' flickering images across the silver screen, and those who lingered devotedly over glorious portraits of their favorites in Hollywood fan magazines.

In its 1938 roster, *Who's Who at Metro-Goldwyn-Mayer*, the studio boasted its "World's Greatest" attributes in a summation brimming with awesome statistics: 117 acres; thirty soundstages; its own police and fire departments; four thousand employees; its own electrical plant, railroad, lumber yards, foundries, machine shops, and mill; a music department library with two million items in it; a research department that answers five hundred inquiries daily; a switchboard that handles more long-distance calls than a city of fifty thousand; and a film laboratory that prints an average of 150 million feet of film for release prints annually. By the following year *The Wizard of Oz* would be one of the most challenging, complicated, expensive, and important films to be processed in MGM's laboratory.

As authors passionate for the subject of *The Wizard of Oz*, we have previously documented the creation and legacy of this cinematic cornerstone in several books. However, our research didn't stop with the publication of each volume. Because so few records survive from the 1938–39 time period, we have striven persistently to unearth novel and relevant information gleaned largely from a wide range of sources original to the period. Our dedication has been akin to the task of assembling a picturesque jigsaw puzzle, painstakingly identifying random pieces that interlock to form a complete and satisfying image.

In compiling this text, our research encompassed new and period interviews with cast and crew; a review of scripts, obscure autobiographies, trade journals, periodicals, and newspapers; and the input of various historians who are experts in their respective fields.

The sheer volume of information made necessary a fresh retelling of *The Wizard of Oz*'s place in entertainment history. In numerous instances our discovery of previously unpublished quotes, anecdotes, and other details revises and dispels longstanding accounts that have, for decades, been accepted as fact. Such inaccuracies include the notion that Arthur Freed was the driving force behind MGM's acquisition of *Oz* as a film property; that Ray Bolger was initially cast as the Tin Woodman before playing the Scarecrow; or that "Over the Rainbow" was a song of entirely original inspiration composed with Judy Garland in mind.

Additionally, for the first time in print, we present a complete account of Samuel Goldwyn's early 1930s Technicolor *Wizard of Oz* that was planned but never materialized. We also document other previously unknown pre-1939 *Oz* productions, including one with a direct association to the Singer's Midgets who would play Munchkins in the MGM film. A veritable day-by-day accounting of the making of *The Wizard of Oz* is covered, punctuated with unpublished, behind-the-scenes stories. Finally, we trace the evolution of MGM's *The Wizard of Oz* from its formidable and largely lauded debut to its theatrical reissues (on the heels of competition from rumored TV versions) and its explosive resurgence as a television special that propelled its players to immortal stature and secured its place in American collective consciousness.

As is true today, motion picture production in the 1930s was very much a *business*, one that could be superficial, duplicitous, and insensitive as much as it was about glorifying excellence in its artifice. By necessity this volume is unauthorized in order to present material that has not been censored or homogenized. Instead, this account is as authentic and as accurate as our research allowed, and in some cases it reveals the realities of studio politics, nepotism therein, and movie-star management. Thus, we present a history that is perhaps unlike any other in its frankness and its comprehensive scope. However, our dual intention is to explore and preserve our inextinguishable fascination and admiration for *The Wizard of Oz*, one that we know is shared by millions the world over.

PART ONE
EVOLUTION

Early Oz

It was not L. Frank Baum's first book, nor even his first children's book. But on the eve of his forty-fourth birthday in May 1900, Baum published a fantasy tale—his sixth book intended for juvenile readers. Several considerations for the title were discarded including *From Kansas to Fairyland*, *The Emerald City*, and *The Land of Oz*, before arriving at the penultimate title, *The Wonderful Wizard of Oz*. The twenty-four-chapter novel became a contemporary publishing sensation and has never been out of print since. Its narrative is as much ingrained in American folklore as Paul Bunyan, Huckleberry Finn, and tall tales about George Washington's cherry tree and his silver dollar.

But unlike American folklore, *The Wonderful Wizard* uses its midwestern setting only as a prologue before transitioning to a wonderland akin to the otherworld traversed by Lewis Carroll's Alice—a mystical, mysterious, and magical parallel universe. In this uncivilized realm the fruited plains are abundant but, commensurate with the land's treasures, its dangers are fiercer than any enemies faced on prairie soil: chimera-like Kalidahs, with their combined features of tigers and bears; belligerent Hammer-Heads, armless beings with retractable, projectile heads used as butting rams; and anthropomorphic trees that clutch and capture unwary trespassers.

Flights of fancy such as creatures with wings, teleportation, telepathic communication, and mechanical devices that prophesized television and robots proliferated Baum's uncharted country throughout *The Wonderful Wizard of Oz* and the thirteen sequels he eventually penned to follow it. Mysticism was an obligatory component of the Oz stories. Unsurprisingly, Baum was not only influenced by the spiritualist movement of the late nineteenth century, he and members of his family were involved in it.

L. Frank Baum's life history has elsewhere been covered extensively by reliable sources, and it is not the intention of this volume to reiterate his biography except to underscore his role as a gentle visionary well ahead of his time. In April 1961 Harry Neal Baum, sole survivor of Frank Baum's four sons, recalled his father's temperament with reverence. "He had a touch of genius. Perhaps more important than that he filled our house with love. He was never stern. There was always laughter in our house. Father was a kindly man, loved people, never swore or told a dirty story. He had no business sense and made many poor investments, but we always had necessities and even luxuries."

The origin of the word "Oz" has often been debated. In 1939 Maud Baum contended that her husband simply imagined the word in the manner that he conjured all of his nonsense names and plots. With the release of MGM's *The Wizard of Oz*, a 1903 account of how Baum coined Oz resurfaced. Ward Farrar, manager of the Loew's theater in Indianapolis, Indiana, contacted James P. Cunningham, columnist for *Motion Picture Herald*, to relay that Baum explained how he arrived at the word "Oz" in a 1903 letter to Bobbs-Merrill of Indianapolis, publisher of *The Wizard of Oz*. Baum's letter, then in the custody of Bobbs-Merrill executive A. H. Hepburn, told how the author was set on using the word "wizard" but was stumped on completing the book's title until he noticed a small filing cabinet divided into drawers marked A–G, H–N, and O–Z.[1] "And Oz it became," wrote the author. Despite an accelerated imagination, Baum could not have envisioned where the word Oz would take him, let alone how the lasting legacy of the word would endure in popular culture worldwide.

---

[1] Another 1939 account stated that Baum obtained the name Oz from the abbreviated symbol for ounce "on the back of one volume of an encyclopedia," further speculating that perhaps the author had known of the village of Oz in Isere, France.

THE ORIGINAL STORY

The Wonderful Wizard of Oz opens on the desolate Kansas prairie and introduces orphaned Dorothy and her black terrier, Toto, who live on a meager farm with Uncle Henry and Aunt Em. One eventful day Henry senses an approaching storm and advises Em to take cover while he tends to the stock. Before Dorothy can join her aunt in the storm cellar, their small cabin is levitated by a cyclone with Dorothy and Toto inside it. Despite the howling winds, their fear eventually subsides, and both the girl and her dog fall sound asleep.

Baum's use of a whirlwind as the catalytic device that transports his protagonist to an unusual realm was not original to *The Wonderful Wizard of Oz*. Richard Mansfield's 1897 nonsense novel *Blown Away* has two sisters, Beatrice and Jessie, carried off by a cyclone to an otherworld replete with talking birds, insects, and an odd assortment of creatures. In *Wonderful Wizard* sequels Baum maintained the use of turbulent transitions to the Land of Oz, such as a storm at sea in *Ozma of Oz* and an earthquake in *Dorothy and the Wizard in Oz*. But the destructive power of a prairie twister was very real to early pioneers. An April 1912 news bit titled "Wizard of Oz Stunt" told of a Broken Bow, Nebraska, country schoolhouse that was swept up by a tornado and carried half a mile with twelve children and their teacher inside. The house was "gently deposited in a wheat field," and only one person was injured.

Dorothy and Toto awaken to discover that the house has settled in the midst of a verdant countryside, known as Munchkin Country, where the girl is mistaken for a sorceress by the elderly Good Witch of the North and three male Munchkins, dressed in blue. The Good Witch tells Dorothy that she freed the Munchkin people from slavery when her house fell on their evil ruler, the Wicked Witch of the East. Dorothy stands to inherit the deceased witch's prideful possession: a pair of Silver Shoes that have a mysterious but unknown charm connected to them.

However, Dorothy desires nothing more than to go back to Kansas, and the Good Witch advises her to seek the resources of Oz, the Great Wizard, who lives in the City of Emeralds at the end of a road paved with yellow bricks. (Dorothy hails from Kansas, the epicenter of her homeland, and, ironically, upon her displacement into the parallel universe of Oz, she must journey to the exact center of that country in order to return home.) The Good Witch cannot accompany Dorothy on her journey, but she vows to "use all the magic arts I know of to keep you from harm." Before vanishing into thin air, the Good Witch bestows Dorothy with a kiss to her forehead that leaves a luminous, protective mark.

Before setting out, Dorothy changes into a clean dress, one made of blue-and-white gingham. She then fills a basket with provisions from the cupboard and decides to exchange her worn leather shoes for the silver ones, which fit her perfectly. After a day of traveling,

Dorothy and Toto spend that evening at the house of Boq, one of the wealthiest Munchkins, who is hosting a celebration in honor of their emancipation from bondage.

The following day Dorothy resumes her journey and, after walking several miles, stops to rest atop a fence near a great cornfield. She is startled when a straw-stuffed scarecrow, attired in worn, blue Munchkin duds, becomes animated and speaks. At his request Dorothy liberates the Scarecrow from his perch, and he reveals that his sole desire is to obtain the brains he lacks. (It was an old crow that told the Scarecrow he would be "a better man" if he had brains.) He joins the party en route to seek Oz's wisdom, much to Toto's chagrin (he growls suspiciously).

After stumbling through a dark forest, they pass the night in an abandoned cottage. The next morning they are surprised to hear a groan and discover a tin woodcutter who has been rendered motionless with rust for more than a year. After lubricating his joints, Dorothy and the Scarecrow explain their mission and the Tin Woodman immediately asks to join them, for he desires a heart. After a time he tells them his story.

He had been a man of flesh and blood, the son of a woodman, who became lonely after his parents died. He was betrothed to a beautiful Munchkin girl who was the maid to an old woman who did not wish to see her marry. The old woman made an arrangement with the Wicked Witch of the East to prevent the marriage in exchange for two sheep and a cow. The Witch enchanted the woodman's axe and, as he set about building his wedding home, a series of accidents befell him by which the axe cut off his limbs. Each gradual amputation was replaced with a metal version made by a tinsmith until, finally, the axe split his torso and he no longer had a heart with which to love the Munchkin maiden. He laments not knowing whether she is still awaiting him.

The group comes to a thicker part of the forest and Dorothy grows anxious after hearing animals growl among the trees. The Tin Woodman reminds her that nothing can harm him or the Scarecrow, while Dorothy is protected by the Good Witch's kiss. They suddenly hear a terrible roar and a lion bounds into their path, knocking the Scarecrow and Tin Man aside. Toto runs barking at the lion, who opens his mouth to bite the dog. But Dorothy intervenes and slaps the brute's nose while scolding him soundly. The lion shamefully confesses to being a coward who has created a fierce facade by roaring loudly at anything that frightens him. After drying his tears with the tip of his tail, he invites himself to join their band in the hopes that the Great Oz will relieve his "simply unbearable" life with a bit of courage.[2]

---

2 The November 19, 1900, review of *The Wonderful Wizard of Oz* in the *Salt Lake (UT) Herald* foreshadows the Cowardly Lion's comedy potential several decades ahead of Bert Lahr's cinematic portrait: "The best of the company, however, is the Cowardly Lion, who roars very loudly to conceal his panic, and wipes his tears of mortification with the end of his tail until he has to betake himself to the sunshine to dry this useful piece of furniture."

Their journey to the City of Emeralds is punctuated with adventures that either color the mettle of those in Dorothy's party or reflect the resourcefulness of each character. When the Tin Woodman accidently crushes a beetle, he is crestfallen and weeps, rusting the joints at his jaws. During a respite from their journey, the Scarecrow thoughtfully fills Dorothy's basket with tree nuts so she will not go hungry. And the Cowardly Lion volunteers to leap the width of a ditch, carrying each of his comrades on his back.

The travelers also face several obstacles that threaten to derail their journey. They narrowly outwit the Kalidahs, hybrid beasts with features of both tigers and bears. When a river impedes their path, the Tin Woodman constructs a wooden raft to cross it; but the Scarecrow is stuck clinging to the pole he was using to steer the raft as the others float away downstream. (A passing stork rescues the strawman after realizing how light he is to carry.)

However, the greatest challenge comes when Dorothy and her friends find themselves in the midst of an expansive carpet of poppies, the odor of which has a strong sedative effect on the girl, her dog, and the lion (not being of flesh and blood, the Scarecrow and Tin Man are unaffected). Dorothy and Toto are carried out of the poisonous flower bed, but the Scarecrow and Tin Woodman lament their inability to rescue the slumbering lion. "Perhaps he will dream that he has found courage at last," notes the Tin Man sadly.

The little party resigns to proceed without their comrade, when a wildcat runs by chasing a gray field mouse. The Woodman takes pity on the mouse and promptly beheads the wildcat. The mouse happens to be the queen of all field mice, who is now indebted to the Tin Man. The Scarecrow devises a plan to save the Cowardly Lion by directing the Woodman to craft a truck on wheels while the queen's minions each gather a length of string. Once the wooden cart is assembled, and each mouse harnessed with string, the Scarecrow and Tin Man haul the Lion onto the truck and together they all roll him out of the poppy bed. The queen mouse gives Dorothy a whistle to call upon her if need be.

After their escape, the party finds the road of yellow brick again and notices that the fences, houses, and clothes of the peasants are green—an indication of their close proximity to the Emerald City. They stop to spend the night at a farmhouse, and the man of the house tells them that the Great Oz is a shapeshifter who can take any form he chooses, referring to the Wizard as "the terrible Oz."

The next morning they notice a green glow in the sky that gets brighter as they approach it until, at last, they reach the Emerald City. Dorothy pushes a bell beside the gate and they are greeted by the Guardian of the Gates, a small man with greenish skin who outfits each of them with a pair of spectacles so as not to be blinded by the glare of the Emerald City.

The man next leads them to a soldier with green whiskers who guards the Palace of Oz. The soldier announces them to the mysterious Oz, who consents to grant Dorothy and her friends a private audience one at a time over as many days. (The soldier later tells Dorothy that Oz was going to send them all away but was swayed when he heard of her Silver Shoes and the mark on her forehead.) They are each taken to separate quarters, and Dorothy finds a number of green dresses made of silk, satin, and velvet; she wears the prettiest gown for her interview with Oz the next morning.

In an emerald-encrusted throne room, she is confronted by a disembodied head "bigger than the head of the biggest giant" on a throne of green marble. The head identifies itself as "Oz, the Great and Terrible." After quizzing Dorothy about her shoes and the Good Witch's kiss, Oz listens to Dorothy's plea for help to return home. The head coldly instructs her to kill the remaining bad witch, the Wicked Witch of the West, in exchange for sending Dorothy home. The girl is devastated when Oz refuses to acquiesce.

Each of her companions is subsequently admitted to the throne room, but to each, Oz takes a different form of appearance. For the Scarecrow, he is a lovely lady with green hair and wings; to the Tin Woodman, Oz is a terrible beast the size of an elephant with five eyes, arms, and legs; and to the Cowardly Lion, Oz manifests as a ball of fierce flames. Each creature makes his plea to be infused with the trait he lacks, but to all, Oz's message is identical. Granting their requests is contingent upon returning with proof that the Wicked Witch of the West has been destroyed. Faced with no other alternative, the little party decides to seek out the witch, who lives in the western territory of Oz, also known as the Land of the Winkies.

The group exits the Emerald City and returns their green spectacles to the Guardian of the Gates. (Shortly thereafter, Dorothy is surprised to notice that her dress is no longer green but pure white.) They are told there is no path to the witch's lair as no one ever wishes to go that way; they are to walk to the west until the Witch spies them and enslaves them all.

They traverse desolate terrain, and the Witch sees them with her single eye, which is as powerful as a telescope. Blowing a silver whistle around her neck, the Witch conjures a pack of forty wolves and instructs them to tear the intruders to pieces. But the Tin Woodman makes good use of his axe and slaughters them all as they attack. Infuriated, the Witch calls a band of forty crows to destroy Dorothy's party. The Scarecrow takes charge next, and as the crows fly at him, he twists the neck of each until they are all dead. The enraged Witch then commands her bee-slaves to swarm at the strangers and sting them to death, but Dorothy, Toto, and the Cowardly Lion are covered with the Scarecrow's stuffings, rendering them indiscernible. Seeing only the Tin Woodman, all the bees fly at him but blunt their stingers against his body and die. The Witch next dispatches a dozen Winkie slaves and arms them with spears to destroy Dorothy and her friends. When the Lion roars at them, the timid Winkies retreat to the Witch's castle, where they are beaten with a strap for failing their mistress.

Confounded for being thwarted on all counts, the Wicked Witch resorts to using the last of three wishes entitled to her by use of a Golden Cap. She dons the cap and enacts the spell that summons the Winged Monkeys, whom she commands to destroy the strangers. The monkeys lift the Tin Man and batter him against sharp rocks; they eviscerate the Scarecrow and throw his clothing into the top of a tall tree; and they bind the Cowardly Lion with ropes and imprison him in the Witch's yard. The leader of the monkeys is about to attack Dorothy when he sees the Good Witch's mark on her forehead and realizes the power of the girl's protection.

The monkeys gently deliver Dorothy and Toto to the Witch before disbanding noisily. The Witch is afraid of Dorothy because of the Silver Shoes but quickly realizes that the girl is unaware of their magic. She puts Dorothy to work while plotting to secure the shoes for her own. One day she trips Dorothy and one of the shoes comes loose. The Witch, gloating in victory, taunts Dorothy that she will soon get the other. Angered, Dorothy douses the Witch with a nearby scrub bucket and is shocked when the Witch melts into a shapeless brown mass before her eyes—water was the Witch's fatal weakness.

Dorothy frees the Cowardly Lion and liberates the Winkies, who deign the day a holiday thereafter. At Dorothy's bidding, the Winkies rescue the Tin Man and Scarecrow and restore them to their old selves. Dorothy admires the Witch's Golden Cap and decides to wear it on the return trip to claim their promises from Oz.

But en route to the Emerald City, the group becomes lost. Dorothy calls the Queen of the Field Mice, who suggests that Dorothy simply compel the Winged Monkeys to transport them using the charm of the Golden Cap. At Dorothy's command the monkeys obey her wish. During the return flight the monkey king tells Dorothy the story of the Golden Cap and how his band became beholden three times to whomever owns it.

The jeweled cap had been commissioned by Princess Gaylette as a wedding gift to her betrothed, Quelala. But just prior to their nuptials, the Winged Monkeys gave Quelala a ducking in the local river. This enraged Gaylette, who spared the monkeys only on the condition that they always obey the wearer of the cap, the first being Quelala until it fell into possession of the Wicked Witch.

When the travelers return to Emerald City, they are made to wait several days to see the Wizard. Having spent their patience, the Scarecrow threatens to call the Winged Monkeys if they are not granted an audience. When they are finally admitted to the throne room, there is no apparition to greet them, only a voice. The Wizard procrastinates in making good on his promises. "You've had plenty of time already," the Tin Woodman exclaims angrily, in a line recited verbatim in the MGM film.

Thinking to frighten the Wizard, the Lion roars loudly, startling Toto, who tips over a screen to reveal hiding behind it a little man who declares himself "Oz, the Great and Terrible." He admits to "making believe" and having fooled the citizenry with his various tricks, including ventriloquism. He explains that he originally hailed from Omaha, Nebraska, and blew into the Land of Oz in a runaway balloon, impressing the natives when he descended from the clouds. He consents to honoring the requests of Dorothy and her companions to the best of his ability.

Oz fills the Scarecrow's head with a mixture of bran and pins and needles, thereby giving him "bran"-new, sharp brains. The Tin Woodman receives a silk heart filled with sawdust, and the Cowardly Lion is giving an elixir to drink that makes him feel "full of courage." The secret, of course, is that each has always possessed the qualities he felt lacking. As for Dorothy, Oz decides to escort her back to Kansas in a balloon that will carry them beyond the deadly desert that borders the country on all sides.

On the day of the balloon's launch, Dorothy rushes to find Toto, who has run into the crowd of spectators to chase a kitten. But before she can board the balloon, the taut mooring ropes crack under tension. As the balloon drifts out of reach, the Wizard calls to Dorothy, "I can't come back, my dear. Goodbye!"—language that would be scripted nearly word for word in the MGM film.

The Scarecrow suggests that Dorothy use the Golden Cap to call the Winged Monkeys to fly her to Kansas. But their leader explains that they cannot cross the desert, and so the second of Dorothy's three charms has been wasted. The soldier with green whiskers tells the crestfallen Dorothy about Glinda, the good witch who lives in the southern Quadling Country. Glinda is "the most powerful of all the witches" and may know how to help Dorothy, but like the original journey to Emerald City, the road to Glinda's castle is fraught with dangers. Dorothy's companions vow to accompany and protect her on the journey.

The first peril the travelers encounter is a row of aggressive, fighting trees that try to block the path through the woods. But the Tin Woodman makes use of his axe to rend the trees' branches, and the company is allowed to pass. The group next travels through the Dainty China Country, the inhabitants of which are all made of fragile porcelain, including a petite princess. In a gloomy forest the Cowardly Lion is revered as King of Beasts by the neighboring animals. He agrees to slay the monstrous spider that has them terrorized and, as the spider sleeps, the Lion pounces and knocks its head from its torso, killing it. The group's final adventure is to pass over a steep hill guarded by the Hammer-Heads, armless men with projectile necks used as battering rams. Dorothy engages the Winged Monkeys for the last time to carry them over the hill to Glinda's castle.

They are granted an audience with Glinda, who agrees to send Dorothy back to Kansas in exchange for the Golden Cap. She intends to use the Golden Cap to transport the Scarecrow to Emerald City, where he will be king, to send the Tin Man to rule over the Winkies, and to return the Lion to the forest, where he will govern the animals. Glinda then reveals that Dorothy's Silver Shoes hold the power to carry her over the desert and indeed could have carried her home the first day she arrived.

After a tearful goodbye Dorothy takes Toto in her arms and enacts the shoes' spell by clapping together their heels three times. In just three steps she finds herself sitting on the

Kansas prairie, reunited with her family, the Silver Shoes having fallen off in the desert and lost forever.

In the authorship tradition of "write what you know," Baum's tale is sprinkled with bits and pieces of prior influences and life experiences. A loping scarecrow that menaced the boy Baum in a recurring childhood nightmare became the docile strawman in Oz. When editing South Dakota's *Aberdeen Saturday Pioneer* in the late 1800s, Baum covered a story about a funnel cloud that extricated an entire house and whirled off with it. In his Our Landlady column for the same organ, Baum humored his readers with a yarn about a farmer who conned his nag into eating wood shavings instead of grass by outfitting the animal with green goggles—a device repurposed when Dorothy and her friends are obliged to don green spectacles before admittance to the Emerald City; the tinted lenses only make the surroundings *appear* consistently verdigris throughout. That fabulous green mecca was most likely inspired by the Great White City of the 1893 Columbian Exhibition in Chicago. (The city was the central attraction at the fair, honoring the four-hundredth anniversary of Columbus's discovery of America.) At night the pristine structures glittered, illuminated by the novelty of electric lights; if viewed through green spectacles, the White City would easily double as the Emerald City.

Baum was also familiar with the works of the Brothers Grimm and Hans Christian Andersen (he references them in his introduction to *The Wonderful Wizard of Oz*). While Baum sought to avoid the traditional yet gruesome manner in which villains were punished or morals reinforced, influences from classic fairy stories crept into *The Wonderful Wizard* such as the concept of three wishes to evoke a charm. Additionally, in a version of *Cinderella* retold by the Brothers Grimm, Cinderella is provided with silver shoes for her second evening at the royal ball. And in Hans Christian Andersen's *The Shoes of Fortune*, magical footwear with teleportation capacity fits their wearer "as though they had been made for him," which is language identical to that which Baum used to describe how the Silver Shoes fit Dorothy.

The Wonderful Wizard of Oz was the second published collaboration for juvenile readers between Baum and illustrator William Wallace (W. W.) Denslow. The narrative and drawings were integral and intertwined, and both author and artist shared the book's royalties. Akin to Sir John Tenniel's *Alice* sketches, Denslow's pictures forever defined how Baum's *Wizard of Oz* characters would be universally envisioned: Dorothy in flowing braids, Toto as a terrier, the Scarecrow with his teardrop nose, the Tin Woodman's funnel cap, and the Cowardly Lion with a ribbon in his mane's topknot. Indeed, it was said that Denslow's prolific and profuse illustrations counted as equally as the book's text when *The Wonderful Wizard of Oz* became the best-selling children's book of 1900.

THE WIZARD TAKES A BOW

The runaway success of *The Wonderful Wizard of Oz* led to its adaptation as a musical-comedy extravaganza for adult audiences, with romance, spectacle, slapstick skits, and memorable songs woven throughout. The show debuted at Chicago's Grand Opera House on June 16, 1902, and relocated to the Broadway stage the following year on January 21, where it played for 293 performances before touring the country in road shows. Most of the humorous antics centered on the odd-couple duo of the Scarecrow and Tin Woodman, which made celebrities out of theatrical partners Fred Stone and David Montgomery, respectively. In 1918 Stone told *Motion Picture* journalist Adam Hull Shirk that he and Montgomery were sent the Frank Baum book while performing in London, with the understanding that they would play the comic leads. "We accepted the proposition," recalled Stone, "and contracted for a salary of $500 a week, for five years, opening at the Grand Opera House, Chicago. That ended our vaudeville work. We played *The Wizard* four seasons."

In the version of the *Wizard of Oz* script held in the collections of the New York Public Library, the show opens on the Kansas prairie, as in Baum's original story. But instead of the isolative existence of Dorothy with her aunt and uncle, there are many farmhands, servants, and others who make up the chorus.[3] The cyclone approaches and everyone rushes offstage. When the lights come up, chorus girls, dressed in blue as Munchkins, remark on the storm and the dilapidated house it blew to their country.

Cynthia, the lady lunatic (she's lost her reason), is led in; the Munchkins believe her to be a sorceress who's caused the havoc. But Locusta, the Witch of the North, intercedes and informs the Munchkins that the house has fallen on the Wicked Witch, whose demise liberates them from a miserable enchantment. Locusta asks Cynthia, "If you are a member of the Sorceress' Union, show your card"—an exchange similar to the scene in MGM's film version in which Glinda questions whether Dorothy is a witch. Cynthia explains that she was engaged to a musician, Niccolo Chopper, who played the piccolo, but he was put under a spell and is now missing. By singing the song he used to play, there is hope of finding him.

Sir Dashemoff Daily enters to tell all that Pastoria, the rightful king of Oz, was also brought back by the cyclone and has instigated a revolution to be reinstated. The current King of Oz had arrived by hot-air balloon; after luring Pastoria into it, he sent Pastoria sailing heavenward and took the throne as his own due to his mystical arts. Pastoria enters and names the Wizard of Oz as the culprit who has swindled him from the throne. Tryxie next enters, having been blown to Oz with Pastoria. She's a saucy waitress from the railroad station in Topeka and is romantically attached to Pastoria, who was working in Kansas as a motorman, being "a fellow that takes life easy" and is a "regular lady killer."

Next, Dorothy, a young woman played by Anna Laughlin, enters with her pet calf, Imogene. Disoriented, she asks, "Well, where am I at? Surely this isn't Kansas." In the wreckage of her home, Dorothy finds Carrie Barry's front door with a note attached to "the princess within" that is a love song. Sir Dashemoff Daily, who is a poet laureate, is the author of the note and, seeing Dorothy reading it, believes her to be Carrie "Caroline" Barry.

When Dorothy is introduced to Locusta, she recoils upon learning she is a witch, to which Locusta replies, "Ah, don't be afraid—I'm not one of the black cat and broomstick kind." Dorothy then asks if she is far from Kansas. The witch informs the Munchkins that Dorothy is under her special protection and, as proof, bestows Dorothy with a magic ring that grants its wearer two wishes. Dorothy immediately wishes to go home, but when nothing changes, Locusta explains that the ring's magic applies only within the borders of the land (similar to the explanation the Winged Monkey leader gives Dorothy in *The Wonderful Wizard of Oz*). Locusta instructs Dorothy to seek the Wizard of Oz as he alone has the power to transport her over the burning desert to Kansas.

---

3 In his third Oz book, *Ozma of Oz* (1907), Baum would concede that Aunt Em and Uncle Henry had "hired men" on their Kansas farm.

After Locusta departs, Dashemoff's mistaken identity between Dorothy and Carrie Barry, "an old maid" who lived below Dorothy's farm (perhaps an inspiration for MGM's Miss Gulch character), is made clear. Dashemoff sings the love song originally written for Carrie, but he now confesses that Dorothy is the recipient of its sentiments. Dashemoff is called away and Dorothy is left alone with Imogene.

Seeing a nearby scarecrow, Dorothy wishes he were alive so she would have company, and by virtue of her magic ring, the wish brings the Scarecrow to life. The Scarecrow explains that he hasn't any brains, only excelsior wrapped in a dish rag. The two exchange banter that was witty for the era as Dorothy helps the Scarecrow down from his post, exclaiming him to be of "loose character" as he wobbles on his legs. Dorothy introduces herself as "one of the Kansas Gales," to which the Scarecrow replies, "That accounts for your breezy manner." (This is the first instance in which Dorothy's last name is revealed. Frank Baum retained it in his *Wonderful Wizard of Oz* sequels and it was also incorporated into MGM's *The Wizard of Oz*.) Dorothy explains her mission and the Scarecrow asks, "Do you think the Wizard would have a set of brains knocking around his place that would fit me?" Dorothy invites him to join her saying, "you'll be no worse off than you are now"—a line lifted from Baum's book and also repurposed in the MGM film. The two exchange more puns before the Scarecrow tells his story in a song.

The next scene is the road through a forest on which Dashemoff encounters Sir Wiley Gyle. Dashemoff asks Gyle to join him in the revolution to restore Pastoria to the throne; but Gyle plans to secure the throne for himself after exposing the Wizard as a fraud, even if it means assassinating him with a bomb.

Cynthia enters identifying herself as "a sweet girl maniac" in search of toast to satisfy her fancy for poached eggs. Cynthia continues her quest for Niccolo; Gyle tells her that the Wizard is really her lost love under an enchantment. Cynthia goes off to find the Wizard.

Pastoria appears with assistants Timothy and General Riskitt, who are to take his photograph for the newspapers. They are momentarily frightened by a roaring lion, whom Pastoria decrees to be a "dandelion." Pastoria takes the lion's picture, which placates the beast. Riskitt informs Pastoria that he is wanted for treason by the Emerald City police. Riskitt and Pastoria conclude they'll both need disguises from here on out. Meanwhile, Pastoria continues on with Tryxie, his would-be queen.

Dorothy and the Scarecrow enter next, exchanging more punny barbs. In a bit inspired by the Baum book, they have a discussion about Dorothy's need to eat while the Scarecrow abstains ("I'm stuffed full now," he says). The Scarecrow also confides that he's only afraid of a lighted match, as in Baum's book, or a cigarette smoker, reference to which appears in an early MGM script.

Hearing a groan nearby, they discover the Tin Woodman, standing rigid with a fife in his hands. "Is that a man or a hardware store?" Dorothy enquires aloud. The Tin Man explains that he is rusted and has been playing the same lovely tune for over a year. He instructs Dorothy to get his oil can to lubricate his joints so he will be "oil right" again. Similar to the MGM script, the Tin Man implores the Scarecrow to "oil my neck a little more. It doesn't turn smoothly." The Tin Man tells them that he was once of flesh and blood and in love with Cynthia, a Munchkin maiden. But as in the Baum book, the Wicked Witch caused his axe to progressively amputate all his limbs—which the tinsmith replaced—until he realized he no longer loved Cynthia because the tinsmith forgot to give him a heart. "That probably came extra," quips the Scarecrow. When Dorothy invites the Tin Man to come see the Wizard for a heart, he asks if the Wizard is a butcher. They end the scene with a song cued by the Tin Man's hopeful prospect of reclaiming his love for Cynthia.

The setting then shifts to a glorious field comprised of a chorus of "thirty or forty young ladies dressed in costumes representing the poppy flower." As the lights come up, the poppy chorus sings of how no mortal can resist the effect of their poisonous perfume. Dashemoff and Dorothy reunite as Pastoria's party enters, disguised as a one-ring circus. Pastoria is dressed as a lion tamer accompanied by the Cowardly Lion; Tryxie is a bareback rider who tends to Imogene.

Dorothy feels sleepy and Dashemoff attributes her sedation to the poppies; Pastoria says he feels "like forty winks," a one-liner later repurposed for the Cowardly Lion in MGM's film. They all succumb to the poppies' aroma, including the animals. The Scarecrow and Tin Man enter and, as in the Baum book, are unaffected by the flowers' perfume. As the duo debate what to do, Dorothy calls out in her slumber for Locusta, the Good Witch. Locusta responds to Dorothy's call, irate at the poppies' treachery. She summons the frozen northern winds to destroy the blossoms and restore from sleep the unconscious victims. In the show's most famous scene, the flowers wilt and wither to the ground as the Snow Queen appears and transforms the poppy field into a wintry tableau.

Act II opens with the Wizard of Oz addressing the chorus. He informs his constituents that he has been the target of an assassination attempt. To appease the crowd, the Wizard performs a magic trick with an egg and a handkerchief followed by making a man in a basket disappear. Sir Gyle is in the audience and calls on the crowd to see that the Wizard is a fraud. Next, Gyle throws bombs, which do not go off, at the Wizard, and the Wizard orders him tossed from the palace. When the Wizard attempts to receive contributions from the crowd, no one responds and the citizens disperse, disillusioned.

Cynthia sees the Wizard and, believing him to be her long-lost lover Niccolo, swoons and fawns with romantic intentions. The Wizard thinks Cynthia is hallucinating and evades her. When she pleads with him to come fly away with her, he retorts, "I will as soon as my wings come back from the laundry." Spurned by the Wizard, Cynthia takes revenge by firing a pistol at him, but he catches the bullet in his mouth.

Dorothy, the Scarecrow, and the Tin Man approach the palace. "Is this where the Wizard does his principal wizzing?" the Scarecrow asks the captain of the guard. Dorothy explains to the captain, "He'd like a few brains and I'd like a pass to Kansas." When Dorothy asks if the Wizard can really honor their requests, the captain is unable to tell; but the Scarecrow pledges his allegiance to Dorothy, saying, "Don't worry, Dottie. If you have to stay here, we'll take care of you," then, to the Tin Man, "You're in on that, pie-plates?" The Tin Man concurs, "That's right, Dottie. With all my heart—when I get it."

The Wizard approaches and greets the strangers. They state their wishes, and the Wizard proceeds to give the Scarecrow his brains, all the while making contemporary quips about politicians and intellect. The Tin Man next tells the Wizard he'd like a heart in six seven-eighths size to which Dorothy openly wonders, "Wouldn't you like to be considered a big-hearted man?" After more punny banter and bargaining, the Tin Man gets his heart at a discount for being secondhand. Dorothy next makes her request, but the Wizard tells her all his passes to Kansas are canceled. "Must I stay forever in this awful country?" she complains, to which the Wizard replies, "How can you call anything awful after Topeka?"

For his miraculous success in fulfilling the Scarecrow's and Tin Man's desires, the Wizard announces he'll throw a ball in his honor. Meanwhile, Pastoria's party, in circus disguise, has arrived at the palace, and their presence is reported to the Wizard. While they are waiting, the Scarecrow, Tin Man, and Cynthia enter. The call comes for Pastoria's circus to give a royal command performance for the Wizard. When the Wizard's confederate official passes through, Pastoria throws a large green cloth over him while Tryxie drugs him with "knock-out drops" wafted under his nose. Pastoria's scheme is to dress in the confederate's uniform and expose the Wizard's fraudulence before the crowd, thus restoring himself to the throne.

As Pastoria and Tryxie carry off the confederate, Sir Wiley Gyle is riling the crowd into realizing that the Wizard is an imposter who has deceived them for many years. Knowing the Wizard will use his disappearing-man-in-a-basket trick to impress the crowd, Gyle nails shut the escape hatch portion of the basket, making the trick ineffectual. Pastoria emerges wearing the confederate's uniform and the Wizard begins his magic basket trick with showman's bravura. Thinking Pastoria is his official, the Wizard "volunteers" him to participate in the trick by entering the basket. Realizing he's been duped, the Wizard stalls but the trick is exposed and Pastoria spills out, denouncing the Wizard and declaring himself the rightful king.

Act III begins at the edge of the domain of Oz, peopled with many soldiers and officials. An officer is looking for escaped prisoners, enemies of King Pastoria, who have eloped from captivity. The fugitives include the Scarecrow and Tin Man, who enter in disguise; the Tin Man is dressed as a chauffeur and the Scarecrow is "attired in many light-colored articles that might be stolen from a clothes line." As the pair cross a bridge, they are detained by a sentry. Both characters engage the sentry in a prolonged banter laden with one-liners to distract him.

The Tin Man is able to exit to go in search of Dorothy and the others. The Scarecrow converses with cooks and waitresses and entertains them with a song until the Tin Man returns, having been unable to locate their party. The sentry enters with the officer, and both highly suspect the Scarecrow and Tin Man to be the runaway rebels. The duo is placed under arrest and led to a cage. Next, the Wizard and Gyle are brought in dressed in convict outfits replete with ball and chain. Pastoria is behind them wearing royal purple robes.

When Pastoria asks the officer if any of the other escapees have been captured, the officer points and says of the Scarecrow and Tin Man, "We've got the What-was-it and the What-is-it in the cage." Pastoria humiliates the Wizard and Gyle by giving them brooms to sweep the streets. Tryxie has a trifle with Pastoria and breaks it off with him, finding him an unsuitable king and longing for her days as a lunch-counter waitress in Kansas. Dorothy and Dashemoff enter and prepare to cross the bridge to freedom. Dorothy wishes to reunite with her friends the Scarecrow and the Tin Man and discovers them both imprisoned.

The Tin Man asks Dorothy for scissors in order to cut apart the Scarecrow and pass him through the cell bars. The Tin Man next advises Dashemoff to bypass the sentry and flee across the bridge, which he does. Dorothy pauses to sing a song about her lover, Dashemoff. The Tin Man, who has finished dissecting the Scarecrow, says, "The Scarecrow is all carved and ready to serve. . . . Will you have some wing or some second joint?" He passes the Scarecrow's limbs to Dorothy as Cynthia enters the scene. Cynthia remarks that something about the "tin gentleman" reminds her of Niccolo, her lost love.

Dorothy and Cynthia carry the Scarecrow's remains in a basket, telling an officer they are going berry picking. Suspicious, he orders the Scarecrow's parts, which he takes to be rubbish, thrown into the river. Dorothy is distraught. Seeing the sentries and guards are nowhere about, the officer charges off over the bridge, leaving behind the key to the cage. The Tin Man climbs down and aids Dorothy and Cynthia to rescue the Scarecrow from drifting downstream. In a theatrical illusion using a shadowbox cabinet, they assemble him part-by-part until the Scarecrow is restored and animated once more. (A similar assemblage occurs in both *The Wonderful Wizard of Oz* and the MGM film after the Scarecrow has been dismembered by the Winged Monkeys.) The Scarecrow declares he feels like a "wet scrambled egg," and asks, "Is my face on straight?" The Scarecrow and Tin Man celebrate their happy reunion and exit offstage.

The sentry overseeing the Wizard and Sir Wiley Gyle enters with both, who lament their sentence as street cleaners. The Wizard muses on his lost political power, "If I ran for king now," he says, "I could sweep the country without any trouble." Gyle counters with, "Wouldn't this be a lovely thing to give up for Lent?"

The Tin Man comes in, followed by Cynthia, who implores him to play the piccolo. He obliges and, experiencing déjà vu, wonders aloud, "I seem to have done this before." After he plays their song, all memories of his love for Cynthia flood back. "Take me to your copper-fastened bosom," Cynthia exclaims. As they embrace, Niccolo, aka the Tin Man, observes, "At last, my new heart has a chance to work."

Dashemoff returns to the Scarecrow, Wizard, and Gyle, having given his pursuers the slip. But they are confronted by Pastoria and his soldiers. Pastoria tells them, "Aha, once more my prisoners. This time I'll take no chances," before he orders the men to be executed—dialogue reminiscent of the climactic confrontation with the Wicked Witch in the MGM film after Dorothy and her friends are surrounded by the Winkie guards. In desperation, Dorothy cries out for Locusta's merciful aid. Locusta intends to create a darkness over the land by which the prisoners might elude Pastoria, but he acquiesces, wanting no part of another cyclone. He grants the prisoners reprieve to depart whenever they wish, as the act comes to its grand finale and the curtain closes.

In theatrical custom the show's book would undergo updating and revision as its run continued. Songs and comedic skits would be swapped out or added, but its plotline

essentially remained intact. *The Wizard of Oz* toured the country in road show companies beginning in 1904 and ran—in one form or another with various casts and musical numbers—as late as 1918. Publicity for the 1939 motion picture estimated that the show played 941 cities. If not an exaggeration, this figure may include repeat performances; when *The Wizard of Oz* began a two-week run at Philadelphia's Garrick Theatre on October 9, 1905, it was *Oz*'s third visit to the Garrick. So pervasive was the acclaim of *The Wizard of Oz* that David Montgomery and Fred Stone, its celebrated clowns, became the equivalent of modern-day rock stars. One of the leading men gave rise to a joke published in *Woman's Home Companion*, February 1906:

"Oh Mr. Stone," said the young lady to the gentleman who played the Scarecrow in *The Wizard of Oz*, "I saw your photograph and kissed it because it was so very much like you."

"And did it kiss you in return?"

"Why, no."

"Then," said Mr. Stone, "it is not at all like me."

The cultural influence of *The Wizard of Oz* was such that its humor and spectacle would be fondly recalled by mature film and theater critics such as Burns Mantle and Walter Winchell when the MGM version debuted in 1939. Additionally, in 1932 actor Ralph Bellamy cited his inspiration to enter show business occurred immediately after his mother took him to see Montgomery and Stone in *The Wizard* as a child.

The critical and popular reception of both *The Wonderful Wizard of Oz* and the hit stage production created a demand for further adventures of the Scarecrow and Tin Woodman. L. Frank Baum was obliged to satisfy the pleading requests of his readers with a series of book sequels though he very much maintained an interest in dramatizing his whimsical creations for the stage. Baum's most ingenious theatrical venture adapted his written fantasies as a multimedia presentation called *The Fairylogue and Radio-Plays*. L. Frank Baum reportedly claimed the word "Radio" in the show's title referred to the surname of a Frenchman who hand-tinted his Oz films for the Parisian company Duval Frères. But in October 1946 Baum historian and NBC Radio employee Jack Snow told *Modern Screen*'s Ben Gross that Baum coined the term after consulting his dictionary for an adjective to describe the radiant projection of slides and film as a novel form of entertainment. Apparently, the definition for "radio" suited Baum best: "emanating on a beam, or ray, of light."

The *Fairylogue and Radio-Plays* program premiered on September 24, 1908, at the Bell Theatre in Grand Rapids, Michigan. *Variety* told of Baum's October 1, 1908, debut at Chicago's Orchestra Hall at which the author, attired in a white Prince Albert suit, narrated the Oz stories in travelogue format (hence the title *Fairylogue*). The production incorporated projections of hand-tinted glass lantern slides, live actors dressed as characters from the Land of Oz, and film footage shot by the Chicago-based Selig Polyscope Company. The entire performance was "garbed in illusions" and "interesting to all, but it is especially excellent entertainment for children." The show proceeded to the Hudson Theatre in New York, where, for three weeks beginning December 13, 1908, Baum gave afternoon presentations on Monday, Tuesday, and Friday.

SILENT-SCREEN OZ

L. Frank Baum's Oz travelogue was well attended but not a lucrative success, and its tour dates, beyond those of New York City, were discontinued after only two months, leaving the author in tenuous financial straits. Hoping to duplicate *The Wizard*'s success, Baum announced in January 1909 that Montgomery and Stone would be reteamed in another musical extravaganza based on his 1907 book, *Ozma of Oz*. The show was slated to premiere the first week of October at Chicago's Studebaker Theater with a score by Manuel Klein and scenic effects by Arthur Veogtlia, whom Baum considered the greatest theatrical painter in America. But the new Oz production was never realized, and by June 3, 1911, Baum filed for bankruptcy, having reportedly invested thirty thousand dollars into the *Fairylogue* show. With liabilities of twelve thousand six hundred dollars and assets of eighty-five dollars, which were said to consist of two suits, a typewriter, and reference books, Baum's humiliation was immediately made public with nationwide headlines that read, "'Wizard of Oz' Author Broke."

To settle his contractual obligation with Selig Polyscope, Baum allowed Selig to produce his Oz tales as a new series of silent films without his direct involvement. *The Wonderful Wizard of Oz* was the first (also advertised as *The Wizard of Oz*), being a short subject of one thousand feet in length. With a March 24, 1910, release date, the picture was timed for the Easter holiday as "one of a series of fairy stories that has taken a small fortune to produce." To intrigue audiences familiar with the Montgomery-Stone extravaganza, the *Oz* film was billed as the "first reproduction of a comic opera ever attempted . . . produced to please grown-ups and children of today." The *Arkansas City (KS) Daily Traveler* informed the public that L. Frank Baum was "more than pleased with the results obtained by the picture people" in translating his *Wizard of Oz* scenario to the screen.

The Selig Polyscope *Wizard of Oz* survives, miraculous as so few films of its era are extant. The opening title and credits are lost, but the picture opens on the Kansas farm with a runaway bucking burro causing a ruckus for the farmhands and (presumably) Aunt Em. Dorothy (played by a child instead of a young woman), the burro, and a cow (all men in animal costumes) encounter a living scarecrow tied to a pole, whom Dorothy frees. A storm blows up and the group of them take shelter by clinging to a large haystack as debris begins to blow. The Scarecrow runs off to carry Toto—portrayed by a live dog—just as the cyclone strikes and the haystack is sent spinning away. A title card next bears the legend, "Blown into the Land of Oz." As Dorothy and the animals extract themselves from the haystack, the Scarecrow wafts in on a breeze. They all set out together.

The scene shifts to the Emerald City throne room, where the ruling Wizard of Oz issues a proclamation abdicating the throne to anyone who releases the citizenry from the evil power of Momba the Witch. His statement also announces his humbuggery and his desire to return to Omaha. But Momba makes a surprise appearance by flying in with her broom and disrupts the proceedings before sailing off.

Back on the road, Glinda appears in the nick of time to transform Toto into a panto-mime bulldog that will serve as an imposing protector for the party just as a lion emerges to attack. The lion is quickly tamed and befriends Toto in his new form. (It should be noted that the scenic backdrop for this sequence includes trees with humanoid faces clearly patterned after the fighting trees in Baum's original book.) The group next finds the Wizard's proclamation posted on a tree; the Scarecrow takes it with him as they all march off together.

On their journey the happy travelers discover the rusted Tin Woodman. Dorothy and the Scarecrow lubricate him as the animals frolic excitedly. Liberated, the Tin Man plays his piccolo, as in the stage extravaganza; Dorothy, the Scarecrow, and the animals dance to the music. They all pair up in couples before marching and singing on their way again.

The next setting is the thatched woodland cottage of Momba the Witch. A winged gob-lin tips her off to the approaching strangers. As Dorothy's party enters, Momba levitates to the ground from her second-story perch and a battle ensues between our heroes and Momba's minions (probably representing the Winkies, as in Baum's book). Dorothy's friends are enslaved in prison cells as Momba, wearing the Golden Cap, orders Dorothy to scrub the floors. Impulsively, Dorothy douses the witch with her bucket of water and, in so doing, Momba dissolves away into thin air. The Winkies enter but the Tin Man raises his axe threateningly and they scatter. The Tin Man frees his companions with the keys from Momba's remains and Dorothy likewise puts on the Golden Cap. The Scarecrow reminds them of the Wizard's proclamation.

They next reach the Emerald City so that Dorothy can claim the crown. The Guardian of the Gate admits them inside amid a procession of guards. The group is escorted into the throne room, where the Wizard is overjoyed when Dorothy gives him the Golden Cap, proof that Momba has been conquered. Dorothy declines the crown, so the Wizard appoints the Scarecrow as king. Amid the celebration the Wizard waves a wand to make himself disappear. He quickly reappears before trotting off arm-in-arm with Dorothy (the Scarecrow and Tin Man remain behind for some brief slapstick buffoonery).

When the clock strikes twelve, a room full of young seamstresses (presumably making the Wizard's balloon) abandon their work and take part in a synchronized dance before tripping away much to Dorothy's amusement. The Wizard is next seen in his balloon preparing to take flight with the citizens of Oz as his audience. He reaches into his top hat and pulls out a white rabbit, then a white dove, before emptying a sandbag that allows the balloon to rise. As another sandbag drops from above, Dorothy emerges from the crowd, reaching heavenward in vain. The Wizard, now fully airborne, sails away. Back on the ground, a parade of horses and camels precedes the Scarecrow and Tin Man in celebrating with an eccentric dance routine as the film closes, paving the way for further adventures of Dorothy in Oz.

The 1910 *Wizard of Oz* film uses elements of the 1902 stage show as well as new material that appears to have influenced the MGM film. Toto first appears as a cairn terrier; Dorothy and the Scarecrow engage in a brief bit of slapstick around a cornfield fence, as in a dance number cut from the 1939 film; Baum's fighting trees are moved out of sequence in the story (perhaps granting latitude to MGM screenwriters to do the same with their fighting apple trees); and a sign posted in the Emerald City ("Union Rules/No Work After 12") probably inspired the carefree lyrics of the song "The Merry Old Land of Oz," which celebrate an impossibly brief workday.[4] Also, the Wicked Witch of the West (aka Momba) carries a broomstick that she uses to levitate in true Halloween custom. Finally, Dorothy providing the Wizard with tangible proof of the witch's demise also factored into the MGM script.

An April 14, 1910, date was announced for the second Selig Oz film, *Dorothy and the Scarecrow in Oz*. The new film was based on the plot of Baum's 1908 book, *Dorothy and the Wizard in Oz*. In it, Dorothy and her companions experience an earthquake and enter the Glass City, where they encounter the dangerous Mangaboos. Jim the cab horse, the Mangaboo Princess, and the return of the Wizard—all elements of the original book—are included, as is the poppy field from *The Wizard of Oz*. Characters from Baum's *Ozma of Oz* are also introduced, and the Scarecrow, Tin Woodman, and Cowardly Lion are finally awarded their desired attributes by the Wizard.

This production was followed by *The Land of Oz* (May 16), with Dorothy and her friends combating a militant-female army in the Emerald City, and *John Dough and the Cherub* (December 19), based on a non-Oz fantasy by Baum, although the film concludes with Princess Ozma in the Land of Oz. *The Land of Oz* was heralded by Selig Polyscope as its "crowning effort," and it was hoped that theater managers would see the picture's merits and run it more than once a day. Unlike the *Wizard of Oz* stage extravaganza, which

---

4 Also, L. Frank Baum wrote in *The Emerald City of Oz* (1910) of the Land of Oz's utopian society, "Every one worked half the time and played half the time. . . ."

appealed to adults and children alike, the Selig series was advertised as fairy stories for the younger set. Interest in the films was fleeting, and it was unusual for them to be screened beyond a single day's engagement. Despite his exclusion from the Selig productions, Baum remained inspired by the illusionist possibilities of the motion picture medium, which suitably complemented the fantasy of his literary exploits.

On April 2, 1914, L. Frank Baum became president and general manager of the Oz Film Manufacturing Company, underwritten by the Uplifters, a group of Los Angeles capitalists who were social colleagues of Baum's. The philosophical premise of the new studio was that of "believing there was a field for a new line of motion picture plays" suitable for entertaining audiences of all ages. Under Baum's supervision the company began making motion pictures as of June 10, 1914. According to *Moving Picture World*'s July 4, 1914, edition, the Oz Film studio occupied a property a block long and a half a block deep on Santa Monica Boulevard, an estate formerly apportioned thirty-five years earlier by Senator Cornelius Cole.

The property's three-story mansion was converted to include a projection room, dark room, and general offices. On the lot was built a stage sixty-five feet by one hundred feet, with another building for dressing rooms, storage, and a carpentry shop. The stage featured a cement trap seven feet deep and sixty-five feet long for disappearances and scenes with rivers. A separate cement vault would house the film and cameras. In all, the studio was described as "the most beautiful in this vicinity," studded with a variety of trees that enhanced the picturesque location. Impending productions were to be *The Patchwork Girl [of Oz]* (based on Baum's 1913 Oz book), *Tik-Tok Man [of Oz]*, inspired by Baum's 1913 stage musical, and *The Wizard of Oz*. In its October 10, 1914, edition, *the Moving Picture World* reported that Baum was passionate for this latest Oz endeavor, arriving at the studio each day by 7:30, rarely breaking for lunch, and working until ten or eleven o'clock every night.

Oddly, a superior remounting of *The Wizard of Oz* was forgone in favor of filmizations of material from Baum's *Wizard* sequels. The July 11, 1914, edition of *Motion Picture News* indicated that while production on the studio's inaugural picture, *The Patchwork Girl of Oz*, was under way, David Montgomery and Fred Stone, the Tin Woodman and Scarecrow of the original Broadway musical hit *The Wizard of Oz*, had been engaged to appear in an Oz Film Manufacturing Company version of *The Wizard* "which will be taken up in the near future." But by October 1914 Montgomery and Stone were back on Broadway in *Chin-Chin*, another successful fantasy operetta, which ran for nearly nine months, after which the duo toured in a road company production for the 1915–'16 season. By then Baum's Oz movie studio was defunct.

The Patchwork Girl of Oz was followed by *The Magic Cloak of Oz*, and *His Majesty, the Scarecrow of Oz*. For the latter film it was reported that Baum was present for its premiere screening and held an informal question-and-answer reception for his youthful admirers. The pictures used state-of-the-art optical effects, a menagerie of pantomime creatures, and the antics of the Scarecrow and Tin Woodman, familiar to theatergoers of the 1902 play and its touring productions. The Oz films were heavily promoted and highly anticipated but, though generally well reviewed, were thought better suited to juvenile audiences.

The Oz Film Manufacturing Company folded in 1915, though an effort was made to sustain the company by Baum's eldest son, Frank J. Baum, and reorganize it under the banner of Dramatic Feature Company. The new studio planned one-reel comedies beginning with *Pies and Poetry*, as well as a feature-length production for adult audiences, *The Grey Nun of Belgium*, to be released through the Alliance Films Corporation, but these efforts failed.

Attempts were made to revive the Oz Film productions into the next decade, and when Mildred Harris, one of the studio's players, married silent-screen icon Charles Chaplin in 1918, Harris's supporting role in *The Patchwork Girl of Oz* was elevated to star status and the picture was retitled *The Ragged Girl of Oz* the following year. Similarly, in January and February 1920, theatrical promoter S. H. "Hopp" Hadley arranged show dates for *His Majesty, the Scarecrow of Oz*, now titled *The Wizard of Oz* and distributed by National Film Corporation. The unique feature of the Hadley bookings was a combination film-and-vaudeville-revue presentation in which the picture's projection would periodically halt for bits of live stage performance. Hadley coined the term "Movical" to define the show and secured comedian Frank Moore, the Scarecrow of the film itself, and a chorus of fourteen "Beauteous Oz Dancing Girls" for engagements in Asbury Park and Trenton, New Jersey, and Scranton and Pittston, Pennsylvania. The act was said to be Broadway-bound but was advertised as "a show for the kiddies," and it went no further.

After the failure of the Oz Film Manufacturing Company, cinematic ventures based on Baum's stories went dormant for nearly a decade, perhaps owing to the author's own disinterest and declining health; Baum passed away on May 6, 1919. But Oz remained a popular subject for pantomime entertainment. In all likelihood, fond memories of the original musical comedy led to Baum's original book being translated into a more manageable play script dramatized by Elizabeth Fuller Goodspeed and first performed by the Junior League of Chicago in January 1923.

When the Fuller Goodspeed script was published by Samuel French in 1928, it was performed by Junior League clubs across the country.[5] The Fuller Goodspeed script is a stripped-down accounting of *The Wonderful Wizard of Oz* absent any formal musical

---

5 The popularity of this version of *The Wizard of Oz* led to script adaptations of Baum's *The Land of Oz, Ozma of Oz,* and *The Patchwork Girl of Oz*—all of which were added to the Junior League repertoire.

numbers or complicated special effects that would prove cumbersome for community and children's theater groups to stage. Instead of Imogene the cow, the Fuller Goodspeed script restores Dorothy's pet dog Toto to the narrative, to be played by a child in costume. Also reinstated is the Wicked Witch of the West, whom Dorothy melts (the stage directions suggest water be substituted with a bucket of white cornmeal). As in Baum's book, the Scarecrow and Tin Woodman are destroyed by the Witch's evil deeds, but for the sake of brevity, they are magically made whole and reunited with Dorothy once the Witch is killed.

The script does incorporate a catchphrase made popular by Fred Stone's Scarecrow from the 1902 show, "I'm so *ne-r-vous!*" and Dorothy uses some contemporary slang such as "goody-goody" and "whoopee!" However, much of the dialogue quotes Baum directly, and the script is notable for being the first to refer to Dorothy's magic shoes as *slippers*, a descriptor repurposed a decade later for the MGM movie script. Similarly, as in the "We're Off to See the Wizard" number, after the Cowardly Lion joins Dorothy's party, the script calls for the group to go "marching off on the road . . . single file, singing a song as the curtain falls." Curiously, in September 1931 a Junior League production of *The Wizard of Oz* was filmed in Indiana, directed by Rosamond Van Camp, with shots taken both outdoors and in the Indianapolis Civic Theatre. The picture was screened at the Civic Theatre on January 2, 1932.

On August 2, 1923, *Film Daily* announced that producer Larry Semon—one of filmdom's highest-paid comedians of the era—had acquired the motion picture rights to *The Wizard of Oz* and put it on his schedule behind several other productions. Semon cast himself as the Scarecrow for his big-budget version of the story. Frank J. Baum, L. Frank Baum's son, was scripting the adaptation.

Frank J. had been involved in his father's business affairs dating to his work as projectionist for the Fairylogue production of 1908. He served as press agent and publicist for the Oz Film Manufacturing Company from New York offices. After a stint in World War I, he joined his family in Los Angeles and kept current with the burgeoning motion picture field, serving as the West Coast representative for the industry journal *Exhibitor's Trade Review* from 1921 to 1923. After L. Frank's 1919 passing, Frank J. represented the Baum estate on behalf of his mother, Maud, in all related negotiations, clearly determined to brand Oz into a lucrative franchise across many media formats. When he trademarked the word "Oz" for the publication of *The Laughing Dragon of Oz*, an original Oz book of his own (copyright 1934 and released the following year), Frank J. was sued by both his mother and the Oz book publishers, and Maud regained control of all Oz interests.

On October 14, 1924, Chadwick Pictures Corporation declared *The Wizard of Oz* its most important production, though at the time, Chadwick, formed in 1915 as a film distributor, had only three of its own original productions under its belt. Expectations were high, and by late October 1924, an advance announcement for Semon's *Oz* touted the

Scarecrow as "universally beloved and admired . . . the greatest character produced on stage and in story in the last generation. He made Fred Stone famous. No actor on the screen today can adequately portray this unique character as Larry Semon, the screen's finest grotesque, fantastic comedian."

Oliver Hardy, then billed as "Babe" Hardy, had been a staple of Semon's comedies since the late teens. To moviegoers familiar with Semon's two-reelers, it was not surprising that Hardy would be cast as Semon's sidekick in *The Wizard of Oz*. One ad highlighted Hardy's casting as the Tin Woodman and foretold of a plotline, in keeping with the stage extravaganza, concerning the Tin Man's lost love, Cynthia:

> Larry Semon in *The Wizard of Oz* will bring back to millions of people the memory of the glorious adventures of the Scarecrow (played by Semon) and the Tin Woodman in the land of the Munchkins. The adventures of the Tin Woodman who goes in search of a heart to restore his love for Cynthia will live forever. With his boiler stomach, his tea kettle face and his funny arms and legs, the Tin Woodman as portrayed by Oliver Hardy will convulse multitudes with side-splitting laughter as he did when he first appeared in the book and on the stage.

On September 9, 1924, Hollywood journalist Wood Soanes reported that Semon went ahead with his new version of *The Wizard of Oz* after Fred Stone declined the opportunity to re-create his famous Scarecrow on the silver screen. Another variation on Stone's participation was recorded by *Exhibitor's Trade Review* in its October 18, 1924, issue. According to that account, Frank J. Baum approached Semon with the thought of launching a live stage production of *The Wizard of Oz* that would travel road-show-style simultaneous to the completion of the photoplay version. Semon would reprise his Scarecrow part from the film as the show would be based on the movie script; but Semon requested that Baum first offer the show to Fred Stone. However, Stone was said to have wired Baum a refusal, "stating that his age makes it impossible for him to dance as limberly as he once did in the role of the boneless straw man." (At the time Fred Stone was nearing fifty.)

With Larry Semon directing and playing a lead role, his production of *The Wizard of Oz* was positioned to be successful given Semon's box-office prowess and the popular history of the Oz books and stage production. But the screenplay—attributed to Semon, "L. Frank Baum Jr." (as Frank J. Baum was billed onscreen), and Leon Lee—strayed so far from its original inspirations that its semblance to *The Wizard of Oz* story and play are unrecognizable.

The picture opens not in Kansas, as did the book and play, but in the workshop of an elderly toymaker (Semon) who is putting the finishing touches on the last of a trio of dolls representing Dorothy, the Scarecrow, and the Tin Man. The toymaker's granddaughter enters and presents to him a copy of *The Wizard of Oz*. Taking the granddaughter in his lap, the toymaker pauses to open the cover, revealing the main titles onscreen (Semon's fiancée, Dorothy Dwan, in the role of Dorothy, receives top billing over her costars).

A placard next sets the stage for the story: "Once upon a time, the people of Oz awoke to find their baby Princess gone. . . ." Years later they gather in the palace. Prime Minister Kruel, a treacherous villain, is the self-appointed ruler of the kingdom. Kruel is aided by Lady Visshus and Ambassador Wikked. Also introduced is the well-loved Prince Kynd, who advocates for the return of the townspeople's rightful queen. Sensing an impending mutiny, Kruel assuages the crowd by calling on the Wizard. The Wizard enters with a top hat, tails, and walking cane and is identified as "just a medicine-show hokum hustler," a description that would be developed for MGM's Kansas charlatan, Professor Marvel.

Kruel suggests that the Wizard stall the crowd by creating distractions to avert their attention ("Do your stuff, Wizzy," Kruel implores). The Wizard proceeds to conjure "The Phantom of the Basket," an ornately costumed transvestite, from an empty wicker trunk, who performs for the awed townspeople.

The scene shifts back to the toymaker's workshop, as his granddaughter rightfully complains, "Oh Grammpy—I don't like that. Read me about Dorothy, the Tin Woodsman, and the Scarecrow." The toymaker turns ahead in the book, and the location now shifts to the Kansas farm. Dorothy is portrayed as an ingenue, in the manner of Anna Laughlin's portrayal in the *Wizard of Oz* stage production. Also introduced is her "mother at heart," Aunt Em; several farmhands (two of whom are played by Semon and Hardy); and Uncle Henry, who is physically aggressive to all. Another farmhand, Snowball, is African American and—in stereotyped tradition—is shown helping himself while loafing in a watermelon patch.

Both Semon's and Hardy's characters vie for Dorothy's affections, sparking a rivalry. Slapstick episodes follow involving broken eggs, a bucking burro, cactus spines, an expectorating duck, and a swarm of bees—all of which add nothing to the plotline and serve only to showcase Semon's gags and mugging. (Interestingly, the latter two effects are done in primitive cartoon animation. A similarly animated bee swarm would be scripted into the fantasy sequence of MGM's *The Wizard of Oz*.)

Aunt Em reveals to Dorothy that as an infant, she was left on their doorstep with a letter stating that an enclosure should be opened only at the time of the child's eighteenth birthday, whereupon wealth and happiness would follow. This has piqued Dorothy's desire to discover her true identity.

Back in Oz, restlessness persists, and Prince Kynd has given Prime Minister Kruel an ultimatum for producing their queen. Kruel directs Lady Visshus and Ambassador Wikked to "get the papers and destroy them, or do away with the girl." Wikked charters a biplane and flies out of Oz. In the toymaker's shop, the granddaughter again pleads, "Aw! Read me some more about Dorothy." And so the scene reverts to Kansas on the occasion of Dorothy's eighteenth birthday. She tells the two farmhands that her uncle plans to tell her "a big, big secret."

But before the big reveal can be made, the biplane lands on the farm and out comes Wikked and his henchmen. Wikked asks Uncle Henry for the sealed envelope, but Henry informs him that only Dorothy can open it. Wikked tries to bribe Henry but is chased off. Wikked next tries to persuade Hardy to obtain the envelope; meanwhile, Uncle Henry unearths the buried envelope but is intercepted by Wikked and his goons. Henry manages to hide the envelope, refusing to give it up. Dorothy is then absconded with, bound with rope, and hoisted to the top of a wooden tower. A fire is set on the ground to burn the anchored rope and cause Dorothy to plummet.

Hardy discovers the hidden envelope and is about to hand it over to Wikked when Semon jumps in and nabs it. Semon is chased by Hardy to the top of twin silos, and, cornered, dives off into a bale of hay. In the nick of time, Semon catches Dorothy as the rope burns through and she falls to earth. Wikked and his crew advance on Dorothy, Semon, Hardy, and Snowball, but the bad guys flee when lightning bolts strike.

The sky clouds over as a windstorm whips up, and more gags ensue involving misplaced lightning strikes (Snowball is impervious to direct hits). Uncle Henry, Dorothy, Semon, and Hardy take refuge in a small hut that is lifted off its foundation by the wind and sent sailing through the clouds. A strong bolt of lightning propels Snowball into the air, dashing toward the hut, which he enters. The hut descends, veers off a cliff, and explodes on impact.

Everyone survives unscathed as they find themselves in front of the Emerald City (Wikked is also shown to have been in the hut). Semon seizes the moment to hand over the envelope to Dorothy; the enclosure reveals she (aka "Dorothea") is the rightful heir to the throne. Prince Kynd, the Wizard, and Kruel come out to see the strangers. The Prince greets them kindly, but Kruel and Wikked accuse them of being trespassers in the Land of Oz to prevent them from entering the city and having Dorothy's identity made public. But Prince Kynd intervenes and reads Dorothy's secret proclamation.

Wikked concedes that while Dorothy may rule the kingdom, he remains its dictator. As Prince Kynd leads Dorothy away, Wikked orders his henchmen after Semon, Hardy, and Snowball. Semon hightails it into a nearby cornfield while Hardy takes cover in a junk pile. Snowball and the Wizard have also been rounded up. When confronted by Wikked, the Wizard declares he has changed the other men and made them invisible (although he earlier said he was a fake who couldn't change a quarter). Meanwhile, Semon decides to disguise himself as the scarecrow who stood sentinel over the cornfield.

Recognizing Semon on his perch, the Wizard seizes the opportunity to demonstrate his "powers" to Wikked by bringing the scarecrow to life. In the brief bit that follows, Semon climbs down and stumbles about in what appears to be a loose-limbed homage to Fred

Stone's Scarecrow characterization. Similarly, Hardy emerges from the junk pile attired as the Tin Man complete with his axe and trademark funnel cap. As the Tin Man advances threateningly, the unnerving sight is enough to cause Wikked and his men to scatter. Semon's party is next attacked when Wikked's men fire a cannon. This is enough to make them surrender, and they march away prisoners of Wikked.

Wikked brings the prisoners before Prince Kynd and demands they be imprisoned in the dungeon for keeping Dorothy from the throne. Kynd agrees to temporarily confine the guilty party. Hardy denies his involvement and blames Semon. But it is Snowball who is sent to the dungeon, the entrance of which is in the palace floor, and finds himself in a den of thieves. Semon follows him and is captured by the same unsavory band of cutthroats. In a whispered aside, Prime Minister Kruel suggests that if Wikked could marry Dorothy, he'd retain his political power.

Happiness reigns, for Dorothy has taken the throne as the rightful queen and is now attired in a fitting headdress and wardrobe. The Tin Man is appointed the "Knight of the Garter" so no metal will touch him (Hardy is now in uniform and is no longer clothed in Tin Man regalia). And the rotund Uncle Henry is made "Prince of Whales."

In the dungeon Semon and Snowball are being taunted by the thieves when the Wizard appears with a lion skin in which Snowball can disguise himself. Semon is to be sent to a den of real lions, but Snowball leaps forward and sends the thieves fleeing by making them believe one of the real lions has escaped. Concerned that Dorothy is being framed, Semon climbs up out of the dungeon and slips into the palace undetected.

Semon is able to warn Dorothy but is called out by Hardy, who rushes Semon with sword in hand. Semon disappears into the catacomb-like dungeon beneath the palace floor with Hardy in pursuit. Hardy enlists Kruel and the thieves to uncover Semon's hiding place; slapstick antics ensue as Semon takes cover in a series of wooden crates. Finally, both Snowball (still dressed as a lion) and Semon think they have outwitted Hardy. But in actuality, they've trapped themselves in the lion's den. From outside the cell, Hardy bids "Mr. Scarecrow" goodbye: "You're not going to have anything to *crow* about, but you're surely going to have lots to get *scared* about."

Confronted by several seemingly ferocious lions, Snowball runs off. Unaware that a real lion has taken Snowball's place, Semon says to the lion, whom he thinks is Snowball, that he is personally not afraid as he's heard "these alley cats like *dark meat.* . . ." The real lion strikes Semon in the seat of the pants and Semon retaliates by kicking the lion in the nose. Meantime, Snowball has returned into view and Semon realizes his predicament. He escapes and reunites with Snowball, but they are stalked by another lion. Snowball is petrified, but for as much as he exerts momentum to move forward, his feet have failed him and he remains in place. Once Semon sees the real lion, he grabs hold of Snowball's tail in a comedic bit that resembles a scene in MGM's *The Wizard of Oz*. Snowball escapes by

leaping through a large chink in the cave wall and plummets down a steep embankment. The lion charges Semon, who is saved when the Wizard leads him away and directs him to the palace.

Meanwhile, Wikked has put romantic designs on Dorothy, who rebuffs his advances. Prince Kynd happens in and both men draw their swords in a duel. As Wikked is about to mortally wound Kynd, Semon, who is above them, causes a huge urn to fall upon Wikked. Semon then jumps a guard who is about to attack Kynd and then runs off as the guard gives chase. Several blasts are fired off-camera and Semon emerges triumphantly wearing the guard's cap (presumably, the guard has been dispatched).

As Kynd and Semon throttle Wikked, Dorothy enters and Wikked pleads a confession, telling them it was he who had hid the infant Dorothy in Kansas to protect her from a hostile faction. Kynd orders Wikked sent away and Wikked is escorted off by palace guards. Semon wipes away his scarecrow makeup and Dorothy acknowledges his heroism with a kiss. But to his disappointment, she walks away with Prince Kynd, to whom she is clearly betrothed.

Just then, Hardy and Kruel enter, still in pursuit of Semon. Hardy pounces on Semon and the two tussle. Semon runs out of the palace and climbs a tall tower (as he did in Kansas). Hardy climbs after him but Semon kicks him off. Simultaneously, Kruel is readying his cannon as Snowball boards a biplane and takes off. The cannon blows apart Semon's tower, but just in the nick of time, he swings to an adjacent tower like a trapeze artist. The cannon is fired again just as Snowball's plane flies by with a ladder dangling from it. Semon catches hold of the ladder as the second tower is destroyed. But the ladder snaps and Semon plummets.

The setting returns to the toymaker's workshop. The scarecrow doll he made falls from its place, awakening the little granddaughter who had fallen asleep and apparently dreamed the entire story. She gathers up all three dolls and, saying goodbye to the toymaker, heads upstairs. The picture ends as Semon takes up the copy of *The Wizard of Oz* again, and a placard informs us that Dorothy and her prince lived happily ever after.

Larry Semon's *The Wizard of Oz* was slated for a December 1924 holiday release, but production only wrapped the week before Christmas. *Exhibitor's Trade Review* noted in its December 27, 1924, issue that a print was en route to the East Coast for an early preview, whereupon the New York critics unanimously praised its riotous comedy; however, the film's West Coast premiere wouldn't be until February 7, 1925, at the Forum Theatre in Los Angeles. (Prior to the screening, a musical-variety act called *An Adventure in the Land of Oz* was presented using wardrobe credited to the feature film.) Its general release would be delayed until April 1925.

The stopgap came with the legal action threatened against Chadwick Pictures Corporation by National Film Corporation, which, *Variety* reported, would "tie-up the countryside presentation of the new Larry Semon production." Days before the Los Angeles premiere of *The Wizard of Oz*, National's president, William LaPlante, claimed his company never relinquished rights to its version of *The Wizard*. National was the new distributor for the Oz Film Manufacturing Company's film *His Majesty, the Scarecrow of Oz*. In February 1915 the film had been retitled *The New Wizard of Oz* and was distributed by Alliance Films Corporation. When National acquired it the title was abbreviated to *The Wizard of Oz*. Under this name, the picture was reissued in 1920 and remained in circulation into 1923. Chadwick was able to file an injunction restraining LaPlante from interfering with the L.A. premiere. Though Semon's film was of identical title, the matter was likely settled when it was proven that the National picture was based on entirely different subject matter and not the original *Wizard of Oz* story.

Of interest to note is that the musical cue sheet for piano accompaniment in movie theaters—officially issued by Chadwick Pictures Corporation—includes samples from the 1902 *Wizard of Oz* stage production as well as Victor Herbert's *Babes in Toyland*, which was inspired by *The Wizard*. Accompanists for *The Wizard of Oz* were cued by the onscreen action or placard titles with notations such as "Lion roar ad lib" and "Work up storm effects, crashes, wind, lightning; cymbal roll when house goes over cliff."

Today, Semon's *Oz* is barely watchable for its belabored gags, racial stereotypes, and plodding story line (which has little to do with the novel on which it is allegedly based). By comparison, *Peter Pan* (1924), the cinematic version of J. M. Barrie's stage pantomime—which was in production simultaneously with Semon's *Oz*—possesses the authentic fairy-tale charm and whimsy absent from the Semon picture.

In 1925 the film took a drubbing from *Oz* book fans. In a letter published in *Photoplay* titled "Mr. Semon, How Could You?" Althea C. Russell of Chicago, Illinois, wrote, "Larry Semon, you owe an apology to the people who have read the Oz books, and do humbly beg the pardon of Frank Baum's memory for the wrong you have done his story." Another *Photoplay* letter, from Wilma C. of Los Angeles, was downright irate: "I possess many Oz books, well thumbed, showing many happy hours spent with them in my childhood. With delight I hailed the advent of *The Wizard of Oz* on the screen. After seeing it, I was disgusted, disappointed and disillusioned. The beautiful fantasy of childhood degenerated into a miserable, third rate, slapstick comedy."

Perhaps the most damning professional review came from the *Los Angeles Times*'s Edwin Schallert, who stated, "More than one producer is probably mad at his own judgment for not selecting to put on *The Wizard of Oz*, and if he isn't he should be. The Larry Semon production has comparatively little to recommend it except the title, because it was done in such a cheaply slapstick way." In 1939 Victor Fleming, who directed MGM's *The Wizard of Oz*, was justified when he judiciously yet accurately described Semon's version as "a free adaptation . . . using the title and little of the story."

Semon's offering was otherwise deemed rollicking good fun but primarily as a kiddie picture—all of which led to Fred Stone receiving letters from across the country imploring him to bring back his *Wizard of Oz*. Stone declined all offers out of respect for his late partner, David Montgomery, who died at age forty-seven on April 20, 1917.

When Larry Semon died at age thirty-nine on October 8, 1928, the press connected his demise to the poor production of *Oz*. "*The Wizard of Oz*, which was to have been his greatest effort," read his obituary, "was a financial failure and ended his career as a producer. Last March he filed a petition for bankruptcy and soon after he suffered a nervous breakdown."

MISCELLANEOZ ENTERTAINMENT

With the Semon film a dim memory, the early 1930s proved especially prolific for *The Wizard of Oz* in a variety of dramatized incarnations. Continuing to represent his mother,

Maud, Frank J. Baum was engaged in plans to bring *Oz* to the radio and movies once again. Previously, arrangements had been made with Reilly & Lee, publishers of the Oz books except *The Wizard*, for various radio stations to read from the Oz books on air. Most notable of these was *Ozmite Club*, heard nationally over station WOKT of Rochester, New York, in spring 1927, and *Topsy Turvy Time*, a children's program hosted by Russell Pratt on WMAQ, Chicago. From 1926 to 1927 Pratt's daily broadcasts featured the Oz series and were heard from Ohio to Oregon. In February 1927 Pratt wrote Reilly & Lee, "I can think of no other stories that would lend themselves so admirably to the wide variety of ages that listen in on our broadcasts. . . . I have received many, many letters from parents and teachers who seem to like the influence of the Oz books." The success of Pratt's efforts did not go unnoticed by Frank J. Baum, and he was soon engrossed in adapting the first dramatization of *The Wizard of Oz* suited for radio and performed with live actors.

In early 1931 a serialization of *The Wizard of Oz* written by "Col. Frank Baum," Baum's World War I military title, was pitched by Baum to radio stations with the suggestion that each affiliate employ its own actors, music, and sound effects using his scripts. The entire series was proposed to cover forty chapters of Oz stories in fifteen-minute segments that could stretch ten to fifteen years at six episodes per week.

In Baum's proposal, received by station KMBC in Kansas City, Missouri, on March 27, 1931, he claimed that the show had already run for twenty-six weeks "in one of the middle western cities" as sponsored by a local milk company, but this was stretching the truth. In reality, Baum had sold the *Oz* program to a radio station in Cleveland, Ohio, but it hadn't yet aired. When *The Wizard of Oz* did broadcast over Cleveland's WTAM, it debuted on July 7, 1931, and ran until February 24, 1932.

Baum's script of Episode One, concerning Dorothy and Toto's transportation to the Land of Oz by a Kansas cyclone, was reviewed by the authors of this book. For the opening signature music, Baum's notation suggests playing "Cinderella's Wedding Day" or "March of the Toys" from *Babes in Toyland*, which the narrator follows by explaining that although the "mysterious Land of Oz" is widely known, few people have been there as it is not located anywhere on earth and is surrounded on all sides by the Great Sandy Desert. Oz is mostly pleasant excepting that "once in a while some old wicked witch will dry up and disappear."

The script begins much as the L. Frank Baum book does, with Uncle Henry warning Dorothy and Aunt Em of the symptoms for an impending cyclone. Toto hides under Dorothy's bed, disallowing his mistress from following her aunt into the cyclone cellar. Once aloft in their airborne house, Dorothy makes a comment to Toto nearly identical to a line later scripted in the MGM film: "We must be right in the very middle of the most terrible cyclone!" Once in Oz, Dorothy is greeted by the three male Munchkins and the North Witch, who explains she is a benevolent sorceress. Curiously, the Good Witch of the North is described as "a queen" in the script notation, foreshadowing the "fairy queen" appearance of the Good Witch in the MGM production.

Also as in the original tale, Dorothy inherits the Silver Shoes of the Wicked Witch of the East; and when the North Witch balances her pointed cap on her nose, it turns into a slate with "Let Dorothy go to the City of Emeralds" written "in big white chalk marks." The Munchkins and the sorceress (whom Dorothy calls "Mrs. North Witch") leave Dorothy and Toto to begin their journey. But before setting out, they first decide to eat and, as "it is not polite to watch people while they eat," the episode closes until Dorothy's "strange and thrilling adventures" continue the following day.

To further demonstrate the *Oz* program's possibilities, Frank J. Baum recorded the first four episodes as samples, circa 1932, in radio impresario Freeman Lang's Hollywood studios under the auspices of Earnshaw Morgan Productions. By this time it appears as though the thought was to produce the series employing Baum's own announcer, actors, music, and sound effects as opposed to the expectation that each radio station do so independently.

A rare surviving sixteen-inch transcription recording of Episodes Three and Four was acquired through the authors' research for this book. (A sixteen-inch disc was the standard transcription format for programs to be played on a special turntable for radio broadcast.) Fortuitously, the performances of the main characters are preserved, as the extant recording encompasses Dorothy's meeting of her three traveling companions en route to the Emerald City. The announcer opens each installment by addressing his prospective listeners with "ladies and gentlemen," instead of "boys and girls," indicating that the show was intended to engage a broader demographic than the juvenile set.

Episode Three opens as Dorothy and Toto assemble the dismembered Scarecrow in the cornfield after a run-in with a charging bull. The Scarecrow's lines are clearly scripted with Fred Stone's characterization in mind; his dialogue is an almost nonstop barrage of puns and jokes. For example, Dorothy says to the Scarecrow, "When we get to the Emerald City, I hope you get a position. What field have you been in Scarecrow?" He responds, "All of them . . . I was moved to the potato patch before I got to the corn." There are also several rather permissive quips, obviously aimed at would-be adult listeners—and similar in tone to future script drafts of MGM's *The Wizard of Oz*. The Scarecrow tells Dorothy how he came to be constructed by a farmer: "Then he painted my mouth but I didn't speak. You see, I didn't know what a mouth was for." Dorothy chimes in, "Gee, I know a lot of men who wish their wives didn't know what a mouth was for." In a succeeding instance, the Tin Woodman discusses the merits of having a heart and falling in love, prompting Dorothy to speculate, "Well if love is half what I hear about it, it must be awfully nice." The Scarecrow follows up with a somewhat risqué retort: "Only half [of] what you hear about it is true. The other half you discover after you're married."

Dorothy and the Scarecrow encounter the Tin Woodman, whom they rescue from his immobilized state. Dorothy repeats the "Is that a man or a hardware store?" line from the 1902 stage production. The Tin Man tells Dorothy his real name is Nick Chopper (as in the Broadway musical and the Oz books); she tells him she's "one of the Kansas Gales"—a bit also repurposed from the 1902 show. The Woodman warns them about the dangerous creatures that inhabit the forest: lions, tigers, and Kalidahs with "bodies like bears," which may have influenced a similar line chanted in MGM's *Oz*. Growling Kalidahs menace the group, and the Tin Man chops down a tree so Dorothy, Toto, and the Scarecrow can safely flee the advancing beasts by crossing a ditch—an incident that occurs in the Baum book only after the Cowardly Lion joins the party. In another bit echoed in the MGM film, Dorothy cries out in distress for "Auntie Em" (in the Oz stories, Dorothy's guardian is only ever called *Aunt* Em).

In Episode Four the travelers are accosted by the Cowardly Lion, who roars but does not speak, as he does in *The Wonderful Wizard of Oz*. When Dorothy declares the Lion a coward, the Scarecrow exclaims, "Hooray! Hooray! I belong to his club. That's the language of the lions and I understand it." Thereafter, the Scarecrow serves as the Lion's interpreter, such as when the Lion "asks" the Scarecrow if the Tin Man is "an auto wreck" after having attacked the woodman. The travelers come to the Emerald River, which they cross by riding on the Cowardly Lion's back (as opposed to the original Baum story in which the Lion carries each of them on his back to leap the width of a gorge). The episode concludes as they are threatened by a snapping black alligator.

The surviving transcription recording for Frank J. Baum's *Wizard of Oz* radio show is a professionally produced program with capable actors, appropriately augmented with music and sound effects. None of the players is identified, but Dorothy is voiced by an adult vocal artist rather than a girl actress, with a Mae Questel "Betty Boop" affect. The Scarecrow speaks in a raspy falsetto, much like character actor Sterling Holloway, and the Tin Woodman is assuredly solid and stalwart in his delivery.

When interviewed for the October 15, 1932, edition of *Hollywood Filmograph*, Universal film actress Gay Seabrook, who would have been thirty-two at the time, said negotiations were under way to bring *Dorothy and the Wizard of Oz* [sic] to the airwaves with Seabrook voicing the lead, Charlie Lung as the Tin Woodman, and Cliff Arquette taking the Scarecrow's part—and it is indeed they who are the actors of the Frank J. Baum show. At the time, Cliff Arquette was remembered from Los Angeles radio for mimicking "Aunt Addie" the anemic evangelist. He would later be best known to TV fans in the character of Charley Weaver. He is the grandfather of actors Rosanna, Patricia, and David Arquette. Charlie Lung was a staple of Los Angeles radio productions, being known as "the man of a thousand voices." Gay Seabrook and her radio partner, Emerson Treacy, made up the popular comedy team Treacy and Seabrook, who bantered in a manner after George Burns and Gracie Allen. In 1933 both Treacy and Seabrook appeared in two *Our Gang* comedies as parents to child actor Spanky McFarland.

Much of the 1932 Oz program's dialogue is Baumian if not verbatim from *The Wonderful Wizard of Oz*, like the Scarecrow stumbling over a hole in the Yellow Brick Road instead of going around it. An exception is the odd decision to make the Cowardly Lion mute, as he was in the 1902 stage production—a silent partner in deference to the Scarecrow and Tin Man. The show was clearly scripted to create a perilous cliff-hanger at the end of each installment to entice listeners to tune in for the succeeding chapter of the serial. It is unknown why Frank J. Baum was unable to sell *The Wizard of Oz* to national radio in 1931–32, but he was simultaneously securing a deal for another serial—of the cinematic variety.

The June 14, 1931, issue of the *Film Daily* noted that work was about to start on a series of twelve one-reel novelty films based on the Oz stories produced by silent film cameraman-turned-director Ray Smallwood, directed by Ethel Meglin, and featuring Meglin's "Wonder Kiddies." (From 1928 to 1962 Ethel Meglin operated a chain of studios for prodigious children who aspired to break into show business. Former students included Shirley Temple, Jane Withers, Mickey Rooney, and Judy Garland.) The first installment was to be titled *The Scarecrow Loses His Throne*, being the initial episode of film chapters inspired by L. Frank Baum's 1904 book *The Land of Oz*. By July 3 the series had expanded to a projected twenty-six Oz films for national release through United Productions under authorization from the L. Frank Baum estate, with Frank J. Baum writing the screen treatments. The film shorts planned to use the Handschiegel Color Process, a primitive green-screen precursor, for tinting of "unusual backgrounds and trick camera shots." (Inventor Max Handschiegel and Smallwood had collaborated in its use since 1926.)

Meglin's young protégées were instructed in singing, dancing, acting, and mastering musical instruments for a thirty-five-piece symphony—all of which were pressed into service for Meglin's debut film short. Eleven-year-old Mary Ruth Boone, a renowned acrobat, who would appear in the films *The Man Who Dared* and *Stage Mother* (both 1933), was cast as Dorothy in a bit of cinematic license, as Dorothy does not appear in *The Land of Oz* book. The narrative is a loosely adapted retelling of the Baum novel. Here, Dorothy is reunited with her friends the Scarecrow and Tin Woodman, and the dramatic dynamic between Dorothy and a wicked witch seems a likely influence for comparable scenes in the MGM film. Song-and-dance interludes by the Meglin Kiddies intersperse throughout the proceedings, which conclude in typical "to be continued . . ." serial formula.

The film's production got under way soon after its announcement and was completed by September 1931. The *Los Angeles Times* heralded the forthcoming fantasy with a still published in the December 6, 1931, edition. The *Times* indicated that the movie's title was now *The Scarecrow of Oz*. But the release was delayed by more than a year, by which time it was

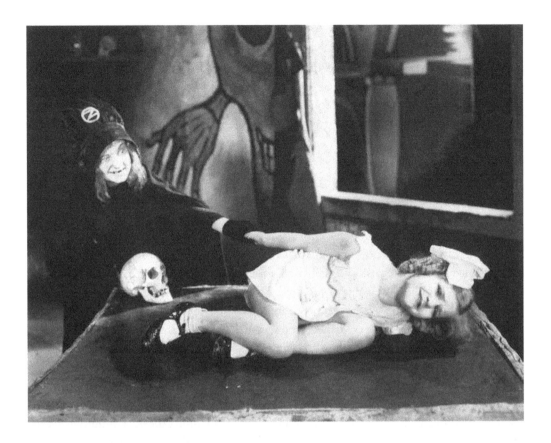

clear no further Meglin-Oz films were to be made. The picture was simply rechristened *The Land of* Oz, now a stand-alone rather than a movie chapter. The Meglin film officially premiered on February 25, 1933, at the Fox Wilshire Theatre in Los Angeles. The film was screened on at least one other occasion, the afternoon of April 1, at the Meglin Pasadena branch studio. Subsequently, *The Land of Oz* was not released nationally as originally intended, although the Meglin Kiddies continued performing in other novelty shorts.

During this period, Fred Stone was asked about reprising his performance in *The Wizard of Oz*, telling Shubert Theatre owner J. J. Shubert:

It can't be done. Dave [Montgomery] is gone and a piece like that can't compare with the big, fast musical shows that are put on today. Why, *The Wizard of Oz* was produced for $30,000. That's the cost of the finale of your first act today. Some of the old-timers might enjoy it, but the younger generation wouldn't sit through it. Oh, if it had a new book and a new score it might run a few weeks but with those changes it wouldn't be a revival—it would be a new show.

But just a year later, Stone was having second thoughts for reviving his greatest stage success. In November 1932, newspaper columnist Chester B. Bahn reported that Stone was in negotiations with Frank J. Baum (representing his mother, Maud) for the rights to the original stage extravaganza with the idea of reviving the show at the 1933 Chicago World's Fair. Charles Dillingham was mentioned as the probable producer, and Stone's eldest daughter, actress Dorothy Stone, would be cast as "the feminine lead." (Father and daughter had just played opposite each other on Broadway in the musical comedy *Smiling Faces*.) Sam Love wrote in his May 26, 1933, New York Inside Out column that Fred Stone had "gone so far as to dig up the [original *Oz*] scenery out of storage." Nothing came of the *Oz* revival, which was still mentioned as late as July 2 when United Press's Mark Barron wrote that the new production, slated for that fall, would star the entire Stone family: Fred Stone; his wife, Allene Crater, whom Stone met in the 1902 *Wizard of Oz* company; and all three of his daughters, Dorothy, Paula, and Carol, making her stage debut. It is unfortunate that Fred Stone's remounting did not transpire, as its timing would've been ideal for cross-promotion with an *Oz* revival over the airwaves.

On July 12, 1933, Maud Baum and Reilly & Lee sold the radio rights to dramatize the *Oz* stories, including *The Wizard of Oz*, to Young & Rubicam Inc. for a serial that would air in fifteen-minute installments three times a week for thirteen weeks. NBC would broadcast the program each Monday, Wednesday, and Friday at 5:45 p.m. from its Radio City studios in Manhattan, with sponsor General Mills promoting its Jell-O gelatin as a tie-in.

Twelve-year-old Nancy Kelly, billed as "the most photographed child in America" for modeling in thousands of advertisements, was selected for the part of Dorothy. Kelly was chosen for her lack of performing experience, the thought being that she would come across as natural and unaffected. No transcription recordings of the *Oz* program are known to exist, but Kelly's delivery must have been engaging. In February 1934 it was noted that Kelly had played her part with such success that when Dorothy returned to Kansas in week eight, and Kelly assumed a different role on the show for two weeks, fifteen thousand letters from children all over the country pleaded for Dorothy's return, which she obliged in week eleven.

Nancy Kelly transitioned to films with notable performances in 1939's *Jesse James* and *Stanley and Livingstone*, and *The Bad Seed* in 1956. Additional *Wizard of Oz* cast members included Junius Matthews as a talking Toto, Bill Adams as the Scarecrow, Jack Smart as the Cowardly Lion, and Parker Fennelly as the Tin Woodman, who is best remembered as Pepperidge Farm's commercial spokesman from 1956 to 1977.

The *Oz* show was intended as the wholesome answer to nationwide parent-teacher group opposition to children's radio programming of harrowing mystery and adventure that "left junior in a state of complete dither, and brought on sleep-wrecking nightmares."

According to a 1934 account, thousands of letters had been received from parents, teachers, and women's club officials praising *The Wizard of Oz* as "the most wholesome, imaginative entertainment for children on the air."

Posed publicity stills were taken of the show's cast attired as their Ozian counterparts, augmented by a fox terrier as Toto; one shot re-creates an illustration from *The Wonderful Wizard of Oz* in which Dorothy offers the Scarecrow some of her bread as Toto looks on. For reasons unknown, the program was widely heralded as the "fortieth anniversary broadcast of *The Wizard of Oz*," erroneously placing the original book's publication at 1893 instead of 1900.

The Wizard of Oz aired beginning September 25, 1933, under the direction of Donald Stauffer with original music by Frank Novak. The series comprised liberal adaptations of *The Wizard* and five of its sequels as a continuous narrative. The *Wizard of Oz* portion of the program followed the Baum book fairly faithfully with some creative license and embellishment.

Bradley Barker, radio's "master of weird imitations," voiced supporting roles and was responsible for the show's unusual vocal effects such as the Cowardly Lion's roars and the buzz of the Wicked Witch's bees. In 1933 Barker said the worst part of his *Oz* assignment was re-creating the noise emitted by embodiment of the Wizard as a ball of fire for the Lion's audience. Sound effects were otherwise handled by Frank Novak, who reportedly used manicure tools to create the "swooping" sounds heard attendant to the Cowardly Lion's appearance and the flapping wings of the talking stork. When Novak needed inspiration to compose his march for the Queen of the Field Mice, he let loose a scampering toy mouse during a rehearsal, which supposedly sent Nancy Kelly scurrying for a table top.

Throughout the broadcast proceedings, narrative interjections were made by Ben Grauer, the on-air announcer, promoting Jell-O and its dessert recipes. As send-away premiums, General Mills printed several short Oz stories first published twenty years before. "The name of this story book, everybody," read Grauer in one instance, "is *The Scarecrow and the Tin Woodman*. . . . The same man who wrote it wrote *The Wizard of Oz* books, so of course it's a swell story!"

After the first episode of *The Wizard of Oz* broadcast, NBC received fifteen phone calls from young listeners demanding to know the exact location of the Land of Oz and refusing to take no for an answer. Similarly, by October 25, 1933, it was said that the brainless "Scarecrow," Bill Adams, was sent "lots of letters of sympathy from youngsters who report they've had trouble passing exams, too."

The entire suite of seventy-seven scripts for the NBC radio program was reviewed by the authors of this book, but for purposes of tracing the development of *The Wizard of Oz* in popular entertainment, only those scripts adapting the original story will be synopsized here.

The premiere episode opens with blaring trumpets as Ben Grauer announces the new program and Dorothy, Toto, the Scarecrow, and the Cowardly Lion introduce themselves to their listening audience. After a Jell-O advertisement, the scene switches to Dorothy's prairie farm at suppertime. Aunt Em and Uncle Henry comment on the darkening sky as Dorothy excitedly notices the grass bowing in the wind. Uncle Henry announces, "By golly, there's a cyclone comin'!" as he leaves to tend to the cows. As in the Baum book, Aunt Em implores Dorothy to join her in the storm cellar, but as Dorothy reaches for Toto, there is a shrieking howl as the twister strikes the house.

As Dorothy openly wonders what's happening, Toto speaks in reply using "a squeaky voice, like a Pomeranian might have," and from here on, Toto becomes Dorothy's wisecracking sidekick. Of interest is that during the cyclone, Dorothy exclaims, "This must be a dream!"—a possible influence on the future MGM script. Also as in the book, Toto falls through the open trap door, but Dorothy rescues him. As the house crashes to the ground, Dorothy and Toto hear somebody screaming, presumably the Wicked Witch of the East.

Emerging from the wreckage, Dorothy and Toto take in the marvelous countryside, of which Toto approves. "Has it all over the Kansas prairies," he remarks, "*I'm* glad we came." They are greeted by a welcoming committee comprised of the Witch of the North and a chorus of Munchkins. The Witch was performed by matronly actress Alma Kruger, whose screen credits include *These Three* (1936), Alfred Hitchcock's *Saboteur* (1942), and a series of Dr. Kildare films for MGM from 1939 to 1942.

The Witch of the North confirms Dorothy's fear that the house did accidentally crush someone by pointing out the two protruding feet of the dead Wicked Witch. "Look at those swell silver shoes she's got on," says Toto. "She must have been somebody important!" The Witch of the North explains that Dorothy and Toto are in the Land of Oz and have liberated the Munchkins. She speaks about the Wizard who resides in the "beautiful, mysterious City of Emeralds," and gifts the magic Silver Shoes to Dorothy. "And . . . they belong to *me* . . . for keeps?" Dorothy asks, but she declines to wear the shoes because they are "too pretty."

When Dorothy weeps at the prospect of being stranded in Oz, the Witch of the North removes her "magic cap," which turns into a "magic slate." As in the Baum book, the slate reveals that Dorothy and Toto should consult the wonderful Wizard of Oz for a solution to their predicament. After the Witch of the North gives Dorothy her kiss of protection, she and the Munchkins vanish in a series of loud explosions, to which Toto cracks, "That's what you call a whirlwind exit!"

Instead of the traditionally identified "road of yellow brick," Dorothy looks for the "Yellow Brick Road" to begin their journey. A first in the history of *Wizard of Oz* productions, the "Yellow Brick Road" is the phrase reappointed in the MGM film, although it was first used in print in *The Royal Book of Oz* (1921). Dorothy takes the Silver Shoes with her, saying, "All right, Toto, come on . . . we're off to find the Wizard of Oz!" as music swells—another allusion to the future film.

The second episode begins as Dorothy and Toto are about to embark on their journey to see the Wizard. But Toto suggests that Dorothy use the Silver Shoes to transport them to the Emerald City instead. Not knowing their charm, Toto improvises a spell that backfires, causing them both to nearly blow away in a storm before the spell is reversed. They next overhear a complaining voice, which they identify as coming from a scarecrow with blue eyes, ears, and hair in a nearby field. After Toto and the Scarecrow engage in some verbal sparring, Dorothy and Toto remove "Mr. Scarecrow" from his perch. After explaining their mission, and upon hearing the Scarecrow's lament for brains, Dorothy invites him to join her. "Don't worry, Mr. Scarecrow," she assures him, "we'll ask the Wizard of Oz to do all he can for you."

In an unexplained, and unnecessary, deviation from the classic narrative, the party encounters a threatening lion whom Dorothy tames with a slap on the nose. As Dorothy scolds him for "being a big bully," the lion speaks, to her surprise. When the lion tearfully expresses his cowardice, Toto assumes the Tin Woodman's line from the Baum book, wondering if the lion has "heart disease." Dorothy suggests the Cowardly Lion come with them to ask the Wizard for courage, but as they start for the road through the forest, they hear the fearsome growls of Kalidahs. Here the episode ends with Ben Grauer assuring young listeners that Dorothy has the Silver Shoes to protect her until the next installment.

In Episode Three Dorothy's group is confronted by the Kalidahs until Toto spies a river they can cross. At the Scarecrow's direction, they escape across a fallen tree that they move over the water. On the other side Dorothy is alarmed to find that one of her Silver Shoes fell off near the Kalidahs, but the Cowardly Lion heroically retrieves it for her.

Their musing over the Lion's valor is interrupted by groans and sighs from the immobile Tin Woodman. When the Woodman asks that his joints be lubricated, Toto quips, "Oil your joints! Have you got rheumatism?" to which the Woodman responds, "I've got Tin-Man-Itis."

After the Tin Man is relieved and nearly chokes the Lion in an elated hug, he tells his story, which follows the plot set forth in the Baum book. After confessing his lost heart, march music is cued as the Scarecrow asks the Tin Man to join their party.

They soon come to another river, and to cross it, they use a raft the Tin Man had previously constructed. Amid quarreling about being overcrowded, the Scarecrow falls into the river and is carried downstream. Meanwhile, the raft starts to break apart as the show concludes until the following episode.

Dorothy and her friends make it to shore in the nick of time and encounter a stork, voiced by Bradley Barker. As in the original story, the stork agrees to rescue the Scarecrow but, here, Toto rides on the stork's back to direct him to the spot. They share several pages of dialogue, during which the stork warns, "Personally, I think you're all crazy—to go hunting for the Wizard of Oz!" The group is reunited and the stork departs, but the Scarecrow is waterlogged and in need of repair. Dorothy puts her magic shoes on the Scarecrow and the Tin Man wishes for fresh stuffing, upon which straw rains from the sky with such velocity that they risk being buried alive, and the episode ends with another cliff-hanger.

As the show returns, the Tin Man says a charm to cease the straw rain and the Scarecrow is restuffed. As in the Baum book, the Tin Man becomes distraught for stepping on a beetle and rusts his jaws for weeping. The comrades next approach the poppy field, and Dorothy, Toto, and the Lion succumb to the flowers' aroma. This sets up a scene in which the Scarecrow and Tin Man bicker back and forth, much as would be scripted in the MGM film. They carry Dorothy and Toto out of the field, hoping to somehow help the Lion.

The Tin Man next intervenes by killing a wildcat that was chasing the Queen of the Field Mice, voiced by radio actress Kay Renwick. As in the book, the Queen's minions bring lengths of string to attach to the truck made by the Tin Man to save the Cowardly Lion. But Toto worries that the Lion may have been magically relocated, concluding this episode.

As the truck advances toward the poppy field, the lead mouse (Bradley Barker) demands some form of payment. The Scarecrow thinks of using the Silver Shoes' charm, and the Tin Man puts on one shoe to wish for cheese, which satisfies the mouse. The Lion is carted out of the poppies and the lead mouse brings Dorothy a silver whistle to summon the mice in the future.

The Yellow Brick Road leads to a wall, beyond which wild-animal noises emanate, frightening the travelers. But the Cowardly Lion bravely jumps the wall in an effort to reason with the brutes on the other side. As he does, the growls and snarls become louder, and the Scarecrow cries out that the wall is impassable to them, leaving the Lion's fate unanswered until the next show.

The Lion returns to tell his friends that the wild animals insist he and the others destroy their enemy the Great Hairy Spider or else Dorothy's party will be attacked by the animals for refusing. Being outnumbered by the animals, the group seeks out the spider and discovers it asleep. As the beast awakens, the Tin Man decapitates it with his axe and is hailed a hero by the others. On the Scarecrow's advice, the Cowardly Lion carries them over the wall on his back. They continue their trek but encounter the Hammer-Heads, who assault them despite the Tin Man's unsuccessful attempts to decapitate one. (At this point the Tin Man questions the incongruence of his gentle demeanor with so much violence!) In desperation, the Scarecrow tells Dorothy to call the field mice as the installment closes.

Thousands of mice converge to greet Dorothy, and the Queen orders them to tickle the Hammer-Heads' legs, rendering them helpless with laughter while the others dash past them. The ploy works, and as Dorothy and her friends emerge from the woods, they see a green glow in the sky ahead—the Emerald City. Delighted, they sing a joyful marching tune:

> Hooray, Hurray, we're almost there!
> To the Emerald City, bright and fair!
> To the Great and Wonderful Wizard of Oz!
> Oh, happiest day that ever was!

Their happiness is short-lived, for they next encounter an army of balloon people that also begins attacking them. Here, the Cowardly Lion's dialogue is strongly reminiscent of that scripted for the character in the MGM film. "I'll see you folks later," he says, to which Dorothy cries, "Lion! Come back here!" "I've got an appointment," the Lion replies. "I'm late already." When he is reminded about the Hammer-Heads, the Lion turns back, conceding, "Well . . . maybe I'll let my appointment go for today." The group deceives the balloon people into drawing closer, only to burst them using straws from the Scarecrow's stuffing. With another obstacle overcome, the travelers finally approach the gates of the Emerald City.

With their destination in full view, Dorothy exclaims, "We're almost to the Emerald City, at last!"—a line nearly the same as in the MGM film. But again, they are delayed, this time by flying umbrella people. With the Scarecrow snatched up, they resort to using the Silver Shoes to disable the new creatures by making it rain, even though the Tin Man will rust. The Cowardly Lion dons the shoes and invokes a charm, causing a thunderous downpour that sends the umbrella people retreating (and causing them to drop the Scarecrow). The Lion casts another spell to cease the rain and restore the Tin Man. At the Emerald City gates, they hear gunshots, prompting more comic riffs from the Cowardly Lion: "So long, folks . . . I have to mail a letter."

A green soldier addresses them, and they explain their purpose in seeking the Wizard. He cautions them about their mission and warns them about getting past the Guardian of the Gates. Just then, a tiger bounces at them through the gates, dangling their fate until next time.

Upon return, the tiger introduces himself as the Hungry Tiger (a character from the Oz books) who resists his penchant for fat babies. The Guardian of the Gates (Ian Wolfe) ushers forth and sends the tiger on his way. Dorothy and her companions each explain their wants but the Guardian chastises them for daring to annoy the Wizard with their foolish errands. After Dorothy appeals to his sympathies, the Guardian outfits them with green glasses and permits them to enter. The Cowardly Lion expresses his second thoughts in dialogue similar to the MGM film. "I've changed my mind about this whole thing," he trembles. "I don't think I care to see the Wizard of Oz, after all."

As they pass through the gates, a deep voice (Ian Wolfe) booms from the Wizard's palace: "Strangers, beware! Beware the Wizard of Oz!" They proceed, assuaging the Lion and taking in the city's startling sights. They are escorted to the palace, where they are accosted by the booming voice as Dorothy enters the throne room alone.

Dorothy has her interview with the bodiless head, which queries her as in the Baum book. The Wizard assigns Dorothy the task of destroying the Wicked Witch of the West, sending her away with the Metro-esque line "Now, *go*! The mighty Oz has spoken!" The Scarecrow and Tin Woodman have their respective audiences with the Wizard, but come the Lion's turn, he goes into hiding. They find the Lion muttering to himself in some bushes and bring him to the palace. The Lion casually explains his absence, saying, "I-I just went for a little stroll."

The Green Soldier tries helping the Lion along after the big cat's legs give out. "Look out! You're pulling my whiskers!" the Lion cries, much as in the MGM film when he pulls his own tail. After being sent away by the Wizard, Dorothy's group resigns to destroy the Wicked Witch. They pass a green horse pulling a green carriage—shades of MGM's Horse of a Different Color—and meet up with the Hungry Tiger again, who informs them about the Wicked Witch and her single, telescopic eye.

Leaving the Emerald City and their green glasses behind, they begin walking westward and encounter an enormous eye in the sky, accompanied by the sound of howling wolves. As in the Baum book, the armies of wolves, crows, and bees are outwitted before the travelers are overcome by the Winged Monkeys. On orders from the Wicked Witch, Dorothy, Toto, and the Lion are taken to the sorceress's castle.

There, the group is presented to the Wicked Witch, described as an old, yellow woman with yellow teeth and a single yellow eye in the middle of her forehead, which gives Toto "the creeps." The Witch makes it plain that she wants Dorothy's magic shoes, but the girl refuses to give them up. It is Toto's idea to try splashing the Witch with water, and after the woman tricks Dorothy out of one of her shoes, the girl throws a pail of water over her, melting her into a puddle. Dorothy, Toto, and the Cowardly Lion rejoice by singing a celebratory song about having conquered the Witch.

They use the Silver Shoes to find their lost friends They are sent shooting across the sky, landing at a foothill in front of the Tin Woodman. The shoes return them to the castle, where the Winkie tinsmiths restore the Tin Man. The Silver Shoes are again employed to locate the Scarecrow, whom the Lion bravely rescues from a tree, and they all magically return to the castle, where the Scarecrow is mended. Dorothy uses the Golden Cap to call the Winged Monkeys, who return them to the Emerald City.

In the throne room they are startled by the Wizard's disembodied voice. They demand he keep his promises to them, but the Wizard makes excuses and procrastinates. The remainder of the episode, from the discovery of the Humbug Wizard (Ian Wolfe) to the gifting of token attributes to the Scarecrow, Tin Man, and Lion, to the launch of the balloon, follows Baum's original narrative.

With the Scarecrow left in charge, he suggests that Dorothy ask the Winged Monkeys to take her to Kansas, but once summoned, their leader explains that to do so is forbidden. The Green Soldier advises that they seek Glinda's aid, so they begin their new adventure. They encounter a forest of talking, moving trees that attack them until the Tin Man uses his axe to destroy the leader, for which the other trees are grateful. They next come to the wall surrounding the China Country and are pelted with marbles. After pleading, they are admitted to enter only if they promise to be careful. But the travelers accidentally damage too many fragile items and are driven out with another onslaught of projectile marbles. They come to a river and begin to cross it on the Lion's back when they are accosted by an army of rubber ducks. After some tense moments, they reach the shore.

In the next episode, Marian Hopkinson voices the part of Glinda. The adventurers finally arrive at Glinda's red castle, where they cross the moat over a drawbridge after the Scarecrow guesses the charm to lower it. Inside, they meet the beautiful witch Glinda on her ruby throne, and they introduce themselves and explain their mission.

As in the Baum book, Glinda uses the Golden Cap to command the Winged Monkeys to relocate Dorothy's friends to their respective kingdoms. The monkey leader infringes on Dorothy's tearful goodbyes with, "Sorry to interrupt this leave-taking—but we monkeys are rather busy today." After their departure, Glinda gives Dorothy the spell to work the Silver Shoes, instructing, "Just stamp your right foot three times, and say, 'Take me home to Aunt Em.'" But Dorothy suddenly realizes she's lost one of the shoes ("That *is* serious," says Glinda), and she and Toto go off in search of it. Thus, *The Wizard of Oz* radio program segues into the next Oz story, *The Land of Oz*, where the original book concludes.

Within its first two months on air, NBC's *The Wizard of Oz* radio show was such a success that by November 28, 1933, *Variety* reported that, effective December 22, General Mills requested another thirteen weeks of episodes—the specified installments were a stipulation of the contract with the Baum estate but also a radio industry standard.

A new round of publicity stills was taken of the Oz characters gathered for a party, at which Jell-O was served, to induct one another into the "Honorable Order of Ozmites," indicating that there may have been a secret society for the show's followers. During the photo shoot Nancy Kelly was said to have consumed an all-important prop: an Emerald City made of green gelatin.

The program's players also turned out for public events. On Saturday, February 17, 1934, Nancy Kelly made a personal appearance in the auditorium of Pittsburgh's Kauffman's department store to host a children's luncheon. The forty-cent menu was Oz-themed, featuring Toto Rolls, Dorothy's Baked Apple, and Emerald City Fruit in Jell-O, among others. On Sunday, March 11, 1934, the entire *Wizard of Oz* cast assembled for a skit under Frank Novak's musical direction as part of orchestra leader Paul Whiteman's live Sunday night concerts at New York's Hotel Biltmore.

Though heavily advertised and endorsed by *The Family Circle* and *Parents* magazines, the *Wizard of Oz* show concluded on March 23, 1934. Four days later Frank Novak announced he was seeking to have his *Oz* songs published, with pictures by Tony Sarg, pending approval from the Baum estate.

On June 19, 1934, in a piece titled "Kids Like Adult Shows Best," *Variety* reported that an advertising agency survey taken of 2,372 juveniles from Newark and Englewood, New Jersey, clearly indicated an overwhelming enthusiasm for the very "blood and thunder" adult programming to which *The Wizard of Oz* was to have been the tame antidote. While Oz rated with parents and teachers, the survey showed that kiddie-themed shows simply didn't hold the interest of their demographic. Of the nearly thirty radio shows ranked by the tykes polled, only eight were designed primarily for child listeners; with just five votes, Oz came in at number twenty-six behind a list that included *Buck Rogers, Little Orphan Annie, Amos 'n Andy, 20,000 Years in Sing Sing, Witches' Tale, Death Valley Days, The*

Lone Ranger, and *Tom Mix*. The demise of the 1933–34 *Oz* radio program would be a cautionary tale for MGM in crafting a screen version that would appeal to all ages.

But another version of *The Wizard of Oz* generated interest in 1934 when Seattle's Cornish School of the Arts produced a marionette operetta under the direction of Ellen Van Volkenburg, with story adaptation by William Kimball and tunes composed by Edward Chambreau. Irene Phillips created the puppets and sets were designed by Mildred Sater, all of which was critically praised for authenticity. A reviewer for *The (ID) Post-Register* remarked, "Pictorially each scene is eye-satisfying. The puppets are exact reproductions of the original illustrations of *The Wizard of Oz*. If you remember, the one in which Dorothy has auburn braids and a blue-and-white checked dress." The show was said to be staged as "lavishly as an elaborate DeMille film spectacle in twelve scenes" with sixteen puppeteers animating thirty-six marionettes. Of the fourteen original songs, the show's theme "Wiz-Wiz-Wizard" was said to be a catchy hit. The concluding scene was "The Balloon Field," thus eliminating the episodic trek to Glinda's castle and providing the same license to MGM for its future screenplay.

Previously, from 1928 to 1929, there was a national tour by Jean Gros's French Marionettes of *The Magical Land of Oz*—featuring nearly life-size versions of the

Scarecrow and Tin Woodman—but that was an original script by author Ruth Plumly Thompson, L. Frank Baum's successor in continuing the Oz series. So though the Jean Gros show was still being performed in the mid-1930s, Van Volkenburg's *Oz* was the first grand-scale marionette interpretation of the beloved Baum book. By 1935 it had been performed 125 times to audiences totaling one hundred thousand in northwestern towns and some East Coast engagements. The show was still given as late as 1937, and the presentation was significant enough to be mentioned in the liner notes for a newly published edition of *The Wizard of Oz* two years later.

Another Oz production ran on the East Coast nearly simultaneous with the Van Volkenburg marionette show. On October 9, 1935, Ethel Barrymore Colt, daughter of actress Ethel Barrymore and niece of actor John Barrymore, took the role of Dorothy in the Jitney Players' children's musical *Adventures in Oz*, thus casting an important "name" in the part for the first time. The theatrical troupe's production was scored by Robert Russell Bennett, who orchestrated *Show Boat*, *Music in the Air*, and *Anything Goes*. The original story was written by Gretchen Dortch and Pendleton Harrison, founded on the L. Frank Baum stories. The show debuted at New York's Girls Commercial High School and toured the eastern seaboard into 1936, appearing in Chapel Hill, North Carolina, Canonsburg, Pennsylvania, and Charleston, West Virginia, before returning to New York at the Brooklyn Academy of Music for a holiday show on December 19.

One of the more promising Oz ventures of the 1930s era was announced by *Film Daily* on October 12, 1932. A Technicolor cartoon titled *The Wizard of Oz* was in development by Ted Eshbaugh's Musicolor Fantasies Company, Eshbaugh's Hollywood studio on North Highland Avenue. Eshbaugh, then nearing thirty, was a graduate of "one of Boston's better art schools," from which he won a scholarship. Upon graduation he went to work as a portrait painter, miniature artist, and sculptor who dabbled in colored animated cartoons.

Eshbaugh had aspirations to apply to animation a color technique he had reportedly developed over a ten-year period.

Eshbaugh's 1931 cartoon *Goofy Goat* is believed to be the first of its kind produced in two-strip Technicolor; previously, cartoons were in black-and-white. *The Snowman*, which followed in 1932 (though copyright 1933), was created in the same method, however, *The Wizard of Oz* was to be the first of a dozen two-reel shorts done in three-strip Technicolor and using the *Oz* characters. Eshbaugh was in charge of production with Carl Stalling as the musical director. (Stalling had scored Walt Disney's earliest Silly Symphony shorts and was later known for his work on Warner Bros.' Looney Tunes shorts.) The rights to produce the *Oz* cartoons were acquired through Frank J. Baum, who received onscreen story credit as "Col. Frank Baum."

Six months later, on April 10, 1933, Hollywood columnist Harrison Carroll announced that Eshbaugh "has finished the first of the *Wizard of Oz* color cartoons," a seven-minute production that would be accompanied by a full musical score. Eshbaugh's cartoon is a vastly truncated retelling of the Baum story in which Dorothy befriends the Scarecrow and Tin Woodman after the cyclone deposits her and Toto in the Land of Oz. They make their way to the Emerald City (sans the Cowardly Lion character), where they encounter the mysterious Wizard of Oz, who entertains them with a display of magic. In cartoon tradition, things go awry when one of the Wizard's tricks backfires and an egg grows to epic proportions, causing distress and structural damage before the spell is broken and all ends happily. With Dorothy remaining in Oz, the open-ended conclusion would lend itself to a serialization of similar misadventures. (Of note to historians of the 1939 MGM film is that monotone hues are used for Dorothy's Kansas farm—as described and depicted in Baum's book—before a clever transition to full color as she and Toto descend into the Land of Oz.)

On June 21, 1933, *Film Daily* noted that the completed cartoon short was brought to New York from the West Coast by Lieut.-Col. J. R. (John) Booth, a Canadian lumber magnate and vice president of Film Laboratories of Canada. Booth had set up headquarters in New York at the Du-Art Film Studios. (Booth receives screen credit as Eshbaugh's co-producer. The animator's films would be released and distributed through Booth's company.) The second installment of the *Oz* cartoon series was slated to begin October 10, 1933.

Concurrent with Ted Eshbaugh creating his *Oz* cartoon serial, a most significant coup for the Baum estate occurred in September 1933 when the live-action photoplay rights to *The Wizard of Oz* were sold to Hollywood film mogul Samuel Goldwyn. The previous year, *Motion Picture Herald* published a list of sixty famous plays tallied by William A. Brady, "the oldest theatrical manager in American theatre." *Oz* was one of only twenty-seven titles ranked "good" as worthy of screen adaptation.

Corbin Patrick, writing for the *Indianapolis (IN) Star*, reported that Frank J. Baum was tendering the *Wizard of Oz* screen rights for seventy-five thousand dollars. Patrick noted that MGM was considering the property as a feature-length vehicle for comic duo Stan Laurel and Oliver Hardy, whose pictures for Hal Roach were distributed by Metro; but, Patrick said, "other studios are bidding." Ultimately, Samuel Goldwyn negotiated acquisition of the screen rights to *The Wizard of Oz* for forty thousand dollars from Frank J. Baum, and the deal became legal on January 26, 1934 (the Baum family and W. W. Denslow's heirs shared in the proceeds).[6] Goldwyn also secured the right of first refusal to option the remaining Oz books for an eighteen-month period, after which the option would be rescinded.

In her September 30, 1933, syndicated column, Hollywood journalist Louella O. Parsons broke the news. "Great news for the kiddies and their parents as well!" wrote Parsons, "*The Wizard of Oz*, Frank Baum's famous fantasy, has been purchased by Samuel Goldwyn for a musical extravaganza to be produced in color." By October 3, *Film Daily* had also announced that Goldwyn was adding Oz to his lineup "as a special musical production separate and apart from his regular schedule for United Artists. Preparation is now underway." (United Artists, or UA, was the successful independent film company established by Mary Pickford, Douglas Fairbanks, and Charlie Chaplin. Goldwyn was one of UA's producers.) The notice indicated that the Goldwyn project would be based on the Baum book and musical comedy in which Montgomery and Stone appeared.

When Goldwyn secured the Oz film rights, Ted Eshbaugh's animated *Wizard of Oz* series was already in development; any live-action picture Goldwyn might have envisioned would be in an entirely different, noncompetitive medium. However, Eshbaugh's branding of an entire franchise of Technicolor Oz cartoons over several years would conceivably present a conflict of interest for Goldwyn in the future—especially if Eshbaugh's shorts caught on and public identification of the Oz characters aligned with the animator's renditions. But a more immediate conflict of interest was that Walt Disney's Technicolor shorts, including his Silly Symphony series, were being released through UA. In fact, it was the success of Disney's 1932 Silly Symphony *Flowers and Trees* that inspired Samuel Goldwyn to pursue a Technicolor *Wizard of Oz*.

By the time Eshbaugh's *Wizard of Oz* was completed, Disney's presence in the animation medium had gained unparalleled critical and popular recognition. In 1932 Disney entered into an exclusive agreement with Technicolor giving Disney a lock on the use of Technicolor in his shorts until 1935. Competing animators were relegated to the use of Cinecolor,

---

6 The transaction delay may have been caused by the $40,000 suit—the precise amount Goldwyn paid for the Oz screen rights—brought by Frank J. Baum in December 1933, against Chadwick Pictures Corp., makers of the 1925 *Wizard of Oz* production, to recover the motion picture rights, originally sold to Chadwick for $12,500.

the less vibrant two-strip color film. (They contested the agreement with Disney, and the following year Technicolor amended the terms.) Disney's Silly Symphony short *Flowers and Trees*, released July 30, 1932, was the first commercially released Technicolor cartoon. Less than four months later, *Flowers and Trees* was the first animated short to be honored with an Academy Award in the category "Short Subjects, Cartoon" at the fifth Academy of Motion Pictures Arts and Sciences ceremony, held on November 18, 1932. It would also be the first of Disney's twenty-two Oscars.

Disney's exclusionary agreement with Technicolor led to a legal dispute where Ted Eshbaugh's cartoon was concerned. On March 27, 1934, *Variety* reported that J. R. Booth, Eshbaugh's financier, had filed a fourteen-thousand-dollar lawsuit in Superior Court against Technicolor for refusing to release the negative and soundtrack to Eshbaugh's *The Wizard of Oz*. Prior to the suit Booth had demanded the return of the negative but Technicolor had refused. Booth was seeking to recover his investment costs.

An attorney himself, Frank J. Baum joined the legal fray. On June 26, 1934, *Variety* reported that Baum had sued Technicolor in federal court for having infringed on the copyright to *The Wizard of Oz* by producing the story as an animated cartoon of the same title. The cartoon in question was ostensibly Eshbaugh's and it was Eshbaugh who would have been accountable for the agreement with Technicolor. By June 8 of the following year, the dispute continued. According to *Variety*, Baum had filed an injunction in the state courts (presumably California and New York, where Eshbaugh and Booth were respectively stationed) to restrain both Technicolor and Eshbaugh from releasing *The Wizard of Oz*. Baum's complaint was that, though he and Eshbaugh had an agreement for the Oz cartoon series, Eshbaugh had failed to honor the time frame for completion of such. Clearly, plans to continue the series were halted.

It is thought that Eshbaugh's animated *Oz* was subsequently released only as a black-and-white version (As evidence of a theatrical release, Oz and Baum historian Fred M. Meyer once saw a predominantly red, white, black, and blue poster for the short in the home of a Baum relation). Thereafter, Eshbaugh continued his animation pursuits, which included the 1945 wartime cartoon *Cap't Cub Blasts the Japs* and sixteen Aunt Jemima TV commercials in 1950.

A Technicolor Dreamland

At the time of his *Wizard of Oz* aspirations, Samuel Goldwyn was one of Hollywood's preeminent producers, making pictures through his Samuel Goldwyn Productions and releasing them through United Artists. (Goldwyn's prior film company, Goldwyn Pictures, had been acquired by Marcus Loew in 1923 and, via corporate merger with Loew's Metro Pictures Corporation and Louis B. Mayer Pictures Corporation, became Metro-Goldwyn-Mayer the following year.)

When Goldwyn purchased the *Wizard of Oz* screen rights, Louella O. Parsons suggested that stage actress Helen Hayes would be an ideal Dorothy in her September 30, 1933, column. Three days prior the *Los Angeles Examiner*'s Harrison Carroll cited W. C. Fields for Goldwyn's Wizard and either Hayes or Mary Pickford for Dorothy. Securing Fields's services was unlikely, as the previous May he had scored megastar status with the release of the hit film *International House*, and Hayes was committed to the New York play *Mary of Scotland*, which would run from November through July 1934. But casting Goldwyn's UA associate Mary Pickford to play *Oz*'s leading role wasn't such a leap. Then forty-one, Pickford had built a silent film empire playing virginal gamines. In February 1933 Pickford completed tests as Alice in Wonderland for Walt Disney that Louella O. Parsons described as remarkable, writing, "She really looks like a little girl." The project was to be a Technicolor combination live-action/cartoon picture but, come spring, the deal was off—Pickford had soured on the twelve-month wait time to create the animations.

Immediately following the announcement of Goldwyn's acquisition of *The Wizard of Oz*, Harrison Carroll publicly applied pressure that it should measure up to Disney's

efforts. "Now that Samuel Goldwyn is going to make *The Wizard of Oz*," Carroll wrote in his October 2, 1933, column, "he'll have to figure out a way to make monkeys fly and trees fight on the screen. What a run of fairy tales *The Three Little Pigs* is starting."[1] (Released the previous May through UA, Disney's wildly successful *Pigs* cartoon short grossed more than ten times its original cost.)

Simultaneous with obtaining the *Wizard of Oz* screen rights, Goldwyn had offered the job of composing *Oz*'s new musical score to Irving Berlin, with lyrics by Moss Hart. The Berlin-Hart collaboration had previously succeeded in creation of the Broadway musicals *Face the Music* and *As Thousands Cheer*. "What's What in Hollywood" columnist Mollie Merrick was ecstatic at the prospect, "What Irving Berlin could do with such charming things as a Kansas cyclone set to harmony and what Moss Hart could do with a lyric about the tin heart of a tin woodman would be nobody's business."

Securing Berlin to score *The Wizard of Oz* would have been a coup for Goldwyn on several fronts. Not only was Berlin the preeminent composer of such musical staples as "A Pretty Girl is Like a Melody," "What'll I Do?" "Blue Skies," and "Puttin' on the Ritz," his publishing firm, Irving Berlin, Inc., issued the sheet music of the songs written for Walt Disney's cartoons, including "Who's Afraid of the Big Bad Wolf" from *The Three Little Pigs* (1933). Thus, public association with Disney's fantasies could be achieved by arranging for Berlin's would-be *Oz* compositions to be published by Berlin's own company. But Berlin was noncommittal. By October 30, 1933, *Variety* reported that Berlin was mulling Irving Thalberg's proposition to join MGM although Thalberg, Metro's head of production, was "not interested" in Samuel Goldwyn engaging Berlin for the *Oz* score. (About a month later it was noted that Thalberg, himself, was "dallying with the idea of filming *The Wizard of Oz*.")

---

1 At this time it was reported that MGM would be making *The Wizard of Oz* in color, but this was quickly retracted.

In his November 24, 1933, Movie World column, journalist Phil M. Scribe reported that Goldwyn was on schedule to fulfill his commitment to UA for the release of five features before August 1934, with *The Barbary Coast* going into production that December, followed by *The Wizard of Oz* in February 1934. In the interim, Goldwyn elevated *The Wizard of Oz* to a status commensurate with its impact as a smash extravaganza on the stage by reiterating it would not only be a star-studded musical, *Oz* would be filmed entirely in color—a costly and ambitious undertaking as the average Technicolor film of the era had a minimum million-dollar budget.

The build-up for *Oz* was not coincidental. It was Goldwyn's answer to the general state of "agitation" that motion pictures had devolved into a cycle of films depicting violence and sexual permissiveness. A typical letter of complaint was published in journalist Helen Worth's newspaper advice column in February 1933. It read, in part, "Like all other children, my two young ones want to go to the movies [but] I simply cannot allow them to see the very sexy and suggestive scenes which appear in practically every picture now produced, but would be glad to take them to see such films as *Alice in Wonderland*, *The Wizard of Oz*, *The Secret Garden* and many other pictures, taken from books which were the delight of all our childhoods." In response to such public outcry, Goldwyn temporarily shelved plans to dramatize *The Barbary Coast*, Herbert Asbury's gold-rush drama, which included drinking, gambling, murder, and prostitution. His *Wizard of Oz* would be the producer's contribution to the plea for family fare and films suitable for viewing by all.

Goldwyn was optimistic that *The Wizard of Oz* would be a Christmas 1933 offering, figuring it an appropriate yuletide entertainment that would especially appeal to children and up its grosses. But nearly a year passed with no concrete activity other than to note that Goldwyn's all-star *Wizard of Oz* was coming and that it "may be Eddie Cantor's next." More specifically, a notice in the *Hollywood Reporter* on June 25, 1934, stated that Goldwyn had purchased *The Wizard of Oz* for Cantor.

At the time, singer-comedian Eddie Cantor was Samuel Goldwyn's golden boy, starring in a cycle of what came to be known as "the annual Eddie Cantor show." Cantor had performed on radio, in Florenz Ziegfeld's stage revues, and in films dating to 1923; but he became a bona fide movie star with 1930's *Whoopee!* which was produced by Ziegfeld and Goldwyn. Thereafter, Cantor starred in a picture a year produced by Goldwyn. Cantor's latest hit was Goldwyn's *Roman Scandals* (1933), a musical comedy in which Cantor imagines himself back in ancient Rome (a scenario also suitable for transporting Cantor to the Land of Oz).

As a preliminary experiment for his proposed *Wizard of Oz*, Goldwyn forayed into Technicolor's extravagance in a sumptuous musical finale to *Kid Millions* (1934) with Cantor transformed into the Willy Wonka–esque proprietor of a fabulous ice-cream factory visited upon by dozens of eager urchins. *Kid Millions* was a black-and-white film but its

Technicolor fantasy sequence ran seven minutes and cost Goldwyn two hundred thousand dollars—money well invested judging from accolades such as that of the *New York Times*, "The lavish ice-cream factory scene, filmed in the new Technicolor process, is the most successful example of fantasy in color that Broadway has seen outside of the Disney cartoons."

But whether Cantor was still to headline Goldwyn's *The Wizard of Oz* became the subject of speculation, as did the picture's production status. While in New York on business, Goldwyn said in February 1934 that his *Wizard of Oz* would have a cast of unknowns. Another February notice, by *Los Angeles Times* columnist Edwin Schallert, indicated that Norman Z. McLeod, director of Paramount's *Alice in Wonderland* (1933), would likely be Goldwyn's directorial choice for *Oz*. In its April 14, 1934, edition, *Motion Picture Herald* announced that Goldwyn's production schedule for the new season would begin on May 1, with *Oz* being among five pictures on the Goldwyn roster. Then a front-page notice in the *Hollywood Reporter* for June 25, titled "'Wizard of Oz' Off," indicated that Goldwyn had dropped *Oz* from his schedule for the year, citing Eddie Cantor's refusal to consider the picture because it "was not his type." Two weeks later United Press staff correspondent Alanson Edwards's July 11 In Hollywood column noted Goldwyn's forthcoming *Wizard of Oz* would cast Cantor in the titular role—one of several notices indicating that Cantor would be the Wizard.

Of her father's proposed casting as Baum's humbug, Janet Cantor Gari suggested in a 2012 interview, "I don't think he was big and blustery enough for the Wizard. . . ." Eddie Cantor was also mentioned for the Scarecrow role—just once—in the *Los Angeles Examiner* of September 27, 1933, but this has been reiterated in *Oz* histories as definitive casting. "I was just a kid and never knew anything about [Cantor's] business arrangements," continued Janet Cantor Gari, "[but] the part of the Scarecrow had to be played by a dancer, and my father couldn't dance." Indeed, given the renown with which Fred Stone was indelibly linked with the role, Cantor as the dancing Scarecrow was entirely unlikely. Even Larry Semon didn't dare dance in his *Wizard of Oz*.

Ultimately, Samuel Goldwyn honored Cantor's disinterest in *Oz* and planned another vehicle for him. On January 24, 1935, *Motion Picture Daily* noted that Harold Arlen, who would subsequently cowrite the score for MGM's *Wizard of Oz*, was to "do the score for Eddie Cantor's next Goldwyn epic," the title of which was unnamed until the following March 19: Clarence Budington Kelland's novel *Dreamland*. The picture was retitled *Strike Me Pink* and it debuted on January 24, 1936. *Pink* would be the last of six Goldwyn-Cantor collaborations.

Absent Cantor, Goldwyn's *Wizard of Oz* may have gone dormant but it wasn't dead. Prior to the release of *Kid Millions*, *Motion Picture Daily* reported on June 25, 1934, that Russian actress Anna Sten, Goldwyn's would-be successor to Greta Garbo, "may appear" in *The Wizard of Oz*. (Sten's three pictures for Goldwyn failed to make an impression and she was released from her contract in 1935.) *Motion Picture Daily* next noted in its July 19 issue that despite Goldwyn having canceled it once, *Oz* still had legs: Goldwyn would "make it this year" once a screen treatment suitable for adult and child audiences was satisfactory, and "tests of key players are underway." That *Oz* was back on, pending an acceptable script, was affirmed by *Motion Picture Herald* in its July 28 edition.

At the time, another actress openly hinted that she wanted *Oz*'s lead role. In July 1934 eight-year-old Cora Sue Collins told Reine Davies, Universal Service staff correspondent, that "Little Dorothy" in *The Wizard of Oz* was her personal favorite and "the role she wishes to bring to the screen some day in the near future." The early 1930s was a prolific period for Collins and she is, today, best remembered for *Queen Christina* (1933) with Greta Garbo, *The Scarlet Letter* (1934), and *The Adventures of Tom Sawyer* (1938).

But a start date for Samuel Goldwyn's *The Wizard of Oz* was postponed yet again. In his August 13, 1934, column, Edwin Schallert reported that it appeared "fairly definite" that Goldwyn's *Oz* would be made within the next six months, putting its inception at early 1935. In the interim, Schallert said, Goldwyn was dickering with various writers for a modern adaptation of the story with the intention of making it "a fairy tale suitable for grownups" given the universal appeal of the fondly recalled Montgomery-Stone musical comedy.

Notices that Goldwyn's version of *The Wizard of Oz* was forthcoming persisted into the following season, with Goldwyn making a pitch for a trend toward film fantasies in a full-page newspaper piece on September 30. In an interview with journalist Dan Thomas, Goldwyn chided those producers who were not cognizant of the call for cleaner pictures and musical fantasies with songs that carry the narrative with realism.

Still, Goldwyn's *Oz* remained idle. On October 14, 1934, the *Charleston (SC) Gazette* ran an article concerning the unpopularity of all-color films and how, cartoons aside, the Technicolor Corporation would now limit such feature films to four per year during the next movie year. Goldwyn's *Oz* was third in line, "postponed from this fall to next spring [1935]." *Variety* for October 16 still listed *The Wizard of Oz* on Goldwyn's 1935–36 schedule, and *Oz* was among impending musicals noted in *Motion Picture Daily*, on January 3, 1935. In an April 4, 1935, report on the annual meeting of the Motion Picture Producers and Distributors of America, its president, William H. Hays, listed *The Wizard of Oz*—"a musical production based on the famous Frank Baum's stories"—as among the anticipated, fine-quality pictures currently in preparation.

The last located report of Goldwyn's *Oz* having any life was Paul Harrison's February 10, 1936, In Hollywood column. Harrison said Goldwyn was making casting plans for the Oz tales and that eleven-year-old child actress Marcia Mae Jones was "likely to be the 'Dorothy' of those fairy stories," though Harrison voted Shirley Temple as the "perfect choice for the role—if she were available." On January 21 Jones had been placed under a

$125-a-week contract to Goldwyn, at which time it was noted that she was "assigned the lead" in Goldwyn's *Wizard of Oz*. This notice precedes Jones's breakout performance in Goldwyn's *These Three* by two months. If there was any substance to this tidbit, it was merely Goldwyn's way of stirring interest in his young protégé, as nothing more came of it.

By April 1, 1936, Samuel Goldwyn's long-rumored *Wizard of Oz* was reduced to the punchline of an April Fool's joke when Paul Harrison said that the producer had signed matronly comedienne Mary Boland (Countess DeLave in 1939's *The Women*) to play "Little Dorothy in the Oz stories." Harrison's circuitous tall tale spun that Boland was casting Goldwyn as the Wizard, and that the Wizard of Oz himself had signed Harpo Marx to direct *The Adventures of Samuel Goldwyn* in Technicolor.

What proved to be the death knell for Goldwyn's *The Wizard of Oz* was the failure of a similar film fantasy played with live actors, Paramount's all-star *Alice in Wonderland*, which premiered on December 22, 1933. The press even hinted that *Alice* stalled Goldwyn's *Oz* when on December 27, Hollywood columnist Chester B. Bahn noted, "Goldwyn's *Wizard of Oz* is held up, [he's] waiting to see how *Alice in Wonderland* fares." Director King Vidor, whose 1934 film *Our Daily Bread* was released through United Artists, chastised Goldwyn in *New Theatre* magazine that autumn. Vidor accused Goldwyn of attempting to play copycat to Disney's efforts with his *Wizard of Oz*, charging that Goldwyn would be forever confused by Disney's success with fantasy while Paramount failed with *Alice*—"a failure which prompted Goldwyn to shelve his plans for Frank Baum's *Wizard of Oz*," Vidor was quoted as saying.

Previously, hopes were high for *Alice*'s success, which would have paved the way for Goldwyn's *Oz* and for MGM to proceed with Charles Kingsley's *Water Babies*, an underwater fairy tale. Within its first weeks in release, *Alice* was off to an auspicious start—enough so for Paramount to announce on January 4, 1934, that Charlotte Henry, who portrayed Alice, would star in *Cinderella*, the studio's next Christmas picture. But the following day, scathing reviews from London film critics were excerpted in the *Hollywood Reporter*, with the *Evening News* proclaiming, "It's over! I have just been through the ordeal of seeing [it]," and calling Henry's Alice "a horrible shock. . . ." In its February 1934 edition, *Motion Picture* magazine published a letter of complaint against *Alice*, "[Why] didn't they turn [Alice] over to the one man in Hollywood who can bring fantastic animal creations to life in pleasing color? The one man who could get the true spirit of Lewis Carroll's masterpiece, the one man who has been working along these lines for years? . . . [the] only man who should have been allowed to come within a mile of *Alice*. Ladies and gentlemen, I give you Mr. Walt Disney!" By mid-July *Motion Picture Daily* reported, "[The] only way exhibitors can be compelled to play *Alice in Wonderland* is by refusing to give them Mae West pictures until they do." Once the receipts were tallied, *Alice*'s weak box office and public drubbing dissuaded Samuel Goldwyn from gambling millions on another little-girl-lost-in-fairyland picture. The irony is that, in advance of *Alice*'s premiere, Charlotte Henry told New York reporter Eileen Creelman that of her next projects, she was interested in Goldwyn's forthcoming production of *The Wizard of Oz*.

DETOURS AND INTERLUDES

Three years later a motion picture version of *The Wizard* was rumored once again. Fred Stone and actress-daughter Paula performed "The Man Without Brains," a number from *The Wizard of Oz*, dressed as the Scarecrow and Tin Man, at the July 1, 1936, Actors' Fund Benefit at Los Angeles's Pan-Pacific auditorium. When photos of them in costume were published, RKO, the movie studio to which Fred Stone was under contract, was flooded with fan requests for an *Oz* revival and, as a result, RKO was reportedly considering a movie version of *The Wizard of Oz* starring both Stones.[2] Nothing more came of this speculation. However, the following year *The Wizard of Oz* resurfaced as viable popular entertainment, albeit of the audio variety that allowed for each listener's unique and imaginative interpretation.

On March 24, 1937, *Variety* announced that the marionette and radio show rights to *The Wizard of Oz* had been secured by brother and sister team Fanchon Simon and Marco Wolff, known professionally as Fanchon and Marco. Previously,

2 Fred Stone had retained copies of his Scarecrow costume and the Tin Woodman wardrobe that had been worn by his late partner, David Montgomery. In November 1926 Stone loaned the latter costume to the Brooklyn Heights Players and the Auxiliary Committee of the Junior League for three local performances of *The Wizard of Oz*.

on October 7, 1935, Louella O. Parsons reported that Marco was planning to bring the post-*Wizard* Baum fables to the screen as Technicolor musicals with a modern score by Ann Ronell, who co-wrote "Who's Afraid of the Big Bad Wolf" for Disney. In 1935 such films were possible because Samuel Goldwyn's option on the Oz book rights expired, though the Fanchon and Marco *Oz* productions did not materialize.

The new *Wizard of Oz* radio show was to be broadcast nationally, and as plans moved forward, Fanchon and Marco commissioned fresh music and dispensed with the idea of using the Ann Ronell *Oz* songs originally written for the screen in 1936. On July 30, 1937, Marco received a call from producer Lester Cowan, Ronell's husband and representative, wanting assurances that the new program's writer, John Alcorn, with whom Ronell had previously worked, was not using any ideas supplied by Ronell. (In 1960 Ronell made an unsuccessful pitch to repurpose her six original *Oz* song compositions for a stage production, film, or TV cartoon show titled *The Wonderful Land of Oz*.)

By April 30, 1937, *Radio Daily* noted that auditions were being held for Fanchon and Marco's serialization of *The Wizard of Oz*. Thirteen-year-old vocalist Estelle Levy was cast as Dorothy in the proposed CBS Radio production. Since 1929 Levy had a relationship with CBS as the cohost, with Patricia Ryan, and performer of the children's fairy tale show *Let's Pretend*. By May 26 *Radio Daily* reported that Levy "was tops as Dorothy in the Fanchon and Marco *Wizard of Oz* production" but that the show was being "auditioned" (for sponsors) and hadn't yet aired nationally.[3]

No record of air dates for the *Oz* program could be located, but the jacket notes for the 1939 photoplay edition of *The Wizard of Oz* indicate that the shows were broadcast in December 1938, although *Radio Mirror* for March 1939 announced, "A unique *Wizard of Oz* air show, with original music motivating the action of the entire program, will be presented simultaneously with the release of MGM's Technicolor version of the Oz stories." Display ads for Estelle Levy in 1938–40 editions of *Radio Daily Annual* reference her performances with Eddie Cantor and Kate Smith, and her part in *Les Misérables* for Orson Welles, but they make no mention of her lead role as Dorothy, suggesting perhaps the *Oz* show hadn't yet broadcast.

Episodes One and Seven of the original 1937 radio transcription are known to survive and were obtained by the authors of this book. The first episode encompasses Dorothy's transportation by cyclone to the Land of Oz and her meeting with the Munchkins and Good Witch; the second extant recording follows the misadventures of Dorothy and her

---

3 Estelle Levy remained with *Let's Pretend* until its 1954 cancellation. Using the stage name Gwen Davies, Levy briefly became a big-band vocalist, touring with Bobby Sherwod in 1943, and later recording with Artie Shaw. She was the voice of Casper the Friendly Ghost in three 1950s cartoon shorts, and in 1963 Levy reprised her role as Dorothy for a children's recording of *The Wizard of Oz* on MGM's Leo label.

friends in the poppy field, the rescue of the Queen of the Field Mice, and the Scarecrow's idea for the Tin Man to build a "go-cart" to move the sleeping Cowardly Lion out of the flower bed. Of significance are nuances that seemingly influenced the 1938 development of Metro-Goldwyn-Mayer's production of *The Wizard of Oz*. (MGM was contractually privy to elements from prior versions of *Oz*.)

Each show opens with the rousing march "How Do You Do? Hello!" as a parade of "weird and eerie" Ozian characters ushers forth singing, in part, "We're off to see the greatest things . . ." not unlike "We're Off to See the Wizard" of the future MGM film. This music also becomes the radio characters' theme song on their journey to the Emerald City.

Also as in MGM's *Oz*, the 1937 radio performance adjusts Baum's Munchkin Country to the more succinct Munchkinland, and Dorothy is greeted by an entire party of male and female Munchkins dressed in green (whom she mistakes for boys and girls) instead of three male Munchkins. Neither does the Good Witch of the North sound like the elderly sorceress of the Baum book. Her voice is melodious, she wields a magic wand, and she identifies herself as "Wanda," perhaps granting leave for MGM scenarists to blend this witch with Glinda, the southern sorceress. (Wanda enchants Dorothy's basket so that its provisions are always magically replenished.) The music that accompanies Wanda's entrance is even similar to that of Glinda's theme in the MGM film.

Unlike Frank J. Baum's 1931 radio show, here the Cowardly Lion speaks—and not only does he talk, his one-liners and exaggerated snores while asleep among the poppies must have had bearing on the inspired casting of Bert Lahr in MGM's *The Wizard of Oz* little more than a year later.

Each episode of the 1937 *Wizard of Oz* closes with credits to John Alcorn, as the writer and director, and composer Charles Paul, and his "Munchkin Music Men," for his original score, before acknowledging "This has been a production of the Columbia Broadcasting System [CBS]."

Oz as subject matter for radio was still a viable prospect beyond 1937–38. On July 15, 1939, a month before the premiere of MGM's *The Wizard of Oz*, the trade journal *Broadcasting* reported that Maud Baum had reassigned the radio rights of *all* the Oz books—including those by Ruth Plumly Thompson—to be represented by Hollywood agent Mitchell J. Hamilburg. But this was to be overshadowed by the spectacular standard soon to be set by the greatest incarnation of *Oz* to date.

FANTASY IN FILM LAND

During the early 1930s, MGM had expressed interest in the cartoon rights to the Oz books, and the press hinted that a cartoon series might piggyback with Samuel Goldwyn's production. Among the last such notices was this entry from the Screen Reporter syndicated column of November 8, 1935: "Famed Oz stories will come to the screen first as animated cartoons as a build-up to a feature with human actors."

But where capturing cinematic whimsy was concerned, the contributions of Walt Disney's vision, power, and purview cannot be underestimated. It was, after all, Disney's *Flowers and Trees* that inspired Goldwyn to acquire the film rights to *The Wizard of Oz*, and it was another Disney success that would renew interest in Oz once again in 1938. On July 28 of that year, Irving Hoffman, writing for the *Hollywood Reporter*, put Disney's contemporary acclaim into perspective:

> We don't believe that Disney's artistry requires any justification. In months it has acquired an appreciation by the public that came to old masters only after years of existence. In their day it is doubtful if any of the great names in art echoed through the halls more loudly than that of Disney does today. His popularity and universal acceptance is sufficient proof that he talks with every tongue and is "Walt" to all the world.

By early 1934 Disney was on the precipice of a major cinematic innovation: creation of his first feature-length animated film. The result was *Snow White and the Seven Dwarfs*, which premiered in Los Angeles at the Carthay Circle Theatre on December 21, 1937. (Director-producer Mervyn LeRoy was among the VIPs in attendance, as was fifteen-year-old singer-actress Judy Garland.) *Snow White* broke nationally in February 1938 and continued playing until April 1939 when it was strategically withdrawn from circulation.

Critics were virtually unanimous in their praise of *Snow White and the Seven Dwarfs*, and seldomly applied laurels like "masterpiece," "classic," and "inspired" were commonplace. In the *Los Angeles Times*, Edwin Schallert called it "a motion picture miracle," and industry trade journal *Boxoffice* declared it "the most important picture from a production perspective since the advent of sound." *Snow White* landed Disney on the cover of *Time* magazine six days after its debut, elevating him to movie mogul status. Within its first three months, *Snow White* was seen by approximately twenty million people.

But beyond critical success, the picture was reaping serious money. Within its first months in domestic release (US and Canada), *Snow White and the Seven Dwarfs* was on its way to grossing upwards of three million dollars in Depression-era money, as *The Film Daily* noted the following June 6 in a piece on the film's record-breaking success. On February 19, 1938, the *Hollywood Reporter* projected that the Disney film could accrue anywhere between six million and eight million dollars in international grosses. (By March 1939 *Snow White*'s international take was made public, adding an estimated $6.5 million more to its domestic gross.) The ensuing proliferation of related character merchandise (dolls, toys, games, and novelties) from 117 companies, combined with its box-office grosses, not only financed Disney's future artistic aspirations, it built his new state-of-the-art Burbank studio—all of which caused the major motion picture studios (and their financial investors and stockholders) to seriously reconsider the viability of film fantasy, so far Disney's exclusive territory.

According to the *Hollywood Reporter* on February 19, 1938:

The success of Walt Disney's *Snow White* has caused all other major producers and distributors to dig around for material and production for one or more cartoon features in color . . . Paramount went into a huddle in New York yesterday and came out with a decision for Max Fleischer to start work immediately on the search for a story that will fit both the child and adult taste for a feature cartoon. . . . MGM, both here and in New York, has been considering such a subject for its program, with the needed production facilities built within its own organization. [MGM had ninety-five cartoonists per the *Hollywood Reporter*, April 8, 1938.]

Not only were cartoons under consideration, live-action fantasies starring film favorites were also being eyed. "All the [film] companies are looking for fairy tales," Virginia Vale summarized in her Star Dust column for March 25, 1938, "and as fast as they find them, all the younger stars from Shirley Temple to Deanna Durbin will be put to work in them."

"Though he had nothing directly to do with it," wrote Kenneth McCaleb in his August 13, 1939, review of *The Wizard of Oz* for the New York *Sunday Mirror*, "Mr. Walt Disney undeniably must take a slight bow for the impetus *Snow White and the Seven Dwarfs* gave to the production of nursery tales. . . . *The Wizard of Oz* might not have been made had not the public accepted *Snow White* so warmly and registered its approval of child classics." And while the Disney influence on Metro-Goldwyn-Mayer's *Oz* is undeniable, new research reflects that the influence was more than incidental.

In *Snow White* Disney offered an innocent and sweetly soprano heroine; dwarfs as comic relief; spooky trees; a scheming, spell-casting witch who—in true fairy-tale tradition—is dispatched in the climax; romance; and a sentimental conclusion. For producers seeking to cash in on replicating *Snow White*'s appeal, sparingly few classics of children's literature could proffer similar plot elements—gnomes, incantations, enchanted woods, witches, and a nubile maiden—and measure up as screen musicals. Still, the rush was on as a slew of literary adaptations were announced. Warner Bros.' animator Leon Schlesinger was interested in *Rip Van Winkle*, another bit of folklore replete with its own horde of bearded imps. Schlesinger got the jump, turning out *Have You Got Any Castles?* in June 1938, his Merrie Melodies riff on famous book characters including its center of interest, Rip Van Winkle.

Two remaining tales with little people might also compete with Disney's wildly popular dwarfs, being *Gulliver's Travels*, with its Lilliputians, and the Munchkins of *The Wizard of Oz*. Both novels either contained—or could be manipulated to contain—satire, romance, heartache, and a good dose of suspense. In fact, by the time of MGM's *Oz*, Prince Denis, one of the Munchkin little people, told reporter W. Ward Marsh that "Mervyn LeRoy, the director-producer, wanted to do *Gulliver's Travels* with us, but that had been taken for the cartoon film." As it happened, *Gulliver's Travels* became the second feature-length animated film, produced by Max Fleischer and released in December 1939.

Walt Disney himself was considering another fairyland production with a young heroine, a cartoon *Alice in Wonderland* true to Sir John Tenniel's classic sketches. In addition, Disney was developing *Pinocchio*, *Bambi*, and *The Little Mermaid*. But even as *Snow White* was in production, the call went out for Disney to add L. Frank Baum to his list. "Of course you can see the almost limitless possibilities in colored animated cartoons," wrote *Pittsburgh (PA) Post-Gazette* columnist Virginia Helene in September 1935. "*The Wizard of Oz* would be a happy choice for a Disney feature." Immediately following *Snow White*'s success, Philip K. Scheuer pleaded with Walt Disney, in his January 2, 1938, Hollywood editorial, to set aside plans for *Pinocchio* and *Bambi* in favor of taking on one of the Oz stories. One anonymous newspaper editor referenced the Oz books in his syndicated speculations for Disney's future animated interpretations on February 11, 1938. "It is pleasant to look ahead of Walt Disney and the things he is doing with his whimsical characters in the amusement world. . . . Remember the Wizard of Oz stories, the Knights of the Round Table, the journeys of Ulysses? A modern whimsical art can bring them to life for millions of children and grown-ups. And somehow it doesn't seem probable the original authors would mind." Also, in 1938 Florence Fisher Parry, writing for the *Pittsburgh (PA) Press*, called for a serialization of *Wizard of Oz* cartoons under Disney's supervision, whom she lauded as a universal storyteller come to earth to lead children into fairyland.

Such public appeal for a fresh remounting of *The Wizard of Oz* did not go unnoticed at Walt Disney Productions. "An analysis of our fan mail over the past two or three years reveals the fact that there are more requests for us to adapt the Oz books than for any other material," began an internal memo to Walt, accompanied by a three-page synopsis of *The Wizard* submitted on February 12, 1938. In an anticipatory move typical of most studios, Disney's story-development department had been engrossed in fleshing out a screen treatment for *The Wizard of Oz* while investigating the other thirteen Frank Baum Oz novels, despite not owning any rights.

As a follow-up to *Snow White*, *The Wizard of Oz* was unanimously deigned best suited in Walt Disney's hands. By early 1938 Disney made it known publically that he was interested in Oz as a future project. "Disney wants to do the story as a feature cartoon," reported the *New Masses*, "but to date has not been able to get the rights." On the heels of *Snow White*'s triumph, *Liberty* magazine also noted, "He would like to get the rights to *The Wizard of Oz*, but Paramount owns them [*sic*], and, so far, refuses to sell." Meanwhile, F. Scott Fitzgerald, novelist of *The Great Gatsby*, was writing scripts at MGM and, in January 1938, Hollywood columnist Sheilah Graham reported that the author wanted to draft *The Wizard of Oz* as a comedy treatment for the Marx Brothers, with whom he was chummy.

The Wizard of Oz, however, was still owned by Samuel Goldwyn, but that was all about to change. By late 1937 United Artists' founding members were scheming to sell off their company stock, buy out Goldwyn as an investor (and one of their independent producers), and sell the business to another film company. A prospective takeover deal by Goldwyn and director Alexander Korda had just fallen through in December 1937 and, by January, no equable resolve was in sight.

During this bitter impasse Goldwyn retreated to Honolulu and entered into a self-imposed hiatus, momentarily disenchanted with the picture-making business. Upon his return stateside in late January, Goldwyn began divesting his story properties, selling to Columbia *Murder in Massachusetts*, New England crime journalist Joseph Dineen's reportorial exposé of police injustice. Most significantly, he also began entertaining offers on *The Wizard of Oz*, and a bidding war fast ensued. By this time Goldwyn had obviously cooled on the notion of an *Oz* picture of his own. As Louella O. Parsons noted, Goldwyn consented to part with the *Oz* rights because he had no juvenile star on his roster, his contract with Marcia Mae Jones having expired without renewal. Goldwyn otherwise had definite plans for producing another fantasy: *Once Upon a Time*, based on the life of fairy-tale author Hans Christian Andersen, a film that was eventually made as *Hans Christian Andersen* starring Danny Kaye in 1952.

THE YELLOW BRICK ROAD LEADS TO MGM

Metro-Goldwyn-Mayer may have been tipped off that Samuel Goldwyn was intending to sell *The Wizard of Oz*, particularly if Goldwyn was aware that the property was prized by Mervyn LeRoy. And there is a likelihood that this may have been so.

In 1937 LeRoy was at the top of his game. He was known as the "genius of Warner Bros." and his attributes, as described by the *Film Daily*, included "young, keen, natural showman, resourceful and progressive"—precisely what Metro needed as a successor to the late Irving Thalberg, MGM's head of production who had died suddenly in September 1936 at age thirty-seven.

LeRoy's films for Warner Bros., like *Little Caesar* (1931), *I am a Fugitive from a Chain Gang* (1932), *Gold Diggers of 1933* (1933), and *Anthony Adverse* (1936), not only enjoyed critical and popular success, they were consistently recognized with Oscar nominations by the Academy of Motion Picture Arts and Sciences. LeRoy possessed technical vision for the medium as well, predicting to the *San Francisco Examiner* in October 1937 that black-and-white movies would eventually give way to all-color films. But by then LeRoy was restless at Warner Bros., seeking greater independence in his creative ventures (that October he purchased film rights to *The Fourth Estate*, a newspaper story that caught his eye). He also desired to escape the undercurrent that he had it soft because he was the son-in-law of Warner Bros. co-founder Harry Warner, LeRoy's wife being Warner's daughter, Doris.

A personal and professional rapport between Samuel Goldwyn and LeRoy dated to 1931 when Goldwyn tapped LeRoy to pinch-hit three weeks of direction for A. Edward Sutherland on *Palmy Days* with Eddie Cantor. The picture was one of the biggest hits of the year, and Goldwyn requested that LeRoy next direct *Tonight or Never* with Gloria Swanson the same year. Of his admiration for Goldwyn, LeRoy said, "I always found Sam Goldwyn to be a man of great taste, and truly one of the finest producers Hollywood has ever seen." In reciprocation Goldwyn affectionately called LeRoy "Mervy," but with Goldwyn's Yiddish accent it came out sounding like "Moiphy."

Personally, the two moguls were known to play poker together, and professionally they swapped writers and players with each other. LeRoy loaned two of his contracted protégés to Goldwyn in August 1937: radio crooner Kenny Baker for *Goldwyn Follies* and teenage sensation Lana Turner for *The Adventures of Marco Polo*. Likewise in August 1937 LeRoy contracted with Goldwyn for the loan of Billy Halop and five other tough boys from Goldwyn's *Dead End* for LeRoy's proposed picture *Heroes of the Streets*.

Goldwyn remained impressed with LeRoy's stellar capabilities well enough to invite the young director-producer to join him in September 1937 as a business partner in a proposed triumvirate Goldwyn-Korda-LeRoy takeover of United Artists during the protracted, months-long tug-of-war with UA's founders (though within a month, LeRoy called his participation in such a deal "very remote").

After rumors circulated in late October 1937 that LeRoy was being courted by RKO Radio Pictures for its head of production, the *Film Daily* announced on November 12, 1937, that LeRoy had signed a contract to join Metro-Goldwyn-Mayer.[4] It was understood that he would serve in the same capacity as Irving Thalberg had, as head of all production activities on the lot, and that he would report directly to Louis B. Mayer, MGM's shrewd, manipulative, and patriarchal vice president.[5] Of LeRoy's transfer to MGM, *Photoplay*

---

4 LeRoy's 1937 contract with MGM was for seven years, and he renewed in 1944.

5 Mayer's reputation has been polarized over time, but in a 1997 interview with the authors, actor Mickey Rooney was adamant: "The only time they can shit and lie about you is when you're dead. 'He's dead. Terrible, awful man!' *He can't defend himself.* He was the *nicest* man in the world."

editor Ruth Waterbury observed on January 15, 1938, "I don't mean to indicate that MGM is grabbing all the production brains, though with the addition of this stalwart they have a good start at it . . . Mervyn did some very fine things at Warners . . . daring things like *They Won't Forget* . . . he is a man of quick, worldly talent, of charm and keen intelligence, and it will be interesting to watch him."

In his newly appointed position and at an unprecedented yearly salary of three hundred thousand dollars, LeRoy would personally oversee production of six features annually, of which he would direct two. LeRoy had been on the Metro lot previously, first in 1930 to direct *Two Little Girls Together* (a project that became 1931's *Gentleman's Fate* with John Gilbert and Anita Page), and, in 1933, Wallace Beery and Marie Dressler for the hit *Tugboat Annie*. His physical transfer to MGM would be delayed until Monday, February 15, 1938, as he still owed Warner Bros. another picture before his contract expired.

But LeRoy may have been distracted. His *Fools for Scandal*, a comedy with Carole Lombard and Fernand Gravet, was a resounding flop for Warner Bros. when it was released the following March, and it was considered a career setback for Lombard. By then Harold W. Cohen, *Pittsburgh (PA) Post-Gazette* entertainment journalist, projected, "Mervyn

LeRoy's *The Wizard of Oz* . . . will make you forget he was the same fellow who made *Fools for Scandal*." In discussions with L. B. Mayer prior to his 1937 contract, LeRoy reportedly mentioned his desire to produce and direct a modern musical version of *The Wizard of Oz*. In 1939 LeRoy wrote, "Shortly after I came to Metro-Goldwyn-Mayer, a studio which is willing to get away from formula pictures and weave expense and time into an idea, I found Louis B. Mayer was 'sold' on the idea. That's all I needed. We started work."

However, LeRoy's first projects under his new MGM unit were *Dramatic School*, a romance with Luise Rainer, Gale Sondergaard, and Lana Turner; and *Stand Up and Fight* with Wallace Beery and Robert Taylor. *The Wizard of Oz* was nameless among "an ambitious group of pictures . . . slated to come under [LeRoy's] jurisdiction during the current year."[6]

In late 1937 Arthur Freed was an MGM lyricist whose hits, cowritten with Nacio Herb Brown, included "Singin' in the Rain," "All I Do Is Dream of You," and "You Are My Lucky Star." Freed possessed a fierce determination to produce films, and his zeal—referred to cynically as overzealousness by some of his contemporaries—allowed him to ingratiate L. B. Mayer's inner circle.

Like LeRoy, Freed claimed he was also keenly interested in *The Wizard of Oz* and foresaw it as both his inaugural project as a film producer and as the breakout vehicle for a blossoming MGM talent in which he held a great personal and professional investment: Judy Garland. But Freed's interest in *The Wizard of Oz* may not have been entirely his own impetus. On April 6, 1938, after MGM had acquired *Oz*, *Variety* noted that the property had been "one of the pet ideas Irving Thalberg had mulled up until his death." Composer Harry Warren recalled, "[Freed] got kind of chummy with L.B. Mayer. And I don't know what happened. Something happened. . . . He kept palling around with L.B. Mayer, and first thing you know . . . they say he said, 'Let's make *The Wizard of Oz*. . . . '" (Following the picture's success, Warren observed that Freed became "L.B. Mayer's fair-haired boy.")

At the time of *Oz*, however, Freed lacked producing experience and was devoid of the pivotal, decision-making clout such experience warranted. L. B. Mayer refused Freed's overtures to produce *Oz*, declined LeRoy's request to both produce and direct the picture, and posited Freed as an apprentice to LeRoy (the two men were acquainted with each other from more than a decade prior). Freed would become LeRoy's unbilled production aide with the understanding that Freed would cut his teeth on *Oz* before launching his

---

6 On March 30, 1938, the weekly edition of *Variety* reported that Bernie Hyman, MGM producer of *San Francisco, Camille, and Saratoga*, would be taking on both *Northwest Passage* and *The Wizard of Oz* as upcoming projects. This was the only time for which Mervyn LeRoy was not mentioned as the *Oz* producer; and as Hyman was associated with neither *Oz* nor *Northwest Passage* (1940), it may be concluded that the report is erroneous.

own production unit at Metro, overseen by LeRoy as production head. Sans LeRoy in the director's seat, *The Wizard of Oz* would need a pilot who could translate its whimsy to the silver screen, not to mention a competent cast of characters who could breathe life into L. Frank Baum's fictional creatures.

Just prior to Samuel Goldwyn auctioning the *Oz* screen rights, Arthur Freed drafted a preliminary cast list for *The Wizard of Oz* on January 31, 1938, and he ostensibly did so with the knowledge that LeRoy would soon be relocating to MGM. Of course, Judy Garland was at the top of Freed's suggested list, as were MGM contract players Ray Bolger and Buddy Ebsen, known primarily for their distinctive, eccentric dance moves and musical-comedy approach (the two were paired in Metro's *The Girl of the Golden West*, released the following March). In particular, Ebsen was described in April 1938 as the "white Stepin Fetchit" for his slow, lazy style of dancing—an allusion to comedian and actor Lincoln Theodore Monroe Andrew Perry, who popularly personified notions of African-American stereotypes in films throughout the 1920s and '30s.

Freed's tentative cast notes were almost certainly an optimistic projection for Metro's acquisition of *Oz* from Samuel Goldwyn, knowing that sale of the rights was pending and that LeRoy would helm the production if MGM successfully purchased the property. Since Kenny Baker was under contract to LeRoy, Freed suggested the singer as "a prince" in *Oz* as it was expected that Baker's crooning talents be exploited where possible. At the time Baker's popularity rated alongside Bing Crosby, Dick Powell, and Nelson Eddy. As *Radio Mirror* reported in 1937, Baker was "tied so tightly by his Mervyn LeRoy contract he practically has to ask permission to sneeze, and the lads on the [Jack] Benny [radio] show delight in ribbing him about his wet-nurse."

In addition to Baker, Fernand Gravet, and Lana Turner, also under contract to LeRoy were composer Adolph Deutsch, actor Allyn Joslyn, and New York photographer's model-turned-actress Vickie Lester.

Previous *Wizard of Oz* histories have magnified the contributions of Arthur Freed to the detriment of Mervyn LeRoy, *Oz*'s executive producer. LeRoy himself was cognizant of a burgeoning imbalance in the retelling of how the picture came to be acquired, especially as Freed claimed that L. B. Mayer green-lighted Freed's desire to purchase the book property, according to Freed's biographer, Hugh Fordin. While Freed may have acted upon Mayer's directive to acquire the property—via mobster-turned-agent Frank Orsatti, a close friend of Mayer's—he omitted that it was for Mervyn LeRoy and not himself.

Toward the end of his life, LeRoy adamantly asserted his place in film history. "Mr. Mayer bought the book for *me*," he reiterated to journalist Aljean Harmetz for her book, *The Making of The Wizard of Oz*. "I wanted to make a movie out of *The Wizard of Oz* from the time I was a kid. I'm getting sick of hearing about Arthur Freed and *The Wizard of Oz*. Arthur Freed's name isn't on the picture. Mine is . . . I never took credit for anything that didn't belong to me. But *I* produced that picture." (LeRoy could well have been remembering a *TV Guide* article that coincided with the March 1970 broadcast of *Oz* in which Freed was described as a "budding producer at MGM" who acquired the film rights from Samuel Goldwyn—with nary a mention of LeRoy.)

LeRoy's near invalidation in modern *Oz* history seems more a campaign to promote Freed's long association with Judy Garland and her MGM career. Freed retained his papers, held in the archives of the Academy of Motion Picture Arts and Sciences; LeRoy did not retain his papers, which skews the perspective of researchers. What is certain is that LeRoy relied upon Freed during *Oz*'s preproduction and generously allowed Freed to take the lead—pending LeRoy's approval—in the areas of casting suggestions and, particularly, script and song development.

While Freed's genius was integral to the creation of MGM's quintessential film musicals, his assistance on *The Wizard of Oz* was very much an internal affair. He is neither mentioned nor quoted in any of MGM's original publicity materials for *Oz* or in periodicals of the day. Only one official *Oz* publicity still pictures him during the preproduction phase, and he was unidentified or edited from it when MGM reproduced the photograph in 1939. And an exhaustive search of national newspaper and trade journal archives dating from 1938 failed to identify Freed's *Oz* connection—except in a singular April 1938 instance—until a 1975 career retrospective, Fordin's *The World of Entertainment*, was published, for which Freed was interviewed.

The notion that Freed had instant carte blanche after *Oz* is also unfounded. A July 29, 1939, write-up about Mervyn LeRoy in *Daily Variety* noted that LeRoy "also had supervision over *Babes in Arms*, on which Arthur Freed was producer," confirming that Freed remained accountable to LeRoy, as head of production, during Freed's tenure on *Babes*. Further evidence of LeRoy's corporate influence over Freed at this time came with the prominent placement of Meredythe Glass, LeRoy's cousin, as an extra among the cast of *Babes*'s teenage performers.

To grant further perspective on how history became distorted, one need only to examine the personalities of Arthur Freed and Mervyn LeRoy. Freed was not universally admired by his colleagues. He has been described by a number of sources as overly ambitious. "If [L.B.] Mayer's ass itched, Freed scratched," noted Harmetz of a Freed detractor. He was also known to be sexually lecherous. Shirley Temple Black's exemplary anecdote in *Child Star*, her autobiography, tells of Freed exposing himself to her in 1941 when she was twelve. Freed was also grandiose: 1952's *Singin' in the Rain* was conceived for the purpose of recycling Freed's songbook. With this awareness, it is not difficult to understand how Freed would have highlighted his contributions to *The Wizard of Oz* to his advantage, especially the property's acquisition, and in reflection of his rise to prominence as MGM's most gifted and prolific producer.

Mervyn LeRoy, on the other hand, was a man of slight stature with a tendency to stutter when he wasn't directing or concentrating. He was variously reported to stand five feet six inches, five feet seven, and five feet seven and a half, although he was likely closer to the foremost measurement in height. In 1937 the *San Francisco Examiner* referred to LeRoy as a "pint of genius," and in his November 28, 1938, column, Hollywood correspondent Ed Sullivan cracked that LeRoy had taken to walking on his tiptoes to avoid being inadvertently photographed in one of *Oz*'s Munchkin scenes. Regardless, it was LeRoy's extraordinary talent that had made him internationally renowned.

The popular and critical reception of LeRoy's *Anthony Adverse* led to a print ad in which he endorsed Dictaphone, a transcription device; and before transferring to Metro, LeRoy would also pitch Bell & Howell's Filmo camera. But his office at MGM was not the digs of someone on a power trip. In 1939 LeRoy's quarters were described by *Photoplay*'s Cal York as "nice, attractive and unpretentious." LeRoy's Thoroughbred racehorse was Mad Sue, who could have just as easily been rechristened Mad *About* Sue; LeRoy's office decor reflected his passion for ponies and featured framed prints of horses on the walls, a couple of lampshades decorated with horse drawings, and a pair of horse-head bookends on his desk. By contrast, Metro makeup artist Jack Young remembered that the commode in L. B. Mayer's office was "constructed of the softest leather which completely surrounded the porcelain bowl. Legend has it that decisions were finalized there during meditation."

At the time, LeRoy was still stuck with an albatross, being long ago nicknamed Hollywood's "boy director" for his adolescent looks. (LeRoy's ubiquitous cigar did little to diminish this perception.) It was a moniker he struggled to overcome as much as he was impelled by a drive to achieve and rise above his destitute beginnings. LeRoy's father had gone bankrupt after the San Francisco earthquake of 1906, and to make ends meet, LeRoy worked as a newsboy who hung around stage doors of the theaters to which he delivered papers. An affinity for singing led to talent shows and the vaudeville circuit. From there he worked his way up in Hollywood as costumer, camera assistant, gag writer, and silent film actor before landing his directorial debut in 1927. In short order, his sense for what made compelling screen entertainment manifested in a succession of acclaimed films.

More than a decade later, the seasoned LeRoy told *Photoplay* journalist Cal York that a good feature is one that will make an audience sit on the edge of its seat. "A good picture either has novelty or dynamite," he told York, adding that he always tries for both. In 1953 LeRoy attributed his success as a director and producer to "hard work and vision and heart." However, pursuing his artifice ventures often required risk-taking. "Mervyn always had the vision," affirmed his cousin Meredythe Glass. "He picked things like *I Am a Fugitive from a Chain Gang* that nobody else would touch in those days and he made them come true." But LeRoy retained the humble demeanor of his roots, as Hedda Hopper observed in her 1941 career retrospective of the producer-director. "There is nothing egotistical about him," she wrote. "He came up the hard way and he knows every knock of the picture business."

Making *The Wizard of Oz* come true had long been an aspiration for LeRoy. His ambition to adapt *The Wizard of Oz* as a lavish, full-color musical was motivated by a boyhood fondness for the Frank Baum book and memories of having seen a road-show production of the theatrical extravaganza. MGM's 1939 publicity serialization about the making of *Oz* noted, "LeRoy had read *The Wizard of Oz* as a boy and had followed it with other of L. Frank Baum's adventures in Oz." More than hyperbole, in a 1974 interview with KCET's *Day at Night* in Los Angeles, LeRoy said, "I always loved the Oz books. In fact, I have the original Oz books that I had when I was eight or nine years old. I still have the books for my grandchildren and my kids." In 1939 LeRoy was tickled that the book was published in the same year he was born and remembered, "The story undoubtedly appealed to me as a boy primarily because it is so human." And he waxed ecstatic about fantasy in general when he told *Australian Women's Weekly*, "The fairy tale offers to harassed modern minds that most tender of virtues, simplicity. It is more elemental and more imaginative than the dramas of the sophisticated. The fairy tale has been humanity's first and most abiding fiction." (LeRoy would have been particularly sensitive to all things reminiscent of childhood during *Oz*'s preproduction. His first child, son Warner, was three years old in March 1938, and his second child, daughter Linda, was born April 17, 1938.)

Pinpointing the precise date when Samuel Goldwyn began auctioning *The Wizard of Oz* is difficult. There was no formal announcement in the trades, but it seems likely the bidding began on or about the third week in February 1938. If Walt Disney was a serious contender, he wasn't showing his hand. On Friday, February 11, 1938, Disney replied to a letter about *Snow White* from screenwriter Frank "Spig" Wead. Wead had also enquired if Walt had ever considered animating the Oz stories. In his response Disney made no mention of trying to obtain the *Oz* motion picture rights and only indicated that every so often he did some serious thinking on the subject but had no definite plans; although Disney acknowledged the fan mail his studio received about the Oz series suggested a keen popularity. Indeed, *Variety* for February 23 reported that *The Wizard of Oz* and *Alice in Wonderland* were tops among the most "highly desirable" of fairy-tale properties sought for cartooning in the wake of *Snow White*'s success.

Where *Oz* was concerned, Edwin Schallert noted in his column for Friday, February 18, 1938, that within the past week, Samuel Goldwyn had received "no fewer than five large offers" for the property, and this was reiterated in *Variety*. It was also mentioned that Twentieth Century Fox, though unequipped to tackle an animated feature, had put in a bid with Goldwyn to buy *Oz* and make it as a "regular feature," not a cartoon, starring Shirley Temple. A February 21, 1938, report in the *Decatur (IL) Daily Review* also supported the probability of a live-action approach: "It seems likely that *Wizard of Oz* will be brought to the screen now, the right to screening having been owned by one studio for five years. It would have flesh and blood actors while *Snow White* has cartoon characters." There was also speculation at this time that Samuel Goldwyn might want to inaugurate a cartoon version of *Oz* himself though UA could confirm no such plans.

If Goldwyn was seriously reconsidering *Oz* or merely bluffing, he readily acquiesced on both counts. Sale of the motion picture rights to *The Wizard of Oz* happened very quickly and within roughly a week's time. By February 18, 1938, an internal MGM memo documented that a deal with Goldwyn "had closed for the purchase by us of *The Wizard of Oz*," although a check to Goldwyn was only cut four months later. Metro's bid of seventy-five thousand dollars had superseded all other offers for the motion picture rights to *Oz*, surpassing Twentieth Century Fox's bid to acquire the story for Shirley Temple. Perhaps Goldwyn was assuaged with knowing that the property went to the studio that still bore his name and would be developed by his friend and colleague, Mervyn LeRoy.

Concurring with the majority consensus that *Oz* should be animated, Hollywood columnist Paul Harrison was miffed. "I hope the ghost of L. Frank Baum gives Samuel Goldwyn a good haunting for not selling the rights to the Oz books to Walt Disney." But Disney was undaunted by the news of Metro's acquisition, as animated cartoons were a distinctly separate medium from live-action motion pictures. In early April 1938, Roy Disney—Walt's brother and business manager—approached Maud Baum, author L. Frank Baum's widow, for the rights to Oz cartoons. But Mrs. Baum found the Disneys untrustworthy; they wanted to buy up the remaining Oz stories only to stave off competitors.

Walt Disney did eventually acquire the screen rights to eleven of the Oz books in 1954, following Maud Baum's death the previous year. The titles not included were *The Land of Oz* and *Dorothy and the Wizard in Oz*, the latter of which was owned by low-budget filmmaker Robert Lippert as of March 30, 1951. On September 21, 1953, *Motion Picture Daily* noted that by the following spring, Lippert planned to produce the Oz book in a joint venture with a German company using Ansco color film. Lippert also intended to alter the book's title to *Dorothy and the Land of Oz* to avoid any conflict with MGM's *The Wizard of Oz*. Lippert's Oz film never materialized and Walt Disney was considering a live-action Oz musical titled *The Rainbow Road to Oz* featuring the popular Mouseketeers of television fame. In December 1956 Disney reportedly paid Lippert as much to acquire rights to *Dorothy and the Wizard in Oz* as he did in total for the eleven Oz books already in his purview in order to preserve the exclusivity of his Oz properties. *The Rainbow Road to Oz* also went unrealized, although three preliminary production numbers from it were televised on *Disneyland* on September 11, 1957.

In 1938, however, Maud Baum was disillusioned by Walt Disney and subsequently negotiated an agreement with Kenneth McLellan, another animator whom she deemed "honest." Ultimately, McLellan was unable to secure financial backing and his Oz cartoons were abandoned.

That Hollywood should tamper with the beloved *Wizard of Oz* once again made Baum devotees nervous. The editor for the *Provo (UT) Evening Herald* took MGM to task on October 12, 1938:

> Let the producers remember this: Millions and millions of men and women grew up reading copies of *The Wizard of Oz* until the books fell apart in our hands. . . . If the movie moguls decide to clutter up the picture with expensive dance routines with lines of undraped beauties and revolving stages it would spoil the whole effect. Still worse would be any attempt to improve the plot by sticking in some silly love story. . . . There is one rule Hollywood can follow . . . keep the entire production simple and unpretentious . . . so that it will be almost as good as the immortal *Snow White*. If that rule is broken, *The Wizard of Oz* may flop.

Decades of TV broadcasts and home-viewing technologies have since brought *The Wizard of Oz* fame and familiarity surpassing that of *Snow White*. Yet such was not the case in 1938 when it was Disney's opus that set the standard by which any future attempts at capturing storybook fluff on celluloid would be judged. Although Mervyn LeRoy's *Oz* was intended to have a human cast, there was general uncertainty as to what extent animation might augment the actors. Comedienne Fanny Brice referred her young protégé, Mrs. Darryl Austin, to Mervyn LeRoy once she learned that Austin painted watercolors of fairy-tale scenes. (Brice had been singled out by Arthur Freed as a prospect for one of Oz's good witches.) LeRoy was intrigued enough to send for Mrs. Austin's art, after which *Motion Picture* magazine reported, "Don't be surprised if a lady called Austin does the cartoons for [Oz]." The July 30, 1938, issue of the *Science Fiction Newsletter* even announced that *The Wizard of Oz* "is being done [in] picture and cartoon form," and indeed several early special effects and an opening-titles concept were to be cartooned.

But in 1938 Metro-Goldwyn-Mayer's animation department was rudimentary in contrast with Walt Disney's efficient and, according to his dissenters, Machiavellian caste system of painters, inkers, animators, and background artists. *Oz* would not, could not, be animated by Metro and still capture *Snow White*'s moviegoing (and repeat-viewing) audience with any timeliness, particularly in an era when motion picture production was fast and furious. *Snow White and the Seven Dwarfs* was three full years in process, and a modernized cartoon unit at MGM was only installed in September 1939, with William Hanna and Joe Barbera at the helm. Between late February and early March 1938, the press revealed what Metro had planned from the onset: that *The Wizard of Oz* would be filmed "with real people." MGM's *Oz* would be a live-action musical *simulating* a cartoon, as its executive producer Mervyn LeRoy decreed, and Metro was prepared to meet the challenge.

It was a risky gamble to rival Walt Disney, held in highest esteem by Mervyn LeRoy, who in later years stated that Disney was one of only two geniuses he had ever met; the other was Irving Thalberg. In fact it was LeRoy who conceived the standard-size Oscar complemented by seven miniature versions when Disney was honored for *Snow White* at the eleventh annual Academy Awards in February 1939. Historically, film fantasies played with actors were tenuous turf. Metro's own *Babes in Toyland* (1934), while a musical fantasy, was essentially another Hal Roach showcase for comic team Laurel and Hardy. Warner Bros.' 1935 *A Midsummer Night's Dream*, though visually sumptuous, did little to further the genre and did less for Warner's entrée into the costly "prestige picture" realm.

Primary to be considered, though, was the resounding box-office failure of Paramount's live-action *Alice in Wonderland* only a few years before—the last such screen fantasy to precede *The Wizard of Oz*. (*Alice* premiered at Christmas 1933 and was still circulating as late as 1936.)

As satire for adults, Lewis Carroll's Alice books have frequently proven unsatisfying as motion picture interpretations, and Paramount's attempt was marred threefold. With little prior experience and limited range, Charlotte Henry in the leading role is pleasant enough but lacks star presence. Instead of a central conflict or advancing quest, *Alice*'s screenplay is a string of disconnected episodes; its minor musical interludes are unmemorable. And its well-known players, including Cary Grant, W. C. Fields, and Gary Cooper (Bing Crosby opted out over a salary dispute), are indistinguishable in grotesque masks and character makeup. As the reviewer for *New Movie* magazine succinctly observed of *Alice*'s actors, "You don't appreciate how important a thing facial expression is until there isn't any."

When Walt Disney announced plans for an animated *Alice* in March 1938, he went public with his disdain for Paramount's version, telling the *New York Times*, "*Alice in Wonderland* should never have been done in the realistic medium of motion picture but we regard it as a natural for our medium." Despite an embedded cartoon segment retelling "The Walrus and the Carpenter," *Alice* was deemed by nearly all to be "a film so bad that it could be counted only as a warning" as Paul Harrison cautioned Mervyn LeRoy about his *Wizard of Oz*.

LeRoy's difficulty was to avoid the pitfalls of *Alice in Wonderland* and manifest a production that would be heralded with similar reverence as *Snow White*, the work that had refueled his impetus for *Oz* as an adult. And the expectation to pull it off came from all directions—Hollywood insiders, stockholders, columnists, and newspaper editors nationwide. From the Hollywood contingent, Louella O. Parsons set the tone in her March 6, 1938, column: "Now it's up to Mervyn LeRoy and Metro-Goldwyn-Mayer to show the world that human stars in *The Wizard of Oz* can do as well as cartoon characters." For mainstream America, Charlie Ellis, entertainment editor of the *Abilene (TX) Reporter-News*, echoed the general consensus in his March 15, 1938, editorial:

> Now comes notice from Hollywood that MGM will screen the old fairy-tale favorite, *The Wizard of Oz*. Such notice would have been met with approval . . . had the announcement been made that *Oz* would be in cartoon form. But it won't be. . . . Why is it that producers can't stick to the most appropriate medium? A full-length cartoon of *The Wizard of Oz* would be hailed probably as the masterpiece that *Snow White* definitely is.

On the same date, March 15, 1938, both *Daily Variety* and the *Film Daily* listed *The Wizard of Oz* as among three upcoming Technicolor pictures planned by MGM—including *Twenty Thousand Leagues Under the Sea*, which was not produced. With the picture on Metro's schedule, Mervyn LeRoy wrestled with the minutiae of its adaptation. As he reflected in a piece written for the *Brooklyn (NY) Daily Eagle* days prior to *Oz*'s East Coast debut:

> Until *Snow White*, full use of imagination had never actually been possible in the making of a motion picture. . . . Everyone who has read *The Wizard of Oz* has his own idea of what places and characters look like, how they sound to the ear . . . That is where the fun began. Brains worked overtime settling problems of pure imagination. After all, there are no tin men or straw men running around to be cornered and studied. No one has ever seen a lion cry. Who has ever been whirled around inside a cyclone and lived to tell what it looked and sounded like inside that twister? And just how does a straw man—or a tin man—sound when he walks?

Regardless of the film medium or the method of production, it was clear that the standard of expectation had been set, and public pressure for LeRoy to match—if not succeed—Walt Disney was on even before a script was drafted.

PART TWO
CREATION

Role Call

Child star extraordinaire Shirley Temple would have been a logical choice to play Dorothy in a live-action production of *The Wizard of Oz* during the mid- to late 1930s. Not only was she at the height of her screen popularity, she could carry a tune with childish charm; could hold her own against the terpsichorean talents of adult costars; and, given her tender years and blonde curls, she was a physical match for the Dorothy of the Oz books. And she was already a Frank Baum fan. In March 1937 *Photoplay* magazine noted, "Shirley's favorite book is that wind-swept thriller of a few decades past, *The Wizard of Oz*," and as late as Christmastime 1938, Temple's "Letter to Santa," published in *Photoplay*, requested "the new *Wizard of Oz* book."

In April 1937 the *New York Sunday Mirror*'s Kenneth McCaleb advocated for Temple as the lead in a production of *Oz* by calling out Twentieth Century Fox's president, Darryl Zanuck: "How about Shirley as 'Dorothy' in a talkie version of *The Wizard of Oz*?" In fact, Temple had been suggested for the role off and on as early as October 1935. One tidbit reported by Harrison Carroll that November announced that she would star in a *series* of *Wizard of Oz* films (not as farfetched as it sounds, as after Shirley's success in 1939's *Susannah of the Mounties*, Twentieth Century Fox unsuccessfully tried to secure the Muriel Denison *Susannah* sequels).

Rumors about the making of *The Wizard of Oz* almost always contain a grain of truth, and one bit of gossip has been a staple of *Oz*'s mythology since its inception. It has often been cited that the success of *Snow White and the Seven Dwarfs* gave *The Wizard of Oz* its impetus. While that may be true in terms of bankability, the call for a modern update of *Oz* can be traced to May 28, 1937, at which time *Oz* was in the top twenty "most called for . . . yet unfilmed" classics recommended for production in a *Film Daily* nationwide poll of fifteen hundred newspaper critics, editors, and columnists. (Hollywood listened: Other recommended titles included *The Adventures of Marco Polo, The Adventures of Robin Hood, Arabian Nights, Bambi, The Blue Bird, A Christmas Carol, Drums Along the Mohawk, Gulliver's Travels, The Mikado,* and *Wuthering Heights*—all of which were made into pictures over the next five years.) CBS Radio's broadcast of a new *Wizard of Oz* serial, announced in March 1937 and recorded for airing on May 12, 1937, probably piqued a renewed public interest in a cinematic version of *Oz.*

If ever there was a time that gave rise to the old Hollywood chestnut about Shirley Temple as Dorothy, the spring of 1937 was it, though it is unknown if the results of the *Film Daily* poll were released to the studios in advance of their May 28 publication. Temple herself recalled the proposed deal in her 1988 autobiography, *Child Star.* The actress's recollection was that MGM had already acquired *Oz* at the time she was making *Heidi* (1937), and that L. B. Mayer dickered with Zanuck for the loan of her services in exchange for Zanuck using MGM's Clark Gable and Jean Harlow in a Fox picture *and* pairing Temple and Gable together in a second film. Gable even surmised that costarring with Temple would sell the public a double dose of dimples. The oft-told versions of the Gable-Harlow-Temple legend all have one thing in common: The deal between MGM and Fox fell through when Harlow died unexpectedly on June 7, 1937. But if the legend were true, it would have been a deal for a differently envisioned *Oz* production than the 1939 version, as in 1937 Samuel Goldwyn still controlled the story's motion picture rights. In 1989, at age sixty, Shirley Temple Black recalled during a TV interview on Seattle's *Town Meeting,* "I would have loved to have played Dorothy in *The Wizard of Oz.* My dad read me the whole Oz book series. . . . But in retrospect, I don't think there could have been a better Dorothy than Judy Garland. She was super."

Where an expensive film like *The Wizard of Oz* was concerned, proper casting was essential. When seeking the right actor for the right part, the motion picture studios had a history of generating publicity and mystique for their impending productions by casting a wide net through talent scouts, regional auditions, and nationwide searches. However, from the point of acquisition in February 1938, *The Wizard of Oz* was intended as Judy Garland's vehicle, and its production was carefully crafted to showcase her singing and acting talents like no movie previously had. "Thus for [MGM's] Dorothy they did not institute a nationwide search for a girl resembling the drawings in the book," reported the *Gazette Montreal.* "They picked a little girl right from their home lot. Judy Garland . . . who needs only years and poundage to become a successor to Sophie Tucker."

The comparison between the two belters wasn't hyperbole. Garland had a taste for "hot," jazzy swing music—her era's rock-and-roll equivalent—but she could also pack an emotional wallop. "She has a greater understanding of lyrics than any child I have ever met during my many years in the theater and on the air," said Tucker herself in praise of Garland's talents.

Judy Garland had come up through the vaudeville ranks as the diminutive standout in a performing sister act before signing with MGM in 1935 at age thirteen.[1] Judy possessed a versatile, powerhouse singing voice mature beyond her years—one that could bring audiences to tears or have them dancing in the aisles, although swing melodies with a red-hot tempo were her forte. Uncertain of how to showcase her, Metro loaned Garland to Twentieth Century Fox for her first feature film, *Pigskin Parade* (1936). She made such a sensation that she was never again considered for a loan-out. Critics took to her and audiences favored her, though she was considered not much to look at. Upon taking in Garland's second picture, *Broadway Melody of 1938* (1937), Mary Marshall, writing for *Modern Screen*, summarized the general consensus:

> My main urge was for the sight of Eleanor Powell's dancing feet. But the hit of the show to me—good though Miss P. was—turned out to be little Judy Garland. Why? Goodness knows, I've heard enough of that general type of hot singing. But young Judy did it so well—she put so much umph behind her songs. Her young voice is powerful and sure of pitch. . . . It's as natural as Judy herself with her snapping black eyes and her wide mouth, which isn't a bit pretty, but which intrigues you and makes you like her, just because it isn't reshaped with lipstick.

Judy Garland was also a pet of L. B. Mayer. In March 1937 Mayer was the guest of honor for the annual Shrine St. Patrick's Day luncheon at the Palace Hotel in San Francisco. Per tradition, Mayer introduced a talented screen newcomer and Garland was his 1937 protégé, fresh from her success in *Pigskin Parade* just several months prior.

In addition to the five MGM films she made in 1937 and 1938, Garland's name was attached to several projects that never came to fruition including Frances Marion's *Molly, Bless Her* (1937) with Sophie Tucker, Reginald Gardiner, and Wallace Beery; producer Lou Ostrow's *Wonder Child* (1938) scripted by Bert Kalmar and Harry Ruby; and producer Harry Rapf's *Circus Days* (1938), which was to have costarred Mickey Rooney, Ronald Sinclair, and Freddie Bartholomew.[2] When Metro announced its cast for *Broadway Melody of 1939* in June 1938, the lineup was a veritable reiteration of that eventually set for *The*

---

1 In a January 21, 1938, trade ad, MGM mythologized Garland's "discovery" as occurring in May 1937.

2 L. B. Mayer continued to see Garland's potential. In early August 1939, after *The Wizard of Oz*, Mayer was quoted as saying that he thought Garland's *Babes in Arms* with Mickey Rooney was "positively going to be a sensation," considering it the top film of the first part of the new picture season. And in December 1951, after both Mayer and Garland had left MGM, Mayer told columnist Erskine Johnson that his first movie away from Metro would be *The Judy Garland Story*. Reportedly Garland was "ready, willing and able to star in the picture."

Wizard of Oz, with Garland, Frank Morgan, Ray Bolger, and Buddy Ebsen.

By early 1938 Garland's popularity was steadily ascending, bolstered by regular radio appearances on *Jack Oakie College* throughout 1937 and Metro's own *Good News of 1938*. Garland's rise to fame climaxed when the film *Everybody Sing* (1938) had its world premiere on Monday, January 24, 1938, at the Paramount Theatre in Miami Beach, Florida. Judy was there in person and was introduced by the management as "a great star," which brought hearty approval from the audience. Her numbers in the picture also brought applause, and after the show, she sang "Dear Mr. Gable" from *Broadway Melody of 1938*, upon which "the audience fairly rose as one to cheer her." The event was covered by editors from the trade journals *Boxoffice*, *Motion Picture Daily*, *Motion Picture Herald*, *Showmen's Trade Review*, and the *Film Daily*, who had nothing but accolades for Garland. At this point *The Wizard of Oz* was the timely and fortuitous momentum that poised Judy for escalation to career stardom.

Mervyn LeRoy contended that Judy Garland was always his first choice for Dorothy, although he thought the girl actress required some physical adjustments. According to a 1943 account in *Photoplay*, by early 1938 LeRoy was observing Garland on the set of her movies. LeRoy saw Garland's potential not only for the *Oz* role but for another of his planned productions, *Topsy and Eva*. "He saw great possibilities in this starry-eyed young girl and he took her under his wing. . . . She was sent to a dentist and porcelain caps were made for three front teeth. Thereafter on the set when a frenzied cry arose for 'Clutch!' everyone knew that Judy's teeth had come 'unstuck' again."

When interviewed in 1953, LeRoy conceded, "I'm crazy about teeth. Before I chose Judy Garland for the lead in *The Wizard of Oz* I asked her to have her teeth fixed. . . . They came down in points." In 1946 Garland recounted this period of her adolescence to *Screenland* magazine. "I was particularly sensitive about my nose and teeth. My teeth didn't all grow at the same time. I thought I was snaggle-toothed, and often used to put my hands over my mouth to hide my teeth. I was like the girl in the ads who was afraid to smile."

Garland's "possibilities" were undeniable, but for the leading role in *The Wizard of Oz*, Nicholas Schenck, president of MGM's parent company, Loew's Incorporated, wanted Shirley Temple as box-office insurance against his company's significant investment. (As of January 1, 1938, Loew's Incorporated had taken over all production activities of Metro-Goldwyn-Mayer Corporation.) Schenck had nothing against Garland. In fact, he was present the night of Judy's triumph with the opening of *Everybody Sing* in Miami. But she had been a supporting player in ensembles up to that time and, unlike Temple, hadn't proven she could carry an entire picture. It wasn't that Schenck didn't have faith in Mervyn LeRoy either. In a December 24, 1938, *Boxoffice* magazine quote, Schenck discussed LeRoy's transfer from Warner Bros. to MGM: "I knew [LeRoy] had a fine reputation as a producer and we were anxious to get him." Nor was Schenck averse to spending money for the edification of cinema arts. As W. R. Wilkerson summarized in his April 2, 1938, Tradeviews column in the *Hollywood Reporter*, "Nick Schenck last year in MGM confabs, in his daily contact with producers, urged them *not* to make cheap pictures, *not* to slice their budgets any, *not* to cut corners in their preparations or actual productions, *but* to get every dollar on the screen by causing the complete elimination of waste in time, effort and money."

Schenck's pragmatic rationale was that LeRoy's big-budget epic required a "star" name to fill theater seats and recoup the roughly three-million-dollar budget—the most expensive picture in Metro's history. And while L. B. Mayer may have reigned over MGM on the West Coast, Schenck most definitely controlled the purse strings from his New York offices, situated above the Loew's-operated Capitol Theatre on Broadway and Fifty-First Street. By example, in late October 1938, Schenck vetoed an offer from the J. Walter Thomson Radio Agency to dramatize MGM's popular Andy Hardy pictures for the airwaves. The deal would have pocketed Metro three hundred thousand dollars for a year's worth of broadcasts, but Schenck feared the shows would detract from the movie series' box-office returns.

To assuage Schenck, Roger Edens, MGM composer and Garland's mentor, dubiously made an appointment to hear Shirley Temple sing on the Twentieth Century Fox lot. He returned to Metro to report that Temple lacked the robust vocal chops required for the extravaganza being prepared, and the part of Dorothy remained Judy Garland's, as intended. (Thereafter, Garland dubbed Temple "Squirly Bumple" in swing-slang terminology.) But modern speculations have fabricated a litany of girl actresses also thought to have been Dorothy-eligible.

Of all MGM's female contract players, Ann Rutherford was the most Oz-conscious and, in 1938, was known to movie audiences as Polly Benedict, Mickey Rooney's best girl in the Andy Hardy film series. Rutherford's 1939 MGM bio listed the Oz books as her favorites. Rutherford learned how to read by sitting in her grandmother's lap while her grandmother recited from *The Wizard of Oz*. Once when her grandmother paused to answer the phone, she returned to find young Ann "about two pages ahead!" When Rutherford's mother critiqued Ann's onscreen hairdo as looking like "a Hammer-Head," Ann explained to a visiting journalist, with a laugh, that her mother "got that from the Oz books." As a schoolgirl, Rutherford would stroll past Ozcot, Baum's Hollywood home, and glimpse his widow Maud tending the flower garden. But at twenty, Rutherford was far too old for the part of Dorothy, and she resigned herself to visiting the Oz soundstage. "I'd go over on the set just to see the Yellow Brick Road—to see what I was missing," she said. "I was happier watching it; there weren't any other girl parts in it but Judy! Everyone else was a witch or Glinda the Good."

Nor was Bonita Granville a contender as has previously been speculated. Though capable enough as an actress (Granville was the youngest performer—at the time—to be Academy Award nominated, for 1936's *These Three*), the part of Dorothy required competency as a singer, which Granville was not. Instead, by the start of *Oz*'s October 1938 production, Granville was set to star in her third Nancy Drew picture for Warner Bros.

Other than Shirley Temple, another viable child star of the era that might conceivably have filled the role of Dorothy was Universal's teenage singing sensation Deanna Durbin. Durbin was not unfamiliar with the Frank Baum stories either; a well-worn copy of *Rinkitink in Oz* occupied a spot next to *Gone with the Wind* on her bookshelf at home. "That was the only Oz book I ever owned," the actress reflected in 1940. "But I read all of them. I borrowed the others from my brother-in-law, who was only a neighbor in those days."

Durbin's May 2, 2013, *USA Today* obituary perpetuated the misconception that Universal's star had been a serious consideration for Dorothy. However, in April 1938 Universal announced that Durbin was slated as the lead in a musical *Cinderella*, Universal's first Technicolor picture. The big-budget feature was to be produced by Joseph Pasternak and directed by Henry Koster, and was set to start the following June. But by April 22 the *Hollywood Reporter* noted that theater exhibitors didn't want Durbin in the proposed fairy tale, explaining, "Objections by exhibitors to having Deanna Durbin appear in *Cinderella* are being seriously considered by Universal. Exhibitor communications to the company state that the young star's popularity at the box office is well over 100 percent right now, and they fear that casting her in a fantasy will injure her drawing power as very few pictures of that type have made any money." Subsequently, Durbin's fairy tale *Cinderella* was canned, although the *Cinderella* story line reemerged in *First Love* (1939), a black-and-white modern retelling starring Durbin. Such feedback about a live-action fantasy could only have added to the jitters felt by the LeRoy Unit at Metro.

Eleven-year-old actress Jane Withers, then in the box-office Top Ten, claimed she took a call recommending her for Dorothy. This was no doubt inspired by Edwin Schallert's reference in the February 18, 1938, edition of the *Los Angeles Times* suggesting Withers for a part in the rumored *Oz* production. "I was under contract to Twentieth Century Fox, so it went no further," Withers recalled. "I was thrilled they chose Judy!" In 1938 Withers publicly expressed her love for *The Wizard of Oz*, a close second to her fascination for comic detective Dick Tracy. The recommendation for Jane Withers as Dorothy may have been advanced by L. Frank Baum's son, Frank J. Baum. At the time, Baum was a fan of Withers and even autographed a set of Oz books for the child star.

When the *New York Times* reported that Twentieth Century Fox had been outbid by MGM for the rights to *The Wizard of Oz* in February 1938, it was because Darryl Zanuck wanted to acquire the story specifically for Shirley Temple, not Withers. In 1939 Zanuck told reporter Wood Soanes, "We buy every story that even suggests a possible Temple picture," inferring that Fox had spent two hundred thousand dollars that year alone on acquiring properties for the child star. Even if Zanuck had bought *Oz*, it was no guarantee a picture would have come to fruition. "Stories don't always jell," Zanuck informed Soanes. "We work them over, assign them to different writers, and keep at them. Then, when they still don't jell, we junk 'em." In 1941 Temple's mother, Gertrude, lamented the oversight to reporter Lucie Neville: "The studio told us it had bought *The Wizard of Oz*—then it turned out Metro owned it." Indeed, Twentieth Century Fox responded by putting Temple in several screen versions of classic tales: *Rebecca of Sunnybrook Farm*, *The Little Princess* (in Technicolor), *Susannah of the Mounties*, and *The Blue Bird* (also in Technicolor), all in under two years.

On the occasion of Shirley Temple's April 23, 1938, tenth birthday (though she was presented to the public as a year younger), Hollywood columnist Paul Harrison noted that Temple had been passed over for the part of Dorothy:

> If there are any fairy stories or fantasies in the movie market within the next year or so, Miss Temple is going to be bidding for them. The greatest disappointment of her brief and eminently griefless career is that she will not be able to play Dorothy in *The Wizard of Oz*. Now and again there was talk of Mr. Zanuck buying the story from Samuel Goldwyn, who had got it from the Baum heirs. But it has now gone to Metro, and the role to Judy Garland.

In 1966 Mervyn LeRoy said of Garland, "She was *my* first choice; she was always my first choice, but the studio wanted me to use Shirley Temple, who couldn't sing and naturally was a great artist in her own right, but she wasn't right for *The Wizard of Oz*, and time has proven we were right when we picked Judy Garland." Noel Langley, whom Mervyn LeRoy handpicked for the *Oz* screen adaptation, agreed. In 1970 Langley squelched rumors that anyone other than Garland had been considered for the role. "That's absurd," he said. "Twentieth [Century Fox] wouldn't have let Shirley be in the picture at any price. Old Louis B. Mayer was determined to make a big star out of Judy Garland if for no other reason than reprisal. Judy and Deanna Durbin were both under contract to MGM and when renewal time came, Mayer decided to keep Judy and let Deanna go. Deanna, of course, went over to Universal where she became one of their biggest box-office stars. Mayer was furious that he had let her get away, but he would never have admitted that he made a mistake. He was determined to make Judy Garland a bigger star than Deanna Durbin just to prove he was right."

Louella O. Parsons broke the news of Judy Garland's casting in her February 24, 1938, announcement of MGM's production of *The Wizard of Oz*. In 1938, however, the selection of Garland as Dorothy was not universally well received. There were reservations that Garland wasn't a physical match for the Dorothy beloved for generations by Oz book readers. In sequels to *The Wonderful Wizard of Oz*, Dorothy was a blonde whom Baum described as "like dozens of little girls you know. She was loving and usually sweet-tempered, and had a round rosy face and earnest eyes." Though Baum does not reveal Dorothy's age, she is estimated to be about six and certainly no more than eight in *The Wizard of Oz*. At fifteen, Garland was too old for the part, but her casting was in the stage and cinematic tradition of the child/woman archetype that included Mary Pickford as Cinderella, Marguerite Clark as Snow White, Betty Bronson as Peter Pan, and Dorothy Dwan as Dorothy in Larry Semon's *Wizard of Oz*. A cleverly designed outfit and a lengthy wig might conceal Garland's maturing breasts such that she could pass for a preadolescent.

The greatest outcry about Judy Garland's casting came from faithful Oz book fans of a certain demographic that besieged author Ruth Plumly Thompson, L. Frank Baum's successor in continuing the Oz series. On May 7, 1938, Thompson told her publishers, "Already the children are writing me indignant letters because they do not like Judy Garland and because she has dark hair and Dorothy light. They do take Oz so seriously, bless their hearts."[3] *Silver Screen* reporter Annabelle Gillespie-Hayek countered public perception and qualified Garland's casting in *The Wizard of Oz* by stating, "Judy isn't as strong on looks as many of our Hollywood girls, but when it comes to personality and ability she's there one hundred percent."

Among the press opposition, *EveryWeek Magazine* called Garland a "buxom singer" and wondered if she would be accepted in the part since "Metro has no star-moppet such as Shirley Temple." Frank Morris, writing for the *Winnipeg Free Press*, was "a little afraid" that Judy would come across as too brash, a sentiment echoed by Hollywood wag Paul Harrison.

"She recently was announced for the role of Dorothy in Metro's version of *The Wizard of Oz*," wrote Harrison in his April 29, 1938, In Hollywood column. "The selection drew

3 Thompson also found herself the recipient of unsolicited bids for parts in the new movie. "Even actors are writing me for jobs in the *Wizard of Oz* film," she said, "As if I had anything to do with it!"

a good deal of adverse comment, and as much from Judy Garland fans as from anyone else. She herself seems a little uneasy about it. The Dorothy of L. Frank Baum's stories was a much younger, simpler girl. The assumption is that Judy will introduce swing music into the Emerald City, and will teach the Scarecrow and Tin Woodman how to do the Big Apple [dance]. Maybe they'll change the title to *The Wizard of Jazz*." Two months later Harrison's disillusionment became reality when the title of Oz's first newly composed song was revealed. He wrote in his June 27, 1938, column, "As this department pessimistically predicted months ago, Judy Garland will sing swing tunes in *The Wizard of Oz*. The first number written for her is called 'Jitterbug.' There'll be truckin' in the Emerald City. And big-applin' in the Land of Munchkins. And whirling in the grave of L. Frank Baum."

Kaspar Monahan, *Pittsburgh (PA) Press* reporter, queried Garland about being cast in Oz—the earliest such interview known—as published in Monahan's February 28, 1938, feature. The journalist met with the actress and her mother, Ethel, in her theater dressing room when Garland was in Pittsburgh promoting *Everybody Sing*. Monahan found Garland reticent to offer much information; she often deferred to Ethel to guide her responses, as was typical of protective stage mothers, noted Monahan. But, he reported, "Judy said she was thrilled over the Oz assignment. . . . She didn't look thrilled . . . she looked tired . . . and her throat was bothering her just a little." But upon revisiting the Garland meeting just before the Oz premiere, Monahan remembered her "enormous delight over her good luck" in being assigned the part of Dorothy.

Though not the *Wizard of Oz* enthusiast that Ann Rutherford was, Judy Garland was familiar with the tale, but she claimed otherwise in a 1967 interview, stating that she never read any of the Oz stories. Though on at least two occasions—in 1938 and 1940—she noted that *The Wizard of Oz* was always her favorite story. And in a 1940 interview with journalist Gladys Hall, Garland recalled that portraying Dorothy "was a dream I'd dreamed ever since Daddy read the Oz stories to me, backstage, when I was just a kid." In a 1938 interview with May Mann, Garland referred to her role as "Princess Dorothy," indicating her familiarity with the *Wizard of Oz* sequels in which the little heroine is bestowed with a royal title.

The press reported that, since being cast in the part, Garland was reading every Oz book she could get her hands on. And she needn't have looked far. Copies of the Oz books abounded in the LeRoy Unit as they provided detailed descriptions of the characters and their personalities beyond *The Wonderful Wizard*. According to one notice, Garland was sent "dozens of them" by her admirers once she was set as Dorothy. (Patsy Bruner, a Garland fan from Kansas, also sent the actress a box of lapel ornaments representing the Scarecrow, Tin Man, and Cowardly Lion.) At the least, Garland was literate in the first book. In a copy of *The Wizard of Oz*, she wrote to her tutor's daughter Virginia, "I'll bet your [sic] going to adhore [sic] this book, as I know I certainly did when I read it. Pretending to be

Dorothy, and going through all her exciting adventures, and all her journeys was too much fun to describe. . . ." Additionally, Garland and her castmates inscribed multiple copies of the Oz books as keepsake souvenirs for admirers during the film's production.

Judy Garland knew that with *The Wizard of Oz*, a lot was at stake. In 1940 she confided to journalist May Mann, "When I was first told that I was to play Dorothy in *Wizard of Oz* with the picture's budget set at three million dollars, I knew that my entire future rested on my ability to play Dorothy convincingly." Thus before cameras began turning on MGM's version of *Oz*, Garland was as poised and prepared as possible.

TOTO

The Wizard of Oz did not go without a publicized talent search. However, it was for a dog to portray Toto. In its 1939 promotional material, MGM claimed that one decision for portraying Toto was, "Should it be a man dressed like a dog?" It was reported in *Variety* on April 6, 1938, that Metro's eastern talent division was scouring the coast for actors that were animal impersonators for a one-time shot to appear in *The Wizard of Oz* in keeping with the portrayal of animal characters in the original musical extravaganza of 1902. Additionally, a preproduction report from 1938 speculated that for *Oz* "even animals, such as Toto, the dog, will have fantastic details added by make-up."

It is not known if the notion of casting an actor to play Toto, like Nana the St. Bernard in *Peter Pan*, was a serious consideration. On February 25, 1938, Arthur Freed had drafted a proposed list of cast and crew for *The Wizard of Oz*. Among his suggestions was a succinct notation that indicated a canine actor for the role of Toto: "Get Judy a Dog." But Mervyn LeRoy decided to put the question to the legions of Baum fans to determine.

Harold Heffernan's March 16, 1938, Hollywood column told of LeRoy's sleepless fits over portraying Dorothy's dog companion. LeRoy, it was reported, "gets jumpy whenever anyone mentions that dog, Toto. What type of animal should play the role? LeRoy would like to know whether he should let Toto talk in the picture." (Toto speaks in the later Oz books and was performed as a speaking role on the 1933–34 radio show.) Heffernan's readers were encouraged to write their opinion to LeRoy in care of MGM.

In his follow-up column of May 8, Heffernan updated his readers, reporting that Mervyn LeRoy received several hundred letters as a result of the previous column's poll. Many of the pleas were from schoolchildren. The rather defensive consensus was that Toto should not be an actor in a costume. Also, Toto should not speak—to which LeRoy rebutted that he only debated the notion because the Cowardly Lion and a host of other strange creatures in the book were vocal, and he couldn't see why Toto should be muffled. And as MGM had made a series of "talking" dog shorts—the *All Barkie Dogville Comedies* of

1929–31—LeRoy had proposed the question, but the producer was now content to let the matter rest. The fans had spoken: Toto would be a real dog with no speaking capabilities.

W. W. Denslow's illustrations definitely picture a terrier of some sort, a cross between a Yorkshire and a Cairn. On September 5, 1938, the International News Service issued a syndicated newspaper casting call for a suitable dog ("Got a Toto?" was the headline), insinuating that it was a money-making prospect with the chosen owner standing to make twenty-five hundred dollars for a sixty-day working schedule. The studio required that Toto "must look something like a Scottie, do tricks, become devoted to Judy Garland and eat an apple before the camera."

Thus, the entire country was searched for Toto, and letters by the hundreds, all carrying photos of dogs, poured into Mervyn LeRoy's office, resulting in the testing of countless canines, mostly Scotties. "Over at MGM, literally hundreds of pooches of all types, breeds and pedigrees are being 'interviewed' and tested for the important role of 'Toto,' the little dog who is Dorothy's pet in *The Wizard of Oz*," read Cal York's account in the December 1938 *Photoplay*. Reportedly, the studio reception room had a steady stream of fortune-hunting men, women, and children with dogs "to see Mr. LeRoy," who personally screened a group of thirty canine hopefuls. In addition to Scotties, noted among the menagerie were an English bulldog and a St. Bernard—the latter accompanied by a little boy, dwarfed by his pet, who insisted to LeRoy that Toto ought to be "a big dog." At the height of the casting craziness, LeRoy received a crate of dog biscuits from his protégé Fernand Gravet with a note attached that read, "Just in case your dogs are hungry."

Milton Harker's September 6, 1938, column suggested that the selected Toto would require the Hollywood treatment, "Any dog taken will have to be 'glamourized,' with the hair of his ears delicately curled and what-not" in order to match the appearance of the dog so uniquely illustrated in the original book. But a trained terrier to fit the bill was virtually in Metro's backyard, having already appeared in movies opposite MGM's Spencer Tracy (in 1936's *Fury*) and Bing Crosby (*Double or Nothing* in 1937).

At the time of *The Wizard of Oz*, San Fernando dog fancier and trainer Carl Spitz, "a diminutive and dynamic German," owned the Hollywood Dog Training School, dubbed by the press as Movieland's most famous "dog house." Spitz's kennels covered ten wooded acres on which was situated living quarters for the Spitz family and Spitz's two "helpers," kennel man Beverly Allen and co-trainer Jack Weatherwax. Three additional buildings represented the training tier for doggie seats of learning: "kindergarten," "high school," and "college." In addition to boarding and training dogs for local clientele, Spitz had a lucrative sideline training dogs for the movies. His prize pedigree was the St. Bernard, Buck, who made a hit opposite Clark Gable and Loretta Young in 1935's *Call of the Wild*. Buck was under a five-year contract to Twentieth Century Fox at three hundred fifty dollars a week with the potential to earn one thousand dollars a week. (Adjusted

for inflation, three hundred fifty dollars is the equivalent of over six thousand dollars in today's currency.)

Carl Spitz also owned a cairn terrier that not only resembled the *Wizard of Oz* book illustrations but was already an experienced "movie dog," having made an auspicious debut in Shirley Temple's *Bright Eyes* (1934). Spitz had trained his dog to replicate Toto's various attributes as Baum described them. It didn't matter that his dog, Terry, was a female and Toto a "he." When Spitz brought Terry to MGM, it was unanimous that they had found the ideal dog.

Terry was undoubtedly put through the paces as described in a 1935 article on Spitz's techniques. "When Carl Spitz is training a dog for a picture role the first thing he asks for is the script. He then returns to his schoolyard where, as he teaches the dog his paces, Carl plays all the other parts himself. It's quite an interesting sight, Mr. Spitz also being something of an actor. It's his boast that his dogs are better up on their lines than most human actors."

The uninitiated might believe that Spitz's dogs would be rewarded with food but such was not the case for Terry, who was "educated with a small rubber ball," as Spitz explained in a June 1939 interview. "Dogs should never be rewarded with bits of food," Spitz said.

"This makes them dull. First, we teach the dog that it's a great honor to be allowed to play with a ball or rubber mouse. Then the dog is rewarded after each trick by being allowed to play with the object for a few seconds."

Judy Garland reportedly became quite fond of Terry and, by one report, Terry became attached to her. MGM noted, "Toto, the cairn terrier pup in *The Wizard of Oz*, flatly refusing to allow Judy Garland to go to lunch without him." But in reality, Terry's time was closely regulated by her handlers. Spitz or Weatherwax sat with Terry off-camera during dress rehearsals, silently cued the dog with hand signals during a take, and took the dog off-set during longer breaks. Terry was simply trained to behave as if she belonged to Garland throughout filming each scene. As Bob Weatherwax, Jack's nephew, asserted, "Jack would have needed to build rapport between Toto and Judy."

Developing such a relationship was likely a facile process. At the time, Garland was said to have several dogs as pets, and held a special affinity for them after an elderly childhood dog committed suicide by walking directly into the path of an oncoming train when Garland's father brought home a new puppy. In June 1941 Harold Heffernan announced that Judy Garland purchased a dog in New York similar in breed to "Toto" after Carl Spitz declined her offer of four hundred dollars—nearly seven thousand dollars when adjusted for present-day inflation—to acquire Terry for her own. (Garland's dog Chou-Chou, a toy French poodle, is pictured with her in publicity stills of the 1941 era.) Evidently, Terry had greater value so long as she was working in pictures.

Cairn terriers can be a temperamental breed, anxious and high-strung. Terry's casting was additionally unusual because male dogs were typically worked in movies as females are more sensitive (for this reason, all the collies portraying Lassie were males). For *The Wizard of Oz*, Terry had to contend with scenes that called for close proximity to open flames and being enclosed in wicker hampers as well as holding her own when the wind machines were turned on full force. When the Wicked Witch interrupts the Munchkinland celebration in a burst of red smoke, Terry was cautiously concealed under the Munchkin barrister's robe until the dog could be scooped up safely by Judy Garland. Once, Terry was put out of commission when she was accidently stepped on by one of the Wicked Witch's Winkie soldiers. Spitz internalized his dog's stress to the point of fainting for the first time in his life.

One would think that Terry would have held a grudge against the Winkies, but it was reported in *Hollywood* magazine that one of the hardest efforts was making Terry bark at the soldiers—the dog had been trained so perfectly, she was taught never to bark on a studio soundstage. Instead, Terry was silently cued with hand signals from out of camera range. Eliciting that first bark allegedly took "a whole day" and finally necessitated bringing in another dog, held off stage (and kept from barking) before Terry responded.

It was Jack Weatherwax who largely worked Terry throughout *The Wizard of Oz*, particularly when Carl Spitz was ill or working a different dog on another picture. Weatherwax never recognized his contribution to film history, training dogs in pictures like *Oz* or *Call of the Wild*. Weatherwax came from humble beginnings in New Mexico and was not formally educated. But when it came to dogs, he was "a genius," as his nephew Bob opined. Weatherwax was taller than most of the males in his family, as well as movie-star handsome, though he was not a healthy man, having suffered hypothermia while working Buck the St. Bernard on location in Mount Baker National Forest, Washington, for *Call of the Wild*. The entire Weatherwax family became renowned motion picture and television animal trainers.

In his 1938 column devoted to the casting of Toto in *The Wizard of Oz*, Milton Harker rightly stated that the canine role was important because it was "one of the few times in screen history where a dog performer is of such consequence to the story," as Toto is featured throughout. Harker figured that the picture, which was to get under way by the second week of September, would be on a sixty-day working schedule, although eighty days was a more likely guess, he concluded. Neither Carl Spitz nor Jack Weatherwax could have foreseen just how shortsighted Milton Harker's timetable would ultimately be as the *Oz* shoot became one of the most notoriously protracted of its day.

THE SCARECROW AND TIN WOODMAN

In *The Wizard of Oz*, Ray Bolger memorably portrays the Scarecrow role, and he was attached to the project from the start. Furthermore, he would soon garner experience working before Technicolor cameras, with Frank Morgan, in Metro's 1938 film *Sweethearts*. Bolger had grown up with the Oz books and was an admirer of Fred Stone's acrobatic dance moves, having seen Stone in the Broadway hit *Jack O' Lantern* (1917).

Ray Bolger's entrée into show business was initially circuitous. While attending Dorchester High School in his hometown of Boston, Bolger specialized in English and economics and excelled in field hockey and track events. After graduating, Bolger tried working in banks and insurance companies. He also sold vacuum cleaners before experience winning amateur dance contests led to his joining the Bob Ott Musical Comedy Repertoire Company and touring New England.

Early in his career, Bolger starred in two two-reel silent films produced by the Red Seal Studios in New York. While performing onstage in a production of *Life Begins at 8:40*, Bolger was given a screen test and, when the show closed, he relocated to Hollywood and signed a contract with MGM Studios. Although *The Great Ziegfeld* was already in production at MGM, special scenes were added to showcase Bolger's famous "rubber legs." (His new dance routines were said to have been inspired by his dreams. Upon awakening he would practice the steps for the rest of the night. Seeing weird shadows in his home after midnight, his new neighbors thought the place was haunted.) After strenuous dancing he was reportedly rubbed down with towels and brushes and covered in "horse liniment," after which trainers walked him around the movie stage until he cooled down. This procedure earned him the nickname "Race Horse." In 1941 Bolger told *Hollywood* magazine that his distinctive choreography was a combination of modern moves and classic ballet, learned from Boston ballet master Senia Russakoff.

Bolger's casting as the Scarecrow was first announced by several journalists in early March 1938. Edwin Schallert's March 7, 1938, *Los Angeles Times* column broke the news with the headline "Bolger Scarecrow in *Wizard of Oz*," which was followed with a recap of Bolger's role in Metro's *Rosalie* (1937) to refresh moviegoers' memories. Schallert also made reference to Fred Stone's Scarecrow when discussing Bolger, and advocated casting Spencer Tracy in the Tin Man role. On March 15, 1938, both the *Film Daily* and *Daily Variety* listed "Ray Bolger and an all-star cast" would headline *The Wizard of Oz* but with no role assignment specified. (These were the only occasions on which Judy Garland was not specifically mentioned for *Oz*.)

Then in his March 16, 1938, column, for which Mervyn LeRoy was interviewed, journalist Harold Heffernan noted, "Dorothy is to be played by Judy Garland and Ray Bolger will interpret the Scarecrow, but the Cowardly Lion, the Tin Woodman, and Toto (Dorothy's treasured canine pet) are more worrisome to LeRoy, he admits, than the old job of cutting ten pounds of the original text of *Anthony Adverse*." A day prior, Charlie Ellis of the *Abilene (TX) Reporter-News* reiterated Bolger's casting in his editorial on the pending production of *The Wizard of Oz*.

Arthur Freed's original January 31, 1938, suggested cast roster for *The Wizard of Oz* lists Buddy Ebsen for the Scarecrow and Bolger for the Tin Woodman. An April 4, 1938, casting notation for Noel Langley's script draft also names Ebsen as the Scarecrow and Bolger as the Tin Woodman. But as Bolger and his wife left for an East Coast trip on April 6, Bolger's understanding was that he was to be the Scarecrow. After a stopover in Boston to visit family and friends, the Bolgers headed to Manhattan for Ray to appear at a benefit. On May 4 the *New York Sun*'s Eileen Creelman published her interview with Bolger in which he again stated that he was set to play the Scarecrow, telling Creelman that he had already met with Fred Stone to discuss the part. Bolger added that the only other cast member known to him thus far was Judy Garland, whom he expected "will play the little girl." Much later, on August 27, 1939, *Citizen Magazine* reported that Fred Stone himself had approved of Bolger's casting in the Scarecrow role. Stone's daughter Paula told the *Cincinnati (OH) Enquirer*, "About five years ago, Dad and I saw Ray Bolger in a picture [MGM's *The Great Ziegfeld*, 1936]. Dad nudged me in the ribs and said: 'There's the only man I've ever seen in movies who could play the Scarecrow.'"[4]

4 The admiration was mutual. Forty years after *The Wizard of Oz*, Bolger contended that Fred Stone was one of his two lifelong idols, the other being dancer and choreographer Jack Donahue.

These announcements of Bolger initially being cast as the Scarecrow revise all previously recorded accounts for the history of the making of *The Wizard of Oz* in books, documentaries, and audio commentaries. Prior accounts have adhered to Arthur Feed's January 1938 casting suggestions verbatim, though it should be noted that on Freed's list there are an equal number of actors who did not appear in *The Wizard of Oz* as those who eventually did. Regardless, this is how Bolger's role was originally announced in the press at large and to Bolger's belief as well, although there would be some internal waffling at Metro about the casting.

In 1938 both Ray Bolger and Buddy Ebsen were under contract to MGM, and neither required new contractual negotiations for their services in *Oz*. David Montgomery and Fred Stone had been the breakout stars of the earlier extravaganza in their respective roles of the Tin Man and Scarecrow, and the two parts were probably seen as interchangeable, although the Scarecrow was the bigger part and the one that brought the greater prestige for its association with Stone. As such, the announcement of Bolger as the Scarecrow was a temporary moment of indecision at a time when *Oz*'s entire production was very much in an embryonic state. For example, on March 15, 1938, a *Boxoffice* magazine blurb about *Oz* noted only that Judy Garland and Kenny Baker "have leads," although Baker would be written out of *Oz* and placed in another Mervyn LeRoy production, 1939's *At the Circus* with the Marx Brothers.

But by the time Bolger and his wife returned to Hollywood from their trip on May 17, 1938, things had changed. In her May 29, 1938, column, Louella O. Parsons confirmed a switch in casting: "Those two long legged, collapsible dancers, Buddy Ebsen and Ray Bolger, are the latest recruits to the cast of *The Wizard of Oz*. . . . Buddy steps into the role of the Scarecrow, created on the stage by Fred Stone, and Ray will use his unruly legs to good effect as the amusing Tin Man."

Both actors began wardrobe tests for these respective characters, but even as production edged nearer to a start date, there remained some ambiguity about Bolger's role. In a 1938 interview with *Modern Screen* journalist Robert McIlwaine, Bolger hinted at some internal debate, saying only that he knew he was slated to appear in *Oz*. "I'm not sure if I'm to play the Scarecrow or the Tin Woodman," the actor said. "Both are swell parts and if they keep it in a light vein, sticking to fantasy, I think [*Oz*] will be a big hit."

Both Ray Bolger and Buddy Ebsen were lean and gangly, and either could have portrayed the loose-limbed Scarecrow. But Bolger was already christened "rubber legs" by the press, and it was he who was better suited to the part due to his terpsichorean style, which he described as "fluid." Indeed, when USC student Gwendolyn Rickard, Bolger's wife-to-be, first laid eyes on the dancer at the Orpheum Theatre in 1929, she thought he resembled "a sublimely homely gazelle."

Decades later Bolger contended in interviews that he persuasively argued for the Scarecrow role and won—though Bolger was known for embellishing the truth to his advantage—telling author Aljean Harmetz in 1976 that his MGM contract specified that he was to be cast as the Scarecrow if ever Metro should make a movie of *The Wizard of Oz*, despite there being no such clause in the original paperwork. However, Gwendolyn Bolger was intimately involved in all decisions pertaining to Ray's career, serving in a pseudo-agent capacity. Bolger always contended that it was the *both* of them who approached Louis B. Mayer to negotiate for the Scarecrow role. In all probability it was Gwendolyn who shrewdly foresaw the Tin Man as the lesser of the two roles; that it would serve Ray to be publicly noted as Fred Stone's successor; and that Ray would also have more screen time in the strawman part.

In any event, the final casting reverted Bolger to the Scarecrow role, with Ebsen taking the Tin Man assignment. Still, the press remained unclear about who was cast as whom. In her October 15, 1938, Going Hollywood column, journalist May Mann referenced both Bolger and Buddy Ebsen among the cast, but indicated that Bolger was the Tin Woodman—though filming was already under way with Bolger as the Scarecrow on the date of publication. Several years after politicking for the part, Bolger told the Associated Press's Franklin Arthur that *Oz* was the "strangest job" he'd ever had, and he only decided he liked the role towards the end of the shoot, after earlier feeling as if he weren't doing it justice.

To simulate the loose-limbed Scarecrow in *Oz*, Bolger was initially at a loss until he remembered from a visit to a museum the elaborate gyrations of which skeletons are capable. He arranged to borrow a skeleton from the Los Angeles Medical School and rigged it to a series of wires and pulleys to study all possible combinations of its actions. Bolger's intention was to shadow the skeleton's nonchalant maneuvers as he perfected the strawman's disjointed gait. With Bobby Connolly, *Oz*'s choreographer, Bolger worked out the movements to be factored into his dance routine patterned after the skeleton's motions. Léonide Massine, resident choreographer of the Ballet Russe, heard of Bolger's unusual Scarecrow dance and asked the comedian to re-create his part in a proposed ballet edition of *The Wizard of Oz* for the New York stage, but such plans went no further.

When Bolger and his wife had guests over to their Beverly Hills home, Bolger hammed it up, demonstrating his new Scarecrow routine across the lawn. "It goes like this," he was overheard saying as he pirouetted around the landscaping before slipping on a pebble and spraining his right ankle. "Serves me right," he sheepishly confessed. "Mother told me it was bad manners to talk with my feet!" Until his ankle healed up, Bolger reportedly shifted his eccentric moves to his left foot when rehearsing with Judy Garland at the studio.

Unlike Ray Bolger, Buddy Ebsen actually began dancing as a child, as his father owned one of the most prestigious dance academies in Orlando, Florida. But by age thirteen, Ebsen gave up dance lessons for baseball because he found dancing "sissified." When he enrolled at the University of Florida, it was with the idea of becoming a doctor. But the 1928 collapse of the Florida land boom impacted the family finances, forcing Ebsen to drop out of medical school.

Ebsen pursued work as a dancer in New York, nabbing employment as a soda jerk at Penn Station. Eventually he teamed with sister Vilma on dance routines, and the two were spotted in a revue at Atlantic City's Babette Club by newspaper critic Walter Winchell, who praised them in his column, launching their careers. As a featured act at the Central Park Casino, the Ebsens were next spotted by a Metro-Goldwyn-Mayer talent scout. In 1935 both Buddy and Vilma were signed to a contract with MGM, where they made their debut the same year in *Broadway Melody of 1936*. Vilma soon retired but Buddy stayed on and was loaned to Twentieth Century Fox to appear opposite Shirley Temple in *Captain January* (1936). Thereafter, Ebsen attained status as one of Metro's featured players, indicating his popularity with the moviegoing public, and had Judy Garland as his dance partner for a number in *Broadway Melody of 1938* (1937). He accepted his casting as the Tin Woodman without qualm. *The Wizard of Oz* was to be Ebsen's ninth film but one that almost cost him his life.

THE COWARDLY LION

After some conjecture it was determined that the Cowardly Lion would *not* be played by a live animal. Instead, the part would be embodied by an actor in a skin suit who would not be expected to cavort on all fours like the lion in the 1902 play or the Larry Semon movie. Metro's Cowardly Lion would be introduced crouching and pouncing on four legs but soon thereafter would saunter erect like a feline biped (the character was informally known as "The Lion Man" among *Oz* crew members). Bert Lahr was the favored choice to fill the role, and casting the comedian was a natural, as Mervyn LeRoy recounted in 1973. "Bert Lahr had been my friend for years, since vaudeville, and he was perfect for the Cowardly Lion. When you thought of a comic with a big mouth who could roar, you just naturally thought of Bert."

At the time, Bert Lahr was reportedly the highest-paid musical-show comedian in New York, earning twenty-five hundred dollars a week for his most recent stage work in *The Show Is On.* His broad comedic style and brash presence were ideally suited to the melodrama of live theater. He sang with dissonance to hilarious effect and had masterfully mimicked foreign dialects for routines and parodies. His brand of physical buffoonery—over-the-top reactions, gestures, and noises—combined with his personal inferiority complex would be well suited for the part of the king of beasts who is just as timid as a kitten.

On the other hand, Tinseltown didn't exactly embrace Lahr. He lacked the striking good looks of a leading man (a trait on which he capitalized), he didn't warble in a traditional manner, and he was not a proficient dancer. Of his unconventional looks, Lahr admitted in 1933 that he wasn't a bit sensitive about his "funny face." "I only have to wear it," he said, "other people have to look at it!"

To date, Lahr had only supporting roles to his filmography credits, which irritated him. "This is nothing distinguished for Hollywood," he remarked in 1938. When asked about making *Flying High* in 1931, Lahr said he could hardly wait to catch a train for Broadway when the film finished. "I got a little hammy," he said. "People in Hollywood didn't show me what I thought was proper respect. So I became sore."

Indifferent about the picture business, Lahr almost forfeited the role for which he will forever be remembered; he wanted a contractual guarantee that he would be employed on *The Wizard of Oz* for five weeks. MGM envisioned requiring his services for just three weeks, as the Cowardly Lion is introduced halfway through the script, but Lahr was prepared to walk. What the movie studio couldn't have foreseen was just how tremendously complex making *Oz* come to life would truly be. In the end Lahr got his guarantee—and worked a total of twenty-six weeks on the picture. He also got assurances that he would be given featured billing "in not later than fourth position" on screen credits and advertising.

When he was cast in *The Wiz-*
ard of Oz, Bert Lahr initially
approached the Cowardly Lion
role from a pragmatic perspective,
reportedly spending hours observing MGM's own Jackie the lion. In
addition to being a staple of Johnny
Weissmuller's *Tarzan* series, it was
Jackie who, as the studio's mascot Leo the Lion, heralded with a
majestic roar the opening of every
Metro picture from 1928 onward.
Lahr's intent was to imitate Jackie's
"voice" and gait. "Jackie has about
twenty different vocal inflections,"
said Lahr prior to production,
"ranging from a whine of protest
to a full-bodied roar. He chuckles
when pleased, grunts approval of
his meals, and even has a wheeling
cry to ask for what he wants."
Lahr's intention was to incorporate
Jackie's intonations into the delivery of his dialogue.

Lahr also drew upon his renown for physicality and rubber-faced guffaws from years on
vaudeville circuits and the Broadway stage. His son, *New Yorker* theater critic John Lahr,
has suggested that the only way Lahr's brand of raucous, physical comedy could successfully translate to film was in the guise of an animal. Indeed, in his 1926 vaudeville act, Lahr's
comedic interpretation of the love song "Peggy O'Neill" was described by *Variety* as "done
in the manner of a sea-lion in amorous mood." And despite film roles before and after *The
Wizard of Oz*, Lahr agreed to another animal imitation in RKO's *Sing Your Worries Away*
(1942). *Hollywood* magazine noted that "Lahr, who did the lion impersonation in *The
Wizard of Oz*, will do an impersonation of a porpoise for an underwater scene. . . ." Lahr
observed his similarity with another creature, adding, "And of course, I'm a jackass quite
often."

Bert Lahr had a reputation for self-deprecation, though it also was part and parcel of
his comedic shtick. In August 1939 the *New York Post*'s Michel Mok wrote, "It has been
known on Broadway for years that Bert Lahr, the doggy-faced clown with the seal bark, is
addicted to worry. He revels in it as a smoker of reefers revels in hashish." Those associated

with Lahr during production of *The Wizard of Oz* have attested to the comedian's seeming insecurity.[5]

Noel Langley remembered Lahr as a chronic worrier not unlike the intrepid pussycat he portrayed. "Everybody was always telling him that the lion was going to steal the picture, but he would moan and shake his head and talk about how horrible he was." In a July 12, 1998, interview, Lahr's eldest son, Herbert, recalled, "He thought that he played a good part but he said, 'Y'know, it's not going to help me much in movies. They didn't see *me*, they saw a lion.' I don't think Dad went out to purposefully steal the picture. It's just that his facial expressions, you empathized with him."

In a May 28, 1998, interview, assistant choreographer Dona Massin remembered Lahr's shortcomings in the dance department. "I can only remember one thing: Bert Lahr. He *hated* it!" she recalled. "The only one I really had to work with was Bert—he wasn't a dancer. He definitely was not! Judy could dance, and Haley, and Bolger was a dancer. Even in rehearsing, [Lahr] had two left feet. Bert was the toughest for me. He just liked to complain, and I don't blame him. I felt sorry for Bert." (At the least, Lahr bonded with Massin's overseer, choreographer Bobby Connolly. It was reported that as soon as *Oz* wrapped production, Lahr and Connolly were trekking to Mexico for a fishing trip.)

Once it was announced in late July 1938 that Bert Lahr would play the Cowardly Lion, artist Paul Terry, of Terrytoons fame, got the jump on Metro by rushing into production his cartoon short *The Newcomer*, which featured a comedic zoo lion voiced by a Lahr imitator. After the cartoon premiered on October 21, a similar lion was seen in two more Terrytoons: *Doomsday* (1938) and *The Nutty Network* (1939). By the time a fourth cartoon, *The Temperamental Lion*, was released in early 1940, Terry's in-house animators referred to the character as the "Bert Lahr lion."

(Whether Lahr was flattered or perturbed by the cartoon imitation is uncertain, although he was known to be fiercely protective of his image. In 1958 MGM attempted to engage Lahr to emcee a children's television cartoon program using his Cowardly Lion voice, but the project did not go forward. Three years later Lahr initiated a five-hundred-thousand-dollar lawsuit against Adell Chemical and Robert Lawrence Productions, claiming their Lestoil commercial imitated his vocals. In 1963 Lahr sued Kellogg's, Screen Gems, and Hanna-Barbera for five hundred thousand dollars over another sound-alike, their popular Snagglepuss lion character. Lahr settled out of court in both instances.)

In any event, Lahr must've been encouraged by the prerelease buzz *The Wizard of Oz* was getting during its long production. As early as January 9, 1939, with two months of

5 As early as 1926, Lahr's inability to feel totally confident is evident when he told Nelson Robbins, dramatic editor of the Baltimore *Daily Post*, "The audience was kinda dumb today. They didn't seem to get me."

filming to go, journalist Paul Harrison was already predicting that Lahr was "about to walk off with *The Wizard of Oz*." By the end of July, Lahr was feeling confident enough to tell the *Brooklyn (NY) Daily Eagle* that "he was hoping to grasp the Academy Award for comedy" for his performance. The overwhelming success of Lahr's performance not only made him the picture's comedic focal point, it forever altered how *Oz* was perceived. It was no longer a showcase for the antics of the Scarecrow and Tin Man duo, and it would be inconceivable to exclude the Cowardly Lion from any future retellings of the tale.

THE WICKED WITCH OF THE WEST

If Judy Garland's casting as Dorothy raised a few eyebrows in Hollywood and beyond, the altered concept of the Wicked Witch of the West would draw protest. The evil crone of L. Frank Baum's story was about to go Hollywood. In *The Wonderful Wizard of Oz*, the Wicked Witch is a minor interruption to Dorothy's journey home. She does not hound the travelers as she does to great dramatic effect in the MGM film. Instead, the Witch is fearsome but, true to Baum's mission to tell a fairy story without "horrible and blood-curdling" morals, she does not torture or devour children as do the hags of the Brothers Grimm. Baum's Wicked Witch of the West is more bark than bite, imbued with a few vulnerabilities to avert childhood nightmares. She wears a patch over one eye, is afraid of the dark, and has a strong aversion to water, hence the umbrella she clutches in W. W. Denslow's ink drawings of her.

Whether Baum's Witch is cognizant of her Achilles heel allergy is uncertain, though she does keep her distance when the enslaved Dorothy bathes. But in Florence Ryerson and Edgar Allan Woolf's June 29, 1938, script draft, the Wicked Witch burns the scrolls that reveal the only way she can be destroyed. As a nod to her original phobia, in a July 25 script revision, Miss Gulch, the Witch's Kansas doppelganger, has acquired an open umbrella that "shades her from the sun." (A closed umbrella can be seen in the final cut of *The Wizard of Oz* across the handlebars of Miss Gulch's bicycle.)

The Wicked Witch of the West was originally conceived as a gruff harridan who doled out withering quips in early script drafts. However, at Mervyn LeRoy's request, on July 27, 1938, *Oz* scenarists Ryerson and Woolf adjusted the Witch from a long-nosed, toothless hag to a sleekly malevolent black-widow type with "a hint of evil beauty." This new characterization would not only evoke the Evil Queen in Disney's *Snow White*, it was in keeping with a cinematic trend toward sensuous yet ruthless villainesses such as Helen Gahagan in *She* (1935), Gloria Holden in *Dracula's Daughter* (1936), and even Elsa Lanchester in *The Bride of Frankenstein* (1935). Thus inspired by the premise that "beautiful women are the most dangerous," Gale Sondergaard was Mervyn LeRoy's logical choice for the *Oz* witch.

Sondergaard was beautiful and competent in her craft, and she had cultivated a reputation as one of the screen's finest female heavies in pictures such as *Maid of Salem*, *Seventh Heaven*, and *Lord Jeff*. Though she was not a witch in *Maid of Salem*, she was convincingly conniving in her role. In 1937 Sondergaard was called "the arch-villainess of the screen" by *Picture Play* magazine, and her characters were described by *Hollywood* magazine as crafty, seductive, manipulative, sex-appealing women, "So powerful and so real . . . that when she moved across the screen you felt like asking an usher to bring you a brickbat so you could knock some of the meanness out of her." Although the actress was conscious of becoming typecast, saying, "I don't want my screen life to be cluttered up with siren parts," she eventually accepted her station. "I'm a witch from way back," she told Hollywood journalist Patricia Clary in 1946. "I was a witch in my first New York play, a dramatization of *Faust*."

Edith Sondergaard adjusted her name after a University of Minnesota girlfriend told her, "You aren't an Edith, you are a Gale!" Sondergaard had come to prominence on the Broadway stage before relocating to Los Angeles with her second husband, director Herman Biberman, whom she had met through the New York Theatre Guild. She had no intention of becoming a motion picture actress until a Hollywood agent convinced her to acquiesce and meet LeRoy, who was casting for the 1936 Warner Bros. adaptation of *Anthony Adverse*.

In 1971 Sondergaard told film historian Leonard Maltin, "I went to talk to him, and I won the role [of Faith Paleologus]. Mervyn LeRoy told me afterwards that as soon as I walked in the door—I had some silver earrings on [such as the character wears]—he wanted me. So all my noble protestations about giving up my career flew out the window, and a whole new career opened up." Under LeRoy's direction, Sondergaard won the Academy Award for Best Supporting Actress—the first year the category was instated.

With LeRoy's transfer to MGM, he put Sondergaard under short-term contract with the intent of placing her and his other discoveries in the productions planned under his unit. LeRoy approached Sondergaard about playing the Wicked Witch in *Oz* concurrent with casting her in a supporting part in *Dramatic School*, circa mid-August 1938. He defined the witch character as a glamorous yet devious villainess, thus appealing to the actress's vanity. As Sondergaard later put it, "In those days, I was not about to make myself ugly for any motion picture." LeRoy described his pitch in a September 3, 1938, Associated Press interview. "Witches, with their hooked noses and long fingers and tall peaked hats, are always the same. I thought we should have a different kind of witch. One with class and maybe sex appeal. Gale Sondergaard will be our witch, a 1938 version."

Altering the idea of a traditional witch was a revolutionary departure. And lest there be any double takes from Oz fans, the title of Harold Heffernan's gossip column for August 12, 1938, delivered it straight: "This Witch is no Scarecrow." Heffernan informed his readers:

If you think the Wicked Witch of the West in *The Wizard of Oz* is going to blossom out on the screen as a hideous, long-beaked old meanie of the *Snow White* variety, you're due for a surprise. Mervyn LeRoy, who'll start making the L. Frank Baum fairy tale September 1, has decided that the cantankerous old woman who menaces Dorothy and her friends on their journey to the marvelous Land of Oz should be treated to just a tiny bit of glamour. With that in mind, he prevailed on Gale Sondergaard yesterday to sign a contract to do this thankless chore. "Don't get me wrong," said LeRoy in explaining his more sightly witch plan. "I'm not going to sacrifice realism for beauty in casting this role. The witch will be repulsive in deeds and manner, but she won't be too hideous to look at. I don't want to scare children away from the theatre."

In LeRoy's capable hands, Gale Sondergaard was game for initial makeup and wardrobe tests on August 27 and September 22, 1938. "We actually did the costumes—a high, pointed hat but of sequins, a very glamorous sequined gown," said Sondergaard. "She was to be the most glamorous but wicked sort of witch. And we got into testing for it, and it was absolutely gorgeous." Indeed, surviving makeup and wardrobe tests show the actress in a formfitting costume that incorporates black sequins, from the cowl covering her head to the tip of her peaked witch's hat. One report contended that even Sondergaard's broomstick would be trimmed in spangles. Her cosmetics complemented the ensemble with long false lashes, dark eye shadow, and dramatic lip rouge. Sondergaard's five-foot-six-inch frame seemed statuesque onscreen, and her delivery as the Wicked Witch might have been as intimidating a presence as her Mrs. Hammond in *The Letter* (1940), especially when threatening young Judy Garland's Dorothy. It is conceivable that at this stage Sondergaard also consulted *The Wizard of Oz* text. "From the moment she is cast in a role," related *Hollywood*, "she devotes every minute of her time to a study of its characterization. . . ."

"Gale Sondergaard, as the Wicked Witch, will provide a new idea in witches, playing the character as a beautiful woman instead of the conventional hag of the fairy story," May Mann announced in her October 15, 1938, Going Hollywood column, belatedly transcribed after her visit to MGM. But as Sondergaard explained it, "Mervyn got to remembering that this was a classic by now, and children who read it, and grown-ups too, were going to say, 'That isn't the way it was written!' And everybody agreed that you could not do that to *The Wizard of Oz*." What likely jogged LeRoy's "memory" was the mounting resistance to the announcements that Sondergaard would play a beautifully wicked sorceress.

Yielding to popular opinion, the decision was made to abandon the glamorous witch and revert to something closer to Baum's original depiction. "LeRoy decided," reported Harold Heffernan, "that the characterization should hold true to fiction." On October 3, 1938, Sondergaard was made up in a false nose and minimal cosmetics to test a series of less

overt wardrobe: a sequinless version of the hooded cowl; a shapely gown with velvet cape and hat; and finally, a long fright wig and a nondescript black cloak. After viewing the new tests, the inevitable became apparent, especially if Sondergaard was to preserve the integrity of her Hollywood image. "And Mervyn said to me, 'I don't want you to be an ugly witch,'" Sondergaard recalled. "So we dropped the whole thing, and of course Margaret Hamilton played the role, and it's a classic."

An award-winning actress, Sondergaard's decision to leave *The Wizard of Oz* was wise; at the time, its production seemed to be in something of a directionless limbo. But Sondergaard was not idle for long. In those days, receiving an Oscar was a distinction that came with enhanced demand and certain longevity. Sondergaard was unfazed by bowing out of *Oz*, saying she lost the role for having "too much sex appeal." On October 22, 1938, the *Hollywood Reporter* announced that MGM was loaning Sondergaard to Paramount for the Martha Raye–Bob Hope comedy *Never Say Die*, after which she would fulfill her Metro contract and freelance. Then, on October 28, the *Hollywood Reporter* noted that Sondergaard had just signed with Warner Bros. for the role of Empress Eugenie in *Juarez*—another role suited to the actress's type.

But by the end of 1939, Sondergaard would take another stab at fantasy, appearing as Tylette the conniving feline in Shirley Temple's *The Blue Bird*—for which no disfiguring makeup was required, as the actress later conceded. "[The] *Oz* character was written as an ugly, horrible, frightening witch," Sondergaard recounted, "and the cat in *The Blue Bird* is after all, a pretty gorgeous creature. So I think it was perfectly natural that she would be glamorous and treacherous."

The Wicked Witch role was recast by October 10, 1938, with character actress Margaret Hamilton. She was already familiar with the tedious peculiarities of working in color film, having appeared in two David O. Selznick Technicolor productions: *Nothing Sacred,* with Frederick March and Carole Lombard, in 1937, and *The Adventures of Tom Sawyer*, released in February 1938. It was also at the time Hamilton signed on that the decision was made to tint the Wicked Witch's skin a poison-green hue, making the character a particularly loathsome villain that would appease Baum diehards. The actress would retain the elongated foam-rubber nose that had been tested on Gale Sondergaard.

In *The Making of The Wizard of Oz*, Aljean Harmetz states that prior to being cast in the MGM film, Margaret Hamilton had played the Wicked Witch twice before in productions of *Oz* put on by Cleveland's Junior League in Ohio, thus setting the stage for predestiny. Hamilton was active with the Cleveland Junior League from 1928 to 1930, and while the players put on *The Wizard of Oz* twice, Hamilton did not play the Wicked Witch—she wasn't even in the cast of either production. In the league's April 1928 *Oz* show, the Witch was portrayed by Mary Foote, whose performance the *Cleveland Plain Dealer* defined as "one of the best character parts in the play." For the December 1929 to January 1930 edition, Mrs. E. P. Prescott took the part of the Witch. Hamilton played the Goblin King in a version of *The Princess and the Goblin*, the Wise Woman in *The Snow Queen*, and Fustian, a curmudgeonly jester, in *The Goose Girl* in addition to reading fairy stories over Cleveland's WTAM radio in October 1928; but by all accounts, she was not in the Junior League's *Oz* productions.

What is true is that Hamilton became a candidate for the Wicked Witch for Mervyn LeRoy after the producer screened scenes of her role as five-time widow Beulah Flanders in *Stablemates* (1938) with Wallace Beery and Mickey Rooney. In 1942 Hamilton recalled the *Stablemates* part as "The only time the movie moguls allowed me a bit of romance [was] when I made eyes at Wallace Beery. But my obvious ogling was obviously unsuccessful," referring to her character's thwarted attempt to woo Beery into becoming her sixth husband.

Hamilton had come up through to Hollywood by way of the Broadway stage. After an auspicious debut in her high school senior play, Hamilton chose her career path. "So that evening at dinner, I announced I was going to attend dramatic school," she recalled more than thirty years later. "Mother never missed a mouthful as she said, 'You'll do nothing of the sort.'" But young Margaret's early theatrical aspirations were funded by her father, Walter J. Hamilton, a prominent attorney in her hometown of Cleveland, Ohio. Six years after teaching kindergarten, and remaining active in local Junior League productions, Hamilton found her calling at the Cleveland Playhouse in shows geared for adult audiences.

She was next cast in *Another Language* at a playhouse in Greenwich, Connecticut, but as Hamilton told it in 1963, that was to be the finale to her theatrical career. "After that play I decided the theater was not for me," the actress told reporter Joan Crosby. "I had a good opportunity to teach at a school in Pennsylvania. The day before I was to sign the contract, I got a call saying the play I had done in Greenwich was coming to Broadway. Did I want to repeat my role?" Hamilton seamlessly segued to the Broadway production of *Another Language*, which became one of the smash hits of the season; she then appeared in the 1933 film version. She quickly cultivated a reputation for playing supporting roles that called for lines with a caustic attitude, which she delivered with aplomb. She mused at the fickleness of audience identification, saying, "It's funny, the things that stick with you. For my first play, *Another Language*, I ate grapes, and for years that was the only thing about me that anyone remembered."

Above all, Hamilton relished comedic turns, especially when performing for a live audience. "There is something about facing an audience and getting people's reactions to your efforts," she noted in 1942. At the time, her favorite role was the part of Ellen in the Lakewood (ME) Players' 1941 summer-stock production of *Ladies in Retirement*. "In comedy," she continued, "you get something you can sink your teeth into, meaty morsels that make the audience sit up and take notice." Hamilton knew it wasn't her looks that would attract attention, saying, "I may not make the male heart beat in faster-than-normal tempo, and I may not have glamour . . ."

But if *The Wizard of Oz* was infused with bits of burlesque comedy, not a shred of it went to Margaret Hamilton. Within a month of shooting the picture, word was out that Hamilton's Wicked Witch was hair-raising. As early as November 26, 1938, the Associated Press put out the advance notice that her performance surpassed prior villains, "For sheer, double-faced, double-tongued, double-dealing villainy, Margaret Hamilton may make other heavies look sissified by comparison. . . . They say her witch will put the hiss in a new key." With the perspective of hindsight, Hamilton recalled twenty-three years later, "I'm sorry they made the witch so nasty . . . but I think they wanted to give the part some zing that adults would appreciate, so they went all out for blood." The actress attributed her effectiveness to the carte blanche afforded her. When called for her screen test, she was told to perform the part as she would interpret the character. "I had a wonderful time," she said. "I loaded myself down with rags and tatters and lots of gook, straggly hair and all."

Meinhardt Raabe, a little person who was cast as the Munchkin coroner, remembered Margaret Hamilton giving each Munchkin player an autographed portrait of herself as she was, without her green witch makeup. "We never saw her like that at the time because she came on the set from the makeup room already fully made up," he recalled with a measure of humor. "So, she gave us these pictures because we had never seen her looking like that at that time."

As of May 1938, Margaret Hamilton was a single mother at a time when such an arrangement was uncommon. She had been married since June 1931 to architect Paul Boynton Meserve, but the marriage unraveled. In divorce court Meserve claimed Hamilton used their house as the site for unruly parties, as many as six nights a week; Hamilton accused Meserve of living off her salary. Following the divorce Margaret Hamilton was granted custody of her young son Toni—short for Hamilton. Thus, by early October 1938 Hamilton was grateful for the continuation of steady work when she won the part of the Wicked Witch in *The Wizard of Oz*.

THE WIZARD

If *The Wizard of Oz* was to imitate the atmosphere and style of Walt Disney's animations, W. C. Fields would have fit right in. A comic character of sorts himself—and readily parodied—Fields had already undergone cartoon caricaturing as Humpty Dumpty in Disney's 1938 short *Mother Goose Goes to Hollywood*, and had appeared as Humpty previously in Paramount's *Alice in Wonderland*, when he was approached to play the Wizard of Oz. Fields was favored for the part by both Arthur Freed, *Oz*'s uncredited associate producer, and *Oz*'s song lyricist E. Y. Harburg. Harburg had even contributed dialogue of the Wizard bestowing gifts to Dorothy's friends with Fields in mind.

But by June 11, 1938, it was reported that Mervyn LeRoy wanted fussbudget comedian Ed Wynn for the Wizard, though Fields could have easily answered LeRoy's call. "I'm looking for a little shrimp," the producer told columnist Harold Heffernan in August 1938, referring to W. W. Denslow's depiction of the Wizard as a small, timid man. "But just any kind of little shrimp won't do," LeRoy continued. "He's got to have ability and personal magnetism. I may have to go into the midget field to get my man." When Hollywood journalist Anne M. McIlhenney interviewed Judy Garland for a lengthy August 5, 1938, article about the actress, Judy expressed great excitement for the impending *Oz* production ("Honestly, I just can't wait.") and offered her thoughts on contenders for the Wizard role. "I just heard today that they're going to get either W. C. Fields or Ed Wynn for the Wizard, and that puts the final touch on it for me," Garland declared, adding, "I'll be so thrilled I won't be able to sing."

Ed Wynn passed on the role, however. In 1970, Mervyn LeRoy told the *Boston Herald*'s Eleanor Roberts, "I wanted [Wynn] badly for the role of the Wizard. He turned it down flatly. He didn't think the part was good enough for him." LeRoy added that he didn't plead with Wynn otherwise. "When an actor thinks a role isn't right for him, he isn't happy in it. And it shows." On September 10, 1938, Louella O. Parsons broke the news that the "incorrigible Bill [W. C.] Fields, one of the best loved men on and off the screen, will sign a contract with Mervyn LeRoy tomorrow for *The Wizard of Oz*. Bill has been juggling the idea just as strenuously as he used to juggle billiard balls on the stage when he was a Ziegfeld star. Today he made up his mind that he would go to work, and so he returns to the movies as the Wizard in Frank Baum's fantasy." Internally, however, Fields was already out, unwilling to yield over a salary dispute as revealed in an August 25, 1938, correspondence to him from his agent:

> Bill, I am really sorry you are not doing *Wizard of Oz*. I can't get the powers that be to go for the ACE [Fields's one-hundred-thousand-dollar asking price]. I can see your point and unfortunately, I can see theirs. It's a short job, about two weeks of actual work. . . . On an actual basis of more than $30,000 a week, it isn't tin, and won't hurt your prestige. With the world acclaim that this opus is going to get, and with the set up it's going to have financially and exploitation, honestly Bill you need it. [Fields declined MGM's counteroffer of seventy-five thousand dollars.]

Noel Langley recalled that Fields felt the part was too small, demanding that it be enlarged (this was prior to scripting several disguises for the Wizard actor in Emerald City). Langley thought Fields would be ideal for the hoaxing magician but noted, "I couldn't do anything more with the Wizard role than I had done. If I had made it more powerful, it would have destroyed the other characters. Fields turned the part down." It has also been variously suggested that the haggling over salary or a scheduling conflict precluded Fields from taking the role, coupled, perhaps, with reticence about tanking in another *Alice*-like picture. "Fields is trying to fit in the [Oz] assignment with his Universal commitment to make *You Can't Cheat an Honest Man*," noted the *Barrier-Miner*'s Hollywood Merry-Go-Round column. "Failing the veteran comedian, the choice will fall between Frank Morgan and Hugh Herbert." (In his January 31, 1938, suggested cast list for *The Wizard of Oz*, Arthur Freed had designated Morgan as ideal for the part of the Wizard.)

For some, however, news traveled slowly. Prince Leon and Gus Wayne were two little people with a boxing act who had previously appeared on Broadway with Ed Wynn in

Hooray for What! (which was scored, coincidentally, by E. Y. Harburg and Harold Arlen, who also would compose the tunes for MGM's *Oz*). Included as part of the publicity for their October 19, 1938, appearance at Jack & Bob's cabaret in Trenton, New Jersey, was this notation: "Your last opportunity to see these two midgets before going to Hollywood to appear [as Munchkins] with W. C. Fields in *Wizard of Oz*."

With Fields definitely unobtainable, it was next predicted, "Charles Winninger looms as the favorite for the title role in MGM's *The Wizard of Oz*. Other candidates include Victor Moore, Hugh Herbert and Frank Morgan." Character actor Winninger could have pulled off the part acceptably enough but not with the refined panache of a Frank Morgan. Hugh Herbert was the leading contender for a September 1938 vaudeville date at Indianapolis, Indiana's Lyric Theatre, a massive four-story showplace with stage acts then breaking records. Corbin Patrick of the *Indianapolis Star* wrote, "[Herbert] has an excellent chance of getting the important title role in *The Wizard of Oz*, a plum for which practically every character comedian in the [movie] colony is reaching. If he gets it, and if production starts soon, Herbert will be unable to tour." Ed Sullivan chimed in with another candidate in his August 23, 1938, Hollywood column. "Don't be too surprised if Robert Benchley gets the title role in *Wizard of Oz*. . . ." At the time, Benchley was best known for MGM's comedic short subjects, *How to Sleep* and *A Night at the Movies*. He also had a role in *Broadway Melody of 1938* with Judy Garland. Wallace Beery was apparently interested in the part as well, the speculation of which led to a misprint in 1939 when R. J. Lea, Ltd., an English tobacco manufacturer, listed *Oz* among Beery's "recent successes" on a collector's card inserted in cigarette packages.

By June 6, 1938, *Oz* screenwriters Florence Ryerson and Edgar Allan Woolf had suggested expanding the Wizard's role, which might've swayed W. C. Fields and further piqued his interest. Prior script drafts had included the "quaint old medicine man" in Kansas who doubled as the Wizard in Oz. But Ryerson and Woolf could foresee someone like Frank Morgan in multiple roles:

We also feel that a great deal is lost by not making more use of the Wizard of Oz throughout the picture. As it stands, he only appears in one scene toward the end. . . . Perhaps he appears as the gateman who lets them into Oz (wearing green whiskers). As the man who drives the "horse of a different color" (wearing purple whiskers). And again as the guard at the door of the audience chamber (wearing red whiskers).

In every case, the audience should recognize him. Not, of course, as the Wizard of Oz, but as the same funny old character we met in the prologue. . . . This would give us a chance to use a man like Frank Morgan without having the audience feel cheated because they didn't see enough of him, which would certainly happen if he is used only once as in the present script.[6] It would also give more importance to the title role of the piece. [In what would have been a historical misstep, the Wizard was also to have been disguised as an Emerald City bootblack, in blackface, who shines Dorothy's shoes.]

W. C. Fields's name would have given *Oz* box office clout, and it is interesting to project how he might have interpreted the part. Of historical curiosity, Fields did scribble a few quips in his *Oz* script to embellish his delivery as the Wizard and Professor Marvel, the kindly Kansas charlatan who convinces Dorothy to end her runaway exile by turning homeward. Author James Curtis quotes from the actor's cursory musings for the Professor Marvel scene in his 2003 Fields biography: "Yes, your aunt wants you back. She wants to put you in moving pictures like Shirley Temple." Ironically, and perhaps fittingly, little more than twenty years later, Fields's voice *was* mimicked as the Wizard for an animated TV series titled *Tales of the Wizard of Oz*.

W. C. Fields and his successor in the Wizard role, Frank Morgan, shared a vice that was as much an addiction as part and parcel of their screen shtick. Both men were notorious alcoholics who drank on set but usually controlled their bingeing professionally. It was Fields to whom journalist Paul Harrison was referring when he wrote in 1939 of Paramount's *Alice in Wonderland*, "[It] was largely played behind full masks which no actor's personality could penetrate. Indeed, it was possible for one player to be drunk as a hoot owl most of the time in the privacy of his disguise, without his condition being outwardly apparent." Frank Morgan's proclivity for the "hair of the dog" ran in his lineage. His family made their fortune as the leading American distributors of Angostura bitters, a blend of alcohol, water, herbs, and spices used to mix whiskey cocktails.

In 1938 Morgan was one of Metro-Goldwyn-Mayer's featured players, a reliable and competent performer who was an audience favorite. Morgan was born Francis Phillip Wuppermann (erroneously spelled Wupperman on occasion) on June 1, 1890, in New York City. Morgan was known in his youth as one of the best boy sopranos in town, singing in the choirs of St. Thomas and All Angels churches. He attended Cornell University but dropped out to pursue sundry and itinerate careers as a brush salesman, advertising man, real estate agent, and cowpoke.

Eventually, Frank determined to emulate the career of his older brother Ralph, who had adjusted his last name to Morgan and made a reputation for himself as an actor in live theater. Frank also adopted the surname Morgan and successfully transitioned to vaudeville

---

6 The reference to Frank Morgan was probably inserted as a pitch by Edgar Allan Woolf, a longtime friend and supporter of Morgan. Woolf had scripted a comedic sketch, "The Last of the Quakers," for Morgan's vaudeville stage debut.

before accruing New York stage credits in *The Man Who Came Back*, *Seventh Heaven*, and *Gentlemen Prefer Blondes*. With his theatrical background and a profile to rival that of professional colleague John Barrymore, Morgan was a natural to transition into silent films in 1916. With the introduction of "talkies," Morgan continued to build a steady film career that included a 1934 Academy Award nomination as Best Actor for *The Affairs of Cellini*.

Noel Langley remembered that Frank Morgan wanted the title role in *The Wizard of Oz* so badly that he agreed to screen-test for it, returning from the vacation he was on after finishing *The Crowd Roars* (1938), directed by Richard Thorpe. At the time, Metro had already declared Morgan "the absent-minded professor of the screen," and noted that audiences equated Morgan's billing in a picture with its comedic success. "[Morgan's] humor is spontaneous, for he doesn't depend upon dialogue," read his 1938 studio biography, "He can make any line funny, even a tragic one."

The timing of Frank Morgan's candidacy for the Wizard of Oz role was fortuitous. By late September 1938, a harried Mervyn LeRoy told Harold Heffernan that come October 1, his long-delayed production would begin—Oz or no Oz—and that he was eyeing Frank Morgan among others. So effective was Morgan's screen test that five minutes afterward, the decision was made to award him the part.

Noel Langley witnessed the test and in 1970 told the *Virginian-Pilot*, "It was one of the funniest things I ever saw. He did a broad, burlesque routine. The director Victor Fleming [*sic*] threw a bucket of cold water on the burlesque.[7] He made Morgan play it straight and it made the man furious. Every time Fleming would shout, 'Is everyone ready?' for a scene, everyone would say 'Yes' except Morgan who under any circumstances would shout 'No.' He protested on every scene."

It seems curious that Morgan was so driven to obtain the Wizard role in reflection of an early-morning interview he gave to the *Brooklyn (NY) Daily Eagle* of June 10, 1939. Colonel Morgan—as he had taken to being affectionately addressed after receiving the distinction from authorities in Georgia—didn't mince words in expressing his disdain-of-the-moment. "I don't like Metro," he said, waking up in his bed at Manhattan's Hotel Plaza. Reaching for his morning egg nog, Morgan explained that he was fed up with "some pretty silly parts" the studio kept handing him, though Morgan prided himself on being equally effective as a dramatic actor. "The company has been making a habit of throwing me into those ridiculous musical comedy parts in the Jeanette MacDonald type of picture." When the uncredited interviewer ventured to ask Morgan, "Doesn't your latest picture, *The Wizard of Oz*, provide you with the high type of comedy that is a move in the direction in

---

7 Langley must have been misremembering or blending memories of separate incidents as Victor Fleming was not associated with *The Wizard of Oz* at the time of Frank Morgan's casting. It was probably Mervyn LeRoy to whom Langley intended to refer.

which you wish to go?" Morgan begrudgingly drawled, "Well, yes, I can see it is. But there will have to be more of that subtle and less of that silly stuff—and dramatic ventures, too."

By September 22, 1938, Morgan's casting was officially announced in the press: "Frank Morgan has been set for the role of the Wizard in *Wizard of Oz*, at MGM." Morgan was said to be so tickled at winning the *Oz* assignment that he celebrated by throwing a boat party on his eighty-one-foot cruiser, *Dolphin*, and junketing with his friends to Catalina.

After it was made public that Frank Morgan had been "drafted for Fields' role," the veteran of vaudeville and debonair leading man of the New York stage and silent pictures brought his own patented spin of confused doublespeak to the part, enhanced, in part, by the portable black cabinet—a miniature stocked bar—that he consulted in his dressing room as necessary in order to project the bewildered milquetoast persona that he had perfected by the late 1930s.

Morgan's imbibing tendencies were well known to the *Wizard of Oz* cast and crew but he was otherwise consummate in his conduct. Margaret Hamilton remembered Morgan as "very loveable, very sweet, very considerate, one of the nicest people I ever knew," adding,

"But he did like his drink." Only once did drink get the best of him on the *Oz* set; on break from the tedium, Morgan, in disguise as the Wizard's throne-room sentinel, was seen sloshed, singing an off-color tune in the guard box.

Frank Morgan brought both chicanery and sensitivity to his performance as the Wizard—the latter aspect being something that might've lacked had W. C. Fields played the part. In reflecting on Morgan's interpretation, Margaret Hamilton found the scene in which the Wizard awards token gifts to Dorothy's companions most touching.

According to Aljean Harmetz in *The Making of The Wizard of Oz*, none of Frank Morgan's obituaries mentioned *Oz* when he unexpectedly died in his sleep on September 18, 1949, at age fifty-nine; but this is a myth. With its first re-release in full swing, *Oz* was included among just four of Morgan's screen appearances by the Associated Press in its official death notice. But at the time, *Oz* was a minor role compared to Morgan's accomplished vitae of nearly one hundred film credits. Included as the most noteworthy was his nomination as Best Supporting Actor for the Victor Fleming–directed production *Tortilla Flat* (1942). In *Flat*, Morgan plays a Spaniard simpleton who presides over a band of stray dogs—among them, the canine who portrayed Toto in *The Wizard of Oz*.

GLINDA

It was Noel Langley who suggested stage comedienne Beatrice Lillie for the part of Glinda the Good Witch. Lillie made movies infrequently and was best known for performing segments of stage revues in which she would parody well-known songs with subtle but exaggerated facial expressions for comedic effect. Lillie was not a great beauty nor was she unattractive—a viable combination for merging Baum's two witches, the mature Witch of the North and the beautiful Glinda. Langley visualized Lillie making her entrance in *Oz* by descending from the sky, supported by piano wire. But as he recalled, "The casting people thought Miss Lillie was too limited in movie appeal and chose Billie Burke instead." Burke was, as Mervyn LeRoy put it in 1938, "an ideally friendly type" for the role. Upon being cast, Louella O. Parsons observed in her September 17, 1938, column that Burke's youthful looks would contrast with the Wicked Witch played by Gale Sondergaard.

In January 1938 *Silver Screen* correspondent S. K. Mook recalled the era when Billie Burke was "the biggest star in New York," contending that the actress looked just the same as she always did, and defining her as "the most glamorous star this country has ever had." Having been one of the first really important Broadway stars to come west for filmmaking, Burke embraced her legacy as show-business royalty. Her regal presence may be traced to the impression left on her as an English schoolgirl, with one of her most vivid childhood memories being the occasion of Queen Victoria's death and the school holiday that followed. But while Burke could facilely affect a British dialect, she was a native of Washington, DC, the daughter of a Barnum & Bailey circus clown, from whom she learned the art of pantomime.

At the time of *Oz*, Billie Burke was the fifty-four-year-old widow of Florenz Ziegfeld, creator of his self-named stage revues, or "follies"—Broadway spectacles of staging and entertainment that jumpstarted film careers for the likes of W. C. Fields, Fanny Brice, Louise Brooks, Will Rogers, and Ray Bolger. Following Metro's romanticized biopic *The*

Great Ziegfeld (Myrna Loy played Burke and William Powell played Ziegfeld), Burke was placed under long-term contract with MGM as one of its featured players. She returned to motion pictures having reinvented herself as a screen comedienne of deft skill and cleverness after Ziegfeld's 1932 passing left her with substantial debt.

In August 1938 Burke explained to reporter Maud Cheatham how she made the transition to screwball comedy:

> I feel that my stage experience gives me a technique that I can put to use now that the peaches and cream of youth have passed me by, yet I realize I am in that in-between period which bars a variety of roles; too old for the romantic heroine, too young for characters. Anyway, I welcome comedy and dearly love these dizzy, daffy characterizations. . . . On the stage, I portrayed glamorous, exciting heroines, and now, on the screen, I play frivolous mothers—the vague, impractical kind that sometimes act as if they believed the stork brings the babies. These ineffectual, flighty women may seem more or less alike, yet each has her own pattern and it is interesting to work it out.

Modern pictures like *Topper* (1937), *Everybody Sing* (1938), and *Merrily We Live* (1938) gave Billie Burke her greatest visibility, but it was her roots on the stage and in silent films that brought her an enduring prominence. She was renowned for her Gibson Girl good looks, with sparkling blue eyes, red tresses, and melodious diction—still pleasing enough in 1938 for her to record her own musical interludes for the *Oz* soundtrack. Indeed, Burke's lack of singing for the screen was lamented in a May 1940 news item, stating, "The noted stage star began her career in musical comedy and has never dropped her singing . . . [but] the only time she has sung in a picture was as the Good Fairy in *The Wizard of Oz*." Burke had been prepared for the opportunity to sing anew, stating, "[I] take lessons and practice just the same. In pictures one never knows."

L. Frank Baum described his benevolent sorceress, Glinda, as a beautiful woman "who knows how to keep young in spite of the many years she has lived." It was perhaps this description that influenced the choice of Billie Burke to portray the film version of the character, especially once both the elderly and youthful witches of Baum's story were blended. Burke was a holistic health advocate ahead of her time. As a matron, Burke preserved her 115-pound figure by standing on her head, turning six somersaults, and taking a two-mile hike before reporting to the MGM studio each morning. In 1952 Burke told King Features Syndicate columnist Ida Jean Kain, "I think age is an illusion in a way. While youth is beautiful, if women could only believe it, there is a beauty that can come with every age. Women should realize they can be lovely looking at fifty and past. Fifty is such a wonderful age."

A notice in the *Tulsa (OK) World* for Burke's 1916 picture *Gloria's Romance* could well have been foretelling of her radiant appearance in *The Wizard of Oz*. "If Billie Burke is to appear in more exquisite gowns than those worn in the first chapter of *Gloria's Romance*, she will have to call in the services of a fairyland sartorial wizard and to use a colloquialism, 'there ain't no such animile.' In *Gloria's Romance* Miss Burke is ravishingly beautiful and more winsome than ever before."

When *Photoplay* journalist Dixie Willson paid a visit to the Munchkinland set, she singled out Burke's ethereal presence as most complementary to the fairy-tale atmosphere, saying, "If ever good fairies lived, this one was the epitome of them all." Willson continued, "As for me, it seemed that all the magic in the world might be accomplished with just one wave of the wand of Miss Burke as the Good Fairy, her elfin Irish smile in the most perfect setting I have ever seen created for it; a cloud of shell-pink tulle, pale silver butterflies poised upon its mesh." In full wardrobe and makeup, Burke declared, "It makes me wish that I were sixteen again . . . that my feet didn't have to touch the ground."

Billie Burke contended that her part in *The Wizard of Oz* was a favorite role because it recalled the grand auspices and resplendent costumery of her early stage performances. (Prior to *Oz* Burke counted her performance onstage in *Becky Sharp* and her hostess role in George Cukor's 1933 film *Dinner at Eight* as her finest work.) In 1938 Burke acknowledged that her charmed life had spoiled her, and referred to herself as a "pampered, luxury-loving woman. . . ." The boudoir of her Beverly Hills home was described as indisputably feminine, decorated with pale-green walls and rug, satinwood furniture, and mauve bed and chairs. On the set of *The Wizard of Oz*, Burke's dressing room was similarly color-coordinated in shades of pastel pink and blue.

Burke's 1938 MGM biography reveals that the mystical themes of *The Wizard of Oz* may have held an especial attraction for her, reminiscent of L. Frank Baum's intrigue with the spiritualist movement of his era. Describing her as a "student of metaphysics," Burke was said to have "always been interested in educational subjects and at the present time is devoting herself to a study of metaphysics. She is of the opinion that the human brain is a natural instrument of communication [i.e., telepathy] and will eventually be developed to replace mechanical devices." Additionally, participating in the production of a children's classic would have been equally appealing. Burke reportedly loved children and, if compelled to work beyond the entertainment industry, noted that she could be fulfilled tending to and training children for working mothers. The part of Glinda would perfectly suit Burke's tenderness for youngsters as the nurturing, mentoring and omnipotent fairy-tale sorceress. And the actress had a Toto-like pet of her own at home, a Scottie aptly named Ziggy after her late husband.

In 1939 Billie Burke reported that "it was fun working on *Oz*," but the actress was hopeful that her role would prove to be the segue to more serious parts in pictures, telling *Script* magazine's DeWitt Bodeen, "I hope I shan't have to go on playing nothing but daffydill ladies and Malaprop mamas. Maybe Glinda will ease me into serio-comedy. After all, Glinda may have been a good fairy, but she wasn't a pixilated [i.e., loony] one." Burke also considered Glinda "a divine part," saying, "There's enough child in all of us to feel thrilled with the settings and feeling of this picture." Like Judy Garland, Billie Burke felt the responsibility of meeting public expectations. "It has me terrified a little to think of living up to the children's idea of what a Good Fairy must be, but I can only hope with all my heart that I don't disappoint them."

At the least, Burke made an impression on one youthful admirer, director Victor Fleming's five-year-old daughter Victoria. She was visiting the *Oz* set on the day that Burke was to film her insert shots for a superimposed montage as Dorothy wishes herself back to Kansas (most of which ended up on the cutting-room floor). Seeing Burke standing alone on the soundstage and illuminated in a circle of arc lights, Victoria was awestruck. "Daddy," she whispered to her father, "do you think I could *touch* the Good Fairy?"

WINGED MONKEYS, WINKIES, AND OZITES

Casting Brooklynite Patrick "Pat" Walshe as Nikko, the Wicked Witch's Winged Monkey confidante, was an example of MGM procuring only the most stellar talents for its production. Then thirty-eight, Walshe had made a career out of imitating chimpanzees on vaudeville stages and in legitimate theater. In a 1920 interview Walshe's height was documented at three feet eleven inches; his diminutive proportions made him bail out of the business world as an adult after his colleagues made him especially sensitive about his stature. After a lengthy illness, Walshe reinvented himself by capitalizing on his size and reentering the vaudeville circuit he had played as a child, circa 1906. As a grown man, Walshe was already a seasoned show business performer, having joined the Follies Bergere as a ten-year-old in 1910. The Follies was the first big cabaret revue of its kind, and Walshe remained with the show for about five years.

On his time off from the theater, Walshe took an interest in the primates with whom he became familiar via circuses and zoos. He began intently studying their mannerisms and "speech," transforming himself into an expert mimic that once tamed a fierce chimpanzee in captivity. Inspired, Walshe had a costumer create a hair suit made to fit him precisely. Augmented with a matching wig worn low on the brow, jutting false teeth (enhanced when Walshe distended his jaw), and gray makeup shaded around the eyes and cheeks, Walshe could become an ape in about ten minutes.

By the time Walshe was secured for *Oz*, he was well renowned for his pantomime portrayals of creatures on the Broadway stage, such as playing a gnome and a squirrel when still a prepubescent in *The Good Little Devil* (1912). But it was Walshe's uncanny impersonation of simians that earned him the nicknames "the human ape" and "the monkey man." Walshe said that he had the "highest admiration for the manifold talents

of the chimpanzee," citing him as the most intelligent of all animal performers. Walshe's respect translated to the accuracy of his portrayals and his ability to entertain—and fool—audiences.

Walshe's stage appearances as apes include the primeval forest scene of *As You Were* (1920); a promotional appearance in Boston for orangutan Joe Martin's film *A Prohibition Monkey* (1921); Jessica's monkey in *The Merchant of Venice* (1923); and a circus scene for 356 performances of *Rain or Shine* (1928) at the George M. Cohan Theatre. In the latter production, Walshe appeared with Betty Danko, who would serve as a stunt double for the Wicked Witch in MGM's *Oz*. Thus, placing Pat Walshe in *The Wizard of Oz* was a logical bit of casting, formally announced in *Screen News* on September 28, 1938. He left New York on Monday, October 3, and trained west, arriving at MGM a week later, ready to report for makeup and wardrobe tests.

Another actor of modest height, four-foot-nine Henry Lewis Stone, had already worked for MGM when he was cast as the commander of the Wicked Witch's monkey fleet, a role often confused with that of Pat Walshe's Nikko. Similar to Walshe, Stone's stature and circus background made him ideal as a stunt double for Tarzan's chimpanzee, Cheetah, playing opposite Johnny Weissmuller. Stone's experience aping the movies' most famous simian made him a natural for *Oz*. Stone prided himself on his physical prowess and agility for such stunt work, owing his fitness to constant workouts and a lifestyle that, in his words, was "kept in sober control by a planned regimen, as if my life depended upon it. And it did! My work demanded it. No drink, no smoke, no late hours."

For *The Wizard of Oz*, Stone was at first hired to test out the piano wires that would enable the Witch's Winged Monkeys to fly. "You can't imagine the number of special-effects technicians the studio hired to work on this picture," he said. "They even had technicians to work small electric motors for the monkeys' wings to flap!" Over thirty years after the fact, Stone could remember working under the glaring Technicolor lights, stating that it was "hot as blazes" in his tight, woolen monkey suit.

Like Henry Lewis Stone, Sid Dawson also found work as a stand-in, double, and stuntman for juvenile actors such as Billy Mauch, Freddie Bartholomew, Mickey Rooney, and Jackie Cooper. Dawson's height—just under five feet—also made him eligible for work as a Winged Monkey. Then thirty-seven, Dawson had been training as a professional jockey until a riding accident ended his racing career after eight months. His frequent presence on the MGM lot and his stunt work led to Dawson being cast as one of the monkeys.

The remainder of the Wicked Witch's army of Winged Monkeys would be portrayed by men of similarly slight stature, including Harry Monty, who would also perform as a Munchkin soldier. Freddie Retter, one of the little people cast as a Munchkin fiddler, was assigned to be Pat Walshe's stand-in and camera double.

To complement the Wicked Witch's evildoings, the sinister sorceress retained her militia of Winkie guards as described in *The Wonderful Wizard of Oz*. But for dramatic tension, MGM's Winkies were now towering figures—about twenty-eight in number—and not the Munchkin-size, timid natives of the L. Frank Baum book. Standing six-foot-two, fifty-eight-year-old actor Mitchell Lewis, one of Metro's featured players in 1938, was selected for the captain of the Winkies, a speaking role that required a commanding presence.

Born the son of matinee idol Manuel Lewis in Syracuse, New York, Mitchell became entranced at the prospect of acting at an early age. Watching his father emote on stage was a compelling childhood memory and young Mitchell learned acting technique directly from the elder Lewis. After theatrical successes in England and the States, Lewis transitioned to parts in silent films and talkies. Lewis's size and gruff persona as the lead Winkie belied his gentlemanly interests as an outdoor sportsman, flower fancier, and would-be politician (his mid-1930s bid for California state assembly was defeated).

Previously undocumented in film history is that Mitchell Lewis was cast in a *second* part in *The Wizard of Oz*—that of the Emerald City's High Priest, or Prime Minister, who presides over the triumphal return of Dorothy after she conquers the Wicked Witch. In an unintentional perpetuation of *Oz*'s doppelganger theme, Lewis was cast as this character for his strength and stature. His ornate costume was said to weigh more than one hundred pounds with its long green robes and train and assorted embellishments. Several players were said to have tested in the wardrobe but were encumbered by its weight and couldn't act naturally. Lewis donned the costume, reported Anne M. McIlhenney, and worked in it as though it were made of feathers. "Ten minutes later he was making  up for the part," she wrote, which included a bald cap, moustache, and goatee. But Lewis was a shoo-in, being another holdover from the cast of Mervyn LeRoy's *Anthony Adverse*.

As Lewis's makeup and wardrobe for his two respective parts in *The Wizard of Oz* was distinctly different, there would be no concern for audience recognition. Lewis's appearance in the Emerald City was deleted, however, when the entire sequence was removed in the editing process, although a scene in which he is pictured was used in advertising. Given his roles in a film fantasy, a note of interest was Lewis's abject belief in superstitions, such that he reportedly wouldn't "look a black cat in the eye."

For their intimidating bulk, the remaining men cast as Winkies reportedly averaged six-foot-one in height and were young athletes recruited from USC, including football star Ambrose Schindler (who was also the Tin Man's stunt double for the cliff-climbing scene). In recent times Schindler's casting as a Winkie has been questioned, suggesting a case of "mis-identification." But on November 29, 1938, notice of Schindler's *Wizard of Oz* assignment appeared in the *Hollywood Reporter* and his name is inked into surviving Winkie wardrobe.

Not all the Winkie extras were without acting experience, however. Julian "Jack" J. Smith followed in his father's footsteps when he was cast as a Winkie. In fact, it was his father, actor Julian Arnold Smith, who recommended Jack for the job. Jack said that the opportunity for extra work in *The Wizard of Oz* came about in a peculiar way. "My dad, first of all, got a part in it and had worked a couple of days when he suggested that I go see the casting director about getting on," Jack recalled before his death in 1998. "He thought there would be a good couple of weeks' work out of it and that I'd be able to make several hundred dollars." As Jack Smith had previously performed in several *Our Gang* comedies and, later, as an extra in RKO's *The Last Days of Pompeii* in 1935, he figured the *Oz* gig would beat mowing lawns, setting up pins in a bowling alley, or preparing salads in a Culver City restaurant. "So I went and talked to the casting director, whom I knew pretty well," said Smith. "And he said, 'Sure, I'll put you on.'

"The first day I went to work, he told me to go down to wardrobe to get made up, then report back to him. In wardrobe they made me up with a green face and gray costume to be one of the Wicked Witch's guards. My dad was already made up as a guard and was on the set. A few other friends were in on it too: Clint Dougherton, Cap Somers, and a couple other guys that I knew real well." Smith was also assigned to lead a bit of choreography involving the Winkies. "When I reported back to the casting director, he said, 'I want you to do something special on this deal. When they start to march into the castle, I want eight of you guys in line to march into the castle and I want you to start them off on the left foot and everybody fall in line military-style.' I'd had ROTC in high school and knew I could do that. He put me up in about four or five different shots. . . ."

After *Oz* Jack Smith found additional work as a wounded soldier on *Gone with the Wind*. With his head heavily bandaged and artificial blood running down the side of his face, Smith was directed to reach up and grasp at the hem of Scarlett O'Hara's skirt while begging for "Water, water" in the famous depot scene. "I did that," Smith remembered, "and think I made about fifty dollars for that because it was lines, although I never saw myself in that. I was never really interested in seeing myself after I did these things." The sole exception was *The Wizard of Oz*, to which Smith took a girlfriend on the occasion of its Hollywood premiere, "It was the only movie I was in that I saw."

As Hollywood was teeming with hopefuls looking to break into pictures, selecting the citizenry to populate the Emerald City was as facile as placing a call to central casting. Some of the Emerald City extras were already acquainted, as Dorothy Barrett, a Wash & Brush Up parlor manicurist, recalled. Many of them simply floated from picture to picture, Barrett said, or got parts through connections or sheer nepotism. For example, Amelia Batchler, another Emerald City extra (and the original model for Columbia's torch-bearing-lady logo), was the sister of Oz's wardrobe mistress, Sheila O'Brien. Lorraine Grey got her first screen appearance in Oz after being a stand-in for her sister, MGM actress Virginia Grey. Likewise, dancer Loie Gaither, also in Oz, was the wife of sound technician Chip Gaither.

Additional identified Emerald City extras include George Beranger, Tyler Brooke, Charles Irwin, Albert Morin, Rolfe Sedan, Gerald Oliver Smith, Carol Tevis, and Bobby Watson. George Beranger had worked in pictures since the silents, having appeared in D. W. Griffith's *The Birth of a Nation* before becoming a star in the 1920s. By the time of *Oz*, his career had been reduced to bit parts. Likewise, Tyler Brooke had played uncredited extras since the 1920s. Charles Irwin was an extra in more substantial pictures such as *The Adventures of Robin Hood* (1938), *The Little Princess* (1939), and *Susannah of the Mounties* (1939). Rolfe Sedan and Gerald Oliver Smith both enjoyed long careers in minor roles. Albert Morin had bit parts as Juan in Metro's *The Girl of the Golden West* (1938) and as Rene Picard in the Atlanta Bazaar scene of *Gone with the Wind*. Carol Tevis was also a vocalist on some of the *Oz* arrangements. Bobby Watson was the befuddled diction coach in *Singin' in the Rain* (1952).

THE MUNCHKINS

In *The Wonderful Wizard of Oz*, the Munchkins, who greet Dorothy upon her arrival in the Land of Oz, are miniature adults roughly the size of Dorothy, "who was a well-grown child for her age," although much older in appearance. Arthur Freed had identified little-person agent and theatrical impresario Leo Singer as a lead contact for convening a cadre of little performers as early as February 1938; and actively gathering little people and animals for the Munchkin scenes rated a top priority in Freed's May 20, 1938, memo to Mervyn LeRoy about preproduction plans.

The Wizard of Oz would not be the first picture to gather a significant number of little people. On April 18, 1938, the *Hollywood Reporter* announced that Abe Meyer would finance production of *The Terror of Tiny Town*, an all-little-person musical western, produced by Jed Buell (Meyer would be associate producer). Both men were said to be "gathering a lot of midget animals in their search for novelties."

But Mervyn LeRoy also considered the plausibility of casting children as Munchkins in the tradition of early stage and screen versions of *Snow White* in which the Seven Dwarfs were portrayed by children—including girls—disguised in stage beards. An April 7, 1938, report about child stars Mickey Rooney and Freddie Bartholomew noted that both were slated to "get the most unusual roles of their careers when Mervyn LeRoy makes *The Wizard of Oz*. He's thinking of having all the child players around represent the Munchkins." Featuring Rooney, Bartholomew, Ronald Sinclair, and other Metro juveniles in cameos might have been a clever bit of self-aggrandizement, akin to Judy Garland's musical ode to Metro's Clark Gable in *Broadway Melody of 1938* (1937). And crowd scenes could easily be fleshed out with kiddie recruits from local dance studios. More likely to be cast as Munchkins with speaking parts would be the recognizable urchins from the successful *Our Gang* shorts.

Hal Roach's big-budget, two-reel Metro musical *Our Gang Follies of 1938* (released December 18, 1937) seems to have been an early influence for the LeRoy Unit, especially if there was a consideration for tapping the talent of show-business kids to portray Munchkins. In *Follies*'s dream sequence, *Our Gang* stalwart Alfalfa Switzer finds himself in a juvenile nightclub that, between patrons and performers, features over a hundred child actors, singers, and dancers. As Alfalfa enters his dreamlike state, spiraling, concentric rings signal the transition—nearly identical to the effect in *The Wizard of Oz* when Dorothy enacts the Ruby Slippers' charm to return to Kansas.

The musical interlude in *Follies* is introduced by Darla Hood, dressed as the "Lovebug," who "stings" the number's participants into declaring musical devotion for their partners. The various "romantics" are shown in theatrical tableaux, the scenery of which is tailored to an insect-size perspective including huge flowers on scale with those in Munchkinland. Some of the juvenile players are presented in brief vignettes in sets of three and in various stereotypes, such as three Park Avenue snobs—akin to how the Munchkin Lullaby League and Lollipop Guild are presented in *Oz*. The three tough boys from "the Bowery" who appear in *Follies* could very well have inspired the Lollipop Guild trio, which was originally named "Three Tough Kids." As shown in a May 11, 1938, conceptual illustration by MGM makeup artist George Lane, the Lollipop Guild is a match for the *Follies* toughs.

The *Follies* vignettes are performed on a curved stage elevated by small, tiered steps, like the design of Munchkinland's civic center. Once the children descend onto the main dance floor, the set bears a striking resemblance to the sweeping spiral of *Oz*'s Yellow Brick Road. Finally, the musical segment is disrupted by black-cloaked meanie Barnaby (actor Henry Brandon reprising his role from Roach's 1934 *Babes in Toyland*), who, like *Oz*'s Wicked Witch, enters stage right and menaces the dreamer-protagonist—in this instance, Alfalfa instead of Dorothy.

Our Gang cast member Tommy Bond has stated that he wanted to be in *Oz* "but I couldn't qualify as one of the Lollipop Guild because I was too tall." Bond recounted in

his autobiography that Mervyn LeRoy "thought that hundreds of children playing the Munchkins would be impossible to control, so they decided on midgets." Indeed, large groups of children could be difficult to manage. For the ice-cream-factory finale of *Kid Millions*, cast member Bond said that "a disgusting concoction of mashed potatoes and cheese" substituted for the less resilient frozen dessert, which wouldn't have lasted long under the Technicolor lights. Creating the illusion that the experience was an enthusing treat was a challenge, and Janet Cantor Gari remembered some of the children vomiting from consuming the faux dessert.

The decision to cast the Munchkins almost exclusively with adult little people would also be cost-effective as there would be no work restrictions for their on-set time as there were for child actors. About a dozen little girls were hired to augment the male little people, but a December 1939 interview attributed to Munchkin Mayor Charley Becker claims there were a hundred children on set, which is inaccurate. MGM anecdotes of the period endure about on-set tutors mistaking some of the little men for their boy pupils when aiding them in the toilet or rounding them up for school, as was wryly retold by Jane Hall in her August 1939 article for *Good Housekeeping*. If based in truth, these may be references to any male little person young enough to still be of school age, such as sixteen-year-old Jerry Maren, as only one little boy is known to have participated. (Maren left high school two months before graduation to appear in *Oz*, and took correspondence courses to earn his diploma.)

According to May Mann, in her January 10, 1939, column, a tutor on the *Oz* set was surprised when she grabbed hold of one youngster who protested, "Madame, before you hustle me off to your school room, perhaps you are not aware I hold two degrees from the University of Iowa." Barney Oldfield, columnist of the *Lincoln (NE) Star*'s Theatre Topics column, suggested that the children working on *Oz* were taking advantage of the confusion. "They duck their study periods between takes by hiding among the midgets which are their size. Teachers have a tough time weeding them out. . . ." In a 1971 interview Jerry Maren explained why the children were indistinguishable from the adult little people. "There were so many Munchkins in the show that they couldn't find enough midgets to fill the parts, so many, many of the Munchkins in the background shots are local children who were hired to portray older midgets."

Suffice it to say, if Disney had seven dwarfs, MGM would have seventy. The actual count of Munchkins was closer to 124, the number originally cited on the July 12, 1938, "Temporary List of People Requiring Costumes" for the picture. In its promotional propaganda, the studio was clear: "Dwarfs or deformed persons were not wanted. Midgets, being perfect humans excepting for size, were wanted." Yet a handful of Munchkin players were clinically considered pituitary dwarfs with enlarged heads and stunted hands and feet, such as actor John George—reportedly a last-minute addition—who had appeared in several

Metro films of the 1920s with Lon Chaney. Most of the Munchkins were indeed perfectly proportioned miniature adults, or midgets as they were commonly called at the time. Not that there was a dearth of little people in Los Angeles. That was a call the Screen Actors Guild could not fulfill. Dorothy's Munchkins would need to be imported to Culver City.

As of September 1, 1938, Viennese impresario Leo Singer was put on a salary of one hundred dollars a week to procure the 124 little people designated for *The Wizard of Oz*. When negotiating his MGM contract, it is unknown if Singer leveraged—or exaggerated to his advantage—a knowledge of the Oz characters as, a few years prior, he had a fleeting connection to the greater Oz saga. Beginning Thursday, March 23, 1933, for five performances (three nights, two matinees), *The Teddy Bear in Oz* was a fantasy-dance segment of the Singer's Midgets program at the Amarillo, Texas, Municipal Auditorium. The new story was presented in two scenes accompanied by original music played on two pianos, and featured fourteen ballet interludes. The narrative was performed by a dozen girls from Elsie Little's dance class, who shared the bill with Singer's Midgets. The story included familiar L. Frank Baum characters such as Dorothy; the Scarecrow; the Tin Woodman; the Wizard; Polychrome, the Rainbow's daughter; and the Patchwork Girl. As the main char-

acters search for and rescue the lost Princess Ozma of Oz, the scenario also introduced the Pink Teddy Bear and the wicked Devil Evil.

Singer reportedly had eighteen little people under personal contract in 1938 but would need to approach talent agents Henry Kramer, Harvey Williams, and Nate Eagle and rely upon word of mouth to drum up the additional little-person extras required. By July 2, 1938, *Boxoffice* reported that Nate Eagle, who conducted the Midget City at the 1933–34 Chicago World's Fair, was awaiting word from MGM to come west from Illinois with his troupe of sixty little people. At the time, production was expected to begin in August 1938, but it would not be until Monday, November 7, 1938, that Singer was to arrive in Chicago to engage Eagle.

The most pervasive plug for casting of Munchkins came when Ed Sullivan announced in his June 21, 1938, syndicated Hollywood column that "Mervyn LeRoy needs 100 midgets for *Wizard of Oz*, address him at MGM." This blurb fed directly into an underground network among little-person entertainers and those who were without show business experience. Munchkin actor Meinhardt Raabe, who hailed from Madison, Wisconsin, remembered how he and others learned about *The Wizard of Oz*. "There was a 'midget grapevine,'" Raabe recalled. "The word came through the channels that MGM wanted to make a picture; they wanted all the little people they could get ahold of. Every little person who walked through the front gate at MGM got a job as a Munchkin, if you were physically able."

It was also through this grapevine that Jimmy Hulse of Circleville, Ohio, learned of *The Wizard of Oz* opportunity. Hulse became acquainted with the grapevine when the Harvey Williams troupe of little people came to his hometown for the annual Pumpkin Show. Hulse joined the troupe in Kansas City in early November 1938, and by January 11, 1939, Hulse had returned home, his work on *Oz* completed. Others, like Adam Kozicki, were already connected to show business for performing in traveling little-person troupes. Even prior to playing a Munchkin in *Oz*, Kozicki received an offer from MGM in 1935 based on a screen test he made at the Capitol Theatre in his hometown of Wilkes-Barre, Pennsylvania. But Kozicki was obliged to decline the invite when his manager wouldn't rescind his contract.

Not every little person in the grapevine was able to participate as planned. Teenager Myrna Clifton's emergency appendectomy caused her to remain in her native Texas and forfeit the opportunity to appear as a Munchkin. Likewise, Sergeant Don Ward, a sixty-two-year-old Helena, Montana, police officer, had to refuse the invitation to appear in *Oz* due to "a serious heart ailment and an attack of arthritis," although he had previously appeared as a pygmy with Johnny Weissmuller in Metro's *Tarzan the Ape Man* (1932). Johnny Roventini, then billed as Johnny Morris Jr. and famous since 1933 as radio's bellhop mascot for Philip Morris cigarettes, reportedly left a Pittsburgh nightclub engagement on November 6, 1938, and headed for Hollywood "to be one of the midgets in *The Wizard of Oz*." The timing of Roventini's departure was synchronous with that of the other incoming Munchkin actors, but nothing came of his *Oz* plans; by December 16 he was making a personal appearance in Roseburg, Oregon, en route to San Francisco.

In addition to disqualifying most people of dwarf stature, MGM kept its Munchkin cast strictly Caucasian and refused to cast minorities—the irony being that the complexion hue of many Ozians was diverse. This didn't deter one African-American hopeful from answering the call for little people. In September 1938 Broadway reporter Regina Crewe told of forty-five-year-old Frankie Brown, described as a dark man "café au lait in color" who originally hailed from Oklahoma. Upon learning of the *Oz* casting call, the forty-inch-tall Brown took leave from his job entertaining at the Glass Hat, the Belmont Plaza Hotel's nightclub, in order to travel west for an interview with Mervyn LeRoy. Though reportedly "perfectly proportioned and well formed," Brown returned to his New York act by October, apparently having been rejected for *Oz*, which was just as well. In the era of Stepin Fetchit, any onscreen appearance by Brown would have been for an undignified gag.

Under the terms of the agreement with MGM, Leo Singer's salary as the little people's representing agent would increase to two hundred dollars per week once production on *Oz* began. (Singer also brought with him his servant and secretary.) All the little actors would receive their compensation directly from Singer as his employees, not Metro's, starting at fifty dollars a week each while waiting for the call to begin work; one hundred dollars a week for rehearsal and filming; and an additional one hundred dollars a week for retakes if needed.

MGM was also compensating Singer up to twenty-five dollars a day for meals, lodging, and travel expenses to transport any little-person actors to Los Angeles from outside of L.A. or Culver City. This included twenty-eight little people who left New York the morning of November 5, 1938, on All American Bus Lines. Coordinating their arrival from pickups in New York, Pittsburgh, Minneapolis, and Chicago—not to mention small towns scattered among all points in between—was an exercise in logistics. Even though the majority of the little people were of age, their typical-size escorts were always distinguished in MGM's paperwork as "adults."

Between November 11 and November 23, 1938, 116 little people had arrived in Culver City. On their first day entering the studio gates, one of the little men, nicknamed Gee-gee the Gunner, walked up to the gatekeeper, held out his hand, and said, "How do you do, Mr. Mayer." Metro's facilities were largely unprepared to meet the needs of the little people, however. It was only after Mervyn LeRoy interviewed the group that he learned of a predicament that required a necessary but humiliating accommodation. Because of their stature, the little people needed assistance to scale the platforms and parallels built for scenes around the rim of the set. LeRoy saw to it that six husky men, at least six feet tall, were on hand as "human elevators" to lift the little people into position. This also reportedly extended to drinking fountains and toilets, although the extent of this humiliation is uncertain. The men in particular resented being picked up as one would a child or a doll.

Some of the little people had already been at Metro since the prior August for preliminary wardrobe, lighting, and Technicolor tests and to gauge their proportions when photographed next to Judy Garland. When *The Wizard of Oz* kicked off its long-awaited production on October 13, 1938, Mervyn LeRoy held a press conference that the little

people who were on-site attended (though their numbers were exaggerated to fifty). The Munchkins reportedly danced, sang, and played instruments for a large crowd. Much mirth was noted when *Oz*'s then-director Richard Thorpe stood in their midst. Standing six feet in height—one of the tallest men in the studio—most of the little people only came up to his knees.

PRAIRIE HOME COMPANIONS

For the roles of Dorothy's worn and weary Uncle Henry and Aunt Em, MGM could draw from its roster of character actors. Tentatively, Arthur Freed proposed Charley Grapewin and May Robson. However, as the Kansas scenes were last on *Oz*'s production schedule, filling these supporting parts was not pressing.

By August 8, 1938, Grapewin had been confirmed for the uncle when MGM announced that Grapewin presented to Mervyn LeRoy his copy of *The Wizard of Oz* theater script, retained from the time Grapewin appeared in a road-show company of *Oz* circa 1908. Grapewin's script was described as much-used and dog-eared but a valuable souvenir nonetheless. One month later *Motion Picture Daily* announced that Grapewin was cast in *Stand Up and Fight*, a Mervyn LeRoy–produced picture.

By mid-December 1938, however, Grapewin announced he was retiring from motion pictures after completing his next role, reportedly in *Ice Follies of 1939*. The press knew not to take Grapewin's pronouncement of retirement too seriously—one wag cracked that it was the actor's forty-seventh such declaration. Grapewin probably didn't take it all too seriously either. It was, instead, a fleeting moment of indecision, as he continued working steadily until just prior to beginning *The Wizard of Oz* in February 1939. But given the critical accolades he received for his portrayal of the elderly patriarch in *The Good Earth* (1937) and the success of *Captains Courageous* (1937), Grapewin may have been content to bow out on top and rest on the laurels of a lifelong career in show business that included stints as a circus acrobat and trapeze artist, vaudeville comedian, and Broadway performer. He was planning to pen a memoir that would cover his history as an actor and the eclectic celebrities and entertainers he had encountered.

When Charley Grapewin declined the role of Uncle Henry, at age seventy, he may have been deterred by the taxing expectation that the farm exteriors would be authentically shot on location in Kansas. On February 7, 1939, the *Hollywood Reporter* noted that another character actor, Harlan Briggs, was cast in *Oz*. But two days later Grapewin committed to the part, perhaps persuaded on several counts. Grapewin likely held admiration for Mervyn LeRoy's production, especially if Grapewin visited the set or previewed rushes, coupled with the opportunity to reunite with his *Captains Courageous* director, Victor Fleming, who was, by then, also *Oz*'s director. The decision to shoot the farm scenes on an

MGM soundstage as opposed to on location in Kansas may have also been an enticement. Additionally, Grapewin was probably swayed by the nostalgic sentiment of his performing roots, as he was a stage history aficionado and collector of old theatrical photographs. Harlan Briggs was thereafter reassigned as Grapewin's *Oz* stand-in, according to the cast contact roster.

By this time May Robson had turned down the Aunt Em role, and on January 31, 1939, Sarah Padden screen-tested for the part as well as posed for wardrobe and makeup stills. Padden modeled at least two different-style aprons in a mock-rural setting that included a white picket fence, assorted shrubs, and a bowl of donuts or crullers, as called for in the script. With her hair in a loose bun and minimal makeup, Padden looks appropriately frumpy but not without a glimmer of tenderness in her eyes.

On February 2, however, the *Hollywood Reporter* announced that Joe Rivkin, actress Clara Blandick's agent, had secured the Aunt Em part for his client. Blandick's portrayal of Dorothy's somewhat stern auntie would recall public identification with her similar roles in film adaptations of Mark Twain's *Huckleberry Finn* and *Tom Sawyer*. The final selection of Blandick would have been Mervyn LeRoy's privilege and he likely opted for her as a nod to her performance in his *Anthony Adverse* in 1936.

What Joe Rivkin didn't negotiate for his client was screen credit commensurate with her costar. Blandick would not receive billing in the opening credits of *The Wizard of Oz*, though Charley Grapewin, as an MGM contract player, would be listed. In the closing credits, Blandick would be ranked after Grapewin, between Pat Walshe as Nikko and Toto the dog. Blandick probably received screen billing after Walshe due to the timing of her casting; Walshe had been set for his role more than four months prior to Blandick. In 1941 Blandick remained annoyed by her absence in the opening credits and commented to a friend:

I have never had the demanding ego that afflicts the stars of our industry. You don't receive a lot of glory playing mothers and aunts and gossips. But now that I am compelled to look back on my movie memories and my eventful week shooting *Oz*, I was a bit bruised by the brushing off I received compared to Charley. He had a less significant "role" in the scheme of things and received no more money. I had appeared with him before and we were always a "good fit." He was a little embarrassed by the slight to me, especially when the [news] feature ran that deemed me "Clara Blandish." That did make me cross. I am, in addition to everything, proud of my family name. [Blandick had combined her middle name Blanchard with her birth surname Dickey to form her stage name.]

The pairing of Charley Grapewin and Clara Blandick as Dorothy's Kansas guardians resonated with readers of the *Fitchburg (MA) Sentinel*, which, on August 19, 1939, reported that veteran theatergoers would remember the actors from local appearances. Grapewin had formerly headlined his own attraction at the Cummings Theatre, and Blandick was a stock favorite in Worcester.

Screen Adaptation

A BAND OF WRITERS

The process of adapting L. Frank Baum's twenty-four-chapter novel *The Wonderful Wizard of Oz* into a screenplay treatment began with locating the proper writers. But it would prove to be a prolonged process in which seasoned scenarists and gag writers would conflict and distort the original source material in efforts to broaden its appeal. As *The Wizard of Oz* was based on a preexisting work, it was possible for Arthur Freed to generate his January 31, 1938, tentative cast suggestions prior to a story draft instead of waiting on an original screenplay conceived as a star vehicle and plugging in supporting cast once the story was written. From a screenplay, all other aspects of the production would be defined: supporting players, songs, set design, special effects, wardrobe, and makeup.

When it was confirmed that Metro had secured the *Wizard of Oz* movie rights, William Cannon, Mervyn LeRoy's Academy Award–nominated assistant director on *Anthony Adverse*, submitted a four-page memo, dated February 26, 1938, comprised of his thoughts about how the Oz characters could be credibly presented onscreen. Cannon's is the earliest such outline known, presumably drafted after he revisited Baum's book.

Though brief, two factors introduced by Cannon remain in the final version of *The Wizard of Oz*. Cannon states that if Frank Baum had written the story in recent times, he would have imbued it with modern contrivances. Thus, argues Cannon, "I think our *Wizard of Oz* background should be a Fairyland of 1938 and not of 1900." (By contrast, Paramount's *Alice in Wonderland* was set in Victorian times.) Cannon also refers to Dorothy's Silver Shoes as "slippers"—a descriptor first used in the 1928 Samuel French play script. According to Cannon, it is the slippers that are impressive enough to gain Dorothy admittance into the Emerald City, unlike in Baum's story in which Dorothy and her companions persuade the gatekeeper about the urgency of their business with the Wizard.

In particular, Cannon felt that the Scarecrow and Tin Woodman characters (no Lion is mentioned) should deliberately be portrayed as humans attired in fantasy garb—as was done in the Larry Semon version—in order to be convincing to modern audiences. Cannon's notions were painstakingly literal. The Scarecrow would be a social outcast unable to comply with any assignment except for the brainless task of monitoring a field as a scarecrow would. But given the Wizard's endorsement of approval, the Scarecrow would be accepted. Similarly, Cannon's human Tin Man was a narcissistic, disagreeable rogue who instigated fights and was deemed heartless by the people of Oz. Encased in a suit of tin, the Woodman was ostracized and tasked with a solitary existence chopping trees. He had tried to see the Wizard prior to meeting Dorothy but was unsuccessful; given Dorothy's protective devices (her magic shoes and the Good Witch's kiss on her forehead), the Tin Man felt an audience with the Wizard was imminent and it would be declared he had a heart.

Cannon cautioned LeRoy about relying too much on the use of magic, "especially when this is used with human beings," and compared Oz's "problem" of believability as comparable to *The Connecticut Yankee in King Arthur's Court*, in which the Yankee dreams he is transplanted in medieval times but introduces modern conveniences.

But LeRoy remained steadfast that his picture would embrace the spirit of Baum's fantasy. He recognized early on that, like *Snow White*, his movie could attract as many adults as children. "I used to think Oz was for children," he said. "Since I've become interested in the [Oz] stories, I talked to dozens of adults who read them. Why, [actress] Kay Francis is one of them. She has a whole series and she's always reading them." Jackie Coogan, Jeanette MacDonald, and Ann Shirley were also among L. Frank Baum's Hollywood fans. Child actor Martin Spellman, who appeared in Metro's *Boys Town* (1938), was a self-proclaimed "*Wizard of Oz* nut" who "read every one of the books" by swapping titles with a friend. (Spellman's curiosity led him to wander onto soundstage 26 as the first set—the Scarecrow's cornfield—was being constructed with its trees, "golden path to Emerald City," and the hill that was built up beyond the field.)

Others among Hollywood's elite were taken with the Baum stories. In May 1937 columnist Jimmie Fidler told how dinner guest Jimmy Stewart overheard Henry Fonda read a bedtime passage from *The Wizard of Oz* to his stepdaughter. After the child fell asleep, Fonda discontinued, which prompted an admonishment from Stewart, "Hey! What's the idea of stopping? Read a couple more chapters—it was just gettin' good." According to *Modern Screen* of November 1939, Bette Davis's two Oscars presided atop a bookshelf in which stood the actress's childhood Oz books.

Scores of adult fans grew up with the Oz books and retained fond memories of the happiness they brought in childhood, with hundreds of admirers continuing to send fan mail to L. Frank Baum—unaware that he had passed on. Striking a balance between Oz book admirers and regular movie patrons was a delicate prospect when planning Metro's version of *The Wizard of Oz*. On March 5, 1938, Hollywood journalist Louella O. Parsons informed her column's readers, "I have heard it whispered that Disney has been asked if he would consider an outside deal to supervise the *Wizard of Oz* script. So much depends upon a right conception of these characters." No formal "outside deal" with Walt Disney is known to have manifested, but it was surely Disney who recommended that Mervyn LeRoy employ his standardized practice for storyboarding, that is, plotting the film's action in advance with a series of interchangeable sketches. As Edwin Schallert told it in the *Los Angeles Times*, "Mervyn LeRoy, producer of *Wizard of Oz*, is taking a leaf from the Walt Disney system in preparing for the production. Scenes are to be re-created in cartoon form first, and then enacted by the players. . . ." That LeRoy followed through is evidenced by one extant *Wizard of Oz* storyboard sequence of graphite panels depicting the chase in the Wicked Witch's castle—an early and complicated episode.

If Disney provided further casual advice to LeRoy, it most likely echoed Walt's statement to *Boxoffice* when asked about editing the horrors from *Snow White* prior to its general release in February 1938. "We have never made pictures for children," Disney explained. "What we really strive for in our productions is to appeal to the child qualities that linger in every adult."

It was a position in keeping with LeRoy's philosophy that any treatment of the source matter should be handled with the awed wonderment of a child. Or as LeRoy put it, in adult terms, "To make a picture like *The Wizard of Oz* everybody has to be a little drunk with imagination." LeRoy maintained this tenet in all future interviews about *Oz*, and it's what guided the producer in his choice (and dismissal) of directors and scenarists.

Thus, William Cannon's outline was set aside in favor of considering treatments contributed by other writers—most of whom felt the need to largely disregard Baum's book in favor of adding extraneous characters and plots.

At the same time Disney's involvement was being rumored, Irving Brecher was assigned to the *Oz* script in early March 1938. Brecher had previously contributed dialogue to Mervym LeRoy's *Fools for Scandal*. But Brecher was hastily reassigned from *Oz* to the next Marx Brothers script, *At the Circus*, which LeRoy was also producing. Then on May 23, 1938, *Motion Picture Daily* reported that Irving Brecher was back on the job, assisted in fleshing out the *Oz* screenplay by Robert Pirosh and George Seaton—presumably to punch it up as the screenwriting duo had previously collaborated on the Marx Brothers' comedy hits *A Night at the Opera* (1935) and *A Day at the Races* (1937).

In the interim Herman Mankiewicz began his three-week stint on March 7, 1938. (Mankiewicz's younger brother Joseph had the script for Paramount's *Alice in Wonderland* to his credit. It was also Joe who, five years later, would have an extramarital affair with

Judy Garland.) Mankiewicz's assignment was announced in *Boxoffice* on March 12, by which time he was immersed in his treatments for *Oz*.

Mankiewicz's drafts, dated March 9–11, 1938, and March 12–19, 1938, are quite literal in terms of honoring Baum's descriptions. Upon arriving in the Land of Oz, Dorothy is greeted by the Good Witch and three male Munchkins dressed in blue and wearing the same round hats that rise to a point with small bells around the brim as Baum described them. The Munchkin dwellings are also the same odd-looking blue houses with domed roofs. Upon learning she has killed a witch, Dorothy's dialogue is direct from Baum: "Oh dear, oh dear! The house must've fallen on her. Whatever shall we do?" As in the book, the Good Witch's hat turns into a slate with writing that instructs Dorothy to seek the Wizard. The Good Witch bestows a protective kiss to Dorothy's forehead, and before embarking on her journey, and as in the book, Dorothy changes into her blue gingham dress and pink sunbonnet and puts on the Silver Shoes that belonged to the dead sorceress.

Mankiewicz also included roles for newly created characters: Princess Betty (MGM's teenage singer Betty Jaynes), who is liberated from a dungeon once the Wicked Witch of the East is vanquished; and Grand Duke Allan (LeRoy's protégé Kenny Baker), to add a romantic subplot to the story. Mankiewicz probably felt at liberty to add the royal characters given that Baum wrote about Princess Gaylette and Prince Quelala in addition to the china princess; and also because of the royalty themes of the 1902 play and 1925 film versions of *The Wizard of Oz*.

At the mention of the remaining bad witch, the scene shifts to the office headquarters of the Wicked Witch of the West, who, like Baum's witch, has only one eye but is a mix of comic buffoonery and villainy, similar to early concepts for Walt Disney's Evil Queen as both portly and conceited.

Mankiewicz's descriptions of the Scarecrow and Tin Woodman mirror Baum's descriptions verbatim, and Mankiewicz indicates a lengthy soliloquy in which the Scarecrow tells of how he came to be constructed, also as in the book. Mankiewicz does, though, suggest that once restored to normal working order after his rescue, the Tin Man goes into a dance routine, as in the final film. Also at this point, Mankiewicz wrote the Cowardly Lion role in a literal sense given ambiguity for how the part would be realized onscreen—as in March 1938 no actor had yet been cast and Mervyn LeRoy was weighing various options that included using a real lion. As in *The Wonderful Wizard of Oz*, Mankiewicz's Lion jumps a chasm that divides the Yellow Brick Road by carrying each of the characters across separately (Dorothy encourages Toto to jump up on the Lion's back).

By March 31 the *Film Daily* noted that Herman Mankiewicz's work on *Oz* was completed. It was said that Noel Langley had collaborated on the script with Mankiewicz, but in actuality Langley and Ogden Nash were both scribing the *Oz* screenplay simultaneously with, yet independently of, Mankiewicz. Langley was a Hollywood newcomer as of 1936, and Nash was known for his whimsical way with poems, rhymes, and verses.

Nash's notes of April 16, 1938—his "suggested outline after meeting with Cowardly Lion"—are infused with sight gags demonstrative of his skills as a humorist. But Nash also draws heavily from ideas in the script of the famous Broadway extravaganza.

As in the opening of the show's Act II, Nash's scenario has the Wizard futilely attempting to impress the citizenry with magic tricks from a special stage outside the palace. Instead of the play's Wiley Gyle, who uses bombs in his efforts to expose the Wizard as a fraud, Nash suggests the Wicked Witch circle overhead on her broom "like a bombing plane" dropping darts to which are attached copies of her ultimatum to the Wizard: Surrender Emerald City no later than noon of the following day or she will destroy it. The crowd expects the clever Wizard is capable of destroying the Witch and averting disaster.

In the interim the Wizard has retreated inside the palace. Dorothy and her friends explain their mission to the Wizard, and he decides to make the Scarecrow and Tin Man his proxies for dispatching the Witch. In a disguise, he goes back onstage to convince the citizenry that the indestructible duo is a better match for the Witch than the Wizard. To prove it, he intends to demonstrate how the Tin Man's armor will repel the Witch's poison arrows and the Scarecrow will deftly catch her enchanted eggs filled with sneezing gas. But the ploy backfires when the Wizard's two stooges thoughtlessly switch places. The arrows strike the Scarecrow, who looks like a porcupine, and the eggs burst against the Woodman, releasing the gas and causing a chain reaction of sneezing among the crowd.

Back in the palace, Dorothy's group demands that the Wizard honor their requests. It is then that he confesses to being a humbug, plotting his escape at dawn in a balloon bound for Omaha. He offers to take Dorothy with him and drop her off in Kansas.

Lizzie Smithers, Aunt Em's Kansas kitchen help, is a romantic foil and MGM's counterpart to the play's Cynthia, also from Kansas. In Nash, Lizzie is a mole for the Wicked Witch, having been promised that she will be a queen once betrothed to Bulbo, the Witch's son, in exchange for gaining the Wizard's confidence. Lizzie quickly becomes the object of the Scarecrow's and Tin Man's affections as they believe she is their lost love (whereas Cynthia was searching for her lost love, Niccolo, the Tin Man). Lizzie infiltrates the group and gets word to the Witch of the Wizard's escape plan.

The Witch summons her Winged Monkeys to thwart the Wizard. Meanwhile, he is bestowing the requested gifts upon Dorothy's companions. In a bit seemingly inspired by Baum's *The Land of Oz*, a dozen field mice scamper out of the Scarecrow when the Wizard opens the strawman's head to insert his brains of pins and needles, also as in the book. The Tin Man receives a heart made of rubber bands, flexible enough to stretch to "hold any number of girls." Delighted, the duo rush off to impress Lizzie. The Cowardly Lion is given a bottle of courage, from which the Wizard sneaks a swig as well.

Through Lizzie's interference, the Wizard's balloon takes off with only Dorothy in it, drifting directly toward the Wicked Witch's western territory. To ensure its destination, the Winged Monkeys capture the balloon. The stranded party sets out to rescue Dorothy, a prisoner of the "gloating Witch," who awaits capture of the others "so they can all be tortured together."

In sight of the Witch's castle, the rescuers are faced with the deadly poppy field guarded on the opposite side by an army of gorillas. Unaffected by the poppies, the Scarecrow and Tin Man lure the gorillas into a chase through the field that renders the simians incapacitated for inhaling the flowers' intoxicating aroma—a contrivance successfully repurposed in Disney's 2013 hit *Oz the Great and Powerful*. The Wizard then catapults across the field and the Cowardly Lion holds his breath and clears the poppies in a dozen leaps.

The group gains access to the castle dungeons, where the Lion proves his bravery against the Witch's creature minions. But they are suddenly launched up a chute and find themselves before the Witch, her son, Dorothy, and the Winkie guards. One section of the floor is red hot, and the Witch becomes a maniacal ringmaster of sorts, cracking her whip and presiding over what Nash calls "a three-ring circus of evil." The Wizard is perched atop a tall chair juggling gas-filled eggs, the Scarecrow and Tin Man must dance, and the Cowardly Lion tries to maintain his balance on a huge ball. Overwhelmed, Dorothy grabs a water bucket marked "For Fire Only" and drenches the Witch with its contents. The evil sorceress immediately melts away with a "wailing cry of fear."

Instantly, the Winkies are freed, the floor cools, and all are reunited to the tune of "The Wicked Old Witch Is Dead," a cue that indicates such a song before the film's composers were ever hired. With their enemy destroyed, the Wizard decides to return to the Emerald City, the Scarecrow will rule over the Munchkins, the Tin Woodman will remain with the Winkies, and the Cowardly Lion will "enforce law and order in the forest." The Wizard informs Dorothy that a single wish is granted to whomever kills the Wicked Witch of the West. She bids farewell to her friends, states her desire to return to her Kansas home, and "through a mystic montage" she is safely back in her bedroom as the picture concludes.

Nash's vision appears to be a comic appeal to those who would recall, and anticipate, the antics of the 1902 musical comedy. As treatments for the *Wizard of Oz* script developed, Nash's suggestions for the balloon attack by the Winged Monkeys, Lizzie Smithers, the Witch's son, Bulbo, and a threatening gorilla remained, incorporated with scenario notations of others, including Noel Langley.

BRAINS, HEART, AND NERVE

As a young novelist and playwright already on staff at MGM, Noel Langley was one of a cadre of eighty-eight writers—by his own estimate—on the lot who were hand-selected by Metro.[1] "You never came to Hollywood looking for a job in those days," Langley recollected in 1970. "You had to be summoned, and you had to be already established to be summoned." Langley's first MGM screenplay was for *Maytime* (1937), but it was his third book, the 1936 children's novel *The Tale of the Land of Green Ginger*, about the exploits of Abu Ali, Aladdin's son, that impressed Mervyn LeRoy and secured Langley the assignment of drafting a *Wizard of Oz* treatment. Olive Roberts Barton, who reviewed *Green Ginger* for the *Bee* (Danville, VA), foretold of Langley's penchant for *Oz*'s adventure, fantasy, and nonsense: "In fact, while the grace and charm of the classic fairy tale are still here, there is something just slightly cockeyed about the whole business that should rock the youngsters with joy . . . humor at its best." Twenty-six-year-old Langley had also shown a comedic flair in his other books, and so would have appreciated LeRoy's desire to retain the whimsy of Baum's prose. He signed on to the project March 5, 1938.

Langley's four script contributions between March and June 1938 earned him screen credit for his adaptation of Baum's book and a co-credit for the screenplay. Mervyn LeRoy was so taken with Langley that by February 4, 1939, *Boxoffice* announced that Langley would be scripting LeRoy's proposed musical, *New Moon* (which went unrealized). Langley adapted the essential elements of the original *Oz* story but, perhaps fueled by a desire to impress, also added extraneous characters and unnecessary fantasy elements not found in Baum's book, among which is the "Horse of a Different Color," a multicolored, *talking* equine—the literal embodiment of an incredulous expression of surprise, "That's a horse of another color!" (Langley may have been inspired by the purple cow mentioned in *The Land of Oz*, Baum's first *Wizard of Oz* sequel.)

Langley's March 22, 1938, draft establishes Dorothy's Kansas dilemma, which provides impetus for the prologue narrative. Dorothy has brought Toto to school with her and the dog has bitten a classmate's hand (it has to be cauterized). Miss Gulch, the teacher, rides her bicycle to the Gale farmhouse to confront Dorothy and dispose of Toto. A similar scenario made it into the final draft of the script, except the victim of Toto's bite is Miss Gulch herself (in Baum's book, Toto, at one point, bites the Wicked Witch of the West). By the final film, Miss Gulch also has a traditional witch's familiar in a "nasty old cat."

Much of Langley's Munchkinland dialogue is very much like the finished film excepting there's no suggestion of "Follow the Yellow Brick Road" as a musical prelude to Dorothy

---

1 Langley's memory, in 1970, of being among eighty-eight writers on staff at MGM aligns precisely with the same figure quoted in Hollywood writer Paul Harrison's June 20, 1938, column.

leaving the Munchkins. She is, instead, escorted to the Munchkinland border at which point the Yellow Brick Road unceremoniously intersects. Dorothy chants to herself, "Follow the Yellow Brick Road and I can't go wrong."

Oddly, by Langley's April 5, 1938, script, there is no mention of Dorothy's magic shoes—a pivotal plot piece—as there had been in William Cannon's four-page outline. Instead of her shoes, Dorothy is protected by the Good Witch's kiss, which impresses the gatekeeper who gains them admittance to the Emerald City. But the dialogue is strikingly similar to that in the finished film:

```
"You can't just walk up to our gate like that and ask to
see the great Oz!"

"Why not?" asks Dorothy.

"Because no one's ever seen the great Oz! They wouldn't
dare!"

"We do, on account of Dorothy's got the mark of the Witch
of the North on her forehead," says the Scarecrow.

"Oh, well then; that's a horse of a very different color;
Why didn't you say so?" asks the little man, and the gate
swings open with him hanging on to it, and it bumps him
against the wall.
```

Noel Langley reinstated L. Frank Baum's Silver Shoes in his May 4, 1938, draft, but ten days later he denoted Dorothy's footwear as "the Ruby Slippers," ostensibly to make them appear more mysterious and mystical in Technicolor. Also to be considered is that, visually, silver contrasting against the Yellow Brick Road of Baum's narrative worked in a literary sense, but silver was unpredictable in Technicolor, requiring a bluish tinge to photograph properly. If not precise, the silver hue would be swallowed up and canceled out against a Yellow Brick Road shaded canary, mustard, or ocher.[2] And where color was concerned, the Yellow Brick Road took priority as a constant set element because yellow could vary if the intensity of lighting was inconsistent. So while it is Langley who is credited with changing Baum's Silver Shoes to the Ruby Slippers, it

---

2 One need only watch Diana Ross as Dorothy wearing Silver Shoes on the Yellow Brick Road in Sidney Lumet's The Wiz (1978) for a cinematic example of this very contention.

is unknown if this was a directive resulting from preliminary color testing or a stroke of Langley's whimsy.

It was also Noel Langley who devised an ingenious device by which to preserve the integrity of the fantasy portion of the story while enhancing the plausibility of the overall plot, which originates in the real world. Langley claimed Mary Pickford's dream sequence in *The Poor Little Rich Girl* (1917) as inspiration. In a sedative state induced by an overdose of sleeping medicine, Pickford's Gwendolyn is reunited with the organ grinder and the plumber, allies from the world outside the confines of her father's estate, in an *Alice in Wonderland*–type otherworld called the Tell-Tale Forest. Her father's stern and uncaring staff show their grotesque and true identities as the literal embodiment of their figurative nicknames: Silly Ass is a mule; Big Ears has ears twice larger than average; Two-Faced Thing has a second face where the back of her head should be; and Snake in the Grass is a loathsome serpent. Gwendolyn's presiding doctor reappears as a magician that implores her traveling party to foresee other realms in his large crystal ball. Upon recovering from her delirium, Gwendolyn encounters some of the real-life vestiges of her nightmare.

For *The Wizard of Oz*, Langley introduced Kansas characters in the prologue not found in Baum's story and reincarnated them into the creature doppelgangers in Dorothy's dream. Over the course of Langley's rewrites, these expanded to include two farmhands, who would double as the Scarecrow and Tin Woodman (as in the Larry Semon picture); the now *Mrs.* Gulch and her son, Walter, who would reappear as the Wicked Witch and her son, Bulbo; and Mrs. Gulch's niece Sylvia and her beau Kenny, who transform into a princess and prince in Oz. (Ethel Hill's and Walter Ferris's screenplay for Shirley Temple's Technicolor version of *The Little Princess*, released March 10, 1939, used the same conceit: real-world characters reappearing as fanciful, otherworld counterparts—including a witch dressed in black—during a dream sequence.)

Noel Langley cleverly found a loophole in Baum's text in order to make the entire trip to the Land of Oz a dream, as in *Alice in Wonderland*. As the cyclone is hurtling Dorothy's house through space, she and Toto fall asleep.[3] Langley rationalized his alterations in terms of box-office insurance in a February 19, 1939, syndicated interview with Lucie Neville titled "So It Wasn't Like the Book, Huh?" which was transcribed during production of *The Wizard of Oz*:

> The patronage of those who want to see an exact movie of the book wouldn't pay for the picture. If one-third of the audiences know the book, it's a good percentage. And

---

3 Additionally, in *The Emerald City of Oz*, fifth of the *Wonderful Wizard of Oz* sequels, Dorothy's Uncle Henry is dubious about his niece's visits to the Land of Oz: "[He] imagined that she had dreamed all of those astonishing adventures, and that the dreams had been so real to her that she had come to believe them true."

we have to please the other two-thirds, who will expect an entertaining picture rather than a faithful reproduction.[4] So we had to compromise by making the first part of the picture in the Kansas setting quite plausible and introducing characters in it that later appear in the Oz sequences. For instance, the Wizard first is seen as a real person, a Professor Marvel, who has a traveling show, and his assistant is a timid, fearful little man who later is the Cowardly Lion [the assistant was later adjusted to become the third farmhand]. In the book, you remember, Dorothy goes to sleep during the cyclone and wakes in the Land of Oz. So making the fairy tale a dream sequence is consistent with the story.

Unbeknownst to Langley, other writers were assigned to review his script and make suggestions for revisions. Mervyn LeRoy brought on Herbert Fields from April 19 to 22, 1938, presumably to interject elements of suitable levity and nonsense as Fields and his brother Joseph wrote the comedy *Fools for Scandal*, LeRoy's last picture at Warner Bros.

But Arthur Freed's April 25, 1938, analysis of what had been submitted to date underscored the theme of focusing on "the main objective" of telling a "real story" that includes fantasy but is primarily motivated by Dorothy's perspective. Freed stressed that the music and comedy could only work against a sound foundation of sentimentality, lacking in what he had seen thus far. As an example, Freed cited the song "Some Day My Prince Will Come" (erroneously referring to the song "I'm Wishing") as Disney's way of propelling the emotional track in *Snow White and the Seven Dwarfs*, and called for a similar setup on Dorothy's Kansas farm.

MGM composer Roger Edens was not specifically signed to *The Wizard of Oz*, but he assisted in pacing the placement of songs in the narrative and even wrote tentative lyrics for certain numbers. The so-called "Kansas Song" began as Edens's "Mid Pleasures and Palaces" before becoming "Over the Rainbow."[5] (Arthur Freed's demand for such a tune was tested when he and Mervyn LeRoy made impassioned pleas to retain "Over the Rainbow" when it seemed as though the song number would be dropped from the final version of the film just prior to its release.)

Accordingly, Noel Langley's May 4, 1938, treatment emphasized the picture's musicality. Langley suggested a cumbersome title sequence that opens on the book cover of *The Wizard of Oz* over which the title credit is superimposed. The book next flips open to a

---

4 In 1938 Walt Disney's story research department learned that about half of the general population was familiar with the story of *The Wizard of Oz*.

5 A 1938 account referencing the *Oz* songs claimed that "Over the Rainbow" would be "sung by Miss [Judy] Garland on a great artificial rainbow." An October 10, 1938, communication concerning the number indicated that Garland was to sing "Rainbow" to Bolger and Ebsen, as the two farmhands, "with an optimistic outlook into the future."

full-page illustration of Dorothy with the caption "Judy Garland as Dorothy," over which Garland was to sing the first two lines of the Kansas Song. Langley proposed that each cast member be introduced similarly, warbling musical couplets by way of introducing their respective characters. The last "page" before the opening scene would be that of Dorothy sitting on a Kansas fence with farmhands Hunk and Hickory. The two men would sing a song about the Land of Oz to which Dorothy would respond with more of the Kansas Song, advocating that Oz "isn't as nice as Kansas."

Perhaps inspired by both Arthur Freed's April 25 Disney reference and a desire to rejuvenate his production team's approach, Mervyn LeRoy decided to revisit *Snow White and the Seven Dwarfs*. Having only seen the picture once before at its premiere, LeRoy contacted Walt Disney and requested the loan of a print, which he screened for the *Oz* unit in an MGM projection room the evening of May 10, 1938. Disney and LeRoy were not only professional colleagues but lifelong good friends, according to Diane Disney Miller, Walt's daughter. A cooperative relationship between Disney and MGM had previously been established with 1934's *Hollywood Party*, which contained an appearance by Mickey Mouse and a Technicolor cartoon fantasy covering a candy-land war, "Hot Choc'late Soldiers," animated by Disney. MGM's *Babes in Toyland* featured Mickey Mouse as well as Disney's Three Little Pigs and their theme song. Further reciprocation led to Disney's Ferdinand the Bull making a cameo in the Technicolor sequence of Metro's *The Women*, which was in development concurrent with *The Wizard of Oz*. Disney also poked playful fun at his MGM association in the December 1938 cartoon short *Mother Goose Goes Hollywood*. Prominently caricatured are MGM's Leo the Lion mascot, stars such as the Marx Brothers, Clark Gable, Spencer Tracy, and Freddie Bartholomew, and Metro films *Mutiny on the Bounty* and *Captains Courageous*.

Subtle repurposing of successful elements from *Snow White* and other fantasy-adventure films were woven into the *Wizard of Oz* screenplay. As in *Oz*, the prologue in *Alice in Wonderland* (1933) introduces real-world characters whose exaggerations the heroine will meet once in Wonderland such as the White Rabbit, the Mock Turtle, and living chess pieces—all of which may have informed Noel Langley, who recalled the 1933 *Alice* in a 1970 interview. An indignant line uttered by *Alice*'s anthropomorphic pudding ("How would you like it if I were to cut a slice out of you?") during the film's climactic coronation sequence resurfaced in *Oz* when one of the humanoid apple trees asks Dorothy how she'd like it if someone tried to pick something off of her.

Some *Snow White and the Seven Dwarfs* redux made it to the screen in *Oz*, such as Toto escaping the Witch's castle to valiantly lead Dorothy's rescue—an obvious nod to the scene in which the forest animals race to alert the Seven Dwarfs of Snow White's imminent danger at the hands of *her* Wicked Witch. And some references were mercifully abandoned like Dorothy daydreaming of her prince charming or fainting at the sight of skeletons in the Witch's closet. Even the pair of nefarious vultures from *Snow White* resurfaced in *Oz*'s Haunted Forest. Upon *Oz*'s release most reviewers made reference to *Snow White*, and parallels between the two pictures did not go unnoticed by some critics. Of *The Wizard of Oz, New Republic*'s unimpressed Otis Ferguson succinctly sniped, "It has dwarfs, Technicolor, freak characters, and Judy Garland." *Motion Picture Herald* similarly observed, "This is whimsy with a wham, a vast and ornate plunge through the breach of prejudice opened by *Snow White and the Seven Dwarfs*, to which [*Oz*] has aspects somewhat akin, not perhaps without intent or design." The *Nebraska State Journal* stated, "The film is *Snow White* all over again with real people. . . . As in *Snow White*, the evil factor is a witch, Margaret Hamilton, and in the dwarf line are the famous Singer Midgets as the Munchkins." Howard Barnes, of the New York *Herald Tribune*, was equally direct: "Like the magnificent Disney film [*Oz*] deals in sorcery and caricature. There are the young girl and the evil crone, the girl's odd supporters and a wild chase in the climax."

Samuel Hoffenstein signed on to rework the *Wizard of Oz* script beginning May 31, 1938. In Hollywood Hoffenstein was best known for writing the original 1931 Frederic March version of *Dr. Jekyll and Mr. Hyde* and *The Miracle Man* (1932). Curiously enough, in the latter film there's a menacing landlord, played by Boris Karloff, named Nikko—the same name given to the Wicked Witch's familiar monkey in *The Wizard of Oz*. Nikko was a fitting moniker for the Witch's sidekick as it's the name of the Japanese town in which monkeys roam freely and is the place of origin for the Three Wise Monkeys that pantomime "See no evil, hear no evil, speak no evil."

ADDITIONAL PUNCTUATION

Hoffenstein's assignment concluded on June 3, 1938, by which time Florence Ryerson and Edgar Allan Woolf were retained to finesse Langley's script, much to his displeasure. "They were good friends of [L. B.] Mayer," Langley said in 1970, "and he had to figure some way to keep them on the payroll." Cynicism aside, if Mayer appointed Ryerson and Woolf to *The Wizard of Oz*, it was probably more tactical than political; they had conceived the screenplay of *Everybody Sing* for Judy Garland. As such, Mayer would have recognized that the duo had an especial sensitivity for developing the character of Dorothy with Judy in mind.

On June 6, 1938, Ryerson and Woolf submitted a four-page critique of their review of the *Oz* material to date. Seasoned and more diplomatic than the younger Langley, Ryerson and Woolf knew how to maneuver studio politics and appease the egos of their supervisors. Ryerson in particular had a laissez-faire approach. She worked at the studio three days a week and two days a week had producers and other writers come to the house she shared with her equally successful husband-writer, Colin Clements.

In their *Oz* review, Ryerson and Woolf indicate that their "few notes" are "merely for discussion," and they proactively back up their criticisms with alternative suggestions. Like Arthur Freed, they felt that Dorothy's emotional desperation to get home should be emphasized so that the various obstacles that prevent her from attaining her goal are more dramatic.

They also felt that the Wicked Witch of the West, who occasionally shrieks from her broomstick, was not menacing enough and should be used to create plot suspense as the Witch sets traps to waylay the travelers. But conscious of the criticisms leveled at Walt Disney for the more frightening elements of *Snow White* (particularly the Evil Queen's demise), they also desired to wean away all traces of implied violence, including having the Wicked Witch of the East morph into a harmless creature instead of having been crushed to death under Dorothy's house. Here, Ryerson and Woolf were likely adhering to the edict set forth by L. Frank Baum in Oz books that succeeded *The Wonderful Wizard* in which the author is abundantly clear in stating that, in the Land of Oz, no living creature can be killed, only transformed.

By June 9, 1938, Ryerson and Woolf were even recommending a new look for the opening credits, one that would require animation:

```
FADE IN ON:

A BACKGROUND—

Which is composed of the signs of the zodiac, the stars,
constellations, etcetera, such as used by astrologers,
fortune tellers, and wizards in their acts. At one side a
little tripod carries a weird burning flame.

The shadow of a wizard with a high, pointed hat is thrown
across this background. We never really see this figure
. . . just the shadow, and one long-fingered hand, with a
full black sleeve.

This hand does various magician tricks . . . and in so
doing makes the titles. There are endless ways this could
be done; the following are merely suggested:
```

First, the long fingers point toward the fire and seem
to draw it forth until the smoke and flame write out the
words, *The Wizard of Oz*. With a wave, the hand wipes this
away.

Next, the hand brings in a hat. From the hat it
materializes a whole flock of doves which fly up to the
screen and turn into more credit titles.

Erasing the credit titles by a gesture, the hand reaches
into the background and plucks one star after another from
the painted sky. As it puts each star down in a row, it
becomes the name of another member of the cast. Perhaps one
star gives trouble, jumps about, refuses to be captured.
When the hand finally plunks it down, it is Ray Bolger or
perhaps Toto the dog.

NOTE: All of the above may sound crazy, but it might
develop into something very unusual and amusing.

In subsequent script alterations and follow-up revisions and notations dated June 4–8,
1938, June 9–18, 1938, and July 25–27, 1938, Ryerson and Woolf did, in equal parts, both
improvement and injustice to Langley's treatments. They retained Langley's two farmhands, Hunk and Hickory (indicated as parts for Buddy Ebsen and Ray Bolger), and
provided them with a plot catalyst. Hickory accidentally starts Hunk's "wind-stopping
machine" and puts it in reverse, thus instigating the cyclone. References to this concept
remain in *The Wizard of Oz* although the anti-wind machine is now Hickory's and not
Hunk's. In a brief exchange, Aunt Em chastises Hickory for "tinkering with that contraption" to which he responds that someday there'll be a statue erected to him—but the
inference that the memorial would be in honor of his invention was excised in the editing
process.

Ryerson and Woolf took Baum's designation of Dorothy's guardians as weary and worn
to the extreme, noting that Aunt Em should be drawn as emotionally inaccessible—a
matriarch who is firm "for Dorothy's own good." They describe her as "a gaunt, grim-
looking individual, with eyes that snap behind her steel-rimmed spectacles. Her hair is
drawn tightly back into an uncompromising knot. . . . Her entrance . . . is as violent as a
cyclone." Aunt Em's mere presence not only intimidates the two farmhands, it sends hen
and chicks, goat and kid, cat and kittens, and doves scattering in all directions.

Ryerson and Woolf also took a cue from Langley's doppelganger premise by introducing Professor Winkle, the carny clairvoyant who mystifies the runaway Dorothy into returning home to Aunt Em. (Professor Winkle becomes Professor Marvel in the final script.) This character would serve as the real-world counterpart to the Wizard of Oz, and in Ryerson and Woolf's earliest script, the Professor's horse-drawn caravan takes Dorothy directly to the front gate of her farm, unlike in the film where Dorothy and Toto hastily retreat on foot. When Dorothy awakens at the end of the story and sees Professor Marvel, she deliriously believes she is still in Oz.

Ryerson and Woolf also saw Dorothy regaining consciousness at the film's conclusion while the cyclone still raged, her vision of Oz having been an instantaneous panorama that has all "passed through her mind in the course of a minute." Like Lewis Carroll's Alice, Dorothy is stirred by hay, twigs, and leaves blowing over her.

The team was clearly conscious of writing for Judy Garland in the lead role. They envisioned introducing Dorothy only after a scene in which Aunt Em, exasperated for being unable to find Dorothy on the farm, openly berates her dawdling niece for "always dreamin' some nonsense." Ryerson and Woolf's description of Dorothy is both an homage to W. W. Denslow's illustration that accompanies the first chapter of *The Wonderful Wizard of Oz* and a consideration of Garland's screen charisma:

```
MEDIUM SHOT—EXT. WHEAT FIELD AND FENCE


Dorothy, her back to the camera, is in much the same position
as in the first picture in the Oz book. She is leaning
against a fence and looking out over the farm. There are
sunflowers growing along the fence. Dorothy wears a simple
checked dress. Her hair is loose and a sunbonnet hangs by one
string down her neck. Under one arm she carries a pile of
school books. She is humming a little tune which fits in with
the rippling of the wheat about her. After a moment she turns
and we get her face for the first time. Her big brown eyes
are dreamy. Her lips are curved in a little smile.
```

Ryerson and Woolf added some charming touches involving Dorothy's dog Toto, whom they described as "her funny, mopsy, little dog." In Munchkinland the Wicked Witch of the West approaches on her broom, the breeze from which dramatically waves the flowers about. Toto takes one look at the Witch and bolts under Glinda's gown as Dorothy exclaims that she wants to go home on the next train. The Witch sees Toto's tail sticking out from under Glinda and grabs him.

By June 10, 1938, Ryerson and Woolf were conscious of appealing to Mervyn LeRoy with a *Snow White* allusion. *The Wizard of Oz* was now to open with Dorothy talking to a "prince" ("Oh—thank you, Your Highness. I shall be honored to open the ball with you."). The camera shifts to show that the "prince" is Toto sitting on top of an old-fashioned stile; his head is cocked and a small daisy-chain crown is perched crookedly over one ear—precisely the sort of cloying treatment to which Noel Langley would later object.

As they progressed, Ryerson and Woolf's insight continued to waver between strokes of brilliance and miscalculation. They claimed to have been feeling as much heat as Mervyn LeRoy to cater to the Frank Baum fans. "We were attacked on all sides by enthusiasts who insisted that certain pet scenes and characters must on no account be slighted or left out. Many of the characters and incidents from forty-odd other Baum books were demanded," they complained.

Taking a cue from the 1902 play script, Ryerson and Woolf, on June 27, 1938, combined Baum's two good witches into a single character, Glinda the Beautiful Witch of the North. (In their notes of June 15, there were still two good witches, Glinda and the Witch of the North, whom Ryerson and Woolf suggested be cast with a character actress akin to a "Laura Hope Crews type."[6]) But then on July 8, 1938, the screenwriting team found Langley's whole Horse of a Different Color sequence—with its crowd of Emerald City extras and the musical procession that begins from Dorothy's entrance and leading to the Wizard's palace—prime for elimination.

Questionable dialogue written for the Scarecrow would have been censored by the Hays Code if it hadn't already been struck in draft form.[7] When the Scarecrow explains to Dorothy that his sole fear is for a lighted match, he adds, "I was crazy about a girl once—I'd have married her only her mother told me she smoked in bed." The Scarecrow confiding his aversion to fire is taken directly from *The Wonderful Wizard of Oz*. But where Baum left this bit of information undeveloped, MGM scenarists employed the Scarecrow's flammability for purposes of suspense. He is, or is nearly, set aflame several times: when the Wicked Witch wields a fireball; when the Scarecrow cowers before the Wizard's throne; and when the Witch uses her broomstick to torch his stuffing in the picture's climax.

Ryerson and Woolf saw fit to retain one of Langley's additions, that of a woodpecker bursting the Wizard's hot-air balloon and thwarting Dorothy's escape home. This bit was

---

6 The reference to Laura Hope Crews is ironic in that Billie Burke, who would play Oz's Glinda, reportedly "set her heart" on playing Aunt Pittypat in *Gone with the Wind*—a role in which Hope Crews was cast. Burke screen-tested unsuccessfully for the *GWTW* part wearing a heavily padded costume, rubber double chins, and cotton stuffed in her cheeks.

7 As president of the Motion Picture Producers and Distributors of America, William H. Hays instituted the Motion Picture Production Code in 1930 to regulate motion picture values via moral guidelines.

actually reported in a plot summary published in 1939 and was thereafter included in the film's official story synopsis retained by the Academy of Motion Picture Arts and Sciences. Another version of the plot synopsis, first published in the *Independent Film Exhibitors* journal on October 22, 1938, also includes the fateful woodpecker and reads as follows:

> Based on the famous children's story. This tells of a little girl who dreams she is wafted from her Kansas farm to the mysterious Land of Oz. Judy Garland plays the young lady. In Oz she enlists the aid of the Tin Woodman and the Scarecrow for directions as to how to return to Kansas. They tell her she must see the Wizard (Frank Morgan). The Wizard decrees that if she can kill the old witch (Margaret Hamilton), he will see that she returns. In a scurry with the witch, Judy accidentally pours a pitcher of water over her. The witch melts away. But then, alas, the Wizard turns out not to be the Wizard, merely a balloonist who doesn't know how to get back himself. Judy is spared further harrowing adventures when with the Wizard she gets into his balloon, starts back to earth only to have a woodpecker make a hole in it and speed up their descent. Like all good dreams—this is where Judy wakes up and realizes that the odd citizens of Oz are actually her friends and workers on the farm.

Ryerson and Woolf provided guidance with respect to visualizing certain imagery and indicating possible musical opportunities. They describe the Emerald City as "a glittering sight of sparkling towers and minarets; a glorification of the Taj Mahal. Every hue of green." When the Wicked Witch tries to pull off Dorothy's magic slippers after Dorothy is unsuccessful in kicking them off, the shoes "suddenly flash like red fire." The Lion's courage is a consumable sauce of Worcestershire and Tabasco. As Dorothy and her companions enter the Cowardly Lion's forest, "sinister, invisible voices" whisper in rhythm, "Watch out for the Witch of the West." They describe a number for the Scarecrow as a "soft-shuffle dance that works up into a wild, leg-flinging burlesque, as only [Ray] Bolger can put over" that gets vocal approval from the crows, "Oh, bravo, Very good. Well done, Sir. More." As Dorothy prepares to leave Oz in the film's conclusion, the Munchkins were to have reappeared to sing the musical chant "There's no place like home."

In Noel Langley's treatments, the Wicked Witch of the West is set on conquering the Emerald City as opposed to securing Dorothy's magic shoes. This aspect of the script shifted with Ryerson and Woolf's revisions but a line remains in the completed film that references the Witch's envisioned takeover when she claims that gaining the Ruby Slippers will grant her the greatest power in all of Oz. Thus, dramatic tension was established from the outset of Dorothy's arrival in Oz by expanding on L. Frank Baum's almost casual notation that "The Wicked Witch had a great longing to have for her own the Silver Shoes which the girl always wore." Given this motivation, the Witch would supplant the assorted dangers on Dorothy's journey—the Kalidahs, and crossing chasms and a river—and the peril of the poppy field would be at her instigation.

Ryerson and Woolf's Wicked Witch implies violence on several occasions, which contradicts the screenwriters' earlier concerns about making the Witch too devious. When the Witch secures Toto separately from Dorothy (unlike in the completed film in which both are abducted together), she tells her Winged Monkey general, "And don't harm her—not so much as a scratch. (with a horrible, ghoulish expression) Leave that to me!" Once Dorothy has been captured, the Witch attempts unsuccessfully to remove Dorothy's Ruby Slippers and threatens to amputate her feet.

One of the Witch's acts of intimidation, which did not end up in the film, was reported in 1939 and may have been influenced by a script draft. In the Emerald City, Frank Morgan, as the Wizard of Oz, was to be seated on an enormous throne while the Wicked Witch "battered at the gates and demanded Judy as her prisoner." This is likely a reference to the threat the Witch skywrites over the town square. The foreboding phrase was originally written in Langley's June 27, 1938, script as "Give me Dorothy and her slippers or I'll destroy your city. W.W.W." Two days later, the skywriting was adjusted to the more succinct "Surrender Dorothy or Die. W.W.W."—actually filmed as such but edited in post-production to only bear the legend "Surrender Dorothy."

The July 27, 1938, version of Ryerson and Woolf's script contains a meandering subplot, the ploy of which is derived from the comedic charades of the 1902 Wizard of Oz stage extravaganza. In this draft the Wizard leaves the Emerald City to join Dorothy's party in search of the Wicked Witch. They infiltrate the "town of the Winkies, with the Witch's castle in the background" disguised as members of "Smith's Circus." Dorothy wears the white tights and ruffled skirts of a bareback horse rider; the Wizard is dressed as a strong man in a leopard skin; the Tin Man is in a ringmaster's long overcoat, top hat, and moustache, which he keeps adjusting to stay on. The Scarecrow is unsuccessful in practicing juggling clubs. Lizzie Smithers, a miscellaneous character transplanted from Kansas, is dressed as a gypsy fortune-teller.

When Noel Langley saw Ryerson and Woolf's revisions to his script, he was vocal in his objections. "It was so cutesy and oozy that I could have vomited. I said, 'The hell with it. Forget the whole thing. Take my name off it.' They actually had that damn little dog [Toto] *talking*. Now, there is a difference between fantasy and whimsy. What they wanted to do was simply silly."

Incensed, Langley stormed off the picture. "I was just twenty-six at the time and they wondered how I could afford to walk out. Even back then, I became known as a pugnacious fighter." Langley's cocky attitude got him blacklisted for two years, not only from Metro but from working at any other studio. Rumors of Langley's diva attitude extended beyond Metro's gates and it is he to whom a Hollywood columnist was likely referring in a 1938 blind item that told of a writer from New York on the MGM lot that was biting the very hand that fed him for being so outspoken in dislike of his superiors. In a 1970 interview with journalist Mal Vincent, Langley recollected his blacklisting was due to L. B. Mayer's refusal to increase his salary from seven hundred fifty to one thousand dollars per week. But Mayer's disdain could be traced to a fatal misstep; Langley's public defamation of Mayer is what got him ostracized. "Out there, as you're called by the top man, so you're called all the way down the line by everyone else," Langley said. "Every time Louis B. Mayer smiled at me, I felt as if a snake had crawled across my face."

Other contributors to the development of the *Wizard of Oz* script, in preproduction or during production, included lyricist E. Y. Harburg, John Lee Mahin, Jack Mintz, and Sid Silvers. Additionally, actors Jack Haley and Bert Lahr reportedly ad-libbed or embellished their lines on set. But regardless of who wrote what, the entire script was subject to scrutiny by the Motion Picture Producers and Distributors of America who applied the Hays Code to film production.

Before *The Wizard of Oz* could begin shooting, it required the approval of censor Joseph Ignatius Breen, who had reservations. On September 26, 1938, Breen sent L. B. Mayer a letter regarding Metro's submission of an August 12, 1938, draft of the *Oz* script, which Breen had vetted. The censor's quibbles included negating a "razzberry" sound (a reference to the Scarecrow taunting the apple trees into slinging their own fruit), the Scarecrow screaming "Fire! Fire!" after being ignited by the Wicked Witch (in the film he cries that he is "burning"), and the advisement that the Cowardly Lion's self-deprecating description as a "sissy" would be excised in Great Britain where it was synonymous with the then-distasteful term homosexual (the word "prissy" was substituted, dubbed into the film's UK release soundtrack). Foremost, Breen expressed concern that the Wicked Witch scenes might be overly intense. "Our experience has shown," Breen wrote, "that such frightening scenes may be deleted by political censor boards, or issuance of a permit for adults only." Pending revision, *The Wizard of Oz* received Breen's stamp of approval, although its script would continue to be honed and refined even as production got underway.

SETTING IT TO MUSIC

The development of songs for *The Wizard of Oz* came as Arthur Freed, Roger Edens and the screenwriters made suggestions for inserting musical and dance numbers as the script developed. Like *Snow White and the Seven Dwarfs* and other Walt Disney efforts, Mervyn LeRoy had already determined that *Oz* would not only feature songs, its musical scoring would serve as an unceasing source of melodic narration for the characters, their actions, and the story events. The *Hollywood Reporter* noted that *The Wizard of Oz* would be "pre-scored throughout for the first time in picture history. It is the method used in making animated cartoons, but has never been done for live music." The *Syracuse (New York) Herald* added, "In order to give the story the quality of a cartooned whimsy, the musical technique of the cartoon will be used."

This meant that *Oz's* onscreen action would be fitted to the songs, as was done in Walt Disney's animations. Trials with this method may have been undertaken, as in September 1939, it was reported that Bill Stewart, an advanced music student in Los Angeles, furnished the musical background for Disney's animated films with his male quartet. The quartet's latest work was reportedly "a series of musical numbers for the pretentious *Wizard of Oz.* . . ." Composing the *Oz* musical score would be undertaken in postproduction by Metro musical director and composer Herbert Stothart; but Stothart would require the specific melodies created especially for the picture from which to parlay compositions that conveyed a range of moods.

The selecting of composers for *Oz's* musical score was overseen by Arthur Freed pending Mervyn LeRoy's approval. Among the songwriters considered were Dorothy Fields (known for "I Can't Give You Anything but Love," "On the Sunny Side of the Street," and "The Way You Look Tonight") and Oscar Hammerstein II (known for *Showboat*). However, Freed at first thought of friend and longtime associate Jerome Kern. Kern was perhaps a logical choice as he had among his Broadway credits *Miss 1917* (1917), which included a burlesque tribute to Fred Stone's famous Scarecrow as imitated by Margaret "Tot" Qualters, and *Stepping Stones*, a 1923 musical fantasy starring Fred Stone and his daughter Dorothy in her Broadway debut.

On March 15, 1938, Louella O. Parsons identified stage and film composer and lyricist Mack Gordon and his songwriting partner Harry Revel as the tunesmiths hired to "write a new score for *The Wizard of Oz*." The musical team was another logical choice as they were to be loaned to MGM from Twentieth Century Fox, where they wrote songs for Shirley Temple pictures. While Parsons had no gripe with the Gordon-Revel assignment, she bemoaned the fact that Metro was apparently dispensing with the score of the 1902 stage production. "Why, will you tell me," Parsons wrote, "do the film companies buy old musical favorites and then disregard the songs that have already proved popular with the public?"

Then on April 8, 1938, the *Hollywood Reporter* noted that Al Dubin and Nacio Herb Brown were assigned to "Mervyn LeRoy's forthcoming *Wizard of Oz* at MGM." Five years prior, Dubin, with Harry Warren, had scored LeRoy's *Gold Diggers of 1933*, which included one of the major breakout anthems of the 1930s, "The Gold Diggers' Song (We're in the Money)." Dubin and Brown were still mentioned as *Oz's* songwriting team as late as *Variety's* April 20 edition. But by the time of LeRoy's May 10 *Snow White* screening at Metro, things had changed. Songwriters E. Y. "Yip" Harburg and Harold Arlen had reported to work on *The Wizard of Oz* just a day prior at a fee of twenty thousand dollars each for ten weeks, with the privilege of converting to twenty-five thousand for fourteen weeks. The duo had officially signed on to *Oz* as of May 3, 1938.

Harburg and Arlen were known as the songwriting team of Earl Carroll's Vanities revues and the Broadway shows *The Show Is On* (1936), *Hooray for What!* (1937), and *Life Begins at 8:40* (1934), on which they composed musical interludes for Ray Bolger and Bert Lahr. As independent artists, Harburg was known for writing lyrics to the songs "Brother, Can You Spare a Dime?" and "April in Paris," while Arlen was best recalled for having written the melodies of "Stormy Weather" and "Let's Fall in Love," in addition to "It's Only a Paper Moon" with Harburg.

How Dubin and Brown were ousted in favor of Harburg and Arlen was the result of Hollywood politics, according to composer Harry Warren. When interviewed in 1972, Warren recollected:

> Originally, when I came out here in '29, the first time, Nacio Herb Brown was the big fellow on the lot, not Arthur Freed. He was the big man, and later on, it turned completely around when the gin rummy craze started! All of a sudden, Arthur Freed and Mervyn LeRoy were playing gin rummy with L. B. Mayer . . . Mervyn LeRoy had a party. And at the party, he invited Harold Arlen and Yip Harburg. And they went to the party, and they . . . I don't know, sort of convinced Mervyn that *they* should do the picture. . . . And it was all set that [Dubin] and Herb Brown were going to do the picture. Until that night at the dinner party, where they switched it to Harold Arlen and Yip Harburg. That's how it happened. I remember it vividly. So politics does enter into it, too, sometimes. I'm not talking about the ability of people but sometimes they happen to be there, and talk to people and people say, "Gee, we ought to use them," you know. So they got the picture.

They not only got the picture, in 1939 the two composers said that working on *The Wizard of Oz* was their most interesting and pleasant assignment to date. Harburg remarked to Philip K. Scheuer of the *Los Angeles Times* that he hoped he accomplished with his lyrics what L. Frank Baum did in the Oz books. Adhering to the principle that the songs should advance the story line, Harburg noted, "We think we've found a way to eliminate stop-plot numbers from the screen." Confining himself to a thirty-two-bar chorus—per public demand for songs in neat, capsule form—Harburg also threw out the 150-word vocabulary expected of Tin Pan Alley (slang for New York's music-publishing street), dispensing with standard rhyming couplets like moon-June and love-above. Instead, Harburg infused his *Oz* lyrics with ingenious, nonsense words worthy of Lewis Carroll or Edward Lear, manipulating "hippopotamus" to rhyme with "top to bottomus," for example.

According to a 1940 summary of their work on *The Wizard of Oz*, the duo's creative process began with them both sitting at a piano keyboard together, searching for a melodic theme to fit the idea for a song they had in mind. The *Oz* music would then be developed and the idea worked into a lyric to fit, similar to the manner in which famed Victorian composers W. S. Gilbert and Arthur Sullivan collaborated.

The first song Harburg and Arlen completed for *Oz* was "The Jitterbug," a jazzy swing number in the style for which Judy Garland was best known, in keeping with Arthur Freed's original notation that Dorothy would be an orphan in Kansas who sings jazz.[8] According to the script, the jitterbug was "a large pink-and-blue spotted mosquito" sent by the Wicked Witch to bite and bother the travelers into musical exhaustion so they'd be spent and thus matchless against the subsequent Winged Monkeys' attack. The song was a double-entendre as the insect of the title may have been inspired by *The Wonderful Wizard of Oz*, in which the Wicked Witch dispatches hordes of bees to terrorize Dorothy and her friends, although there was already a similar bee scene in the MGM *Oz* script. Another inspiration may have been the "Lovebug" who prompts musicality in those she stings in *Our Gang Follies of 1938*.

But as a song, a new dance was already being called "jitterbug" and the upbeat tempo of the *Oz* number was in keeping with the trend. By December 1938 it was reported that Judy Garland and Mickey Rooney had "organized their own jitterbug [dance] club. . . ." Reporter Robbin Coons happened to wander into the MGM recording stage to watch Garland, Ray Bolger, Buddy Ebsen, and Bert Lahr sing the "Jitterbug" tune, which, Coons explained, "will match with their progress [when the film is shot later] through a scary, enchanted forest."

Snow White and the Seven Dwarfs was hailed as much for its artistic achievements as for its great music, and its catchy songs by Frank Churchill and Larry Morey became nationwide hits. Harburg and Arlen's subsequent contributions mirrored Disney's pacing in *Snow White* to a degree. Per Freed's recommendation, there was "Over the Rainbow," a ballad of longing for Dorothy in the prologue as in Snow White's "I'm Wishing." (Snow White filling her scrub bucket at the well for "I'm Wishing" would have been imitated in a scene dropped from the *Oz* script in which Dorothy reprises "Over the Rainbow" while filling her scrub bucket at the Wicked Witch's courtyard fountain.)

"Ding-Dong! The Witch Is Dead" was surely conceived in the same rousing spirit as Disney's anti-Depression anthem "Who's Afraid of the Big Bad Wolf." In fact, come October 31, 1939, Sara Lemon, a syndicated columnist, observed that for Halloween that year, children were singing "Ding-Dong! The Big Bad Witch Is Dead."

---

8 In its August 24, 1938, edition, *Variety* reported that the third Harburg-Arlen song completed was "The Merry Old Land of Oz."

The Seven Dwarfs' marching song "Heigh Ho, Heigh Ho" likely inspired "We're Off to See the Wizard" sung by Dorothy and her friends, which was tentatively titled "The Marching Song" in script drafts. The non-Disney derivative for "The Merry Old Land of Oz" number was the British phrase "Merrie Olde England," a euphemism for utopian life-style, as reflected in the *Oz* song's lyrics—fittingly performed by a Cockney cabby in the Emerald City. (Harburg also included in the lyrics the word "jolly," a traditional English adjective.)

Paul J. Smith and Leigh Harline's incidental background score reworked the leitmotifs for *Snow White's* characters to heighten the mood of specific scenes. The frenzied version of "Heigh Ho" as the dwarfs race to rescue Snow White from the Wicked Witch was one example. Likewise, a distorted arrangement of *Oz's* marching song, "We're Off to See the Wizard," served as the Wicked Witch of the West's theme. This now-classic leitmotif was as close to a musical number as the Witch would come, which was duly noted in a July 1939 write-up on the film's songs and its composers in Pennsylvania's the *Harrisburg Telegraph*: "Every member of the cast excepting the Wicked Witch sings a solo." Even the Witch's Winkie guards were given a military march, to which they chanted, "O-ee-oh, e-oh-ah!" the inspiration of which could be attributed to "Coo-ee-oh," a cruel queen's name in Baum's 1920 book, *Glinda of Oz*.

Unlike "The Jitterbug," Harold Arlen revealed in a 1947 interview that the melody of "Over the Rainbow," Dorothy's Kansas solo, was written for the character but wasn't composed with Judy Garland's personality in mind. "Judy Garland has never sung any-thing as straight or melodic as that," Arlen said, "but it won the Academy Award and has been identified with Judy ever since." Not only did "Over the Rainbow" become Garland's signature theme, it became a popular standard in the American songbook, culminating in its 2001 appointment as the number-one "Song of the Century" in a Recording Industry Association of America poll. In 2004 a similar survey by the American Film Institute, titled "100 Years . . . 100 Songs," ranked "Over the Rainbow" as the greatest movie song of all time. And in 2017 "Over the Rainbow" as sung by Judy Garland in *The Wizard of Oz* was declared worthy of preservation by the Recording Registry of the Library of Congress for its significance to America's audio heritage.

Curiously, *Oz's* most famous tune was predated by a fairyland operetta of the same title. *Over the Rainbow* was a two-act libretto written in 1915 by Edith Sanford Tillotson with music by Fred W. Peace, and published in New York by Tullar-Meredith Co. The plot is similar to a scenario right out of the Oz books (one of Frank Baum's popular characters was Polychrome the Rainbow's daughter). In *Over the Rainbow*, four little sisters day-dream in their playroom on a rainy afternoon. Having grown bored with their books and toys, the children fall asleep, though the youngest struggles to remain awake in the hopes of seeing a rainbow.

The sun appears and, like MGM's Glinda, the Rainbow Queen enters "beautifully dressed in white, draped with the rainbow colors carrying a staff and wearing a golden crown." The Queen has heard the children's talk about the rainbow and invites them to visit her fairyland "beyond the rainbow." In the second act, the Queen accompanies the four sisters through fairyland, introducing them to its fantastic inhabitants: the four winds, the painters, sun and moon beams, dewdrops, and fireflies—all of whom introduce themselves to the children with musical interludes. The color scheme of the fairyland act was to be done in rainbow hues to contrast with the dreary weather of the first act. The sixty-minute *Rainbow* operetta was popularly staged by students across the country until at least 1948.

As Irwin Hochberg, his given name, *Oz* lyricist E. Y. Harburg had been bitten by the performing bug in his youth and had won amateur acting prizes as a student at New York's Public School 64. In 1939 he recalled being the "best little goddamned actor" on the East Side. *Over the Rainbow* was performed in Brooklyn at the Bushwick Avenue German Presbyterian Sunday School by a cast of fifty over two nights on April 15 and 16, 1915. At the time, Harburg would have still been a teenager and, given his thespian ambitions and the location of the presentation, it is not inconceivable that Harburg would have known of the operetta in his youth and recalled the production's fairy-tale theme and title when writing "Over the Rainbow" for *The Wizard of Oz*. If not, then he almost certainly became aware of *Over the Rainbow* commensurate with MGM's preproduction survey of musical fantasies comparable to its *Wizard of Oz*.

But then, as now, there were tremendous corporate safeguards mounted to deflect any liability of third-party influences. For example, when Victor Fleming's *Test Pilot* (1938) became a smash hit and top moneymaker, Dolores Lacy Collins filed a million-dollar lawsuit against MGM/Loew's claiming plagiarism of her late husband aviator James H. Collins's 1935 memoir of the same title. Though a judge ruled in Metro's favor, the process was burdensome.

If Harburg knew of the *Over the Rainbow* operetta, he wasn't saying, at least not publicly—especially as the most darling of the operetta's main characters is named Dorothy and Act One closes with a song titled "Over the Rainbow." However, the phrase "over the rainbow" was included in all of Harburg's draft titles from the very start. In later years Harburg owed his song title's inspiration to the idea that a rainbow would have been the only thing of significant color in Dorothy's otherwise arid Kansas existence, and, he said, "I thought that the rainbow could be a bridge from one place to another." The simplistic musical bridge of "Over the Rainbow" is reminiscent of "Twinkle, Twinkle Little Star," which may have inspired Harburg to write the lyric "Someday I'll wish upon a star."

Despite these influential thoughts, all of the *Wizard of Oz* musical numbers were original, though the melody of "If I Only Had a Brain" was recycled from an unused tune

Harburg and Arlen had written for *Hooray for What!* There was no consideration given to reappointing songs written for previous Oz productions; L. B. Mayer was too shrewd to aggregate royalties payable to anyone other than his own studio. For this reason, Ruth Plumly Thompson's overtures to Mervyn LeRoy about reusing her songs from an Oz "playlet" that traveled to department stores across the country in 1924 fell on deaf ears. Nor was repurposing songs from the Montgomery-Stone play a consideration, to Louella O. Parsons's chagrin. The script for the Broadway musical comedy was obtained for review by MGM but its political jabs and inside jokes were outdated and its songs were virtually unrelated to the story, as was typical of the era in which it was composed. However, in his column tracking the film's development, Douglas W. Churchill noted, "To arouse memories in old-timers, fragments from the musical-comedy [score] will be heard now and then . . .," but this did not come to pass. After *The Wizard of Oz* premiered in 1939, Mrs. George Frenger, cousin of Paul Tietjens, who cowrote numbers for the play, went public with her partiality, saying, "The music in the film version has been entirely changed and . . . lacks the musical value of the original."

On September 30 and October 1, 6, 7, and 11, 1938, in advance of the start of production, Judy Garland joined Ray Bolger, Buddy Ebsen, and Bert Lahr to prerecord "If I Only Had a Brain/Heart/Nerve," "We're Off to See the Wizard," "The Jitterbug," "Over the Rainbow," and "If I Were King of the Forest." Herbert Stothart and Georgie Stoll capably conducted the MGM orchestra. These recordings would be pressed into discs for on-set playback, to which the actors would lip-synch, as well as for incorporation directly into the complete soundtrack.

One anamoly reportedly surfaced while making these recordings. It was discovered that if Bolger, Ebsen, or Lahr had any loose change in their pockets, the microphone would pick up the clanking noise and ruin the take. "So a rule was made," wrote Anne M. McIlhenney in her Filmland Rambles column. "If any of the boys forget to empty their pockets before doing their film chore, they had to buy coffee and refreshments for the recording and camera crews. Glumly they report that Lahr has bought three times, Ebsen two, and Bolger once. And even with low score, Ray claims a foul—he insists that it was a dollar bill that crackled in his pocket and a 'crackle' wasn't a 'clank'—but the technicians insisted that it was an offside noise just the same. And they're bigger than Ray, so he bought."

Another precaution was made when Bert Lahr recorded his comedic "If I Were King of the Forest" number. He had an unconscious tendency to sway back and forth while singing, so he was asked to stand behind a chair placed into position before the microphone and hold on to it firmly with both hands. This eliminated the swaying, which had changed the recording distances between his vocals and what the microphone captured.

It was also at this time that an uncredited vocalist garnered mention when an October 16, 1938, news bit noted that Adriana Caselotti was destined to remain invisible in films.

Caselotti was the singing and speaking voice of Disney's Snow White. In *Oz* Caselotti was engaged to sing the "woodland voice which joins that of Tin Woodman Buddy Ebsen as he sings to Judy Garland, 'If I Only Had a Heart.'" Thus, with most of the musical numbers recorded, *The Wizard of Oz* was prepared to go before the cameras.

THE SHOOTING SCRIPT

Despite the third-party influences and creative liberties, the *Wizard of Oz* script essentially kept L. Frank Baum's story line intact. The final shooting script is dated October 10, 1938—seventy-two hours prior to the start of production. Mrs. Gulch had reverted to *Miss* Gulch as she had been originally, and her son Walter (also the character Bulbo in *Oz*) was excised. The distinction of *Miss* Gulch was also more becoming of Gale Sondergaard, who was to have played this part in addition to the Wicked Witch of the West.

In Bulbo's place, and in true witchcraft tradition, the Wicked Witch gained a familiar, a monkey named Nikko whose wings the Witch has clipped short in order to keep him as her servant. Extraneous characters including Lizzie Smithers, princes and princesses, and a dragon had all been cut as the final-version script was honed and streamlined. But in it, a new character remains and another, who appears in the finished film, is absent.

The script, credited to Langley, Woolf, and Ryerson, is also noted as "Okayed by Mervyn LeRoy." Oddly, the screenplay doesn't open on Dorothy as does the Baum book and, eventually, the finished film. Instead, the camera pans through the Kansas farm to dillydallying farmhands Hunk and Hickory, the Ray Bolger and Buddy Ebsen characters. Hunk plays his harmonica as he absent-mindedly churns butter with his foot. Hickory is "tinkering with a weird contraption" consisting of old hot-water boilers, stovepipes, funnels, and a bent teakettle; this is his wind-stopping invention described as "worthy of Rube Goldberg." (Goldberg was a cartoonist known for his depictions of complicated, convoluted gadgetry the product output of which was illogically simplistic.)

The two itinerates are chastised by Aunt Em who, despite a grimness on the surface, has a "softness underneath." Allusions to the Ozian characters each farmhand becomes are obvious in Aunt Em's admonishments, particularly when she warns Hickory (later the Tin Man) that his joints will rust and he might fall asleep standing up. The scene then shifts to a country road, in the distance is Dorothy riding her pony home with Toto trotting along- side. She stops to straighten a scarecrow's hat before charging into the barnyard through a flock of geese.

(The notion that Dorothy would ride a pony must have been an expectation even after production got under way—and in advance of shooting the Kansas scenes. The December 25, 1938, edition of the *San Antonio [TX] Light* noted that "Judy Garland is spending

spare time from *The Wizard of Oz* set at MGM on horseback. The young singing star has been promised a horse by her mother if she shows sufficient proficiency at riding. . . ." By the time of making *The Harvey Girls* (1946), Garland was reportedly "deathly afraid of horses," perhaps tainted by the experience of learning to ride for *Oz*. In the final film, Dorothy and Toto are solo and on foot as they race home.)

Dorothy tells Hunk and Hickory she has been expelled by the schoolmarm Miss Gulch. Toto has bitten Miss Gulch and Dorothy has retaliated Miss Gulch's meanness by calling her "a nasty old witch." (Miss Gulch had previously referred to the dimwitted Hunk as brainless.) The farmhands caution Dorothy about Aunt Em's wrath, and Dorothy advises them that she longs for "a place where you don't always get into trouble." This cues her singing of "Over the Rainbow," which is performed for Hunk and Hickory—rather than to Toto, as in the final film—and includes alternate lyrics from those in the final recorded version.

The setting shifts to Miss Gulch peddling down a narrow lane as the strains of "Over the Rainbow" are still heard softly, instead of the now-classic Miss Gulch/Wicked Witch leitmotif. Uncle Henry, described as "a mild, ineffective little man, with a kindly face," is painting the fence and has put up a "Fresh Paint" sign as Miss Gulch pulls up. Startled, Henry backs up against the fence, which imprints white slat marks on his backside. Miss Gulch is there to confront him and Aunt Em about Dorothy, with dialogue identical to that in the final film.

Everyone is convened in the "typical old-fashioned farmhouse parlor" with flowered wallpaper, family pictures on the wall, plush furniture, and gilt bulrushes in the corner. The scene unfolds as it does in the final film with Miss Gulch (still identified as "the teacher") threatening a damage suit if the family does not relinquish Toto to her so that he may be destroyed as per sheriff's orders. Dorothy goes "suddenly berserk" and calls Miss Gulch a witch for the second time that day.

Toto is imprisoned in a basket Miss Gulch has brought to contain him and, as she pedals away with the basket strapped to the rear of her bicycle, she does so with an "expression of smug satisfaction upon her face." Toto works open the clasp on the basket and bolts home, where he leaps through the open window to Dorothy's bedroom and catches her "full on her chest." As in the movie, Dorothy decides they should run away from home and special emphasis is given to how small and forlorn they look against the immensity of the Kansas prairie.

Weary from their exile, Dorothy and Toto come to "COTTONWOODS AND SPRING," where they spy an encampment of two wagons. The first is a small cage-wagon with tarnished gilt carving, like old-fashioned circuses used for their animals (which was to contain a mangy-looking lion in an earlier script). The second, larger wagon is dusty and shabby and gaudily decorated with mystical symbols and icons. The latter is Professor Marvel's abode, an "old carnival fakir" who gives psychic readings from his crystal ball and also performs juggling and sleight of hand. (In the final film there is only Professor Marvel's caravan.)

Dorothy hears music and traces it to Goliath (later to be the Cowardly Lion), who is playing an accordion. The Goliath character was to have been a dwarf named Joe at one point; he is here described as "a timid-looking man in a bowler hat and striped jersey," to be portrayed by Bert Lahr. Professor Marvel is "cooking wienies over a camp fire" as he does onscreen. The exchange between Professor Marvel and Dorothy is identical to the final film except for insertions that define Goliath's character as fearful.

Goliath is terrified of Toto sniffing at him and gives a "whiney of alarm" as Dorothy assures him that her dog is harmless. But Goliath is afraid of all animals, especially lions. When Dorothy explains that she and Toto are running away because Toto bit Miss Gulch, Goliath screams in fright and the Professor decrees that Goliath "just hasn't any courage at all."

Professor Marvel concedes that he and Dorothy must consult his crystal ball for guidance. He gives Goliath a silent cue as they enter his caravan, and while the Professor distracts Dorothy, Goliath riffles through her belongings. Goliath finds a photograph of Dorothy with Aunt Em and discretely passes it to Professor Marvel, thus giving the fortune-teller a point of reference for his false prophecy about Aunt Em's attack of brokenheartedness. (In the final film it is the Professor who discovers the photograph during the moments he has advised Dorothy to close her eyes.) There is also a brief reference to poppies on the wallpaper of Dorothy's bedroom—dialogue that was shot but excised from the final film. (Also in Dorothy's bedroom are a washbasin and pitcher, a doll, and a framed print of a foreign city with towering turrets.)

Believing that Aunt Em is truly ailing, Dorothy decides to turn back and rationalizes that she can entrust Toto to Hunk's care in order to avoid further confrontation with Miss Gulch. As Dorothy heads home with Toto, there's a close-up of Professor Marvel and Goliath as the Professor, still holding Dorothy's picture, muses, "I'd give a lot to know what the old lady's *really* doing."

(It is interesting to note that in this script there is no third farmhand named Zeke, a part later written for Bert Lahr. As the Kansas scenes were to be filmed last according to the shooting schedule, there were still scripted revisions to be made that would tweak the prologue and do away with Goliath. As such, a reference to Dorothy's friendship with just the two farmhands known to her—per this script version—remains in the final film, the scene of which was shot in November 1938. In it Dorothy has a moment of déjà vu in which she wonders how it is that her new best friends, the Scarecrow and Tin Woodman, seem so familiar to her, as if she's known them all along. Dorothy never makes a similar remark to the Cowardly Lion character.)

Back on the farm a windstorm is blowing up, which is just the opportunity Hickory's been waiting for. Heedless of Uncle Henry's calls to take cover, Hickory tries to activate his anti-wind machine, which blows up in a loud explosion. Aunt Em is frantic for not being able to find Dorothy.

Dorothy and Toto reach the farm gate as the wind lifts both of them off their feet. Toto is blown back past Dorothy, who is able to grab him in time. This bit may have been inspired by a tense incident in *The Wonderful Wizard of Oz* in which Toto falls through the open trapdoor in the house floor during the cyclone. Dorothy rescues him by grabbing his ear and dragging him back inside.

Dorothy tears through the house calling for her guardians, but, unlike in the final film, she does not check the outside storm cellar. Instead, she cowers on her bed as a blast of wind blows out the window, striking her unconscious with delirium. What is next designated as "the first scene of our fantasy" is a long shot of the funnel cloud hitting the farm as the house goes whirling up into the air.

As she revives and sees debris flying past the window, Dorothy exclaims, "Toto! We're not on the ground anymore!" which causes Toto to retreat under the bed. Similar dialogue was filmed but snipped in editing, creating a continuity issue in the final film. One moment,

Toto is on the bed, with Dorothy, barking at an airborne cow, and the next moment, he is peeking out from under the bed. Among the various personages that are also airborne is Miss Gulch peddling her bicycle. As in the final film, she morphs into the Wicked Witch of the East but the script description was composed with Gale Sondergaard in mind: "First of all her hat begins to grow long and thin, her dress turns into a slinky black robe with flying sleeves which suggest the wings of a bat."[9]

As the Witch flies off into the distance, cackling on her broom, there was to be a special-effects shot of the funnel cloud parting company with the house, which then plummets to earth. Dorothy opens the front door slowly, and the script is specific in stating that this is the first time Technicolor is used, as all the Kansas scenes were to be in "grey washes" in keeping with Baum's multiple use of the adjective "grey."

Dorothy takes in the colorful sights about her "with an expression of delighted amazement." When she says to Toto, "We must be over the rainbow," as in the final film, it is

---

9 Sondergaard's earliest wardrobe tests include a gown with elongated, floor-length sleeves.

because an insert shot of "a beautiful rainbow overhead" was to precede this line. Glinda enters in a crystal bubble but is still described as a "plump, kindly, cheerful little woman" and not the graceful sorceress portrayed by Billie Burke. Dorothy's line about witches being "old and ugly" aligns verbatim with Baum's description of Blinkie the witch in his 1915 book, *The Scarecrow of Oz*.

The Munchkinland dialogue continues much as it is in the final film, with the Munchkin natives happily spreading the glad news of the Wicked Witch of the East's demise—she was crushed under Dorothy's house. During "Ding-Dong! The Witch Is Dead," the town crier rings the doorbell on a Munchkin hut. In response, a funny bearded man throws open the shutters on an upper window and asks, "Which old witch?"—dialogue that was actually recorded. The crowd below chants, "The Wicked Witch!" in a bit edited from the final film. The Lollipop Guild toughs give Dorothy a floral lollipop instead of an authentic one as in the final version of the film.

The celebratory proceedings are interrupted by the appearance of the Wicked Witch of the West, who vows vengeance on Dorothy once Glinda magically places the dead witch's ruby shoes on Dorothy's feet. In making her threats, the Witch twice refers to Dorothy as "my little pretty," which was scripted as an allusion to Judy Garland's original blonde appearance. The dialogue continues much as in the final film except there is no "Follow the Yellow Brick Road" lead-in to "We're Off to See the Wizard." Instead, five little Munchkin fiddlers lead Dorothy and Toto to the boundary of Munchkinland, at which point the Yellow Brick Road is found.

The scene dissolves to Dorothy chanting to herself, "Follow the Yellow Brick Road," as she and Toto come to a crossroad. Dorothy mistakes the nearby Scarecrow for a signpost to the Emerald City. Their exchange differs a bit from the final film, with banter about the Scarecrow being stuffed and therefore "stuck up" (on his perch). Once Dorothy frees him, he confesses his want for a brain in his song-and-dance number, which garners the approval of a half a dozen crows. In dialogue similar to the final film, the Scarecrow joins Dorothy's trek and they march off together singing "We're Off to See the Wizard."

They come to an apple orchard and, unbeknownst to them, the Wicked Witch is in the shadows behind one of the trees "watching the two approach with an expression of great malignancy." The intended implication is that the Witch had enchanted the trees to set a trap to capture Dorothy. The scene continues as in the final film, with Dorothy and the Scarecrow encountering the ornery apple trees, denoted as speaking "in a wooden voice that issues from a knothole that works like the mouth of Charlie McCarthy [Edgar Bergen's famous ventriloquist dummy]." Once insulted by the Scarecrow, one of the trees winds up "like a pitcher" to pelt its apples at them.

Their hunt to gather the thrown apples leads to the accidental discovery of the rusty Tin Woodman, whose oil can is not resting on a nearby stump, as in the final film, but is, instead, "fixed to his hip, in the same manner that a flask would be." This designation was apparently retained up until the scene for the Tin Man's discovery was first photographed. The oil can in the surviving stills is of the small, thumb-pump variety as worn on the hip by Buddy Ebsen in a wardrobe test just prior to commencement of production. After the scene was officially filmed (with Ebsen's replacement, Jack Haley), the footage was discarded and reshot because the Tin Man had appeared shiny and polished, not rust-corroded. For the reshoot, the oil can was replaced with a larger version that featured a handle and pump lever.

Dorothy and the Scarecrow liberate the Tin Man and he goes into his song number about longing for a heart. When Dorothy suggests he join them, he is doubtful in a bit of dialogue cut from the final film: "To the Emerald City? That's a long and dangerous journey. And it might rain on the way. . . ."

What follows is the scene in which the Wicked Witch unexpectedly appears on the roof of the Tin Man's cottage. She tries to intimidate Dorothy's friends by threatening to stuff a mattress with the Scarecrow's innards (in an era when some mattresses were stuffed with straw). She also tells the Tin Man she'll use him for a beehive, and after the Witch's disappearance, bees begin to magically pour forth from his mouth, ears, and the funnel tip of his cap. This scene was indeed shot but cut from the final film; the bee effect was done using a combination of live bees (a bee wrangler was called for) and animated bees for the swarm that was to issue from the Tin Man.

The Scarecrow and Tin Man pledge their allegiance to Dorothy despite the Wicked Witch's attempts to dissuade them, and they all march down the Yellow Brick Road, arm in arm. As they enter an eerie forest, still singing, about fifteen or twenty voices were to chant, "Watch out for the Witch of the West," which prompts Dorothy's line in the final film about not liking the dark and creepy forest.[10] The Scarecrow worries that they may meet hay-eating animals, but the Tin Man suggests the wild animals would mostly be lions, tigers, and bears—an allusion to Baum's half-tiger, half-bear Kalidahs.

There is no pseudo-song indicated for what would become the characters' recitation of "Lions and tigers and bears, oh my!" Instead, as the Cowardly Lion makes his entrance and advances upon them, they retreat, step-by-step, to musical chords. In a 1970 interview Noel Langley said that once he learned Bert Lahr would play the Cowardly Lion, it was easy for him to insert Lahr's comical dialogue. The shooting script bears Langley's handicraft in the description of the Lion striking a boxer's pose, and waltzing toward Dorothy's companions "with his fists up like a boxer, doing some very fancy shadow boxing," while

---

10 As of October 3, 1938, just ten days prior to the start of production, the musical chant by a chorus of voices, "Watch Out for the Wicked Witch," as it was now titled, was set to be rehearsed in advance of recording four days later.

egging them on to put up their dukes. After chastising the Lion for bullying them all, Dorothy invites him to join their party, and after he sings his song, there is a "musical fadeout," although another round of "We're Off to See the Wizard" is not specified.

The scene cuts to the Wicked Witch with Nikko, her "familiar chimpanzee," spying on them in her crystal globe and creating the poisonous poppy field. As the group emerges from the woods, they glimpse the towers and domes of the Emerald City "in the far distance, shrouded mystically in a haze of mist." When they run through the poppies, there was to be a slow-motion insert shot of Toto running after them with his tongue hanging out (the implication being that, as the smallest and closest to the ground, Toto would be the first affected by the poppies' effects). Dorothy was to then sleepily tell him he mustn't go to sleep before succumbing herself. The other characters then have a brief exchange, wondering what's happened to Dorothy. It is likely that these shots were filmed but cut for time in the editing process. As in the 1902 stage production, Dorothy remains subdued among the flowers instead of being carried to safety by the Scarecrow and Tin Man, as in the Baum book.

The scene then proceeds as in the final film, with the Cowardly Lion falling asleep as well and Glinda answering the distress calls of the Scarecrow and Tin Man by summoning a snow shower (also as in the stage production) to squelch the poppies' poison and break the Witch's spell. In the interim Nikko, the monkey, has retrieved the Golden Cap at the Witch's instruction so that the Witch can command the Winged Monkeys to steal Dorothy's slippers. This portion of the scene was cut from the final film, with no explanation given for the appearance of the Golden Cap. In a fit of anger, the Witch flings the cap across the room before deciding to fly on her broomstick herself to intercept the travelers at the Emerald City.

Dorothy and her friends tramp out of the snow-covered field to the musical accompaniment of "Optimistic Voices." At the Emerald City gates, their call is answered by the doorman, who is described as reminiscent of Professor Marvel but with a pointed cap (like an old-fashioned nightcap), a scrubby moustache, and a funny red nose. As in the final film, Dorothy's Ruby Slippers impress the doorman enough to gain them all entry through the gates.

The script next sees Dorothy and her friends make their way down three or four marble steps to a buggy made of emeralds and green glass (in the final film, it is a standard-appearing carriage). The cabby "is also Professor Marvel" in a different makeup and beard; he is "as Cockney as a costermonger." The cabby makes no mention of taking them anywhere, but they all board the buggy and, to Dorothy's amazement, the cream-colored horse has now turned a shade of purple, being the Horse of a Different Color. This leads into the "Merry Old Land of Oz" number during which the steed transforms its hue one last time. In the final film, the horse changes from white to purple to red to yellow. A sequence with the

horse also colored blue was filmed but not used. Thus, the horse's hues were to represent the predominant colors of the four countries surrounding the Emerald City in the Oz books: Gillikins (purple), Quadlings (red), Winkies (yellow), and Munchkins (blue).

The scene next shifts to the "Wash and Brush Up Co., Ltd., Inc." (which gets abbreviated to "Wash & Brush Up Co." in the final film) in which the Scarecrow is stuffed with fresh excelsior, a boot polisher spiffs up the Tin Man, Dorothy is given a facial massage, and a manicurist tends to the Cowardly Lion's claws. In the final film Dorothy instead receives a new coiffure and she and Toto are perfumed; and five attendants cater to the Lion. They all strut out of the shop singing one line from "We're Off to See the Wizard," which Dorothy does in the final film. The procession is interrupted by a rumble of thunder as the Wicked Witch swoops overhead, black smoke trailing from her broomstick, skywriting a call for Dorothy to surrender. The Tin Man nervously quips, "Can't that female take no for an answer?"

Fearful, the townspeople descend upon the Palace of Oz with Dorothy's group in tow. At the entrance to the palace is "a funny guard" who is also the Professor Marvel character in a different disguise with a "fiercely turned-up moustache." As in the final film, he bellows at the mob to disperse but Dorothy and her friends insist on seeing the Wizard. At the call of a bugle, the sentry pauses for the changing of the guard, during which he marches importantly into the guard box, turns around, and marches out with his moustache now turned fiercely downward—a bit of comic nonsense shot but cut from the final film.

Upon learning that the girl is the same Dorothy the Wicked Witch is pursuing, the guard agrees to announce their presence to the Wizard. Their jubilation leads into the Cowardly Lion's musical number "If I Were King of the Forest," which contains some additional lyrics edited from the final film, resulting in a bit of a continuity gap in how Bert Lahr is posed for the next scene. The guard interrupts the Lion's song to decree that the Wizard has instructed him to turn Dorothy's party away. In a line cut from the final film, the Lion interjects, "Would it do any good if I roared?" Dorothy's disappointed weeping affects the eavesdropping guard, who blubbers through a downpour of soggy tears that he'll get them in to see the Wizard.

In what was to be a lap dissolve, instead of the palace doors simply opening as was shot for the final film, Dorothy's group finds themselves in a palace corridor that stretches for miles and is "high and narrow and grotesquely decorated." There was a bit of business when the Cowardly Lion reconsiders meeting the Wizard and Dorothy tells him, "Come on—we'll soon find the Wizard." Her last two words were to echo and become louder and more distorted in pitch until they blare, "The Great and Powerful Wizard of Oz!!!! Oz!! Oz!! Oz!! Oz!!" As the throne room doors open, the Wizard's booming voice orders them to come forward, to which the Tin Man comments weakly, "That'll be us, folks"—a line cut from the final film.

The script's description of the throne room is very specific: a huge, lofty hall beautifully decorated in green and silver glass with glistening emeralds everywhere, but everything is dim and eerie. On either side of the throne were to be black velvet curtains and large screens with weird designs, with a notation that the placement of the screens was crucial to a later scene. An indistinct form occupies the throne itself, making Toto whimper and bolt behind some curtains. In the script, it is only after Dorothy begins addressing the Wizard that two large urns by the throne flare up, and through the smoke two bright-green eyes peer out. This is what was to prompt Dorothy's line in the final film, "Jiminy Crickets!"

Next, a shadowy mouth appears, calling the others forth. When the Lion faints—as he does in the final film—the script calls for him to briefly revive and make boxing motions before realizing where he is and passing out again. The scene continues as in the final film, with Oz commanding that their wishes will be granted when they return with the Wicked Witch's broomstick. When the Tin Man exclaims that they'd have to kill the Witch to get the broom, the Wizard replies with a line cut from the final film: "That's the little idea I had in mind. . . ." The scene ends as it does in the final film with the Cowardly Lion running out of the throne room, down the corridor, and taking a swan dive by crashing through a plate-glass window. But the script makes it seem as though the window would be open and the crashing sound heard would only occur after a pause when the Lion "reaches the street."

In the subsequent setting, Dorothy's party is en route to find the Wicked Witch by making their way through the creepy Haunted Forest, so designated with a signpost that reads, in part, "Witch's Castle, One Mile"—grammatically correct in the script but misspelled as "Witches Castle" by the prop department for the on-camera sign. The group enters carrying pseudo weapons of protection. The Scarecrow has a water pistol and a long stick that bends like rubber in the middle; the Tin Woodman has a huge spanner wrench in addition to his axe; and the Cowardly Lion holds a fishing net and an exterminator's spray pump with "Witch Remover" printed on it.

After interpreting the signpost's annotation, "I'd Turn Back If I Were You," the Cowardly Lion tries to make a break for it but is retrieved by the Scarecrow and Tin Man, as in the final film. Looking up, they all see—in quick succession—two black owls, two bats, and two crows with red eyes, all glaring at them from different trees. (In the film they see two owls and two vultures with flickering red eyes.)

A brief exchange follows that was edited from the final version of the film in which the Tin Man states they're on enemy ground and that Dorothy ought to have something with which to protect herself. The Lion offers his Witch Remover. Dorothy doubtfully asks if it works, and the Lion replies that it's only good for threatening. Perturbed, the Scarecrow grabs the spray can and tosses it away. As it hits the ground, it vanishes as they look at one another incredulously. This prompts the Scarecrow to say, "You know something?" to which his comrades shake their heads and listen, leading to his next line, as heard in the final film, "I believe there's spooks around here." The rest of the scene proceeds as seen in the final film with the Tin Man being suddenly levitated before violently crashing back to earth—perhaps an allusion to the way he is battered on rocks by the Winged Monkeys in Baum's story.

The locale cuts to the Witch's tower room, where she's been gleefully observing the paranormal activity in her crystal. With her are Nikko and, on the window ledge, the leader of the Winged Monkeys, whom the Witch has apparently summoned using the Golden Cap seen previously. At the Witch's direction the monkey leader gives a shrill whistle that causes a rustling and chattering in the air that grows louder by the second. As in the final film, the Witch assures the monkey leader that their victims won't put up a struggle as she's already sent "a little insect on ahead to take the fight out of them!" As she continues giving instructions to bring back Dorothy, her dog, and, especially, the Ruby Slippers, the Witch has to shout in order to be heard over the screaming and chattering of the bat-like army flying past her tower room window.

The scene switches back to Dorothy and her friends in the Haunted Forest for "The Jitterbug" song and dance number, which was shot but excised from the final film. In it, the group cautiously advances step-by-step as the whine of the jitterbug comes over the soundtrack. A large mosquito-like insect bites the Lion's neck, then Dorothy's ankle and the Tin Man's cheek before attacking the Scarecrow. As the music grows louder and spookier, the forest trees quiver their branches to the rhythm, and the group sings their song while "jittering," or shivering, along the path.

As the "Jitterbug" number breaks up, the group hears a weird chattering and whistling and, looking up, sees the Winged Monkeys coming at them in flight formation. As the monkeys swoop down, there is panicked dialogue from Dorothy's friends—unheard in the final film—during which two monkeys grab Dorothy and start up with her. As Toto looks up after Dorothy, "barking and howling with excitement," a third monkey seizes him and disappears into the sky.

There is next a fade-in on the interior of the Witch's tower room, instead of an exterior establishing shot of the castle itself, as in the final film. The Witch's dialogue was obviously written with Gale Sondergaard's deliciously evil characterization in mind:

```
Witch (with diabolical sweetness)
Why, this is quite an unexpected pleasure!

CAMERA DRAWS BACK to show Dorothy who is looking very
frightened.

Witch (contd.)

It's so kind of you to take pity on my loneliness and visit
me.

CAMERA DRAWS STILL FARTHER BACK showing that Nikko is going
towards the door with a basket containing Toto. Whines and
cries are coming from the basket.

Dorothy (in great distress)
Where are you taking my dog? Give him back to me!

Witch
All in good time, my little pretty, all in good time.
```

The scene continues as it does in the final film with the Wicked Witch trying unsuccessfully to remove the Ruby Slippers from Dorothy's feet, and Toto escaping from the basket, just as he did back in Kansas. In a bit not in the final film, Toto dodges out from under the arms of two Winkie guards as a squealing Nikko collides into the guards for what sounds like a bit of comic relief. Toto leaps off the rising drawbridge and runs into the forest. The scene concludes with the Witch—incensed at being foiled—giving Dorothy an hour to live and imprisoning her alone in the room.

In the clearing where Dorothy was abducted, the Tin Man, now heavily dented, and the Cowardly Lion are restuffing the Scarecrow when Toto enters barking furiously and tugging at them urgently. The Scarecrow realizes that Toto will guide them to Dorothy and they follow his lead, but—in a bit not in the final film—the Tin Man's legs give way and he rattles to the ground saying, "My legs, my legs! I'm buckled! Oil me quick!"

Back in the Witch's tower room, the segment of another edited scene begins with the musical strains of "Over the Rainbow" as Dorothy tries the door and, finding it locked, falls crying with her head on her arms. Lifting her head, and in between sobs, she plaintively sings several bars from her Kansas Song before calling out for Aunt Em, which is where the final film picks up. The Witch's crystal "begins to swirl and smoke restlessly" as a vision of Aunt Em appears within. Dorothy cries out to her in dialogue precisely as in the final film only to have the vision fade, replaced with that of the Wicked Witch herself, mocking Dorothy's terror.

Meanwhile, Dorothy's companions have scaled a hillside of boulders and slippery shale when they see the Witch's castle with its "great pointed towers . . . silhouetted against the sky on the peak of the mountain. There is a full moon which makes it almost as bright as day." The others convince the Cowardly Lion that he's capable of rescuing Dorothy ("You're going to be brave and like it!" says the Tin Man in dialogue not in the final film), as all three are sneak-attacked from behind by three Winkie guards. Through insert shots not in the final film, the assault is witnessed by a distraught Dorothy from the tower window. Recycling the "disguise" routine from the 1902 play, our heroes emerge victorious and don the uniforms of their assailants, the implication being that "the Winkies have been vanquished, if not killed, by Dorothy's friends," as indicated by the script.

The three infiltrate the changing of the guard at the entrance to the castle with "the last one being the Lion, who is having a dreadful time with his tail"—a comedic bit that is one of the classic moments in the final film. In fact, the exchange and patter of the three male characters throughout these scenes veers toward emulation of Metro's Marx Brothers, which is precisely what an unnamed *Oakland (CA) Tribune* reviewer noted upon seeing the completed film. Once inside, the group breaks off from the marching procession of Winkies and, seeing Toto scratching at a door, call to Dorothy. More cut lines follow as they try to open the door in vain by tugging on it; but the Lion gets in the way of their progress, and the Scarecrow smacks his paws. Finally, the Tin Man rends the barricade with his axe, freeing Dorothy. They grab her and run down the corridor.

Just as Dorothy and her friends reach the doors to exit the castle, they are trapped by the Witch and "about thirty or forty" of her Winkie guards.[11] There's a brief deleted exchange as the Tin Man presses the Cowardly Lion to "Do something! Roar at them!" but as the Winkies advance, the Lion closes his mouth, hopelessly saying, "What'll it get us?"—unlike in the Baum book in which the Lion does indeed roar loudly enough to cause the Winkies to retreat. As the Winkies close in on the captives step-by-step, the Scarecrow observes that the huge circular iron candelabra hanging above them is anchored by a rope tied to a cleat a few feet from them.

With a cry of "Seize them!" the Wicked Witch throws the hourglass with which she marked time in countdown to Dorothy's death. It "explodes like a bomb in a flash of red smoke" as the Winkies rush them. The Tin Man raises his axe as the Lion says, "Here we go boys!"—which is another line edited from the final film. But in the nick of time, the Scarecrow jerks the Tin Man's axe causing it to sever the rope that tethers the candelabra, which crashes with a rusty screech on top of the Winkies.

They begin their escape attempt anew, commenting excitedly along the way in lines cut from the final film, such as the Scarecrow's remark, "It's no good trying the doors again! Look for a window!" and "Keep straight on!" Eventually, as in the final film, they are recaptured and a fracas ensues. As such, there is no climactic tension in which the Wicked Witch corners them and threatens to destroy them one by one. Instead, in the midst of the mob scene, the Witch sets the Scarecrow on fire and Dorothy extinguishes the fire and simultaneously douses the Witch with a bucket of water. The Witch then melts away and the script description reads just as L. Frank Baum wrote it. The Witch begins to shrink and shrivel and deteriorates into "a brown, shapeless mass, already half melted. A bubbling groan comes from her."

With the Witch vanquished, the Winkies and Winged Monkeys start to sing and dance, shouting, "The Wicked Witch is dead - Which Witch? - The Wickedest Witch!" This dissolves into a parade through the Emerald City as Dorothy and her companions return triumphantly; the Scarecrow carries the Witch's broomstick (all of which was filmed but trimmed from the final version). This dissolves to the throne room with the great green head facing them from the throne with a notation that the room arrangement is as before.

The scene proceeds as it does in the final film except that, as in Baum's book, Toto pushes over a nearby screen—instead of drawing back a curtain—to reveal the Wizard in human form. The four friends demand to know who the man is, and when he declares himself to be the Wizard, the Scarecrow says angrily, "I don't believe you! We've *seen* the Wizard—over there, in smoke! You're just trying to stop us seeing him!"—lines not in the final film. More

---

11 Curiously, the July 12, 1938, "Temporary List of People Requiring Costumes" for *The Wizard of Oz* indicates only the Winkie general and six other soldiers.

deleted lines follow as the faux Wizard tries to impress and distract them with sleight-of-hand magic tricks, which motivates the Tin Man to fiercely say in a Baumian tone, "Shall I chop off his silly little head?" to which the Scarecrow and Lion shout, "Yes!" (Among the publicity stills taken of the *Wizard of Oz* cast, there is a pose of the Tin Man threatening the Wizard with his raised axe, after the W. W. Denslow book illustration.)

As the frightened man begs for his life, he turns a row of flags of all nations into a bunch of flowers—which are visible on the Wizard's console in the final film, even though these lines were deleted. (Frank Morgan reportedly worked closely with a professional magician to perfect the sleight-of-hand effect.) The final version of the film picks up with the Scarecrow declaring, "You humbug!" and the Wizard dispensing the token rewards to each of Dorothy's companions with great and blustery ceremony. The Wizard also resigns to take Dorothy back to Kansas in the balloon that carried him to "the heart of this noble city" originally. In another edited line, he tells them of his predicament when the balloon cut loose the first time: "There I was, floating through space, a man without a continent."

The setting next wipes to the city square, where rests a decorated platform housing the Wizard's balloon with himself and Dorothy in it. The Scarecrow, Tin Woodman, and Cowardly Lion stand near, in charge of the mooring ropes. The fanfare proceeds as it does in the final film, with the Wizard's proclamations until Toto "suddenly cocks his ears and growls," distracted by a small girl—not a glamorous ingenue as in the final film—holding a kitten. As the Wizard says "Now if you will be good enough to cast off that rope," Toto jumps out of Dorothy's arms to rush into the crowd. The preceding line was cut from the final film, creating a continuity issue as it appears the Tin Man is deliberately unlooping the mooring rope in his charge instead of acting on the Wizard's command.

Dorothy runs after Toto, who has been caught by a guard in the crowd. As the guard hands the wriggling dog to his mistress, Dorothy pauses to tell the guard, "Oh thank you—very kind of you—thank you," a bit cut from the final film (Dorothy is only seen returning to the platform with Toto already in her arms). In the meantime the loosened balloon goes shooting into the air as the Wizard drifts out of sight.

Just when all seems lost, Glinda magically appears and the subsequent scene is verbatim to the final film as Glinda reveals the charm of the Ruby Slippers and Dorothy bids a sad farewell to each of her beloved comrades. The exception is that, at the point at which Dorothy tells Glinda she's finally ready to leave, the surrounding crowd begins to softly sing, "The Merry Old Land of Oz," which doesn't occur in the final film. It has previously been stated that when Dorothy tells the Scarecrow she'll miss him most of all, this is an allusion to a script draft in which the inklings of a romance between Dorothy and Hunk, the Scarecrow's Kansas counterpart, were suggested. But Baum's text clearly indicates Dorothy's partiality for the Scarecrow at the point of her tearful departure: She kisses the Tin

Woodman and Cowardly Lion goodbye but instead hugs the Scarecrow's soft body—as she does in the film, the Scarecrow having been her first and oldest acquaintance.

To enact the Ruby Slippers' spell, Dorothy must tap her heels three times while repeating "There's no place like home." As the incantation begins, "the noise of a whirlwind comes in and the screen begins to swirl and twist like spinning smoke." What follows is a montage of imagery from Dorothy's adventures—which was filmed, assembled, and included in the preview versions of the movie but deleted from the final cut. The montage was to be superimposed over a close-up of Dorothy's face, and it included all of the colorful Ozian personages she encountered before shifting to the gray washes of familiar Kansas images such as Aunt Em, Uncle Henry painting the fence, Hickory's wind machine, a flock of ducks, a cow, etc. During this, a chorus of voices was to be singing "Over the Rainbow" in the background as the montage fades to black with only Aunt Em's voice on the soundtrack, imploring Dorothy to awaken from her nightmare.

Dorothy starts to revive, but upon recognizing Aunt Em asks, "Is it really you, or are you still in the Witch's crystal?"—a line not in the final film. Also not considered for the final film is the following sequence of events: Thinking Dorothy is delirious and in need of a doctor, Uncle Henry rushes outside. There's next a cutaway shot of the roadway outside the Gale farm as Professor Marvel and Goliath steer their caravan, urging the horses at full speed, obviously concerned for Dorothy's safety. Recognizing the farm from Dorothy's photograph, they stop and encounter Uncle Henry, who blurts that Dorothy's in need of a doctor, to which the Professor says, "Good. I'm just in time!" Dumbstruck, Uncle Henry asks Goliath if the Professor is really a doctor and Goliath replies, "Mister—there ain't nothing he *ain't*."

The Professor and Goliath poke their heads in at Dorothy's window and, seeing them, she thinks the Ruby Slippers' spell didn't work as she believes she must still be in Oz. The two farmhands, Hunk and Hickory, have been presiding over Dorothy as well, and when Hickory spills a bowl of water on Dorothy, she becomes more lucid. Dorothy looks up to see Hunk, his hair tousled with straw, and she starts to call Hickory "Tin Man." With the full realization of her surroundings, Dorothy exclaims to Toto that they truly are home. Aunt Em embraces Dorothy and cradles Toto in her other arm. With everyone gathered at her bedside and with a beautiful sunset visible in the background, the music swells as Dorothy philosophizes that "This is the most beautiful place in the whole world!" and the picture ends.

(It is curious to note that instead of ending with a close-up of Dorothy's beaming face, as does this version of the screenplay and as does the final film, an October 7, 1938, rendition of the film's conclusion has the camera pan past Dorothy and out the window to settle on Professor Marvel's lion in a cage before fading to MGM's trademark Leo the Lion.)

This near-final version of the script preserves the most salient elements of the L. Frank Baum story, and remarkably so, given the number of different scenarists who contributed outlines, critiques, drafts, and rewrites. The central fantasy portion of the screenplay would remain intact for the most part; the Kansas scenes, however, would require extensive reworking. If John Lee Mahin rewrote or otherwise improvised portions of the script on set, particularly lines for Bert Lahr, as he told Aljean Harmetz, it would had to have been mainly for the Kansas sequences as the October 10, 1938, script (written before Mahin came on *Oz*) is otherwise largely true to what was committed to film. Significantly, Mahin created Zeke, the third farmhand, thus neatly including Lahr's Kansas counterpart in the farm scenes.

Expunged from the *Wizard of Oz* adaptation were the most superfluous characters and subplots from Baum's narrative. The many obstacles Dorothy and her friends encounter en route to the Emerald City were compressed to include the poppy field episode (minus the field mice), made famous in the early stage musical, and the new menace of the Wicked Witch of the West. The fighting trees from the anticlimactic trek to seek Glinda in the book were retained and supplanted along the journey to the Emerald City. Other incidents, like the encounters with the Kalidahs, the stork that rescues the Scarecrow, the Hammer-Heads, and the Dainty China Country, were unceremoniously discarded as unessential to the advancement of the story. There was also a limit to what special effects were manageable in 1938, being as though the script already called for enough technical headaches to solve as is.[12]

But beyond filmmaking mechanics, the final shooting script also had heart that would speak to audiences universally. In September 1938 Mervyn LeRoy told the Associated Press of *Oz*'s substance: "The story has a lot of 'stuff.' The lion thinks he's cowardly, but he has courage without realizing it. The scarecrow is always asking for brains, yet he figures things out for himself. The woodman wants to do many things; without knowing it, he accomplishes much." The stuff of which LeRoy spoke worked. At an August 9, 1939, Los Angeles press screening of *The Wizard of Oz*, the emotion was palpable. As the projection room lights came up, the critics were weepy, "crying with the young star, Judy Garland, at her farewell to the people of the wonderful Land of Oz."

Of course, no one could have predicted this outcome nearly a year prior—or that it would take as long for *The Wizard of Oz* to make its debut. MGM was reaching to suggest that *The Wizard of Oz* would be released for Christmas 1938 early on in its development. When *Silver Screen* magazine announced in its December 1938 issue that MGM had cast Judy Garland as Dorothy, also indicated was that *Oz* was "a picture designed for Christmas release."

---

12 Oddly enough, a *Wizard of Oz* scarf, licensed by MGM in 1939, incorporates several images associated with the Baum book in its movie-inspired design including a pointed Munchkin hat, the stork, the Golden Cap, and Toto wearing his Emerald City spectacles.

So competitive were motion picture studios at the time that regular reports on their production schedules—and which were tied or lagging—were published in film industry trade journals; that *Oz*'s start date was repeatedly rescheduled did not go unnoticed. On September 10, 1938, *Boxoffice* reported that production would get under way on September 15, but by September 17 *Oz* was only "nearing the starting mark." Then on September 24 the *Hollywood Reporter* announced, "Mervyn LeRoy will gun *The Wizard of Oz*, big Technicolor special at MGM in three weeks. Frank Morgan has been set for the lead with top spots going to Judy Garland, Ray Bolger, Buddy Ebsen, Billie Burke, Gale Sondergaard and Charles Grapewin. Richard Thorpe will direct." But the hurdles of adapting and honing the screenplay and songs would only be matched by the challenges and frustrations of bringing the production to cinematic fruition. Within a month, two actors in the *Hollywood Reporter* lineup would be off the picture, and *Oz* would be without a director.

Looking the Part

"Jack Dawn was quite a man," wrote MGM makeup artist Jack Young in his unpublished memoir. "To be with him, one would not guess he was in the makeup end of the business. He was a big man and a rough man . . . a tyrant, and we were scared to death of him in those days. He would come growling through and when I say growl, he growled. He had a jaw that stuck out four feet and when he started to snap it, boy, we jumped."

Dawn had become head of Metro's makeup department in 1937 the hard way, running away from his Kentucky home at thirteen to elude his alcoholic, abusive father. Dawn escaped to Covington and trudged back and forth to Cincinnati, Ohio, across the old John A. Roebling Suspension Bridge, looking for errands and odd jobs. There, Dawn found work as a Western Union messenger boy and a bellhop at the Havlin Hotel. It was in Cincinnati that Dawn was first attracted to the allure of show business. "I used to go to Keith's [Theatre] and sit in the gallery," he told journalist Teet Carle in 1939. "It was at the old Walnut Street Theatre that I first saw the stage presentation of *The Wizard of Oz*, on which I am now working, with Montgomery and Stone. I can still remember many of the make-ups."

After migrating west Dawn's wanderlust took him to San Francisco, where he got a job aboard a South Seas freighter. He next relocated to Los Angeles where, as a ranch hand, he befriended a movie cowboy who got him into pictures. Dawn worked his way through the Hollywood ranks as a stuntman, extra, and actor, including a stint as a Keystone Kop with Fatty Arbuckle. His knockabout existence made Dawn the perfect artist to imagine solutions to the complications *The Wizard of Oz* would bring because, as Jack Young characterized him, "His whole principle was that if you can't do it, do it anyway; whether it was with plaster or whether it was with a brush. His knowledge was limited, so consequently in the limited knowledge there was nothing that stood in the way. Out of twenty things that would go wrong, he would come up with one that shouldn't have happened and it would blossom like the damndest flower you ever saw."

Despite Jack Dawn's abrasive demeanor, Jack Young defended him. "[Dawn] made make-up have guts. . . . He gave it dignity, uncouthly, but he gave it a voice." Dawn's innovations in makeup artistry allowed for the *Oz* actors to have a voice as well, brilliantly so. It is, perhaps, one of Hollywood's most disgraceful oversights that Jack Dawn has never been formally recognized for his achievements.

Just prior to *The Wizard of Oz*, Dawn estimated that in a year his department required more than one thousand large cans of face powder, three thousand pounds of grease paint, five hundred pounds of false hair for beards and wigs, twenty gallons of spirit gum adhesive, and fifty pounds of assorted waxes and plastics for modeling. In preparation for megaproductions such as *The Good Earth* and *The Wizard of Oz*, Dawn expanded the makeup department staff to meet the demand. "When I recently wished to add six members to my staff," he wrote in 1938, "I interviewed more than 500 applicants, and each one I picked had graduated from an art institute, though some of them had drifted rather strangely into other work. . . . But the importance to me of this group of youngsters I have taken under my wing is that they are being trained from the start on the new lines of screen make-up. It is being impressed on them that their knowledge of facial contour, anatomy, sculpture, and painting is of vital importance."

The process of creating individual facial molds for all actors and extras involved painting on a gelatinous prep called Negacol, over which plaster of paris would be slathered. This made a precise impression of each person's features from which a bust could be made to experiment with foam-rubber appliances without the need to tax the actor's time. Jack Young described the preparations involved, suggesting that *Oz* "could not have been made without the aid of a make-up department and a prosthetic laboratory," recalling that Jack Dawn "went all out" with an unlimited budget. "We did countless sketches of the many characters before each one was finally agreed upon: the many changes of Frank Morgan as the Wizard, the involved make-up of the Scarecrow, the Tin Woodman, Margaret Hamilton as the Wicked Witch [to whom Young was specifically assigned], the Munchkins, the [Emerald City] townspeople, the flying apes, and, of course, Judy Garland and the Good Witch, Billie Burke."

Depending on the day's call for *The Wizard of Oz*, effecting the transformation of the principals as well as hordes of extras was akin to "a real mass production line," as Jack Young called it, one that also included readying Metro's stars and supporting players working on other pictures. Among the crowd of extras requiring individualized makeups were the Munchkins and Emerald City citizens. Each of the male Munchkins wore facial

prosthetics, such as a button nose, and a bald cap on which was glued a sculpted yak-hair wig. Jack Dawn probably felt at liberty to tint the Munchkin hairpieces in bizarre hues, owing to the Whimsies, another race of characters in Baum's *The Emerald City of Oz* (1910), whose hair was colored blue, pink, green, and lavender. The notion of facial appliances to enhance the female Munchkins did not get beyond preproduction.

Taking a cue from Henry Ford's motorcar assembly line, Jack Dawn assigned specific makeup applications to select makeup artists for the Emerald City scenes, in which three hundred people all required cosmetics, thus creating an application "chain." The townsmen of the Emerald City were outfitted with a bald cap, over which black paint was directly brushed to create a unique hairline for each. By February 12, 1939, it was reported that *Oz*'s "tin soldiers" had a beef with the makeup department—the bald caps were causing their hairlines to recede, conceivably limiting their work elsewhere. Jack Dawn's initial intentions to tint green the hair and cheeks of girls in the Emerald City—as in the Baum book—were tabled as overly ambitious.

One believe-it-or-not tidbit that became part of *Oz* lore and concerned makeup was the unlikely tale of Margaret Hamilton keeping her witch nose in her pocketbook. When a purse snatcher nabbed it, the nose was returned to her in the mail with a note: "Wow! So this is Hollywood!" There may be some validity to the story after all, however. It first appeared in Harrison Carroll's March 3, 1939, column (shortly after the *Oz* shoot had wrapped) in which readers were told that the purse theft occurred near Grauman's Chinese Theatre. Hamilton had reportedly taken in a show at Grauman's on a Saturday evening following a day's work at the studio. Carroll made a public plea on behalf of Hamilton for the handbag to be returned to the actress care of MGM as it contained the "fake nose Miss Hamilton wears for her role as the Wicked Witch in *The Wizard of Oz*." Hamilton was known for her comedic timing and so, if the story is true, it can only be speculated that Hamilton retained the nose as a gag or perhaps as a souvenir to show her son at home.

Hamilton's artificial proboscis was publicly described as being cast in metal or, more specifically, made of tin, although this was probably to preserve the secrecy of its true composition. Writing for the 1938 English publication *Behind the Screen*, Jack Dawn was cautious when discussing his use of foam-rubber appliances: "I cannot go into too much detail about this at present as I have patents pending for the formula." Indeed, in a filmed promotional segment for *Of Human Hearts* (1938), Dawn is shown re-creating his makeup for John Carradine's Abraham Lincoln using common plastiline putty. When interviewed by Anne M. McIlhenney in August 1938, Dawn referred to his secret formula only as "No. 6," so named for both the number of years he experimented and his previously unsuccessful trials. (Dawn was so guarded for feeling competition with Universal's Jack Pierce and Perc Westmore of Warner Bros.)

The Wizard of Oz was, as Jack Young said, "a tremendous spectacle," owing to its aura of whimsy the success of Jack Dawn's makeup designs. Such sentiments were echoed in 1972 by fellow apprentice Jack Kevan, who, without hesitation, rated *Oz* the best picture on which he had ever worked. "I put more artistic effort into it than any other film," said Kevan. "There was the Cowardly Lion and the Scarecrow and the Tin Man to make up, and the elves—all midgets from Germany. It was fun, real fairy tale work."

From the outset of preproduction on *The Wizard of Oz*, thirty-five-year-old Adrian was designated as the film's wardrobe designer. Though Sam Kress oversaw Metro's wardrobe department, Adrian was its leading fashion designer from 1928 to 1941. In this capacity his iconic creations for MGM's cinema queens, including Greta Garbo, Norma Shearer, Myrna Loy, and Joan Crawford, influenced style ideas in women's couture worldwide in an era when films made fashions and actresses set trends.

In 1937 Adrian was described as a temperamental yet imaginative bachelor with an estate in the affluent Toluca Lake neighborhood of Los Angeles, replete with a peacock "for atmosphere." Any untoward queries about Adrian's effete, bon vivant persona were sufficiently concealed by his August 1939 marriage to MGM leading lady Janet Gaynor.

Born Adrian Adolph Greenberg, he was known as Gilbert Adrian, combining his first name with that of his father's. But he was best recognized by the sole, distinctive signature "Adrian," a rather exotic title probably inspired by his early idol and MGM predecessor designer Romain de Tirtoff, who was known professionally by the pseudonym Erté. "Gowns by Adrian," Greenberg's onscreen credit, was more a sophisticated reflection of his New York and Parisian schooling than his New England roots as the son of Jewish immigrants and millinery shop owners.

The Wizard of Oz was a creative relief from costume pictures such as *Romeo and Juliet* for which Adrian designed gowns by consulting paintings of the masters such as Botticelli, Benozzo Gozzoli, Fra Angelico, Bellini, and Signorelli. The oft-repeated anecdote about Adrian taking inspiration for his *Wizard of Oz* designs from boyhood sketches may be traced to August 1938 when journalist Weston East reported that Adrian was "having fun whipping up extraordinary outfits" for the Land of Oz characters, and that "he sent to his old hometown—Naugatuck, Connecticut—for his old schoolbooks. As a kid he read the Oz books and sketched costumes for the strange inhabitants of the imaginary land. He wants to prove he was bright even at an early date." Indeed, Adrian's studio biography indicates that "from childhood his bent was artistic and purely creative," but the anecdote about doodling imaginative designs in the margins and flyleaves of his textbooks may have been embellished to be made *Oz*-specific as a similar account—minus the *Oz* reference—was published a year earlier.

Writing for *Behind the Screen*, Adrian defined his approach to wardrobe design:

> My first task is to make pencil sketches of costume ideas—only a silhouette, the "body line" upon which the costume will be developed. Then the details of the neckline, sleeve treatment, and trimmings are drawn in, and the costume adapted as a whole.

At this point, I work the pencil sketch out in watercolors in the approximate tones in which the costume will be made, with color contrast and details as they will appear in the finished costume. Sometimes swatches of the fabrics to be used are attached to the finished sketches, so that the texture and color contrast may be visualized clearly.

Adrian only designed wardrobe. He had an aversion to handling fabric and never measured, cut, or sewed. He also had a tendency to destroy his sketches, ripping them in half with dramatic flair. But his fanciful designs for the Munchkins must have appealed to him—they are the only of his paintings known to have survived from *The Wizard of Oz*. When Hollywood journalist Hedda Hopper told of stopping by Adrian's studio in late June 1938, she remarked on several of the unusual wardrobe sketches for the Munchkins, adding, "He's having more fun over *Wizard* than a trip to Europe."

Although Adrian received screen credit for *Oz*, given the scope of the project coupled with other assignments, he most certainly had staff support for the creative envision of wardrobe for minor players such as Emerald City citizens or Munchkins—all pending Adrian's final reworking before presentation to Mervyn LeRoy for approval. Lee Batchler, nephew of women's wardrobe dresser Sheila O'Brien, spent long hours discussing the behind-the-scenes politics of filmmaking with his aunt (Batchler himself is in the movie business). Even though O'Brien, then thirty-six, was on very good terms with Adrian, said Batchler, given the massive workload on the *Oz* wardrobe department, "Sheila probably designed a good many costumes herself. But it would have had to have been with Adrian's blessing, and given the time crunch, maybe even at his behest. That's how things worked. That's how things still work today. Uncredited visual effects artists create this or that individual shot, yet come awards time just the handful of visual effects supervisors get nominated. Imagine 130 artists taking the stage to accept an award for *Jurassic Park*. Assistant designers often do signature work in films that goes uncredited. . . . If Adrian was hired to give the film's costumes their signature look, whatever Sheila designed would have been conceived and executed to harmoniously blend with Adrian's work so that the overall result appeared to be the work of a single designer."

Batchler's speculation is supported by Adrian himself who, at the time of *Oz*, wrote, "At any big studio there is a huge staff of experts in the art of cutting and tailoring, exclusive fur workers, needle-women, and hand embroiderers—each to do his or her specialized bit in creating these costumes for the screen, to make the finished fashion satisfy the fastidious stars in every minute detail. . . . In conclusion, let me go on record as saying that the story of any gown worn before the cameras is a history of untiring work, skilled technicians, expert planning, and flawless execution."

Adrian's temperament *and* talent would be tested on *The Wizard of Oz*. His glorious period pieces for costume pictures such as *Romeo and Juliet*, *The Gorgeous Hussy*,

Camille, and *Marie Antoinette* called for the combined expertise of beautiful presentation and academic accuracy. *Oz* was pure fantasy, the boundaries of which would be determined by the mercurial eye of the Technicolor camera.

THE LOST PRINCESS OF OZ

Like Snow White, L. Frank Baum's heroine Dorothy was a storybook princess, having been bestowed that distinction ever after in Baum's 1907 book, *Ozma of Oz*. *Ozma* was the second of Baum's thirteen *Wizard of Oz* sequels and marked Dorothy's first return to Oz. At the book's conclusion Dorothy is "presented with a pretty coronet and made a Princess of Oz." Indeed, succeeding Oz books refer to "Princess Dorothy," and the girl is often pictured wearing her gold coronet, as she does on the cover of several succeeding Oz books. Dorothy's royal lineage had also been a plot device of Larry Semon's *Wizard of Oz* when it was revealed that Dorothy—now an eighteen-year-old ingenue—was secretly a princess of Oz, dethroned and covertly displaced in Kansas as an infant.

During preproduction on MGM's *Oz*, Mervyn LeRoy was absorbed in reading the Oz books and was clearly influenced by the notion of Baum's Princess Dorothy. LeRoy's original vision of the Dorothy character matched illustrator John R. Neill's sketches of a slender, blonde girl. The decision to portray Dorothy as a blonde instead of a brunette as depicted in *The Wonderful Wizard of Oz* would have been made almost immediately: A gorgeous Max Factor wig, painstakingly handmade one strand at a time, was created for Judy Garland to wear for her initial *Wizard of Oz* makeup test on April 29, 1938—little more than two months after MGM secured the story rights.[1]

Judy had previously appeared heavily made-up in a 1935 Technicolor short called *La Fiesta de Santa Barbara*, but *The Wizard of Oz* would elevate the medium's artifice. Garland's cosmetics were also in keeping with the princess look: generous rouge and heavy base to imitate the thick, flat tints of cartoon paint; a subtle piece of foam rubber covered the gap on the bridge of her nose. Subsequently, Judy Garland's artificial appearance suggested an animation come to life, in keeping with Mervyn Leroy's intention that life should imitate art. "If Disney can reproduce humans with cartoons" he said, "we can reproduce cartoons with humans."

Judy was taken by her new appearance and the opportunity for glamour it brought. Magazine writer Katherine Hartley informed readers of the October 1938 issue of *Hollywood* that Garland was looking forward to *The Wizard of Oz*. "Mervyn LeRoy selected

---

1 About two months would have been the amount of time required to create a full-length, high-quality wig.

her for the prize-plum part of Dorothy and Judy is beaming, not only because the part is wonderful, but because the picture is to be in Technicolor and she is going to be wearing a light wig with long golden curls." Judy added, "Of *course* I want to be beautiful! And Adrian—he's doing my costumes—says I *am* going to be beautiful in this one!"[2] A syndicated news brief of November 13, 1938, indicated that the wig, its flowing hair tied with a ribbon, was to emulate the appearance of Dorothy in the Baum stories, and that Garland was so intrigued she could hardly keep from staring in the mirror, "Just to make sure it's me." Looking ahead to Thanksgiving, the actress told newspaper reporter Pauline Gallagher that she was grateful "for the chance to be a blonde in *The Wizard of Oz*."

As originally envisioned, Adrian's wardrobe designs for Judy Garland adhered to L. Frank Baum's 1910 designation that Princess Dorothy should dress in a manner befitting the dignity of her position. Adrian created a series of frocks to test on Garland that were a sophisticated spin on contemporary girls' dresses with puff-sleeves and suspender straps. The final selected wardrobe was in keeping with this basic style, but the blue fabric that made up the skirt and bodice had a satiny sheen to it, accented by a polka-dot bow at the throat of the blouse, which was all more in keeping with a special-occasion "party dress."

While the change from Dorothy's Silver Shoes to Ruby Slippers made a striking Technicolor contrast against the Yellow Brick Road, it also preserved an authentic connection to the Baum canon that might appease Oz book fans liable to protest the switch. A pair of red shoes that conceal magical powers is central to the plot of *Rinkitink in Oz* (1916)—the only other Baum-Oz story to feature enchanted footwear. As illustrated in the book, the *Rinkitink* shoes are identical to Adrian's Arabian design for a jeweled version of the Ruby Slippers that were tested on Garland, from the low heel and curled toe to the decorative, curved flaps at the front and rear of the shoe collar. However, this ornate design was abandoned in favor of a standard pump augmented with bugle beads that would catch the light for a shimmering effect.

Because Judy Garland was a minor, California child labor laws mandated that a total of eight hours a day could be spent at the studio, half of which were designated for schooling and recreation (three hours and one hour, respectively). As MGM makeup artist Jack Young explained it, for a child actor like Garland, that meant "two hours for makeup and hair, half an hour for wardrobe, and, with rehearsals, that left very little time for filming. Someone up front came up with a brilliant idea which the legal department checked out and found no flaws. Simple: send a makeup artist and hairstylist to her home and do her there, thereby saving preparation time and adding to shooting time."[3]

---

2 Weston East, writing for the August 1938 edition of *Screenland*, also noted, "You know that Judy Garland has arrived when Adrian is assigned to costume her picture."

3 Web Overlander was assigned to apply Judy Garland's makeup on *The Wizard of Oz*. Overlander later became the exclusive makeup artist to western star John Wayne.

Playing the blonde and beautiful Princess Dorothy of Oz meant Judy Garland had to slim down. The camera added weight and, on her four-foot-eleven frame, every pound showed. Garland appears anything but overweight when viewing her pre-*Oz* films against the cultural values and social mores of today's society. But the 1930s was the era of the wasp waist and the pencil-thin silhouette—neither of which Garland possessed.

Garland's weight loss was achieved through a combination of several undertakings. A 1943 account of how Judy got the role of Dorothy told of a studio conspiracy to—literally—mold her to the part:

> After the day's tests [for *Oz*] loud and mournful was the wailing from the projection room, "What are we going to do about these curves on little Judy?"
>
> Princess Pudge was ordered to get the heck on a reducing diet.
>
> "But I'm starving," Judy protested and went right ahead lapping up banana splits.
>
> In Hollywood news gets around. Out at MGM a call came through for wardrobe.
>
> "This is Madam So-and-So," a foreign voice announced. "I hear you have a problem on your hands concerning Judy Garland's figure. Now I have a garment. . . ."
>
> The wardrobe department literally pricked up its ears. Madame arrived and in due time created an odd-looking contraption which Judy swore was made of iron. Miracle of miracles, though, the curves disappeared. All through *The Wizard* when Judy danced blithely down the Yellow Brick Road underneath the innocent-appearing gingham dress was a complicated invention, the likes of which were never seen in the wonderful Land of Oz.

Despite the corset to blur her silhouette, Garland's attempts at binge dieting were undisciplined thanks in part to unwitting enablers like L. Frank Baum's granddaughter Florence. Then a frequent visitor to the *Oz* set, Florence Baum recalled, "Judy had an ongoing weight problem . . . and the studio kept her on a strict diet. We had become friends by now, and Judy would have me—her hopeless slave—go to the commissary at noon and order a double portion of mashed potatoes and gravy, and sneak it to her on the set. We did this for quite a while, and to my knowledge the studio heads never found out." Florence Baum, then fifteen, was understandably naïve to misjudge MGM to be so obtuse when it came to its star investments; the studio was already implementing another strategy that served a dual purpose.

To get Garland reducing, Metro assigned Barbara "Bobbie" Koshay as Judy's personal athletic conditioner. Koshay put Garland through a regime of regular exercise that included badminton, swimming, hiking, and tennis. As a trainer, Koshay was more than qualified, being disciplined enough to have made the Olympic swim team ten years prior. Garland was no slouch herself, just a growing girl with a healthy appetite (chocolate cake was said to be a personal weakness); at the time of making *The Wizard of Oz*, she spoke of horseback riding and desiring to learn how to ski. According to an interview she gave to Hollywood reporter James Reid, Garland also talked her mother into letting her get a motor bike but that was short-lived. "Somebody phoned the studio," Garland recounted. "'Your Judy Garland is going up and down [Sunset Boulevard] at what looks like eighty miles an hour.' That was the last straw. A few executives had nervous breakdowns, what with *The Wizard of Oz* not yet finished, and I had to give up motor biking." Once, while boating off Balboa bay with her mother Ethel and Koshay, Garland impulsively dove overboard and swam for the opposite shore, yelling back for them to follow. Ethel's shouted pleas to turn around went unheeded, and Judy swam the width of the bay, approximately one mile.

Beyond personal training, Bobbie Koshay was also Judy Garland's *Wizard of Oz* stunt double and filled in on the set for tests and setups.[4] The two became chummy to the point of spending social time together after hours, which was an odd arrangement in that Koshay was pushing thirty and Judy was sixteen. Indeed, in 1939 Garland cited seventeen-year-old actress and dancer Delia Bogard as her closest friend. The two had known each other from attending Hollywood's Lawlor Professionals School for performing children in the early 1930s. (Bogard also knew Mickey Rooney from Lawlor's as well as from playing Tomboy Taylor in Rooney's Mickey McGuire comedy shorts.) At the time, Garland was also girl-friends with another same-aged peer, actress Patti McCarthy.

Knowingly or not, Bobbie Koshay fulfilled the same function as one of Metro's infamous star spies, paid to portend an alliance and expected to report any noncompliance. Between time on the *Oz* set and workouts and "girlfriend-dates," Koshay kept Garland under virtual surveillance. The relationship continued through Judy's next picture, *Babes in Arms*, by which time MGM was satisfied with Judy's weight and Koshay's "duties" were retired. The job of keeping tabs on Judy Garland's extracurricular activities then fell to Judy's duplicitous new "best friend," MGM publicist Betty Asher—who was big-sister age at just five years Garland's senior. Garland's stand-in duties were subsequently assumed by red-haired Bernice "Bunny" Webb.

To expedite the dieting process and suppress her appetite, Garland was also prescribed chemical stimulants by a studio physician, specifically Dexedrine, as Meredythe Glass recalled in a 2011 interview. (Glass was an extra in the Emerald City and of Hollywood pedigree by relation; she got the *Oz* gig because Mervyn LeRoy was her mother's cousin.) Dexedrine tablets were new to the market as of 1937, used to treat narcolepsy, depression, and obesity—not that Garland was obese by any stretch. A shade older than Judy,

---

4 Though Koshay took Garland's place on camera, dancer Caren Marsh and actress Rhoda Cross, daughter of lightweight boxing champ Leach Cross, were lighting stand-ins for Garland on *Oz*, with Cross segueing directly from serving as such on Garland's *Listen Darling* (1938).

Meredythe Glass conceded they were very young at the time and still carrying baby fat, "We were both kind of chubby." While the Dexedrine provided pep, unknown was its potential for addictive misuse and adverse side effects including paranoia and insomnia. Said Glass, "I tried one and was up all night. I said the heck with that! The energy that [Garland] spent dancing should have done it. Then, they'd knock her out at night with sleeping pills."

Whether it was an amphetamine side effect or self-consciousness instilled in Judy by published comments like, "[Judy's sisters] are pencil-slim and Judy is anxiously hoping that she soon will be, too," Garland's burgeoning paranoia was evident to reporter Paul Harrison when he lunched with Judy and Ethel in the MGM commissary. In his April 29, 1938, column, Harrison informed readers that for her *Wizard of Oz* role, Judy was "still on a diet. I had lunch with her and her mother the other day and she was grumbling about it. 'Everybody in the restaurant is watching to see that I don't snitch an extra dessert or something,' she said. 'At least I feel that everybody's watching. Maybe it's my conscience.'"

Strangely enough, Judy's weight—and what she ate—became a near preoccupation and running joke in the press during the making of *The Wizard of Oz*. Alice L. Tildesley of the *Oakland Tribune* interviewed Garland in the MGM commissary "eating a baked potato filled with creamed chicken and ham," noting that Judy was mindful of "settling her blue gingham dress carefully." In December 1938 Hollywood writer Grace Wilcox told readers of her own luncheon with Garland, whom she said was "a little too fat." In what Wilcox described as a gustatory event, Garland allegedly consumed soup, double lamb chops, a baked potato, string beans, a glass of milk, muffins, chocolate ice cream, and a cup of coffee.

These accounts are at odds with those that suggest Garland was deprived. For example, "Judy Garland Diets to Keep That Girlish Figure for Her Child Star Character Parts" was the headline of a rather humiliating piece by Paul Harrison. Another report claimed Garland was ordered to reduce three inches from her hips before starting *Oz*. Jimmie Fidler thought his readers "might get a chuckle out of Judy Garland's plight" when he told of how Metro czars were determined to trim Garland's waistline: "Every day, no matter where she sat in the commissary, the same waitress appeared to take her order. And every day the same thing happened. Judy ordered half the items on the menu—and the waitress, after carefully writing down each item, went to the kitchen and brought her a bowl of thin soup. After five days, Miss Garland gave up—and ordered soup."

Such reports only conspired to perpetuate Judy's image as a comical paradox of sorts: immensely gifted but physically awkward and unattractive by Hollywood standards. The working title for Garland's 1938 film *Everybody Sing* had been *The Ugly Duckling*, a reference to her part in the picture. And a March 1938 endorsement for Coldspot refrigerators, titled "Movie Star Loots Refrigerator," pictures Judy on her knees raiding the icebox, her arms overflowing; a box marked "Pure Lard" is front and center. Even a year after Garland achieved renown for being "Dorothy, the girl with the braids down her back, in *The Wizard of Oz*," as Milton MacKaye wrote for *Ladies' Home Journal*, she was still described as "an ounce or so on the plump side." MacKaye noted, "When I lunched with her she had a cottage-cheese salad as a dieting gesture and chocolate ice cream because she wanted it."

In 1948 gossip maven Louella O. Parsons recalled Judy as "the little fat girl I first met on the set of *The Wizard of Oz* . . . She was so embarrassed about her plumpness then, and did everything to disguise it. . . . Judy was always lamenting that she loved to eat, and just couldn't keep her weight down. . . ." In 1945 Sheilah Graham was blunt in recollecting, "In those days, Judy was not only fat, but homely." Adding insult to injury, some reviewers considered Garland "fat-cheeked," "pudgy," "well-fed," or "plumpish." The perception of Judy as a flawed commodity that required refinements was insensitive at best and devastating to her fragile psyche. Such subjective critiques made during her formative years haunted Garland into adulthood. Of her *Oz* ordeals, she told *American Weekly* in 1961, "I was studied like a piece of merchandise. It didn't occur to anyone that I might have feelings."

In 1970 *Oz* screenwriter Noel Langley recalled that the studio was "always after [Garland] to keep her weight down. I think that was her tragedy—the fact that she was always made to be something she wasn't. She was actually *meant* to be a very fat woman." Makeup artist Howard Smit was empathetic for the young actress while working on *The Wizard of Oz*. "I felt sorry for Judy Garland," Smit told the *National Enquirer* in 1975. "Even then, she had a weight problem and the people at MGM would hardly permit her to eat anything. I'll never forget the envious way she looked at the cast and crew while they downed their lunches. Then she'd just stare disgustedly at her own small plateful of lettuce and tomato salad."

Even after she blossomed into a swan, Judy could never quite fathom herself as alluring or desirable. The psychological damage to her self-perception had been instilled by MGM long before. In a 1972 interview Bette Davis, an actress whom the young Judy Garland admired, said of the movie industry's obsession with physical perfection in the 1930s: "It was absolutely heartbreaking . . . I was defeated. And this really does catastrophic things to your ego, and I didn't have a lot of ego and never have had lots anyway, which is a big misnomer about actors. We have very little ego basically." Garland was feeling the effects in 1938 when she confided, "[I] want to grow up to be very beautiful too. Only I probably won't. But I do try. I take awfully good care of myself. I won't ever smoke or drink—I hate anything that has even the littlest fizz to it, even Coca-Cola. And I pay a lot of attention to my hands . . . I cold cream my feet every night, just like I do my hands and face!"

Ann Rutherford, MGM contract player, *Andy Hardy* costar, and friend to Judy Garland, recalled Judy's struggle with self-image during wardrobe fittings. "She was a little girl; she was shaped like a little barrel. The wardrobe people were pinning and prodding to the point where tears were running down one side of Judy's cheek. She told them, 'I don't have a waistline—don't try to give me one!'"

MGM further compromised Garland's physical shortcomings with public disclosures like that of makeup chief Jack Dawn. In a June 18, 1939, syndicated feature, Dawn pointedly remarked, "[Judy's] eyebrows dipped down too close to her nose, making her forehead too high and her nose too short for the rest of her face. After the brows were raised and there was more space between them, the features were in good proportion." Dawn also commented that Judy's hair was all wrong for Technicolor and added, "Judy Garland had to lose some weight [for Oz] because everybody photographs heavier than they actually are." Oz makeup artist Jack Kevan agreed. In a 1965 interview he recounted, "As Judy Garland began to mature—that horrible stage between child and woman—she still had the child's pudginess. We used contouring to make her look older and to give her the same shape face as, say, Joan Crawford. Crawford has a very fine, symmetrical face."

Acts of humiliation were as much a part of the daily business of picture-making as they were integral to the Metro machine that regulated and controlled its corporate "properties." In Judy's case its aftereffects endured all her life. At the time of The Wizard of Oz, she was still trying to live down the "horrible example" of MGM's error for having retained her instead of Deanna Durbin when the studio decided between the two singers. This was not only internal knowledge (Ed Sullivan told of how people on the lot would smugly point her out), it was known publicly as well. Thus, in 1939, Judy's mother, Ethel, affirmed that Garland possessed no diva attitude. It was, in fact, Ethel's rules for a successful stage career that Judy adopted as her own precepts, "I will try to emulate, but never imitate, other stars; I will learn something new in each role; I will never complain about roles given me, knowing any role stands out if properly handled; I must never be discouraged by failure nor become conceited with success." (When it came time for Garland to pass along show-business advice to daughter and budding performer Liza Minnelli, Judy distilled Ethel's guiding words into the oft-quoted, "Be a first-rate version of yourself, not a second-rate version of somebody else.") Shortly after Oz, Ethel told reporters, "Happily, there is no part of the conceit in Judy. No affectation, but a sense of humility. She is happy about her success in The Wizard of Oz . . . but untouched by it. No 'conquering hero' resides in our home!"

Which was all just as well. MGM was not above deflating any swelled heads that might ask for an untimely or unreasonable raise or—in the ultimate act of defiance—sue the studio. Stage mothers of minors, like Judy Garland's mother Ethel, were in particular seen as nuisances as they were almost always on set, prepared to run interference on their child's behalf. Indeed, in a series of behind-the-scenes shots taken during Oz, Ethel can be seen sitting off to the side, in her reading glasses, with Judy's copy of the script in her lap as she monitors her daughter's rehearsals.

To keep its stars in line, Metro kept a stable of second-string "lookalikes," less talented, less charismatic players who bore a fleeting resemblance to its "A" performers such that the studio—in a passive-aggressive manner—subtly suggested that any star whose ego grew too grandiose was not indispensable. In the early 1940s, for example, actor James Craig was the studio's Clark Gable look-alike, said child star Margaret O'Brien, who had her own look-alike. Associated Press reporter Bob Thomas wrote that MGM's Rosalind Russell and Franchot Tone were potential proxies for Myrna Loy and Robert Young, respectively. At Warner Bros., Errol Flynn's "replacement" was Ronald Reagan, according to actor Martin Spellman.

From MGM's perspective, a Judy Garland look-alike was negligible; but a *sound-alike* was entirely different. Commensurate with preproduction on *The Wizard of Oz*—and Garland's top billing—the studio publicly promoted its juvenile newcomer Janice Chambers as its newest sensation, "a twelve-year-old combination of Judy Garland and Deanna Durbin." Chambers's agent Zeppo Marx, of the famed Marx Brothers, discovered her through Chambers's vocal coach at the Chicago Conservatory of Music and arranged her

MGM audition and screen test. The March 29, 1938, press announcement of Chambers's Metro contract indicated she was twelve though she was, in fact, less than two months' shy of fifteen. Chambers was subsequently groomed with acting bits in *Young Dr. Kildare* (1938) and *The Adventures of Huckleberry Finn* (1939), but she also had pipes. With an operatic vocal range, Chambers was said to reach F above high C but, like Judy Garland, she could capably cover jazz and swing. The prodigy also sang in six different languages and did comedic impressions, including imitations of Jenny Lind and Beatrice Lillie. By November 22, 1938, an MGM publicist noted that Janice Chambers "scored a sensational hit at Victor Hugo's [nightclub] Sunday night. The gal's amazing voice and personality made the audience clamor for four encores."

For a 1938 publicity portrait sitting, MGM went so far as to attire Chambers in one of Judy Garland's costumes from *Love Finds Andy Hardy*, and announced that she was slated to appear in *Babes in Arms* with Garland. On downtime from picture making, Chambers even stood in on tests intended for her better-known teenage counterpart, as she recalled prior to her March 2016 passing. "I also did a lot of tests for Judy Garland," Chambers told author Laura Kennedy. "She was so beautiful and terrific. Mickey Rooney was there too, but Judy was my favorite." Chambers's sister Dale Barker remembered that Chambers was actually a contender for the role of Dorothy in *The Wizard of Oz*—a claim Chambers questioned. "I don't think I was really considered," she said, "but I did a lot of tests with the actors, especially Bert Lahr, the Cowardly Lion."

Any unspoken insinuation that Janice Chambers was Judy Garland's standby for *Oz* would have emanated directly from the studio as a tactic to enforce Garland's humility and Ethel's compliance. But Chambers's presence at MGM was merely a smokescreen. Metro had no intention of replacing Judy Garland who, unlike Chambers, had already proven her national appeal. Chambers made a third picture, *Sergeant Madden*, in 1939, before the studio allowed her contract to lapse.

Garland was not without her supporters, of course, including those beyond the studio walls. She was as likeable as she was liked. Ray Bolger was delighted to be cast with her, and in 1938 he told reporter Robert McIlwaine, "Judy Garland is to play Dorothy, the little girl blown from Kansas to the Land of Oz. There's some marvelous songs in [*The Wizard of Oz*], so she should be perfect!" In February 1939 director King Vidor told Judy she was "a swell actress." Judy's *Wizard of Oz* hairdresser, Beth Langston, considered Judy and Greta Garbo her "pets." (Langston was Garbo's hairdresser on 1939's *Ninotchka*.) Sheila O'Brien, women's wardrobe mistress—who was surely privy to Judy's physical shortcomings—was "Mama II" to Judy, whom O'Brien called "her little gal."

Rose Carter, Judy's on-set tutor, referred to her as "my star student." Over the course of the *Oz* shoot, Carter and Garland had developed what was described as "a warm friendship," the result of Carter having been assigned to Garland by Mary MacDonald, MGM's lead in-house educator. Carter's loyalty was questionable however; in August 1940 it was announced that since Garland had graduated high school, Carter was free to collate the material she'd retained into a book titled *The Life Story of Judy Garland*.

Actress-turned-gossip-columnist Hedda Hopper was a great Garland fan and admirer who consistently praised Judy and, in later years, came to her defense when warranted. L. Frank Baum's grandson, Stanton, recalled of his visits to the *Oz* set, "Judy was tremendous at memorizing things. She was always very friendly and very nice." Indeed, Garland impressed the *Wizard of Oz* company by memorizing three new words every day and trying them out on cast and crew. As proof positive, in 1990 Judy's daughter Liza Minnelli described Garland as an amazing raconteur with an immense vocabulary.

Famed journalist Adela Rogers St. Johns also paid a visit to the *Oz* set, during the second week of January 1939, while on a mission to write a *Photoplay* series on MGM stars. At the time, Rogers St. Johns was described as "one of Judy Garland's most enthusiastic fans." Rogers St. Johns was also chummy with director Victor Fleming who, years prior, had been her taxicab chauffeur when she was a Los Angeles society girl.

Despite the burden of MGM's humiliations going into *The Wizard of Oz*, Judy Garland clearly had a dearth of fans and supporters as her devoted allies. And according to contemporary accounts, she was excited about *Oz*. In March 1940 she was quoted as saying, "The next thing I knew, I was playing a role I had always dreamed of—'Dorothy' in *The Wizard of Oz*. Here I was actually seeing the Emerald City, the Land of the Munchkins, the flying monkeys and all the rest. My, I was happy!"

MEN OF CHARACTER

In retrospect, it was the outrageous costumes designed by Adrian and Jack Dawn's makeup appliances for the Scarecrow, Tin Woodman, and Cowardly Lion that were singled out as notoriously unbearable to endure. Of the male leads, journalist Harrison Carroll observed, "[They] can go on for hours about the trouble they've had with their costumes," while the *New York Times* asserted, "Any one of the three would cheerfully gag Mr. Dawn with one of his own rubber faces. They itch."

When interviewed by Aljean Harmetz, Ray Bolger claimed he knew he was cut out to play the Scarecrow before swapping roles with Buddy Ebsen (who didn't mind the switch so long as he was still attached to the picture). But preliminary tests for Bolger as the Tin Man and Ebsen as the Scarecrow had already taken place prior to the switch, and in Bolger's case, initial thought was given to his range of motion by devising a rubber Tin Man suit that would offer some flexibility. Then, a September 1938 account by the Associated Press declared that Bolger's rubber suit had been shucked in favor of "a suit of armor made of tin cans" because the rubber outfit "looked phony." When Bolger met visiting reporter Anne M. McIlhenney in the studio commissary, he was concerned that the sweltering Tin Man outfit was causing him to lose weight. "Imagine dancing in boiler underwear," Bolger complained. "By the time I finish the picture they can use me for skeleton shots."

In the same AP article, an early test of Buddy Ebsen's scarecrow outfit is described: "They gave [Buddy] some raggedy clothes and had tufts of straw sticking out here and there. He said he felt like he was going to a party. The suit has been remade, of quilting, and

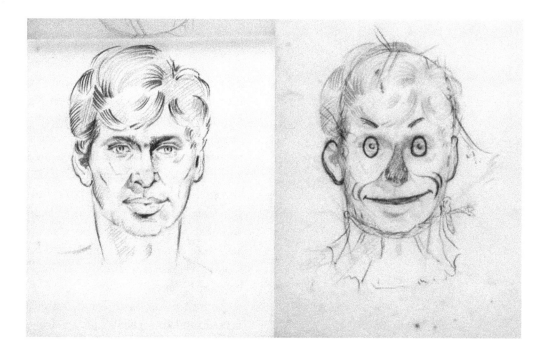

the straw seems to be falling out of it. Shaggy-haired Ebsen actually looks like a scarecrow (although an awfully well-fed one) now."

Having learned from the failure of Paramount's *Alice in Wonderland*, Jack Dawn's intent was to transform the *Oz* actors into fantastic creatures using foam-rubber appliances—not masks—to augment and exaggerate their facial features as subtly as possible. Makeup artist William Tuttle had designed a Scarecrow makeup for Buddy Ebsen that began with a sketch of the actor's face with a tracing paper overlay on which the Scarecrow features were drawn. The design essentially remained the same once Bolger took on the role, a burlap-textured sack that covered the actor's head and tied at the neck. Hand-applied black circles around each eye mimicked the style of Fred Stone's original interpretation. The burlap sack would be made of a thin foam-rubber sheath that encased his head, delicately adhered around his facial features with spirit gum.

If carefully removed after use, the pliable prosthetics of Bolger and others could be used a second time, but after forty-eight hours the foam rubber would stiffen and crack, making it unusable. After the first thirty masks, Bolger joked to reporter Grace Wilcox, "Another two weeks of shooting and I'll be challenging [Boris] Karloff's title as the Man of a Thousand Faces." One story about Bolger's makeup told of its removal "with a quick jerk like a piece of adhesive tape." The actor supposedly soothed the aftereffects on his skin with lemon cream, warm water, and moisturizing oils each night.

In 1941 memories of what Bolger termed "a tedious and unpleasant process" were still fresh when the actor explained the complicated makeup to four members of the British Royal Air Force visiting the set of Bolger's film *Sunny*. Not only did Bolger wear a rubber mask, he said, it was all covered with a thick, gooey paint that would also stick to his arms and legs. But Bolger's chief complaint about the makeup was that he couldn't hear because his ears were covered. He compensated by looking to assistant director Al Shenberg for his cues.

As the Tin Woodman, Buddy Ebsen's makeup and, in particular, his wardrobe were the subjects of significant experimentation. In July 1946 *International Projectionist* recounted the trial-and-error efforts to construct the Tin Man wardrobe as "a major studio worry" that fell to studio property men, tin-working men, metal experts, and even makers of metal armor. Following wardrobe tests on August 27, 1938, Charles G. Sampas noted in his September 8 *Lowell (MA) Sun* Hollywood column, "Buddy Ebsen will wear a costume of aluminum for his appearance as the Tin Woodman in *The Wizard of Oz*."

Getting into the aluminum costume was also painstaking and complicated, prompting Ebsen to quip to the syndicated Behind the Make-Up column, "I guess I'm the only actor in Hollywood with a tinsmith for a maid." Present for the fitting were Mervyn LeRoy; Joe Cook, unit production assistant; dance director Bobby Connolly; and musical director Herbert Stothart. As reported by Anne M. McIlhenney in her Filmland Rambles column, the metal costume was fitted to Ebsen by *two* tinsmiths "who began to snip here and there with shears to mold the metal chemise." "You look like a new kind of hamburger stand," Stothart was heard to say. The snipping went on, the shears finally working on the metal around Buddy's neck. "Gosh!" drawled Ebsen, "Do I get nervous when a guy shaves me!" With the fitting completed, there was only one casualty: While Ebsen was testing a knee joint, one of the tinsmith's fingers was caught and cut by the metal.

In a May 20, 1993, TV interview, Ebsen recalled the impossible logistics of performing in a veritable suit of armor on this occasion:

Well, the first problem was the wardrobe. The wardrobe department had never made a tin suit before. So on the theory that "tin" means tin, they made me one out of stove pipe. Now, just between you and me, there's very little "stretch" in stove pipe, especially in the "southern regions" of the suit. So there I was in the suit for the first time, and the MGM brass sitting out front to be shown, and the director [i.e., LeRoy] said to me, "Walk." So I walked. I sounded like a junk wagon coming down a bumpy road. And he said, "Dance." So I did a little dance. He said, "Do a big step," so I did a hitch kick and almost gave myself an ad-lib sex change. So I yelled in pain, explained to the director; he says, "Get him out of there! The part doesn't call for a soprano."

The aluminum suit not only lacked mobility, it was much too noisy to be practical for filmmaking. The assignment was taken to Sam Winters, in MGM's studio tailor shop, who devised a noiseless suit made of a bamboo frame covered in buckram and a layer of authentically silvered leather. By September 7, 1938, Arthur Freed assured Mervyn LeRoy that Ebsen's outfit was "getting into shape."

Meanwhile, Ebsen was working out his dance steps based on the theory that the Tin Man was constructed by a plumber and his joints would imitate the motion of a plumber's wrench in action.[5] Additionally, it was announced that the dancer would make 240 intricate steps in the space of fifty seconds for one of his *Wizard of Oz* scenes (a logistical improbability).

As the Cowardly Lion, Bert Lahr was dubious about his own transformation, telling Hollywood journalist Duncan Underhill, "Those producers don't mind making me win the hard way. In *The Wizard of Oz* they handicap me with a sixty-pound costume and five pounds of false jowls and a part called *The Cowardly Lion*." Lahr's estimation of his wardrobe's weight was consistent with sixty or "about seventy pounds," as he told the *New York Times*'s Bosley Crowther, although other accounts range from fifty to ninety pounds. In an August 1939 interview, Lahr said his lion costume "weighed sixty pounds, complete with mane and football pads in the shoulders. It was awfully hot. . . ."

In 1941 Lahr explained the sweltering conditions caused by wearing the lion suit. "The heavily padded costume I had to wear as the Lion in *The Wizard of Oz* . . . took me an hour and a half to get into . . . then for Technicolor they have to use ten times the amount of light they use in other pictures, so we had ninety arc lights beating down on us . . . it was really tough." Lahr wore long johns under the stifling getup, which itched the comedian, as he told reporter Robbin Coons: "And if you think that wearing a lion's hide over my underwear wasn't burleycue, you should have had to do my scratching!"

---

5 In Frank J. Baum's script for his proposed 1931 *Wizard of Oz* radio program, the Tin Man makes mention of the plumber who poured hot solder down his neck.

Lahr probably had a sense of what he was in for, however. By October 2, 1938, he was said to be working with Adrian on designing a costume that would conform as much as possible to a real lion's anatomy. Previously, *Variety* of September 7, 1938, had noted that instead of a real lion suit, Lahr would wear a synthetic replica "assembled hair by hair." Indeed, only two weeks before production on *The Wizard of Oz* began, Lahr tested in an alternate lion outfit made of plush and accented with faux fur. But this wardrobe was rejected in favor of a costume constructed of two actual African lion pelts, its gloves and shoes fashioned from real paws.

Lahr had already tested the authentic skin suit but perfecting its construction supposedly took two months. According to United Press correspondent Frederick C. Othman, MGM had to diffuse the rumor that its trademark, Leo the Lion, was killed to make Lahr's costume. When filming, the actor reportedly had to remove the suit every twenty minutes in order to cool down despite the addition of small holes punctured throughout for ventilation. Indeed, once production got under way, the *Oz* set became known as "the Mervyn LeRoy sweat shop" for enduring conditions that Lahr defined as like "working in a furnace."

Jackie Ackerman, of MGM's prop department, manually operated Lahr's lion tail throughout *The Wizard of Oz* with the use of a fishing-line filament from the catwalk overhanging the soundstage. But early tests were conceived to allow the tail to wag independently. Fred Gabourie, a studio technician, created an electric motor that would power the tail to wag an average of 960 times per working day, with a range of motion from three feet to seven feet wide. The motor was also said to operate the tail in order to reflect the Cowardly Lion's emotions, from a puppy-like wiggle to a majestic sweep. For reasons unknown, the motor was dispensed in favor of old-fashioned manpower.

Synchronizing the tail with Lahr's performance required practice, according to Hedda Hopper. "The other day [Lahr] caught the tail in his mouth and they had to get a pair of pliers to pick the bristles out of his teeth." The leonine appendage was said to have attracted the curiosity of a studio cat as the actor strolled about the stage rehearsing his lines. When Lahr walked faster, the cat pounced harder at the costume's tail until Lahr could stand it no more and retreated to his dressing room. "At last I am beginning to live my role!" he called out as he firmly shut the door.

Lahr's tawny ruff and mane was a wig created by Max Factor. According to a May 19, 1945, *Saturday Evening Post* article, the lion wig was complicated to make in order to complement Lahr's makeup and took a month alone just to manufacture. The actor's overhanging, foam-rubber jowls made smoking difficult, and cigarette ash littered the wig and wardrobe such that when the lion skin was sent to the studio cleaners, Lahr attached a note that read, "Since wearing this blinking thing, I've developed the mange. Can you do anything about it?" Opening his mouth wide enough to eat was also problematic. Lahr told *New York Post* reporter Michel Mok in August 1939: "[I] ate soft foods, mostly soups through . . . a tube." Even so, Lahr actually *gained* weight while playing the part, something that still mystified him in January 1940 when he told the Associated Press, "[I] am still losing the weight I gained in Hollywood."

It has long been part and parcel of *Oz* lore that the lead actors were asked to leave the MGM commissary due to their unsettling appearances. A version of the anecdote was first reported in January 1939, but the locale had been relocated from Metro's restaurant to the Hillcrest Country Club in Los Angeles. The story was that Bert Lahr invited Ray Bolger and Jack Haley to dine in the mode of "come as you are" so the actors could "go directly to the club from the stage without removing their weird outfits, as that chore alone would take more than their lunch hour." As this was Hollywood, it was said that no one at the club batted an eye. In her book *Me and My Shadows: A Family Memoir*, Lorna Luft, Judy Garland's daughter, relates that her mother said the primary objection from commissary diners came when the men removed those pieces of foam-rubber appliances that would permit them to eat freely at luncheon; the remnants of adhesive on their faces resembled strings of mucous. It was after complaints were registered that Bolger, Haley, and Lahr took their meals in separate quarters.

But the sanction didn't occur as immediately as what may have been believed. The actors *were* permitted in the studio restaurant at least through the first two weeks of production and perhaps periodically thereafter. On October 27, 1938, screenwriter Richard Connell Jr., best known for the short story "The Most Dangerous Game," was on the lot doctoring the script for *Balalaika* when he wrote home about his encounters with Ozites in the commissary:

Tell Richard a lion ate lunch at the next table to me today. He ate poached eggs. He was a very real lion, tho his skin had zippers. Under his whiskers he is the comedian, Bert Lahr playing in the pic, *Wizard of Oz*. Other strange inhabitants of that fabulous land—scarecrows, tin men, fiends with green faces [Winkies], may be seen these days in the studio lunch room.

Jane Hall, writing of her visit to the *Oz* set for *Good Housekeeping*, mentioned that Ray Bolger was always friendly to her when she saw him in the commissary, and in his column of November 29, 1938, Jimmie Fidler told of bumping into Jack Haley, in his Tin Man getup, while "at the Metro commissary." But at some point the *Oz* makeups created enough of a distraction for the other patrons that an option was proposed between Frances Edwards, proprietress of the restaurant, and the *Oz* unit to provide the actors with their meals in a location outside the commissary. In a 1939 *New York Post* interview, Ray Bolger explained that the rationale for the lunchtime accommodations was twofold. "Eating was quite a problem. We didn't eat in the commissary, but in a little room by ourselves. . . . There were two reasons for it. In the first place, the studio didn't want to have our costumes and makeups seen by anyone who wasn't connected with the picture. And, besides, even if they had permitted us to have lunch in the commissary, we wouldn't have done it because we were too much of a sight."

During her visit to the *Oz* set, journalist Dixie Willson came upon the three actors waiting for luncheon to be served in their dressing room. The actors had shed their wardrobe for bathrobes but retained the countenances of a burlap-bag face, tawny lion's mane, and a silver visage accented with rivets. As Willson stood silently gaping, Ray Bolger grinned, "I know what you're thinking. . . ."

THE GREAT AND POWERFUL OZ

During the making of *The Wizard of Oz*, Frank Morgan's trademark moustache—or the lack thereof—persistently made news. In April 1939 *Photoplay* reported on the actor's melancholy, pining for his lost moustache, noting, "He had it for ten years then *The Wizard of Oz* made him shave." By July 1939 *Radio Mirror* told of Morgan's proposed remedy: "Frank Morgan, as you know, has been going around lately without his moustache—much

to the consternation of news photographers and autograph hounds. They have failed to recognize him. Frank cut off the facial adornments to play his role in *The Wizard of Oz*, but he is growing a bigger and better moustache 'like a toothbrush bristle,' says Frank."

Dispensing with the facial hair was Morgan's concession to the variety of beards and matching hairpieces he would don for multiple disguises. When portraying the palace guard, the actor was originally tested in a huge, green beard, like the soldier with green whiskers in Baum's book. As the coachman, he was envisioned to be clean-shaven and as the bald Wizard, Morgan was to wear "only a lock of hair over his forehead that moves when he is agitated." For Kansas's Professor Marvel, Morgan's own hair was used, though he grew it out "so long it curls at the end" to achieve a rural, backwoods look.

An oft-told believe-it-or-not tale from the *Oz* set concerns the overcoat worn by Morgan as Professor Marvel. The script called for a coat of the "gay nineties vintage." The coat was selected for Morgan, from a job lot purchased by MGM from a secondhand dealer, for its black broadcloth lined in Skinner satin with a worn, velvet collar and handwoven buttons. Coincidentally, the coat was said to have originally belonged to L. Frank Baum, who had resided in Hollywood in his last years. Presumed to be publicist fiction, the story has been given veracity in a newly uncovered detailed account from 1939: "Director Victor Fleming, inspecting [Morgan's] coat, noticed the letter B embroidered in yellow thread near a lining pocket. Peering inside he saw a label in faded ink. On it was written the name L. Frank Baum, with the date, Oct. 25, 1899, and the order number, 5182. The coat bore the label of Harry Berger & Co., Chicago."

Another version suggests that it was Frank Morgan who made the discovery, noticing the label after testing in the coat. In either case, Morgan reportedly shouted for Mary Mayer, press agent on *The Wizard of Oz*. Everyone present was apparently incredulous. Cameraman Harold Rosson vouched for the legitimacy of the coat in a 1971 interview, when he stated, "The coat had come from Chicago. It had been made for L. Frank Baum . . . you know, I stood there, or sat there, and looked at this label, and read it and commented about it, and didn't believe it because it was just too incongruous. It just couldn't happen."

Unfortunately for Miss Mayer, none of the news outlets she contacted would pick up the story, calling it "fake." When Mayer encountered visiting reporter Frederick C. Othman, she made the journalist try on the overcoat and see for himself. Othman was both suitably impressed and sympathetically moved—as Mary Mayer was near tears of frustration—to be the sole newspaperman to print the whole extraordinary tale. According to MGM's campaign material for *Oz*, the coat was presented by Judy Garland to Maud Baum after its use.

GOOD VS. EVIL

Billie Burke's character, Glinda, was noted in the script as "the Beautiful Witch of the North," which suited Burke's mantle as a famous beauty of stage and screen. However, her character was most often referred to simply as "the Good Fairy" by most all associated with *The Wizard of Oz*. An ethereal gown layered in coral-hued tulle was designed by Adrian, accented with a butterfly motif and scattered with metallic stars and glittering snow crystals. Burke's full wig, which recalled her own renowned glorious auburn tresses, was crowned with a shimmering headdress, above which miniature stars supported on filament appeared to hover.

It has been stated that Burke's wardrobe was merely repurposed, originally a gown worn by Jeanette MacDonald in *San Francisco* (1936), but this is purely speculation. While costumes were reused when and where appropriate, suggesting this was done for *Oz* minimizes the grandeur of the production and its innovative designer. And a close comparison of the two costumes reveals they are not of identical construction. Furthermore, in a May 1939 article on designing for Technicolor, Adrian singled out his Glinda design, writing, "It's a grand opportunity for Billie Burke, as the beautiful good witch, to array herself in the loveliest of rainbow hues."

At fifty-four, Billie Burke's Glinda appeared ageless. But her onscreen look was achieved with a common beauty aid of the time: cosmetic lifts. MGM makeup man Jack Young explained the process, stating, "In the early days of motion picture makeup, when plastic surgery was in its infancy, a system was developed to create the illusion of youth. It was a physical act that could make the individual younger, an act that was impossible with makeup. They were called 'lifts,' and are still in use today." Essentially, as Young explained it, the lifts were two-inch-long pieces of chiffon, one-half inch wide. Affixed to each chiffon piece was adhesive tape from which extended thread that was tied to a rubber band. Once the lifts were glued to the skin in front of each ear, pulled taut, and secured under the wig, Burke appeared magically rejuvenated, as befitted her character.

At first, Margaret Hamilton's Wicked Witch of the West was slated to appear simply as a distorted version of her Miss Gulch counterpart, as if Miss Gulch had simply unknotted her bun, grew a wart, and developed a pervasive case of gangrene. It was this makeup—a Max Factor specialty blend, tinted green—that would later prove particularly problematic; its hue came from the copper used in its chemical base.

There was no traditional or historical precedent in making the Wicked Witch green. The depiction of witches in pre-1938 popular culture rarely had unnaturally tinted flesh, and when they did it was orange or red. Nor did L. Frank Baum distinguish his Witch's skin as unusual in hue. A plausible explanation for making MGM's witch green instead of a deathly blue pallor, a sallow yellow, or an angry red can be traced to Walt Disney. During the 1938 period in which Mervyn LeRoy was in direct communication with the animator, all of Disney's correspondence would have been on his elaborate *Snow White and the Seven Dwarfs* stationery. Disney's full-color letterhead pictures Snow White and the dwarfs across the top, and at the bottom of the page is the Wicked Witch at her cauldron. In *Snow White*, the skin color of Disney's witch is normal but on his studio stationery, her face and hands are a ghoulish green. If LeRoy were looking for inspiration to match the menace in *Snow White*, he needed look no further than the correspondence from his mentor in fantasy.[6]

---

6 *Snow White* preproduction sketches also picture the Wicked Witch with greenish skin, although LeRoy wouldn't have been privy to these.

To heighten Margaret Hamilton's menacing portrayal of the Wicked Witch, a foam-rubber appliance was made to enlarge her considerable, natural nose. A special greasepaint with a green foundation was painted over the false nose, and highlights and contours were painted on her face in dark and light green. Hamilton also began the *Oz* production wearing a pageboy-style wig with bangs, similar to that worn by Gale Sondergaard for her "ugly witch" tests. Unlike Sondergaard's original costume, Hamilton's wardrobe was decidedly unglamorous. It was standard witch fare, all in black from her conical hat to her cape, which would flow dramatically in the breeze.

CREATURES BIG AND SMALL

As dictated by the script, the Wicked Witch's Winkies were transformed from L. Frank Baum's diminutive men to monstrous giants. In designing the wardrobe of the Witch's foreboding sentries, Adrian drew inspiration from the uniforms of the Hungarian hussar cavalry, particularly the hussar's busby, a military headdress fashioned of fur into a cylindrical cap. (Adrian supplanted the busby's traditional red plume with a black raven's wing.) The Winkie costumes were also of an identical color scheme: black, buff, gray, and red with metallic accents. The saddle coverings of the Prussian hussars were black with red scalloped edging, which Adrian clearly adapted into the design of the Winkie's flared kilts, under which were worn loose-fitting trousers for chase sequences.

The Winkie wardrobe was of ornate felt construction, the weight of which was perhaps rivaled only by Bert Lahr's lion pelt costume. As Winkies, Jack Smith and his father, Julian, not only endured the sweltering wardrobe, their makeup came with handicaps as well. When Margaret Hamilton was cast as a hideous, green-complexioned witch, the Winkies' makeup was revised to reflect the identical pallor as their mistress, including a similarly hooked nose. Jack Smith recollected an amusing incident involving his father's elongated proboscis:

> Once when dad and I were in make-up with the big noses and green faces, we drove home for lunch about four blocks from the studio. We were driving down Washington Boulevard and people were almost driving off the road when they saw these two green critters in a car. They probably thought we were from Mars or something. When we got home, my dad, he liked to have a hot cup of coffee so my mom poured him one. He was drinking his coffee, not paying much attention to what he was doing. His nose was getting into the hot coffee and it was starting to bend down, down, down. When we got back to the studio, he had to go back to make-up to fix his nose.

When Julian Smith returned to the makeup department, he was chastised for damaging the makeup and was instructed to drink his coffee through a straw from then on, which he did.

Adrian's wardrobe design for the Witch's army of Winged Monkeys was in keeping with the Winkies' military influence and for consistency utilized the same color scheme. W. W. Denslow hadn't dressed the monkeys in anything other than to distinguish their king with a cap, but Adrian attired each of MGM's monkeys with a short jacket and gave a similarly styled cap to Nikko and the monkey leader. (It has become part of *Oz* mythology that *every* monkey wore a cap but this is untrue.) An early report suggested that the Winged Monkey suits were originally going to be made from authentic simian hides, like the Cowardly Lion outfit, and that the suits would be "Technicolored." "All available monkey fur is being bought by MGM for use on the strange creatures of the Winged Monkeys in *The Wizard of Oz*," it was noted. "The monkey fur they insist must be in a neutral shade so that dyeing in bright hues is possible." MGM's wardrobe department was said to have requisitioned "three truckloads" of monkey fur.

Unlike the Winkies, the monkeys' flesh was not green but a ghastly postmortem gray that tended toward a bluish tint when photographed in Technicolor, which would reflect the hue of the original W. W. Denslow color plates. The monkey makeup was otherwise consistent from one simian to another. Each monkey wore a yak-hair wig sculpted into a central, curved crest. Foam-rubber appliances covered the brow, nose, and upper lip. The appliance was hinged to cover the lower jaw in a manner that allowed some flexibility for the monkeys—Nikko especially—to emote by opening and closing their mouths. Don Cash was an eighteen-year-old makeup assistant on *The Wizard of Oz*, but when he worked on *Planet of the Apes* thirty years later, he was assigned to re-create Roddy McDowall's makeup as the chimpanzee Dr. Cornelius on a daily basis. The *Apes* makeup was said to have been inspired by the success of the Winged Monkey makeups designed by Jack Dawn for *The Wizard of Oz*.

After conceptual paintings were rendered, the makeup procedure for transforming little people into Munchkins was the same as for any MGM star: Sit for a plaster life mask. Once a "positive" cast was made, it allowed the makeup artists to experiment with plastiline modeling clay directly on the life mask. In this manner, the high cheek bones, bulbous noses, and elfin chins could be imagined into being. In at least one instance, an early test was done on a child actor. Show-business children could also be unruly, especially if over-indulged by stage mothers. MGM makeup artist Del Armstrong recollected making up one such ornery youngster for a Munchkin test using a bald cap:

I was unlucky enough to draw a very spoiled obnoxious brat to get in my [makeup] chair. He continually yelled, fussed and wiggled about saying I was pulling his hair. After a very long day, I was also very tired and very irritated at this little monster. So, as a parting gesture, I took out my electric hair clippers and mowed a firepath up the back of his head. Needless to say, there was hell to pay when his Hollywood mother saw her little darling.

The next day, I was called into Jack Dawn's office. There was the irate mother and her little imp. Jack Dawn went up one side of me and down the other—for the benefit of mama. Then he called Skip Borden (our wig maker) in and measured the little brat for a wig. Mr. Dawn had a quiet conversation with Skip, then told mama to come in the next day for the wig. I wondered why Mr. Dawn didn't take a sample of the kid's hair, a normal procedure.

The next day, Mr. Dawn called me into his office and said, "What you started, you can finish." Mama and the smirking little brat were there. Mr. Dawn gave me the hair piece. There was a *snow white* streak up the back of the wig. It served the little skunk right. I almost couldn't keep a straight face as I pinned it on the kid. Mama didn't say a word but stomped out of the office. I turned to Mr. Dawn—he was smiling. For a tough guy, he wasn't without a sense of humor.

The boy in question could have been nine-year-old Bobby Coleman of Crestline, Ohio. On December 31, 1938, after the Munchkinland scenes had finished filming, the child actor, who had relocated to Los Angeles three months prior, was identified as among the children chosen for the cast of *The Wizard of Oz*. The Mansfield, Ohio, *News Journal* reported that Coleman had appeared in local amateur productions before crashing the Hollywood studio gates. Coleman was also appearing with Bing Crosby in Paramount's *The Star Maker*, which followed *Oz*'s release.

Meinhardt Raabe recalled the makeup application of each Munchkin performer, regardless of their age:

Jack Dawn created the make-up for each Munchkin. Then they took a still picture and that they put in the file. So next morning, we went to work, [they'd] get your picture out of the file and make you up exactly like Jack Dawn had done the day before. [Dawn] couldn't himself do 130 [*sic*] Munchkins every morning. Everybody had a master picture, a still, taken after Jack Dawn had worked on them individually. Some had higher cheekbones, moustaches, then some had a skull cap and whatever hairstyle they wanted over the top. It was glued in over the skull cap, over that they'd put the hairpiece. I'm slightly color blind so I can't tell whether mine is red or brown.

The bald caps also served to contain body heat and perspiration, which made it particularly unpleasant performing under the hot lights as each day wore on. Jerry Maren, one of the Lollipop Guild tough boys, remembered the skull caps in no uncertain terms during a June 14, 1998, interview, calling them, "Very pain in the neck! Under the hot lights . . . it was hot and sweaty! They [makeup men] would look for [perspiration] leaks!" Maren's comments were affirmed by makeup artist Charles Schram. In addition to being assigned to re-create Bert Lahr's Cowardly Lion makeup throughout *The Wizard of Oz*, Schram was also appointed to watch from behind the camera on set in order to touch up makeups as needed or to adjust bald caps that were slipping from perspiration.

Raabe recalled the procedure for the wardrobe design of each Munchkin performer:

[Adrian] and his staff measured every individual Munchkin—asking what lines they had or what their part was—designed a costume individually for every Munchkin according to what their position was going to be. My costume was heavy felt. Because, you see, over a long period of shooting, we had it on and off every day, and of course under these heavy lights it had to stand up; it couldn't be flimsy material. Let's put it this way, we all had a little perspiration involved! It took the wardrobe department about five or six weeks to produce all these [Munchkin] costumes. Meanwhile, they were rehearsing so by the time rehearsals were complete, the costumes were ready to shoot. They were perfectionists as far as the details were concerned.

That strive for perfectionism extended to the selection of the proper director and nearly derailed production of *The Wizard of Oz* altogether.

The Directors:
Take One and Take Two

It was not unusual in 1938 for motion picture directors to pinch-hit by filling in for one another due to illness or conflicting schedules. But the succession of directors on *The Wizard of Oz* at the very start of production was cause for concern. Norman Taurog was the first so designated to steer the picture, having secured a long-term contract with MGM on May 13, 1938. The following day *The Wizard of Oz* was identified as among the first of Taurog's vehicles in the Hollywood trade papers, but oddly enough, announcement of his assignment was delayed in the general press until August 21, 1938, at which time Judy Garland was erroneously listed as playing "Alice."

In the interim, on June 20, Louella O. Parsons had reported that Mervyn LeRoy was hoping to get Busby Berkeley to direct *Oz* once Berkeley wrapped up *Comet Over Broadway* at Warner Bros. Parsons noted that LeRoy wanted Berkeley "for the intricate special numbers," which was probably the reality as opposed to Berkeley directing *Oz* in its entirety. Berkeley had designed, staged, and choreographed four song-and-dance sequences in LeRoy's smash hit *Gold Diggers of 1933*. But Berkeley fell ill while making *Comet* and there were no further notices that *Oz* would be directed by anyone other than Taurog, although Berkeley was brought in to choreograph the Scarecrow's dance sequence in spring 1939.

Norman Taurog's uncredited assistant director on *The Wizard of Oz* would be Alfred Shenberg, Louis B. Mayer's nephew by marriage to his wife Margaret Shenberg. In 2015 Al Shenberg was described by family members as "a gregarious character with a big personality. He was well liked and did not seem to suffer the fates of others who have gained from nepotism. There must have been a little trepidation on Al's part about working at MGM being the nephew of Louis B. Mayer."

At the time of *Oz*, Norman Taurog was best known for coaching juvenile actors into stellar performances and was dubbed "Hollywood's ace director of children" by *Screen Children* magazine. Taurog had, himself, started in show business as a child actor, making an auspicious New York stage debut at age eight in *The Good Little Devil*, sharing the bill with Mary Pickford and Dorothy and Lillian Gish. By 1916 he appeared in silent pictures produced by the Independent Moving Pictures (IMP) Co. and L.K.O. Studios. When he saw himself onscreen for the first time, he quit acting in favor of becoming a property boy, assistant director, and cutter and, later, director.

As an adult, Taurog gained renown for directing child stars such as Jackie Cooper (Taurog's nephew by marriage) in *Skippy*, *Huckleberry Finn*, and *Sooky* (all in 1931), Deanna Durbin in *Mad About Music* (1938), and *The Adventures of Tom Sawyer* (1938) with Tommy Kelly. Indeed, the February 15, 1938, *Film Daily* review of *Tom Sawyer* noted, "Taurog . . . has always been distinguished for his handling of young actors." In May 1933 Taurog had been announced as the director of Paramount's *Alice in Wonderland*, an assignment that ultimately went to Norman Z. McLeod.

For the July 1938 edition of *Screen Children* magazine, Taurog attributed his success with children to treating them like grown-ups. "I try to win their confidence first," the director told journalist Girard Comstock. "I appeal to their sense of fair play. I never break a promise to them, and as a result, I get loyalty and obedience from them. A growing child is as much an individual as a grownup, and is entitled to certain independence of thought and action. If children are intelligent enough to be in the movies, they're intelligent enough to think for themselves."

But behind the scenes Taurog's methods could be questionable. When tears wouldn't come to Jackie Cooper for a crucial scene in *Skippy*, it was Taurog who infamously ordered Cooper's dog to be executed off-set. The ploy worked: After a gunshot rang out, Cooper became hysterical and Taurog got the take he wanted. The dog was then revealed to be unharmed, but Cooper never forgave Taurog of the betrayal.

Taurog won the Academy Award for his direction of *Skippy* and, just prior to *Oz*, he was about to score his biggest hit—and subsequently snag another Best Director nomination—for *Boys Town*. To inspire child actor Martin Spellman to openly sob for a pivotal scene in *Boys Town*, Taurog got clearance to have Spellman's mother leave the set so the director could coach Spellman into imagining that the boy's mother was in a terrible accident, was hospitalized, and died before Spellman could be reunited with her.

Where *The Wizard of Oz* was concerned, Taurog had a unique connection. He had directed most of Larry Semon's comedy shorts from 1920 to 1922 and certainly would have been aware of Semon's *Wizard of Oz* production. It is likely that he, Mervyn LeRoy, and other members of MGM's *Oz* unit revisited the Semon picture early on, mostly as a precaution for what to avoid and also to mine any elements that could be repurposed in an updated version.

Taurog also probably prepared by reviewing selections from the Oz book series by Baum and Thompson (texts that he later had rebound and stamped with his daughter Patricia Ann's name), though these were mostly contemporary printings and not from Taurog's personal collection of notable first editions. The blueprint for the "Exterior Crossroads" set was drafted under his supervision, indicating that Taurog would have blocked and staged the first scheduled scene—that of Dorothy's encounter with the Scarecrow. Another set, "Interior Miniature Cyclone" (not used in the final film), also bears Taurog's name as drafted on July 27, 1938. Taurog had oversight on preliminary makeup and wardrobe tests for which the cast participated on August 27, in addition to Technicolor tests that included Judy Garland and several Munchkins.

Also at this time, the cast rehearsed their dance routines while attired in preliminary wardrobe. Both the Scarecrow and Tin Woodman would have individual dance numbers in homage to Fred Stone and David Montgomery of the original stage production. There was also a group routine to "The Jitterbug" to be worked out. As initially choreographed, this number called for an exchange of backslaps between the actors, but given the strenuous pace, Buddy Ebsen was suffering from heat, encased in his Tin Man outfit. During a break, he took a playful jab at Judy Garland in her thin gingham frock. "It's okay for you," he grouched, "but it's killing me." Unbeknownst to Ebsen, Garland was suffering herself, having returned from a Lake Arrowhead vacation with an overdose of exposure. With a forced grin, Judy reportedly bared her back. "You big softie," she retorted, "you ought to try getting your back slapped—when you've got a sunburn like mine." It is probable that Norman Taurog had input into the direction of these dance routines as they correlated to the action of their respective scenes.

But days thereafter, Taurog was replaced by director Richard Thorpe. According to Mervyn LeRoy it was because "[Taurog] didn't quite understand it, and asked to be taken off, and I admire him for it because he realized that he didn't appreciate what he was doing and could not get the best." Taurog was quickly reassigned to *The Adventures of Huckleberry Finn* with Mickey Rooney. According to a notice published in *Variety* on September 14, 1938, the switch in directors was made so that Taurog could "start preparations for *Huckleberry Finn*." Ed Sullivan stirred the pot in his Hollywood gossip column of October 11, 1938, portending of obstacles to come: "Why did MGM give *Wizard of Oz* to Dick Thorpe after Norman Taurog had been announced as director?"

RICHARD THORPE: THE EFFICIENT

Richard Thorpe not only had a reputation for bringing in pictures on schedule and within budget, he was also known for being thoroughly prepared. Like his brilliant contemporary Alfred Hitchcock, Thorpe came to the set with any guesswork eliminated, the result of having worked out the day's scenes the night before. The director's proficiency was noted in his ability to capture a scene in one or two takes. In 1937 Thorpe was described by MGM as quiet, calm, and unruffled. The result was an "unusual morale" in his company. "[He] never raises his voice," reads his MGM bio of the era, "never becomes excited, and is always absolutely sure of what he plans to do." Once, during production of *Tarzan Escapes* (1936), a herd of elephants stampeded but Thorpe quietly contained any burgeoning hysteria among cast and crew by chuckling at the pachyderms. "Poor silly things, they're afraid of a flapping piece of canvas," he remarked. The *Tarzan* company began laughing along with him, and any panic was diffused. The elephants were corralled by their handlers and shooting resumed as though nothing had happened.

Thorpe's level head and steady hand was precisely what was needed for a costly project such as *The Wizard of Oz*. And like Dorothy, he hailed from Kansas, having been born in Hutchinson and schooled in Wichita. In 1937 Thorpe was quoted as saying he believed he had yet to make his best picture. Given the importance being accorded to *Oz*, Thorpe's opportunity to top himself loomed large.

During preproduction Thorpe approved blueprints for the initial sets. These included the Emerald City and Wizard's Throne Room; the Lion's Forest; the Poppy Field; the Witch's Castle; and locations in and around the Kansas farm set, the earliest of which is dated September 12, 1938. The Kansas scenes also called for the central staging of the whirlwind twister that whisks Dorothy's rustic cabin to the Land of Oz.

For such an ambitious undertaking as *The Wizard of Oz*, MGM not only had a plan A, it had backup plans as well for various facets of production. One example of this was the Kansas setting. Right up until the week before filming commenced, it was being reported that a location shoot in Kansas was planned. The *Hollywood Reporter* noted on October 8, 1938, "Richard Thorpe will shoot the musical numbers completely before going on location in Kansas and starting the dramatic scenes." (Based on a budget expense line item, MGM had previously dispatched a camera crew to Kansas to scout locations.) At the same time, Thorpe, assistant director Al Shenberg, and unit production assistant Joe Cook took a day trip to scan Southern California for a setting rural enough to serve as the Kansas locale.

Shooting films off the lot and on location—including out-of-state settings using juvenile actors—was not unheard of. In May 1938 Norman Taurog and members of the *Boys Town* unit spent a week in Omaha, Nebraska, at Father Flanagan's orphanage compound. On November 7, 1938, Richard Thorpe, unit manager Art Smith, and cameraman John Seitz returned from Northern California, where they selected locations for MGM's *Huckleberry Finn*. And *The Yearling*, acquired by MGM in May 1938, was slated to be filmed in Florida. But a location shoot involving juveniles was complicated by child labor laws.

According to an October 30, 1938, report from the Hollywood bureau of the Associated Press, it was estimated that Judy Garland would be scheduled for one day's shooting outdoors on location (for the "Over the Rainbow" number). But the Southern California location selected by Thorpe as the site of the Kansas farm was fifty miles from MGM, making the commute one hour and forty minutes one-way. Garland would be provided with a portable schoolroom, the same as when making a picture at Metro. But with four hours combined for school and recreation, shooting on location would leave her with only forty minutes of work time out of a total four-hour work-time maximum. "It wasn't worthwhile," concluded the AP article, "so the location [will be] re-created at the studio."

In addition to weighing the options for a location shoot, blueprints had been drafted for the farm set exterior (interior scenes could be shot on a soundstage). As filming progressed, plagued by delays and added expenses, the notion of trekking to Kansas for an authentic location shoot was also nixed in favor of erecting the farm on a soundstage according to the backup plan.

What remained, however, was the intent to manipulate the film medium by starkly contrasting the Dust Bowl farm with the Technicolor fantasy of Oz, thus adhering to L. Frank Baum's description—and W. W. Denslow's accompanying pictures—of Dorothy's homestead and surroundings as gray and barren. John Nickolaus, head of MGM's film lab, intended to use "Technicolor black and white" stock (standard black-and-white film printed in sepia tones) in order to create prairie landscape that was as monochromatic as Baum described it. Nickolaus had already experimented with the sepia platinum toning process on *The Good Earth* (1937) and *The Girl of the Golden West* (1938). In December

1938 Howard Dietz, head of MGM's advertising and publicity department, heralded Nickolaus's development as one of Metro's great innovations of the year.

But before this process could be employed for *The Wizard of Oz*, special permission was required from David S. Shattuck, treasurer of Technicolor Motion Picture Corporation. On September 20, 1938, Shattuck sent MGM executive Eddie Mannix a letter that read, "This will confirm our agreement in respect only of your forthcoming photoplay *Wizard of Oz* that . . . you may photograph the so-called Kansas sequences of such photoplay . . . on your own black and white negative."

Finally, on October 8, 1938, the *Hollywood Reporter* announced that

production of *The Wizard of Oz* was set to begin: "Production on *The Wizard of Oz* starts Wednesday [Oct. 12] at MGM with the first musical number featuring Judy Garland and Ray Bolger being photographed." The original budget breakdown for *The Wizard of Oz* also records the official start date of production as October 12, 1938. This is supported by an existing still of Ray Bolger's Scarecrow facial makeup taken on this date, although this may have been for an on-set dress rehearsal. The *Hollywood Reporter* for October 14, 1938, carried a notice that "*Wizard of Oz* went into production yesterday [October 13] at MGM under the direction of Richard Thorpe." October 13, 1938, is the start date officially recorded by MGM.

Richard Thorpe was expeditious indeed. Within two weeks shooting *The Wizard of Oz*, Thorpe had filmed Dorothy's introduction to the Scarecrow and all the events in and around the Wicked Witch's castle. A scene on the latter set included a long, gliding shot—150 feet in length—of the principals rushing down a staircase. The shot was filmed with cinematographer Harold Rosson manning the Technicolor camera, which had an underslung mount nicknamed the "sloth camera" by Judy Garland after the creature that hangs upside down. The unique mount was designed for use with a big camera crane that allowed for operation of the camera from within six inches of the floor to thirty-five feet in the air. (When it came time to film the Emerald City, Rosson reportedly became seasick from being hoisted about a set swimming in hues of green.)

According to reference stills, photographed to preserve continuity of each set's appearance, it is possible to pinpoint the dates for some of the scenes filmed by Thorpe. The Scarecrow scenes lasted from October 13 to 14, 1938. In this sequence Dorothy rescues the Scarecrow, he goes into his song-and-dance number, and they march off together down the Yellow Brick Road. Harold Heffernan described the sequence for his readers:

> The dance opens with the Scarecrow, released from a pole in a cornfield, sitting beside Judy Garland. . . . He sings the song "If I Only Had a Brain." As he finishes, he doubles himself up, rolls down a bank, then gradually pulls himself upright, going into a tap step. As he dances, the Scarecrow gains confidence and tries to pirouette. But his legs twist like pieces of rope. Judy untangles them and away he goes again, this time in a series of soft-shoe steps, punctuated by near-collapses, a "split" from which he gradually raises himself and odd gyrations with his large cotton gloves.

Of his routine, Bolger said, "We had to work out this business a step at a time because it was a matter of characterization. We're trying to keep the scarecrow illusion always before the audience."

Among the first in a series of calamities to hinder the start of production was an incident that reportedly occurred during the Scarecrow's song. Midway through a take, one of the immense overhead arc lights developed a short circuit and began popping and crackling, raining a shower of sparks down upon the actors. Ray Bolger instinctively bent over Judy Garland to shield her from harm while his back bore the brunt of the sparks. Though Bolger's costume was supposedly inflammable, his exposed straw stuffing was not, and Richard Thorpe is credited with having grabbed a fire extinguisher to wet Bolger from head to toe. The scene recommenced once Bolger changed into a duplicate costume, and he was hailed a hero by the company for the quick-thinking actions that protected Judy.

On October 15, 1938, scenes with the Wicked Witch threatening Dorothy in her tower room were taken. October 17 was Dorothy's tearful reprise of "Over the Rainbow" while a prisoner in the Witch's castle. For this and similar such scenes, Judy Garland required no artificial means of generating tears like those actors who smelled onions or used glycerin drops. She told reporter May Mann she simply thought of sad things. The ability to emote so authentically is a credit to Garland's preternatural talent, and her on-set sobs affected the crew observing her from behind the camera. More so, this was the same sequence in which Dorothy glimpses a vision of Aunt Em in the Witch's crystal globe. The script identifies this as a "TRICK SHOT," and indeed it would have to be achieved in postproduction as a double-exposure or insert shot as Clara Blandick was not yet cast in the role (further testament to Garland's abilities as she had no actual "person" to visualize).

In 1981 Margaret Hamilton reminisced about performing opposite Judy Garland for the first time on the set of *The Wizard of Oz* during the initial period under Richard Thorpe's direction. "No one impressed me quite as much as Judy did those first days," Hamilton said. "She had those marvelous, expressive eyes, and there was a feeling of wonder displayed in that little face. Her enthusiasm was contagious . . . once we started to work with her, we realized there was something special about her."

On October 19, 1938, Dorothy's rescue by her companions from the Witch's imprisonment was filmed. October 20–21 was the chase of Dorothy's party by the Winkies through the Witch's entrance hall. October 20 also saw exterior shots of the Winkies outside the drawbridge, possibly for Toto's escape. Scenes of Dorothy's companions disguised as Winkies on the rocks overseeing the Witch's castle were made on October 25. In 1938 there was a six-day workweek; October 16 and 23 were Sundays so no filming occurred.

As a director himself, Mervyn LeRoy initially kept his distance, giving Richard Thorpe some breathing room while also allowing the actors to adjust to their uncomfortable routine. Ebsen's chin piece gave him a stiff neck, Bolger's textured-burlap mask was painted

a color that made him nauseous to look in the mirror, and Lahr's yellow-rubber upper lip prevented him from chewing. "And you'll notice that Mervyn LeRoy, the producer, is nowhere to be seen," Lahr muttered to United Press correspondent Frederick C. Othman. "The reason is easy to find," continued the comedian. "He's scared to come down here. He doesn't dare. He knows there's a Cowardly Lion here that would bite his leg off." (Othman qualified Lahr's threat by suggesting it sounded none too real and that the actor was enjoying himself playing in a picture as no grown man had played before.)

Though production was advancing at a steady clip, Othman advised his readers not to expect *The Wizard of Oz* before February or March 1939. At the time of Othman's visit, Richard Thorpe had already begun rehearsing scenes in the apple orchard leading to the discovery of Buddy Ebsen as the Tin Man. But shortly thereafter, production was suddenly halted. Mervyn LeRoy had finally reviewed the "dailies"—raw, unedited rushes from each day's takes—and was dissatisfied with Thorpe's straightforward approach. With so much at stake, LeRoy made the executive decision to dismiss Thorpe from the picture. In a 1966 interview, the producer recalled, "[Thorpe] didn't quite understand *The Wizard of Oz* either, because I guess you've got to have the heart and mind of a kid to make *The Wizard of Oz.*" In his 1974 autobiography, *Mervyn LeRoy: Take One*, LeRoy referenced Thorpe's dismissal by noting, "There's too much hasty firing around this business but, of course, there are times when it is essential to the integrity of your film. As a producer . . . I had to replace a director and it wasn't easy but it had to be done."

In hindsight, Thorpe told Aljean Harmetz he already sensed his days on *Oz* were numbered but, at the time, Thorpe was probably caught off-guard. When MGM executive Eddie Mannix took the stand before the National Labor Board for a Screen Directors Guild hearing in September 1938, Mannix stated that at MGM some directors rarely if ever look at the rushes during the making of a picture and have little to do with the cutting. Thorpe's last day was noted by MGM as October 24, 1938.

A number of still photographs survive from Thorpe's time as director, some of which were erroneously used to publicize the picture on the occasion of its debut and subsequent re-releases. These stills are interesting to analyze in that they reflect staging and other details different from what appears in the finished film.

For example, the Scarecrow's cornfield set—with its stylized clouds, patchwork of rolling hills, swaths of flowered sward, and oval-shaped yellow bricks painted directly on the stage floor—looks like something repurposed from Walt Disney's *Flowers and Trees* cartoon. In these scenes Judy Garland does not carry a basket as she does in the final version (and as Dorothy does in the Baum book).

In the Wicked Witch's castle, Margaret Hamilton peers into her crystal globe and later intimidates Dorothy all while seated on her throne, emphasizing her station as the ruler of western Oz. When the Witch leaves to skywrite her threat over the Emerald City, she dramatically glides the length of the set on her broom and sails out the window. In the final version she stands at the window at which point the film cuts to a miniature witch on a broom circling the exterior tower before zooming off. (Given that this scene was restaged, scenarist Noel Langley inserted the original staging for the witch in 1961's *Snow White and the Three Stooges*, which he cowrote.)

When the Wicked Witch summons the Winged Monkeys, only the monkey leader appears in the Thorpe scene. Unlike in the final version, the shot is from the outside looking in, probably to highlight a June 22, 1938, special effect in which "Winged Monkey Captain Appears in Puff of Blue Smoke." Toto's escape from the castle was more perilous than the final version; he must first leap across the moat from the rising drawbridge and outmaneuver parallel rows of spear-wielding Winkie guards. During Dorothy's rescue her three companions (who have infiltrated the castle disguised as guards) do not shuck off their costumes but remain in them during the subsequent chase. When reshot, the three friends shed the Winkie wardrobe, likely to avert the confusion of audiences thinking Dorothy had been recaptured.

The October 29, 1938, edition of *Boxoffice* magazine reported that "sudden and serious illness" had befallen Richard Thorpe. Another press notice of the same date suggested that Thorpe had come down with a cold from cranking up the soundstage air-conditioning in order to keep the twenty-eight men sweltering in their wool Winkie wardrobe from suffering heat prostration. The November 2, 1938, edition of *Variety* said that Thorpe was "stricken with flu and ordered to the desert for treatment," which was a partial truth. Thorpe was sent to Palm Springs for damage control, to avoid the prying queries of the Hollywood press. But by November 15 *Motion Picture Daily* accurately noted that Thorpe had been "relieved of the direction of *The Wizard of Oz*," and that he would be taking over direction of *Huckleberry Finn*, replacing Norman Taurog yet again.

Coinciding with Richard Thorpe's dismissal, Buddy Ebsen succumbed to the respiratory issues inflicted by inhaling the aluminum powder used for his Tin Man makeup. In a 1993 interview Ebsen remembered the complications brought on by his Tin Man disguise:

> Anyway, the next problem was the makeup. They got me in the studio at eight o'clock in the morning. They glued a rubber cap over my hair, glued on a rubber nose, glued on a rubber chin, covered the whole thing with clown white [makeup] and then took a giant step in the wrong direction. They powdered me with aluminum dust . . . very finely ground aluminum dust. Well, after you work on a picture for ten days, they powdered you maybe a dozen or two dozen times a day. Stuff gets in the air, you're going to breathe some of it; I breathed enough to coat my lungs with it. I collapsed, they took me to the hospital—I spent six weeks in the Good Samaritan Hospital under an oxygen tent—and that is the story of my short visit to the Land of Oz.

That was late October 1938, and a few weeks later, it was widely reported that Ebsen had to relinquish the Tin Man role due to "an attack of pneumonia" and would recuperate in Palm Springs. Poetic justice was served fourteen years later when Ebsen was cast as the Scarecrow in a theatrical production of *The Wizard of Oz*, based on the MGM movie, at the Fair Park Auditorium in Dallas, Texas. The show was such a great success there was talk of touring it.

Oddly, in his November 14, 1938, column, Harrison Carroll didn't indicate that Ebsen was off the picture, noting that Buddy "was threatened with pneumonia but is better now." Carroll also wrote that Ebsen wears "one of the most uncomfortable costumes in Hollywood history," stating that "He's the Tin Woodman in *The Wizard of Oz*." But at the time of publication, it was almost two weeks since Ebsen had to be replaced in the role.

GEORGE CUKOR: THE TEMP

In great haste, the directorial seat was assumed by George Cukor, as announced on October 28, 1938, by the *Film Daily*. Although Ralph Wilk reported that "George Cukor will direct *The Wizard of Oz* for Metro," Cukor was not intended to helm *Oz* long-term. Louella O. Parsons wondered how Greta Garbo would get along as she had wanted Cukor to direct her in *Ninotchka*, but in reality he was already involved in preproduction to direct *Gone with the Wind*—Hollywood's most important and highly anticipated motion picture production. Nor was *Oz* subject matter that appealed to Cukor's directorial taste. He was long lauded as one of Metro's top-ranking directors. The financial, artistic, and critical successes to his credit included *Dinner at Eight* (1933), *Little Women* (1933), *David Copperfield* (1935), *Romeo and Juliet* (1936), and *Camille* (1936). Even if he wasn't already committed, Cukor would have sniffed at the notion that he should direct what was essentially considered a live-action cartoon, no matter how grand its production values. Noted for reenvisioning classics for the screen, Cukor thought *Oz* subpar literature. Curiously, though, stills exist, taken during Richard Thorpe's direction, that bear a typed caption erroneously indicating that *The Wizard of Oz* was "directed by George Cukor and produced by Mervyn LeRoy."

George Cukor's contribution to *The Wizard of Oz* was that of a seasoned and intelligent resource. He had a penchant for detail and was noted for having cultivated a rapid grasp of filmmaking problems. Despite his misgivings, Cukor approached *Oz* similarly to his mounting of *Romeo and Juliet* two years prior. The trajectory of Shakespeare's star-crossed lovers includes banishment, murder and suicide over the course of just four days. Cukor told *Photoplay*'s Frank Small, "[T]o meet the demand of the public for reality, for events that seem possible and credible, we had to prepare a good many explanatory scenes . . . America would not under any circumstances swallow the accepted melodramatic portrayal and the usual presentation of the play. Offering the story so that its effect might be one of reality meant a careful segregation of the prose from the poetry."

On *The Wizard of Oz*, George Cukor aided Mervyn LeRoy by assessing the overall production, troubleshooting the obstacles thus far, and recommending revisions for the appearance and delivery of the actors—the latter being a specialty of Cukor's since he was considered a superior director of dialogue. As such, it could well have been Cukor who recommended a rerecording of Bolger's "If I Only Had a Brain" number. In the original September 30, 1938, rendition, Bolger's interpretation has a subtle, awed quality that may have come across as trite onscreen, which was precisely what Cukor sought to remedy. Although the number was reshot in early November, the song was eventually rerecorded in February and April 1939, and filmed again under Busby Berkeley's direction thereafter.

Cukor also felt Bolger's Scarecrow makeup should be better defined and that Margaret Hamilton's Wicked Witch would appear more sinister with a different wig that could expose a sharper nose and extended chin. (Prior to Cukor's consultations, Hamilton had tested a similar hairdress on October 8, 1938—a loose bun with tendril-like tufts in front of each ear.) The Witch's Winkie sentries were given platform shoes to elevate their height and effect a uniform, imposing menace.

In particular, Cukor found Judy Garland's "Princess Dorothy" appearance and mannerisms to be cloying and inappropriate. In early sequels to *The Wonderful Wizard of Oz*, Dorothy speaks with a childish lisp, and it seems this influenced how Garland should portray the part. Cukor coached her into simplifying her performance to seem authentic, less conspicuous. By December 1938 Garland confided her valuation for Cukor's insight to journalist Grace Wilcox, saying, "I learned more in the two days he was on *The Wizard of Oz* than I ever learned at any one time before." Cukor initiated a new round of hairdressing and wardrobe tests to reflect a more realistic approach for the Dorothy character. On October 26 and 31, 1938, Garland made new tests before auburn schoolgirl braids were decided upon on November 3. Production was due to resume the following day.

Coinciding with the New York premiere of *The Wizard of Oz* in August 1939, *Women's Wear Daily* provided its readers with an exacting description of Garland's hairdress, specific enough to be duplicated:

> Judy's haircomb as Dorothy is attractive, reviving a style popular with girls when the book came out in the late '90s [*sic*]. The hair is parted in the center, rolled high on each side, and worn in two braids that finish halfway down with curled ends. A small bow is tied at the top of the curl. For a school coiffure it is charming and practical and could be recommended highly as just right for the plaid and checked ginghams that are going back to school this fall.

Judy Garland's hair was reddened with a henna rinse to match the hue of Dorothy's locks as depicted in the color plates of *The Wonderful Wizard of Oz*. Garland primarily retained this auburn shade until making *The Clock* (1945), although on *Oz* her natural tresses would be augmented with a wig for length enough to create Dorothy's flowing braids. Bob Roberts, a wig designer at Max Factor, was instructed to make Garland appear as a "young, early teenager of twelve to fourteen . . . and I think she was only about sixteen at the time anyway." Working from sketches, Roberts created a three-quarters wig that matched Garland's hair color, had length to create braided extensions, and was affixed to the back of her head. As Roberts explained it, "The [wig] hair was tied by hand into a skull-fitting foundation and secured to a wig band which was pinned tight over her own hair."

Adrian revised Judy Garland's wardrobe in keeping with the new, subdued approach to her character. "Great splashes of color, vivid greens, sparkling blue, scintillating reds, will blaze across the screen in . . . *The Wizard of Oz*," he wrote, "And little Judy Garland, as the beloved Dorothy, will offer a smart contrast in her clean blue-and-white checked little girl dresses." The new frock was a modern echo of L. Frank Baum's original description and featured a hidden pocket for Dorothy's handkerchief (not for stowing cigarettes, as a modern-day auctioneer of one of the jumpers has claimed).

The bugle-bead construction of the Ruby Slippers also underwent revision. The beads were replaced with sequins and jeweled bows were added at the toes of Garland's slippers, perhaps to emulate the appearance of Snow White's dainty footwear. Likewise, the patent-leather Mary Jane shoes Garland would have worn in Kansas, and in which she had tested, would be changed out for simple black leather lace-ups.

It was also George Cukor—and not succeeding director Victor Fleming, as has been previously cited—who suggested adjustments to the Scarecrow's cornfield set to dispense with its stylized, cartoonish appearance in keeping with his disdain for the overall setup to date.

To revise the set, Cukor consulted Herbert Ryman, an early choice of Cukor's to serve as his art director on *Gone with the Wind*. Ryman was an MGM staff artist who also taught a course on motion picture design techniques once a week at Chouinard Art Institute in Los Angeles. Ryman had previously contributed conceptual designs for *The Wizard of Oz*, but Cukor was well familiar with Ryman's work, having successfully collaborated with the artist on *David Copperfield* and *Romeo and Juliet*.

According to John Stanley Donaldson, Ryman's biographer, "His last work for MGM was the Emerald City segment for *The Wizard of Oz* . . ." but the timing of a November 8, 1938, news bit about Ryman coincides with Cukor's time on *Oz*. In it, Ryman's sister, Lucille, said that "he recently has been working on *The Wizard of Oz*.[1] Thus, the cornfield set was overhauled over the course of several days, replacing the painted cobblestones of the Yellow Brick Road with Masonite tiles that more closely resembled actual bricks.

---

1 Shortly thereafter, Ryman left MGM to work for Walt Disney on *Pinocchio, Fantasia, Dumbo,* and *Bambi* before becoming a top designer for the Disney theme parks.

Curbing added a modern, urban touch in contrast with the dirt roads in rural Kansas. The authentic cornstalks, which had authentically withered under the intense lighting required for Technicolor filmmaking, were replaced with a glistening and resilient celluloid cornfield. The scenic backdrop was softened to appear naturalistic instead of like a stylized cartoon sketch; a row of fences, in diminishing perspective, was added for depth.

According to Noel Langley, George Cukor also revised the *Oz* script, saying, "What we have here simply will not work cinematically." But at that point, the script was essentially intact as a working document, largely as it would translate to the screen. What Langley was likely referring to was Cukor's vision for discarding the entire exaggerated "cartoon" approach, which would have been disastrous onscreen, particularly the surreal incongruence of Judy Garland's appearance on a Depression-era Dust Bowl farm.

By November 1, 1938, it was being reported that Cukor was recalled from his loan-out by David O. Selznick to continue preparations for directing *Gone with the Wind*. At the same time, Nicholas Schenck had arrived in town from New York for a week of conferences with studio executives. Ostensibly, Schenck's agenda included serious discussion about the future of *The Wizard of Oz* and whether it was feasible to proceed or cancel it and cut his losses. Mervyn LeRoy must've been both passionate and persuasive; Schenck left earlier than expected for the return trip to New York. On November 5, *Boxoffice* noted that Victor Fleming was next in the "pilot's seat" as fourth in a succession of directors on *The Wizard of Oz*. But Fleming had already taken up shooting *Oz* the day prior—the very day Nick Schenck left MGM, likely feeling placated with rejuvenated confidence in both LeRoy's and Fleming's abilities to pull off *Oz* successfully.

VICTOR FLEMING: THE REDEEMER

In its December 3, 1938, summary of the *Oz* production to date, *Motion Picture Herald* suggested that Victor Fleming's selection as director was one of extraordinary care: "*Captains Courageous* and *Test Pilot*, stories vastly different in conception than *The Wizard of Oz*, were more than successfully brought to the screen by Victor Fleming. Assignment of Fleming to bring this production to screen realism in all its beauty and charm should serve as a worthy exploitation item."

Victor Fleming was indeed a timely choice to take over the troubled *Wizard of Oz* production. In his six years at Metro, Fleming had cultivated a reputation for handling megastars such as Jean Harlow, Spencer Tracy, Wallace Beery, Myrna Loy, and Clark Gable, MGM's king of the lot, with the respectable but down-to-earth ease of a mentoring pal or an older brother. While lunching with Ed Sullivan at the Brown Derby, Fleming told the entertainment journalist that the hallmark of a great performer is an almost animal intelligence in grasping a character and knowing instinctively how to project it so that an audience will understand it. "All of the great performers," said Fleming, "are emotionally unstable, and have such heights and depths that they live in a world apart from most of us."

In particular, Fleming had a personal and professional affinity for Clark Gable, and the two often spent time after hours engaged in outdoor sportsman's activities. MGM child actor Martin Spellman described the two men's charismatic relationship as being "like twins with larger than life personalities." Fleming oozed a masculine virility that matched Gable's own machismo, and Gable put his camaraderie with Fleming ahead of MGM protocol. The actor bucked the studio's caste system—which dictated that stars shouldn't commingle with either extras or production staff—and sat with Fleming at the director's table in the studio commissary. (A gambling dice cage sat center on the director's table and was spun when the bill came due; the loser picked up the tab for the entire table.)

Fleming also had an aptitude for rehabilitating floundering productions with the aid of his friend and trusted collaborator, screenwriter John Lee Mahin. As president of the Screen Playwrights, an early screenwriters' union, Mahin was possessed of the same stalwart resolve as Fleming and on February 17, 1938, went so far as to write the Academy of Motion Picture Arts and Sciences to withdraw his nomination for *Captains Courageous* when he objected to the Academy's discriminatory tactics. (Director Frank Capra, Academy president, told Mahin his position for winning the award was immaterial. "We don't care whether you accept it or throw it away....")

Mahin's innate sense of fairness came to bear upon the *Oz* production as well. By March 23, 1939, as a rough cut of *Oz* was being assembled, Mahin would be called upon to intercept a dispute between Noel Langley (who was threatening arbitration) and Edgar Allan Woolf and Florence Ryerson concerning their respective screen credits. By March 29, the disagreement was settled when Mahin, Woolf, and Ryerson viewed the picture to ascertain how the billing should read.

Together, Fleming and Mahin had finessed the scripts of several previous Fleming-directed films that were successes: *Red Dust*, *Bombshell*, *Treasure Island*, *Captains Courageous*, and *Test Pilot*. Fleming had most recently salvaged *The Great Waltz* (1938), and though Julien Duvivier received screen credit, it was show-business knowledge that Fleming had taken the reins necessary to whip the picture into shape. On November 3, 1938, the *Hollywood Reporter* noted that the cinematic duo of Fleming and Mahin would do "their stuff again" for the studio, "this time on *Wizard of Oz*, Mahin's third important ailing patient in a row [following *Test Pilot* and *Too Hot to Handle*] and Fleming's second."

In 1971 Ray Bolger remembered Fleming's take-charge approach, stating, "You can't imagine the manpower and lack of brainpower when you get assembled with a group like that. I really don't know how they finished the picture. But they had such discipline on that set that this Victor Fleming had created. He put up with no nonsense and it worked."

Fleming's directorial competence was otherwise considered unremarkable for the period. In 1997 Mickey Rooney recalled his disbelief upon learning of Fleming's assignment sixty years prior. "Fleming directed me in *Captains Courageous*," said Rooney. "I couldn't believe that they would pick *Victor Fleming*, who was a former boxer!" Noel Langley was likewise disenchanted with Fleming for *The Wizard of Oz*, asserting, "He knew little about fantasy. He was in a rush to get through the picture so he could direct *Gone with the Wind*. I remember, he would let the actors rehearse and then they'd shoot it all rather informally." When asked to name Metro's top directors while testifying under oath in December 1938, MGM producer Hunt Stomberg listed Fleming last, preceded by Richard Thorpe and King Vidor among others. Fleming's 1939 salary of one hundred fifty-six thousand dollars was matched by that of Norman Taurog but exceeded by MGM directors Sidney Franklin, Robert Z. Leonard, and W. S. Van Dyke.

Totaling over $2.5 million when adjusted for today's inflation, Fleming's earnings hardly seem compensation enough when one considers his directorial efforts on both *The Wizard of Oz* and *Gone with the Wind* in 1939. A September 3, 1939, United Press piece on Fleming dubbed him "Hollywood's Big Spender" for having "splurged" more than ten million dollars making movies (*The Great Waltz*, *Oz*, and *GWTW*) since the previous January. "No other director ever turned out so many big-time movies in so few months. Nor has any director quit the movie business as often as he has." By January 3, 1940, *Variety* hailed Fleming as the "year's epic director," in terms of biggest-grossing pictures. *Oz* was then projected to tally five million dollars and *Gone with the Wind*, upwards of ten million, which made Fleming "the top coin-getting director of all times."

In May 1973 Mervyn LeRoy told UPI correspondent Vernon Hall, "I suggested Fleming to Louis B. Mayer [to direct *Oz*], and then all of us at MGM began working on him to do the picture. Finally he agreed." When Victor Fleming was interviewed by *Good Housekeeping* reporter Jane Hall (for Hall's August 1939 visit-to-the-movie-set recap of the previous February), he was ambivalent about having directed *The Wizard of Oz*. "They made me [direct it]. You don't think I wanted to do it, for Gossakes? I want a vacation." As of January 23, 1939, Fleming was still engrossed in shooting *Oz* when the *Hollywood Reporter* projected that Fleming would be "tied up on *Wizard of Oz* until late spring," thus shelving production of what was to have been Fleming's next film, *The Yearling* with Spencer Tracy and Gene Reynolds.

At the time of Jane Hall's *Good Housekeeping* interview, Fleming was in the midst of directing *Gone with the Wind* and was, understandably, worn. When Hall complimented Fleming on his fine work for *Oz*, he became terse, "How could you hear that? Picture isn't even put together yet." But before Hall left, Fleming obligingly acknowledged that *Oz* was the "most interesting picture I ever directed." By November 1939, after *Oz* had debuted and he was still engrossed in postproduction on *Gone with the Wind*, Fleming was succinct in stating, "I have no hesitation in admitting that *The Wizard of Oz* provided more little problems, along with the big ones, than any picture I have directed."

In January 1940 Fleming reflected on this prolific yet daunting period, "I went to work on *Gone with the Wind* with the headaches of pure imagination from *Wizard of Oz* still ringing in my ears," he stated. "I had felt that picture was quite a problem, but now I began to see something Utopian in an audience which didn't know what a Munchkin was, nor how an Emerald City might look. I was down to the bedrock of reality [on *GWTW*], with millions of voices shouting, 'Hew to the line, mister.'"

In March 1939, a month after Fleming's work on *Oz* had wrapped, columnist Sheilah Graham caught up with him on the *Gone with the Wind* set and asked, "I thought you were taking a vacation after *Wizard of Oz*?" to which Fleming cracked, "I'm not here." Graham pressed, "How did you come to take over this picture?" Fleming grinned, "I said the wrong word at the wrong time." How George Cukor came to be released from *GWTW* so that Fleming could be taken off of *Oz* and transferred as director to *GWTW* is one of those infamous eleventh-hour brokering deals for which Hollywood is renowned. The irony in Fleming twice succeeding Cukor on two consecutive projects is that both directors were said to have been "the best of friends."

Ten days after Fleming left *Oz* in February 1939, Harold Heffernan told readers of his Hollywood column that the decision was made at three in the morning at Mervyn LeRoy's Santa Monica beach home. Fleming's buddy Clark Gable had the male lead in *GWTW* and Gable was dissatisfied with Cukor's professional direction and personal style. That night, Gable, producer David O. Selznick, and Eddie Mannix had viewed *GWTW* scenes at Selznick's compound and concurred with Gable that a change was necessary. Earlier that week another columnist, Harrison Carroll, summarized the difference in approach of each director, calling Fleming a sharp contrast with Cukor: "He is taciturn where Cukor is suave. His forte is action. Cukor has an eye for subtleties."

Heffernan said that LeRoy held the key to the whole deal as Fleming was directing *Oz*, which gave LeRoy the right of first refusal. Selznick, Mannix, and Gable sped over to LeRoy's home. Awakened by a commotion at his front door, LeRoy called out, "I'm in bed—what do you mean busting in at this hour of the night?" to which Selznick barked, "We want your director—we've got to have Victor Fleming."

It was at dawn that LeRoy finally gave his consent to permit Fleming to relinquish *Oz* after much discussion and telephoning to other studio officials—final approval was granted by L. B. Mayer. Selznick and Gable drank a toast to LeRoy before taking their celebration out into the light of day. The irony is that as *Oz* was winding down its production schedule, Fleming anticipated a fishing vacation. Described as gray-haired, seamy-faced, and possessed with a work ethic of "a concentration achieved by few other Hollywood directors," Fleming solemnly informed the press, "After [*Oz*] I'm going away where no one can find me—not even me." Unable to refuse his closest ally, Fleming accepted *GWTW* as a personal favor to Clark Gable.

It was John Lee Mahin who, in later years, suggested that Fleming agreed to direct *The Wizard of Oz* with paternal instinct as his motivation, finding appeal in the opportunity to craft a cinematic valentine for his two young daughters. Fleming himself retained the adventuresome spark of youth, telling Alexander Kahn of the United Press: "It is not difficult for adults to accept the [Oz] story and enjoy it as much as children. For, as you know, we are all Peter Pans to some degree."

But Fleming's connection to the subject matter ran deeper than manufacturing an ode to his children. In his youth the director reportedly encountered L. Frank Baum on several occasions. In an MGM press release, Fleming acknowledged being introduced to the author when Baum vacationed at the Hotel del Coronado in San Diego, where Baum wrote *Dorothy and the Wizard in Oz* (1908), *The Road to Oz* (1909), and *The Emerald City of Oz* (1910). Fleming was also said to have known Baum when Frank and Maud relocated to Hollywood (also in 1910) and Baum was active with the Oz Film Manufacturing Company. In 1939 Fleming was quoted as saying, "I was a youngster then, intensely interested in the show business. Naturally when introduced to the author, my first remark was about his [Oz] story and the stage show." The encounter left a lasting impression. "Throughout

[Fleming's] career," reads the press release, "he remembered the Oz stories but he never dreamed that he would one day be chosen to direct one." Fleming was, in particular, intrigued by the novelty of *The Wizard* in popular culture. "*The Wizard of Oz* is the only musical show I know of that lived on the stage for thirteen years," he noted in 1939, "and the principal reason was that it was an original idea"—or at least that was the explanation Baum gave Fleming when they met.

Originality aside, Fleming told Alexander Kahn that, with *The Wizard*, he hoped to balance the picture's fantasy with a measure of realism in order to present a satisfying entertainment. "Such attempts at pure fantasy have been tried without success," said Fleming, "but in *Snow White*, we found fantasy that could be realistic. For the time being the audience actually could believe in dwarfs, a witch and a poisoned apple. Disney was using real characters and outside of a little magic they did real things."

KING VIDOR: BRINGING IT HOME

With Fleming's transfer to Selznick International Pictures, *The Wizard of Oz* was again left without a directing pilot. The paradox of assigning King Vidor to finish the film with its Kansas farm scenes and violent twister is that Vidor's 1913 motion picture debut was *Hurricane in Galveston*, inspired by his real-life boyhood experience of having survived the devastating Galveston hurricane of 1900, which he subsequently wrote about for *Esquire* in 1935. In addition to Ball High School in Galveston, Vidor attended private schools, Peacock Military Academy in San Antonio and Tome School for Boys at Port Deposit, Maryland. Afterward, Vidor settled in Houston with the intention of writing for magazines and motion pictures but ended up producing and directing three short films while there.

When Vidor next relocated to Hollywood, he received a well-rounded orientation to the motion picture business, selling some of his stories, working as a movie extra, and working as a script clerk at Universal. It was at Universal, where Vidor had advanced to scenario writer, that he met filmmaker Judge Willis Brown. Brown was an author and lecturer on boys' delinquency issues, having served as a judge of the Utah Juvenile Court system. Brown was impressed with Vidor and offered Vidor the chance to direct films based on Brown's work.

As a director, Vidor was golden at MGM. His *The Big Parade* (1925) became the studio's greatest commercial success at that time and was critically hailed as an important document of World War I. But Vidor would never commit to a long-term contract at MGM, preferring instead to freelance for other studios. His two most recent successes just prior to *The Wizard of Oz* were *Stella Dallas* (1937), with Barbara Stanwyck, Samuel Goldwyn's talkie remake of a 1925 melodrama; and *The Citadel* (1938), an English film with Robert Donat and Rosalind Russell for which Metro-Goldwyn-Mayer was distributor.

Part of Vidor's appeal to complete *Oz* was that he was already experienced with the peculiarities of working with Technicolor cameras as the primary director of Metro's *Northwest Passage* in 1938 (the theatrical release of which would be delayed until 1940). In addition to overseeing *Oz*'s Kansas scenes, which included Dorothy's encounter with Professor Marvel, Vidor oversaw Technicolor "pickup shots," or retakes, as needed for continuity. He also directed Technicolor scenes for "Exterior Witch's Castle Gates" (a March 16, 1939, retake); "Smoke Ring Effect" (the spiraling, superimposed "smoke ring" during

Dorothy's transition back to Kansas); and "Good Witch in the Sky" for the superimposed shots of Billie Burke during the poppy field scene.

Reference stills of the Kansas farm set taken on February 10–11, 1939, include live animals—cows, horses, and chickens. However, Victor Fleming was not officially relieved of *Oz* until February 18. It is unknown if these set stills were for dress rehearsals or if Vidor began these scenes with a second unit while Fleming continued some Technicolor work. (There were some minor bits involving the farmhands that could be shot without Judy Garland, and Bolger and Lahr are visible in a Kansas set still in which Vidor is also present.) It is also possible that a *sixth* director stepped in momentarily. In a 1974 TV interview with Los Angeles's *Day at Night*, Mervyn LeRoy claimed, "I directed a few little scenes in [*Oz*] after Victor Fleming had to go away."

Unlike the fantasy scenes under Fleming's direction, in which the camera fluidly floated, King Vidor's direction of the Kansas sequences was straightforward. Vidor was apparently nonplussed at taking over *Oz*, adhering to his edict "keep it simple," as he reflected in a 1948 interview. "For a dozen years," he told the International News Service, "I have followed that motto in my life and my work. If you let things get unnecessarily complicated you run into trouble which should have been avoided in the first place."

As was customary in the studio system, Vidor received no screen credit for pinch-hitting on *Oz*, but that was to be expected. In latter-day interviews Vidor indicated that Fleming was a friend and colleague and that he never disclosed his participation on *Oz* until after Fleming died in 1949 (although Hedda Hopper had announced it publicly in her February 17, 1939, column). In lieu of his many laudable directorial contributions, Vidor remained proud of having staged Judy Garland singing "Over the Rainbow" with unsophisticated simplicity yet fluidity of motion as Dorothy meanders and muses about an untroubled life beyond her own backyard.

The Shoot: Capturing Fantasy on Celluloid

A June 8, 1938, temporary schedule for the shooting sequence of MGM's Production #1060—as *The Wizard of Oz* was officially designated—indicates not only the tentative order of scenes but also the scene numbers (as broken down in the script), how many pages each scene covered, the actors required for each scene, the accompanying songs (if any), and any special effects or trick shots required.

As it was when *Oz* originally began production under director Richard Thorpe, the first scenes were to take place at the Yellow Brick Road crossroads and cornfield in which Dorothy meets the Scarecrow. But unlike Thorpe's shooting schedule, which next captured scenes in and around the Witch's castle, the June 8 schedule calls for the *Oz* unit to convene to the set of "Forest with Apple Trees and Road (Tin Man's House)," where Thorpe was preparing to progress before his dismissal and reassignment. From there, the scenes were to flow in sequential order, with the Munchkinland scenes following those in the Witch's castle; followed by scenes in the Wizard's throne room and the Wizard departing in his balloon (for which a woodpecker was still needed). As had been the plan from the onset of production, all the Kansas scenes were to be filmed last, including Dorothy's song ("Over the Rainbow"), with Buddy Ebsen as Hickory providing accompaniment on his harmonica. But the *Oz* shooting schedule would be thrown off by Richard Thorpe's abrupt termination as director and Ebsen's unexpected illness, which caused him to sacrifice his role as the Tin Woodman.

Once Ebsen recovered from his near-fatal condition, he reported for work on *Four Girls in White* (1939) followed by *The Kid from Texas* (1939), after which his five-year contract with Metro was fulfilled and Ebsen left to freelance at other studios. He later found his

greatest success on television as George Russell, Fess Parker's sidekick on *Davy Crockett* (1954–55), as the patriarch of *The Beverly Hillbillies* (1962–71), and as the homicide sleuth *Barnaby Jones* (1973–80).

In hindsight, at six-foot-three, Ebsen as the Tin Woodman, topped with a funnel cap, would probably have appeared physically disproportionate to his costars while traipsing down the Yellow Brick Road onscreen. No matter, by November 17, 1938, the troubled *Oz* production's difficulties were summarized in the press and Ebsen's departure was distilled as follows: "Buddy Ebsen wore the Tin Woodman's metal suit for two weeks, then had to bow out of the cast, complaining of a severe chest pain. . . . If MGM had to do [*Oz*] all over again it probably wouldn't."

A REFURBISHED TIN WOODMAN

When it quickly became apparent that Buddy Ebsen would not recover in time to return to his *Wizard of Oz* role, MGM hastily contracted another actor with comparable song-and-dance talents, Jack Haley, on loan from Twentieth Century Fox. It was not the first time Haley would play proxy on account of another actor's ailment. In 1935 he was tapped to replace Eddie Cantor, who had taken ill and required a stomach operation, for a Vinton Freedley Broadway production under development.

In 1939 Haley told the *New York Sun* that he had never read the L. Frank Baum book in his childhood nor did he have time to read it once he was cast as the Tin Woodman, explaining that "working at the studio all day, you just don't have time for reading." So he only read the script. But his young son's nurse read the story to Jack Jr., who in turn kept his father informed of the fictional narrative. After conferring with others, Haley concluded that the novel wasn't solely for juveniles. "Funny how grown-ups seem to get just as much enjoyment as children out of that book," he said in August 1939. "There's a lot in it for grown-ups."

Haley was set to start on *Oz* no later than November 4, 1938, but by this time he had already begun prepping for his role and had recorded, on October 30, a new version of "The Merry Old Land of Oz" number. On December 22, 1938, Haley recorded another version of "The Jitterbug." The recording schedule noted, "Charley Haley [*sic*] replacing Buddy Ebsen's singing . . ."

In the interim, Jack Dawn altered the composition of the Tin Man makeup from a powder to a paste, thus circumventing Haley from inhaling the aluminum dust. The safe use of the powder in paste form was vetted by the Laboratory of Clinical Pathology and the Overton Laboratories. Internally, however, the chemical ingredients were still considered hazardous to wear such that when the paste was applied to Haley's face, paper shields were used over his eyes and, on set, a makeup artist was assigned to shadow him to daub away with cotton packs any sign of perspiration to avoid the aluminum seeping into his pores or running into his eyes (although exactly this did happen, leading to an eye infection that sidetracked Haley for the better part of a week).

At thirty-nine, Haley was an old vaudeville trouper. However, *The Wizard of Oz* proved to be an unimaginable grind. Haley's tedious makeup required up to two hours early each morning in order to be on set by eight in the morning. As production progressed, makeup application was honed to seventy-five minutes, according to an interview Haley gave Eileen Creelman of the *New York Sun*. Another forty minutes was needed to remove the makeup after the conclusion of each day's shoot. Haley estimated that, before the picture wrapped, he would spend a total of 540 hours in makeup alone.

Once filming began for the day, Haley was confined to a stifling costume that didn't allow him to sit down—although, like Buddy Ebsen before him, Haley was expected to dance in it. In 1939, Behind the Scenes in Hollywood columnist Harrison Carroll described the actor's predicament: "Haley's Tin Woodman suit is really made of leather, but it's like wearing a heavy suitcase for a coat and two leather golf bags for trousers." In hindsight,

Haley told Philadelphia journalist Mildred Martin that he suspected David Montgomery, Broadway's original Tin Man, had it worse. "His costume was really made of tin. Mine was made of buckram and cellophane. Even so I couldn't sit down in it."

Fifty years later Jack Haley Jr., who was five when he visited the *Oz* set, remembered, "When I first saw my father dressed in the Tin Man outfit, he had his [tin] pants off. I remember it so vividly, because going on to that set was like being at Disneyland. When they were shooting close-ups of him, they didn't have to put the whole bottom on. He couldn't sit down in that costume." More specifically, Haley was prevented from assuming a seated position because of his drum-shaped torso and "had to take the whole top off to sit down," as he complained to Eileen Creelman in August 1939. "The only time I was able to get out of that costume was when Judy Garland went to school. And I was glad when it was time for school!"

A consummate trouper, Jack Haley offset his chagrin for playing the Tin Man with one-liners about being vacuum-packed or needing to carry a can opener in case he fell and couldn't get up. Haley told Hollywood insider Jimmie Fidler, "Just today I opened a can of sardines. The one on top looked up at me and started to laugh . . . 'I'm just wondering,' it cracked, 'how long *you're* in for?'" On another occasion Fidler wrote that Haley was still grumbling. "Thought I'd been through the worst of it," Haley said, "but now they are adding insult to injury. Last evening some dizzy dame caught me standing on the curb [in costume] and tried to mail a letter in me!"

The actor was also the brunt of good-natured ribbing from friends. Tom Fizdale, columnist for *Marysville (OH) Tribune*'s Listen to This, told readers, "Now that Jack Haley's wearing silver make-up and his Tin Woodman armor for the *Wizard of Oz* film, he's ducking lots of wise cracks." Among them, "Why do people leave rusty old tin cans around?" and "Look for the date on the label." By December 1938 Haley had made it his New Year's resolution to "get out of my Tin Woodman armor before warm weather."

Concurrent with *Oz*, Haley juggled another assignment. Beginning October 14, 1938, Haley starred in his own weekly radio series broadcast over CBS, *The Wonder Show* (sponsored by Continental Baking Co., makers of Wonder Bread and Hostess Cakes), accompanied by regulars Lucille Ball, Haley's female foil; announcer Gale Gordon (later Ball's television costar); comedian Artie Auerbach; and singer Virginia Verrill.[1] It was a grueling schedule as, by day, Haley was the Tin Man, and evenings, Haley collaborated with his *Wonder Show* writers on scripting the succeeding week's radio program. By the fourth show on November 4, 1938 (by which time Haley was cast in *Oz*), the entire script parodied Haley's exhaustion working in pictures and on radio. Haley recalled the draining

---

1 Haley's contract for *The Wizard of Oz* stipulated that Metro would not hold him past three o'clock on one day of each calendar week for his radio appearances.

combination: "That was quite a winter. By the time we did the show Friday night, I was physically exhausted. Emotionally, however, I was very satisfied. I loved doing that radio show."

Haley's dual assignments provided unlikely fodder for a contemporary CBS plug. On November 19, 1938, it was reported that Haley, dressed in his "weird tin costume and silver paint that he wears for his role in *The Wizard of Oz*," showed up to a *Wonder Show* rehearsal in full *Oz* attire, inducing the page boy to believe that CBS "was re-creating the Mars broadcast for television!"—a reference to the October 30, 1938, CBS broadcast of Orson Welles's controversial radio dramatization of *The War of the Worlds* presented by *The Mercury Theatre on the Air*. By the fifteenth installment of *The Wonder Show*, on January 20, 1939, Haley's work on *Oz*'s Technicolor scenes had about wrapped, and he celebrated the occasion by incorporating an *Oz* sketch into the program.[2]

During the strenuous *Wizard of Oz* shooting schedule, Haley napped whenever possible to make up for sleep lost at night. Because lying prostrate in his Tin Man outfit wasn't practical, Haley leaned on a reclining board—which, to the layperson, resembled an angled ironing board—used by actors for relaxation when attired in unwieldy wardrobe. A 1946 account noted that "Jack can go to sleep at the drop of a nightgown anywhere, anytime, anyplace but one of his greatest performances in that respect was when he was playing his celebrated role of the 'Tin Man' in the famous picture *The Wizard of Oz* on the MGM lot. During any pauses in the shooting of the picture, Jack would wander off in his cumbersome costume, sit down somewhere and go sound asleep. They almost had to use a can opener to awaken him for his scenes."

Haley's ability to check out effortlessly drew the envy of Bert Lahr. According to columnist Leonard Lyons, the perturbed Lahr would turn to Ray Bolger and sarcastically quip, "And I can't even sleep nights in a silk-covered, soft bed." Such banter was more a matter of comedic one-upmanship than unprofessional regard. All three actors knew one another from the vaudeville circuit and legitimate theater, and maintained morale with practical jokes in what was termed "a gagging feud." As reported by Jimmie Fidler on February 1, 1939, Haley apparently bribed the hairdresser who was marcelling Lahr's lion wig to short-circuit the curling iron, giving Lahr a shock that "made him break all high-jump records." Lahr retaliated when Haley snoozed on a reclining board in his Tin Man suit and Haley awoke to discover his outfit papered with tomato-can labels.

During this period, Jack Haley added something more to his brimming plate. Hollywood in the 1930s was a welcome diversion for the workaday public from the toils of the Depression, and its movie star elite were both revered and emulated as social models. At

---

2 Haley's work on *The Wizard of Oz* officially concluded on February 25, 1939, after the actor filmed his portions of the Kansas sequence.

a time when appearances mattered and publicity could advance (or kill) careers, the Haley household welcomed a child whom the press called "adopted." Adoption by celebrities was not unheard of. In 1935 Loretta Young famously camouflaged her lovechild with Clark Gable as an adoption; Wallace Beery adopted Carol Ann, daughter of his second wife's cousin, and in December 1939, Beery was said to have adopted a seven-month-old baby girl, the intentions of which he had announced to Harrison Carroll at the *Wizard of Oz* premiere; and in 1940, Joan Crawford adopted Christina, the first of her four adopted children. But the Haleys' new addition wasn't an infant. Simultaneous with *The Wizard of Oz*, the Haleys became parents to "Jimmy," a ten-year-old orphan with a reputation for being unadoptable in welfare circles. (Jack and his wife Florence were already biological parents to son "Jackie" Jr. and daughter Gloria.)

To promote Haley's role as the Tin Woodman, a photo shoot was arranged in the Haleys' Beverly Hills home. The setup was for Haley to pose while reciting a passage from

The Wizard of Oz novel to Jimmy and Haley's nephews Robert (a future congressman) and Donald Dornan. Jackie would be seated closest to his father on a sofa while the others looked on. According to a 1939 notice in *Modern Screen*, Jimmy was considered Haley's boy: "It looked like Jack Haley's role of the Tin Woodman in *The Wizard of Oz* was going to prove too much to survive. Every night on arriving home his three children and two visiting nephews would demand to hear the entire day's events and the most exciting scenes reenacted."

What might've been "too much to survive" was Jimmy, who was reportedly a royal hellion. Already a veteran of previously unsuccessful placements, he was described in 1939 as a ruffian who "sometimes nicked furniture and broke an occasional vase and ran around the house like a little Indian." For the *Oz* publicity portrait, he wears a Black-Foxe Military Institute uniform. From its 1928 inception, Black-Foxe, located on Wilshire Boulevard in L.A., was the era's tough-love academy otherwise known as a dumping ground for Hollywood offspring, especially the unruly ones. Beyond 1939 Jimmy's fate is unknown but his fleeting, failed adoption by the Haleys was quickly hushed up and forgotten. He was cropped out of the official portrait released by MGM of Jack Haley reading from *The Wizard of Oz*. The still, as it is now known by *Oz* fans, is a tight shot of Haley with only Jack Jr. Nor is Jimmy mentioned in Haley's posthumous autobiography, which collected the actor's personal and professional remembrances. Apparently, Jimmy was simply too much for the Tin Man's heart to bear.

A FRESH START

It was at about the time that Richard Thorpe was replaced as *Oz*'s director that MGM divided into two camps, those who unconditionally supported Mervyn LeRoy's vision and those jaded studio veterans who resented LeRoy as a Johnny-come-lately for receiving an irrational and disproportionate salary. Published reports of LeRoy wearing dollar shirts and imported silk underwear, or paying a thousand dollars for a lifetime membership to Earl Carroll's new restaurant, didn't ingratiate LeRoy to the studio's laborers, technicians, and tradespeople.

Among this faction, LeRoy was referred to cynically as "Mr. Brink," the personification of death from the successful Broadway play *On Borrowed Time*—the screen rights to which Metro acquired in June 1938, and the screenplay of which was under development simultaneous to *Oz*'s production. LeRoy was so named because his enemies gloated that he was ruining *Oz* with the "kiss of death." The introduction of Victor Fleming, considered the studio's troubleshooter, was surely a source of embarrassment for LeRoy, proof positive that he was every bit as much "up a tree" as was the Mr. Brink of *On Borrowed Time*.

Amid uncertainty for the future of *The Wizard of Oz*, a lone journalist came to Mervyn LeRoy's defense. In his November 12, 1938, column, *Boxoffice* editor Ivan Spear devoted his entire write-up to the Hollywood rumor mill that predicted "a literal avalanche of 'it-can't-be-dones'" from doubting Thomases in the film-making community. Spear contended that LeRoy was a showman in the true sense of the word who was attempting to capture the "warmth, sentiment and fantasy of the Baum original and, at the same time, make it appealing both to the children of the present day and those adults who enjoyed the [Oz] books as kids at the turn of the century." Citing LeRoy's intelligent, painstaking preparations for *Oz*'s production, Spear advised confidence in the producer and accurately foretold that LeRoy's expensive trip to fairyland would "pay dividends to all concerned—studio, exhibitors and theatre patrons alike."

With Victor Fleming at the helm, work on *The Wizard of Oz* cautiously progressed, and on November 4, 1938, the film resumed production. The scenes shot were of Dorothy's first encounter with the Scarecrow, remaking the same scenes originally filmed by Richard Thorpe. This was reportedly the day on which yet another holdup occurred. Jimmy, a trained raven, was to have a big-screen cameo but ended up bringing the company to a standstill when he decided to fly up into the rafters and refused to be coaxed down, thus bringing the day's shoot to a halt. (From then on, Jimmy had a raven standby named Coco as backup.) Production took up the following day on the same set, which was officially titled "Crossroad/Land of Oz."

With Judy Garland's new appearance as Dorothy now set, MGM photographer Virgil Apger took publicity photographs of her posing with Toto the following day, November 5, 1938. Portraits from this early sitting would eventually become widely disseminated in the press, reprinted in pictorial layouts and advertisements for *Oz*.

Thus, under the directorial reliability of Victor Fleming, *Oz* proceeded but behind closed doors. MGM's policy on studio visitors infiltrating its soundstages was definitive, as pointedly stated in a 1939 brochure, *Your Visit to Metro-Goldwyn-Mayer*, which notes that the admission of those "privileged to tour the lot" is a "precarious undertaking." There was only one daily tour, which began at two thirty weekdays with a no-cameras-permitted policy. Even so, the *Oz* set was strictly closed to all outside visitors, especially press during the tenuous transition of directors. Sleuthing journalists could only get vague fragments of what was going on behind the stage walls. The Hollywood reporter for the *Mail* (Adelaide, South Australia), said the set was closed because "officials don't want the chicaneries of film making in this special instance revealed to the public. Judy Garland is the dreamer [in *Oz*]. I saw her later strolling round, and she merely hinted at the wonderful magic that was going on behind those sealed doors." May Mann of the *Ogden* (UT) *Standard-Examiner* told readers of her December 9, 1938, column that despite the moratorium on visitors, she peeked in the door even though *Oz* was still a closed set. Mann was able to see Jack Haley in his Tin Man getup, but Haley would only comment on his "heavy and stiff" costume.

November 6–11, 1938, found the company shooting scenes in the apple orchard and Tin Man's cottage sets. In keeping with L. Frank Baum's description that the Ozian countryside was populated by birds of rare and unusual plumage, MGM rented additional, uncommon avians from the Los Angeles Zoo as part of the attraction's successful plan to raise funds for food and care of the animals (elephants, bears, and deer were also leased for work in pictures). The birds, reportedly the largest group to be trained for the movies, would lend an otherworldly ambience to the settings. In a couple of instances, a sarus crane nearly upstaged the actors on the Tin Woodman set by spreading its substantial wingspan on camera, and catching Ray Bolger off-guard by attacking his straw filling—which caused the dancer to beat a hasty retreat.

Jack Haley was still acclimating himself to maneuvering about the set in his wardrobe and had to exercise special precautions. In 1939 it was reported that during the scene in which Haley struts down to the Yellow Brick Road from the wooded glen where his Tin Man is discovered, he lost his balance and fell over backwards. Unable to right himself in the cumbersome costume, Haley was rescued by Pop Arnold, head camera grip. "The tin shirt was pinching my windpipe and I couldn't get my breath," Haley gasped. "I hope that doesn't happen again—at least not when I'm alone some place." Victor Fleming took due precaution, saying, "From now on, Arnold, you watch Jack wherever he goes. A sort of keeper of the Tin Woodman."

The *Wizard of Oz* shoot was belabored for its use of Technicolor and trick effects but also for Metro's obsessive attention to minute detail. In 1978 Ray Bolger noted, "We had to match everything that had been filmed the day before. In my case, the straw had to be precisely placed to match the way it was in the last shot we had made—but the very second that I moved, the straw would be dislodged. Perhaps no one would ever know the difference, but that's the way they worked in those days." According to an August 1939 interview Jack Haley gave New York journalist Eileen Creelman, so much of the time lost on *The Wizard of Oz* was spent either waiting for adjustments to be made to the huge lights necessary for Technicolor photography or waiting while Judy Garland broke away from the company for tutoring sessions. "Time is what ate up all the money on that picture," Haley informed Creelman. "Sometimes we'd all have to sit around for an hour—I'd be reclining on that board—while Judy was studying social science or something like that." In one specific instance, however, the delay was entirely avoidable and, as fate would have it, the incident involved Haley and occurred on or about the morning of November 11, 1938.

In his December 29, 1938, column, Frederick C. Othman recapped the alarming circumstances and quoted Jack Haley as saying, "They put me in [Buddy] Ebsen's tin suit and I carried on. For three days I worked in a shiny suit of tin with a sparkling tin nose, a bright tin strap around my chin, a glistening tin pot on my head and a coat of brilliant tin paint on my face. I glittered to no end—for three days." This was all before, as Othman called it, "somebody got to reading the original book once more. As he read *The Wizard of Oz* once more, his heart sank. The script called for the Tin Woodman to have been caught in the rain two years before [*sic*], and to be covered with rust."

From the set, director Victor Fleming called Mervyn LeRoy, who gave the edict that *The Wizard of Oz* would be done right or not at all. With the executive decision made to reshoot the prior three days of filming, the previously shot footage with Haley was scrapped at a costly loss, estimated at sixty thousand dollars, which translates to over one million dollars when adjusted for today's inflation. (This figure was derived from the production per diem rate of a twenty thousand dollars minimum.) Immediately, Haley's makeup was removed and his costume was taken to be chemically spackled so to appear authentically corroded.

With little to do during the wait time, Jack Haley had the afternoon off and wandered over to the MGM commissary, where he vented his predicament to Ed Sullivan. New makeup and wardrobe tests were done with the actor on November 12, 1938, and retakes of the Tin Man scenes took place from November 15 to November 19, with Haley now appearing rusty. These scenes included the "If I Only Had a Heart" song and dance and the reprise of "We're Off to See the Wizard."

The next scenes were those performed on the Lion Forest set on November 21–22, 1938. On November 26 the famous dance down the Yellow Brick Road departing the forest took place. The notion that Ray Bolger, Jack Haley, and Bert Lahr deliberately crowded out Judy Garland to their own advantage for this shot, as Garland told it to TV host Jack Paar in 1962, is a falsity. The original blueprint for the Lion Forest set clearly shows a significant widening of the road where the encounter with Lahr's character occurs and a narrowing of the pathway where the principals exit the scene. There simply wasn't space enough for each to dance comfortably four abreast in the unseemly wardrobe. For the long shot of the quartet exiting the scene, Bob Weatherwax, nephew of Toto's co-trainer Jack Weatherwax, recalled that Jack was in the bushes to the left of the actors, and after they passed he pushed the dog out of the shrubs and into camera range on the Yellow Brick Road.

Tuesday, November 29, 1938, was a rare day for which Judy Garland was not required to be on set. The scene was that of Dorothy's friends at the top of the cliff overlooking the Witch's castle. Though final shots were done on a soundstage, Alexander Kahn of the United Press claimed an exterior set in a rear corner of MGM's back lot was used. The set in question was a group of outdoor cliffs known as the "Leper Rocks," originally constructed for the leper sequence of *Ben Hur* (1925). Kahn wrote that the cliffs were most recently employed "for the mountain climb of Bert Lahr, Jack Haley and Ray Bolger in *The Wizard of Oz*." It is unknown if there was initial thought given to shooting this scene outdoors, or if the Leper Rocks were used for blocking or rehearsing the scene pending construction of the set.

The following day, November 30, 1938, scenes in the courtyard of the Witch's castle were shot, and December 1–3 was for scenes in the entrance hall of the Witch's castle. The Witch's melting scene is also believed to have been shot during this period. Judy Garland told *Oakland (CA) Tribune* journalist Alice L. Tildesley that she found the witch-melting act tedious. "I've been pouring water on the old witch in *Wizard of Oz* all morning," scoffed Judy. "It might have been fun once. But it gets tiresome." Garland's expression of boredom was echoed by that of Jack Haley, who recalled that most often the actors were taxed with feigning fear.

It was also at this time that the *Oz* rumor mill received some much-needed damage control. Alexander Kahn's December 5, 1938, column served as a mini–history lesson for those unfamiliar with L. Frank Baum or the acclaimed *Wizard of Oz* Broadway show. Kahn declared that the film version "is expected to achieve feats which Baum only described in fancy," noting "even the Kansas cyclone becomes a realistic thing as created by a Hollywood wind machine." Kahn's timing was both a fortuitous and welcome reprieve for the LeRoy Unit, especially as the Munchkin scenes—the picture's most involved segment—were pending.

For December 9–10, 1938, filming took place in the expansive poppy field set. In 1949 electrician Floyd Porter recalled his biggest job at MGM was lighting the 300-by-200-foot indoor set for *The Wizard of Oz*. Much irony was made in 1939, as the field required forty thousand artificial blossoms while thousands of acres of real poppies bloomed not far from MGM. Following these scenes, production was preparing for the extensive Munchkinland sequence.

WELCOME TO MUNCHKINLAND

When actress Billie Burke's services for another picture were being negotiated for a loan-out to Hal Roach in mid-October 1938, it was projected that her commitment to *The Wizard of Oz* would last from approximately November 9 to December 5, 1938. But it wouldn't be until December 17, 1938, that the Munchkinland scenes were ready to be filmed with Burke as Glinda. According to a February 2, 1939, interoffice memo, on December 29 and 30, 1938, Victor Fleming was shooting the very first part of the Munchkin sequence, which included the shot of Dorothy opening her farmhouse door. These two days of filming concluded the Munchkin scenes.

Previously, between December 14 and 16, 1938, the vocal tracks for the Munchkin music were recorded with Judy Garland and Billie Burke, with other vocal artists taking the part of Munchkins. Among such "specialty" performers voicing various Munchkin roles were two freelance mimics with a connection to Walt Disney, Pinto Colvig and Billy Bletcher. Bletcher was the voice of Pete, Mickey Mouse's bully-rival as well as the Big Bad Wolf in Disney's *The Three Little Pigs*. Colvig was the speaking voice of Disney's Practical Pig in *The Three Little Pigs* and the voices of Sleepy and Grumpy in *Snow White and the Seven Dwarfs*. But in 1938 Colvig's best-known character vocal was for Disney's anthropomorphic dog Goofy. On *Oz* Colvig's "wild dialogue," meaning speaking parts without musical accompaniment, included the deaf Munchkin asking "Which old witch?" and one of the three Lollipop Guild characters. Bletcher's included solo parts such as declaring that Dorothy will be "his-tory" and that she'll "be a bust" in the Munchkin Hall of Fame. The voices of both men would be distorted to a "pip-squeak" pitch as one might imagine issuing from a Munchkin.

By March 1939 Colvig had compiled his memoir and recalled recording musical takes with actual little people and not just professional "cartoon vocalizers," as he referred to himself and Bletcher. As Colvig recalled it:

Never have I worked with a happier and more willing group of show-people than those little troupers. One of them was celebrating his fifty-fourth birthday with a quart of Scotch (half his own size) which had been given to him as a present. The little fellow was feeling "high, wide and squeaky" and getting into everybody's hair with his quips and pranks, but not wanting the [musical] director to know of his condition, he kept hiding himself in the center of the group chorus.

During the recording of "The Witch Song," one piping voice stood out above the rest. The possessor of the voice was sought out and told, with good reason, to go home and sleep off the effects of his birthday celebration and to forget about singing that ding-donging song about how the witch had turned up dead. The problem was this: for "the Witch Song," the little guy had gotten his B's and W's mixed!

As a validation of Colvig's recollection, there exists a notation on the December 15, 1938, "Daily Music Report" for Oz that indicates "3 midgets" were recorded on thirteen different takes—where most other takes seldom went beyond a half dozen.

With The Wizard of Oz on track and in good form in Victor Fleming's capable hands, Munchkinland was the first major set open to Metro's stars as well as select studio visitors in December 1938. It was a glorious affair in miniature, with its central pavilion, lily pond, guard house, civic center, and rows of thatched huts that resembled mushroom caps. Cellophane hollyhocks, rising high about the dwellings, accented the environment in keeping with Baum's description that "banks of gorgeous flowers" were prevalent throughout the countryside. On December 14, 1938, Variety proclaimed Munchkinland "the tallest interior set" in MGM history with a "central tower ninety feet high."

The reception to Munchkinland was so encouraging that Mervyn LeRoy told news reporters he was planning to re-erect the entire miniature village at the impending 1939 World's Fair in New York. In fact, the January 4, 1939, edition of Variety reported that LeRoy had completed negotiations to operate a "Wizard of Oz concession with 116 midgets" at the fair, and that the Munchkin village set would be dismantled and shipped in sections to Flushing, New York, for rebuilding on the fairgrounds. There was a little-people village at the 1939 World's Fair in which some of the extras who were Munchkins participated, but the attraction was not known to have had a Wizard of Oz connection.[3]

Telling the little people apart from children could prove difficult. As makeup man Del Armstrong said, "The type of makeup made them all look alike except when one walked by smoking a long cigar." This also caused confusion for extended family of the makeup

3 By December 28, 1939, Charles Grutzner Jr. of the Brooklyn (NY) Daily Eagle reported that when the fair reopened in May 1940, the ailing kiddie-concession area would be transformed. "A glittering Emerald City, like that in The Wizard of Oz, may be one of the innovations in the general rebuilding of the Children's World. There's nothing certain yet, but Warner Brothers [sic] are dickering to take over the concession and put some life, including a Cowardly Lion, Tin Man, Scarecrow, and the Wizard himself, into the place."

234

artists. During production of *The Wizard of Oz*, Ethel Miles, wife of Ray Bolger's makeup man Norbert, heard the doorbell one day and, looking out through a window in the door, saw no one. The doorbell rang again and when Ethel opened the door, she found some children calling on her son Terry, who also worked on *Oz* as a makeup artist. She told them they couldn't see him and closed the door in their faces, wondering why a bunch of little kids would want to talk to her adult son. As it turned out, the "children" were some of the Munchkins!

Actress Rita Johnson, en route to work in Metro's *Broadway Serenade*, was similarly duped. One December morning while driving to the studio, she saw a boy with his thumb in the universal hitchhiking position. Johnson stopped, thinking she was giving a school-child a lift, but to her amazement, the tiny person turned out to be a fellow coworker and one of the little people performing in *The Wizard of Oz*.

Five-year-old Jack Haley Jr. had his own foolproof mode of discernment. "It was easy to know who the adults were," he recalled in 1989. "You see, as a child, I hated eggs. In the morning when the Munchkins came on the set some of them would have egg in their moustaches. I knew they were adults in spite of their size because I rationalized that no kid would eat eggs for breakfast."

Donna Jean Johnson was among the little girls who could perform well enough to pass for female Munchkins, primarily in background shots. Her agent at the time was Sue Carol, actor Alan Ladd's wife. It was Carol who notified Johnson's mother about the *Wizard of Oz* opportunity and facilitated her getting the gig. For Johnson, filmmaking was a trying ordeal, as she remembered it in 1998:

> I was blonde and tiny for six, and I could sing and I could dance . . . I was terrified the whole time I was on the set because of the midgets. They were mean! They would bump into you and say mean things to you . . . ask me who I was going to be when I grew up. "You sure think you're cute, don't you?" I remember those comments. I remember the odor of the midgets sweating. Kids don't sweat like adults do . . . I was scared the whole time I was on the set. There were people everyplace, people yelling—almost like an otherworld feeling. It was also the largest set I'd ever been on.

Aside from the professionally trained children, teaching over a hundred little people to dance for the Munchkinland musical sequence was another challenge. Given the restrictions of their limbs, *Oz* choreographer Bobby Connolly started by measuring the length of the little peoples' strides to determine the dance moves of which they might be capable. To accomplish this, he put chalk on the soles of several of their shoes and had them walk the floor of his dance studio at different speeds. Once the average length of their dancing strides was established, routines for the entire group were developed. Because the steps of typical-size dancers are longer, no normal dance routines could be used as a model for the Munchkin dancers.

Many of the little people were relatively inexperienced, as Connolly asserted in a 1939 interview. "Most of them knew nothing about dancing," said Connolly, "so we had to lay out chalk lines on the stage floor to guide them in getting into position for formations. Then we trained them for days in the lockstep, in order that they would learn to keep time to the music. And finally we worked on individual steps."

According to Margaret Pellegrini, who played a Munchkin villager, one of Connolly's assistant choreographers took over once the steps were set. In a 1994 interview, Pellegrini remembered, "Dona Massin showed everyone the steps. Those that could do it were put in the front [of the crowd scenes]." Prince Denis, another Munchkin actor, recalled that most of the hard work involved coordinating the choreography with lip-synching to the lyrics of "Ding-Dong! The Witch Is Dead." "We never used our own voices," he said in 1980. "They were dubbed in. Somebody else said our lines which were then re-recorded to make them sound that way [i.e., high-pitched]." Australian reporter Lon Jones told of watching over a hundred little people trying to learn the tune, as Clark Gable also looked on. When Gable cracked to the rehearsal pianist, "Why don't you use halftones for these little fellows?" the Munchkins gave him the raspberry.

Apparently even Toto required Bobby Connolly's services. "The dog had to take its cues from its trainer," Connolly said, "and that would have been all right except that the trainer was stone [i.e., tone] deaf. So I'd give him his beats just a fraction of an instant ahead of time, and thus when relayed to the dog, the beats came out on time. It required a lot of figuring." This statement is validated by a March 1939 report that noted Connolly "taught the dog Toto to dance on his [sic] hind legs," and by Bob Weatherwax, who confirmed that his uncle Jack did, in fact, teach dance routines to dogs.

While Toto is not seen actually performing in any dance sequence in the finished film, there may have been a tidbit deleted in which the dog keeps time with the Munchkin army. The scene in question occurs at the reprise of "Ding-Dong! The Witch Is Dead" in Munch-kinland. As the music begins, Toto—for no apparent reason—trips down the steps of the town hall, where he has been standing with Dorothy, and falls in line behind the marching Munchkin soldiers. This may have been the lead-in for the dance moves to which Connolly was referring.

With Busby Berkeley unavailable, Bobby Connolly was Mervyn LeRoy's second choice as dance director for *The Wizard of Oz*. Connolly's selection also had a Warner Bros. con-nection, as it was he who staged "The Boy From Harlem," a musical nightclub sequence in LeRoy's *Fools for Scandal*. While it was Connolly who got the press—and the screen credit—for choreography on *Oz*, including the elaborate Munchkinland sequence, it was Dona Massin and, particularly, Arthur Appell who picked up the slack. Appell was known as "Cowboy," the nickname given to him by entertainer Jack Oakie during their time on a Montana ranch.

According to Appell's daughter Victoria in a 2014 interview: "[Appell] did most, if not all, of the dance choreography himself on the picture as Bobby Connolly was not around much due to heavy drinking, and Arthur Freed promised him the credit for the picture if he would take over the choreography. This Arthur Freed did not do. My father was so well loved and liked by all and he was not one to boast or exaggerate his accomplishments as some in the industry did, so I fully believe this was true." Arthur Appell bitterly remarked that he'd be surprised if Connolly worked an entire week on *Oz*. Thereafter, Appell was very disillusioned by what happened with his lack of credit, and never particularly wanted to see *Oz* when it was shown on TV years later.

On occasion, the purported antics of a few of *Oz*'s little people came into question, perpetuated most famously by Judy Garland herself. Garland referred to the lot of them as "little drunks," claiming the Munchkins "got smashed every night," as she told talk show host Jack Paar during an interview televised in 1967. Similarly, *Oz* screenwriter Noel Langley bluntly summed them up as "The wildest, little whoring rascals you ever saw," adding, "They had to put up guards around the chorus girls to keep order on the set."

In 1970 Langley recounted an infamous anecdote that even in 1939 made the rounds in print, albeit in discrete jargon. A Munchkin scene was delayed until one of the little actors could be dislodged from having fallen into a regular-size toilet, allegedly inebriated. In his January 3, 1939, column, Harrison Carroll's blind item alluded to the incident, "Get Whitey Hendry, head of MGM studio police, to tell you the hilarious mishap that occurred to one of the midgets in *The Wizard of Oz*." In 1971 Ray Bolger recalled what happened next. "We were all looking for him. And we found him too! Apparently, he drank his lunch, sat on the stool, fell into it and couldn't get out. There he was with his head and legs stuck up!" Whether truth or fiction, Hedda Hopper identified the little person in question as Billy Curtis and, tongue-in-cheek, said that actor Nelson Eddy, MGM's prize baritone, had rushed in to rescue Curtis from drowning.

Oz makeup man Jack Young remembered some of the Munchkin rabble-rousers also. "The [Oz] Christmas party was really a ball," penned Young in his unpublished memoir. "I will never forget two little midgets, really loaded, staggering down the studio street, each one clasping a bottle of champagne almost as big as they were. Whitey Hendry, the studio Chief of Police, had to bail out two female midgets charged with prostitution."

Then in his late twenties and rather the playboy, Young was no saint himself. "One little one made a play for me," he wrote. "She was about three-foot, eight-inches tall. She said she was twenty-three. I couldn't get it out of my head that she was just a baby. When we talked, I would lift her up and set her on the table. Her voice was high and she had a European accent. She was trying to lure me to her apartment and I, amused, played along. The conversation went something like this":

I said, "If I did come up, what would you do?"

She replied, arching her eyebrows and looking quite coquettish, "I would mix you a cocktail."

"And then what would you do?"

"I would cook you a great Christmas dinner."

"Then?"

She lowered her eyelashes and sort of giggled, wiggled her little body, and murmured, "I'm twenty-three."

Prior Oz histories have documented Judy Garland's promotion from contract player to star at the time of shooting the Munchkinland sequence. MGM ceremoniously presented her with a mobile dressing room of her own—a symbol of having attained a critical, popular, and financial status at the studio. But this was not Garland's first and only portable dressing room. *Motion Picture* for February 1938 told of Garland's pride for her "tiny square green-room on wheels—nothing elaborate or fussy," that had previously belonged to actress Marie Dressler. However, the Oz trailer was larger and the first custom-decorated for Garland's exclusive use. Munchkin player Margaret Pellegrini was among the extras who recalled that Judy generously allowed the little people to walk through her new quarters. Six months later, though, Garland nearly burned down her new trailer when she was cooking on an electric plate and the curtains caught fire, damaging her dressing table before the flames were put out.

Decades afterward Judy Garland was still fondly recalled by surviving Munchkin players who enjoyed their on-set rapport with the child star between takes. Charley Becker, who played the Munchkin Mayor, remembered his camaraderie with the actress in 1962: "Of course, Judy Garland was the real star. She became a favorite of mine." Jerry Maren defined Garland as "a typical teenager" who would always greet the Munchkin group with a friendly wave and a "Hi gang!" "She loved us as much as we loved her," he said. "We fell in love with her."

Production of the Munchkin segment for *The Wizard of Oz* was the first time any little-person group had been gathered in such a great number, anywhere—a unique precursor to Little People of America conventions. Jerry Maren recalled his awe in 1971: "Until I arrived in Hollywood, I had seen only one other midget in my entire life. It was great to see all those other little people and to know that I wasn't really that different."

Most others were consumed by the magnitude of the Hollywood opportunity, even those who had previously appeared onscreen. In February 1940 Munchkin performer Prince Denis reflected, "*The Wizard of Oz* was the biggest picture we were ever in. We think it is the biggest picture ever made. Before it, both my wife and myself had appeared in *The Terror of Tiny Town*." Charles Royale, who, with his sisters Helen and Stella, was also among the Munchkin clan, said in June 1939 that the excitement trumped the grind: "Out there in Hollywood we had to get up at five in the morning when we were working on the picture! But even at that—we liked it!" And Harry Doll, who appeared in *Oz* with his three "little" sisters, concurred: "It's really going to be a nice picture . . . Judy goes to sleep, you see, and when she wakes up, why she's in the land of the little people . . . and in Technicolor, too!"

As daughter of *Oz* alum James "Chip" Gaither, the picture's sound technician, and dancer Loie Gaither, Michelle Kutasi said her mother recalled that everyone loved the little people. "Ninety-nine percent of the studio personnel loved working with them. They had so much fun!" L. Frank Baum's grandson, Stanton, remembered the Munchkins' playful camaraderie. "If they were supposed to have a little group line up to greet Dorothy, they would just leap-frog up to her. Of course that wasn't in the movie!" In 1998 MGM actress Ann Rutherford recalled that the Munchkin players "had such an enthusiasm because they had never encountered anything like the glamour of a studio."

Indeed, most of the Munchkin clan were duly starstruck; one of the young lady little people supposedly swooned when she saw Clark Gable. The closest sixteen-year-old Margaret Pellegrini got to Gable was seeing his double, Philip Harron, who portrayed a Winkie in *Oz*. Pellegrini also mistook stunt double Bobbie Koshay for Judy Garland, saying, "I thought she *was* Judy—that's how much I knew!"

On December 23, 1938, Milton Harker, International News Service correspondent, quipped that MGM's movie stars were going to spend Christmas with writer's cramp now that the Munchkins had all become "autograph conscious." According to Harold Heffernan, Billie Burke visited the Munchkinland set before filming her own scenes and was beset by fifty little people seeking her autograph, including one who seemed awkwardly silent. Another little person piped up, asking Burke, "Will you please sign for this chap? He can't ask you because he can't talk." To the surprise of those present, Burke responded by engaging with the nonverbal man using sign language, and the two were said to have had an animated conversation. Afterward, Burke explained, "Haven't talked sign language since I went to school. We mastered it as kids and used it behind our books."

Milton Harker reported that Billie Burke signed all autograph books in one day and that "Judy Garland, Jack Haley, Joan Crawford and Wallace Beery have been doing a lot of signing." Harker added that all the little people were patiently awaiting face time with Robert Taylor, Norma Shearer, and Clark Gable. Victor McLaglen posed for pictures and Norma Shearer supposedly lost a poker game to some of the little men. On another occasion, Shearer brought her children Irving and Katherine to see Munchkinland—it was the children's second visit to a movie set, the first having been to see their mother on the *Marie Antoinette* soundstage. Spencer Tracy brought daughter Susie to the set, but she only sighed and pined to look like actress Hedy Lamarr when she grew up.

It is uncertain if the offspring guests of MGM's elite were random visitors or if there was a select opportunity set aside by which the studio threw open the Munchkinland set for a festive occasion. The latter scenario was recalled by studio carpenter Lester Dranbur, who reunited with Margaret Hamilton on the set of television's *Car 54, Where Are You?* in 1963. "Do you remember the party they had for our children on the Munchkinland set before it was torn down?" Dranbur asked the actress. "I remember every detail," Hamilton replied, "but my son, who was three-and-a-half then, doesn't even remember being there."

Ed Sullivan observed that when Wallace Beery visited the Munchkinland set, he was "discussing the weather with a group of *Wizard of Oz* midgets." Apparently, a number of the little people were taken off-guard by the California climate. During a torrential downpour, they were seen gingerly stepping on boards to cross puddles while loudly complaining. "This is nothing," Billy Curtis told them. "If you'd been here last year when it really rained, you'd all be washed down the drain pipes."

Not surprisingly, the little-person invasion became the butt of similar jokes. One that circulated about the studio went like this: "I didn't get a wink of sleep last night on the train. There was a midget pacing the berth above me." Accustomed to name-calling, this sort of ribbing would have generally been taken in stride, but the group was collectively adamant about posing for gag photographs. "They refused," reported *Stage* magazine, "to be pictured in any way but the most conventional still formation."

Silver Screen reporter Paul Karel found the Munchkins most fascinating during his visit to the *Wizard of Oz* set. "Over two hundred [*sic*] of these tiny people are secreted away in apartments in Culver City during the day and work only at night so as not to arouse too deep a curiosity. Each of these small characters presents a unique makeup problem. They are given apple cheeks, bulbous noses, pink, green and magenta beards." Ed Sullivan, accustomed to all manner of startling sights in Hollywood, confessed his astonishment when visiting MGM; he rounded a corridor and found the passageway "jammed with little men." Grace Wilcox found the little people totally unappealing when complaining of her encounter in Gotham Delicatessen and Restaurant on Hollywood Boulevard, gibing that she nearly stepped on four or five of them when they got underfoot, adding, "Out of make-up, they look anything but Sweet Sixteen. Some of them have enough wrinkles to make a map of Czechoslovakia, in its revised form."

Some published reports about the Munchkin actors served as primitive educational primers for the public at large. They bought their clothing in children's departments but had their shoes specially made; a store in New York catered to their scaled-down needs, even to miniature furniture; their stomachs are child-size but "they eat as much as a normal adult"; and some of them start growing again at any age, "which is why the Lilliputian fraternity never checks a midget's official height until he dies."

Those little people who received press by name included Billy Curtis; Charley Becker, the Munchkin mayor, who reportedly served as the chef for the group lodged at the Culver City Hotel; and Jerry Marenghi, later shortened to "Maren," who at the time was supposedly sweet on little Jeanette Fern, playing a Munchkin villager. It was said that the pair met "under a toadstool" while making *Oz*, and Maren remarked that Jeanette was "pretty as a doll."

While the press made much of the unique cadre of little people, another incident, well-known to *Oz* aficionados, was largely suppressed. A timing mishap during Margaret

Hamilton's fiery exit in Munchkinland on December 28, 1938, caused the actress's witch hat and broom straws to ignite and scorch her face and hand severely. According to a January 5, 1939, memo, Hamilton "suffered first degree burns on her face and second degree burns on her hand." MGM provided that "Miss Hamilton is not to be taken off salary during the period she is incapacitated" and estimated that "she will be able to resume her work in a week or ten days." The studio also absorbed the ninety-dollar doctor bill from Hamilton's attending physician, Dr. Stanley W. Immerman.

Makeup artist Charles Schram recalled that prop man Mack Johnson also suffered burns (and required heavily salved bandaging) for beating out Hamilton's flames with his bare hands as makeup man Jack Young and an assistant worked to gingerly remove Hamilton's wig and makeup. In retrospect, Stanton Baum recalled how crowded the set was, making it "kind of easy to understand [how the accident could have occurred]; they were fighting so much for space."

One would think that MGM would have hushed up the incident to avoid any further negative press about its troubled *Wizard of Oz* production, but Hedda Hopper informed readers of it in her January 13, 1939, column: "Margaret Hamilton as the Witch made her entrance through a trap door with flames shooting up a shaft and had her face badly burned while doing it."

Another Oz-related malady requires clarification. On March 10, 1939, Billie Burke, who portrayed Glinda the Beautiful Witch of the North, tripped leaving the set, reportedly breaking two bones in her ankle, and was hospitalized at Cedars of Lebanon for a week before being released with a cast. The incident was announced in the press-at-large with accounts of Burke's daughter, Patricia, chartering a plane after learning of the accident by radio; how cast and crew sent a huge bouquet of spring flowers to Burke's hospital room; and how Burke's look-alike double, Estelle Ettere, filled in on camera as needed. The picture, however, was not *The Wizard of Oz*, as has been previously reported, but *Maiden Voyage* (released on May 26 as *Bridal Suite*).

Any confusion about on which movie set the injury occurred can be traced to Billie Burke herself. In July 1939 she erroneously told journalist Inez Wallace, "My last work was in *The Wizard of Oz*. While working on that picture I tripped over a cable on the set and broke my ankle. The studio was very nice about it—they 'shot around me,' as we say, until I was better." The Oz connection also bears true in the postponement of retakes for Judy Garland and Burke. A notice in the *Hollywood Reporter* on May 6, 1939, indicated that, though Herbert Stothart and Georgie Stoll finished the musical scoring of Oz on May 5, the "feature will get an editing polish after washup shots of Billie Burke, who has been laid up with a leg fracture, and Judy Garland." Likewise, the *Fitchburg (MA) Sentinel* clarified on May 16, 1939, "Billie Burke expects to discard the cast from her injured ankle soon and will then finish work on two scenes of *The Wizard of Oz* which were being delayed pending her recovery."

After the Munchkinland scenes concluded, additional opportunities were presented to certain members of the Munchkin ensemble. But not every *Oz* little person was attracted to the lure of show business. In 1981 Parnell St. Aubin, a Munchkin soldier, found the movie industry anything but glamorous, saying, "There were too many distractions in Hollywood and I didn't go for it." Some of the little people stayed in Los Angeles and took temporary assignments doubling as Munchkins for *Oz*-related events or appearing as extras in *Tarzan Finds a Son!* It was announced that a group of male little people would be made up as pygmies for *Tarzan*, but the roles were changed to chimpanzees. Yvonne Moray, one of the Munchkin Lullaby League ballerinas, found work as a singer and dancer at the Jade Club in Hollywood.

Prince Denis and his wife, Ethel, both Munchkins in *Oz*, said that they toured for several weeks at openings of *The Wizard of Oz* and played repeat dates in larger cities when *Oz* went into second-run theaters. They also appeared in a sideshow operated by Johnny Bejanno, right-hand man of Robert Ripley, of "Ripley's Believe It or Not!" Billed as "*The Wizard of Oz* midgets," the Denises appeared in the huge, circus-style show alongside fourteen attractions, including Lionel, the boy with the face of a lion, and "Sea Tiny," a mermaid. As early as December 1940, however, Prince Denis began deceptively claiming he played opposite Judy Garland in *Oz* as the Munchkin Mayor, Charley Becker's role.

When *The Wizard of Oz* premiered in Philadelphia, Maurice Gable of the Boyd Theatre arranged for several little people, wearing Munchkin wardrobe on loan from MGM, to ride throughout the city, attracting attention and drumming up business. One of the little people, Colonel Casper, had appeared in the film and had worked with Fred Stone; but it is not known whether the others were Hollywood imports.

Other Munchkin little people found work in vaudeville or nightclubs, playing up—to exaggeration—their *Oz* connection. Cynthia Nickloy appeared onstage at Shine's Glove Theatre, Gloversville, New York, before the August 27, 1939, premiere screening of *Oz* to discuss the "rather trying time" making the picture, especially the high-powered lights that made it "terrifically hot on the set." "Little Jean," Jean LaBarbera, made her debut at Lou's Tavern in Asbury Park, New Jersey, in October 1939, "direct from Hollywood" having been "featured with Judy Garland in *The Wizard of Oz*." Prince Leon and Gus Wayne, now billed as "Mickey Rooney's Midget Pals," returned to Jack & Bob's in Trenton, New Jersey, in January 1939, where it was noted that the pair had "leading parts with Judy Garland and Frank Morgan" in *Oz*. The following December they appeared as "The Midget Twins" for a Wilkes-Barre, Pennsylvania, food and household exposition, for which they were advertised as "recently starred in *The Wizard of Oz*." Murray Wood, one of the Munchkin dignitaries, sang at the C-Bar-C Ranch in Elverson, Pennsylvania, and was promoted as "Star of MGM's Super Production *Wizard of Oz*." Wood and his wife, Jean

Lanier, appeared as "Famous *Wizard of Oz* Midgets" in the park theater of the Williams Grove Speedway, outside Harrisburg, Pennsylvania.

Meinhardt Raabe returned to his gig as Little Oscar in Madison, Wisconsin, and served double duty by promoting Oscar Mayer products and *The Wizard of Oz* when he made the rounds to give fifteen-minute speeches prior to local screenings of the film. Raabe told of his behind-the-scenes experiences making the picture and wowed his (largely juvenile) audiences. "*The Wizard of Oz* used the most lights, the most electricity, of any picture that had ever been made . . ." he extolled from the stage. He continued:

> This picture was made without any outdoor sets—completely indoors. For instance, the poppy field scene, if you look at it in the picture, it looks just as natural as outdoor sunlight. It was all done indoors. Chris Brown was the chief architect of the electrical set-up. Of course in our part [Munchkinland], we had all the thatched cottages and the huge artificial flowers. So we had a fireman going around with a meter all day long checking to see if there were any "hot spots." And he would find a hot spot and say, "Fan out that light" to lessen the concentration of light on that particular spot [and avert spontaneous combustion].

Raabe's elocution skills proved effective. According to a *Wisconsin State Journal* write-up on August 25, 1939, Raabe kept two thousand children "speechless and almost awestricken," sitting on the edge of their seats, fascinated by his magical Tom Thumb–like appearance. One little girl broke the tension with a squeaky quip, "He looks almost real," to which her neighbor whispered, "If you don't keep quiet he'll disappear in the sky." The mothers were as thrilled as the children and listened just as intently as Raabe told of his encounters with other Munchkins and Judy Garland in Hollywood. The setup worked, and after the screening one middle-aged woman commented, "That land looks better to me now than it did when I read about it as a child."

SPOOKS AND THE HORSE OF A DIFFERENT COLOR

Following the Munchkin sequence, scenes in the Haunted Forest took place January 3–4, 1939, and included the Winged Monkeys' attack. Henry Lewis Stone, one of the monkey troupe, recalled the airborne shots were compromised when some of the small men cast as monkeys got inebriated on cocktails at lunchtime or were too afraid of heights to enact the flight trajectory while suspended midair on wires. Adjusting the monkeys' aerial wiring to avert obvious detection was painstakingly tedious, as Stone recounted:

We had problems of the kick-back into the cameras . . . called halation. What the cameras caught was a sort of thin beam of bright light out there in the thin air of the glimmer of light that the wires sort of tossed off as the cameras panned or moved horizontally, but not the up and down movement. We couldn't (with our eyes) see the wires when the set was properly lit. But, the cameras caught and picked up this eerie refraction of the great amount of light that had to be used for the color picture being photographed. It was so maddening to the cameramen. Just those tiny glints of sparkling, shimmering light that the human could only see occasionally; but the cameras would pick [it] up as a hazy glare only for an instant, but long enough to spoil the "take." The only way to overcome the effect was to shoot straight down into the set and never move or pan the cameras.

There were generally two cameras shooting in case one film buckled, or a camera failed to get the whole three- or four-minute shot. . . . Each time the wires were drawn through the pulley shim (either up or down), they had to be touched with a sponge wet with some kind of gunk (that dried out in seconds) covering up any shiny spot or spots that might kick-back that halation refraction of amazingly short duration but bright as a star twinkling where there never should have been any light.

January 5, 1939, saw the company perform the "Merry Old Land of Oz" number in the Wash & Brush Up Co. interior, which was done in one continuous camera pan from right to left. For casting of the six leggy chorines featured in the sequence, it was reported that measurements used by Florenz Ziegfeld to judge female leg perfection, twenty years prior, were revived, as the roles required attractive girls with slender, shapely gams of identical proportions. Two hundred girls were said to have auditioned for the onscreen bit parts before it was narrowed to a dozen who had eighteen-inch thighs; twelve-and-three-quarter-inch calves; thirteen-and-one-quarter-inch knees; eight-inch ankles; and size five and one-quarter shoes. Dona Massin, assistant dance choreographer, was among the six chorus girls chosen, though she was handpicked by Mervyn LeRoy, who knew her from his Warner Bros. days. Victor Fleming was said to have chosen the other girls, listed as Frances Dietz, Laura Knight, Mary Jane McKinnon, Katharine Snell, and Virginia Carroll.

Scenes in the Jitterbug Forest, a subset of the Haunted Forest, including the deleted "Jitterbug" song-and-dance number, were taken January 6–9, 1939. In keeping with Yip Harburg's lyrics, which reference "bats in the trees," ten bats were trapped in Northern California and trained to sit on a tree branch swaying and wriggling to the "Jitterbug" music for a close-up insert shot. In a January 11, 1939, United Press interview, Jack Hinds, MGM property man, said that the bats were docile and easily tamed. The same drill was also required from a row of birds.

As the "Jitterbug" routine kicked into high gear, wind machines were used for added effect, whipping up leaves and dust as the living trees swayed to the music. After Victor Fleming called "Cut!" the players began rubbing dust out of their eyes. Jack Haley groaned dismally, having already endured one eye infection thus far. "Blink your eyes fast, that gets the dust out," Judy Garland was heard to advise him. "That's all very fine," answered Haley, "but how the dickens am I going to blink my nose?"

A brief scene that ended up being deleted was shot on January 12, 1939. In it, the principal characters follow the Yellow Brick Road out of the poppy field and dance toward the Emerald City. This was filmed on a completely different set, "Set No. 27," from that which is seen in the final film. The shot followed Glinda's snow shower and called for the group to dance past a weeping willow and assorted ferns and shrubs as the snowflakes that cover them melt in the sunshine. Incidentally, the snowfall was created using crushed gypsum and not asbestos as has been so widely reported. The use of gypsum to simulate snow in motion pictures dates to the silent era, although inhaling the mineral too deeply could prove hazardous to actors.

January 14–17, 1939, scenes covered the group's arrival at the Emerald City gates and the Horse of a Different Color carriage ride through the city streets. (The United Press presumed to rechristen the multihued horse "The Morning After" in reference to hangover symptoms akin to pink elephants and little green men.) Somehow, journalist Whitney Bolton completely misconstrued the scene setup: "The Cowardly Lion, at one point, will be reading. The yellow horse will look over his shoulder. The Scarecrow will say to the Cowardly Lion: 'There's a yellow horse reading over your shoulder.' 'That,' the Cowardly Lion will say, jumping up, 'is a horse of another color.' And the yellow horse will turn white." Also, in the final film a continuity error occurs in this sequence. As the principals disembark from the carriage, it drives off with Toto still in it, although in the next scene he is sitting in Dorothy's lap.

During this period an open invitation to visit the *Oz* set was extended to the Hollywood press—a first since production began. Harrison Carroll recounted in his February 1, 1939, column that he was taken on a personally conducted tour of the Emerald City by Mervyn LeRoy. LeRoy, "leaning against an imitation emerald star about twice his height," explained to Carroll the difficulty of bringing fantasy to the screen. "We figure the picture has to be more than just a fairy tale, so we are treating it like a Ziegfeld show—having the characters sing and dance." Carroll's visit made for good press. The journalist left impressed, his curiosity satiated by having glimpsed what he termed one of Hollywood's mysteries: "*The Wizard of Oz* set opens up, and a few of us are given a chance to see where MGM is pouring all those dollars—more dollars than on any other picture since the fabled *Ben Hur.*" Visiting Louisville, Kentucky, reporter Boyd Martin agreed, writing, "[I] can assure you that the picture will be a riot of color and the unusual. I visited particularly the

Emerald City which had all the 'atmosphere' of Baum's description and W. W. Denslow's illustrations."

Another Hollywood journalist, Mitchell Woodbury, was also on hand for the filming of the Horse of a Different Color sequence. But unlike Harrison Carroll, Woodbury was most intrigued by the downtime when Victor Fleming called, "Print!" after four or five takes, and the actors dispersed. Judy Garland, whom Woodbury described as wearing "a wig of flaming red hair with pigtails," dashed for her portable dressing room. Bert Lahr sat down and unzipped his skin suit in an effort to cool off, while Jack Haley made for his vertical reclining perch. Only Ray Bolger was sociable, stopping to momentarily chat with Woodbury. Bolger confided that his morning makeup application lasted an hour, but by midafternoon it began tightening up and pulling on his skin.

Then, at noon, Woodbury encountered "a weird sight" at luncheon: dozens of Emerald City extras, all attired in green with "black patent leather-like skull caps," resembling Orson Welles's Martian characters. That was, in fact, the joke around the studio, as Woodbury put it: "Mars attacks the MGM commissary." Elsewhere, Hedda Hopper decreed that lunch hour in the studio's restaurant resembled St. Patrick's Day, with two hundred extras costumed in varying shades of green.

January 1939 proceeded with additional work on the Emerald City set. During this period MGM star Wallace Beery visited the Oz set again, this time cutting his lunch hour in half to take daughter Carol Ann to see the Emerald City. Scenes outside the Wizard's chamber, site of the "If I Were King of the Forest" number, were made on January 19. January 20 comprised scenes of the Wash & Brush Up Co. exterior. Publicity portraits of Bert Lahr and Ray Bolger in full wardrobe and makeup were taken on this date by studio photographer George Hommel. Similarly, on January 28, 1939, Judy Garland posed in her Emerald City ringlet coiffure for publicity portraits, also by Hommel.

Whitney Bolton, Hollywood columnist for the *Philadelphia Inquirer*, was witness to the procession sequence in which Dorothy's party returns to the Emerald City after successfully vanquishing the Wicked Witch (a scene that was excised in editing). Bolton only gained admittance to the set after "passing four stern policemen," and was overwhelmed with the grandeur of the setting and costumery as the Emerald City citizens lined the street, cheering and singing as the principals marched victoriously, four abreast. "It was a beautiful, stunning scene," Bolton wrote, "with a magnificent marching song for tempo."

Between shots of this sequence, Bolton observed, the huge arc lights were cut for conservation and comfort, and recordings were aired over the soundstage playback system to soothe and entertain the crowd on break. With everyone relaxed in semi-darkness, "suddenly a phonograph began playing a hot Louis Prima number," Bolton noted. In spontaneous reaction to the music, Judy Garland and Ray Bolger launched into an impromptu jitterbug swing session. Overhead on the catwalk, an electrician turned on a single arc light that cut a ray through the gloom and spotlighted the dancers. "And for four-and-a-half minutes they danced a 1939 whooperoo amid an ages old fairyland setting," Bolton said. "Unfortunately, there was not a single camera on the set except for the one used in the production. It would have made a swell exploitation short."

The workweek of January 23, 1939, was set for the Wizard's balloon departure in the Emerald City town square, followed by Glinda's reappearance and Dorothy's return home. Given the tightly monitored restrictions on Judy Garland's work time, close-ups of her otherwise unidentifiable body parts were covered by doubles, and the insert shot of Dorothy tapping her heels together was no exception. The model for such close-ups remains unknown, but it was quite possibly Bobbie Koshay or even Claire Meyers, who was a leg double for Joan Crawford, Virginia Bruce, and "other MGM stunners," according to a 1938 behind-the-scenes account by journalist Jeanne Sprague.

Of the more than one hundred Emerald City townsmen, two—appearing only in Glinda's scenes—are distinguished with bright red, not black, hairlines. Plants of this nature can be indicators of an inside joke. The Glinda scenes were shot simultaneous to the January 26 opening scenes of Scarlett O'Hara and the Tarleton Twins in *Gone with the Wind* at Selznick International Pictures, which was a major industry event as these were the first scenes taken after a highly publicized search that resulted in casting Vivien Leigh as Scarlett. Given this degree of awareness, it seems likely that one or more mischievous young makeup artists intended the two red-headed townsmen as Ozian counterparts to *GWTW*'s ginger-haired Tarleton Twins. Beyond speculation, it should be noted that prior to its December 1939 premiere, *GWTW*, as a pop culture phenomenon and forthcoming motion picture epic, was referenced or parodied in films such as *Broadway Melody of 1938* (1937), *The Awful Truth* (1937), *King of Gamblers* (1937), *Hollywood Hotel* (1937), *A Yank at Oxford* (1938), *Babes in Arms* (1939), and *Second Fiddle* (1939).

February 3, 1939, was designated for scenes in the Wizard's throne room, and it was after these scenes that a tragedy befell the *Oz* company. Makeup artist Charles Schram recalled that Bert Lahr's on-camera stunt double for the Cowardly Lion's impulsive dive through a plate-glass window in the Emerald City was killed in a motorcycle accident during production. And while not a tragedy, Paul Adams, Frank Morgan's longtime stand-in, gave up the movie business to become a state patrol officer in New Mexico.

Scenes in the Witch's tower room also took place on February 3, 1939, possibly with a second unit. Revised staging meant retakes for Toto's escape from the Witch's castle on February 7. Special precautions needed to be taken where fire was used in several scenes, especially one in the Witch's castle in which Ray Bolger gets torched by the Wicked Witch.

The shot in question ran about five takes and, though Bolger was attired with asbestos undergarments, two firemen with extinguishers and a group of attendants with wet

blankets stood at the ready off-camera. Two contemporary accounts of the day's shoot make it possible to cobble together a virtual transcript of the proceedings:

In her grey, grim castle the Wicked Witch of the West was trying to set Ray Bolger on fire. "That's right," director Victor Fleming encouraged her, "get your broom aflame and then light him as if he were a cigarette."

The Wicked Witch (Margaret Hamilton in a fearsome getup) looked with distaste at the broom, and with apprehension at Ray Bolger. As the Scarecrow in *The Wizard of Oz*, he was stuffed with straw and had burlap wrapped around his head. "Go on," he said, "what's the matter? Don't you want me to be a hot number?"

"I'm s-scared!" Margaret squeaked.

Nevertheless, she applied flame to the broom and applied the broom to Ray, who began to burn briskly. The cameras turned. By and by some fellows with fire extinguishers put Ray out. "Let's try it again," director Fleming suggested, "and Miss Hamilton, please look as if you *enjoyed* it."

Margaret Hamilton . . . let a make-up man add some more green to her green face, wrapped her long black cloak around her and stepped in front of a number of huge men, who with green faces and fantastic costumes represent the Winkies.

Miss Hamilton looked across at Judy Garland as Dorothy, Bert Lahr as the Cowardly Lion, Jack Haley as the Tin Woodman, and Ray Bolger as the Scarecrow.

"All right," said director Fleming, "we'll make it." He reached in back of him and picked up a fire extinguisher.

Cameras whirled and Miss Hamilton, shrieking in her wrath, shouted that she will finish the four, one by one. She lifted her broom to a torch on the wall, lighted it, and thrust it at Bolger.

The comedian's straw-stuffed costume blazed up.

"Cut," cried Fleming. The men with wet sacks rushed in and put out the blazing costume. The straw was renewed, a fresh broom brought in, and the scene filmed again. Four times [more] did Miss Hamilton set fire to Bolger before the director was satisfied.

"Sit down and rest, Ray," Fleming said.

"I'm okay, "Bolger said, "I didn't worry."

"I-I need the rest," said Miss Hamilton. "The strain was all on me. I-I feel faint."

They did the fire incident five times. At the end, Ray Bolger said he felt perfectly dandy—it was Margaret Hamilton who fainted!

Hamilton had good reason to be queasy about the fire incident. The actress had only just recovered from burns suffered on the Munchkinland set several weeks prior.

Scenes in which the humbug Wizard is exposed were filmed on February 9, 1939, before the company moved to the Kansas farm set the next day. A Line on Hollywood gossip column noted that Ray Bolger, Jack Haley, and Bert Lahr were "trading their fancy costumes for overalls" for the real-life portion of the Oz plot. February 11, 1939, was for Judy Garland's scenes with Professor Marvel, which Garland had thoroughly rehearsed with Frank Morgan after hours at the actor's Holmby Hills residence.

The Kansas scenes were intentionally filmed in sobering black-and-white, later processed in a sepia tint, and without the lighting intensity required for Technicolor. However, the contrast between Kansas and Oz—and the novel moment of transition—was divulged to the public in its entirety by "On the Lots" candid reporter J. D. Spiro in his February 12, 1939, feature. Elsewhere, the transition scene from sepia to Technicolor was touted as a first in film history. "When Judy Garland's home lands in Oz, she and the house interior is in black and white. Through the door, covering only a portion of the film, the Land of Oz is seen in Technicolor."

On February 18, 1939, Victor Fleming was officially relieved as director of *The Wizard of Oz*, replaced by King Vidor. Vidor shot scenes in Kansas, including the "Over the

Rainbow" number, from February 19 to February 24, 1939. The following day, February 25, cast publicity portraits in full costume and makeup were taken in the MGM portrait gallery by famed photographer Clarence Sinclair Bull. These include a series of photographs of the actors individually, as a group, and posed with an oversize prop edition of L. Frank Baum's *The Wizard of Oz*.

WRAP PARTY

By February 27, 1939, production on *The Wizard of Oz* was considered closed, pending retakes, which began the following day. Retakes concluded on March 10, with the exception of pickup shots involving Judy Garland and Billie Burke on June 30, 1939. The unusually taxing production had been as bittersweet as it was bonding for the company.

But most of the *Wizard of Oz* cast and crew were young and spirited. Jackie Ackerman, who wagged Bert Lahr's tail from the catwalk above the sets, had worked in the film industry since he was a teenager with only a stint in World War II as a hiatus. He recalled the camaraderie of the *Oz* set, saying, "When you're in a studio like that, it's a big family." As Judy Garland's on-set guardian, Mama Ethel Gumm was part of the gang too, and cast and crew celebrated her forty-third birthday on November 17, 1938, at the party Judy threw for her.

Such familiarity also led to practical joking. Surrounded by a cast of professional comedians and habitual gagsters, Judy Garland was not immune from razzing. In an interview published on October 8, 1939, Garland said her *Wizard of Oz* costars plotted to haze her with pranks on an almost daily basis. "Once I lay down for a nap in my dressing room," she told Lupton A. Wilkinson, "and someone—never mind who—had put smudge pots under my bed. They slipped in and lit them, then ran out and yelled 'Fire!' When I stumbled out through the smoke, they threw water in my face."

Another case of ribbing occurred on the latter part of the *Oz* shoot. Assistant director Al Shenberg made news when he reportedly dissuaded an ornery pig from bothering Judy Garland on the Kansas farm set for the scene in which Dorothy balances along the fence of a pen before toppling in (as this was technically a stunt, the incident may have happened to Judy's double instead). When the same pig tried to charge Toto, Shenberg rushed to the rescue again. The next day the entire company presented Shenberg with a jar of pickled pigs' feet and a medal made of a ham rind hanging from a dime-store necklace, which they insisted he wear—until it started to stink. David Selditz, Al Shenberg's grandson, thought his grandfather would have been game for possessing "a large personality and an elevated sense of humor. Of course the irony of the pig is that we're Jewish."

Director Victor Fleming took a shine to Judy Garland, calling her "Ange," though in October 1940 she couldn't account for the nickname's origin. But the admiration was mutual. When Fleming left the *Wizard of Oz* company to take over David O. Selznick's *Gone with the Wind* in mid-February 1939, Garland reportedly took it personally. Given her so-called "violent" crush on Fleming, she was smarting from his presumed disloyalty, and it wasn't safe to mention Vivien Leigh's name in her presence for a time. But Garland recovered to orchestrate Fleming's farewell party. The festivities wrapped with a jokey send-off when the crew turned on five huge fan machines to blow Fleming off the set and away "with the wind," over to Selznick's studio a mile away.

The wind-machine incident may have inspired a *Wizard of Oz* anecdote attributed to Judy—though probably ghostwritten—and published on August 17, 1939, in Pennsylvania's *Harrisburg Telegraph*. Telling stories from the *Oz* set, Garland "writes":

> Only one thing happened on account of me. At least, they all laughed and said it was my fault. I wanted to treat the company to ice cream cones one day when we were working on the farm set. We were doing the first wind of the cyclone that day. Well, I ordered the cones and the poor waiter got on the set just as they turned on the big wind machine. Did that ice cream fly out of his hand. Whew! All over the stage. All of us got some ice cream on us and the only one who really enjoyed it was Toto, the dog, who ran here and there lapping up ice cream until his tongue was almost frozen.

Though clearly embellished to enhance the charm factor, the timing of the reported incident, the Kansas scenes, would have placed it in February 1939—coinciding with Fleming's departure from *The Wizard of Oz*—while also preserving anonymity with regard to the change in directors from Fleming to King Vidor, whose work on *Oz* included the farm scenes.

To grant perspective on the tremendous preparation, planning, and production schedule for *The Wizard of Oz*, a 1938 *Film Daily* list of statistics indicates that the average feature took twenty-two days to shoot. The scope of the *Oz* production was apparent in preproduction when on September 7, 1938, Arthur Freed urged Mervyn LeRoy to ensure that Judy Garland's radio appearances be postponed until after the picture, taking into consideration "that [since] she is a child and we are limited in the number of hours we can work with her anyway, any additional loss of time can get us into real difficulties." In a September 9, 1938, contract with radio-broadcast sponsor Lord & Thomas, Garland's agent, Victor Orsatti, was optimistic in supposing that *Oz*, which was to start "very shortly," would "be finished around the end of October, or early part of November." But the picture far exceeded all projected deadlines.

Come August 1939 it was officially tallied that *The Wizard of Oz* was eighty-six days in production (with fifty-three days originally estimated) and twenty-two days for retakes. Judy Garland was fifteen when she was cast as Dorothy and began wig and makeup tests;

she was sixteen throughout the majority of filming; and according to the assistant director log for *Babes in Arms*, Garland's next film, she would have been seventeen on June 30, 1939, when it was noted "Judy Garland working on *Wizard of Oz* retakes." An August 23, 1939, statement of Judy Garland's earnings reflect that she made five hundred dollars a week for a total of $9,583.31 on *The Wizard of Oz, or approximately $172,000 in modern currency.*

The arduous task of bringing *The Wizard of Oz* to fruition in a manner befitting the book's loyal following and classic status, coupled with Metro-Goldwyn-Mayer's reputation for quality filmmaking and unparalleled resources, was achieved in a process rarely duplicated before or since. The confluence of myriad arts and crafts, combined with the novelty of Technicolor photography, proved particularly challenging. Sundry accoutrements fell by the wayside as the *Oz* settings were developed, such as the November 1938 notation that "Fancy hedge trimmers will practice up on making freak formations out of hedges." All of the sets were built on soundstages, and copious reference stills were taken from every angle to ensure continuity between takes and to also have precise documentation in case of retakes. On *Oz*, this proved fortuitous when in February 1939, a portion of the Scarecrow's cornfield needed

to be rebuilt for retakes after the original set had been struck. The blueprint notes that the field was to use "celluloid corn as before" and advises "check stills" for accuracy.

Dressing the *Oz* sets also meant that decorations had to be created and could rarely be requisitioned or taken out of storage in the property department, as were the various sickles and pruning equipment used to spruce the Scarecrow's straw in the Emerald City, for example. The most prominent repurposed prop was the basket used for the Wizard's balloon, once the property of Jack Thomas, a professional balloonist. It was brought to MGM in 1925 when King Vidor's *The Big Parade* was filmed, and had last been rented for the hilarious ascension scene in the 1927 comedy *Rookies* in which the anchored balloon breaks free, levitating the leading man, his girlfriend, and her uncle until they parachute to earth. After its use in *The Wizard of Oz*, the basket and equipment were said to have been permanently acquired by MGM.

Early on, Hollywood scribe Paul Harrison noted that MGM's harried production was fraught with obstacles such that "they were so jittery about their problems that for three months no visitors were permitted on the sets." By February 1939 Harrison—a premature dissenter of Mervyn LeRoy's opus—became a convert, placating his column's Oz book fans. "If the customers have been worrying about what the movies are doing to *The Wizard of Oz*, I can assure them that the story is well in hand—and in very sympathetic and capable hands, too."

Harrison's public assertion was a welcome sentiment in the LeRoy Unit. When Mervyn LeRoy bumped into Ed Sullivan at a preview of Twentieth Century Fox's *Rose of Washington Square* in April 1939, he said of *Oz*, "So help me, I think we've got it licked." Substituting for the vacationing Frederick C. Othman, United Press's Hollywood correspondent, LeRoy reflected on the mammoth undertaking *Oz* presented in a July 1, 1939, editorial:

L. Frank Baum created marvelous characters and events from pure imagination. . . . It was our job to make every strange character live, every fantastic event transpire. . . . Before we got through with it, we were all sweating blood but Ray Bolger still looks like a scarecrow, Jack Haley like a tin woodman and Bert Lahr like a cowardly lion. . . . It even took weeks of tests to select the right hairdress and farm-girl frock for Judy Garland, the correct make-up for Frank Morgan, the green face of Margaret Hamilton and the fairy costume of Billie Burke. But more troublesome than all of these was the task of finding the Munchkins. . . . Try to find 120 of them in the United States. It took months. . . . Yes, you can see what a merry job this was becoming. Remember, everything had to be made to order; nothing could be taken out of stock.

What also couldn't be taken out of stock were some of the most striking effects to be conceived, not only for *The Wizard of Oz* but for any motion picture to date.

Conjuring Magic

From the point of acquisition, it was evident that *The Wizard of Oz* would be a complicated project by virtue of its fairy-tale locale in which magical events were commonplace. Making trees come to life (a la Walt Disney), monkeys fly, and witches vanish and reappear were among the problems to be solved. But the turbulent funnel cloud that whisks away Dorothy and Toto to the Land of Oz was a crucial illusion; the believability factor required total authenticity.

So far as the actual twister was concerned, Arnold "Buddy" Gillespie, Metro's special-effects department head, had been experimenting with possibilities since August 1938. The result was nothing short of spectacular. In its review of *The Wizard of Oz, Time* magazine compared the picture's tornado with the twenty-minute storm sequence in Samuel Goldwyn's *The Hurricane* (1937). But there was also special-effects creator Fred Sersen's "sand devil" funnel cloud of Twentieth Century Fox's *Suez* (1938)—the closest thing to the *Oz* cyclone to date—which cost more than three hundred thousand dollars.

Gillespie, who was never seen without a pipe, was adept at making miniatures, anything from a battleship to an airplane. Though known for his technical expertise and problem-solving capabilities, the Kansas cyclone, at first, had him stumped. One of Gillespie's early experimentations with a plaster of paris funnel cloud has been previously unrecorded. Anne M. McIlhenney, *Buffalo (NY) Courier-Express*'s Hollywood reporter, told of her stop to the Metro plaster shop on August 13, 1938, where she was invited to a glimpse of the tornado prototype. "'A cyclone!' I gasped," McIlhenney wrote, "and couldn't wait until I saw it with my very own eyes. Sure enough there was a huge plaster cone hanging from the ceiling, inverted and looking very much like a saffron colored icicle." "LeRoy is just experimenting," a sculptor told the journalist, "It's for *Oz* and we can't get the real thing you know. You can order a lot of things but not a cyclone."

Experimentation continued to proceed, and on August 20, 1938, Gillespie photographed a test of a water vortex in a tank—a clever thought at the time though impractical. This was followed by unsuccessful simulations using a large rubber cone (which lacked fluidity) before hitting upon the idea of a cloth "tube" that was tested the following November 5. Additional tests were made in January 1939 before successfully capturing the proper effect on film between then and mid-February.

Gillespie explained that *Oz*'s onscreen storm cloud was a thirty-five-foot elongated canvas sleeve shaped like the funnel of a real tornado (*not* a lady's silk stocking as has been misreported, though the concept was similar). A mechanized crane that traveled the length of the stage was hung from the bottom of the roof trusses. The crane supported the canvas cone, which was then rotated by a D.C. motor on a speed-control dial. The motor assembly was also arranged to tip at an angle. The base of the canvas cone was attached to another car on the stage floor that would travel a predetermined course.

When compressed earth and dust, wind fans, and cotton clouds attached to shifting glass panes were added to the setup, the effect of a Kansas cyclone was complete. This footage could then be rear-projected onto a background screen while Judy Garland and the other actors fought against its "life-size" winds in the foreground for a single camera shot. Bill Vogel, trick and stunt cinematographer, devised the Flexible Lacquer Screen for rear-projection shots on such scenes in *The Wizard of Oz* as well as for *Ali Baba Goes to Town*, *China Seas*, and *Test Pilot*.

Melting the Wicked Witch of the West was far more simplistic for Gillespie. MGM contended that three professional magicians were consulted to learn their special-effects secrets and indeed the Witch's gradual disappearance is in keeping with the old trick of a trapdoor in the stage floor. As Margaret Hamilton recollected forty years later, a property man took half a pail of water and threw it at her from out of camera range for the close-up of the water splashing the Witch full on. Hamilton was positioned on a hydraulic elevator that would slowly descend beneath the stage floor as dry ice emitted a steam effect. "If I stuck my head out too far, it was possible to catch my [prosthetic] nose on the edge of the elevator," the actress remembered. Hamilton's dress was tacked to the floor so as to contain the air flow caused by the elevator and allow her to slip out of her robes and leave them behind. An oversize version of her witch's hat gave the impression that her head was shriveling. In typical publicist fashion, the melting effect was summarized as follows: "Before your very eyes a woman of flesh and blood melts like a snowball at a jitterbug party—and Dorothy gets possession of the 12-cylinder broomstick to carry her back to the other side of the rainbow."

During Margaret Hamilton's recovery from the burns she suffered on the Munchkinland set, the *Oz* crew shot scenes around her. But upon her return on February 11, 1939, Hamilton was confronted with the prospect of another special effect with potential for a similar risk. She was expected to ride the Witch's broomstick from which black smoke would issue at the press of a button for the shot in which the Wicked Witch skywrites an aerial threat over the Emerald City. Hamilton firmly declined, understandably gun-shy about another accident, and deferred to her stunt double, Betty Danko.

A self-proclaimed "fatalist," Danko had been in the movie business since the late 1920s. At the time of *The Wizard of Oz*, Danko was thirty-five and attractive, though she had no desire to be an actress. In 1935 she said her preference was to continue doing "bump work," which meant taking the dangerous jolts and falls for stars such as Jean Harlow, Joan Crawford, Irene Dunne, Madge Evans, and Thelma Todd. Danko's repertoire of stunts ranged from tripping down a flight of stairs to jumping off an ocean cliff. As such, she found herself in steady demand for stand-in work, which paid eleven dollars a day, as well as stunt work, which paid as much as thirty-five dollars a day. In January 1939 Lloyds of London, the famous insurance broker, selected twenty-five movie daredevils as good risks and offered them annual coverage against death and dismemberment, which lowered the insurance costs of film studios. Betty Danko was among the select performers—and one of only three women—chosen for Lloyds's charter stunt work policies.

In identical makeup and wardrobe, Danko would pass for Margaret Hamilton's Wicked Witch undetected in brief takes. Makeup artist Charles Schram recalled the shot's setup, "[Danko] was suspended with fine piano wires about ten feet above the floor on the black process stage. She was flying sitting on her broomstick and supposedly skywriting a message to Dorothy. Below her, under her skirt and broomstick, was a cartridge that expelled a stream of white smoke like a rocket." But in short order, something went awry.

In 1944 Danko recalled that *The Wizard of Oz* was the only picture on which she had ever been injured, to date, in her twelve years of film stunting. Reporter Erskine Johnson recounted the accident that ensued in his In Hollywood column:

> [Betty] was doubling for the witch in *The Wizard of Oz*, flying through the air with the greatest of ease on a broomstick [for the skywriting scene]. The broomstick was suspended from the soundstage ceiling with invisible wires. Betty was supposed to press a button to release some smoke during the scene, but something went wrong and there was an explosion. She was really flying through the air—minus the broomstick. Betty started grabbing at things, cut up her arms on the wires and darn near busted her back when she hit the cement floor. She went to the hospital for two weeks, but came out good as new.

Not quite. Danko was so seriously injured when her broom exploded during the aerial stunt that she required a hysterectomy from the blast's damage to her internal organs.

While she was laid up, the cast and crew sent over a copy of Baum's *The Wizard of Oz* as a get-well present, inscribed with notes to cheer her. "Get well quickly" and "Speedy recovery" were Judy Garland's contributions. Sheila O'Brien, chief women's wardrobe dresser, quipped, "Stay off those brooms and quit tearing up the wardrobe!" And Margaret Hamilton wrote, "Between fire and explosions, it's been fun! Thank you, Betty dear, for all you 'took' for me. Much love—Mag the Hag." Thereafter, Danko was nicknamed "Broomstick Betty." (Stuntwoman Aline Goodwin completed the shot.)

The inclusion of the skywriting sequence was one of the modern touches to update *The Wizard of Oz*. Commercial skywriting in the United States was only established in 1932; onscreen, it would still be viewed as something of a novelty. Under Buddy Gillespie's supervision, tests of the aerial message were made each month from January through May 1939. According to Gillespie, a six-foot-square tank that was four inches tall was filled with two inches of water made opaque with milk. The tank was raised twelve feet above the stage floor so that the camera could shoot up into it. A stylus was made using a hypodermic needle upon which was affixed a black silhouette of the Wicked Witch, "about the size of an old-fashioned postage stamp," as Gillespie recalled it. Under slight manual pressure, the stylus would release the "smoke," which was sourced from a container of black sheep dip, an animal delouser. The operators creating the lettering wrote in reverse so the camera would read the message properly. Wind drift was made by slightly fanning the milky water. The completed illusion was double-exposed against a Technicolor-blue sky.

Another updated addition to *The Wizard of Oz* was the Wicked Witch's use of a crystal globe as her oracle (it would also echo Professor Marvel's use of such in the Kansas sequence). The globe was filled with water for scenes in which action is viewed in it; film of the action was angled to project into the globe for a single shot.

Like most every special effect on *The Wizard of Oz*, creating the grotesque, disembodied Wizard's head, with its enlarged, superior cranium, green complexion, and pointed fangs, required experimentation. This spellbinding effect began with sculptor Joe Norin making a small prototype in clay based on Jack Dawn's sketches. Once the design was approved, a plaster cast was taken from which a model facade was made in plaster of a half-inch thick. Makeup artist Charles Schram helped paint it realistically and it stood about eighteen inches high. A test was made using footage the special-effects crew shot on Stage 14 of the Wizard's palace in miniature with smoke and flames issuing from the throne.[1] They

---

1 Stage 14 was reserved for shooting movie scenes for which sound and dialogue would later be dubbed due to the noise of various machinery needed to create special effects. The Kansas cyclone in miniature was also shot on Stage 14.

photographed the head separately and superimposed it over the film of the miniature throne. But this approach was unsatisfactory because the stationary mouth wasn't covered by smoke as much as anticipated. Next, animation was superimposed over the mouth, but then, as Schram recollected, they "couldn't have a motionless face with the drama of Frank Morgan's voice." The same was true for a larger-than-life version of the head used in long shots with the actors—it simply appeared too static.

In 1997 Charles Schram further explained, "As I remember, we did the scenes with the actors [with] a big loud speaker set up next to the camera with Frank Morgan's voice. Colored sheets of gelatin over the lights gave the effect of fire projected [on the actors' faces in reaction shots]." An anonymous actor, made up as the Wizard's hideous head, lip-synched Frank Morgan's recorded dialogue while photographed against an all-black velvet background for which only the actor's face was visible.

Given how heavily made-up the actor was, there was no need to consume Frank Morgan's time with the tedium of the shoot in makeup that would render him indistinguishable and over which smoke and flames would obscure his face. The actor was possibly Morgan's double Paul Adams. But then, as now, most staff working behind the scenes desired to work in front of the camera, and the phantom Wizard could even have been portrayed by one of the makeup artists such as Norbert Miles (also spelled Myles), Ray Bolger's makeup man, who still listed "actor" as his 1940 census occupation and had sixty motion picture roles to his credit, mostly silent shorts. Likewise, Bolger's stand-in, Stafford Campbell, also dabbled in acting, appearing on Broadway with Al Jolson and serving as Errol Flynn's stand-in, according to Campbell's daughter Sue.

The footage of the gigantic Wizard's head was superimposed with shots of the throne—not projected onto the actual smoke and steam on set, as it was originally envisioned—to create a complete and highly effective illusion. The special, colored smoke for these scenes—and others on *Oz*—was devised by Anthony D. Paglia, formerly of New Castle, Pennsylvania, whose hobby of experimenting with fireworks and pigmented powders landed him the *Oz* gig after MGM responded to his one-dollar classified ad. Paglia's powder "produced a faster and clearer smoke of various colors. Since the picture was produced in Technicolor, the smoke effect had to be as perfect as possible." Paglia spent six months on *Oz*, dividing his time between the set and his job as a telegrapher on a railroad.

Another double-exposure effect was that of Glinda's translucent bubble from which the sorceress could mystically emanate and retreat at will. This comparatively "simple" effect was in concession to Glinda's mode of transportation as cited in the Oz books, an airborne chariot drawn by either swans or storks. Life-size bubbles as transportation were employed in Baum's *The Road to Oz* (1909) as well as in the seventy-second installment of the NBC *Wizard of Oz* radio program. In the latter production, magic, colored bubbles deliver Dorothy and her friends to the Emerald City; the Scarecrow is encased in a pink bubble, like MGM's Glinda.

According to a July 8, 1938, memo from art department chief Cedric Gibbons, in which Gibbons cites cartoon and double-exposure tricks, the double-printing of Glinda's bubble would not be done in the MGM lab but would be turned over to Technicolor for processing. Initial tests included a shot of the set and a shot of the floating bubble as well as "another piece of film of the bursting bubble, and another one of a figure standing in position [to simulate actress Billie Burke]." The bubble itself was to be shot against a black background—in 1938 black velvet was the equivalent of today's green screen for use in creating double-exposure illusions.

To make the Winged Monkeys soar through the air, men of small stature, attired in fur suits reportedly made by Max Factor, were suspended over the stage. Their wings flapped by means of battery packs concealed under their jackets. By September 7, 1938, Arthur Freed advised Mervyn LeRoy that the wings-and-motor mechanics would be imminently available for his approval, assuring LeRoy that all seemed "not only beautiful, but practical." As Charles Schram recalled it in 1997, "[For] one shot of the flying monkeys, just before they capture Dorothy and Toto, they wore leather harnesses under their costumes that supported a pulley on their backs. They slid down from high overhead, on stretched

piano wires, to just in front of the camera. They landed and ran after Dorothy and captured her." (The shot of the monkeys actually levitating with Dorothy required that stunt double Bobbie Koshay take Judy Garland's place.)

Creating the flying effect for the Winged Monkeys was another instance of MGM having one or more backup plans. The shot of the simians descending into the Haunted Forest was at first done as a cartoon sequence. However, the animation was inconsistent with the intercut of the principal characters reacting to, and fleeing from, the monkeys, and the cartoon footage was scrapped.

But cartoon animation was used for the jitterbug in the Haunted Forest. The insect was at first shown as a miniature replica for the shot of it landing on the Cowardly Lion's nose and then biting his neck before switching to a cartoon version buzzing about. As reported by the *Santa Cruz (CA) Evening News* of November 3, 1938, the task of envisioning the replica model that would fly from a tree to land on Bert Lahr fell to Harry Edwards, one of the property masters on *Oz*. Though the script called for a mosquito-like creature, Edwards pored over microscopic pictures of germs and research department images of various insects before surveying members of the cast. Judy Garland suggested that the jitterbug should resemble a big beetle with claws like an eastern lobster's. Buddy Ebsen envisioned a moth with rainbow-colored wings and a beak like a mosquito, and Ray Bolger thought it should be like a flying caterpillar with an auger-like beak. "I suggest something soft and fluffy, like a flying powder puff, with no claws or beaks or anything of that kind," was Bert Lahr's contribution. "You see, it's my nose it's supposed to land on." Once the jitterbug model design was finalized by William Horning, associate art director, the animation department could cartoon the rest.

Similarly, cartooned bees would swarm from the Tin Man after the Wicked Witch makes good on her threat to transform his hollow innards into a bee hive. But instead of vanishing from the cottage rooftop in a puff of smoke, as she does in the final film, the Witch was to have flown away in cartoon form as well, as Gibbons noted: "We pull the witch off the roof with wires, cut back to our people [i.e., Judy et al.], then back to the bees in cartoon. The witch follows them in cartoon."

Where Oz's special effects were concerned, Metro only revealed enough information to generate mystique, despite Jimmie Fidler publicly calling for the studio to spill the beans. MGM's pat response was to state, "The illusions were of course filmed behind locked doors." Closer to Oz's release date, MGM acquiesced slightly. "Most of the fantastic effects, tried for the first time in this film, are kept secret, but Metro-Goldwyn-Mayer consented to reveal the secret of the talking trees," reported *Pic* magazine. The anthropomorphic tree effect was intended to rival their animated counterparts in Walt Disney's memorable short *Flowers and Trees*.

For the two argumentative apple trees and the trees of the Jitterbug Forest, eight of Hollywood's tallest extras were chosen. Rubber suits, cast from authentic tree bark, were molded for them with face screens and moveable branches that were brought to life by each operator slipping into them like arm-length gloves. Each rubber tree had a zipper closure in the back. Not only could the operators within not see or hear, the conditions were said to be so stifling that the men inhabiting them could only work twenty minutes at a time before the cameras. Bobby Connolly worked out a system of coordinating the Jitterbug Forest trees' dance rhythm by rigging lights inside each tree and tapping a control, which flashed the lights, to convey when the operators should sway and clap the branches like hands. Director Victor Fleming was impressed by the musical synchronization of the trees, commenting, "We peopled trees with human beings who waved their limbs and danced with remarkable rhythm."

In his April 18, 1939, column—and four months before Oz's theatrical debut—Jimmie Fidler did reveal how the Horse of a Different Color was done by painting two white steeds with vegetable dyes—a task assigned to makeup department chief Jack Dawn, and not Arnold Gillespie. Hollywood insider Erskine Johnson called this one of the most strenuous makeup jobs in recent years because the horses needed to be pigmented from head to hoof. After Dawn consulted with Max Factor to devise a nontoxic makeup for the horses, Technicolor tests were made in autumn 1938.

According to Fred Gilman, the horses' handler, both animals were longtime teammates, having worked on other pictures; but once dyed, they balked at one another. "Any horse," said Gilman, "can tell you there's no such thing as a blue horse. This looks like the end of a beautiful friendship." (Gilman knew horses, having been a popular cowboy star in a slew of 1920s western melodramas.) After the scene was shot, makeup artist Charles Schram recalled that both horses were rinsed off in the Pacific Ocean but did not come completely white again for some time.

In describing the Horse of a Different Color effect, Hollywood columnist Frederick C. Othman said that Jell-O was used to pigment the two steeds, having met Humane Society approval because it "washed out easily." This has become the widely accepted explanation when, in fact, in 1939 there was no flavored Jell-O to account for the purple or blue coloring of the horses; only raspberry, lime, lemon, strawberry, cherry, and orange Jell-O was sold.

Not every special effect on *The Wizard of Oz* was a tedious one. High-voltage electrical "juice," *not* apple juice as the Internet has purveyed, was used to create the illusion of protective sparks emitting from Dorothy's shoes as the Wicked Witch tries to abscond them. But every special effect would require coordination with composer Herbert Stothart to enhance the gaiety, suspense, and the awesome wonders of Oz.

POSTPRODUCTION:
SCORING, SOUND EFFECTS, AND WARREN NEWCOMBE

With principal photography completed and its cast dispersed (but on call for retakes), postproduction for *The Wizard of Oz* centered on synchronizing, dubbing, and looping its soundtrack. Simultaneously, the musical scoring was composed by Herbert Stothart to complement a rough cut of the picture in April 1939. Stothart delegated sundry portions of the scoring to his associate conductor, Georgie Stoll, as well as to musicians Leo Arnaund, George Bassman, Murray Cutter, Paul Marquardt, and Robert Stringer. As originally conceived, *Oz* was to have underscoring from start to finish, which was 60 percent higher than other MGM musicals such as *Sweethearts*, and 30 percent more than straight dramas like *Mutiny on the Bounty* or *Marie Antoinette*, previous record holders for background music.

According to a 1936 *Photoplay* essay on the cinema arts, it took an average of four days to score a picture; although *Oz* was a far more complicated and involved undertaking, the process was no different. To begin, Stothart would have viewed a cursory edit of the film repeatedly while making notes for the placement of certain musical movements. For example, he and Stoll had to plan for surprise "breaks" and vibrato harmonies by penciling in such unconventional music effects as "bumps," "rachets," "peanut wagon whistle," "klinknobs," "races," "squeals," and "crashes." "There is no musical term for most of the effects," Stothart explained to the *Buffalo (NY) Courier-Express*, "so we just had to list them, adding the approximate key and the timing."

Then, an arranger would modify and orchestrate the melodies for continuity's sake, ensuring that the score segues smoothly from one scene to the next. In the third segment of the process, Metro's private equipment would print the orchestra's sheet music, designated by whatever instruments were required. The final step was to rehearse and record the score with a seventy-piece orchestra, timing the beginnings and endings with a stop watch so that all musical interludes fit the picture with mathematical precision.

For *Oz*, Stothart deftly incorporated the Harburg-Arlen melodies as incidental leitmotifs for the main characters. Said Stothart, "The songs are among the cleverest I have ever handled, and show a wide versatility from lilting whimsy to the melodious ballad 'Over the Rainbow.'"

Controversy over the near-deletion of Dorothy's theme song following initial previews of *The Wizard of Oz* is well documented in Hollywood lore. Absent "Over the Rainbow," the picture's repetition of this theme would have caused an aura of cinematic musical ambiguity—which is precisely what occurred when Alfred Newman's "Someday You'll Find Your Bluebird" number was dropped from Shirley Temple's comparable film fantasy *The Bluebird* the following year. Had "Rainbow" been permanently removed from *Oz*, it probably would have resurfaced in another Harburg-Arlen score.

Further, Stothart's musical strains for each of Dorothy's three companions echoes "If I Only Had a Brain/Heart/Nerve" respectively; Professor Marvel / the Wizard / the Emerald City reflects "The Merry Old Land of Oz"; Glinda's six-note theme is a derivative of "We're Off to See the Wizard" in reverse; and the Miss Gulch / Wicked Witch of the West score is a discordant rendition of "We're Off to See the Wizard" that becomes increasingly maniacal as the picture proceeds.

Beyond merely reiterating the Harburg-Arlen tunes, Stothart was conscious that each character's musical accompaniment should authentically reflect his or her persona. "We tried also to musically explain the Baum philosophy behind the characters," he rationalized. "The Lion turns out to have the finest kind of courage, because he accomplishes things even though afraid to attempt them; the Scarecrow has a brain because he thinks himself out of emergencies without having any conceit about it; and the Tin Woodman, because he is capable of a great loyalty, really has a heart. And the end of the rainbow Judy is hunting for is her own home, the one place where she finds real happiness. It was intensely interesting to work out these ideas in music."

As was customary in motion picture scoring, Stothart wove samples from classical compositions as "mood music" for dramatic effect, though he publicly denied such sampling. "For instance, where the Wizard appears as a great ball of flame," Stothart observed, "it called for something like Wagner's fire-music. But to have used that would have been fatal. People would simply say we stole it. It was up to us to try to do it with a different form of musical structure."

Even still, classical pieces Stothart reworked for *The Wizard of Oz* include Felix Mendelssohn's Scherzo Opus 16 no. 2 for Toto's thrilling escape from the Wicked Witch; Modest Mussorgsky's "Night on Bald Mountain" for Dorothy's rescue in the Witch's castle; "Gaudeamus Igitur," traditionally associated with universities, for the presentation of the Scarecrow's diploma; and Mendelsohn's "Spring Song" to emphasize the levity of the Cowardly Lion's sissified lament, the music to which was deleted in editing. Incorporating passages from classical compositions was not only a movie tradition, it was an Oz tradition where dramatizations were concerned. Frank J. Baum's intro and closing for his 1932 *Wizard of Oz* radio pitch includes fragments of "Funeral March of the Marionette" and "In the Hall of the Mountain King." Likewise, the 1933 Ted Eshbaugh cartoon incorporates Camille Saint-Saens's "The Swan." The 1937 CBS Radio production of *The Wizard of Oz* uses "Rock-a-Bye Baby" during the cyclone when Dorothy and Toto are being swayed to sleep by the gale winds.

In keeping with *Oz's* overall theme of homespun Americana, Herbert Stothart lifted fragments of well-known but simplistic melodies of childhood tradition. "The Happy Farmer Returning from Work" accompanies the opening shot as Dorothy and Toto breathlessly rush home; "The Whistler and His Dog" (or "Oh Where, Oh Where Has My Little Dog Gone?") for the scene in which Dorothy plans her runaway exile with Toto; Johannes Brahms's "Lullaby" plays as Dorothy becomes sedated in the poppy field; and the sentimental strains of "Home, Sweet Home" yield a bittersweet tone to the scenes in which Dorothy bids farewell to her Ozian companions, continuing through to her reawakening in Kansas.

Despite his reliance on the Harburg-Arlen songs and the sampling of familiar musical compositions, the citation of these influences does not suggest that Stothart's score for *The Wizard of Oz* was not inspired in its own right. Stothart's triumphs include the majestically haunting main titles overture, the dirge-like March of the Winkies, and finessing the rousing accompaniment for the cyclone scenes, for which George Bassman had oversight.

Stothart was also charged with carefully considering how the music could support the visual narrative in a manner befitting of its whimsy. When interviewed by Bruno David Ussher in May 1939 for *Hollywood Spectator*, Stothart remarked on the pressure of preparing complete scores for both *Balalaika* and *The Wizard of Oz*. "Musically, I am living in two different worlds," said Stothart. "*Balalaika* is of a charmingly realistic [Russian] atmosphere. And, of course, in *The Wizard*, music and sound must be highly imaginative, unreal as well as super-realistic." The ordinarily tranquil Stothart revealed an uncharacteristic edge to his demeanor when he recounted that he had recently informed a "certain MGM executive" (perhaps an anxious Mervyn LeRoy) that while music could be heard in two places at once, he could not defy the law of physics by being in two places at the same time to juggle both scores! *Balalaika* was in the vein of film operettas for which Stothart arranged and directed, such as *Naughty Marietta*, *May Time*, and *Rose Marie*; and Stothart also scored the sweeping period sagas *Romeo and Juliet*, *Mutiny on the Bounty*, *The Good Earth*, and *Marie Antoinette*.

If Stothart was pressed for time, he was not above repurposing his own compositions. The entire score of the climactic chase through the Witch's castle—from the moment the chandelier descends on the Winkies until Dorothy and her companions are cornered—was lifted note for note from the scene in which the French Revolution is declared in the previous year's *Marie Antoinette*, though the piece is actually employed to greater dramatic effect in *Oz*.

The Wizard of Oz required that Stothart's minute attention be closely coordinated with sound engineers to relate the music to sound effects such as the tinkering clanks of the Tin Woodman's motions (created by banging a piece of steel rail). Already, MGM had reportedly catalogued thousands of feet in soundtrack that comprised an estimated two hundred thousand noise effects—enough for a two-and-a-half-hour picture. Sifting through this mass of recordings, and synchronizing with Stothart's music the most illusionary of those selected, was another laborious accomplishment that prolonged *Oz's* postproduction. Come April 1939, Mervyn LeRoy revealed to reporter Harrison Carroll that *Oz* would be another seven weeks in the making due to factoring in the appropriate noises, which involved, for example, as many as ten men to imitate the Tin Man's clanks and squeaks, and a dozen others to synchronize the Scarecrow's rustling swishes.

Wild bird calls were recorded at the Bird Park aviary on Catalina Island, off the California coast in the Gulf of Santa Catalina, home of up to eight thousand rare and exotic species. The rustling of the flying monkeys' wings was "really the recorded sound of the flight inland of thousands of sea gulls during a storm," according to journalist M. Lewis Russel. Reportedly, one parrot almost shanghaied the sound crew's Catalina Island work when it persisted in flying past the microphone muttering, "Hey you so-and-sos, get the hell outta here!" Los Angeles newspaper editor W. E. Oliver wrote that it took some tricky editing to cut the parrot's expletives without sacrificing the other bird calls, such as the hornbill, which "roars."

Additionally, hoot owl noises were needed to augment the Haunted Forest. A bird wrangler was consulted to figure out the problem of recording an owl on cue. He experimented by bringing an eagle close to an owl, without endangering the smaller bird. The owl reacted terrifically, so two days later the handler brought both birds to MGM's sound department with the intention of repeating the experiment. The owl was set on a perch under a microphone and then the eagle was brought close. But the owl wasn't even bothered and wouldn't screech, not even a peep. However, some splendid eagle cries were secured. The following day, a substitute owl was brought in—with success.

To grant the Kansas cyclone's roaring winds authenticity, MGM hired O. O. Ceccarini, deemed one of America's five greatest mathematicians by Albert Einstein, to arrive at the formula for the exact noise inside a funnel cloud. Ceccarini's calculations were submitted to Mervyn LeRoy in a report gleaned from studies of air velocity, pressure, and friction as well as elements gained from the United States Weather Bureau. The conclusions called for blending percentages of roar, whine, whistle, static electricity crackles, and air friction rustle, although, as Ceccarini added, "Though these noises would be generated, a human being would not hear them, as the air rushing past the ears would insulate them from all sound whatsoever." Despite this caveat, MGM exercised creative license to great effectiveness.

For *The Wizard of Oz*, it was reported that as many as ten sound tracks at a time were juggled by sound engineers to synchronize the effects. In reel five technicians blended fourteen separate sound tracks into one, encompassing regular dialogue, "voices" of the apple trees (specially added), sounds of the tree's apples being plucked, the branch slapping Judy Garland's hand, apples thudding on the ground, the Tin Man's jaws and joints squeaking, rustling noises from the Scarecrow, animal noises (Toto the dog), and the squirt of an oil can.

In another example, two takes of "Jitterbugs Attack" were recorded on May 6, 1939. Both takes lasted about a minute, timed to cover the duration of the characters' dialogue as the insect stings them just prior to "The Jitterbug" song-and-dance number. It was reported that "MGM's idea of what a Jitterbug sounds like is the combined sound tracks of (a) the buzzing of a mosquito, (b) the noise of a hummingbird, (c) the squeak of a dry axle, (d) the sound of a whistle and steam."

The synchronization of scoring and preliminary sound effects editing led to a May 8, 1939, re-recording of Judy Garland and Ray Bolger performing "We're Off to See the Wizard" for the Scarecrow scenes. On May 17, 1939, "phony heart beat effects" were recorded for the Tin Man. The *swoosh* as the Witch flew on her broomstick to skywrite "Surrender Dorothy" was created by setting off dozens of real skyrockets, accounting for six hundred feet of supplies, and blending the recorded sound with that of aerial bombs. On May 23, 1939, a recording to accompany the sequence whereby the Witch turns the Tin Man into a beehive (deleted in editing) was made by "scratching on cans for effect of bees hitting Tin Man's insides."

Like L. Frank Baum's Wizard, Frank Morgan was an accomplished ventriloquist. But more than clever vocal illusions were required to replicate the thundering proclamations of the Wizard's phantom presence, towering above the palace throne in the form of a disembodied head. The script had directed that "Oz's voice is hollow as if spoken through a long, hollow tube, giving it a booming and echoing voice," and so the sound technicians obeyed those instructions literally. They gathered in an underground tunnel that ran the length of the MGM compound (a common design to access buildings on an expansive campus in inclement weather or emergency) and then, using Frank Morgan's prerecorded lines, funneled the audio through a concrete tube a quarter mile away. The successful result, modified with a small electrical soundboard on-site, was picked up by microphone and rerecorded into a final soundtrack. When played back on set, it was reported in February 1939 that the bellowing effectiveness of Morgan's Wizard lines were completely frightening to Toto the dog.

Other sound issues required rerecording or dubbing due to "poor intelligibility" of actors' voices, wind machines, set noises (such as footsteps) and "those for which cue tracks were made," a reference to an indication for when a specialty noise should be inserted. Examples of these types of tedious synchronization included the need to add the distorted voices of the apple trees; Judy Garland's first line in Munchkinland (considered "bad due to set noise"); the introduction of the Tin Man up until his song (set noise and wind machine); poppy field dialogue due to "paper flowers" sounds; the steam effect when the Witch melts; and the sound of the peeping chicks on the Kansas farm, which, according to the log, "overload the valve and sound out of proportion to scene." In particular, Margaret Hamilton's shrill voice was noted to have "overload quality . . . particularly scene 192 in which Toto escapes from basket."

MGM was notorious for its keen attention to artistic detail, infusing even its short subjects and "B" pictures with enough panache to justify the studio's reputation as Hollywood's gold standard. "*The Wizard of Oz* . . . has been in production so long that only Hollywood veterans remember the starting date . . .," Jimmie Fidler dryly quipped. This was echoed in Len G. Shaw's theater column for the *Detroit (MI) Free Press* when he learned of the picture's near completion in June 1939, "It begins to look as though that long promised old-time stage spectacle might be coming along some day in screen form." Indeed, Judy Garland's studio-issued biography of February 5, 1939, stated that *Oz* was "due for release around Easter," which was reiterated in a press notice of March 15: "Sometime around Easter we should get a glimpse of *Wizard of Oz*." But *Oz*'s release date was overextended by perfecting its illusions in postproduction.

The most closely guarded of all MGM's technical secrets was that much of the Land of Oz (and even a portion of Kansas) seen in long shots was rendered in two-dimensional paintings, from the craggy cliffs and foreboding battlements of the Wicked Witch's castle to the towering turrets of the Emerald City. It was neither practical nor financially feasible to invest time and resources in erecting exteriors and facades that would be viewed briefly onscreen. To compensate, live-action scenes identified for these trick shots would be filmed on portions of sets; the remaining backgrounds would be added using paintings rendered in pastels, pencil, and crayon. The paintings left blank the area estimated for the live-action footage, which would be inserted via double-exposure to form a complete and seamless scene. The man responsible for creating such effects was Warren Newcombe, of MGM's art department.

Newcombe got his professional start as a portrait painter, book and magazine illustrator, and theatrical costume and set designer. While in New York, Newcombe partnered with Neil E. McGuire in the art of applied "settings and title effects in color or black and white" for films such as *Kismet*, *Vendetta*, and *The Four Horsemen*. In 1947 Newcombe won the Academy Award for Best Visual Effects for *Green Dolphin Street*.

As early as March 27, 1939, an outline of scenes requiring the insertion of so-called "Newcombe" shots was generated by Newcombe to Charlie Chic, who oversaw the *Oz* unit's production. Each scene would require a separate painting (in some cases, only a stationary image was needed), all of which would be filmed in Technicolor to complement the live action already photographed. Unused takes and test roll footage of Newcombe shots for *The Wizard of Oz* were held in reserve at Technicolor pending a final edit of the picture, after which Technicolor was given the okay to destroy it all on September 21, 1939.

Some of the Newcombe shots were deceptively subtle, including the interior corridor leading to the Wizard's throne room or the long shot of "Tin Man, Straw Man and Lion

Man creep up and look over rocks at Winkies doing their march in the courtyard." For Newcombe's shots of the Wicked Witch's castle, Metro imported Candelario Rivas, a Mexican-born artist known for his adept skill in rendering architectural structures. An all-over painting was used for the exterior of the castle at night with the notation for "flickering torches" as an added effect. Still further Newcombe shots were in process on April 4, 1939, when it was noted that Scene #118, of the "four principals going towards Emerald City after leaving poppy field," was screened as a test for Mervyn LeRoy's approval, which LeRoy viewed and okayed (as he would on all remaining takes).

The art department at MGM was also responsible for designing the Land of Oz dwellings and landscape, including an Emerald City that reflected the futuristic art moderne style of similar, otherworldly metropolises in contemporary films like *Things to Come* (1936) and *Lost Horizon* (1937). For this, MGM staff indicated that they did not use the Baum Oz books as reference but instead relied upon their own imaginations. After rejecting grandiose sketches of what resembled the Taj Mahal, it was determined that the Emerald City exterior would be comprised of a series of tiered, domed spires—a modern take on the turreted fairy-tale castles of old. This design was echoed in the decor surrounding the Wizard's throne, similar to a majestic cathedral pipe organ—appropriate for an audience with a mysterious entity.

As technical postproduction work behind the scenes continued into spring 1939, a steady stream of *Wizard of Oz* publicity bits and "coming soon" teaser ads served to entice moviegoers prior to the picture's unveiling.

Public Premiere

During *The Wizard*'s lengthy shooting schedule, tidbits about the production and its staff and players were trickled to the press to arouse public anticipation for MGM's forthcoming Technicolor epic. Some of the notices seemed to almost root for the picture's failure by reporting any setback, no matter how minor. On November 10, 1938, the *Hollywood Reporter* said that Mervyn LeRoy had a severe cold and would be confined to his home for a few days. (LeRoy's ailment was possibly stress-related as this was about the time that days' worth of Technicolor footage was scrapped in order to reshoot the Tin Man scenes.) On January 20, 1939, the *Reporter* noted of *Oz*'s shooting schedule: "Pic was shot around Judy Garland yesterday [Thursday, January 19] when she doubled up with arsenic poisoning from an artichoke," which may have been code for severe menstrual cramping as, a month later on February 13, the *Reporter* indicated that Judy was again off work. (Studio Notes, a news column, noted on February 20, that Garland's illness provided Jack Haley with a break from his Tin Man costume for the first time in four months, but he had in fact had respite from the role during the Munchkinland sequence as well.) At the same time, Ray Bolger became ill. "Ray Bolger went home Thursday [February 9]," noted the *Reporter*, "hampering work for the remainder of the week. Bolger is scheduled to report today."

Additional reports from the *Oz* set were benign curios, such as Judy Garland planning a housewarming party once her newly built Bel Air home was finished. When Garland, her mother, her grandmother, one of her sisters, and a butler and maid moved into the house, circa April 1939, the actress polled her friends for appropriate titles to christen the residence. "So far, she looks with favor upon those names based on the stories of Oz," the press noted.

Among other tidbits were that Frank Morgan was "changing his makeup four times a day for his role in *The Wizard of Oz*"; Ray Bolger was cutting paper caricatures of his fellow castmates; and Bert Lahr was "being his own stand-in during the illness of his regulation stand-in." Bolger was said to have lost up to twelve pounds from his 149-pound frame, while Lahr was said to have gained twenty-nine pounds "under the cumbersome garb of the Cowardly Lion." Judy Garland pitched Christmas Seals on December 21, 1938, for the National Tuberculosis Association (and got a deep paper cut on her hand from wrapping presents). Attired as Dorothy, Garland posed before a broken mirror for a "spooky" Friday the 13th portrait to run on Friday, January 13, 1939.

As an advance attraction, MGM cooperated with the crafting of a floral *Wizard of Oz* float as Culver City's entry in the 1939 Tournament of Roses "Golden Memories" parade. The festivities were held on Monday, January 2—not on January 1 as has been previously cited—in keeping with tournament tradition when New Year's Day falls on a Sunday. The Oz float was peopled by Munchkin actors and movie star doubles authentically made up and attired in full fantasy wardrobe. The most expensive—and irreplaceable—accoutre-

Old Man Hoodoo Leaves His Mark

The Friday the 13th hoodoo frightened JUDY GARLAND, M-G-M juvenile, today. She stepped up to this mirror to admire herself in her pretty new frock and found that Old Man Hoodoo had been there before her and left his intimidating mark. Once again in 1939 will Friday fall on the 13th, but if you get through today safely you won't have to worry about the awesome combination again until October.

ment on the float was the wig worn by Bobbie Koshay as Dorothy. For this event, Koshay donned the blonde wig that she shared with Judy Garland during the initial weeks of tests and filming so as to preserve the chestnut-colored wigs currently in use at the studio. Likewise, the Cowardly Lion outfit used on the float was a backup version and not Bert Lahr's wardrobe. Shirley Temple was the parade's Grand Marshal and, upon viewing the passing *Wizard of Oz* float, was said to have exclaimed, "It seems like fairyland, Mother." Prior to dismantling, the float was among the others on a post-parade display taken in by a throng of thousands on January 3.

At around this time, Judy Garland told a reporter on the *Wizard of Oz* set that, immediately upon wrapping the picture, she anticipated a European vacation with her mother—their first overseas trip—on which she planned to sightsee the countryside on bicycle (though Ethel was "not as enthusiastic about this part of the trip"). Also while on the *Oz* set, Frank Morgan announced that he, too, was definitely sailing to Europe in July; but then the comedian had made the same prediction for the past four years and those plans were always waylaid in favor of accepting roles that he couldn't pass up. As it happened, neither Garland nor Morgan ventured to Europe due to looming war concerns. Instead both actors remained on US soil and traveled to New York—Morgan to take in the sights at the World's Fair with fellow actor Bill Gargan, coinciding with a press preview of *Oz*, and Judy on a combination personal appearance and holiday.

POST-OZ REPRIEVE

Judy Garland's popularity would be catapulted commensurate with *Oz*'s release, but she was becoming increasingly conscious of the cost of fame. On March 28, 1939, Judy Garland, her mother, and Rose Carter, Judy's tutor, trained east to New York for several weeks of personal appearances culminating at Manhattan's Loew's State Theatre. The following morning Garland awoke to the news that the night she left Hollywood, her girlhood friend Delia Bogard had been brutally beaten by a serial assailant and left for dead. (Bogard rallied to full recovery and her attacker, who had previously killed another young woman, was executed.) In less than a year, Garland would herself be the target of a thwarted kidnapping plot, on March 7, 1940.

Thoughts of Bogard's assault must've rattled Garland when she tangled with overzealous New Yorkers. Garland was caught off-guard by a new Manhattan fan trick of pulling off celebrities' hats while yanking out strands of hair as souvenirs (she offered ten dollars and an autograph for the return of her hat). Garland's savior was reportedly one of the little people with whom she had become a favorite while making *The Wizard of Oz*. Identified as Frederick Stout—though no known Munchkin had that name—the forty-inch man offered to be Garland's New York bodyguard and would see to it that the actress was not manhandled by pushy Manhattan crowds. "Outside of helping him into taxis and up curbings and steps, the idea worked swell," Garland was reported to have said.

Between taking in five Broadway shows, touring the World's Fair, and playing the Loew's theater circuit, Garland met with *New York Post* reporter Irene Thirer in the actress's Sherry-Netherland suite for one of her earliest post-*Oz* interviews. After reporting to work on the same picture for six months, Garland felt entitled to a vacation. "It took from last April until the start of the picture for the wardrobe department and the makeup department to do their part—and no less than seven directors got started on it before Victor Fleming stepped in and turned it out," she explained.[1] Still, Garland was no less enthusiastic for making the picture, saying, "I got really scared at times, but I laughed myself sick at Bert Lahr's lion face and Ray Bolger's scarecrow. And Billie Burke is simply beautiful in Technicolor."

For her Loew's State performances, Judy planned to debut a long gown—a career first onstage—which, she conceded, was in contrast with her upcoming appearance as Dorothy. "I go back a few years [for Oz]," she said, "and play a child of twelve." Garland estimated that her physical maturation might translate into a professional maturation. "Oh, if I were only nineteen," she mused, "maybe I'd have a chance to try for *Rebecca* [the David O. Selznick–Alfred Hitchcock production]. There's a part I'd adore to play."

The New York excursion also brought Garland another benchmark of notoriety. The landmark Reuben's Restaurant and Delicatessen in Manhattan was inspired to name a sandwich in her honor, as per its tradition of christening menu items after celebrities. The press reported that Judy was sending New York postcards back west to "all the crew who worked with her in *The Wizard of Oz*." Upon her return to Hollywood in late April, Garland began work on *Babes in Arms*, which was to be her second hit musical production of 1939.

Despite being momentarily annoyed with MGM's pick of roles for him, Frank Morgan continued working steadily after *Oz*, next appearing with child actress Virginia Weidler in the western *Henry Goes Arizona* (1939) before he was finally cast in the dramatic parts he openly bemoaned were lacking on his film vitae: *The Shop Around the Corner* (1940) and *The Mortal Storm* (1940). Morgan also played opposite Billie Burke in two comedies in 1940, *The Ghost Comes Home* and *Hullabaloo*—an unsurprising coupling as both actors were MGM contract players specializing in farce, though the two shared no scenes in *The Wizard of Oz*.

Given his top billing in *Oz* (listed third behind Garland and Morgan), Ray Bolger was poised for a successful season. But on April 3, 1939, the *Hollywood Reporter* announced that MGM had allowed Bolger's studio contract to expire without renewal. According to Bolger, he asked to be released from his contract. Bolger may have grown weary of Metro giving him the short shrift. Two of his dance numbers, in *Rosalie* and *The Girl of the Golden West*, ended up on the cutting-room floor as would an elaborate routine that accompanied "If I Only Had a Brain" in *The Wizard of Oz*. (By 1985 Bolger had completely forgotten having filmed the lost *Oz* scene at the time of its inclusion in the compilation film *That's Dancing!*)

Two months later Bolger and his wife Gwendolyn were slapped with a fifteen-thousand-dollar Supreme Court lawsuit by Select Theatre Corp. that charged the Bolgers with

1 If Garland's recollection was accurate, her citation of seven *Oz* directors could include the contributions of Mervyn LeRoy and Busby Berkeley as well as Taurog, Thorpe, Cukor, Fleming, and Vidor.

wrongful detention of three books containing 286 dramatic sketches used in Schubert plays. Bolger didn't make another picture until *Sunny* (1941) for RKO, for which he received second billing after Anna Neagle. Instead, after *Oz* he returned to his first love: the vaudeville stage. In a piece published in *American Cinematographer*, Bolger evinced discontentment with the picture-making process: "Having come from the Broadway stage, where I created everything myself, I found it difficult to adapt to the regimentation of the film medium, of having to hit a little chalk mark on the set in order to end up before the camera in a close-up. This didn't give me the sense of freedom or release that I liked to have. I wanted to roam and let the camera find me, instead of me finding the camera." As further evidence that Bolger had soured on motion pictures, he specified that he was an "actor—theater" for the 1940 census. Throughout 1940 the dancer embarked on a national tour of major cities headlining a revue with other acts, and all the newspaper ads pictured and referenced Bolger as the "loveable Scarecrow" from *The Wizard of Oz*.

When Bert Lahr married for the second time on February 11, 1940, the press photo of him and his bride, former showgirl Mildred Schroeder, was widely circulated with the heading "Cowardly Lion's New Mate." Lahr's personal contentment was not equaled by professional satisfaction, however. When asked what became of his movie career, Lahr replied, "You see, I played the Cowardly Lion so well that they don't think of me as anything but a Cowardly Lion. And how many Cowardly Lion parts are there?" In typical Lahr fashion, he added, "and I won't play with Tarzan." (Lahr's 1953 version of the retort was that the only remaining lion part of significance was in George Bernard Shaw's *Androcles and the Lion*.)

More than a dozen years later, Lester Shurr, Lahr's agent, responded to the recommendation that his client should star in a television series using his Cowardly Lion character from *The Wizard of Oz*. "On the face of it," Shurr commented, "there might be some merit in the suggestion, but you could never get the rights. The picture is still a goldmine for MGM. The studio re-releases it for a few weeks or months almost every year and it's good for a million bucks every time out. Even if only one character in it was released for TV use, that would cut into the future profits of the picture because TV is a medium of quick saturation." After *Oz* wrapped, Lahr returned to New York having accepted the comic lead in Cole Porter's musical *DuBarry Was a Lady* (1939), with Ethel Merman and Betty Grable.

Jack Haley's concerns that his *Oz* role might unduly influence his career were as similarly blasé as Bert Lahr's attitude. "I can't expect to find any more roles like that," he told the *New York Sun*'s Eileen Creelman. "Hardly likely that I can spend a lifetime playing Tin Woodmen, is it?" Like Lahr, Jack Haley also left Hollywood for the New York stage, appearing in Rodgers and Hart's *Higher and Higher*, which opened at the Shubert Theatre on April 4, 1940. Haley did not become outwardly bitter about his Tin Man role until the 1970s, but his temporary disdain for picture-making was apparent. He didn't return to

Los Angeles—and films—for eighteen months, until January 1941. When Haley did make another picture, *Moon Over Miami* (1941), it was performing before the Technicolor cameras once more, although completely unencumbered this time.

Following *The Wizard of Oz*, Terry the cairn terrier recovered and continued working in pictures such as *Bad Little Angel*, also released in 1939. As in *Bright Eyes*, Terry's name in *Angel* was "Rags," but off-camera Terry was now referred to exclusively as "Toto" after her famous screen counterpart. Commensurate with *Oz*, Terry began receiving fan mail, but according to an October 1939 account, it wasn't until *Angel* that the dog was besieged by autograph hounds.

> In answer to the crowds of children that waited outside MGM each night hoping to see the stars and get their autographs, Terry's handler, Jack Weatherwax, carried an ink pad with him when he left with the dog. "Then, when stopped by the fans, Toto gravely dips one paw in the pad and Weatherwax plants the paw on the proffered autograph book. Because of their uniqueness, these paw prints are bringing top prices on the autograph bartering 'curb.'"

In addition to *Bad Little Angel*, two other films Terry made after *The Wizard of Oz*—previously undocumented—are *Love Crazy* (1941), with William Powell and Myrna Loy, and *Back from the Front* (1942) with the Three Stooges. But before *Oz* had wrapped production, Terry received a call for employment that would take her to the Great White Way—a first for a movie dog. Theatrical journalist George Ross reported that while filming the Kansas scenes, Charley Grapewin became so impressed with Terry that he wrote a part especially for her in *Red Tape*, a play he was developing for a spring 1940 Broadway mounting. Grapewin's play is not known to have been produced, however, and both Grapewin and Terry continued making motion pictures instead.

On July 29, 1939, *Daily Variety* reported that Mervyn LeRoy, eager "to return to piloting," would become a producer *and* director for Metro, with L. B. Mayer's approval. Referencing *The Wizard of Oz*, and his initial desire to direct it, LeRoy told Hollywood columnist Robnbin Coons in March 1940: "I'd work sixteen hours a day in a picture and yet I'd know all the time I couldn't be really happy unless I was out there on the set directing it too. It wasn't that I found fault with the direction—I had Victor Fleming, one of the very best. It was just that I had been a director, and I needed to keep on being one—it's the job I like best." First up on LeRoy's schedule was to be *Ziegfeld Girl* starring Hedy Lamarr, Margaret Sullavan, and Lana Turner—a film that would not be made until 1941, with Judy Garland replacing Sullavan in the cast lineup and without LeRoy's participation.

Victor Fleming's unparalleled output in 1939 would position him to take the Academy Award for Best Director for *Gone with the Wind*, but he was pensive when it came to the success of his contributions to *The Wizard of Oz*. In late 1939 Fleming was premonitory in stating, "There have been many color pictures and we are becoming accustomed to them. But I earnestly believe that *The Wizard of Oz* attains something even beyond the expectations of those who made it."

COMING ATTRACTION

In a November 1939 interview with the North American Newspaper Alliance, Victor Fleming remarked on his *Oz* producer's demagogic undertaking, "Mervyn LeRoy had a job I didn't envy and I imagine he was never envious of mine as director." In advance of editing *The Wizard of Oz*, Fleming offered a chivalrous concession. In deference to LeRoy's devotion, Fleming's sportsman's gallantry was evident when, on May 31, 1939, he posted a letter to the Screen Directors Guild waiving his right to the last title card of the picture's opening credits, transferring such right to LeRoy instead—although the adjustment went unimplemented.

In March 1939, after the film had wrapped its production (save for retakes), attention was given to the look of its opening and closing credits. According to MGM, thirty-five main title sequences for *Oz* were considered or created, apart from the aforementioned book-opening routine suggested by Noel Langley, and the Florence Ryerson–Edgar Allan Woolf sorcerer's shadow idea. Metro's Leo the Lion, reclining in full-body profile, was the background for one version, with the title *The Wizard of Oz* rendered over the top of it. This style was reportedly tested in various color versions. One simplistic approach was to introduce each word of the movie title as a separate image in a distinctly elegant font. Another main titles concept was filmed on March 23, 1939. A large glass ball filled with white liquid, and with the title *The Wizard of Oz* painted on it, was dropped from high above Stage 14 onto the floor, covered in black cloth. Once photographed, the footage was printed in reverse to give the illusion that the intact crystal ball manifests from the shattered glass and liquid. These were all ultimately negated in favor of a monotone cloud montage that could simply have been rear-projection footage repurposed from Victor Fleming's aviator opus, *Test Pilot*.

After the special effects, matte shots, scoring, and titles were factored in, Mervyn LeRoy, Victor Fleming, and Blanche Sewell accommodated Fleming's *GWTW* day schedule and worked evenings to edit *The Wizard of Oz* into a theatrical-length feature. Because *Oz* had a musical underscoring that was virtually complete throughout the entire picture, editing was a particularly painstaking process without creating hash out of Herbert Stothart's compositions.

Blanche Sewell was a masterful cutter who would arguably have made a brilliant director. But this promise was unfulfilled, eclipsed by her indispensable editing deftness. Employed at MGM since 1921, Sewell had an affinity for military-themed pictures and was a favorite editor of Irving Thalberg. She also took a hands-on approach, making suggestions on the soundstage while a film was in production.

Dubbed a "barber of drama," Sewell's editing enclave, as overseen by Margaret Booth, was described by *Photoplay*'s Howard Sharpe as "a cluttered room lined with film racks containing reels, re-winders, sprockets for keeping film and soundtrack in correct juxtaposition, and what all—the floor crinkled with fallen film as you walked, film fountained out of waste baskets, film came loose from numbered rolls and tickled your neck as you sat." In 1936 Sewell told Sharpe of her profession's special challenge:

A cutter . . . must transform hundreds of unrelated pieces of action into a smooth-running story with no jumps or breaks. He must create out of muddled scenes and sequences an hour and a half of rhythm—the camera changes its position constantly but the audience must not be aware of this. Dramatic scenes must be pointed up with close-ups, stale ones necessary to the plot must be hurried.

Our worry is that we can't always tell how the theatre patrons are going to react. When we work with comedy we leave everything in and wait for the preview; the gags that get a laugh are saved, those that flop get cut. Sometimes an audience likes a banal scene because of exceptional acting—sometimes the climaxes we've planned and worked on for months fizzle miserably in a theatre. These have to come out.

Mervyn LeRoy's choice of Blanche Sewell to edit *The Wizard of Oz* was not by random selection. Skilled as she was, Sewell was also Walt Disney's sister-in-law by marriage. (Blanche's brother, Glenn Sewell, was married to Hazel Bounds, and Hazel's sister was Disney's wife, Lillian.) According to author John Stanley Donaldson, Disney surreptitiously consulted Sewell after hours from MGM while *Snow White and the Seven Dwarfs* was edited. Sewell possessed, in Donaldson's language, an infallible grasp of the *emotion picture*—an intuitive ability for cinematic pacing to strike the proper tempo and temperament. It was her insightful whittling that coalesced the best of *Snow White*'s artistic triumphs and shaped them into an instantly acclaimed motion picture masterpiece. LeRoy was hopeful Sewell would work such wizardry a second time.

Prior to previewing *The Wizard of Oz* with the public, it was screened in-house for a very discriminating constituency: MGM's roster of child actors. An August 12, 1939, notice emphasized the weight of opinion these juveniles carried, especially given their acclimation to the mechanics of film construction. "Children in the studio school previewed the sets and scenes and when they had evinced satisfaction with them, Victor Fleming, director of the picture, was satisfied. They constitute the audience he was aiming at. 'People may be sixty when they come into the theatre,' he said, 'but they'll be six while they are looking at the picture.'"

Thereafter, private screenings and select previews for *The Wizard of Oz* were planned for June 1939, after which further tweaks and edits were made to trim its running time and tighten its narrative prior to its public reception at large. In 1955 Mervyn LeRoy told Hollywood correspondent Bob Thomas, "Previews are indispensable. You can put your heart and soul into a picture, but you never know if it's good until you play it before an audience." *Oz* cameraman Harold Rosson noted that the primary purpose for the previews was to elicit comments from audiences that would guide "the final true editing of the picture." It was a procedure crucial to the cutting process of any "A" picture but more so for *Oz*. As noted in the July 11, 1939, edition of the *Manitowoc (WI) Herald-Times*, "MGM is staking a lot on the public's reception

of Mervyn LeRoy's *The Wizard of Oz*, which will be previewed this month and then held up for cooler weather release. Fantasies are always problem children of the movie minds and the critics can't yet forget Paramount's fancy but profitless splurge on *Alice in Wonderland*."

Prerelease audience feedback was crucial to how the final version of any "A" picture would be edited, reshot, or augmented with new scenes. Putting over *Oz* in a manner that would delight and entertain the masses and appease followers of the Oz books was as much a balancing act as it would be for David O. Selznick's production of *Gone with the Wind*. Immediately following the *Wizard of Oz* sneak peeks, audience members would be given printed preview questionnaires to solicit constructive commentary with questions such as "How did you like the picture?" and "What did you think of the cast?" Other queries were of a more technical nature, including, "Was the sound entirely clear and could you understand the dialogue? If not, do you recall which parts were not audible?"

Because it was thought that certain audiences around Los Angeles were jaded by too-frequent previews, the major studios went far afield to gauge fresh reactions. In separate interviews, both Mervyn LeRoy and *Oz* cameraman Harold Rosson accurately remembered the first preview for *The Wizard of Oz* in San Bernardino, which took place on Sunday, June 4, 1939, at the Fox Theatre. According to Rosson, the night of the San Bernardino preview was tense with anticipation because the picture was a "huge gamble, because it's an unbelievable story" and that fantasy onscreen was successfully portrayed "very seldom."

That evening, as Rosson recalled, he, LeRoy, Fleming, Herbert Stothart, and L. B. Mayer "would leave the studio in a private car . . . that would take us downtown to where we hooked on to the inter-urban line. . . . It was the first time the picture had ever been shown to the public in general. . . . The studio was now laying all their money on the line. And this was a very important picture. So there was a lot of excitement. Is it going to go over, or is it not going to go over? Is it going to go over big or only small?"

Mervyn LeRoy had a method for attending previews. He disdained preview comment cards, preferring to tune in to the spectators' pulse. "You don't need cards," he told Bob Thomas. "You can get the feel of the audience just by observing them. I like to sit in the balcony and look down on them. If they sit forward in their seats, I know the picture is going well. If they slump back and get fidgety, that means trouble."

Immediately following the San Bernardino preview, Ed Sullivan told his readers on June 6, 1939, that Mervyn LeRoy had already sliced the picture down to two thousand feet and that Judy Garland and Bert Lahr "do a pretty good job of stealing the flicker." The film was readied for its second preview at the Fox Theatre in Pomona on Friday, June 16. In addition to the requisite studio brass, Judy Garland also attended this advance screening. After the show the *Pomona Progress* noted that "the little songstress obligingly autographed everything handed her as she made her way from the theatre."

Roy Lindsay, a Fox Theatre associate, put entertainment journalists on notice with postcards bearing the legend: "Just previewed *Wizard of Oz*. It's great; don't miss it." However, "O.H.K.," the *Pomona Progress* movie critic, had reservations for the picture's tense moments, writing, "Make no mistake folks . . . the movie is not for children, at least not in the form previewed last night to a near capacity audience at the Fox. But it's so exceedingly well done, every type of normal grownup should like it. It's horrific but amusing, and ends happily." O.H.K. went on to say that *Oz* was not recommended for children because it left little to the imagination, citing, as an example, "the Kansas twister which almost gets the little girl is too realistic," but commenting that "Margaret Hamilton as the bad, green-faced witch was a howling success."

The Pomona audience was ecstatic over *Oz*, however. Nine hundred fifty-one completed preview cards were turned in, each a rave for the picture. Among the aspects that the audience found most pleasing were the antics of the Munchkins in their respective musical sequence.

The print screened in Pomona ran 112 minutes in length; another eleven minutes would be shorn as the *Oz* narrative was further edited. Another, final preview was held on

Tuesday evening, June 27, in San Luis Obispo. Mervyn LeRoy distinctly remembered that at this preview *Oz* clicked. In 1973 he told United Press International journalist Vernon Scott, "I'll never forget our sneak preview in San Luis Obispo, California, where the audience sat in silence for almost a minute at the end of the screening. That can mean the picture is very good or awfully bad. Then they broke into cheers."

Resulting from the round of three previews, various bits were edited from *The Wizard of Oz* in order to trim its running length to a tolerable 101 minutes. Anything that was not viewed as essential was liable to end up on the cutting-room floor. This included minor bits of dialogue that added little or nothing to the plot (as noted in the preceding analysis of the October 10, 1938, script) and excising some of Margaret Hamilton's more fearsome threats. But in several instances, entire musical numbers were dropped.

Cut from *The Wizard of Oz* was an extended and fantastically athletic version of Ray Bolger's "If I Only Had a Brain" song, which necessitated reshooting portions of the scene for continuity. Also trimmed was the triumphal parade through the Emerald City after the Wicked Witch had been conquered—a musical segue of "Ding-Dong! The Witch Is Dead" that transitioned the action from the Witch's castle to the Emerald City in a glittering bit of pageantry featuring three hundred extras feting Dorothy and her friends upon their victorious return.

On at least one occasion, "Over the Rainbow" was excised before its final restoration to the completed cinematic narrative. Both Arthur Freed and Judy Garland recollected this coincided with the Pomona preview. In 1952 screenwriter Ben Hecht claimed it was he who nearly caused the song's deletion, saying, "I almost convinced Mervy LeRoy to throw 'Over the Rainbow' out of *Wizard of Oz*." The oft-cited rationale for cutting the song— that it was undignified for Judy Garland to perform a musical number in a barnyard—was the excuse for a greater argument. A number of reviewers for *The Wizard of Oz* would criticize the overall lagging pace of the Kansas prologue, and it is conceivable that some preview audience members made similar complaints, especially as one of the important questions asked on the comments survey would have been "Did any parts seem too long? If so, what parts?" "Over the Rainbow" was the only Kansas scene that could be trimmed in its entirety without creating serious continuity issues. In 1970 Mervyn LeRoy affirmed this rationale, recalling that studio executives thought the opening Kansas scenes took too long and that the film's pace could be accelerated by dropping the number.

Most significantly deleted was "The Jitterbug," the song-and-dance routine in the Haunted Forest that included synchronization to the music with humanoid trees that swayed and clapped in tune. Had "The Jitterbug" been retained, it may have been rebuked as old-fashioned by the public—depending on the era in which it was viewed—before becoming embraced as nostalgic. On October 3, 1938, the *Hollywood Reporter* noted that Paramount had canned a film based on the life of Benny Goodman and the trendy jitterbug dance craze for this very reason: "Execs figure jitterbug craze might be a thing of the past by the time the band leader is available."

The theory that "The Jitterbug" was eliminated to retain *Oz*'s aura of timelessness is supported by the recollections of Jack Haley and Margaret Hamilton. In 1956 Haley noted, "I remember at the time they cut a jitterbug routine for fear it would give away the period it was made. So now there's nothing to give a clue since it's all in costume." Similarly, in 1961 Hamilton said, "I had no idea the movie would become a classic. I don't think any of us did, but the people who made it perhaps thought so. There is a jitterbug number in the original musical [score] and it was filmed in a complete sequence and then cut." Although "The Jitterbug" was deleted from *The Wizard of Oz*, an instrumental rendition was repurposed for a tap dance sequence in "Time Out for Lessons," an *Our Gang* short released December 2, 1939.

Ultimately, the final cut of *The Wizard of Oz* preserved the humanistic element of L. Frank Baum's narrative in a motion picture–length retelling—more authentic than any previous interpretation. But public opinion still awaited *Snow White*'s heir apparent—and where pedestrian tastes in entertainment were concerned, the public could be fickle.

LAUNCHING "LEROY'S FOLLY"

By the end of July 1939, MGM's film-processing laboratory worked overtime to produce 550 prints of *The Wizard of Oz*. When *Oz* was entered for copyright with the Library of Congress on August 7, 1939, it was registered not with a print of the film but with a cache of production stills (which remain in the Library's collections to this day) as was protocol then.

The finished theatrical trailer for *Oz* was readied for national distribution by August 11. Presented in travelogue format, its main titles announced, "A Metro-Goldwyn-Mayer TravelTalk—The Wonderful Land of Oz." The narration set up the tour beginning, "Many, many miles east of nowhere lies the amazing Land of Oz. . . ." It continued with requisite hyperbole, "Metro-Goldwyn-Mayer, joining the world in the celebration of the Golden Jubilee of Motion Pictures, climaxes a half century of entertainment progress by presenting its miracle in celluloid, the Technicolor extravaganza, *The Wizard of Oz*." (This last bit was subsequently deleted as obsolete from future re-release versions of the trailer.)

The original trailer for *Oz* was a bit lengthier than would be its succeeding re-release trailers, and included shots of Margaret Hamilton, Billie Burke, the Munchkins, and an outtake of the Witch threatening the group from the Tin Man's cottage. In addition, the Filmack Trailer Co. of Chicago created five different specialty trailers designed to promote *Oz* from every conceivable angle, from a special children's performance of the picture to the suggestion that *Oz* would offer carefree respite from worries over the European Nazi invasion.

By April 22, 1939, the *Boxoffice* trade journal indicated that *The Wizard of Oz* was slated for limited-engagement theatrical road shows; that is, select screenings (usually two a day) with reserved seats at premium prices. The July 8, 1939, edition of *Daily Variety* announced that *The Wizard of Oz* would have its official premiere at the Carthay Circle Theatre on August 16 or the following week at seventy-five cents per ticket (three times the national average). The Carthay had the reputation as the launching site of important pictures and the projected several-month run of *Oz* at the Carthay would uphold an aura of prestige for the succeeding road-show premiere of *Gone with the Wind*. A July 28 *Daily Variety* update changed the *Oz* event to "around August 10," and shortly thereafter the Los Angeles press confirmed that the Carthay-*Oz* opening was now slated for August 9, 1939, preceding show dates at both Grauman's Chinese Theatre and Loew's State on August 16. These announcements also indicated that two special guests would be "one of the highlights" of the event—former Broadway Scarecrow Fred Stone and Maud Baum, L. Frank Baum's widow.

Then on August 3, 1939, Wood Soanes divulged, "August 10 is set as the world premiere of MGM's *Wizard of Oz* at the Carthay Circle in Hollywood." But the August 10 date was postponed for a week later. Next it was reported, "The scheduled opening of *Wizard of Oz* for August 16 at Carthay has been definitely canceled. The MGM production will open at a later date at Grauman's Chinese." Such premiere musical chairs was not unheard of. Metro's *The Women*, which followed *Oz* on the studio's release schedule, endured similar logistical snafus.

There was also consideration given to double-billing *Oz* with another picture, but by August 12, 1939, *Daily Variety* noted that *Oz* would be single-billed. "Decision to solo," it was said, "was reached late yesterday, and is prompted largely by similarity of picture's appeal with that of *Snow White and the Seven Dwarfs*, which was single-billed almost exclusively through this territory."

By August 5, 1939, it was decided to dispense the road-show angle and switch to, in *Daily Variety* lingo, "day-daters"—or more-accessible-to-the-masses showtimes and prices. The *Wizard of Oz* premiere was officially rescheduled for Tuesday night, August 15, 1939, at Grauman's Chinese Theatre, necessitating an early termination of its booking for *Stanley and Livingstone*. *Oz*'s trailer was adjusted accordingly and a tag was superimposed over a long shot of the Witch's castle that stated, "Because of the intense, wide-spread interest, *The Wizard of Oz* is being given a general and early exhibition throughout the world, so that everybody may see this superb and long-awaited attraction at popular prices!"

The scheduling roulette accounted for *Oz*'s debut in scattered regional play dates—largely shore resorts—ahead of the Grauman's August 15, 1939, screening but commensurate with

August 10, the date originally set for the West Coast premiere. These included Green Bay, Wisconsin, on August 10; Cape Cod, Massachusetts, and Kenosha, Oshkosh, and Appleton, Wisconsin, on August 11; Oconomowoc, Wisconsin, on August 12; Portsmouth, New Hampshire, and Escanaba, Racine, Rhinelander, and Sheboygan, Wisconsin, on August 13; and Chicago, Illinois, and Gaffney, South Carolina, on August 14. With no further justification, on August 5, 1939, the *Appleton Post-Crescent* simply relayed, "Appleton has been selected as one of the few cities in the United States for the premiere release of *The Wizard of Oz*. . . . The picture will be shown [in Appleton] almost a whole week before it will be opened in New York." Harrisburg, Pennsylvania, also enjoyed a special midnight preview of *Oz* at its Loew's Regent Theatre the evening of Friday, August 11.

This didn't prevent several other locations from laying claim to the "World Premiere Showing" of *Oz*, among them Bluefield, West Virginia (August 18), and Spirit Lake, Iowa (August 17), which covered the gala via the resort town's first-ever radio broadcast. Also staged was a kickoff event at Fremont, Michigan's so-named Oz Theatre, a newly constructed thirty-thousand-dollar "official Oz theatre." Elsewhere, *The Wizard of Oz* was set for its official national release on August 25, 1939.

The *Wizard of Oz* premiere at Grauman's epitomized Hollywood at its most decadent, and no expense was spared in mounting it. The 1937 *Snow White and the Seven Dwarfs* premiere at Carthay Circle had re-created in three-dimension the dwarfs' cottage, mill wheel, diamond mine, and foreboding trees. Little people costumed as Mickey and Minnie Mouse, Donald Duck, and, of course, Grumpy, Dopey, and the remaining dwarfs, greeted all who attended. Two of the little people who masqueraded as dwarfs were Billy Curtis and Major Doyle, both of whom went on to be cast as Munchkins in *Oz*.

Similarly grandiose plans were announced to transform Grauman's courtyard with decor direct from the *Oz* sets. Elmer Sheely of MGM's art department (and who also worked on the picture) was in charge of decorations. The theater forecourt was converted into a green celluloid cornfield complete with a scarecrow (a mannequin in Ray Bolger's duds) through which a yellow brick road extended to the theater entrance. A "live" tin man robot was flown down from San Francisco as a point of interest for photo opportunities. Larger-than-life green-glass spires were transplanted from the Emerald City as were flat cutouts of Munchkin huts, used to create the illusion of depth in the background of the Munchkinland set.

Grauman's ushers were attired as citizens of the Emerald City, and several Munchkin players, made up and costumed for their parts, were to be on hand to lend atmosphere and to mingle with the guests. The *Long Beach (CA) Independent*'s Harriet Trane, columnist of Tidbits by Trane, informed her readers that one of the Munchkin impersonators, Victor Wetter, page boy of the Long Beach Hilton hotel, would be on leave from his position in order to attend the premiere, noting that Wetter had a very important role in *Oz* as the

"captain of the army who leads Dorothy through Emerald City." (Wetter was actually the Munchkin army captain.)

Amid the juggling of premiere dates, MGM offered *Wizard of Oz* advance tickets by mail order beginning on August 4, 1939, with in-person ticket sales set to open on August 9 at a special box office installed in the Grauman's forecourt. Would-be pedestrians desiring to attend *The Wizard of Oz* premiere were cautioned that only a limited number of seats were being offered to the public. Advance requests by stars and motion picture personalities got priority, ensuring that "virtually every film celebrity is expected to attend." The house was sold out by the morning of August 14, but Grauman's had erected bleachers outside the theater for throngs of fans that would gather for the following evening's premiere. By three o'clock on the afternoon of August 15, the bleachers were already jammed to capacity with more than five thousand people. Although most brought their own boxed lunches, it was said that street vendors made a small fortune peddling sandwiches and soft drinks.

A live broadcast of the premiere event was scheduled to air over KMPC starting at eight thirty the evening of the premiere. (The broadcast concluded at nine o'clock and the picture started a half hour afterward.) An orchestra played selections from the movie's score as the stars arrived at the theater. A crowd of twelve thousand spectators mobbed Hollywood Boulevard four hours before showtime and reportedly broke through police barricades in a fan frenzy when MGM beauty Hedy Lamarr emerged from her limousine. Not every celebrity appreciated the aggressive show of admiration, and some of the stars hid their faces behind curtained car windows until the theater was reached. As those cars passed the bleachers, boos and raspberries arose from the crowd. *The Wizard of Oz* was the first time horseback police had been used at a Hollywood premiere to contain the excitement and protect the stars from overzealous admirers.

The previous Saturday Lana Turner had collapsed while making *Dancing Co-ed*, the result of nervous exhaustion from working (and playing) too hard. She expected to attend the *Oz* premiere but was under doctor's orders to rest and recover. Hollywood correspondent Harold W. Cohen chastised Joan Crawford for being conspicuously absent at an event for her own studio before describing the ensuing electrifying excitement of the evening in his August 20, 1939, column:

> Thousands of flags floated lazily in the breeze; a band kept playing the tunes from the picture as the stars stepped before the microphone to speak their little pieces. [Only those celebrities with MGM affiliations were permitted to be interviewed on air.] Mile-long limousines spilled their beglamoured cargoes at the curb in an endless stream while the bleacherites roared like Brooklyn baseball fans at a ninth-inning Dodger uprising; a dozen search lights flashed crazily back and forth across the skies and the air was charged with a thousand and one excitements. It was a Hollywood opening to end all Hollywood openings.

The Wizard of Oz marked the first time children of screen stars were specially invited to a Hollywood premiere, and Bing Crosby, Andy Devine, Virginia Bruce, and Dick Powell were requested to accompany their progeny to the gala. Among the celebrities who are known to have brought their own children were Harold Lloyd, Wallace Beery (who got the biggest cheers), and Eddie Cantor, who brought his youngest daughter, Janet. When Beery's Carol Ann said, "My daddy told me if I was a good girl and took a nap, he'd take me to see *The Wizard of Oz* tonight." Cantor quipped, "Janet told me if I was a good boy and took a nap, she'd take me to see *The Wizard* tonight." Attending offspring of the Hollywood press were Ed Sullivan's daughter Betty and Harrison Carroll's son.

As a guest of honor that night, Maud Baum was perhaps genuinely overwhelmed and oblivious amid the glamour and excitement. According to Maud's granddaughter Ozma Baum Mantele, Maud appeared "engulfed" in the revelry to the point of forgetting about her own relatives. Ozma and her family had not been invited to the event but, instead, bought tickets and were lined up at the curb. When "Grandmother Baum" was being interviewed at the premiere dais located outside the theater, the Baums filed by and waved. As Ozma Baum Mantele recounted in later years, Maud "never batted an eyelash" at them, and the incident was never discussed.

Ozma did not go entirely unnoticed that evening, however, and a press mention of her presence included a family anecdote: "When she was born, she was the first girl born in the family for three generations. Her delighted grandfather presented the baby with a diamond necklace. 'You are a little princess and will wear diamonds,' he remarked, and asked that she be named, Ozma, after the Princess of Oz in his books."

If Maud Baum felt especially distinguished that Hollywood evening it may have been augmented by the general knowledge that "she has a large circle of friends among the pioneer families of this once-exclusive residential suburb of Los Angeles," and that she was decreed "the happiest woman in the crowd."

Fred Stone, the fondly recalled Scarecrow of the original stage show, made an appearance at *The Wizard of Oz* premiere with his daughter, actress Paula Stone. Fred Stone had already seen the picture at a private screening, and in December 1938 it was noted that Paula, then playing Beulah, one of Clark Gable's chorines in MGM's *Idiot's Delight*, was a frequent visitor to the *Oz* set. Paula surreptitiously kept her father apprised of the goings-on, as he was on the East Coast appearing in a Broadway revival of the comedy *Lightnin'*, saying, "Dad is anxious to come back here. He wants to see what they're going to do with *The Wizard of Oz*."

The reunion of Fred Stone with L. Frank Baum's widow at such a spectacular celebration was a bittersweet occasion; the two shook hands and chatted for several minutes. Stone had outlived his *Wizard of Oz* sidekick, David "Tin Man" Montgomery, but Montgomery's niece, actress Goodee Montgomery, another VIP in attendance, was his proxy as one who shared a connection to the musical comedy. Tragically, Anna Laughlin, the 1902 show's original Dorothy, committed suicide at age fifty on March 6, 1937, by turning on the gas jets of the oven in her apartment after leaving a three-page letter in which she claimed her daughter, singer and actress Lucy Monroe, had "forsaken her."

Among the MGM *Wizard of Oz* cast present were Billie Burke and Ray Bolger, who, according to one fan, sat in near proximity to each other. The fan, who nabbed autographs from both celebrities, noted: "Sat behind them at the world premiere. . . ." No known photographs show Frank Morgan in attendance, but he was reportedly present and may well have slipped in; as of July 5, 1939, he was working with Metro to schedule the *Oz* premiere and avoid a conflict with the grand opening of a grocery he was constructing in Beverly Hills. Bert Lahr was also on hand, "in a tuxedo instead of the genuine lion skin suit he wears in the picture," noted the United Press recap of the events. It was also mentioned that Herbert, Lahr's eleven-year-old son, missed the premiere.

Actress Joan Bennett's two daughters, Diane and Melinda, were said to have been fascinated with the Munchkins as they made their way into the theater. But five-year-old Melinda had suddenly become too sophisticated for such frivolity after seeing the picture. Upon their departure a radio announcer stopped the Bennett party and asked little Melinda what she thought of *The Wizard of Oz*. "I didn't like it. It's for children," she was said to have remarked. Similarly, when the twelve-year-old daughter of composer Deems Taylor was asked if she liked *Snow White* better than *Oz*, she replied, "No, not better but as well."

The evening's press coverage extended even to the after-party. Following the opening, members of the *Oz* camp, including Victor Fleming and Mervyn LeRoy, reconvened at the Café Trocadero nightclub to bask in the evening's success and belatedly celebrate Bert Lahr's August 13 birthday. When Lahr arrived LeRoy was so ecstatic that he greeted Lahr with kisses on both cheeks. LeRoy was also said to be so excited that he forgot to order dinner for his guests, but Mrs. Darryl Zanuck and the wife of producer William Goetz stepped in as hostesses.

Hedda Hopper overheard Eddie Cantor remark to Ray Bolger, "Ray, I hated to see you standing on the sidelines in *The Wizard of Oz*, while all those others danced," which led to Hollywood journalist Harold W. Cohen cornering Mervyn LeRoy to enquire why there was no scarecrow dance in *Oz* as a tribute to Fred Stone and the old-timers who were endeared to him. LeRoy explained that such a routine had been shot but he had to cut it out because the picture was too long. The Trocadero festivities continued well beyond midnight, with anyone connected to *Oz* congratulating one another for having silenced the chorus of naysayers that predicted the film's failure as recently as a month before.

The *Wizard of Oz* premiere was such a smash success that, the next day, the Associated Press projected that *Oz*'s worldwide revenue was destined to top five million. All day-after reviews were raves, showering accolades and superlatives as much for the exciting star-studded evening as for the picture itself. *Daily Variety*'s Alta Durant erred when she included Judy Garland among the attending "top players of the picture" in her recap of the events. Garland missed the Grauman's festivities for being in New York to launch *Oz*'s East Coast debut with MGM costar Mickey Rooney. By January 21, 1940, Lucie Neville noted that Judy still "never has seen all of *The Wizard of Oz*, though it was playing when she and Rooney . . . made a joint appearance in New York." But Garland made certain she was there in spirit, wiring a telegram expressing her good wishes to Victor Fleming. During *Oz* she had developed a personal and professional veneration for the director, as she admitted the previous April. "If I ever get to the stage where I can have my choice of directors," she told journalist Irene Thirer, "I'll make nothing but Victor Fleming productions."

It wouldn't be until the following July that *The Wizard of Oz* was screened for Garland in an MGM projection room, where she finally saw the completed film for the first time in its entirety (she had seen only a rough cut for the Pomona preview). Metro's screening of *Oz* for Judy made national news as a premiere a year late: "The reason the starlet has never been able to see the picture was due to her personal appearance tour coming at the same time as the release."

Immediately following the Grauman's premiere, Maud Baum waxed ecstatic over *The Wizard of Oz*, proclaiming, "The picture is beautiful—and I have never seen such reviews." Another opinion of the film from a Baum family member came from Leslie Gage, Frank Baum's niece. In September 1939 Gage's sole critique was for Judy Garland's casting. She quibbled "that the little girl of the books might have been somewhat too grown up in the picture version." By late October even Maud's perception had grown a tad jaded. She reportedly was "well satisfied" with the film except that she wished there had been more music in it, and that there had been no witch, claiming that her late husband would have taken exception with the terrifying aspects of Margaret Hamilton's performance. If Maud was at all off-put by the Witch, she would have vehemently disapproved of the following scripted scene cut prior to filming:

```
CLOSE-UP OF WITCH'S HANDS
Pulling roughly at the slippers. They suddenly flash like
red fire.
The witch shrinks back, staring at the slippers and nursing
her hand.


WITCH
Ouch! They burnt my fingers!


DOROTHY
I'm sorry. I can't help it.


WITCH (suddenly has an idea)
I'll cut them off!
(she reaches toward a wicked-looking knife which is on the
wall, then changes her mind)
```

In its July 15, 1939, issue, *Publishers Weekly* announced that *The Wizard of Oz* would have its East Coast premiere at New York's Astor Theatre "shortly after Labor Day" with a national release "two or three weeks later." Similar to juggling the West Coast premiere, those plans were revised. A month later both the New York premiere date and venue had been adjusted to August 17, 1939, at the Capitol Theatre.

The opening of *Oz* at the Capitol Theatre was a publicity coup orchestrated by the Loew's New York team of promoters led by Oscar Doob (who took to signing his name *Ozcar*) with Ernie Emerling and Eddie Dowden handling the details. The tie-up was a four-fold stunt devised to generate excitement for the personal appearance of Mickey Rooney and Judy Garland on the theater stage as well as to promote *The Wizard of Oz*, entice moviegoers to see Rooney's picture *Andy Hardy Gets Spring Fever* in circulation at other Loew's-owned theaters, and create buzz for the impending Rooney-Garland film *Babes in Arms*, which would be released that October.

The buzz was buoyed further by Ben Serkowich, press agent of the Capitol's publicity department. Serkowich was so impressed by *Oz* at an advance screening that on August 4, 1939, he wrote of his enthusiasm to film critics of the New York press. "I saw [*Oz*] yesterday," he wrote, "and, putting aside my interest as an employee, have no hesitancy in saying that I think it is the finest motion picture entertainment I have ever seen in my 25 years of association with the industry. I have never said that before. In fact, I don't think anyone has ever had the nerve to say it. When you see it, I hope you'll say it in print, and I believe you'll come close to saying it. It is really the kind of thing people will want to see again and again."

On August 6, 1939, Mickey Rooney and Judy Garland departed Los Angeles with the Capitol as their final destination. *Movie Story* magazine reported that the duo's mothers were sent as chaperones to ensure that "Mickey was to be Andy Hardy at all times; Judy was to be Dorothy of *The Wizard of Oz*." Indeed, Rooney's manic energy couldn't easily be contained. MGM makeup artist Charles Schram remembered that Rooney would spontaneously go off on tangents, picking up a pair of drum sticks, for example, to instigate an impromptu jam session. This "bit" was incorporated into the Rooney-Garland stage show, and made to appear as equally impulsive as it had been at MGM.

Personal appearances were planned en route to Manhattan to polish the song-and-comedy act Rooney and Garland were to perform between screenings of *The Wizard of Oz* at the Capitol. Among the stops were Washington, DC, on August 9, where their appearance diverted traffic and prompted the decree that "no adult stars had ever brought out such a mob of Washingtonians." The Washington bureau of the *Film Daily* reported that three thousand fans turned out to greet the stars as they were welcomed by the president of the Board of Commissioners of the District of Columbia flanked by thirty uniformed ushers and thirty "Roxyettes."

A "Standing Room Only" sign was posted at the theater an hour before the show, by which time the street was blocked by a crowd of five thousand. *Hollywood* magazine expanded that figure by an additional thousand patrons and dubbed Rooney and Garland the Prince and Princess of Hollywood when it reported that the first audience of the day yelled and cheered for an hour. This prompted the house manager to take the stage to announce that the teen performers were finished for that show as he implored seat holders to vacate the theater so the throng outside could be admitted in.

Sara Morrow, writing for Pennsylvania's the *Harrisburg Telegraph*, was among the press represented as Rooney and Garland arrived in Washington for a luncheon held in the Crystal Room of the Hotel Willard, hosted by Carter T. Barron, East Coast manager of Loew's Theatres. After the two celebrities had about ten minutes to eat, they spent the rest of their lunch hour answering questions from the journalists in attendance.

According to Morrow, Rooney thrived upon the adulation. "I just love it," he said. "I like to get away from home. At home, the other kids just treat me like any other person, and no one stares but it certainly is different here." Morrow described Garland as "the pretty red-haired little singer" who was lovely, charming, and polite. Garland told Morrow that the personal appearance grind was already taking its toll, saying that she had never before in her life been so tired.[2] However, the reporter noted that Garland was "not concerned about herself, her attention is centered on Mickey," who was always raring to go. During their performance the pair had a code, "22-14," that each called out to the other as a good luck greeting. When Morrow specifically asked Judy about *The Wizard of Oz*, the actress replied, "It is very beautiful technically. Of course you know it is a fantasy, but I hope that everyone will like it."

Paul Walker, columnist of the *Harrisburg Telegraph*'s Reviews and Previews feature, said that the reception audiences gave Rooney and Garland "puts a lump in your throat and a tear in your eye—just plain, unadulterated, genuine admiration." Like Sara Morrow, Walker also found Rooney to be cocky one-on-one but was thoroughly entertained once the pair took to the stage, describing the "pandemonium for two full minutes" that greeted the celebrities. According to Walker, after Rooney's imitations of Lionel Barrymore and Clark Gable, and Garland's songs, and dances and patter with Rooney, there was "curtain call after curtain call" of applause coming in invisible waves. "I've never seen anything so spontaneous," Walker wrote. "The crowd is on its collective feet, and as it settles back, a woman stands up and shouts, 'Mickey, you're a fine boy.'" Rooney was fueled by the adoration while Judy was seen to be panting in the wings, reiterating, "I've never been so tired." Rooney's response was to give her a friendly shove and an encouraging "Come on, Jutes" before taking repeated bows.

From DC, Mickey Rooney and Judy Garland went on to make appearances in Bridgeport and New Haven, Connecticut, before heading to Manhattan. When the pair arrived at New York's Grand Central Station on August 14, 1939, they were mobbed by over ten thousand fans, some of whom were the high-school-age winners of a ballot contest to serve on an official reception committee.

---

2 On August 30, 1939, *New York Post* reporter Michel Mok remarked of his interview with Garland: "She sounded rather sleepy and looked a little tired."

On Friday night, August 11, a participating boy and girl from each of the seventy-four Loew's theaters was selected from an estimated two hundred thousand entries to welcome Rooney and Garland at the train station, escort them to the Capitol, and share a luncheon with the pair on August 16 in the Empire Room of their hotel, the Waldorf-Astoria. There, all contest winners obtained autographs from the Hollywood pair and each was given the new edition of *The Wizard of Oz* book. Jack Haley, in town for an engagement of his own at Loew's State Theatre, served as the luncheon's toastmaster; and band leader Guy Lombardo provided the music.

At the Capitol, Rooney and Garland played five shows a day, six on Sunday, between screenings of *The Wizard of Oz* in a house that seated fifty-four hundred. Mickey Rooney reveled in the outpouring of fan and press attention. Garland was accustomed to Rooney's antics and boundless zeal, described by *Radio and Television Mirror* in 1939 as "that adolescent combination of genius and holy terror." He reportedly made Loew's officials and the Capitol management sick with worry at the start of their daily shows by bursting through the stage door just as the band struck up their overture—nearly to the point of being late. Garland was said to have taken it all in stride, confident that Rooney wouldn't let down a fellow trouper.

Hollywood Spectator had previously, and erroneously, listed Mickey Rooney among the *Wizard of Oz* cast, as did Virginia Vale, commentator for the column Star Dust, when she indicated that both Judy and Mickey played the picture's leading roles. Robert Gardner, columnist for *Hollywood Red Ink*, wondered, "Everybody from a black-face comedian to a Shakespearean actor and Mickey Rooney have come up for the lead in *The Wizard of Oz*." But the Capitol's Ben Serkowich clarified Rooney's connection:

> Fun history for New York will probably date from Thursday, August 17th, when Metro-Goldwyn-Mayer brings *The Wizard of Oz* to the Capitol Theatre. Although this event in itself is expected to be enough to make it a red-letter day on anyone's calendar, the Capitol will also present Mickey Rooney and Judy Garland, in person, on the stage, between performances of the film. Judy is the little Kansas girl blown by a cyclone to the land of Oz. Mickey is not in *Oz* but he does come along on the screen a few months hence with Judy in *Babes in Arms*.

On opening day, August 17, 1939, the *Film Daily* reported that lines began forming at five thirty in the morning with patrons showing up at the Capitol box office with hot coffee and doughnuts. By eight forty-five the line was six-deep around the entire block, and ticket sales were suspended until eleven o'clock to relieve congestion. In addition to box-office sales, ushers were sent out into the crowd to sell tickets. At three that afternoon the theater was still completely encircled and additional police reserves were called out.

The total number of patrons for the day was said to be thirty-eight thousand. Suffice it to say, Rooney and Garland were rock stars before the phrase was coined. "Nothing like it has happened in New York since *Snow White and the Seven Dwarfs*," the papers decreed. At the Capitol first-week grosses were seventy thousand dollars, or 167 percent over the normal take.

In February 1940 little-people performers Prince Denis and his wife, Ethel, both of whom appeared in *Oz*, claimed that fifty Munchkins were at the Capitol's New York premiere. Among Rooney and Garland's celebrity visitors was heavyweight boxing champ–turned–restaurant entrepreneur Jack Dempsey. Dempsey brought his young daughter Joan to see *The Wizard of Oz* and stopped backstage afterwards to meet and greet the Hollywood pair and to exchange autographs.

After their August 30 evening show, Mickey Rooney returned to the West Coast as, the following day, live performances continued with Judy Garland and her *Wizard of Oz* costars Ray Bolger and Bert Lahr. For the stint, Lahr made thirty-five hundred dollars and Bolger, fifteen hundred dollars. Before *Oz* Bolger and Lahr had a history on the stage, and both appeared in the Broadway show *Life Begins at 8:40*. Between takes on the *Oz* set, they regaled each other with tales from the vaudeville circuit. One such anecdote, as Lahr told it, occurred in Portland, Maine. The theater manager told Lahr, "Think you're funny? Last week we had a comic named Rubberlegs Bolger who killed the people."

For the Capitol engagement, Bolger flew into New York on American Airlines. Lahr took the Super Chief streamliner, but the "Train of the Stars" promptly misplaced the comedian's luggage, sending Lahr into a nervous dither. "Why let it bother you?" Bolger asked. "Buy yourself another pair." Lahr groaned, "But my diamond studs are in them," to which Bolger needled, "What swank! You mean you wear diamond studs in your trunks?" "Gawd, how you talk," wailed Lahr. "I lost my trunks, my baggage, my luggage, and there you sit gagging like it was funny. It's awful, I tell you awful!" Lahr's frustration was only piqued by his dissatisfaction with tracing his luggage by phone. "Lemme talk to somebody that understands the English langwidge," he roared into the receiver. "*I'm going to sue. Can you hear me? I'm going to sue!*"

Onstage the teasing Garland took from the actors during the making of *The Wizard of Oz* continued. Once, while in the midst of singing one of her numbers, Lahr turned out the lights and grabbed the microphone out from under her. But Garland could dish it back, and retaliated during Lahr's "Song of the Woodman" routine by dumping a bushel of wood chips over the comedian, crowning him with the basket, and squirting seltzer water on him.

Ever the trouper, Garland performed the last two shows at the Capitol with a limp, having sprained her ankle. Upon Garland's return to the West Coast in early September, her cook splurged—diet be damned—by welcoming the starlet home with her favorite dessert: chocolate cake with thick fudge icing topped with homemade custard ice cream.

Following the Mickey Rooney–Judy Garland cross-country junket, a second tour began almost immediately. A *Wizard of Oz* caravan embarked on its nationwide itinerary from New York on August 25, 1939, to coincide with the Capitol Theatre opening. The tour was supervised by Metro's veteran caravan captain Volney Phifer. The caravan consisted of a Chevrolet motor van adorned with Oz decor and, in its trailer, a mobile stable to transport the two miniature black Shetland ponies that steered the picture's Munchkinland phaeton, which was on loan from MGM. Before departing New York, the carriage took center stage for photo opportunities with Mickey Rooney at the reigns and Judy Garland seated in its carved floral coach.

The horses' color was said to be a rarity, and four-year-old "Wizard" and five-year-old "Oz" each stood thirty-seven inches high at the shoulder and weighed three hundred pounds. They were also veteran performers, having appeared in pictures before and post-Oz. One of the ponies infamously threw Bonnie Blue Butler's character to her death in *Gone with the Wind* (little person Freddie Retter, who was a Munchkin fiddler in *Oz*, was actress Cammie King's stunt double for the dramatic shot).

At each stop on the *Wizard of Oz* tour, child-size versions of the movie costumes were outfitted for those lucky children chosen to don them for the local press, and to pose with the ponies and lead a parade. MGM provided the copy for newspaper publication that read, in part: "Just think of it! You may be riding in the same carriage which Judy Garland, the screen's outstanding young actress, rode in when she entered the wondrous Land of Oz." Phifer and the traveling van returned to New York on October 18, 1939, after which *Motion Picture Daily* noted that Long Island and New Jersey towns were next on the itinerary.

In addition to the traveling caravan and the Rooney-Garland personal appearances, there was a third, previously undocumented tour that coincided with East Coast openings of *The Wizard of Oz*. Since publication of *The Wonderful Wizard of Oz* in 1900, a number of women named Dorothy claimed to have been the inspiration for L. Frank Baum's plucky heroine. For example, at the turn of the century, Dorothy Brandt's widowed mother ran a clipping service in New York City, subscribing to national newspapers and clipping book reviews for well-known authors including L. Frank Baum. When the family relocated to Walton, in central upstate New York near the Delaware River, Baum is reported to have visited the girl in her home. He became a favorite guest, one day telling her that he was writing a story about a little girl who traveled to a fairyland, whom he would name Dorothy after her. In 1957 Frank J. Baum refuted all such rumors by flatly stating, "There is no truth to any of the stories," contending that his father selected the name Dorothy simply because he liked it.

But on September 1, 1939, the *Bessemer (MI) Herald* noted that Mrs. Laud Jacobs, nee Dorothy Stickley, was the original Dorothy, having lived next door to L. Frank Baum in Grand Rapids, Michigan. "Baum became acquainted with his young neighbor," the *Herald* reported, "and the idea of writing a fantasy for children occurred to him. He would build the tale around Dorothy." There are holes in the Dorothy Stickley story, however. The *Herald* relates that Baum lived next door to the Stickleys "shortly after 1900," meaning post-publication of *Oz*. Moreover, Baum is not known to have resided in Grand Rapids, although he did vacation in Macatawa on Lake Michigan, about thirty miles from Grand Rapids, and he debuted his *Fairylogue and Radio-Plays* in Grand Rapids in September 1908. Apparently MGM believed Mrs. Jacobs's story to be authentic. She was put on an East Coast personal appearance tour throughout the month of September "as the girl who inspired the heroine of the Oz books." Her travels were arranged for and underwritten by MGM.

PROMOTION AND RECEPTION

MGM designated two hundred fifty thousand dollars for its *Wizard of Oz* advertising campaign, and plans for publicizing the picture began in early April 1939 with a target date of July 1 to begin breaking coverage nationally in the August issue of movie magazines—though some photos slipped out as early as the prior February. Thus well before, and coinciding with, both East and West Coast premieres, *Wizard of Oz* newspaper and fan magazine coverage ranged from colorful advertisements to Kodachrome layouts to Sunday paper rotogravures, all of which served to fuel intrigue for the most highly anticipated motion picture since *Snow White*. In fact, it was the rare ad or feature that did not reference *Snow White* in some respect. In an unusual and unprecedented ploy, MGM had *condoned* the comparison by touting *Oz* against *Snow White* on its posters and publicity materials.

This led to some confusion as reported by the *Fairbanks (AK) Daily News-Miner*: "First of all we'd like to clear up an idea that seems to be in the minds of quite a few people and that is, that this picture is not a cartoon. We were quite surprised at the number of people who were under the impression that this picture was done in the style of *Snow White*. . . ." For those unaware, some theaters added "Not a Cartoon" to their *Oz* newspaper advertisements. The reviewer for the *Portsmouth (OH) Times* even advised, "Don't go to see *The Wizard of Oz* thinking you are going to be treated to a Walt Disney color cartoon." Sterling Sorensen, the stage-and-screen editor for the Madison, Wisconsin, *Capital Times* wasn't so certain. "The strangest thing about *The Wizard of Oz* . . . is that it resembles a color cartoon by Walt Disney," he wrote. "It seems at times to have been drawn, rather than enacted on solid stages with living people. . . . Judy Garland as the little girl is sweet and as pretty as Snow White." The critic for the *Knickerbocker News* (Albany, NY) predicted that Bert Lahr's Cowardly Lion would surpass *Snow White*'s Dopey in popular affection.

As *The Wizard of Oz* began playing in four hundred first-run theaters across the country from late August into September 1939, the reviews came pouring in. Most were sensational, ravishing accolades for the sets, trick photography, songs, and cast. Of all the actors, it was unanimous that Bert Lahr's performance was most memorable. "As a matter of fact," wrote Hollywood journalist Harold W. Cohen, "it is Mr. Lahr's picture. He steals it lock, stock and barrel. His 'King of the Forest' song is something to cherish always, one of the screen's top moments in comedy. . . ."

In particular, *The Wizard of Oz* was Judy Garland's breakout role and it was the rare critic who was disenchanted by her performance. Herbert Cohn, writing for the *Brooklyn (NY) Eagle* of August 18, 1939, revised September 29, was one of those uncommon reviewers. (He was also one of the first to misidentify Garland's song from the picture as "*Somewhere* Over the Rainbow.") Having caught *Oz* at the Capitol Theatre the day it opened, Cohn's critique of Garland read:

> Judy Garland is, of course, Dorothy, the schoolgirl, who looks for the Land of Heart's Desire and is catapulted, instead, into the Munchkins' Technicolor Land of Oz. To this observer, she is not quite so convincing as the rest . . . she is just not the right choice for the naïve youngster. She is too much on the jitterbug side to be mixed up seriously with witches, good or bad, and a shift of scene that transports her from the Capitol "mike" and a scalding hot version of "Comes Love," to a romp through the Wizard's palace comes a little too quickly for our imagination.

Oz's box-office returns were generally commensurate with the glowing praise it received. Oddly enough, in its August 30, 1939, issue, field news staff for the New England edition of the *Exhibitor* trade journal noted that *Oz*'s debut in first-run theaters was doing "spotty" box office, noting, "Some openings big but show not generally doing gross it should, considering investment." But elsewhere, *Oz* was accruing excellent box office in its first run, as reported by *Motion Picture Daily* the following week. In Minneapolis, Minnesota, *Oz* "did fine" at the State Theatre with a take of nine thousand dollars over the average forty-four-hundred-dollar gross, while in St. Paul the picture was the "best business getter" at the Paramount Theatre with a gross of six thousand dollars, over the typical four-thousand-dollar take. Also for the week ending August 30, *Oz* "scored well" with a gross of eighty-two hundred dollars at the Fifth Avenue Theatre in Seattle, Washington, where the usual gross would be seven thousand dollars. In Ohio *Oz* was proclaimed the "Cleveland Winner" at the Loew's Stillman with a gross of six thousand dollars compared to its average of four thousand dollars.

The picture even got a Kansas seal of approval when two members of the Emporia Better Films Council publicly endorsed *Oz*, noting, "Kansas [culture] gets its share of laughs but no harm is done." (In further regard to Kansas culture, there was apparently no attempt to have the *Wizard of Oz* cast imitate midwestern dialect with the exception of pronouncing the word aunt as "ant"—and not "ont"—as in Aunt Em.) Gladys E. McArdle, manager of the Owl Theatre in Lebanon, Kansas, was initially reticent about *Oz*. "Personally, I do not like this type of show and expected to be bored," she told *Motion Picture Herald*, "but it is so good in every way no one can help liking it."

The Wizard of Oz was regarded with annoyance by some other Kansans, though. *Hutchinson News* columnist J.P.H. went expecting to see the picture of the year but ". . . as far as we're concerned only Bert Lahr as the Cowardly Lion saved it from being a complete washout. When it comes to fantasy . . . we'll take Mickey Mouse." A similarly defensive position was taken by Marion Ellet of the Lawrence *Daily Journal-World*. "Walt Disney need not worry about competition yet" she wrote, complaining that *Oz* "reeks of moral platitude." In a closing jab, Ellet sharply summarized, "With a little less slang and a little less intrusion of mundane reality, it might have been a second-rate drama of the land of make-believe. But, as it stands, it's a belabored hybrid which is about as near to *Snow White* as I to Hercules." (Ellet overlooked that all previous *Oz* dramatizations incorporated a measure of contemporary slang and modern humor.)

Rolla C. Clymer of the Kansas industrial development commission took exception with a technicality, and informed MGM that the state had been "maligned" and that Kansas is not "the cyclone state." Clymer backed up his contention with sixty years' worth of weather records reflecting much more severe tornadoes in other states, concluding, "Kansas would have it known that it has far more winsomeness than warts." Mervyn LeRoy responded, "There should be considerable satisfaction to all Kansans that when we came to film the cyclone there was not one available anywhere in the state. We had to make one and I assure Kansas we made it as winsome as possible." LeRoy also said that Clymer's beef was actually with the original *Oz* author. "With all due respect to the state," LeRoy asserted, "I would like to point out that the complaint is thirty-nine years late—the complaint should have been made to L. Frank Baum who wrote the story in 1900." (The neighboring *Kansas City (MO) Star* offset the commotion in Kansas by underscoring *Oz*'s general appeal: "Don't miss this movie. You may want to see it every day this week.")

There were also concerns expressed that *Oz*'s Wicked Witch was overwhelmingly terrifying to very sensitive children, in the way of the witch in *Snow White*. But this was countered by *Detroit (MI) Free Press* columnist James S. Pooler, who took two youngsters to see *The Wizard of Oz* and claimed both were unfazed by the witch, writing, "The boy said, 'Why doesn't somebody sock her?'" before acknowledging that the kids knew enough to distinguish fantasy from reality. "They didn't fancy [the witch] and her mean ways," he said, "but they weren't afraid and they knew everything was going to come out all right. Besides, it was just make-believe."

Those patrons and critics who were irked by *Oz* seemed either protective of Walt Disney or bothered by liberties taken with the Baum original. It was surely childhood memories of the Oz stories that prompted Margaret Connell of Des Moines, Iowa, to pen a prizewinning letter to *Modern Screen* magazine as published in its January 1940 issue. In her commentary, Ms. Connell states that "*The Wizard of Oz* disappointed me greatly," writing that "the story was almost entirely different from the Oz books I read and reread as a child." (The irony is that MGM's version was the most faithful film adaptation of the several attempts to date.) Ms. Connell conceded that many people seeing the picture have not read the books but she was upset that Dorothy didn't remain in Oz (as she does in *The Emerald City of Oz*) instead of returning to her drab Kansas home at the film's end.[3] Ms. Connell concluded by appealing to Hollywood screenwriters about altering classics like *Oz*: "If a story is good enough to achieve undying fame, doesn't it stand to reason that people want to see it brought to life minus Hollywood improvement?"

Overall naysayers were far and few, but those reviewers who were critical were cutting. *Glamour* magazine chided Mervyn LeRoy with a double-edged compliment, calling the male leads "comic props" and suggesting ". . . there was too much of an atmosphere of fear, too little of joy and gaiety . . . but we do thank you and urge you to continue your experiments. . . ." Animator Max Fleischer, of Betty Boop and Popeye fame, publicly stated

---

3 The point that Margaret Connell overlooked, as can be said of those journalists and critics who have decried Dorothy's choice of Kansas over Oz, is stated clearly by L. Frank Baum in *The Emerald City of Oz*. Dorothy enjoys the luxuries of life in Oz but preferred to be in Kansas because her family loved her and needed her with them.

in November 1939, "I believe animated pictures are the greatest medium for fantasy there is. *The Wizard of Oz*, for instance, would have been a much finer picture if it had been told not through the medium of flesh actors but in animated figures." But then, Fleischer had also taken a swipe at *Snow White*, calling it "too arty." By the end of 1939, MGM agreed with Fleischer. In a January 3, 1940, *Variety* piece on the burgeoning profitability of feature-length cartoons, it was reported that Metro executives were seriously considering an animated picture of their own since "the expensive *Wizard of Oz* fell short of Walt Disney's *Snow White*." The consensus at Metro was that, artistically and financially, *Oz* would have been more successful as a cartoon.

Others felt MGM's show of grandiosity was overblown, like Grace Wilcox of the syndicated *Screen & Radio Weekly*, who wrote, "Frank Baum, the author, was a master of brush strokes, but MGM laid it on with a trowel." The New York critics were far more discriminating in their impressions of *The Wizard of Oz* than those based in Los Angeles, likely spurred by nostalgic recollections of the Montgomery-Stone Broadway extravaganza. The most disparaging of these was the *New Yorker*'s Russell Maloney. Among his lambastes, Maloney cited the "raw, eye-straining Technicolor, applied with a complete lack of restraint." ("Beverly Hills," reviewing *Oz* for *Liberty*, also found the picture's lavish hues to be "perhaps in too garish color.")

Another Gotham critic, Howard Barnes, was equally unimpressed in his August 19, 1939, *New York Herald Tribune* review. Barnes found *Oz* resplendent pictorially, "richly caparisoned in Technicolor," but felt the show missed "a great many of the fabulous accents of the original [play]," and found it "rarely has the power to bemuse one." Jesse Zunser, reviewing *Oz* for *Cue*, New York's metropolitan magazine, called the picture a "solid hit" and a "pleasant evening's entertainment" but qualified the proceedings by writing, "MGM, not content with leaving well enough alone, has seasoned and occasionally soured, this lovely dish with $2,000,000 worth (it all shows) of Technicolored, candy-sticked, Hollywood splendiferousness."

(Despite these 1939 critiques, it is *Oz*'s outstanding color cinematography that has contributed to its modern-day longevity. As Jack Haley remarked in 1971, "We were lucky, though, because color had just come in when the picture went into production. Oh, yes, there had been other color pictures, but the color hadn't been good. Because *The Wizard of Oz* was made in good color, it became a classic. If it had been in black and white . . . well, it might not have held up so well.")

Though complimentary of *Oz*, *Motion Picture Daily* reviewer Alfred Finestone felt the rub lay in the updated translation. "Weakness is apparent in the whimsy itself," he wrote. "Dating from the year 1900, it may or may not appeal to sophisticated adults in the year 1939. Valiant attempts have been made to inject a modern note, and while in itself it clicks tremendously, in the surroundings it appears quite out of place." Howard Barnes echoed Finestone's assessment, though Barnes found *Oz* "far better" than *Alice in Wonderland*

and *A Midsummer Night's Dream*, noting that when the Wicked Witch "starts doing sky-writing in warning the Tin Woodman, the Scarecrow and the Cowardly Lion to surrender Dorothy, the spell snaps rather badly." W. Ward Marsh, reviewing *Oz* for the *Cleveland (OH) Plain Dealer*, made a similar remark. "When it is good, it is very good, and it is at its best in its gayer moods. When it lets down, as it often does," continued Marsh, "too much reality has crept in, songs are continued beyond a point of suspense and interest sags."

Some critics felt the merrymaking in the Land of Oz had been unnecessarily waylaid by the prolonged Kansas scenes. *Pictures Reports* for August 16, 1939, found this element to be *Oz*'s singular fault, citing, "About the only criticism that can be offered against the picture is that valuable time is wasted in getting Dorothy off to Oz. Quite unnecessary is the establishment of the farmhands in Kansas as the prototypes of the Scarecrow, Tin Woodman and Lion. It is footage that could be eliminated in favor of more gorgeous bits of business of the ilk of the Horse of a Different Color." In its August 26 issue, *Film Bulletin*'s reviewer, "Barton," praised the film's makeups and Technicolor pageantry but noted that it was "a bit tiresome in the early sequences," and that aside from "the slow beginning," the film was directed splendidly. The *Fox West Coast Bulletin* for August 12, 1939, was succinct: "Though the sepia sequences drag, the color sequences fascinate."

According to some, the picture's opening scenes would have benefited from excising "Over the Rainbow." In his August 16, 1939, summary of *The Wizard of Oz* following its Grauman's premiere, Harrison Carroll found Dorothy's song number in the prologue objectionable for causing "a needless delay in the story." Nancy Grimes of the *Portsmouth Times* suggested "Dorothy's first song should have been eliminated." Robbin Coons of the Associated Press agreed in his August 26, 1939, *Oz* review, in which he noted, "The picture could have been speeded more at its beginnings, especially by the elimination of Judy's first song." Additionally, at the Allied Theatres of Michigan convention the first week of October 1939, *The Wizard of Oz* was listed as an example of "excessively long screen credits"—fifth in a discussion of eight main points addressed by the convention.

In lieu of all the hype for Metro's big-budget sensation, *The Wizard of Oz* took another hit, this time from the *Harvard Lampoon*. In its recap of movie "worsts" for 1939, the college humor organ distinguished the picture as "most colossal flop of the year."

Syndicated columnist Virginia Vale took note of the minor controversy, observing that practically everybody liked *The Wizard of Oz* and those who didn't were "almost violent on the subject. . . ." Citing *Oz* as September's "movie of the month," Associated Press special-features writer Robbin Coons summarily quelled any uneven temperaments, "It may or may not be Oz as L. Frank Baum created it but, if memory serves, it's close enough, and it's a lot of show for anybody's nickels."

The majority of other film critics and newspaper reviews exhausted all adjectives in lauding *The Wizard of Oz* as the most fascinating and enjoyable picture of the year. Not only did "The Greatest Technicolor Show-World Miracle since *Snow White*" dispel any hint of a coattails imitation, it fast established an identity as a unique screen entertainment on its own substantial merits.

Dick Spong, "Hometown Fan Fare" columnist for the *Harrisburg (PA) Evening News*, boldly took Walt Disney fans to task in his August 14, 1939, *Oz* review. "Disney, the first artist to take advantage of the tremendous possibilities for fantasy the screen affords, has had until now, the edge in the none too friendly rivalry that exists between him and Hollywood," Spong wrote. "With the release of *The Wizard of Oz*, however, Mr. Disney is no longer peerless. Working with human clay, director Victor Fleming has achieved the sort of artistic miracles Disney creates with pen and air-brush, and this department is inclined to consider Fleming's chore the more difficult . . . *The Wizard of Oz* is no slavish imitation of Disney, nor is its appeal to adult or child either increased or diminished by the fact that *Snow White* preceded it. It is now a great picture, and it would have been equally great if a man named Disney had never lived."

"Penetrix," the reviewer for *The Movies . . . and the people who make them*, lauded the picture's escapism:

> Today I have been sitting in a comfortable seat in a moving-picture theatre watching the Munchkins, and the straw man who wanted a brain, the tin man who wanted a heart, the lion who wanted courage. . . . I flew through the air with the greatest of ease on the wicked witch's broomstick . . . and I listened with childish awe to the Wizard of Oz . . . I quite forgot that he was Frank Morgan and that the beautiful fairy who looked and spoke just as a beautiful fairy should, and did in the days when I consorted with them, was really Billie Burke.

More than any other Hollywood columnist, Pennsylvania's Paul Walker of the *Harrisburg Telegraph*'s Reviews and Previews feature, was arguably *Oz*'s greatest champion. On virtually a daily basis between July and November 1939, when he ranked *Oz* among his top ten picks of the year, Walker made references to *Oz* and Judy Garland. When it was announced that Mickey Rooney and Judy Garland would be making a stop in Washington, DC, for a personal appearance en route to *Oz*'s New York premiere, Walker enthusiastically told his readers he would be present and would make certain to ask Judy about *Oz*. In response, a press agent sent Walker a making-of-*Oz* account ghostwritten for Garland, addressed to Walker and signed "Your friend, Judy Garland." (The same letter was also sent to other newspaper entertainment editors nationwide.)

Walker devoted most of his August 14 column to a review of *Oz*, which, like fellow columnist Dick Spong, he had seen in Harrisburg on August 11, and advised all readers: "Put it on your list—NOW!" Local expectations for the 1939 version of *Oz* were high as the Montgomery-Stone extravaganza had played Harrisburg at the Lyceum Theatre on October 29, 1903, and was hailed as "one of the most colorful plays I ever saw on stage," by a city man. When *Oz* played its last night on August 23, Walker admonished the populace for not giving it the same glowing reception he had, noting that kiddie day business was grand but night business, aimed at adults, fell off. "It's only telling the truth to say that the writer is more than a little disappointed at the rather cool reception Harrisburgers gave one of the best—and certainly the most unusual—films to be created in Hollywood."

Among motion picture theater men (movie house owners, operators, and managers), *The Wizard of Oz* ranked tops in record-breaking box office. One enthusiastic rave affirmed, "A perfect picture in every way and one of the world's masterpieces in picture making and one of the leading pictures of the year . . . good for a return date any old time." (Another theater owner was in the minority when he said, "I personally would have preferred the *Tik-Tok Man of Oz* [the 1913 stage musical] plot to this one but my hat is off to Mervyn LeRoy for this great accomplishment.")

Small theaters with rural patronage that screened pictures on one or two nights didn't fare as well with *Oz*. "Very poor draw in small towns for this kind of picture," wrote John Leveck, manager of the P.T.A. Theatre in Benoit, Massachusetts. "Picture is excellent but the crowd won't take it." B. W. Merrill, with the Lyric Theatre in Edgar, Nebraska, praised the overall production but noted it "did not draw as well as expected." At the Ritz Theatre in Mapleton, Minnesota, manager Harry Blubaugh thought *Oz* had "swell color" and "good music" but ticket sales "were only fair." Elsewhere, in Piqua, Ohio, it was noted that at least 75 percent of the audience members at the premiere showing of *Oz* were children.

Overall, *The Wizard of Oz* was a box-office hit and an artistic success. If Mervyn LeRoy's gamble on the picture was ever mocked or dismissed, he was, henceforth, exonerated. The day of the Grauman's premiere, Ed Sullivan declared *Oz* a new high in Hollywood artistry that would confound LeRoy's hecklers, and, within a week, George E. Phair of the *Hollywood Reporter* summed up Tinseltown's sudden change in attitude: "Since *The Wizard of Oz* clicked at the box office, Mervyn LeRoy is the Wizard of Hollywood, in person. Not so long ago the boys were calling him a crackpot. The fellow actually had the impudence to try something different."

Other reviewers and critics followed suit, showering LeRoy with praise; but the producer couldn't have been more tickled than when he received a complimentary letter on August 23 from Walt Disney—the undisputed king of film fantasy. In part, Disney wrote to LeRoy, "The sets were swell, the color was perfect for the story, and the make-ups far exceeded anything I thought possible. . . . All in all, I think you turned out a fine picture and you have my congratulations." As proof of the picture's youthful barometer, Disney concluded his note to LeRoy by humbly pointing out that his daughter Diane considered *Oz* "as good as *Snow White*."

PART THREE
LEGACY

Laurels of Distinction

Like *Snow White and the Seven Dwarfs*, the score of *The Wizard of Oz* served to enhance its popularity. "Over the Rainbow" was the breakout hit. Meredythe Glass first heard the song as a recording broadcast over the playback system while appearing as an extra on the Emerald City set, circa January 1939. She remembered that during a break, Judy Garland was seated in the Emerald City coach, in conference with Mervyn LeRoy and other executives. Glass and her fellow actors in the three hundred–odd crowd were treated to a sneak preview of the song. "All of a sudden we heard 'Over the Rainbow,'" she said. "We heard Judy singing and we all got quiet. There was that beautiful number. No one had heard the song before. That was a moment in history in my mind. Then, we all clapped."

The ballad caught on equally with the public, especially after its official debut on the June 29, 1939, *Wizard of Oz* edition of the *Good News* radio program. Following the show, the *Hollywood Reporter*'s Bill Bloecher predicted, "Harold Arlen's and Yip Harburg's 'Over the Rainbow,' warbled so terrifically by Judy Garland on *Good News*' *Wizard of Oz* preview, is a cinch for the hit class." In its July 5, 1939, review of the *Good News* episode, *Variety* commented that "some fault may be found with the prolonged building [i.e., a dramatized introduction] of 'Over the Rainbow,' but [it is] forgivable in Judy Garland's hands," calling Garland's reprise of the song "excellent."

According to *Daily Variety*, "Rainbow" was among the numbers in orchestra leader Paul Whiteman's August 9, 1939, radio broadcast of *Oz*'s "complete score." The performance was carried live on CBS from Milwaukee, where Whiteman's orchestra was in the midst of his tour of midwestern cities.

To prime other musicians for the *Oz* tunes, MGM invited 125 local musical experts, band leaders, and radio program musical directors and producers to a special screening of *The Wizard of Oz* at the studio on August 14. Also on this date, *Daily Variety* noted that "Over the Rainbow" ranked first in "network plugs," with sixty-eight plays for the week prior. For the week of August 19–25, the song came in second in an analysis of combined plugs on NBC and CBS radio. "Rainbow" was back at number one for the week of August 26 through September 1 with forty-three plugs, and "Ding-Dong! The Witch Is Dead" rated number twenty-five with fifteen plugs.

"Over the Rainbow" and the other *Oz* tunes also figured into the first-ever theatrical dramatization of the movie story. On August 20, 1939, evangelist Aimee Semple McPherson put on "heavy competish," per *Daily Variety* lingo, with local movie houses. McPherson staged a version of *The Wizard of Oz*, sanctioned by MGM, in Angelus, her Los Angeles temple. Major scenes and songs from the film were enacted using an elaborate choir and orchestral effects. Members of McPherson's congregation took the principal roles and McPherson narrated the fantasy. Over four thousand people were said to have jammed the temple seats and aisles, and the event was broadcast via McPherson's radio station.[1]

World-champion figure-skater-turned-actress Sonja Henie was so taken with the song's popularity that she performed an "Over the Rainbow" finale to her 1939–40 Hollywood Ice Revue national tour. The "Rainbow" program entry was said to be reminiscent of Henie's *Alice in Wonderland* segment of the previous year's tour. Press for the show's Cleveland, Ohio, stop noted: "The great finale is *The Wizard of Oz* on ice, with a towering spiral slide reaching the roof of the arena." Other accounts suggest that the "Rainbow" finale wasn't necessarily *Oz*-specific but provided the musical theme for a trip through a candy shop at Christmastime, with many fairy-tale characters including the Three Little Pigs, the Big Bad Wolf, Donald Duck, a Halloween witch, Peter Pan, Puss in Boots, and assorted "living" candies, such as peppermint sticks and gumdrops.

In September 1939 Decca Records issued a four-disc album of songs from *The Wizard of Oz* rerecorded by the Ken Darby Singers with Judy Garland vocalizing "The Jitterbug" and "Over the Rainbow" (no other *Oz* cast members participated for the Decca recording). By December the sheet music to "Over the Rainbow" had sold nearly five hundred thousand copies. The *Mason City (IA) Globe-Gazette* nominated *The Wizard of Oz* "which boasts the hit 'Over the Rainbow'" for Best Motion Picture Score in its 1939 year-end tally of meritorious musical achievement awards (Larry Clinton's cover version of "Deep

---

1 McPherson wasn't the only one to find potential in *Oz*'s spiritual implications. The reviewer for the *Kossuth County (IA) Advance* saw Biblical characters represented in the narrative's "strange underlying religious theme." And Reverend Alfred Swan of Madison, Wisconsin, used *Oz* as a parable for his September 17, 1939, sermon.

Purple" took Best Song). Clearly, the song's impression was indelible and it would only grow more so in the coming years.

"THE WHOLE TOWN'S OZ-IFIED!"

With the nation thoroughly saturated in all things Oz, various masquerade parties, debutante balls, and community events adopted *The Wizard of Oz* as a timely theme. In July 1939 actual costumes used in *Oz* were reportedly borrowed from MGM and worn by local women for a two-day festival in Omro, Wisconsin. Billie Burke received a similar request from her hometown, when a DC socialite wanted the loan of her Glinda gown for one similar such soiree. And on September 7, 1939, the Wisconsin *La Crosse Tribune and Leader-Press* advertised, "Showing Duplicate of Billie Burke's *Wizard of Oz* Gown" informing readers, "Remember the gorgeous pink formal with silver stars that Billie Burke wore in *The Wizard of Oz*? A duplicate of this gown is to be modeled in the second annual Beta Sigma Phi sorority style show and coffee Sunday afternoon at Hotel Stoddard."

Also in September 1939, and by sheer coincidence, a *real* Professor Marvel made national news. Professor C. S. Marvel, director of the University of Illinois's organic chemical laboratory, was engaged in experiments to extract amino acids necessary to someday create a hypothetical "pill" that could contain a complete meal—identical to L. Frank Baum's Land of Oz character, Professor Wogglebug, who invented "Square-Meal Tablets" for his students.

When four little lion cubs were born on October 4, 1939, at the Philadelphia Zoo, they were each named after an *Oz* character: Dorothy, Scarecrow, Tin Woodman, and Cowardly Lion. Similarly, the previous July a lion cub was flown from the 1939 World's Fair to Hollywood in honor of Bert Lahr's Cowardly Lion.

The Wizard of Oz was still well within national consciousness when an enormous, seventy-foot inflated Tin Man—perhaps the most readily identifiable Oz character—joined the character balloons and floats for the Macy's Thanksgiving Day Parade on November 25, 1939. Designed by illustrator and puppeteer, Tony Sarg, the balloon was later repainted in yellow and green, and the Tin Man, repurposed, became "Laffo the Clown" the following year. Although the 1939 parade featured balloons of Pinocchio, Uncle Sam, Santa Claus, and Superman, it was press photos of the Tin Man that made the papers.

Further evidence of a mounting *Oz* awareness came in December 1939. Ruth Swanton, a home economics instructor from Emmetsburg, Iowa, made national news when she advised creaming the eggs and sugar of a cake recipe four hundred strokes to the tune of "We're Off to See the Wizard." It was also reported that the African-American basketball team the Harlem Globetrotters had earned the timely—but now racially inappropriate—title

"Dusky Wizards of Oz," for their ability to "make the basketball do everything but explode in a routine of nifty tricks and comic antics."

A couple of Oz-related scammers also received news coverage. Thirty-seven-year-old Vaughn Purgson, Ada, Oklahoma, resident occult seer (billed as "The Wizard of Oz") and newspaper columnist of "The Wizard of Oz Question Box," was sentenced to eighteen months prison time for performing an abortion on a seventeen-year-old sandwich stand carhop for whom his crystal ball had predicted "trouble." One wayward pet owner used Oz awareness to procure his own media attention. On February 1, 1940, the *San Antonio (TX) Express* reported "Police Hunt Dog Featured in Movie" as Harry W. Hall enlisted the aid of local law enforcement "to help him find his lost Scotch terrier 'Toto' which Hall falsely claimed was featured in *The Wizard of Oz*." (How Toto ended up in Texas as a Scottie and in Harry Hall's possession was unexplained!)

Judy Garland's performance in *The Wizard of Oz* was skilled enough to quiet those critics who initially decried her miscast for being "hotcha" and overly exuberant. In a favorable review of the picture, "L.O.P." penned, "The little Garland girl is very good. At times she may seem a little robust for Dorothy, but she really subdues her buoyant, vivacious young self sufficiently to be an acceptable little heroine." Kaspar Monahan of the *Pittsburgh (PA) Press*, was also conciliatory of Garland when he wrote, "But for the minor drawback that she's a bit too large to play Dorothy, Judy Garland in all other respects measures up to her assignment."

Given her elevation to star status commensurate with *Oz*, Garland also found herself in greater public demand. On August 8, 1939, a Western Union telegram was sent from "Judy" to the Logansport, Indiana, *Press* to accompany a trophy sent by MGM for the Logan Theatre's "most popular baby" contest just prior to *Oz*'s debut there. The telegram read, in part, "Just learned of the baby popularity contest . . . Wish I could be in Logansport to award a trophy . . . Good luck to all the babies."

On Saturday, December 2, 1939, Judy Garland and her eldest sister, Sue, were taken by one of MGM's sixteen-cylinder limousines to St. Joseph's Hospital at Anaheim for a two o'clock appointment to visit eight-year-old Natalie Norris, a local child. Norris had been felled by what was described as an unidentified "strange disease" for which major surgery was required. As she was recovering, the little girl was babbling in her delirium about Dorothy in *The Wizard of Oz*—the last picture she had seen just before being stricken, as Harrison Carroll recorded in his December 16 column. Dr. John W. Truxaw, Norris's doctor, suggested an unusual remedy that involved Judy Garland, believing "that a call from the motion picture songstress would assist Natalie in her recovery."

Natalie's mother contacted MGM to request Garland's presence. Touched by the child's illness, it was reported, Garland agreed to "visit the sick little girl in the very costume she wore as Dorothy." Judy told Mrs. Norris, "I'll come as soon as I can," and in advance of the scheduled trip, sent Natalie one of the *Wizard of Oz* dolls created and dressed in Garland's image together with photo stills from the movie. The care package was accompanied by an inscribed letter:

Dearest Natalie:

I want to write you this note to tell you to hurry and get well so you can write to me and tell me all about yourself. I had a wonderful time "Over the Rainbow," and if I go back to the Land of Oz I'd like to take you with me. I shall close now and be waiting for your letter. I hope you will write to me when you are well which I know will be soon. And don't forget we have a date. You and I and Toto.

[signed]
"Dorothy" (Judy Garland)

Meanwhile, Natalie was all smiles contemplating the visit. "I have a date with Judy," she explained. When Judy entered Natalie's room on the chosen day, the youngster's face lit up in instant recognition. "My goodness," she reportedly exclaimed, "Where is Toto?" Garland stayed and talked as long as the doctor would allow before warbling an impromptu rendition of "Over the Rainbow," which brought Natalie's mother to tears. Harrison Carroll noted that, best of all, "the youngster has shown definite improvement since the visit." (Norris also recovered inspired. By 1962, after studying music in Vienna for eight years, she was put under contract to the opera house in Linz as the lead contralto.)

MGM did not attire Judy in her Dorothy ensemble for the visit, as had been announced, though Garland's hair was described as red and she wore a simple frock and modest pumps. But given Natalie Norris's immediate recognition of Garland, the singer might as well have been fully made up as her *Oz* character. An October 1940 *Modern Screen* rendition of the incident is that Natalie's mother contacted Garland to request an autographed picture of Judy as Dorothy for her ailing daughter. "Judy did better than that," reads the account, "She took the autographed picture to the hospital herself. And when the little girl came out of the fever, there was the living Dorothy standing by her bed."

Afterward, the Garland sisters and Mrs. Norris posed with Natalie's portrait and the bouquet the Norris family presented to Judy in appreciation. Then, as now, charitable acts by Hollywood celebrities received front-page press and the attention reflected well on Garland and, of course, MGM.

In spring 1940 the graduating class of Paris (MO) High School sent Judy Garland a letter from their class president explaining that *The Wizard of Oz* was being staged as the class play and begging her to attend and be the guest of honor. Instead, MGM sent a floral bouquet in proxy that Metro claimed was Mickey Rooney's idea. The huge arrangement of California flowers occupied Garland's chair of honor at the graduation banquet. At the same time, the planning committee of an eastern university's banquet sent Garland its *Wizard of Oz*–themed placeholders and menu with dishes that included "Tin Woodman Soup" and "Over the Rainbow Salad."

By this time, seventeen-year-old Garland lamented the strong association the public had made between her and the character of Dorothy to reporter James Reid. "Ever since *The Wizard of Oz*, I've been accused of being twelve years old," she sighed. "You should see some of the disappointed looks I get when people lay eyes on me in person. They expect someone in gingham, with braids, to come out singing 'Over the Rainbow.' And I come out, instead. I think some of them are pretty angry with me, too, for not wearing braids, and not dressing like Dorothy, and not being eleven or twelve. They've written in [to MGM] about it. I don't get any sympathy from anybody. People I've trusted all my life tell me, with perfectly straight faces, that I ought to feel flattered. 'It isn't every actress that people are willing to believe younger than she is.'" But any reservations Garland may have had about typecasting were soon to be assuaged by greater recognition of her talents.

AWARDS AND ACCOLADES: THE ACADEMY AND BEYOND

While the performances of Judy Garland and Bert Lahr were most frequently singled out by critics for their contributions to *The Wizard of Oz*, others in the cast received recognition too. Billie Burke's performance has been the subject of parody since the 1970s, when *The Wizard of Oz* had attained legendary status through its TV broadcasts. In particular, the inflection of a trill in her dialogue with lines such as "Toto too," has made her Glinda easily criticized by modern reviewers as saccharine or disingenuous. But to appreciate how restrained and understated a performance Burke gives in *Oz*, one need only watch her skill as a comedienne in such MGM classics as *Dinner at Eight*, *Topper*, or *Everybody Sing*. In these films, Burke is at her best playing perpetually befuddled, melodramatic high-society matrons. Ted Reed, reviewing *The Wizard of Oz* for the *Harrisburg (PA) Telegraph*, took notice of the distinction in the actress's delivery as Glinda, writing, "Billie Burke is amazing as 'the good witch'—it has been so long since she has played anything but foolish, rattle-brain women."

In her portrayal of Glinda, Burke projects a benevolent sweetness that exemplifies her character's all-knowing and serene grace. Glinda does not betray Dorothy in negligence by allowing her undue tribulations, which thus circumvents the often-raised question, "Why didn't Glinda tell Dorothy the way to get home right away?" The point is that, in her wisdom, Glinda's clairvoyance foresees the outcome of Dorothy's journey and knows no serious harm will befall her; sans the journey, Dorothy's maturity remains stagnant. This precise plot device is revealed at the conclusion of Baum's book *The Patchwork Girl of Oz*, in which Glinda has been magically monitoring another of Dorothy's (sometimes perilous) adventures knowing full well the safety of the outcome.

As validation for her effectiveness, by February 6, 1940, the newly formed Newspaper Film Critics of America nominated Billie Burke's Glinda in *The Wizard of Oz* as best performance by a female supporting player of 1939 alongside nine other nominees including Greer Garson in *Goodbye, Mr. Chips*, Rosalind Russell in *The Women*, and Geraldine Fitzgerald in *Dark Victory*.

As hellish a trial as it may have been, Jack Haley's portrayal of the gentle, romantic man of tin won over at least one fan who, prior to *Oz*, had been indifferent. In December 1939 *Photoplay* published an open letter from Kalamazoo, Michigan, resident Alice Oman. Moved by Haley's performance, Oman's confession summarizes the Tin Man's ability to touch hearts—qualities that endure with repeated viewings of *The Wizard of Oz* decades later:

Dear Jack Haley,

I never thought I'd be writing a fan letter to *you*, of all people. You've always been just another comedian. Oh, your bright eyes were rather cute, but who'd ever remember you? Or go to a picture because your name was on the marquee?

And then I saw you in *The Wizard of Oz*. I sat there as popeyed as you were when you first beheld the mighty Wizard. Could this appealing Tin Woodman, searching so wistfully for a heart, really be Jack Haley? Heart or no heart, his tin countenance clearly registered emotion: the openmouthed fear that made his tin knees clank together, the overpowering desire for a heart, his affection for Dorothy. Then, when he had found his heart, only to feel it break as Dorothy was leaving, our hearts broke with his for a moment. When an actor's breaking heart causes a temporary fracture in our own, then we call that actor great.

So, Jack Haley, I salute you—a new dramatic star. If MGM doesn't star you in some serious roles worthy of all the pathos you brought to the Tin Woodman, then you'd better find a boss who will. Because you certainly have what it takes.

On September 15, 1939, Haley wrote a fan in Philadelphia with a gracious and restrained perspective: "It is always a great pleasure to know that my work has brought pleasure and satisfaction to people. The part of the Tin Woodman was one that I enjoyed and felt a sympathy for, and if this feeling was conveyed to my fans, I am more than grateful." True to the era, however, Haley's sentiments were probably ghostwritten by a studio secretary.

However, when substituting for New York columnist Leonard Lyons, Haley wrote, "[I] guess I'm getting back to the six-year-old stage in my costume of the Tin Woodman. I got a kick out of doing it. . . ."

Terry the cairn terrier's *Wizard of Oz* performance impressed more than a few reviewers, but one in particular thought the canine actor's showing deserved formal recognition. On August 21, 1939, Bob White, writing for the Benton Harbor, Michigan, *News-Palladium*, summarized the general perception of Terry. "You remember Toto, Dorothy's adoring and adorable little dog. It's about time some Motion Picture Academy awards were handed out to animal actors, and Toto is entitled to a solid gold license tag and a sirloin steak banquet with testimonials."

White's prediction came to fruition when on February 27, 1940, it was reported that Terry was formally honored for her performance. The event was the first annual Academy Award meeting of the Tailwaggers, a national dog-enthusiast society. At the ceremony three movie dogs received bronze "Boscars," the dogdom equivalent of Hollywood's Oscar award. Asta, the wire-haired fox terrier from the *Thin Man* series, was named best male dog actor; Daisy, the mongrel from the *Blondie* series, took best female dog; and Toto was named "most promising dog actor of 1939" for *The Wizard of Oz*. (Toto's offspring, "Rommy," later continued the acting legacy in movies and television.)

By the close of 1939, *The Wizard of Oz* brought Mervyn LeRoy further laurels and accolades. The National Screen Council bestowed LeRoy with *Boxoffice* magazine's Blue Ribbon Award for September 1939, and LeRoy won the *Parents Magazine* annual award for best picture produced for family audiences. *Photoplay* magazine included *The Wizard of Oz* on its list of "Outstanding Pictures of 1939" Gold Medal Award nominees, and *Oz* made 1939's top-ten lists for *Film Daily* and *Showmen's Trade Review*—for which it placed among the top twenty-five moneymakers of 1939. There were a couple of rare exceptions. *Oz* was not top-ranked by *Motion Picture Review Digest* on its list of "Ten Best American Films," but it was included on the *Digest*'s "Second List" of runners-up alongside such notables as *Bachelor Mother, Destry Rides Again, Golden Boy, Idiot's Delight, Intermezzo*, and *The Women*. When the Associated Press released its list of "most likely to be considered" best pictures, *Oz* was absent, though it was expected that there would be "some additions by studios wanting recognition, or more, or better recognition. . . ."

Given these preliminary prizes, it was anticipated that *The Wizard of Oz* would make a respectable showing when the Academy of Motion Picture Arts and Sciences announced its annual award nominees if for nothing other than Hollywood politics; Mervyn LeRoy was chairman of the ceremony's program committee and was designated to present the Best Director award.

But there had already been buzz in critics' reviews about recognition for, at the least, *Oz*'s technical achievements. In his August 10, 1939, review for *Motion Picture Daily*,

Alfred Finestone praised not only Bert Lahr for turning in "the No. 1 performance" but rightfully noted, "The make-up job calls for a special award." In her August 28 column, Dorothy Kingsley, who would become an MGM screenwriter, was also of the opinion that Lahr "should get some kind of a special Academy Award." Harold W. Cohen agreed, stating that Lahr's turn as the Cowardly Lion "should force the Academy into establishing a new Oscar for comedians." Louella O. Parsons singled out the Jack Dawn makeups, and felt Judy Garland's performance "puts her in line for the Academy Award." Len G. Shaw, writing for the *Detroit (MI) Free Press*, applauded both Garland and Lahr, "Judy Garland really comes into her own . . . but we think you will agree that Lahr, strikingly realistic in jungle make-up, is especially good as the terror-stricken big cat, a blend of comedy and emotion that stands close inspection." And come January 6, 1940, Harrison Carroll listed Bert Lahr as a contender for best supporting performance by an actor against Walter Brennan in *Kentucky*, Thomas Mitchell in *Stagecoach*, and Wilfrid Lawson in *Pygmalion*. But there was no formal nomination for Lahr, Garland, or Jack Dawn come awards season.

Twelve-thousand ballots were cast by Academy of Motion Picture Arts and Sciences constituents and, upon tabulation, *The Wizard of Oz* was indeed one of ten films nominated for Best Picture in keeping with the previous critical distinctions accorded to it. *Oz* was also nominated for Best Song ("Over the Rainbow" by Harburg and Arlen), Best Original Score (for Herbert Stothart's brilliant scoring that incorporated the Harburg-Arlen melodies), Best Cinematography Color (Allen Davey and Harold Rosson), and Best Special Effects (A. Arnold Gillespie)—the first year for this category.

The Academy's twelfth annual awards banquet and ceremony for 1939 was held on February 29, 1940, in the Coconut Grove nightclub of the Ambassador Hotel, Los Angeles. The event was the first of nineteen hosted by Bob Hope, who would crack that the ceremony was a "benefit" for David O. Selznick as his *Gone with the Wind* began accruing wins and Selznick received the Irving Thalberg memorial award.

As was expected, *Gone with the Wind* took the Best Picture award. Had *GWTW* not won, the honor would have most likely been a tight race between either *Goodbye, Mr. Chips* or *Mr. Smith Goes to Washington*. For its era, *The Wizard of Oz* was not a serious contender for Best Picture. It was a whimsical musical laden with technical bravura and heralded as a novelty; but only dramas or romantic comedies were deemed worthy of the Academy's pinnacle prize in those days. Instead, *Oz* was 1939's self-indulgent showcase for MGM's resources, opulence, and capability—the studio's way of asserting its superiority in the film industry with a roar not unlike that of its own mascot, Leo the Lion—just as *Marie Antoinette* had been the 1938 prestige offering, *The Good Earth* the year before that, and *The Great Ziegfeld* in 1936. The Hollywood correspondent for the *Fairbanks (AK) Daily News-Miner* explained Metro's stance: "Incidentally the producers don't plan on making a profit on this picture. They figure this one a 'prestige' picture. Seems to me that three million is a lot of money to gamble on prestige . . . but if Mr. and Mrs. Audience can see pictures like this at popular prices it is certainly okay by us . . . nothing pleases us more. So more power and prestige to the producers of *The Wizard of Oz.*"

The Wizard of Oz did not go empty-handed. It received Academy recognition by winning both music awards for which it had been nominated. Responding to a note of congratulations from MGM executive Eddie Mannix, Harold Arlen wrote on March 5, 1940, "*The Wizard of Oz* was one of the most delightful assignments I've had to date and the studio's great appreciation of our work certainly played an important part in the creation and success of 'Over the Rainbow.'" Arlen also had the sheet music of all the songs he co-wrote for *Oz* professionally bound as presentation copies.

Almost immediately, however, Herbert Stothart's Oscar win was the subject of contention and controversy. There were dissenters who decreed that his "original musical score" was not entirely original but was, instead, an adaptation of the works of several other composers. Cited as previous cinematic examples were Erich Korngold's incorporation of Mendelssohn's music for Warner Bros.' *A Midsummer Night's Dream*, as well as Stothart's use of Nikolai Rimsky-Korsakov's ballet suite for "Scheherazade" in Metro's *Balalaika.*

Fred Sersen's realistically simulated earthquake and flood for Fox's *The Rains Came* took the special-effects honor over both *The Wizard of Oz* and *GWTW*. Technicolor Corporation received a special trophy for its contributions to successful filming in three-color production, which encompassed Technicolor pictures culminating in two of the 1939 Best Picture nominees, *GWTW* and *Oz*.

Mickey Rooney presented Judy Garland with a miniature Oscar "for her outstanding performance of present day juvenile roles"—the terminology used by the *Film Daily* and MGM when lauding the award results.[2] The juvenile award was given irregularly by the Academy, and both Rooney and Deanna Durbin had been its recipients the previous year. Garland scored a hit with Rooney in 1939's *Babes in Arms*, but it was generally acknowledged that her award was in recognition for so competently carrying *The Wizard of Oz*. By November 1940 MGM summarized Garland's achievement as unique to *Oz*: "Judy won her most prized recognition after her appearance in *The Wizard of Oz*. The characterization of Dorothy won her the gold statuette given by Motion Picture Academy of Arts and Sciences [*sic*]." The recognition would also buoy Garland to her first role starring solo in

2 This was the only occasion in Garland's storied career for which she was so honored by the Academy of Motion Picture Arts and Sciences. She was subsequently nominated as Best Actress for *A Star Is Born* (1954), but the award was given to Grace Kelly—a win Garland herself had predicted in February 1955, telling Hollywood correspondent James Bacon that she believed Kelly would take the prize though she remained hopeful. Garland was nominated as Best Supporting Actress for *Judgement at Nuremberg* (1961) but lost to Rita Moreno in *West Side Story*.

1940's *Little Nellie Kelly*. After accepting her Academy Award, Judy Garland obliged the audience by singing "Over the Rainbow."

In its May 1940 recap of that evening's events, *Photoplay* rated Judy Garland's receipt of the juvenile award from Mickey Rooney tops among highlights of the ceremony. "Mickey Rooney handing Judy Garland her statuette for the best performance of a juvenile during the past year," the prestigious publication noted, ". . . was charming to watch . . . with his new-found dignity upon him . . . and then forgetting himself and kissing [Garland] with kid enthusiasm . . . Judy was never more persuasive than when she crooned 'Over the Rainbow,' the year's prize-winning song, into the mikes, with a suspicious little quaver in her voice."

In 1952 Garland recalled that evening. "[*The Wizard of Oz*] is ever the reminder of the most sensational moment of my career—the night of the Academy Award dinner when Mickey Rooney presented me with the golden Oscar. The lump in my throat was so big when I sang "Over the Rainbow" that I sounded more like Flip the Frog than the most excited girl in all Hollywood. And I'll never forget how Mickey came to my rescue, for I was so nervous I thought I'd faint. He practically held me up through the second chorus."

Although "Over the Rainbow" was recorded by other artists, it was most closely associated with Garland and became a signature of her musical repertoire. Both Harold Arlen and

Garland were present for the Golden Gate International Exposition Music Festival in San Francisco the evening of September 24, 1940. Accompanied by Arlen at the piano, Judy sang "Over the Rainbow" for an extraordinary evening of live performances that included a veritable who's who of Americana's great composers and classic tunes, among them "Take Me Out to the Ball Game," "Singin' in the Rain," "Smoke Gets in Your Eyes," "Summertime," "I Can't Give You Anything but Love, Baby," "Star Dust," and "God Bless America."

By 1942 music critic Janice Rhea already considered the tune a near-standard for its exceptional beauty and charm. The same year, "'Over the Rainbow' sung by Judy Garland in *The Wizard of Oz*" was ranked the all-time motion picture number by Barry Wood, host of radio's *Your Hit Parade*, the nation's favorite song barometer. During her first tour entertaining army camps in 1942, Judy noticed that the troops wanted "Rainbow" over any other song. "We did four shows a day," she told Walter Winchell that August, "one at the reception center where the newly inducted boys gather, one in the hospital, and two in the auditorium. At each show I sang two set songs [multiple songs to a set] and then did request numbers. It seems the boys favor the old songs and in my case the two outstanding requests were 'Over the Rainbow' and 'Dear Mr. Gable.'" (A wild story that swept the camps had Judy literally over the rainbow when a rumor circulated that she, Deanna Durbin, and Bette Davis perished in a plane crash!) In 1943 Garland reprised "Rainbow" for a broader listening audience on the Armed Forces Radio Service's *Command Performance* program, hosted by Bob Hope.

Coinciding with Garland's July 20, 1943, appearance to entertain the troops stationed at Fort Indiantown Gap Military Reservation, near Lebanon, Pennsylvania, the singer caught up with the *Harrisburg Telegraph*'s Hollywood columnist Paul Walker at the Penn-Harris Hotel. Garland had arrived in Harrisburg by train from New York, after she and her mother, Ethel, who joined her on a succeeding train, got separated. The last time Walker had encountered Garland, she was appearing in Washington, DC, with Mickey Rooney five years prior in advance of opening *The Wizard of Oz* at the Capitol Theatre in New York. When Walker recalled the event, Judy reminisced, "We certainly had fun on that trip."

Walker told Garland he had been listening to her spot on *Command Performance* the night it aired, hoping out loud she would sing "Over the Rainbow," and the next moment she did, to which Judy replied that she did "sort of believe in mental telepathy." Garland admitted that she loved to sing for the soldiers and insisted on eating with them at Indiantown Gap, declining officers' invitations to eat with them privately and remarking, "I want to entertain the soldiers and not be entertained by the officers." When Walker mentioned "Rainbow," Judy—more than five years after first performing it vocally—said of the *Oz* song, "That's my favorite, too. I can sing it anytime and it's one that I always like to hum. The soldiers like it too; it's one they always call for."

Postwar Reprise

A BURGEONING CLASSIC

The World War II years were a sobering period in American history, particularly after the United States officially entered the international fray in December 1941. But the recent success of *The Wizard of Oz* made the story's themes ripe for patriotic parody when the 7th Division US Army staged *The Wizard of Ord* on Saturday and Sunday, May 10–11, 1941, at the War Memorial Opera House in San Francisco—the first army camp presentation of its kind. The performance was a success and the San Francisco newspaper critics raved, so a second mounting was offered May 28–29 at the State Theatre in Monterey, billed as an all-soldier operetta with a cast of one hundred. The two-hour show, now with a cast of two hundred, was reprised a third occasion for an audience of thirty-five hundred at the Hollywood Bowl amphitheater, June 6–7, 1941, after which it garnered a complimentary review in *Variety* ("*The Wizard of Ord* measured up to professional standards.")

The *Ord* production may have been inspired by memories of sarcastic battle cracks from "Headlights" columnist Lew M'Clenrghan. On February 26, 1940, M'Clenrghan suggested that if *The Wizard of Oz* were to be made again, its songs would be revised as "We're Off to Bomb the Wizard" and "The Terrible Witch Is a Red," while "Follow the Yellow Brick Road" would serve as instructions to air raiders.

The three-act *Wizard of Ord* show, with an eighteen-number musical program by Colin McDonald and Carl Arnold, concerned young enlistee John R. Smith, who meets up with three hoboes, the Scarecrow, Tin Man, and Cowardly Lion, while en route to the Fort Ord Military Reservation in Monterey Bay, California. After the four encounter troops of the 7th Division on military maneuvers, Johnny finally reaches the headquarters of the great maker of men, the wonderful Wizard of Ord. On the journey, the men, supported by dozens of their compatriots, sang morale-rousing numbers such as "Remember Your Uncle, Our Uncle, Uncle Sam," "You're Never Bored at Ord," and "Gone with the Draft," a nod to *Gone with the Wind*. The army production did not acknowledge Metro-Goldwyn-Mayer nor were any of the *Oz* songs interpolated into the show, but "Keep Looking for a Rainbow" was sung in the first act and "Everybody Rates a Rainbow" was a featured solo by John Smith in the third act. The entire cast sang "Wonderful Wizard of Ord," a parody of "We're Off to See the Wizard," also in the final act.

In 1942 MGM was solicited for official permission to use "Over the Rainbow" and all the other *Wizard of Oz* songs in a stage production of the story put on by the prestigious St. Louis Municipal Opera. Though the Harburg-Arlen *Oz* songs were incorporated (as well as "Some Day My Prince Will Come" from *Snow White*, performed as "Some Day My Love Will Come"), the new script was based on the L. Frank Baum story. The show was scheduled for a six-day run, from August 10 to 16, 1942, before it was supplanted by *Show Boat*. Still, the Muny's production was popular enough for other troupes and community theaters to stage their versions throughout the 1940s and beyond—including a 1947–48 English production at London's Strand Theatre—serving to sustain sentimental reminisces for the 1939 film and its enduring musical numbers.

In November 1946, Hunt Stromberg Jr., son of MGM producer Hunt Stromberg, announced he was mounting a Broadway production of *The Wizard of Oz*, adapted from the screen version, to follow his successful revivals of *The Red Mill* and *The Front Page*. Rumors of such a stage version of *Oz* continued to circulate into the next decade. In March 1947 it was producer J. H. DelBondio who was contemplating the show's revival for an October debut, with Ray Bolger in the leading role. By October 1951 Broadway columnist Dorothy Kilgalen reported that actor Ray Malone was being considered for the Scarecrow in the proposed stage re-mounting. The last located notice of such a show was in February 1953, when Harold W. Cohen wrote, "Broadway may see *The Wizard of Oz* again next season, the first time since the old Fred Stone–David Montgomery production back in 1903." However, despite what appears to have been concerted efforts, a modern stage version of the MGM film never materialized.

In the years following *The Wizard of Oz*, Judy Garland finally attained status as one of MGM's glamour girls, appearing in the company of Hedy Lamarr and Lana Turner in *Ziegfeld Girl* (1941). Through dieting (to the point of near-anorexia), skillful makeup (the angle of her eyebrows changed), and carefully lighted and posed publicity portraits, Judy was reinvented from the girl next door to a leggy, alluring ingenue. The jacket copy from the MGM-authorized novelty book *Judy Garland and the Hoodoo Costume* (1945) explained the transformation: "Introduced as a musical comedy star, Judy has proved her talent in the dramatic field as well. Her unforgettable role in *The Wizard of Oz* marked the height in her career as a child star. Now she is starring in more sophisticated roles, with at least one straight drama a year." Despite having parted ways with MGM, Garland still recalled *Oz* as a signal occasion in 1951. "One day . . . Mr. Mayer called me into his office," she informed reporter Michael Drury, "[he] told me Mervyn LeRoy was going to produce *The Wizard of Oz* and wanted me to play Dorothy. It was my first big break. I got a special Academy Award for that film. . . ."

During the war years, the days of extravagant prestige pictures such as *The Wizard of Oz* were over for the duration. (The minimum budget on a Technicolor picture of the era was one million dollars.) Some productions were shelved, such as Victor Fleming's *The Yearling*, or had budgets reduced, as the war put a moratorium on any future production of such costly "colossals," as Robbin Coons coined them in his September 18, 1939, Hollywood Sights and Sounds editorial. "Meanwhile," Coons essayed, "the American movie fan can look forward to a goodly flock of peace-made local 'colossals,' typical of which are *Gone with the Wind*, *The Wizard of Oz*, *Elizabeth and Essex*, *The Rains Came*, and *The Women*. Any of these should provide the movie-goer with a little forgetfulness of the times the world moves through."

BIG-SCREEN COMEBACK

Fond recollections of *The Wizard of Oz*'s sumptuous Technicolor treats lingered into the 1940s. The picture was on a three-year release schedule, which ended in 1942. In April of that year, the Squire Theatre in New York booked *Oz* for a weeklong engagement. To boost patron intrigue, it was reported that the original costumes worn by Judy Garland, Frank Morgan, Ray Bolger, and Jack Haley were shipped from MGM for display in the lobby. *Oz* was still sporadically screened in theaters as late as 1943. By then, it was usually on a double bill with Walt Disney's *Dumbo* or booked with a serial such as *G-Men vs. Black Dragon*, and supplemented with cartoons, before MGM retired it from circulation.

But beginning March 18, 1943, veteran Hollywood correspondent Jimmie Fidler called for a revival of MGM's *The Wizard of Oz*, reminding Metro that, with *Oz*, they were "sitting on a goldmine" and requested a reissue for the benefit of children. The following November 7, Fidler again advocated on behalf of "dozens of kids" who'd requested an *Oz* reissue, and who "comprise at least 50 percent of the habitual movie patrons." Harrisburg, Pennsylvania's Paul Walker, another Hollywood newspaper editor, made several public requests in 1943, writing, "We'd like to see *Wizard of Oz* again."

On July 13, 1944, Fidler listed *Oz* among his choices to be re-screened in honor of MGM's twentieth anniversary, suggesting that such "banner offerings . . . would gross almost as much money today as they did when first released." Fidler made a fourth public plea in his June 23, 1945 column, citing *Oz* as "undoubtedly the best kids' picture ever filmed."

Rival Tinseltown reporter Hedda Hopper took up the crusade as her own on October 11, 1945, though she referenced Fidler's appeals in her opening line:

> Well, you fans who've been begging for another look at *The Wizard of Oz* may get your wish around Christmas time. I had a look at it the other night—it's really delightful; fresher than when it was first made. The difference in Judy Garland rather astonished me. She was so young, so round, so fully packed. After seeing Ray Bolger, Bert Lahr and Jack Haley, I wonder why they haven't been teamed again.

By October 10, 1946, Hopper reported, "My campaign to have *The Wizard of Oz* re-released has borne fruit. As soon as Metro can get enough Technicolor prints, it'll be put back on the screen." A month prior Hopper questioned why *Oz* was not among other upcoming MGM reissues, asserting, "That was one film that was way ahead of its time." But by this time, *Oz* was indeed slated for a Metro reprise but within the parameter of a corporate strategy.

On July 3, 1946, the *Film Daily* announced that MGM had created a new department especially to market reprints of its past successes, acknowledging that the studio had a library of "masterpieces" yet unseen by rising generations. The plan was not to flood the market with dozens of pictures worth reviving but to limit their release to five or six per year. *The Wizard of Oz* was on the roster of prospective reprints as well as *The Great Waltz, Gone with the Wind*, and *Mutiny on the Bounty*.

But when an *Oz* reissue was not forthcoming, Hedda Hopper followed up twice more with her call in 1947, and again on February 26, 1948, when she reported, "*Philadelphia Story* is being reissued, but not *The Wizard of Oz* which the fans are clamoring for. Metro can't get enough Technicolor prints for the latter." (Disparity of *Wizard of Oz* prints in the United States may be attributed to most copies circulating in foreign countries, where *Oz* was only just debuting after World War II.)

Meanwhile, a new edition of the original Decca recordings for *The Wizard of Oz* was issued in 1947—and again in 1949 and 1954—and the accompanying sheet music received plain wrappers more dour in appearance than reflective of the joyful contents. From 1950 onward the *Wizard of Oz* songs were an inseparable component of any kiddie-record release of the story on vinyl.

Hedda Hopper reiterated the appeal for a re-release on November 18, 1948. "Letters are pouring into my desk from parents urging me to beg Metro to reissue *Wizard of Oz* again over the holidays." Finally, on November 29, 1948, Wood Soanes announced that MGM would reissue *The Wizard of Oz* for postwar audiences and a new generation of youth ("The Wonder Show for the Whole Family!" proclaimed the ads).

Others who joined in besieging MGM to bring back *Oz* included manager George Peters of Loew's Theatre in Richmond, Virginia. Peters partnered with *Times-Dispatch* drama editor Edith Lindeman to ask, "Like to See *Wizard* Reissue? Speak Up! Perhaps You May." Shortly after the newspaper column ran, Lindeman called Peters to report that several hundred of her readers had replied affirmatively. In Cleveland Omar Ranney of the *Cleveland Press* wondered in his daily column how many of his readers would like to see *Oz* again. He got more than three thousand requests!

At MGM all pleas for a reissue of *The Wizard of Oz* were fielded by Mildred Kelly, of its special services department, who said the studio received yearly requests to recirculate the picture. Apparently the collective fan campaign worked and Metro promoted *Oz* as the "most requested" of its hits from years past. Jimmie Fidler expressed his gratification on December 7, 1948:

> I believe everyone must approve of the announcement that MGM is going to reissue *The Wizard of Oz*. The kids who cheered that classic a decade ago have grown up now and been succeeded by another set of youngsters who will find ecstatic pleasure in the adventures of Dorothy, the Tin Woodman, the Scarecrow and all the other creations of Frank Baum's wonderful imagination. The release date of that particular reissue will be a red-letter day for kids everywhere, and let me confess that I'm going to circle the date on my own calendar. I want to see it again, too.

"Lyons Den" columnist Leonard Lyons offered an official time frame for the re-release on January 31, 1949: "MGM will reissue the ten-year-old musical *Wizard of Oz* for the Easter trade." But in her March 26, 1949, column, Hedda Hopper proclaimed the re-release a personal victory: "For years I've been urging Metro to reissue *Wizard of Oz*. Now they'll do it—at Easter time. The studio will take advantage of three of their stars—Ray Bolger, Bert Lahr, and Jack Haley—each of whom is starring in his own play on Broadway. In *Wizard of Oz* you'll see Judy Garland at her tip-top, singing that haunting melody 'Over the Rainbow.'" By April 1 Jimmie Fidler reiterated the appeal: "Better make it a point to tell parents who have been bewailing the dearth of pictures 'ideal for kid audiences' that MGM is giving them a real break by reissuing [one] of the greatest juvenile favorites of screen history—*The Wizard of Oz*. . . ."

MGM may have also felt pressured to re-release *Oz* sooner rather than later. The modern television medium was fast becoming fodder for the Frank Baum stories, beginning with a September 29, 1948, *Variety* notice that Robert Stanton Baum, second of the *Oz* author's four sons, now representing his father's estate, had signed an agreement with Alfred Levy and David Susskind of Century Pictures for broadcasting rights to twelve of the Oz books. But the *Variety* notice would conflict with the rumor of another television project.

When MGM announced a definite *Wizard of Oz* reissue in March 1949, the news came soon after word of direct TV competition from one of its own players. On September 16, 1948, Edwin Schallert reported that actor-singer Dick Haymes, featured in Metro's *Words and Music*, which would debut that December, was now making a deal for the television rights to the Oz books. Haymes partnered with Bill Burton to form Beverly Television Productions Inc. and signed Sonny Burke and Paul Francis Webster to compose original songs for the proposed series. By the end of February 1949, the International News Service said the Haymes television show remained viable, noting Haymes's intention to present the stories as a combination of live action and animation, with actress Peggy Cummins (best known for her "bad girl" part in 1950's *Gun Crazy*) playing a leading role in the first installment.

Then, on August 8, 1949, actor Johnny Downs, who had just wrapped his role as the Tin Woodman at Pittsburgh, Pennsylvania's Civic Light Opera production of *The Wizard of Oz*, told *Post-Gazette* reporter Harold W. Cohen that *he* was trying to arrange for an Oz TV series, so taken was he with the story. Later that year, on December 5, *Broadcasting* announced that television rights to the Baum series were acquired by TeeVee Film Company in Hollywood and that puppeteer Burr Tillstrom, creator of *Kukla, Fran and Ollie*, was engaged for a series of half-hour episodes beginning with a marionette version of *The Land of Oz*. Of these various TV projects, only the Tillstrom pilot is known to have been produced. However, there was clearly a growing interest—and public demand—for televised Oz material, making MGM's plans for a theatrical re-release of its *Wizard* particularly timely.

A test booking of *The Wizard of Oz* for the Easter season opened at New York's Mayfair Theatre on April 16, 1949, and quickly proved to be overwhelmingly successful. The ads enticed, "Come 'Over the Rainbow' and find wonderful Easter entertainment," and noted that Judy Garland's costars were simultaneously appearing on Broadway: Ray Bolger in *Where's Charley*, Bert Lahr in *Make Mine Manhattan*, and Jack Haley in *Inside U.S.A.* Other ads asked, "Is Your Husband Cranky?" and "Is Your Wife Grouchy?" suggesting that a trip to see *The Wizard* was the antidote. "We promise you'll love the grand Technicolor musical . . . you'll have fun or your money back!" The prestige of *Oz*'s director and producer was highlighted as well. "Considering that *The Wizard of Oz* was directed by Victor Fleming, currently represented on the screen by Ingrid Bergman's great success, *Joan of Arc*, and was produced by Mervyn LeRoy, whose recent productions include *Little Women* and *Homecoming*, it is easy to see why this musical remains one of the screen's finest creations." Judy Garland's greatest MGM hit at the time had been *Meet Me in St. Louis*, released in 1944, and many of the ads and posters played upon that association by using a portrait of Garland not as Dorothy but as Esther Smith, her *St. Louis* role.

By April 19, 1949, *Motion Picture Daily* projected that the Mayfair's business concluding the first week of the reissue was expected to take in fifty-five thousand dollars. (In its second week *Oz*'s Mayfair gross was a "handsome" thirty thousand dollars; by its fifth week, the gross had dropped to a "moderate" fourteen thousand dollars.) Syndicated Broadway columnist Walter Winchell advised his readers, "Don't miss it this time." Eileen McConnell, of WMGM New York's "For Children Only" radio program stirred further interest by initiating a contest in conjunction with the screening. Her listeners (of all ages) entered by submitting their drawings of the wizard from which three winners would be announced. The prizes were passes to see *The Wizard* at the Mayfair and records of the show's songs.

The Mayfair's owner and general manager Harry Brandt wrote an open letter, published in New York papers, "written with a grateful heart about a wonderful picture." In part, Brandt wrote:

> In my thirty-five years as a showman, I have never seen any entertainment evoke such a response from the public as has MGM's *The Wizard of Oz*. It is simply thrilling to stand in back of the theater and hear the waves of laughter, the applause and the enthusiasm that greet every showing of this film. . . . Believe me, I feel it is a privilege to be part of all this joy. . . . I know that I'm very proud to bring back *The Wizard of Oz* for thousands of New Yorkers to see.

By May 1, 1949, *New York Times* film critic Bosley Crowther, known for his acerbic bite, made *The Wizard of Oz* the theme of an editorial—the lead article on page one of the *Times*'s Amusement Section. In his essay Crowther waxed nostalgic for the escapism *Oz* offered, not only for its entertainment value but for a "sweet forgetfulness" of a bygone era. "But we speak of this film with affection of one who saw it ten years ago," Crowther reminisced, "and who looks at it now with vagrant memories of much that was happening then and has happened since. And despite the infiltration of these painfully realistic thoughts, called up by the mere association, it is still a delightful experience." Crowther praised the picture's "Technicolored candy realms" as the region of "fanciful people and fairy queens." He lauded "the wistful song 'Over the Rainbow'" as well as "We're Off to See the Wizard." And of the sole cast member he noted by name, Crowther wrote, "Dorothy is still the wide-eyed symbol of the spirit of the eternal child, beautifully represented by Judy Garland in fresh, round form and lyrical voice."

A second site was selected by MGM for another test booking of *The Wizard*, one that would be more telling of mainstream America's reception for an *Oz* revival. Howard Burkhardt, manager of the Midland Theatre, Kansas City, Missouri, took full advantage of the opportunity by attiring three men in duds like the unusual trio of star characters in the picture with orders to parade the business streets on opening day. Burkhardt furnished albums of the *Oz* songs to disc jockeys of several city radio stations, which resulted in a local revival in popularity for "Over the Rainbow." Burkhardt scored his greatest promotional coup by arranging for MGM starlet Jane Powell to make a personal appearance at his theater for afternoon and evening showings of *Oz*. (Powell was in town to sing at a pop concert with the Kansas City Philharmonic Orchestra at the Municipal Auditorium.) Powell's star attraction was such that in its May 21, 1949, edition, *Showmen's Trade Review* noted that "the old film [*Oz*] drew near capacity audiences. Business for the week bettered the average."

With the Mayfair and Midland exceeding all expectations, advance screenings of *The Wizard of Oz*, called "trade shows," were held for theater owners in thirty-one major cities on May 19, 1949. The trade show screenings of *Oz* were intended to gauge exhibitors' reactions globally, and the response was glowing. Once the picture released nationally the following July 1, box-office returns for "MGM re-presents *The Wizard of Oz*" were such that the film earned back its original costs not recouped in 1939. Oddly enough, the State Theatre in Syracuse, New York, debuted the re-presentation of *The Wizard of Oz* on March 10, 1949. Citing the picture as one of the top reprint requests of MGM, the Syracuse engagement was more than a month ahead of the two test bookings and nearly four months before the nationwide re-release.

In her September 26, 1949, column, Hedda Hopper was self-congratulatory. "For years I begged Louis B. Mayer to reissue *Oz*, but said he, 'Don't bother me.' I mentioned the matter once to Dore Schary [MGM's chief of production as of 1948], and four weeks later the picture opened in New York. I hear that it's already taken in over three million dollars."

In between her moments of bravura, Hopper also made a professional misstep by writing in her September 10, 1949, column that Mervyn LeRoy was taken off *Oz* as director.

On September 13, Arnold M. Grant, LeRoy's attorney, sent Hopper a letter requesting that she retract her humiliating claim, which Hopper reluctantly did on September 26, saying, "[I] inadvertently did in Mervyn LeRoy by saying he was taken off *The Wizard of Oz* as director. Mr. LeRoy produced the picture; and it goes without saying that a producer couldn't fire himself." In his 1974 autobiography, LeRoy wrote that he felt vindicated in making Hopper eat crow, having endured her potshots for years.

On the occasion of its national re-release, *The Wizard* received publicity and promotion on par with a new debut, and it nabbed rave reviews all over again. Among these, *Time's* May 9, 1949, issue informed its readers, "*The Wizard of Oz*, dusted off and reissued, proves that true wizardry, whether in books or on the screen, is ageless. In the Magical Land of Oz, nothing changes." Jane Lockhart, film critic for the *Rotarian's* August 1949 edition, agreed: "As fresh as when it was first released, its tunes and dances as sprightly and spontaneous as ever, its Technicolored sets lavish and beautiful. Except for sensitive children who may be frightened by the ugly witch, the whole family will find this *delightful entertainment*." Upon revisiting the picture, Dan S. Terrell, movie critic for *Household* magazine, declared, "*The Wizard of Oz* shares honors with *Snow White* as Hollywood's most successful retelling of a well-loved fairy story—as fresh and entrancing as it was in 1939." When *Oz* returned to theaters in Los Angeles on July 8, 1949, the *Los Angeles Daily News* simply reprinted its original, favorable review from August 16, 1939.

An anonymous reviewer for the Syracuse, New York, *Post-Standard*, marveled at *Oz's* staying power. "Even though the picture was made ten years ago, its color effects have never been surpassed, its surprising camera angles topped, or its superb direction, fine acting and catchy tunes bettered." Another Syracuse critic, Marjorie Turner, of the *Syracuse Herald-Journal*, pronounced *Oz* without peer since 1939 with the exception of *Snow White* "which was in a slightly different pattern," and suggesting those who saw *Oz* originally would feel a nostalgic stir to take another look. Chief among Turner's praise was Judy Garland "just out of the 'brat' classification" then, but currently "garnering the garlands in Hollywood as a grown-up lady star of some magnitude." Symptomatic of how MGM's *Oz* had yet to pervade our cultural consciousness, however, Turner misidentified Garland's Dorothy character when she observed, "Judy never did anything better, young or adult, than her Margaret in this one."

Following her child-star days, Judy Garland's reputed physical and emotional struggles were sensationalized in the press such that Stuart Awbrey, of the *Hutchinson (KS) News-Herald*, qualified the *Oz* reprise:

Judy Garland is coming back to town. Not the Judy of divorces and nervous breakdowns and temperamental fits. But the Judy of ten years ago. . . . And the Judy whose song was "Somewhere [*sic*] Over the Rainbow," a lyric that really is more in keeping with the American spirit than the national anthem. . . . Judy Garland as Dorothy is still as wide-eyed and wistful as we remember her. It has been a painful ten years since *The Wizard of Oz*. . . .

In further acknowledgment of the changes brought about by the intervening decade, Jack Lait Jr. was reverential in his March 9, 1949, Hollywood column, informing readers that patrons who intended to see the forthcoming *Wizard of Oz* reissue might be interested to learn that three people who had important parts in its production had all died within a short period of time that year: director Victor Fleming, composer Herbert Stothart, and film editor Blanche Sewell.

As evidence of its growing status as a contemporary classic, the Academy of Motion Picture Arts and Sciences selected *The Wizard of Oz* for its twelfth series retrospective of Academy Award–winning pictures. Between October 16 and November 27, 1949, seven films so honored in 1939 were screened at the Academy Award Theatre on Melrose Avenue in Hollywood; *Oz* represented 1939's Best Song and Best Original Score when it was shown at eight thirty at night on Sunday, November 20. Of the picture's enduring score, critic Harold W. Cohen wrote, "Never again will *Oz* be quite the same without 'Over the Rainbow' or the mournful laments of the Scarecrow, the Tin Woodman and the Cowardly Lion."

Oz's assorted terrors also withstood the test of time with fresh potency. Students at an Akron, Iowa, elementary school saw the show with mixed results. The third grade reported, "Most of us enjoyed it, but there were a few who got frightened," while the fourth grade noted, "Some of us did not like the looks of the bad witch." The *Syracuse Herald-Journal*'s Marjorie Turner wrote of how "frighteningly real" *Oz* was: "Indeed, at one point the rear of the theatre was crowded with tots who refused to sit cooped up in a theatre seat while the Wicked Witch got her comeuppance, or the trees talked and clutched, or the Wizard bellowed through sheets of fire and smoke." Actor Gene Kelly even complained to the Associated Press's Bob Thomas, "I took my little girl to *Wizard of Oz* and she had nightmares for weeks."

In lieu of its nightmares, in 1950 the National Children's Film Library Committee recommended *The Wizard of Oz* for its high entertainment value after screening it for 102 schoolchildren. The Committee called *Oz* "an exquisite screen offering," noting "the entire audience was vociferous in its approval."

Riding the crest of the *Wizard of Oz* revival, the Lever Brothers Company, makers of Lux soap products, through its agent, J. Walter Thompson Company, engaged Judy Garland to reprise her role as Dorothy for a one-hour radio version of the MGM screenplay. The contract, dated December 18, 1950, was received by the William Morris Agency in Beverly Hills, Garland's representative, and remunerated the actress in the amount of five thousand dollars (minus agency commission) pending Lever Brothers' ability to secure the broadcasting rights "at a reasonable cost."

Clearances were obtained and *The Wizard of Oz* aired as a *Lux Radio Theatre* Christmas Day 1950 special. The show was performed and broadcast from the CBS studios in Los Angeles, station KNX, from six to seven o'clock Pacific Standard Time. The program's script was adapted by S. H. Barnett and is nearly verbatim throughout in keeping with the 1939 film. An original copy of the script was obtained by the authors of this book and was compared with the surviving audio transcription of the program.

The story was presented in three acts, with "frameworks" inserted in between for patter related to Lux soap products or Hollywood news. (Fred Stone's daughter Paula, by this time a writer-producer for MGM radio attractions, participated in one such spot, though no reference was made to her father or any *Oz* association.) Given the tight time frame, Barnett's narrative deleted most of the Munchkinland festivities, although parts for the Munchkin Mayor, Lawyer, and Doctor were portrayed. Also dropped were episodes involving the apple trees, the poppies, and the Winged Monkeys. The Wizard does not offer to fly away with Dorothy in his balloon but instead remains in Oz; nor does Glinda require Dorothy to tap her heels as a requirement for returning to Kansas.

Though no other original *Oz* cast members participated, Judy Garland was complemented by top vocal impressionists of the day. Cast as the Scarecrow was Hans Conreid, soon to be Captain Hook in Walt Disney's *Peter Pan* (1953). Herbert Vigran, the Tin Woodman, was a radio favorite of comedians Bob Hope, Jimmy Durante, and Jack Benny, and went on to appear in hundreds of television programs of the 1950s and 1960s, including *I Love Lucy*. Betty Lou Gerson, who impersonated Glinda, would become best known as the voice of Disney's Cruella de Vil in *One Hundred and One Dalmatians*. Additional players rounding out the cast included film actor Ed Max as the Cowardly Lion, Herbert Butterfield as the Wizard, giving it his best Ed Wynn impression, and Noreen Gammill (one of the gossiping elephants in Disney's *Dumbo*) was the Wicked Witch of the West.

The show's musical director was Rudy Schrager, who made the most of the film's score, and Judy Garland's star presence, by including "Over the Rainbow" twice (a reprise by Garland came at the story's conclusion) and "We're Off to See the Wizard" (now sung by Garland *with* the Munchkins instead of solely performed by the Munchkins, as in the film). The individual songs of longing for each of Dorothy's three male companions were retained as was the Munchkins' singing of "Ding-Dong! The Witch Is Dead," which was also warbled by a chorus of Winkie guards after the Wicked Witch has been melted. Deleted from the musical program were "The Merry Old Land of Oz" and "If I Were King of the Forest."

Judy Garland seemed to seamlessly slip into the role she essayed over a decade prior, and many of the inflections she gives in the delivery of her lines are identical to her 1939 performance. The occasion was also marked by the attendance of the actress's four-year-old daughter, Liza Minnelli. Liza's single scripted line, "Goodnight," at the close of the show, was cut for time, as was the roster of supporting cast members. Highlighted by Garland's appearance, the Lux broadcast was a delightful holiday treat. In all, the 1949–50 return of *The Wizard of Oz* was precisely the relief for what ailed postwar moviegoers of all ages.

ANOTHER RE-RELEASE

The 1949 *Wizard of Oz* reissue wrapped its official show dates in 1951, though it continued to be shown intermittently through 1954, largely as a single-day kiddie matinee with cartoon extras. Still, MGM announced on June 3, 1955, that *Oz* would again be brought back to theaters heralded with a new campaign. Broadway columnist Dorothy Kilgallen inferred Metro was seizing the opportunity to profit after the re-release of Greta Garbo's *Camille* (1937) stunned the movie industry by breaking attendance records at New York's Normandie Theatre. The success of *Camille* showed there remained a demand and an audience for "oldies-but-goodies" from the Metro vault. The Normandie was selected to screen *Oz* in its 1955 East Coast "re-premiere," where it came "close to record holder" in terms of box-office returns and was predicted to be "off to a long run." Simultaneously, *Oz* would also screen at Salt Lake City's Capital Theatre, where it played three weeks and brought in three times the average re-release business.

A new campaign was devised to promote *The Wizard of Oz* in accordance with its latest theatrical reissue. Billing it as "the neatest trick of the season," MGM proclaimed it was bringing back *Oz* for a whole new generation that wanted to see it and those who wanted to rekindle happy memories of it. The trailer was adjusted accordingly, reflecting an appeal to those who never saw *Oz* in its past releases: "If you've never seen it—you've got a rare treat in store!" The trailer added, "If you've seen it before . . . you'll get a lift all over again!" and emphasized, "All the magic, the spectacle and beauty . . . better than ever in wide screen!" The last tag was a reference to the 1955 reformatting of the original picture ratio to accommodate the novelty of an elongated projection, making movies seem even larger than life in a ploy to attract more patrons away from watching television at home. Radio spots played up this angle too, citing *Oz* as "the delightful comedy about the little girl who was transported to a magical land where nights are gay with love and laughter. . . . Now you can live those joyful adventures on the wide screen. . . ."

Two of the picture's stars were enjoying renewed success in 1955, and publicity deigned they should be singled out when advertising *The Wizard of Oz*. Sample copy played up Judy Garland's triumph in her recent motion picture comeback: "[Garland] won an Academy Award nomination for her performance in *A Star is Born*. Capitalize on this fact by calling attention to it in as many ways as possible." Ray Bolger was similarly promoted for his Thursday evening TV series by which strategically placed commercials could remind viewers "that Bolger can be seen in one of his greatest screen appearances as the Scarecrow in *The Wizard of Oz*."

Showmanship exploitation was much as it had been for the 1939 and 1949 engagements. Theater managers were encouraged to partner with local businesses to promote Oz cooperatively. A display of Oz titles was recommended for bookstore and library tie-ins, and a travel agency ad was suggested to read, "Happy Land of Make Believe to Happy Land of Sunshine!" Select screenings were recommended for high school and college newspapers as well as teen councils. Film societies and women's clubs were to be notified. Playing "Over the Rainbow" on each theater's P.A. system would "plug" the picture several weeks in advance. Film critics and movie editors were asked to review Oz again for their respective newspapers. And it was also suggested that enterprising managers tie-up with a popular local children's TV show for a contest, the prize for which would be free tickets to a Saturday morning showing of *The Wizard of Oz*. At the Loew's Stillman in Cleveland, three young men dressed as the Scarecrow, Tin Man, and Cowardly Lion and paraded the streets in a bit of ballyhoo repurposed from the previous Oz campaigns.

In its first three weeks, *The Wizard of Oz* was "doing new picture business" in Indianapolis, topping many of the new attractions from the previous year, while in Columbus it was bringing in twice the average re-release business. However, in the era of such childhood diversions as Howdy Doody, Peter Pan, Roy Rogers, and the *Disneyland* TV series, *The Wizard of Oz* was largely billed as a double feature or a kiddie show with plenty of cartoon fillers. Though Oz's strongest box-office competition was Disney's *Davy Crockett* and *Lady and the Tramp*, even the most hardened juvenile was nonetheless entranced by Judy Garland, as exemplified in an anecdote shared by the Hollywood branch of the Newspaper Enterprise Association:

A "reader" writes: "Thought maybe you'd like an outside Hollywood picture of what happens when Judy Garland sings. My four-year-old blonde is slightly cold-blooded. The only sentiment she has ever shown has been for Davy Crockett, a Davy Crockett rifle, and a galloping horse at the pony track which almost parts her head from her shoulders.

I took her to see *The Wizard of Oz*. Judy's 'Over the Rainbow' song was less than a minute old when she started sobbing—tears running down her cheeks. I still don't believe it—but I saw it. Is it genius or hypnotism?"

It's genius, ma'am.

Still, there were those who only saw Judy Garland's shortcomings. Mrs. Walter Ferguson, reflecting on *Oz* for the *Albuquerque (NM) Tribune*, was unduly fatalistic:

When that long lost little girl, Judy Garland, sang "Over the Rainbow," there was a big lump in my throat. I had forgotten how fresh and pretty she was then. . . . But adults who remember Judy Garland as a young girl will suffer through the film. To see what time and life can do to one brings on nostalgic pains and heartache. It must be torture for the middle-aged to see herself as she was, in the first bloom of youth. It is not the loss of beauty and freshness alone that is so terrible—but the loss of our dreams—the evidence of failure to become what we had once hoped to be.

An anonymous editor for the *Baytown (TX) Sun* was equally unforgiving, reminding readers that *Oz* was made "long before Judy Garland ever had two marriages, two divorces, [a] nervous breakdown, attempted suicide and a fat figure. . . ."

The movie editor for the *Paris (TX) News* put Judy's career in proper perspective, observing, "*The Wizard of Oz*, which has gone down in Hollywood history as one of the greatest musicals ever made . . . started Judy Garland off on a spectacular career culminating in her recent triumph in *A Star is Born*, and one of the songs she sings, 'Over the Rainbow,' remains a popular favorite with vocal artists throughout the world. . . . You don't see many pictures like *The Wizard of Oz*. It presents the magic of filmmaking at its best."

Despite the accolades, the 1955 theatrical outing of *The Wizard of Oz* proved less lucrative than the 1949 re-release. Moreover, by early August 1955 the announcement of another *Wizard of Oz* TV series threatened to dissuade ticket-buying patrons who might otherwise wait for the Oz stories to come to television. Hollywood journalist Eve Starr reported that Maple Productions was formed on August 8 for the express purpose of creating a series of thirty-nine half-hour TV movies made from the Baum and Ruth Plumly Thompson Oz books, specifically *The Wizard of Oz*. Starr admonished the new film company, writing, "I hope they know what they are doing. . . . And I hope they realize they are tampering with the childhood memories of thousands upon thousands of people. This is not a proposition to be taken lightly." (Starr got her wish as nothing further came of the proposed Oz TV series.)

Perhaps to entice would-be moviegoers into theaters, Metro allowed excerpts from *The Wizard of Oz* to air on two television programs. The first was *Remember 1938*, a ninety-minute retrospective hosted by Groucho Marx, which aired June 19, 1955. The show was advertised as featuring two scenes from *Oz*. A thirty-second clip from *The Wizard of Oz* was shown on the second episode of Metro's new TV series *MGM Parade* on September 21, 1955. The weekly program starred former studio alum George Murphy, who hosted segments from MGM's greatest hits (a small-screen version of *That's Entertainment!* nearly twenty years before its time). Though the TV journal *Broadcasting* panned this installment of the show as "tired and spiritless," "a long, long trailer," and essentially a "commercial" for MGM, the reviewer noted that *Oz* was the first clip introduced by Murphy at the top of the program. It was the scene of Judy Garland and her costars singing "We're Off to See the Wizard," a number which *Broadcasting* declared "immortal."

In 1949 MGM had included another "We're Off to See the Wizard" excerpt from *The Wizard of Oz* in its self-congratulatory theatrical short *Some of the Best*, which honored the studio's twenty-fifth anniversary; but the *Remember 1938* and *MGM Parade* programs were the first occasions for which clips from *Oz* were shown on network television. Within a year MGM would revisit this burgeoning medium and *Oz* would subsequently soar to unimagined heights of popularity by securing enduring proclaim beyond anything envisioned in 1939.

Legend

Television brought *The Wizard of Oz* to national prominence once more when in 1956 MGM leased its film property to CBS Television to air on the Ford Motor Company's Ford Star Jubilee program. On March 5, 1955, NBC-TV drew a rating of sixty-five million viewers for its color telecast of Mary Martin in *Peter Pan*—a television record at the time—and the live *Pan* show was remounted for a January 9, 1956, TV reprise. Advertising insiders projected that *The Wizard of Oz* could radically alter the attitudes of admen wary of Hollywood movies on TV in a manner similar to *Peter Pan* because the picture was American-made, was slated for a time slot that was prime viewing, and was pitted against normal competition. Expectations for *The Wizard of Oz* were high as this first-ever feature film sale to television would pave the way for the sale of more Hollywood pictures to TV—this coming at a time when a definite square-off between motion pictures and the stay-at-home entertainment of television viewing was at its most crucial.

There is ambiguity about the amount CBS committed to MGM to show *The Wizard of Oz*. The July 25, 1956, issue of *Motion Picture Daily* and the August 6, 1956, issue of the trade journal *Sponsor* noted that CBS paid a reported nine hundred thousand dollars for the right to air *Oz* four times for a deal that was inked four days prior. (The intention for CBS to sign with MGM was publicly disclosed on July 24.) *Motion Picture Daily* for July 25, 1956, reported that Charles C. ("Bud") Barry represented MGM in the negotiations, but in *The Making of The Wizard of Oz*, Aljean Harmetz cites Metro attorney Frank Rosenfelt as the lawyer who "assisted in the negotiations for MGM."

The contract to broadcast *The Wizard of Oz* permitted CBS to cancel the agreement after the first two presentations of *Oz*. Thus before it even aired, it was determined to repeat the picture several occasions beyond its premiere TV showing. For CBS, the cost of each showing was two hundred twenty-five thousand dollars (a figure confirmed by Harmetz), but other reports suggest the price was two hundred fifty thousand dollars, such as that of *Variety*'s July 25, 1956, edition. Journalist Otto R. Kyle, writing for the *Decatur (IL) Daily Review* two days after *Variety*'s publication date, stated that CBS would debut *Oz* at Christmas and had paid five hundred thousand dollars for the privilege of that broadcast and a subsequent airing in 1957. (Kyle also said that the film would be edited to ninety minutes for television.) A week before the *Oz* broadcast, Rex Polier, writing for the *Philadelphia Bulletin*, noted, "CBS recently purchased the TV rights to the movie for $200,000. . . . It is the first time that such a build-up and huge audience have been made available for an old movie."

But the old movie would turn out to be evergreen. Polier must've been working from memory when he informed viewers in advance that, "In the story, a twister whirls Dorothy into the sky, taking with her her dog, three farmhands, a grouchy neighbor who was about to take her dog, and a carnival mind-reader. Once in Oz, each is transformed." Another TV critic, Grem Octopada, writing for the *Salinas (KS) Journal*, appreciated the opportunity to "introduce a whole new generation to the twin magic of *The Wizard of Oz* and the lusty little girl who sings about bluebirds flying over rainbows." Octopada was also conciliatory about broadcasting a vintage film. "I've always believed television should strive for the new, for things especially tailored to the medium. But in the case of Judy and *The Wizard*, I'll concede a point. The show is worth repeating for the youngsters, old and young, who have never seen it."

The Wizard of Oz aired on Saturday, November 3, 1956, getting a nine-day lead on the broadcast of NBC's musical version of *Jack and the Beanstalk*. Despite *Oz* starting at nine o'clock at night and concluding at eleven, forty-five million viewers tuned in. (CBS had originally suggested showing *Oz* on a Friday night from seven thirty to nine o'clock, but the network had given the Ford Star Jubilee program the right of first refusal for its regular nine-to-eleven time slot.) Contemporary newspaper ads had given parents fair notice: "Let the kids stay up with the entire family to watch the first television broadcast of the brilliant musical fairy tale set in the enchanted Land of Oz."

CBS advised new color TV owners to expect the initial scenes of the picture to be in black-and-white "so they won't think something is wrong with their set." But the average color television set cost in the neighborhood of five hundred dollars and the majority of viewers watched *The Wizard of Oz* in monochrome on their black-and-white sets. The novelty of *Oz*'s transformation scene was a hearty holiday plug for the new color technology, especially in anticipation of a repeat showing. *Broadcasting* quipped in its November 12, 1956, edition:

If CBS had deliberately set out to whet color-starved appetites by color-casting a richly-remembered Technicolor film to homes predominately equipped for black-and-white, it couldn't have done a better job. The Great Oz, or more conveniently, Santa Claus, should be getting a flood of new requests—asking, not courage for a cowardly lion, or a heart for a tin man—but a TV set that will picture the Emerald City beyond the rainbow.

In 1956 it was unheard of to round out the nearly twenty-minute gap created by *Oz*'s 101-minute running time with commercial advertising in order to fill a two-hour time slot. Thus began the tradition of television and film stars acting as hosts for the CBS-TV special. As Judy Garland was unavailable, Bert Lahr was engaged to share hosting duties with Liza Minnelli, Garland's then ten-year-old daughter, from the CBS studios in New York. (Jack Haley was also hired by CBS to promote the broadcast in press interviews.) The program opened with an introductory announcement in which the narrator called *The Wizard of Oz* "a motion picture classic" and "a masterpiece of literature which has fascinated children and adults for years. . . ." In the scripted banter, Lahr explained Garland's absence, noting, "she's appearing at the Palace Theatre in New York in her wonderful, wonderful [concert] show. . . ."

Lahr went on to inexactly recall that in the picture he was about to eat up Minnelli's mother but couldn't for being the Cowardly Lion (Lahr noted that he had only seen *Oz* once before—at its 1939 premiere). Lahr told the girl that all the actors felt as though they "were living in the wonderful Land of Oz" at the time and mentioned how "cute" Toto the dog was. The pairing of the veteran comedian and the young Hollywood progeny was charmingly nostalgic for adults and appealing to the demographic of kids close in age to Minnelli. On a side note, Judy Garland told columnist Leonard Lyons that she rehearsed Liza for three weeks prior to her TV debut. "I behaved just like a stage mother, doing everything wrong," Garland said. "Never again."[1]

Film industry reservations for the power of "event" programming, such as *Oz*, to enthrall even in black-and-white TV proved to be founded. *Motion Picture Daily* reported in its November 7, 1956, issue that ticket sales in the Broadway motion picture district were unaffected by the *Oz* telecast, but elsewhere movie theaters saw a national loss of two million dollars the Saturday night *Oz* aired, according to Sindlinger & Co.'s November 17, 1956, weekly activity report of theater grosses (movie house grosses were restored to normal the following week).

MGM also made out with its *Wizard of Oz* soundtrack album, pressed on its MGM Records label, as a 33-1/3 LP and a boxed set of 45s, and released to coincide with the

---

1 Six years later Minnelli voiced and sang the part of Dorothy for a feature-length animated musical that would eventually be released in the United States as *Journey Back to Oz* (1974).

1956 TV broadcast. The recording comprised selections from the original motion picture soundtrack (the "Merry Old Land of Oz" number is deleted and there is no reference to the Ruby Slippers). The *Oz* soundtrack album was reissued in 1959 with corporate sponsor Pepsi-Cola's emblem printed on the back cover. For Christmas 1961, the record sold over one hundred thousand copies as a Duncan Hines premium, through TV sponsor Procter & Gamble. (In keeping with *Oz*'s newfound fame through its highly rated TV showings, the original cast album got a makeover in 1962 with a gatefold jacket, revised liner notes, and new cover art by prolific children's book illustrator Sheilah Beckett.)

So great was the impact made by the 1956 *Wizard of Oz* telecast that, in February 1957, Judy Garland was nominated for an Emmy award in the category "Best Actress-Single Performance" by the Academy of Television Arts and Sciences. But cries of protest ensued for this and other inequities that year, and the Academy hastily withdrew Garland's nomination as it was not a performance original to the television medium.

Speculation about another showing of *The Wizard of Oz* began soon after the initial, successful CBS broadcast. The February 1957 issue of *Radio-TV Mirror* said that the network was flooded with letters requesting an encore broadcast, noting that CBS had paid four hundred thousand dollars for two airings. In April 1957 *Sponsor* magazine ranked *Oz* fourth on a list of five color fairy tales that had proven hits for network TV, according to Trendex, an audience measurement service similar to the Nielsen rating system, qualifying that *Oz* had aired "when the average moppet is in bed." Both telecasts of *Peter Pan* rated tops, followed by *Jack and the Beanstalk*. The March 31, 1957, TV broadcast of Julie Andrews in *Cinderella* rounded out the list. Throughout the summer of 1957, it was variously reported that CBS would schedule another showing of *Oz* "as a Christmas present to viewers," but the network failed to repeat the broadcast that year.

Sponsor's August 16, 1958, issue indicated that CBS-TV "has a nut of $250,000 to work off" and was looking to reschedule *The Wizard of Oz* for the upcoming season but thus far had no bites from corporate sponsors. But sponsors were secured (Pepsi-Cola and Schraft's Candy) and *The Wizard of Oz* returned to network television on Sunday, December 13, 1959. Because there had been quibbles about the 1956 showing beginning at nine o'clock and concluding at eleven—well past the bedtime of the average youngster—CBS rebroadcast *The Wizard of Oz* from six to eight o'clock. Comedian Red Skelton, then in the ninth season on his self-titled CBS series, was appointed the show's emcee. Like the pairing of Lahr with Minnelli, Skelton cohosted the program with his eleven-year-old daughter, Valentina. Both were dressed in Victorian-era attire with Skelton as the "storyteller," a la L. Frank Baum, who introduced various "chapters" of the famous tale.

On the occasion of *Oz*'s second television broadcast, Judy Garland was hospitalized in New York, where she'd been recovering from acute hepatitis since November 18. Garland watched the show from her room and, as husband Sid Luft told the press, "sang the songs along with the soundtrack." Afterward, Garland phoned Joe and Lorna Luft, her two young children, who had tuned in to *Oz* from their home in Los Angeles, to reassure them that "Mommy was okay and the Witch didn't really get her." The picture's realism had overwhelmed the children, who became hysterical believing the Winged Monkeys had absconded with their mother. "All the fantasy had the little one [Joe] crying, and worried about his mother," Luft said. "But he was fine after Judy talked with him."

For the 1960 autumn TV season, Shirley Temple rebooted her popular storybook anthology series from two years prior, this time entirely in color. Temple kicked off the NBC series with an adaptation of Baum's *The Land of Oz*, with Temple playing two parts: "Tip," the boy protagonist, and Princess Ozma. The Scarecrow and Tin Man featured in the show are made up and costumed identical to their MGM counterparts, and the program aired three months in advance of the scheduled broadcast of *The Wizard of Oz* on CBS that year. The Associated Press's Cynthia Lowry slammed the show the day after it aired for daring to emulate Metro's original production: "It's hard to figure out why the producers elected to start off with *The Land of Oz* when there's a fine motion picture called *The Wizard of Oz* available for broadcast again. . . . Shirley Temple played a dual role Sunday night but even two Shirley Temples don't equal one Judy Garland. Missing was the fine trick photography, the singing and dancing in the motion picture."

When *The Wizard of Oz* did air on December 11, 1960, it was actor Richard Boone, of CBS's *Have Gun, Will Travel*, who hosted with his seven-year-old son Peter. Their segment began with Peter peering through a telescope in the den of the Boone homestead, wondering about a voyage to the moon. Richard decides to tell young Peter about a different voyage, that of Dorothy's trip to the Land of Oz; and they sit down in front of their TV set to enjoy *The Wizard of Oz* together.

On December 10, 1961, and December 9, 1962, Dick Van Dyke, then enjoying extraordinary success with his CBS show, introduced *The Wizard of Oz* with three of his four children, Barry, Chris, and Stacey. The Van Dyke clan gathered for publicity portraits on both occasions, posing with an oversize edition of the *Wonderful Wizard of Oz* book, seated on huge toadstools with a shining castle in the background, and preparing to sail off to see the wizard in a hot-air balloon. For the 1962 broadcast, Van Dyke told the press he was thirteen years old when MGM released *Oz* and that he still listed the picture as one of his all-time favorites. The firestorm of media attention given the November 22, 1963, assassination of President John F. Kennedy postponed *The Wizard of Oz* for the holiday season that year, and it did not air again until January 1964.

In December 1961 Associated Press TV-and-radio writer Cynthia Lowry denoted *Oz* as "an old, old movie that seems to gain rather than lose charm with annual repetition. One only hopes that they don't decide to make that one again with some new kid taking Judy Garland's place." Lowry's observations were in keeping with the times; the 1960s was a tumultuous and transitory period in national history, and artistic expression was revolutionary. The motion pictures (and actors) of *Oz*'s era did not receive widespread appreciation until 1974's MGM retrospective *That's Entertainment!* Instead, the films of yesteryear became ready fodder for parody and ridicule as hokey, out-of-fashion, and old hat. That *The Wizard of Oz* not only survived but *thrived* as it was discovered by a new generation did not go unnoticed by newspaper columnists and TV editors. The popularity of *Oz*'s television career also piqued the interest of the undisputed purveyor of childhood entertainment. Inspired by *Oz*'s ratings success, it was reported in April 1961 that Walt Disney would be adding an Emerald City attraction to his Disneyland theme park.

Preceding *Oz*'s 1964 outing, the *San Antonio (TX) Light* praised the film's "endless fancy, the exciting adventure and the brilliant acting of the immensely talented crew," and applauded *Oz* as a "special treat . . . for the new and old generation." A few years later another columnist quipped, "This one has been shown so many times everyone would be disappointed if 1967 went by without it. . . . Great stuff, even after almost 30 years." Also in 1967 editor Maryann Buczek thought *The Wizard of Oz* a "lovely bright movie . . . of World War II vintage but retains its charm and appeal for 'children' of all ages."

Simultaneous with Cynthia Lowry's 1961 comments, William E. Sarmento, TV critic for the *Lowell (MA) Sun*, waxed nostalgic, calling *Oz* a "joy." He further articulated the essence of *Oz*'s staying power:

Everything is right with the world once more. Well at least it seems that way after viewing for the umpteenth time Judy Garland, Ray Bolger, Jack Haley and Bert Lahr following the Yellow Brick Road to see the Wizard of Oz. Maybe Congress could pass some sort of law that would compel the CBS network to show this classic film every holiday season forever. . . . Just when one is about to give up hope on television something comes along like *The Wizard of Oz* that makes you feel that all is not lost. I'm sure that many parents remember toddling into one of the downtown theatres some twenty-odd years ago to see little Dorothy fly over the rainbow. It must be a real kick for these same grownups to sit with their children in front of the television set and make that magical journey all over again. . . . I'm sure you join with me in a sincere plea to the powers that be to keep Dorothy, the Tin Man, Scarecrow and the Cowardly Lion together, singing and dancing into the hearts of all of us through all the years to come.

The last of the CBS TV hosts was entertainer Danny Kaye. Then starring on *The Danny Kaye Show*, the actor was also known for playing in a similar musical fantasy, Samuel Goldwyn's production of *Hans Christian Andersen* (1952). Kaye, who cautioned young viewers of *Oz* not to fear the MGM lion's roar at the start of the picture, taped his segment as host in 1964. (At the time, Judy Garland's weekly CBS series was simultaneously promoted.) By then CBS had shifted the showtime to January 26, 1964, after the holidays. The TV network also reused the same segments of Danny Kaye over the next three years. (After CBS declined to pay MGM one million dollars per each future airing, NBC consented to pay MGM eight hundred thousand dollars to telecast *Oz* from 1968 to 1975, after which CBS regained the TV rights once more and aired *Oz* for another twenty-two years.)

Because so few Americans owned color televisions at the time, CBS broadcast *Oz* in black-and-white in 1962; but prior to *Oz*'s 1964 return, the *San Francisco Examiner*'s Dwight Newton provided cautionary instructions for those who had purchased color sets in the intervening years. Newton's advisement is nostalgic of an era when television programming was transitioning to take advantage of the new technology:

> The last time around, in 1962, CBS televised it in black and white only. Tonight it will be in black and white partly, and in color mostly. WARNING: If you have a color set that seems to be working properly, don't fiddle with the dials when the *Wizard* color goes off and on. The show will run something like so: Danny Kaye will introduce it in color. The show title and credits will be in color [*sic*]. The next twenty minutes, or less, when Dorothy is in Kansas and until the twister lifts her to Oz, will be in black and white. The rest of the show will be in color except the last two minutes which will be in black and white in Kansas again. All commercials will be in black and white except the one in the third position, which will be in color. Got that? Good.

At the time, the *Examiner* recalled how in 1939 its film critic, Ada Hanifin, had been charmed by the picture and the effect it had on a "house full of children [that] yelled and applauded when the story began to unfold on the screen, and their enthusiasm was unbounded when it finished." Hanifin called *Oz* "the most engaging fantasy of its kind," and predicted it would be as important to children as Santa Claus. In 1964 the *Examiner* noted that while World War II had long since ended, *The Wizard of Oz* was still with us, already calling it "probably the most widely viewed movie of all" due to its five previous network television exposures.

It may be difficult for younger fans to appreciate the anticipation of the annual *Wizard of Oz* broadcasts of the 1960s and 1970s; since 1980 they've had instant access to it via VHS cassettes or DVD and Blu-Ray editions. But in the days of three-network TV, *The Wizard of Oz* was an *event*. A frequent sponsor of the *Oz* telecasts, Procter & Gamble summarized the status *Oz* had attained by 1967 stating, "*The Wizard of Oz* has been adapted for stage plays, radio shows, puppet shows, and musical comedy but the adaptation we think of first is the motion picture! Television has brought the *Wizard of Oz* movie its greatest success. This annual TV classic has become a tradition."

IMMORTALITY

Judy Garland died unexpectedly at age forty-seven on June 22, 1969, the result of over-ingesting sleeping tablets. A lifelong reliance on prescription medication had taken its toll. Ray Bolger was the first of Judy's *Oz* costars to be interviewed within hours of the news, commenting that her star charisma was evident during the film's production. At the time, Garland's actress-daughter Liza Minnelli was making the film *Tell Me That You Love Me, Junie Moon*. Her makeup artist was Charles Schram, who had worked on *The Wizard of Oz* and who did Garland's makeup on her MGM pictures both pre- and post-*Oz*. At Minnelli's express request, Schram agreed to make up Judy Garland one last time. Alone with her corpse overnight at Frank E. Campbell Funeral Home in New York, it was something he later said he would not want to experience twice. The *New York Times* estimated that twenty thousand people filed past Garland's glass-enclosed casket to pay their respects. Among the celebrities in attendance were Bolger and composer Harold Arlen, who had written "Over the Rainbow" just over thirty years prior. Bolger proclaimed, "Judy didn't die. She just wore out."

In a June 27, 1969, editorial for the *Roselle (IL) Register*, journalist Rick Friedman eulogized Garland in a manner representative of her admiring and nostalgic constituents. Titled "Thank you, Dorothy, for a Dream," Friedman wrote, in part:

Through all of our growing up years she would always be there, growing up a little bit ahead of us, a part of the visual literature we read over and over up there in black and white and sometimes in Technicolor on that big screen. . . . Thirty years ago and just last Christmas and the last few Christmases before that as children of our own now sat before a television screen so they, too, could kill the Wicked Witch of the West, follow the Yellow Brick Road, oil the rust out of the Tin Man, put the Scarecrow back together again. . . . Thanks to you, Dorothy, we all have.

It was decided to plan a tribute to Judy Garland for the next airing of *The Wizard of Oz* on the NBC network on March 15, 1970. The film wouldn't be hosted as it had been in prior years, but there would be a moment of reverence for Garland's legacy leading in to the film. *Oz*'s producer, Mervyn LeRoy, directed actor Gregory Peck, who was president of the Academy of Motion Picture Arts and Sciences at the time, for a one-minute tribute to Judy. A regrettable concession was that LeRoy was compelled to excise sixty seconds from *Oz* to make up the time difference and not sacrifice valuable commercial advertising. LeRoy chose to edit a gratuitous tracking shot of Munchkinland as it contained no dialogue. Otherwise, LeRoy had no interest in rewatching the film but for the first few minutes. "I look only to see if the print is right," he said. "Sometimes TV is careless about using an old print. But why should I see it all the way through? I know the story and I viewed it all at least thirty times in editing before it was released." LeRoy did concede, however, that there wasn't a single scene he would alter if he were making the film anew.

Corporate sponsor the Singer Company—of sewing machine fame—pulled out all the stops in honoring Garland's and *Oz*'s legacy with newspaper and magazine advertisements as well as giveaway posters. (In the late 1960s, Singer had sponsored TV variety shows and concerts for Herb Alpert, Don Ho, Tony Bennett, and Elvis.) Surviving cast members Margaret Hamilton, Jack Haley, and Ray Bolger were reunited by *TV Guide* to reflect on their roles, the film's impact, and their relationships with Judy in interviews and a photo shoot specifically for this "special encore telecast" of *Oz*. More than corporate hype, the media buildup to the 1970 *Wizard of Oz* telecast was philanthropic, as Mervyn LeRoy noted. "The Singer Company, which is sponsoring the broadcast this year, has agreed to donate a cottage at the Motion Picture Country Home [a retirement village for aged and ailing actors] this year in the name of Miss Garland," LeRoy explained. "Norman Rockwell's painting of Judy with her dog, Toto, will go on the front of the cottage."

In this era the professional camaraderie forged by Bolger, Haley, and Lahr prior to *Oz* became, post-*Oz*, the kind of trench-mate, blood-brother bond that unites wartime survivors. Bolger literally bore battle scars decades after the fact. In 1971 he reportedly still had slight impressions on both cheeks resulting from the nightly removal of his Scarecrow makeup. Jack Haley Jr. remembered the union among the three troupers, noting that, when growing up, "Uncle Bert Lahr would always stay with us when he came out to do a movie in Hollywood."

The kinship between Haley and Lahr would be tested by Jack Haley Jr. in 1940 during the run of his father's Broadway show *Higher and Higher*. Jack Jr. boasted of his father's *Wizard of Oz* celebrity to some neighborhood peers. "You know, my father was the Tin Woodman . . ." to which the other kids responded with a skeptical, "Oh yeah!" "Yeah," said young Haley, "and furthermore his best friend played the Cowardly Lion." But the other boys dismissed him with "Go away, we're busy." That night Jack Jr. asked his father, "Pop, how well do you know Bert Lahr?" After being assured both players knew each other quite well, Jack Jr. made a request. "There are some kids that need a lesson. Put on your Tin Woodman clothes and get Bert Lahr to dress up as the Cowardly Lion and come over to Central Park tomorrow at three o'clock."

Jack Haley Jr. also recalled that whenever Ray Bolger started to rhapsodize about *The Wizard of Oz* during joint interviews in the 1970s, his father would interrupt with, "Would you stop! For God's sake, you know what we all went through every day. We all hated that picture and couldn't wait to get off it!"

With the passage of time, Haley felt at even greater liberty to set the public straight. As early as the 1956 television broadcast of *The Wizard of Oz*, Haley tempered any romanticizing—despite cumbersome costuming and uncomfortable makeup—that filmmaking was a party, telling James Devane, of the *Cincinnati (OH) Enquirer*, "I had to carry all that makeup and costume around for months and months and it was horrible, just awful." After *Oz* had garnered legendary status in the 1970s, Haley distilled the experience to a succinct, "Like *hell* it was fun!" during a TV segment with *The Tomorrow Show*'s Tom Snyder. In 1989 Jack Haley Jr. reiterated his father's position when interviewed by *Lefthander* magazine, "My father hated doing that picture. He said it was the toughest job he ever did in his life. He just wanted to get it over with."

But Ray Bolger remained steadfast in his affinity for *The Wizard of Oz*, at least publicly, and often with the embellished clarity of hindsight. In 1971 he told Barry Conrad of the *Hamilton (OH) News-Journal*, "I always felt that if there was a fantasy that would live, it would be this one. . . . Not everybody can say they belong to a classic." Bolger then underscored his universal renown by citing a recent example: "I got off a plane at Orlando for the Disney [World] opening and the little girls who were working there suddenly realized I was the Scarecrow and about six of them ran across the street and said, 'Hey, will you sing 'If I Only Had a Brain'?"

Bolger re-created his Scarecrow routine on television for the Christmas Eve episode of his variety show in 1954. Viewing the segment today, Bolger appears remarkably fit and limber fifteen years after the fact. Attired in his original MGM wardrobe, he sings "I Whistle a Happy Tune," from *The King and I*, to cheer two lost youngsters (the rights to use

"If I Only Had a Brain" proved too costly for the show's budget). Bolger then loosely prances about the stage before tripping into his famous "rubber legs" split. Throughout, Bolger emulates his moves from the deleted dance sequence, directed by Busby Berkeley, that originally accompanied the extended version of "If I Only Had a Brain" in *The Wizard of Oz*. The reaction from TV viewers was so enthusiastic that Decca Records wanted Bolger to perform some of the less familiar Oz stories for an album.[2]

Bolger again reenacted the Scarecrow dance on TV in 1957, 1966, and 1968 but would otherwise do nothing to besmirch his status in the eyes of children of all ages. In 1965 he turned down a reported fifty thousand dollars to portray Ralston Purina's Checkerboard Scarecrow in Corn Chex cereal commercials. Declining the offer was a no-brainer for the actor, who stated he didn't think it would be fair to his young fans if the Scarecrow showed up in a commercial instead of the Land of Oz (the role went to Bobby Van). The following year Jack Haley, Bert Lahr, and Bolger would all refuse the paltry sum MGM offered them to lend their voices to the Oz animations the studio was developing for its 1967 television series "Off to See the Wizard."[3]

Instead, Bolger focused his attention on the development of "The Wonderful Wizardland of Oz," a proposed theme park that would "out-Disney Disneyland." Even though a similar attraction had just opened in North Carolina's Land of Oz at Beech Mountain, Bolger was undeterred in his vision to capitalize on the Oz theme by launching parks in "the Los Angeles area and probably Florida." In 1970 Bolger told Associated Press writer Gene Handsaker, "Disneyland has characters—Mickey Mouse, Donald Duck and so on, but we have a theme; that everyone has a heart, brain and courage. And that by using them properly, you reach the pot of gold, which is home." Wizardland's prospects seemed promising for the moment, with a yellow brick road leading through Scarecrow Land with a farm-like petting zoo, Tin Man Land featuring mechanical attractions, and Cowardly

2 The Decca Records project did not materialize, but in 1965 Bolger narrated an adaptation of L. Frank Baum's *The Scarecrow of Oz* for a Disneyland Records illustrated book and record set.

3 The Oz actors' voices were intentionally imitated for an officially authorized 1990–91 Saturday morning cartoon series inspired by the MGM film.

Lion Land with its wild animals. There would also be Dorothy's house in Kansas with a cyclone effect and castles for the Wizard and Witch. An odd juxtaposition is that the park would also have a communal living area for retirees over age fifty-five. Despite working with a San Francisco contractor and a Utah construction company, Bolger's theme park was never realized.

In her later years Margaret Hamilton was dogged by the spectre of her chilling performance as Oz's Wicked Witch, saying, "Sometimes I think I have never done anything but ride a broomstick." Chagrined, she downplayed the part by saying, "I don't feel it was any great piece of acting. After all what do you do with a witch but the obvious?" She also found herself routinely justifying her part in The Wizard of Oz as just that—a role, albeit a dual role. Like most of the principal Ozians, Hamilton had a Kansan counterpart in Miss Gulch, the wealthy spinster. In a 1970s note to a concerned young fan, Hamilton attempted to rationalize Miss Gulch's position and her drive to settle a score with the Gale family:

I did not try to hurt "Toto"—honey—I played a part called Miss Gulch—and it was Miss Gulch who was so cross and mean. No matter who played Miss Gulch—she would be played that way—cross and mean—a little like a witch—don't you think? The Witch didn't try to hurt the Lion! Only the Scarecrow! But she (the Witch) never managed to do any of the things she wanted to do! Neither did Miss Gulch—the dog Toto—got away—remember? I hope you are all over being scared. . . . So many things look and seem one way—and are not really that way. I expect if we could really know Miss Gulch she wouldn't be so nasty—and we'd find out why she was so upset over Toto. She tho't he tried to bite her! We think Toto wouldn't bite anyone—but Toto did bark and maybe scared Miss Gulch! There are lots of things to think about.

As the media-at-large increasingly portrayed Judy Garland as a tragic figure in the years following her fatal overdose, Hamilton did due diligence by consistently redirecting reporters. In 1970 she told the New York Daily News's Margaret McManus:

There were no signs then [1938–39], of all the troubles to come, at least as far as the rest of us could see. Of course, as soon as she [Garland] was finished with her scenes, she went off to the school room on the studio lot, to study her lessons, so how much could we tell? But she was the happiest, most enthusiastic sixteen-year-old, just a darling, gay child. And she was so full of excitement about her part. She loved playing Dorothy.

Ray Bolger also defended Garland but with typical melodramatic embellishment. "Judy never heard a lullaby, and she never saw a rainbow that wasn't manufactured in a film studio. All she did was work, work, work! She can't be blamed for ending the way she did." Jack Haley vacillated between comments such as, "She didn't get love and discipline. It broke my heart," while in other instances he was less sensitive, defining Garland as a "poor sucker" who got "hooked" on pills. According to an anecdote recorded by Garland ally and confidante Jack Paar, there was little love lost between Judy and Haley in post-Oz years. Allegedly, Garland "hated" Haley though Paar claimed, "I don't know what it's all about." Perhaps it is best to accept at face value Haley's earliest reaction to Garland's passing in an August 2, 1969, interview: "I felt a great sadness, not only for Judy, but for the millions of young people to whom Dorothy in *The Wizard of Oz* was a kind of symbol. The whole substance of the film was the belief that Dorothy wanted to get home; that's why it has such great appeal." For what it's worth, in 1939 Haley had told the *New York Sun* that Garland was "a darling" and that he was enchanted by her, as was everyone connected with the picture.

The mid-1970s saw resurgence in *Wizard of Oz* popularity for another generation. In 1974 toy manufacturer Mego Corporation obtained a license from MGM to produce a line of *Wizard of Oz* dolls and began a yearlong research survey of day-care centers and nursery schools to ascertain children's familiarity with the movie characters. Beginning in 1971, Mego had introduced eight-inch, fully articulated action figures and play sets patterned after motion picture, TV, and comic book characters including *Planet of the Apes* and *Star Trek*. But the expertly modeled *Oz* figures superseded the popularity of all others, aided by a masterful promotion that would reunite the original film cast once more.

Mego's *Wizard of Oz* line launched at New York's annual Toy Fair trade show on February 10, 1975. The publicity kickoff, held at the Waldorf-Astoria's grand ballroom, gathered surviving *Oz* alum Mervyn LeRoy, Margaret Hamilton, Jack Haley, and Ray Bolger for a screening of select scenes from the picture (always "on," Bolger sang along out loud). The actors posed with their doll likenesses, and all reminisced about *Oz* once again. Mego president Marty Abrams had personally invited over one thousand toy buyers, who were duly starstruck. By the end of Toy Fair, Mego had over twenty million dollars in retailers' advance orders for the *Oz* figures.

Kathleen Carroll, film critic for the New York *Daily News*, was on hand for the *Oz* cast reunion, and transcribed the impromptu banter of the Hollywood veterans during an after-hours luncheon at Sardi's in her March 2, 1975, *Sunday News* piece: "It's Old Home Week for *The Wizard of Oz*." The grumbling, one-upmanship, and good-natured barbs the actors traded were a throwback to the vaudevillian camaraderie that sustained them during the intensive 1938–39 *Oz* production.

Jack Haley mostly remembered the torture of wearing all that makeup as the Tin Woodman, saying he had "no fun at all," and that his only reprieve was during Judy Garland's tutoring time. As Haley proceeded with the rant, he quipped that Bolger "got high" from sniffing the glue used to affix his makeup mask, which brought a huge laugh from the entire table.

Mervyn LeRoy recalled that Bert Lahr had tremendous anxiety over his part, and approached LeRoy during production with tears in his eyes, saying, "I think I should get out of the picture." But LeRoy noted the actors "were always on time," to which Ray Bolger interjected, "I don't know why we're still speaking to him," referencing their early-morning call.

Haley brought up Judy Garland, questioning her reliability when Garland claimed the trio of vaudevillians upstaged her. "It just wasn't true," he said. "After a while, I guess, she just started to believe it."

LeRoy praised Victor Fleming as a "great man," and reiterated the legend about how "Over the Rainbow" was nearly deleted by executives who didn't understand the picture. "They were afraid of it," he conceded.

As Bolger was served his order of spaghetti, he quipped, "It's Italian straw," to which LeRoy chimed in, "He's still the strawman." At this point, Margaret Hamilton leaned over and whispered to Kathleen Carroll, "You are in the midst of two nuts, one supernut. They're always on," advising the reporter not to take their remarks too seriously.

When Bolger offhandedly said of Hamilton, "We never saw her when we were working," Haley reminded him that he was present for the melting scene and accused Bolger of sniffing glue again.

The lunch at Sardi's would be the last time the surviving *Oz* alum would be gathered together. Just four years out, Jack Haley would die at age eighty on June 6, 1979. Margaret Hamilton's tongue-in-cheek quip about her obituary reading "Ding-Dong! The Witch Is Dead" would be honored by some in the media who headlined her May 16, 1985, passing at eighty-two. The last survivor of the main cast, Ray Bolger, would succumb at age eighty-three on January 15, 1987. Mervyn LeRoy died at eighty-six, September 13, 1987. (Previously, comedian Bert Lahr was seventy-two when he passed on December 4, 1967, and Billie Burke died at age eighty-five on May 14, 1970.) The Yellow Brick Road survivors were well aware that *The Wizard of Oz* would outlive them and all expressed gratitude for the immortality it brought them in a business that often treats its veteran performers with indifference and disregard, especially if they are no longer relevant.

But *The Wizard of Oz* remained relevant, further buoyed by a nationwide media and merchandising blitz for its 1989 fiftieth anniversary. By the 1990s any ancient comparisons between the achievements of Walt Disney and *The Wizard of Oz* had long since dissipated in favor of Judy Garland and company courtesy of *Oz*'s status as a television institution and video icon. However, one last gasp of competitive rivalry was pitched in the 1996 promotional material for *Oz*'s "Available for the last time this century!" video campaign. *Oz* was noted as having a "higher purchase intent than *Snow White*" which, at the time, had a video premiere following its final theatrical release.

Most recently, *The Wizard of Oz* enjoyed its milestone 75th anniversary celebration, which began a year early in 2013. On that occasion, the film had its gala "re-premiere" at the TCL Chinese Theatre, formerly Grauman's Chinese Theatre, site of *Oz*'s original 1939 debut. Hollywood celebrities turned out for the family event marked by the appearance of several surviving cast members who had portrayed Munchkins. Of special note is that this was the unveiling of a transformative technology that allowed *The Wizard of Oz* to be viewed for the first time in 3-D.

The irony is that, in 1939 film critic Wood Soanes was among those who didn't foresee *Oz* having any lasting value when compared with the work of Walt Disney and Max Fleischer, who held fast to his conviction that film fantasy was the private realm of the cartoon. "MGM is making money," wrote Soanes, "but not history with *The Wizard of Oz*." Happily, time has proven otherwise.

Bibliography

*Please note the distinction between *Variety* (a weekly publication) and *Daily Variety*.

"About 'The Wizard of Oz,'" *Emporia (KS) Daily Gazette*, September 23, 1939.

"Academy of Tailwagger Awards," *Ottawa (Ontario, Canada) Journal*, March 16, 1940.

Adrian, "The Importance of Color," *Murray Pioneer* (Renmark, South Australia), May 4, 1939.

"Ahead of Mr. Disney," *Clearfield (PA) Progress*, February 11, 1938.

"A Heavy High Priest," *Detroit (MI) Free Press*, January 20, 1939.

"Air Ya Listenin?" *Mason City (IA) Globe-Gazette*, December 30, 1939.

"A Line on Hollywood," *Harrisburg (PA) Telegraph*, February 21, 1939.

"A Line on Hollywood," *Harrisburg (PA) Telegraph*, September 5, 1939.

"A Line on Hollywood," *Dunkirk (NY) Evening Observer*, March 11, 1939.

"A Line on Hollywood," *Camperdown Chronicle* (Victoria, Australia), Tuesday, March 14, 1939.

"A Line on Hollywood," *Dunkirk (NY) Evening Observer*, April 1, 1939.

"A Line on Hollywood: Judy Garland Planning Her First Trip to Europe," *Dunkirk (NY) Evening Observer*, February 18, 1939.

"A Line on Hollywood: Original 'Oz' Script Is Gift from Actor," *Hollywood News and Features*, MGM, August 8, 1938.

"All Girls 16 or Under!" *Daily (Lawrence, KS) Journal-World*, September 7, 1939.

"Alliance Release New Oz Film," *Motion Picture News*, vol. 11, no. 5, February 6, 1915.

"All the Way From Oz," *Portsmouth (NH) Herald*, November 28, 1939.

"The Amusements," *Sunday Record-Herald* (Chicago), June 29, 1902.

Anderson, Arthur. *Let's Pretend and the Golden Age of Radio*, Boalsburg, PA: BearManor Media, 2004.

Anderson, Nancy, "LeRoy's Lions Refused to Eat Christians," *Mt. Vernon (IL) Register-News*, June 30, 1973.

Anderson, Nancy, "Oz's Tin Woodman Surviving All Eras," *The Argus* (Fremont, CA), October 4, 1971.

"Anna Sten, Importation from Russia, Presented in First American Film," *Oakland (CA) Tribune*, February 4, 1934.

"Ann Shirley," *Hollywood*, vol. 25, no. 7, July 1936.

Ardmore, Jane, "Judy," *American Weekly*, October 1, 1961.

Arthur, Franklin, "Ray's Making Love to Anna Neagle, Now," *Baltimore Sun*, February 16, 1941.

"Ashley Midget Visits Parents," *Wilkes-Barre (PA) Record*, July 17, 1935.

"At Least One Movie Fan Likes Judy Garland's Picture Work Better Than Spencer Tracy's," *Mansfield (OH) News-Journal*, December 13, 1939.

"At the Movies," *Manitowoc (WI) Herald-Times*, September 9, 1938.

"At the Movies," *Manitowoc (WI) Herald-Times*, November 17, 1938.

Awbrey, Stuart, "We're Off to See the Wizard, the Wonderful Wizard of Oz," *Hutchinson (KS) News-Herald*, November 20, 1949.

Bahn, Chester B., "Fred Stone May Revive Baum Play," *Syracuse (NY) Herald*, November 28, 1932.

Bahn, Chester B., "Goldwyn's 'Wizard of Oz' Is Held Up," *Syracuse (NY) Herald*, December 27, 1933.

Bahn, Chester B., "Industry Statistics," *The 1939 Film Daily Year Book of Motion Pictures*, 1939.

Bahn, Chester B., "'Mr. Chips' Voted Best of 1939," *Emporia (KS) Daily Gazette*, January 20, 1939.

Ball, Linda, "Mercer Islander Traveled the Yellow Brick Road," *Mercer Island (WA) Reporter*, November 30, 2011.

Barabak, Mark, "Munchkin Fondly Recalls His Favorite Engagement," *Salina (KS) Journal*, April 27, 1980.

"Barbara Koshay Is Opening a Swimming School in Hollywood," *Salt Lake (UT) Tribune*, July 29, 1939.

"'Barbary Coast' Put on Shelf by Goldwyn," *Motion Picture Daily*, vol. 35, no. 147, June 25, 1934.

"Barber Shop Quartet," *San Antonio (TX) Express*, January 8, 1939.

Barnes, Howard, "The Screen," *New York Herald Tribune*, August 20, 1939.

Barron, Mark, "Paula Stone Has One Part; Rumor Has It 'Wizard of Oz' to Be Revived in Fall," *The Tennessean* (Nashville), July 2, 1933.

Baum, L. Frank, *The Emerald City of Oz*, Chicago: Reilly & Britton, 1910.

Baum, L. Frank. *The Wonderful Wizard of Oz*, Chicago: George M. Hill, 1900.

"Baum Slaps Suit on 'Wizard of Oz' Tinter," *Variety*, vol. 118, no. 8, May 8, 1935.

"Behind the Make-Up," *Wilkes-Barre (PA) Record*, September 29, 1938.

"Berlin Just Social," *Variety*, vol. 112, no. 5, October 10, 1933.

"Berlin Mulls MG Bid," *Variety*, vol. 112, no. 8, October 31, 1933.

"Bert Lahr Has Share of Ideas," *Ames (IA) Daily Tribune*, February 15, 1954.

"Bert Lahr Impersonates Porpoise," *Hollywood*, vol. 31, no. 2, February 1942.

"Bert Lahr Is Hamlet Off Stage," *Indianapolis (IN) Star*, January 21, 1940.

"Bert Lahr Kidding with Phil Plant and Marjorie King at the Paradise Restaurant," *Syracuse (NY) Herald*, August 7, 1939.

"Bert Lahr Succeeds Rooney in NY P.A.'s," *Daily Variety*, vol. 24, no. 71, August 28, 1939.

"Bewitching Witch," *Ames (IA) Daily Tribune*, November 5, 1938.

"Big Drive on 'Wizard of Oz' by Chadwick Exploiteers," *Moving Picture World*, May 2, 1925.

"Billie Burke Expects to Discard Cast," *Fitchburg (MA) Sentinel*, May 16, 1939.

"Billie Burke Hurt," *Altoona (PA) Mirror*, March 11, 1939.

"Billie Burke Is Ex-Stage Singer," *Santa Ana (PA) Register*, July 27, 1940.

"Billie Burke Trips on Set, Breaks Ankle," *Oakland (CA) Tribune*, March 11, 1939.

"Biography of Judy Task for Teacher," *Harrisburg (PA) Telegraph*, August 5, 1940.

"Birds and Beasts Work for Zoo Home," *Harrisburg (PA) Telegraph*, December 5, 1938.

"Bitter Court Fight Pending Over 'Wizard of Oz' Rights," *Variety*, vol. LXXVII, no. 12, February 4, 1925.

"'Blackmail' Suits Made by 'Oz' Scion," *Harrisburg (PA) Telegraph*, September 20, 1939.

Blakeslee, Howard W., "High Cost of Living: Food Priced at $900 a Pound," *Pantagraph* (Bloomington, IL), September 3, 1939.

"Blandick to 'Oz,'" *Hollywood Reporter*, vol. XXXXX, no. 1, February 2, 1939.

"Bleachers to Seat Crowd at 'Wizard of Oz' Opening," *Los Angeles Examiner*, August 14, 1939.

"Block Booking Not at Fault, Asserts Mayer," *Motion Picture Daily*, vol. 36, no. 9, July 12, 1934.

Bloecher, Bill, "Hollywood on the Air," *Hollywood Reporter*, vol. LII, no. 28, July 1, 1939.

"Bob Hope and Judy Garland Feature New Pepsodent Show on WIBA at 9," *Capital Times* (Madison, WI), September 26, 1939.

Bodeen, DeWitt, "Our Cover Girl," *Script*, vol. XXI, no. 517, July 29, 1939.

Bogue, Jesse, "Business Utilizes Music," *New Castle (PA) News*, December 10, 1963.

Bolger, Ray, "'The Wizard of Oz' and the Golden Era of the American Musical Film," *American Cinematographer*, vol. 59, no. 2, February 1978.

"Bolger Says Judy Never Got Chance," *TV Tab*, March 21–28, 1979.

"Bolgers Sued for $15,000 by Select Theatres," *Hollywood Reporter*, vol. LII, no. 31, July 6, 1939.

Bolton, Whitney, "Scenes on 'Oz' Set," *Philadelphia Inquirer*, February 5, 1939.

Bond, Tommy, *Darn Right It's Butch*. Wayne, PA: Morgin Press, 1994.

"Branch Reiterates Appeal for Code in Michigan Meet," *Showmen's Trade Review*, vol. 31, no. 11, October 7, 1939.

Brooks, Marla, "Jack Haley, Jr.: Growing Up in the Land of Oz," *Lefthander Magazine*, vol. 14, No. 3, May/June 1989.

"Brown-Dubin Teamed," *Variety*, vol. 130, no. 6, April 20, 1938.

Brown, Kingdon, "There's No People," *Raleigh (WV) Register*, April 22, 1961.

Bruno, Charles, "Star Flashes," *San Mateo (CA) Times*, November 29, 1938.

Buczek, Maryann, "Serendipity," *Arlington (IL) Heights Herald*, February 19, 1967.

Bullock, Ginny, "'Wizard of Oz' Producer Blames Hollywood's Lack of Glamour and Mystery on Big Business Takeover," *National Tattler*, December 9, 1973.

Burdette, Jay, "In Hollywood," *Press Democrat* (Santa Rosa, CA), July 16, 1939.

Burdette, Jay, "In Hollywood," *Press Democrat* (Santa Rosa, CA), August 31, 1939.

"B. Wood Lists 'Parade' Bests," *Mason City (IA) Globe-Gazette*, August 22, 1942.

Calvin, Paul, "'The Wizard of Oz' Should Make Parents Cheer," *Family Circle*, vol. 3, no. 14, October 6, 1933.

"Cal York's Gossip of Hollywood," *Photoplay*, May 1939.

"Capitol Adds Flesh for Opening of 'Wizard,'" *Daily Variety*, vol. 24, no. 48, August 1, 1939.

Carle, Teet, "Local Boy Makes Good," *Cincinnati (OH) Enquirer*, July 30, 1939.

Carle, Teet, "Odd Jobs for Oz," *Winnipeg (Manitoba, Canada) Tribune*, November 5, 1938.

Carroll, Harrison, "Behind the Scenes in Hollywood," *San Mateo (TX) Times and Daily News-Leader*, April 10, 1933.

Carroll, Harrison, "Behind the Scenes in Hollywood," *Bristol (PA) Daily Courier*, October 2, 1933.

Carroll, Harrison, "Behind the Scenes in Hollywood," *San Mateo (TX) Times and Daily News-Leader*, August 30, 1934.

Carroll, Harrison, "Behind the Scenes in Hollywood," *Evening Independent* (Massillon, OH), November 14, 1938.

Carroll, Harrison, "Behind the Scenes in Hollywood," *Evening Independent* (Massillon, OH), December 28, 1938.

Carroll, Harrison, "Behind the Scenes in Hollywood," *Evening Independent* (Massillon, OH), January 3, 1939.

Carroll, Harrison, "Behind the Scenes in Hollywood," *Evening Independent* (Massillon, OH), February 1, 1939.

Carroll, Harrison, "Behind the Scenes in Hollywood," *Call-Leader* (Elwood, IN), February 23, 1939.

Carroll, Harrison, "Behind the Scenes in Hollywood," *Bristol (PA) Daily Courier*, April 24, 1939.

Carroll, Harrison, "Behind the Scenes in Hollywood," *Call-Leader* (Elwood, IN), July 6, 1939.

Carroll, Harrison, "Behind the Scenes in Hollywood," *Morning Herald* (Uniontown, PA), September 18, 1939.

Carroll, Harrison, "Behind the Scenes in Hollywood," *Evening Independent* (Massillon, OH), November 2, 1939.

Carroll, Harrison, "Behind the Scenes in Hollywood," *San Mateo (TX) Times*, March 11, 1940.

Carroll, Harrison, "Ill Youngster Better After Judy Sees Her," *Winnipeg Free Press*, December 16, 1939.

Carroll, Harrison, "In Hollywood," *Wilkes-Barre (PA) Record*, January 6, 1940.

Carroll, Harrison, "'Wizard of Oz' Scores Lustrous Triumph," *Los Angeles Evening Herald and Express*, August 16, 1939.

Carroll, Harrison, "'Wizard of Oz' Stands Up With 'Snow White,'" *Los Angeles Evening Herald and Express*, August 10, 1939.

Carroll, Kathleen, "It's Old Home Week for 'The Wizard of Oz,'" *New York Sunday News*, March 2, 1975.

"Cartoon Field Looks Lush to Metro, Will Turn Out Full-Length Fantasy," *Variety*, vol. 137, no. 4, January 4, 1940.

Chandler, Jack, "Always Judy and Bright," *Picturegoer Weekly*, June 3, 1939.

"Chat About Books and the Makers of Books," *New York Herald*, September 9, 1900.

"Chatter," *Variety*, vol. 115, no. 2, June 26, 1934.

"Chatter—Hollywood," *Variety*, vol. 112, no. 14, December 12, 1933.

Cheatham, Maud, "Glorifying the American Matron," *Screenland*, vol. XXXVII, no. 4, August 1938.

Cheatham, Maud, "Judy Garland's Musical Memory Book," *Movie Life*, August 1952.

"Child Recovers; May See Actress," *Santa Ana (CA) Register*, December 2, 1939.

"Child's Book Made Into Adult Film," *Pomona (CA) Progress*, June 17, 1939.

"Child Star of 'Wizard of Oz' Scores Major Triumph," *Kokomo (IN) Tribune*, February 10, 1934.

"Children's Play to be Presented," *Daily Notes* (Canonsburg, PA), October 3, 1936.

"Children's Reading Needs Topic of Author-Librarian," *Bakersfield Californian*, November 23, 1938.

"Child Star Returns to the Screen/Nancy Kelly's Career," *West Australian* (Perth, West Australia), April 6, 1939.

Churchill, Douglas W., "Disney's Philosophy," *New York Times Magazine*, March 6, 1938.

Churchill, Douglas W., "'Wizard of Oz' Returning," *Baltimore Sun*, February 12, 1939.

Churchill, Winston S. *Their Finest Hour*, Boston: Houghton Mifflin Company-Riverside Press Cambridge, 1949.

"Cinémarks," *Boxoffice*, vol. 33, no. 21, October 15, 1938.

"Cinémarks," *Boxoffice*, vol. 35, no. 12, August 12, 1939.

Clary, Patricia, "Bad Gal Gale Frightens Kiddies," *Salt Lake (UT) Tribune*, February 10, 1946.

Cohen, Herbert W., "Hollywood," *Pittsburgh (PA) Post-Gazette*, August 21, 1939.

Cohn, Herbert, "'Wizard' Fine Fantasy, Helps to Pack Capitol," *Brooklyn (NY) Daily Eagle*, August 18, 1939.

"Color Cartoon Series Also to be on 16 MM," *Film Daily*, vol. LX, no. 87, October 12, 1932.

"Colorful Parade to be Climax of Festival at Omro," *Oshkosh (WI) Daily Northwestern*, July 20, 1939.

Colvig, Pinto. *It's a Crazy Business: The Goofy Life of a Disney Legend*. Theme Park Press, 2015.

"Comedian's Coach Is Real Life Lion," *Zanesville (OH) Signal*, October 2, 1938.

"Comments on the Films," *Moving Picture World*, vol. 6, no. 14, April 9, 1910.

"Comments on the Films," *Moving Picture World*, vol. 6, no. 22, June 4, 1910.

"Comments on the Films," *Moving Picture World*, vol. 7, no. 26, December 24, 1910.

Comstock, Girard, "Taurog at Work," *Screen Children*, vol. VII, no. 7, July 1938.

Conrad, Barry, "Local 'Wizard of Oz' Fan Traces Tiny Actor," *Journal News* (Hamilton, OH), June 4, 1974.

Conrad, Barry, "Ray Bolger Recalls His Days as Scarecrow of 'Oz,'" *Journal News* (Hamilton, OH), November 5, 1971.

Coons, Robbin, "Behind the Scenes in Hollywood," *Wilkes-Barre (PA) Record*, September 10, 1943.

Coons, Robbin, "Hollywood Sights and Sounds," *Big Spring (TX) Daily Herald*, September 18, 1939.

Coons, Robin, "Hollywood Sights and Sounds," *Record-Argus* (Greenville, PA), March 1, 1940.

Coons, Robbin, "Hollywood Sights and Sounds," *Big Spring (TX) Daily Herald*, September 26, 1940.

Coons, Robbin, "Hollywood Speaks," *Mansfield (OH) News-Journal*, October 25, 1938.

Coons, Robbin, "Judy Garland Looks Back on 'Long' Career," *Pampa (TX) News*, July 12, 1942.

Coons, Robbin, "'Wizard of Oz' a Choice Movie," *Monitor-Index and Democrat* (Moberly, MO), August 26, 1939.

Cooper, John M., "Radio Ringside," *Daily Times* (New Philadelphia, OH), February 28, 1949.

Corbett, Walker, "The Story Behind a Hit: Tune Makes Top Quickly," *Green Magazine* (Boston), September 10, 1939.

"Cornfield Feature set for 'Oz,'" *Daily Variety*, vol. 24, no. 60, August 15, 1939.

"'Cracked Ice Follies' Thrilling Ice Spectacle at Local Arena, *Lethbridge* (Alberta, Canada) *Herald*, February 29, 1940.

Creelman, Eileen, "Charlotte Henry, of 'Alice in Wonderland,' in Town for a Few Days" *New York Sun*, December 12, 1933.

Creelman, Eileen, "Jack Haley Eats Ice Cream and Talks of 'The Wizard of Oz,'" *New York Sun*, August 16, 1939.

Creelman, Eileen, "Ray Bolger Happy Over the Prospect of Making 'The Wizard of Oz,'" *New York Sun*, May 4, 1938.

Crewe, Regina, "Broadway Ballyhoo," *Times-Union* (Albany, NY), September 11, 1938.

"Critics' Forum," *Film Daily*, vol. 71, no. 125, May 28, 1937.

Crosby, Joan, "Wizard of Oz Witch Pursues Actress," *Bristol (PA) Daily Courier*, May 18, 1963.

Croughton, Amy, "Scanning the Screen," *Rochester (NY) Times-Union*, August 18, 1939.

Croughton, Amy, "Scanning the Screen," *Rochester (NY) Times-Union*, April 4, 1940.

"Cukor Drops Assignment on 'Oz' for 'Wind' Job," *Boxoffice*, vol. 33, no. 24, November 5, 1938.

"Cukor Keeps 'Oz' Moving," *Variety*, vol. 132, no. 8, November 2, 1938.

"Cukor Takes Over," *Boxoffice*, vol. 33, no. 23, October 29, 1938.

Curtis, James. *W.C. Fields: A Biography*, New York: Alfred A. Knopf, 2003.

"Cycle of Cartoon Features on the Way Following 'Snow White's' Click," *Variety*, vol. 129, no. 11, February 23, 1938.

"Cyclones Go Under the Microscope," *Boxoffice*, vol. 33, no. 14, August 27, 1938.

"'Cyclone State' Protests 'Wizard of Oz' Twister," *Bakersfield Californian*, September 2, 1939.

Daly, Phil M., "Along the Rialto," *Film Daily*, August 3, 1939.

Davies, Reine, "Schnozzle Durante Yearns to Play Title Role in 'King Lear,'" *Syracuse (NY) American*, July 15, 1934.

"Deanna as 'Cinderella' in Technicolor Picture," *Boxoffice*, vol. 32, no. 22, April 23, 1938.

Denton, Ralph, "A Filmgoer's Diary," *Picturegoer*, March 2, 1940.

Devane, James, "'Wizard of Oz' Film Plugged," *Cincinnati (OH) Enquirer*, October 30, 1956.

Dingle, Cornelia, "Man Tells How He Became a 'Monkey,'" *Boston Sunday Post*, December 12, 1920.

"Does It Again," *Sunday Times-Signal* (Zanesville, OH), November 26, 1939.

"Doings at Los Angeles," *The Moving Picture World*, vol. 20, no. 13, June 27, 1914.

Dooley, Susy, "Make-Up Is to Attract Men," *Des Moines (IA) Register*, September 28, 1965.

"Dopey Gets More Fan Mail Than Snow White," *Minneapolis (MN) Tribune*, February 6, 1939.

"Dots and Dashes," *The Mail* (Adelaide, SA), Saturday, February 18, 1939.

"Dots and Dashes," *The Mail* (Adelaide, SA), April 8, 1939.

"Dream World: Trip to Land of Make-believe Planned for Orphans, Saturday," *Winnipeg Free Press* (Canada), September 14, 1939.

Drury, Michael, "Judy Garland's Own Story! Her First Big Film Break," *The Independent* (Long Beach, CA), January 31, 1951.

"Dubin-Brown Paired," *Hollywood Reporter*, vol. XXXXV, no. 8, April 18, 1938.

Dugas, David, "The Witch of Oz and Her Name Is Margaret Hamilton," *Photoplay* (British edition), June 1974.

Dwiggins Worsley, Sue, with Charles Ziarko. *From Oz to E.T.* Lanham, MD: Scarecrow Press, Inc., 1997.

East, Weston, "Here's Hollywood," *Screenland*, vol. XXXVII, no. 4, August 1938.

"The Editor's Letter Bag," *Nottingham* (Nottinghamshire, England) *Evening Post*, July 24, 1941.

Edwards, Alanson, "In Hollywood," *Olean (NY) Times-Herald*, July 11, 1934.

Ellet, Marion, "Mugwump Musings," *Daily (Lawrence, KS) Journal-World*, October 7, 1939.

Ellis, Charlie, "Picture Fantasy Misses Fire Outside Cartoons," *Abilene (TX) Reporter-News*, March 15, 1938.

"Employed Lichtman Foreseeing Him as Ultimate Loew's Chief," *Boxoffice*, vol. 34, no. 5, December 24, 1938.

"Eshbaugh to Produce Color Cartoon Series," *Hollywood Reporter*, vol. XII, no. 47, January 16, 1933.

"Everyone Sings in 'Oz' but Bad Witch," *Harrisburg (PA) Telegraph*, July 28, 1939.

"Experts Hear 'Oz' Tunes," *Daily Variety*, vol. 24, no. 50, August 14, 1939.

"Fanchon and Marco's 'Wizard,'" *Variety*, vol. 126, no. 2, March 24, 1937.

"Fantasy in Oz," *Brooklyn (NY) Daily Eagle*, September 29, 1939.

Ferguson, Mrs. Walter, "In Happy Land of Oz," *Albuquerque (NM) Tribune*, July 25, 1955.

Fidler, Jimmie, "In Hollywood," *Amarillo (TX) Globe-Times*, May 19, 1937.

Fidler, Jimmie, "In Hollywood," *Santa Ana (CA) Register*, January 18, 1939.

Fidler, Jimmie, "In Hollywood," *Nevada State Journal*, February 1, 1939.

Fidler, Jimmie, "In Hollywood," *Muscatine (IA) Journal and News-Tribune*, February 16, 1939.

Fidler, Jimmie, "In Hollywood," *Nevada State Journal*, February 17, 1939.

Fidler, Jimmie, "In Hollywood," *Santa Ana (CA) Register*, February 21, 1939.

Fidler, Jimmie, "In Hollywood," *Chronicle-Telegram* (OH), April 18, 1939.

Fidler, Jimmie, "In Hollywood," *Joplin (MO) Globe*, September 23, 1939.

Fidler, Jimmie, "In Hollywood," *Chronicle-Telegram* (Elyria, OH), March 5, 1940.

Fidler, Jimmie, "In Hollywood," *Joplin (MO) Globe*, December 4, 1942.

Fidler, Jimmie, "In Hollywood," *Nevada State Journal*, March 18, 1943.

Fidler, Jimmie, "In Hollywood," *Joplin (MO) Globe*, November 7, 1943.

Fidler, Jimmie, "In Hollywood," *Joplin (MO) Globe*, July 14, 1944.

Fidler, Jimmie, "Movieland: It's People and Products," *Appleton (WI) Post-Crescent*, October 3, 1938.

Fidler, Jimmie, "Movieland: It's People and Products," *Appleton (WI) Post-Crescent*, August 16, 1939.

Field, Hana S., "Triumph and Tragedy on the Yellow Brick Road: Censorship of *The Wizard of Oz* in America," *Baum Bugle*, vol. 44, no. 1, Spring 2000.

"Film 'Big Parade' Features Midgets," *Portsmouth (OH) Daily Times*, November 13, 1938.

"Film Fantasy Runs Up Bill of $3,500,000," *Cincinnati (OH) Enquirer*, August 20, 1939.

"Film Fantasy/The Wizard of Oz/Elaborate Scenes," *Maitland* (Australia) *Daily Mercury*, December 28, 1938.

"Film Midgets to Appear at Fair," *Port Arthur (TX) News*, January 1, 1939.

"Film Shorts," *Goulburn Evening Penny Post* (NSW), October, 25, 1939.

"Film Villains Prove Scarce," *Arizona Republic*, November 27, 1938.

Finch, Christopher. *Rainbow: The Stormy Life of Judy Garland*. New York: Grosset & Dunlap, 1975.

Finestone, Alfred, "The Wizard of Oz," *Motion Picture Daily*, vol. 46, no. 28, August 10, 1939.

"Finish First 'Oz' Short," *Film Daily*, vol. LXII, no. 69, June 21, 1933.

"First of Oz Films Is Underway," *Motion Picture News*, vol. X, no. 1, July 11, 1914.

Fisher Parry, Florence, "'Snow White' Calls for a National Holiday; All Children, Old and Young, Should See It," *Pittsburgh (PA) Press*, March 13, 1938.

"550 'Oz' Prints," *Daily Variety*, vol. 24, no. 45, July 28, 1939.

Flamini, Roland, *Scarlett, Rhett and a Cast of Thousands*. New York: MacMillan Publishing Co., 1975.

"Fleming Has Tried Several Times to Get Away from It," *Charleston (WV) Daily Mail*, September 3, 1939.

"Fleming to Meg 'Oz,'" *Boxoffice*, vol. 32, no. 13, November 19, 1938.

Fleming, Victor, "Color and Sound in Movies," *Winnipeg (Manitoba, Canada) Tribune*, November 11, 1939.

Fleming, Victor, "Director Tells of Filming 'Oz': Wife of Author Supplied Story's Background," *Citizen Magazine*, August 27, 1939.

Fleming, Victor, "Keeping Faith with Those Who Read Famous Book," *Wisconsin State Journal*, January 31, 1940.

"Follow Up Comment," *Variety*, vol. 135, no. 4, July 5, 1939.

"For Art's Sake," *Belvidere (IL) Daily Republican*, November 21, 1938.

"Former Belleville Midget Knows Show Business Greats," *Belleville (KS) Telescope*, February 15, 1962.

"Former New Castle Man Provides Smoke Color Effects for Movie Scenes," *New Castle (PA) News*, August 16, 1939.

"Frank Morgan, Actor, Dead," Associated Press, September 19, 1949.

"Frank Morgan Has Appeared in Many Plays Since Stage Debut," *Hammond (IN) Times*, March 12, 1939.

"Frank Morgan's Peeve," *Brooklyn (NY) Daily Eagle*, June 10, 1939.

"Freddie and Mickey May Get the Most Unusual Roles of Their Careers," *Hammond (IN) Times*, April 7, 1938.

"Fred Stone Stands Watch in Making of 'Wizard of Oz'" *Cincinnati (OH) Enquirer*, August 14, 1939.

Fremon, Mori, "She Never Gets Her Man," *Hollywood*, vol. 31, no. 3, March 1942.

Friedman, Rick, "Thank You, Dorothy, for a Dream," *Roselle (IL) Register*, June 27, 1969.

"From Circus to 'Rain or Shine,'" *Brooklyn (NY) Daily Eagle*, May 27, 1928.

Fuller Goodspeed, Elizabeth, *The Wizard of Oz: A Play in Three Acts*. New York: Samuel French, 1928.

"Gab by Alta Durant," *Daily Variety*, vol. 24, no. 33, July 14, 1939.

"Gab by Alta Durant," *Daily Variety*, vol. 24, no. 57, August 11, 1939.

"Gab by Alta Durant," *Daily Variety*, vol. 24, no. 61, August 16, 1939.

"Gab by Alta Durant," *Daily Variety*, vol. 24, no. 62, August 17, 1939.

Gallagher, Pauline, "Why They Are Thankful," *San Antonio (TX) Light*, November 20, 1939.

Garland, Ethel, "Hollywood Can't Hurt My Judy," *Sunday Times* (Perth, Australia), June 30, 1940.

Garland, Judy, as told to Gladys Hall, "Judy Garland's Gay Life Story," *Screenland*, vol. XLII, no. 3, January 1941.

Garland, Judy, "Judy, Now a Star, Finds World Good," *Cleveland (OH) Plain Dealer*, March 14, 1940.

Gillespie, A. Arnold. *The Wizard of MGM: Memoirs of A. Arnold Gillespie*. Duncan, OK: BearManor Media, 2011.

Gillespie-Hayek, Annabelle, "Personality Comes in All Sizes," *Silver Screen*, vol. 9, no. 2, December 1938.

"Goldwyn Adds Musical to Lineup," *Film Daily*, vol. LXIV, no. 2, October 3, 1933.

"Goldwyn Completing Lineup by April 1," *Film Daily*, vol. LXIV, no. 43, November 21, 1933.

"Goldwyn May Do at Least 8 for '36." *Variety*, vol. 116, no. 5, October 16, 1934.

"Goldwyn May Do Oz," *Motion Picture Daily*, vol. 36, no. 15, July 19, 1934.

"Goldwyn Pantries Yarn on Andersen's Life," *Daily Variety*, vol. 24, no. 57, August 11, 1939.

"Good News Closes Season Tonight With a Preview of 'Wizard of Oz,'" *Capital Times* (Madison, WI), June 29, 1939.

"Gowns by Adrian," *Montana Butte Standard*, October 31, 1937.

Graham, Sheilah, "Hollywood Today," *Indianapolis (IN) Star*, March 19, 1941.

Graham, Sheilah, "Hollywood Today," *Winnipeg* (Manitoba, Canada) *Tribune*, July 4, 1945.

Graham, Sheilah, "Says Joan Fontaine, Nagel, Not Engaged," *Lincoln (NE) Evening Journal*, January 18, 1938.

Graham, Sheilah, "Touring the Picture Lots with Sheilah," *Winnipeg* (Manitoba, Canada) *Tribune*, March 16, 1939.

"Grann Film Saga," *Allers* (Swedish), no. 51, July 1939.

"Greeks Didn't Have Words for Judy's Fans 'U-b-i-q-u-i-t-a-r-y,'" *Uniontown (PA) Morning Herald*, October 16, 1937.

Grigsby Doss, Helen, "Judy Garland," *American Girl*, November 1939.

Grimes, Nancy, "Looking Over the Shows," *Portsmouth (OH) Times*, September 27, 1939.

Grutzner Jr., Charles, "The World of Tomorrow," *Brooklyn (NY) Daily Eagle*, December 28, 1939.

Hackett, Walter H., "Midgets Now Visiting City in New Film, 'Wizard of Oz,'" *Lansing (MI) State Journal*, June 8, 1939.

Handsaker, Gene, "'Wizardland,' Ray Bolger Brain of a New Project," *News-Palladium* (Benton Harbor, MI), August 26, 1970.

Harker, Milton, "In Hollywood," *Kane (PA) Republican*, September 6, 1938.

Harker, Milton, "Midgets Becoming Autograph Conscious," *New Castle (PA) News*, December 23, 1938.

Harmetz, Aljean. *The Making of the Wizard of Oz*. New York: Alfred A. Knopf, 1977.

Harrison, Paul, "Buddy Ebsen Plays a Tin Type," *Lowell (MA) Sun*, October 6, 1938.

Harrison, Paul, "Don't Worry, Wizard of Oz Fans, Harrison Assures Us the Tin Woodman Will Be Tinny and Straw Will Stick Out of Scarecrow's Garb in Faithful Version," *Port Arthur (TX) News*, February 14, 1939.

Harrison, Paul, "Frank Morgan Can Toss the Quick Quip Even After Cameras Are Cut," *Olean (NY) Times-Herald*, March 3, 1939.

Harrison, Paul, "In Hollywood," *Lancaster (OH) Eagle-Gazette*, February 10, 1936.

Harrison, Paul, "In Hollywood," *Daily News* (Frederick, MD), March 16, 1938.

Harrison, Paul, "In Hollywood," *Daily News* (Frederick, MD), April 29, 1938.

Harrison, Paul, "In Hollywood," *Laredo (TX) Times*, May 6, 1938.

Harrison, Paul, "In Hollywood," *Daily News* (Frederick, MD), June 21, 1938.

Harrison, Paul, "In Hollywood," *Ironwood (MI) Daily Globe*, February 21, 1939.

Harrison, Paul, "In Hollywood," *Olean (NY) Times-Herald*, July 6, 1939.

Harrison, Paul, "In Hollywood: Blue Horses Pull an Emerald Coach in the Wizard of Oz Color Film," *Hope (AR) Star*, November 29, 1938.

Harrison, Paul, "Judy Garland Diets to Keep That Girlish Figure for Her Child Star Character Parts," *Sandusky (OH) Star-Journal*, April 30, 1938.

Harrison, Paul, "Screen Chats," *Shamokin (PA) News-Dispatch*, April 1, 1936.

Harrison, Paul, "Screen Writing Couple Upsets Tradition by Acting Normal and Being Happily Wed Without Any Professional Jealousy," *Kingsport (TN) Times*, September 14, 1939.

Harrison, Paul, "Shirley Temple Is Getting to Be a Big Girl Now," *Daily News* (Frederick, MD), April 23, 1938.

Harrison, Paul, "Sound Effects in the Movies: How It's Done," *Lowell (MA) Sun*, May 9, 1939.

Harrison, Paul, "'Wizard of Oz,' Which Started Out as a Movie 'Bust,' Blooming Into First Class Fairyland Entertainment," *Kingsport (TN) Times*, August 4, 1939.

Hartley, Katherine, "Judy Keeps a Date," *Hollywood*, vol. 27, no. 10, October 1938.

"Hedda Hopper," *Los Angeles Times*, September 19, 1949.

"Hedda Hopper's Hollywood," *Cincinnati (OH) Enquirer*, June 30, 1938.

"Hedda Hopper's Hollywood," *Los Angeles Times*, February 9, 1941.

"Hedda Hopper's Hollywood," *Lowell (MA) Sun and Citizen-Leader*, July 18, 1941.

"Hedda Hopper's Looking at Hollywood," *Harrisburg (PA) Telegraph*, October 11, 1945.

Heffernan, Harold, "On the Flicker Front," *St. Louis (MO) Post-Dispatch*, June 26, 1941.

Heffernan, Harold, "Grace Hayes as Successor to Dressler," *Winnipeg* (Manitoba, Canada) *Tribune*, February 27, 1939.

Heffernan, Harold, "Ray Bolger Loses Weight in 'Oz' Scarecrow Role," *Indianapolis (IN) Star*, November 24, 1938.

Heffernan, Harold, "Three Ex-Heroines of Films Are Happy to Play Bits Now," *Indianapolis (IN) Star*, May 9, 1938.

Heffernan, Harold, "'Wizard of Oz' Gives Director Nightmares," *Des Moines (IA) Register*, March 16, 1938.

Hellman, Jack, "1st Coast Camp Show Highlighted by Tuneful Score; 'Wizard' Well Produced," *Variety*, vol. 143, no. 1, June 11, 1941.

Henderson, Jessie, "On 'The Wizard of Oz' Set," *Hollywood*, August 1939.

"Highlights in Selling Features," *The Exhibitor*, vol. 22, no. 16, August 30, 1939.

"High on Sex Appeal, Gale Tries Comedy," *Pittsburgh (PA) Press*, April 15, 1939.

"Hilly Branch School Finals and Farmers Meeting," *The Robesonian* (Lumberton, NC), April, 14, 1932.

Hoffman, Irving, "Tales of Hoffman," *Hollywood Reporter*, vol. XXXXIII, no. 29, January 15, 1938.

Hollis, Richard, and Brian Sibley. *Walt Disney's Snow White and the Seven Dwarfs and the Making of the Classic Film*. New York: Simon and Schuster, 1987.

"Hollywood," *Daily Notes* (Canonsburg, PA), October 30, 1947.

"Hollywood," *Variety*, vol. 112, no, 6, October 17, 1933.

"Hollywood Canines Have Doggy Affair," *El Paso (TX) Herald-Post*, February 27, 1940.

Hollywood Newspaper Enterprise Association column, *Progress-Index* (Petersburg, VA), August 21, 1955.

"Hollywood Newsreel," *Hollywood*, vol. 28, no. 11, November 1939.

"Hollywood Plans to Limit Output," *Charleston (WV) Gazette*, October 14, 1934.

"Hollywood Roundup," *News-Herald* (Franklin, PA), January 11, 1939.

"Hollywood's Animal Actors," *Popular Mechanics*, vol. 79, no. 6, June 1943.

"Hollywood Small Fry," *Modern Screen*, vol. 24, no. 2, January 1942.

"Hollywood's 'Red Hot Mamma,'" *The Mail* (Adelaide, SA), Saturday, August 10, 1940.

"Hollywood to Fairbanks," *Fairbanks (AK) Daily News-Miner*, July 26, 1940.

Hopper, Hedda, "Hedda Hopper's Hollywood," *Cincinnati (OH) Enquirer*, November 24, 1938.

Hopper, Hedda, "Hedda Hopper's Hollywood," *Cincinnati (OH) Enquirer*, January 14, 1939.

Hopper, Hedda, "Hedda Hopper's Hollywood," *Cincinnati (OH) Enquirer*, January 14, 1939.

Hopper, Hedda, "Hollywood's Hopper," *Los Angeles Times*, January 26, 1939.

Hopper, Hedda, "Hedda Hopper's Hollywood," *Los Angeles Times*, February 17, 1939.

Hopper, Hedda, "Hedda Hopper's Hollywood," *Los Angeles Times*, August 25, 1939.

Hopper, Hedda, "Looking at Hollywood," *Salt Lake (UT) Tribune*, September 28, 1946.

Hopper, Hedda, "Looking at Hollywood," *Portland (ME) Press Herald*, April 25, 1947.

Hopper, Hedda, "Looking at Hollywood," *Portland (ME) Press Herald*, December 4, 1947.

Hopper, Hedda, "Looking at Hollywood," *Portland (ME) Press Herald*, November 18, 1948.

Hopper, Hedda, "Movie Bits," *St. Louis (MO) Post-Dispatch*, December 24, 1938.

"Horse Rainbow for Wizard of Oz," *Ogden (UT) Standard-Examiner*, October 21, 1938.

"Hot from Hollywood," *Stage, the Magazine of After Dark*, May 1, 1939.

Hubbard, Keavy, "Screen Life in Hollywood," *The Register* (Sandusky, OH), October 20, 1932.

"Hulce Youth Returns After Work in Film," *Daily Herald* (Circleville, OH), January 11, 1939.

"Independent Exhibitors Film Bulletin / Production Record," *Independent Film Exhibitors*, vol. 4, no. 21, October 22, 1938.

"In Hollywood," *Charleroi (PA) Mail*, August 16, 1939.

"In Hollywood," *Charleroi (PA) Mail*, August 31, 1939.

Inman, Julia, "'Wicked Witch' of 'Oz' Is Really Very Nice," *Indianapolis (IN) Star*, July 24, 1961.

"In New York with Dale Harrison," *Zanesville (OH) Signal*, November 10, 1939.

"Inside Stuff" Column, *Movie Story*, November 1939.

"Inside Stuff—Legit," *Variety*, vol. 112, no. 7, October 24, 1933.

"Interesting Developments in 'Wizard of Oz' Plans," *Brooklyn (NY) Daily Eagle*, October 29, 1926.

"Jack Haley, 'Tin Man of Oz,' Returns to Films," *La Crosse (WI) Tribune*, August 2, 1969.

Jackson, Michael, "Protecting the Future of the Greatest Little Star," *Photoplay*, March 1937.

"Jimmie Fidler," *Monroe (LA) News-Star*, December 7, 1948.

"Jingling of Coins Halts Film Dance," *San Antonio (TX) Express*, January 27, 1939.

"Jitney Troupers to Present Two Programs Today," *Daily Tar Heel* (Chapel Hill, NC), April 5, 1935.

"Jitterbug Proves Puzzle to Screen," *Santa Cruz (CA) Evening News*, November 3, 1938.

Johnson, Erskine, "Around Hollywood," *Pampa (TX) News*, December 7, 1943.

Johnson, Erskine, "Behind the Make-Up," *The Times* (San Mateo, CA), May 19, 1939.

Johnson, Erskine, "In Hollywood," *Ironwood (MI) Daily Globe*, February 21, 1944.

Johnson, Erskine, "Louis B. Mayer May Film the Judy Garland Story," *Fresno (CA) Bee*, December 20, 1951.

Jones, Lon, "Netting Money with Hair," *The* (Brisbane, Australia) *Telegraph*, January 14, 1939.

J.P.H., "This and That," *Hutchinson (KS) News*, September 20, 1939.

"Judy," *Music Makers of Stage, Screen and Radio*, September, 1940.

"Judy Garland and Buddy Ebsen," *Appleton (WI) Post-Crescent*, September 16, 1938.

"Judy Garland Gets Wig in Film," *Rochester (NY) Democrat and Chronicle*, November 13, 1938.

"Judy Garland, Glorifier of Teen Age on Screen, Afraid of Glamour," *Cumberland (MD) Evening Times*, October 4, 1940.

"Judy Garland Increasingly Popular Young Lady of the Movies," *Winnipeg (Canada) Free Press*, January 18, 1939.

"Judy Garland Memorial Set," *Richmond (VA) Times-Dispatch*, March 13, 1970.

"Judy Garland, MGM Studio, Present Cup for Baby Contest Winner," *Logansport Indiana Press*, August 10, 1939.

"Judy Garland on Mend but Progress Is Slow," *Kansas City (MO) Times*, December 15, 1959.

"Judy Garland Plans Visit to Stricken Anaheim Child," *Santa Ana (CA) Register*, November 30, 1939.

"Judy Garland Plays Her First Solo Starring Role in *Little Nellie Kelly*," *Amarillo (TX) Globe-Times*, November 22, 1940.

"Judy Garland Sings for Soldiers at Gap," *Lebanon (PA) Daily News*, July 22, 1942.

"Judy Garland Stars in 'The Wizard of Oz' in 'Lux Radio Theatre' Yule Offering," CBS Holiday News press release, December 18, 1950.

"Judy Garland's 'Wizard of Oz' Repeats Triumph," *Paris (TX) News*, October 30, 1955.

"Judy Garland Wants to Play Great Drama," *Australian Women's Weekly*, March 9, 1940.

"Judy Hopes to Ride Bicycle in Europe," *San Antonio (TX) Light*, March 19, 1939.

"Judy Knits Sweater," *Wisconsin State Journal*, December 4, 1938.

"Judy Learns Riding," *San Antonio (TX) Light*, December 25, 1938.

"Judy Returns," *Des Moines (IA) Sunday Register*, March 15, 1970.

"Judy Seeks Name," *San Antonio (TX) Light*, April 30, 1939.

"Judy Sees Oz," *Chillicothe (MO) Constitution-Tribune*, August 3, 1940.

"Judy Sent Gifts by 'Oz' Book Readers," *Harrisburg (PA) Telegraph*, February 17, 1939.

"Judy's Guard Only Forty Inches Tall," *Harrisburg (PA) Telegraph*, May 30, 1939.

Kahn, Alexander, "Bits of Gossip About Hollywood Film Folk," *Vidette-Messenger* (Valparaiso, IN), February 11, 1939.

Kahn, Alexander, "Bits of Gossip About Hollywood Film Folk," *Vidette-Messenger* (Valparaiso, IN), March 9, 1939.

Kahn, Alexander, "Bits of Gossip About Hollywood Film Folk," *Vidette-Messenger* (Valparaiso, IN), June 5, 1939.

Kahn, Alexander, "Hollywood Roundup," *Oshkosh (WI) Daily Northwestern*, December 5, 1938.

Kain, Ida Jean, "Keep in Trim," *Lethbridge* (Alberta, Canada) *Herald*, February 21, 1952.

Kaufman, David B., "Movie Parade," *Mason City (IA) Globe-Gazette*, September 1, 1939.

Kaufman, J. B. *The Fairest One of All: The Making of Walt Disney's Snow White and the Seven Dwarfs*. San Francisco: Walt Disney Family Foundation Press, 2012.

Kavanaugh, Simon, "Make Up Man Recalls Great Stars," *El Paso (TX) Herald-Post*, August 5, 1972.

Keavy, Hubbard, "Screen Life in Hollywood," *The Register* (Sandusky, OH), October 20, 1932.

"Keep Life Simple, Says King Vidor," *Evening News* (Harrisburg, PA), November 17, 1948.

"Kelland Yarn for Cantor," *Motion Picture Daily*, vol. 37, no. 65, March 19, 1935.

Kendall, Read, "Around and About in Hollywood," *Los Angeles Times*, September 20, 1938.

"Kids Like Adult Shows Best," *Variety*, vol. 115, no. 1, June 19, 1934.

Kilgallen, Dorothy, "Voice of Broadway," King Features Syndicate column, August 22, 1942.

Kilgallen, Dorothy, "Voice of Broadway / Gossip in Gotham," King Features Syndicate column, March 14, 1955.

Kingsley, Dorothy, Untitled Hollywood column, *Wisconsin State Journal*, August 28, 1939.

Kohrs, Karl, "I'm Glad I'm Homely," *Parade*, October 7, 1951.

Krug, Karl, "The Show Shops," *Pittsburgh (PA) Press*, September 20, 1931.

Kyle, Otto R., "By the Way," *Decatur (IL) Daily Review*, July 27, 1956.

Lait, Jack Jr., "Hollywood," *Brooklyn (NY) Daily Eagle*, March 9, 1949.

Lambert, Stanley, "What the Picture Did for Me," *Motion Picture Herald*, vol. 136, no. 13, September 23, 1939.

"Lana Turner Collapses," *Schenectady (NY) Gazette*, August 16, 1939.

"Lana Turner to MGM," *Hollywood Reporter*, vol. XXXXIII, no. 41, January 29, 1938.

Lane, Lydia, "Noted Director Defines the Elements of Beauty," *Big Spring (TX) Herald*, July 5, 1953.

Lane, Virginia T., "How to Break Into the Movies," *Motion Picture*, vol. LV, no. 6, July 1938.

"Larry Semon as the 'Wiz,'" *Exhibitor's Trade Review*, October 18, 1924.

"Larry Semon, Screen Comedian, Is Summoned by Death; Pneumonia and Breakdown Closes Eventful Career," *Mansfield (OH) News*, October 8, 1928.

Lemon, Sara, "Hallowe'en 1000 Years Ago Similar to Today's Fracas," *Press-Gazette* (Hillsboro, OH), October 31, 1939.

"LeRoy Becomes Producer-Director," *Daily Variety*, vol. 24, no. 46, July 29, 1939.

LeRoy, Mervyn, "Imagination at Premium," *Brooklyn (NY) Daily Eagle*, August 13, 1939.

LeRoy, Mervyn. *It Takes More Than Talent*. New York: Alfred A. Knopf, 1953.

LeRoy, Mervyn, "LeRoy Promises Fans Wizard of Oz Film to Follow Baum Tale," *Courier-Journal* (Louisville, KY), July 2, 1939.

LeRoy, Mervyn. *Mervyn LeRoy: Take One*. New York: Hawthorn Books, Inc., 1974.

LeRoy, Mervyn, "With the Hollywood Reporter," *Middlesboro (KY) Daily News*, July 1, 1939.

"LeRoy Back to Coast Without Making Deal," *Film Daily*, vol. 72, no. 96, October 22, 1937.

"LeRoy Guns 'Wizard' in 3 Weeks, Morgan Tops," *Hollywood Reporter*, vol. XXXXVII, no. 42, September 24, 1938.

"LeRoy's Ambition Is Coming True," *Winnipeg Free Press Magazine Section*, September 23, 1939.

"LeRoy's 'Oz' at Fair," *Variety*, vol. 133, no. 4, January 4, 1939.

"LeRoy to Make Six Annually for Metro," *Film Daily*, vol. 72, no. 115, November 13, 1937.

"LeRoy Will Join Metro at Expiration of His Present Warner Bros. Contract, *Film Daily*, vol. 72, no. 114, November 12, 1937.

Lewis, Dan, "Ray Bolger: Scarecrow Promoting 'Wizard of Oz' in Memory of Judy Garland," *TV Time and Channel*, March 14, 1970.

Lipke, Katherine, "Looking Them Over," *California Sports*, vol. 2, no. 11, December 1924.

"List Ten Best 'Scene-Stealers' in 1939 Movies," *Capital Times* (Madison, WI), December 31, 1939.

"Literature Note," *The Constitution* (Atlanta, GA), April 19, 1903.

"'Little General' Jerry Maren in Show Business 32 Years," *News Journal* (Hamilton, OH), March 19, 1971.

"Little-Known 'Real' Wizard of Oz Created Small Girl and Land That Have Never Died," *Bridgeport (CT) Post*, April 9, 1961.

"Little Man Has Busy Day," *Independent Record* (Helena, MT), October 13, 1940.

"Living Film Players Steal Their Work Away from the Cartoon Creatures," *Australian Women's Weekly*, December 2, 1939.

"Lloyds Protects Film Stunters," *Rochester (NY) Democrat and Chronicle*, January 15, 1939.

"Loew's Officially Takes over MGM," *Hollywood Reporter*, vol. XXXXIII, no. 25, January 11, 1938.

"London News Letter," *Hollywood Reporter*, vol. XVIII, no. 45, January 5, 1934.

Lowry, Cynthia, "4 New TV Shows Not Too Exciting," *Indiana (PA) Gazette*, September 19, 1960.

Lowry, Cynthia, "Good Movies Not Always Good on TV," *Hope* (Arkansas) *Star*, December 11, 1961.

Lyons, Leonard, "Broadway Medley," *The Times* (San Mateo, CA), November 10, 1956.

Lyons, Leonard, "The Lyons Den," *Salt Lake (UT) Tribune*, January 31, 1949.

Lyons, Leonard, (Jack Haley substituting) "Our New York Column," *Minneapolis (MN) Star*, August 29, 1939.

MacKaye, Milton, "Rooney, Garland, Durbin: The Mighty Atoms of Hollywood," *Ladies' Home Journal*, vol. LVII, no. 9, September 1940.

Maltin, Leonard, "FFM Interviews Gale Sondergaard," *Film Fan Monthly*, no. 118, April 1971.

Manners, Mary Jane, "The Ugly Duckling Who Became a Swan," *Silver Screen*, June 1940.

Mann, May, "Going Hollywood," *Ogden (UT) Standard-Examiner*, October 15, 1938.

Mann, May, "Going Hollywood," *Ogden (UT) Standard-Examiner*, December 9, 1938.

Mann, May, "Judy Garland Loses Fear as Fat Role Is Assigned," *Ogden (UT) Standard-Examiner*, June 4, 1939.

Mann, May, "Judy Garland Wants to Be New Bette Davis, She Says," *Ogden (UT) Standard-Examiner*, August 10, 1940.

Mann, May, "Judy Waits Three Years - Crashes Films on Her Own," *Ogden (UT) Standard-Examiner*, October 23, 1938.

Mansfield, Richard, *Blown Away: A Nonsensical Narrative Without Rhyme or Reason*, L.C. Page & Co., 1897.

"Many Take Part in Wizard of Oz Broadcast Here," *Spirit Lake (IA) Beacon*, August 24, 1939.

"Marionette Show Here Today," *Helena (MT) Daily Independent*, September 27, 1935.

Marshall, Mary, "Personality Better Than Beauty," *Modern Screen*, December 1937.

Marsh, W. Ward, "One Moment Please: Leaders of the Munchkins in *The Wizard of Oz* Talk About Films and Film Making," *Cleveland (OH) Plain Dealer*, February 28, 1940.

Marsh, W. Ward, "One Moment Please: Noted Director Hits at Producer's Sins," *Cleveland (OH) Plain Dealer*, October 14, 1934.

Marsh, W. Ward, "'Oz' in State, Excellent Fantasy," *Cleveland (OH) Plain Dealer*, August 19, 1939.

Martin, Boyd, "Out-of-the-Ordinary Promised Those Who See 'Wizard of Oz,'" *Courier-Journal* (Louisville, KY), August 17, 1939.

Martin, Mildred, "Jack Haley Finds Comedy Very Serious," *Philadelphia Inquirer*, September 4, 1939.

"May Mann's Going Hollywood," *Ogden (UT) Standard-Examiner*, December 22, 1938.

"May Mann's Going Hollywood," *Ogden (UT) Standard-Examiner*, January 10, 1939.

"May Mann's Going Hollywood," *Ogden (UT) Standard-Examiner*, December 1, 1939.

"May Mann's Going Hollywood," *Ogden (UT) Standard-Examiner*, June 4, 1939.

McCaleb, Kenneth, "I Visit with Shirley Temple," *Sunday Mirror* (New York), April 25, 1937.

M'Clenrghan, Lew, "Headlights," *Belvidere (IL) Daily Republican*, February 26, 1940.

McFee, Frederick, "Dancing Demon," *Hollywood*, vol. 30, no. 7, July 1941.

McIlhenney, Anne M., "Filmland Rambles," *Buffalo (NY) Courier-Express*, August 15, 1938.

McIlhenney, Anne M., "Filmland Rambles," *Buffalo (NY) Courier-Express*, August 18, 1938.

McIlhenney, Anne M., "Filmland Rambles," *Buffalo (NY) Courier-Express*, August 28, 1938.

McIlhenney, Anne M., "Filmland Rambles," *Buffalo (NY) Courier-Express*, September 12, 1938.

McIlhenney, Anne M., "Filmland Rambles," *Buffalo (NY) Courier-Express*, September 16, 1938.

McIlhenney, Anne M., "Filmland Rambles," *Buffalo (NY) Courier-Express*, September 28, 1938.

McIlhenney, Anne M., "Filmland Rambles," *Buffalo (NY) Courier-Express*, September 30, 1938.

McIlhenney, Anne M., "Filmland Rambles," *Buffalo (NY) Courier-Express*, October 3, 1938.

McIlhenney, Anne M., "Filmland Rambles," *Buffalo (NY) Courier-Express*, October 11, 1938.

McIlhenney, Anne M., "Filmland Rambles," *Buffalo (NY) Courier-Express*, October 20, 1938.

McIlhenney, Anne M., "Filmland Rambles," *Buffalo (NY) Courier-Express*, October 30, 1938.

McIlhenney, Anne M., "Filmland Rambles," *Buffalo (NY) Courier-Express*, January 23, 1939.

McIlhenney, Anne M., "Filmland Rambles," *Buffalo (NY) Courier-Express*, January 25, 1939.

McIlhenney, Anne M., "Filmland Rambles," *Buffalo (NY) Courier-Express*, February 12, 1939.

McIlhenney, Anne M., "Filmland Rambles," *Buffalo (NY) Courier-Express*, July 28, 1940.

McIlhenney, Anne M., "Movieland's 'Sculptor of Faces' Remolds Players Into Any Character with His Magic Plastic Material," *Buffalo (NY) Courier-Express*, August 21, 1938.

McIlhenney, Anne M., "Screen's Young Songstress Thinks Stage Tops Movies," *Buffalo (NY) Courier-Express*, August 5, 1938.

McIlhenney, Anne M., "Wizard of Oz Brings Funds to Local Man," *Buffalo (NY) Courier-Express*, August 16, 1939.

McIlwaine, Robert, "He's Not Movie Minded," *Modern Screen*, November 1938.

McIlwaine, Robert, "Sweet Sixteen," *Modern Screen*, vol. 19, no. 3, August 1939.

McPhee, W. E., "What the Picture Did for Me," *Motion Picture Herald*, vol. 136, no. 13, September 23, 1939.

McPherson, Colvin, "The Screen in Review," *St. Louis (MO) Post-Dispatch*, August 20, 1939.

Meehan, Jeanette, "Leading a Dog's Life in Filmland," unidentified newspaper clipping, 1935.

"Meglin Kiddies' Own Motion Picture," *Meglin Kiddie News*, vol. 1, no. 1, April 1933.

BIBLIOGRAPHY

"Memo from Mars," *Belvidere (IL) Daily Republican*, November 19, 1938.

"Merrick, Mollie, "What's What in Hollywood," *Winnipeg* (Manitoba, Canada) *Tribune*, October 31, 1933.

"The Merry Men from 'Down Under,'" *Brainerd (MN) Daily Dispatch*, April 18, 1941.

"Mervyn LeRoy Set to Enter U.A. Deal," *Film Daily*, vol. 72, no. 71, September 23, 1937.

"Metro and Paramount Licensing Manufacturers, Expect $600,000," *Motion Picture Herald*, vol. 136, no. 10, September 2, 1939.

"MGM Drops Bolger," *Hollywood Reporter*, vol. LI, no. 2, April 3, 1939.

"MGM Is Staking a Lot on the Public's Reception of Mervyn LeRoy's 'The Wizard of Oz,'" *Manitowoc (WI) Herald-Tribune*, July 11, 1939.

"MGM Loans Sondergaard to Para for 'Say Die,'" *Hollywood Reporter*, vol. XXXXVIII, no. 16, October 22, 1938.

"MGM Trade Shows May 19 / The Wizard of Oz," *Motion Picture Herald*, May 14, 1949.

"Mickey and Judy Take $3,000,000 'Oz' to Broadway," *Motion Picture Herald*, vol. 136, no. 9, August 26, 1939.

"Mickey, Judy Toasted by Fans," *Brooklyn (NY) Daily Eagle*, August 16, 1939.

"Midget Footsteps in Dance Measure," *Pittsburgh (PA) Post-Gazette*, October 18, 1938.

"Midget Studies to Get College Degree," *Salt Lake (UT) Tribune*, July 26, 1939.

"Miscellany," *The Movies . . . and the people who make them*, vol. 1, no. 19, May 11, 1939.

Mok, Michel, "Lahr the Lion Roars for Railroad Blood - He Lost His Baggage and Diamond Studs," *New York Post*, August 30, 1939.

Monahan, Kaspar, "'Oz,' 'Four Feathers' are Early Bookings," *Pittsburgh (PA) Press*, August 2, 1939.

Monahan, Kaspar, "'There Goes Judy' Wish Comes True," *Pittsburgh (PA) Press*, February 28, 1938.

Mooring, W. H., "Hollywood Once-Over," *Picturegoer and Film Weekly*, vol. 10, no. 516, April 12, 1941.

"Morgan Again Wants Trip to Europe," *Harrisburg (PA) Telegraph*, March 18, 1939.

"Morgan Can Buy at Own Grocery Store," *Winnipeg* (Manitoba, Canada) *Tribune*, July 5, 1939.

"Morgan Discovers Old Wizard Coat," *Harrisburg (PA) Telegraph*, March 25, 1939.

"Morgan to Ride in Famed Film Balloon," *Daily Times* (New Philadelphia, OH), February 4, 1939.

Morriss, Frank, "Mirth and Fantasy," *Winnipeg Free Press*, September 23, 1939.

Mosby, Aline, "Demand Grows for Old Time Favorites," *Baytown (TX) Sun*, July 19, 1950.

Mothershead, Finis, "Midgets—Gay and Somber, Young and Old, Rowdy and Restrained—Invade City for All Night Stop," *Abilene (TX) Reporter-News*, January 6, 1939.

"The Movies by T.H.C.," *Kossuth County (IA) Advance*, September 19, 1939.

"Movies Yield to Education," *Twin Falls (ID) News*, October 30, 1938.

"The Movie World," *Pathfinder*, August 26, 1939.

"Moving Picture News," *Variety*, vol. XII, no. 5, October 10, 1908.

Mulholland, F. J., "Why Didn't They Give 'Alice' to Disney?" *Motion Picture*, vol. XLVII, no. 1, February 1934.

"Munchkin Prefers to Tend Bar," *Indiana (PA) Gazette*, August 21, 1981.

"Music-Comedy and Extravaganza," *Sunday Record-Herald* (Chicago), June 22, 1902.

"Music Leads Studio Trend for New Year," *Motion Picture Daily*, vol. 37, no. 2, January 3, 1935.

"Network Plugs," *Daily Variety*, vol. 24, no. 59, August 14, 1939.

"Network Plugs," *Daily Variety*, vol. 24, no. 71, August 28, 1939.

"Network Plugs," *Daily Variety*, vol. 24, no. 75, September 5, 1939.

Neville, Lucie, "I Want to Be an Actress" *Lima (OH) News*, June 18, 1939.

Neville, Lucie, "So It Wasn't Like the Book, Huh?" *EveryWeek Magazine, Laredo (TX) Times*, February 19, 1939.

Neville, Lucie, "They Call Judy Garland a New Film Star," *Salt Lake (UT) Tribune*, January 21, 1940.

Neville, Lucie, "What Have They Got That You Haven't Got?" *Lima (OH) News*, June 18, 1939.

"New Books," *Salt Lake (UT) Herald*, November 19, 1900.

"News and Gossip of the Studios," *Motion Picture*, vol. XLVII, no. 1, February 1934.

"News from Hollywood," *World's News* (Sydney, NSW), December 10, 1938.

"New Stars Are All Very Young," *The Mail* (Adelaide, SA), October 28, 1939.

Newton, Dwight, "Color Magic for Wizard of Oz," *San Francisco Examiner*, January 26, 1964.

"Nicholas Schenck Here," *Hollywood Reporter*, XXXXVIII, no. 24, November 1, 1938.

Niemeyer, H. H., "Return of the Wizard of Oz," *St. Louis (MO) Post-Dispatch*, July 7, 1939.

"NFCA Film Nominations Reflect 1939 'Ten Best,'" *Film Daily*, vol. 77, no. 26, February 6, 1940.

"1939 Hollywood Toppers," *Variety*, vol. 137, no. 4, January 3, 1940.

Noble, William, "What the Picture Did for Me," *Motion Picture Herald*, vol. 136, no. 11, September 9, 1939.

"Noon Hour at MGM," *Pic*, vol. V, no. 2, January 24, 1939.

"Notes from Dec. 9 Rerun of Classic," *Sandusky (OH) Register*, December 1, 1962.

"Obituaries (Anna Laughlin)," *Variety*, vol. 126, no. 4, April 7, 1937.

Octopada, Grem, "Wizard of Oz Coming Back via Video," *Salina (KS) Journal*, October 28, 1956.

"Off to See the Wizard," *Baytown (TX) Sun*, November 11, 1955.

Oldfield, Barnet, "Theatre Topics," *Lincoln (NE) Star*, January 8, 1939.

"$120,000 Worth of Dogs," *The Reporter* (Le Grand, IA), December 12, 1940.

"Operetta 'Over the Rainbow,'" *Alma (KS) Signal*, April 4, 1918.

"Orchestra Records 102 Tunes for 'Oz,'" *Winnipeg (Manitoba, Canada) Tribune*, July 5, 1939.

Orphan Outing with the Wizard of Oz," *Winnipeg (Canada) Free Press*, September 18, 1939.

Othman, Frederick C., "Hollywood Day by Day," *Morning News* (Danville, PA), October 27, 1938.

Othman, Frederick C., "Hollywood Day by Day," *Morning News* (Danville, PA), February 22, 1939.

Othman, Frederick C., "Hollywood Fantasy: Tin Pants for 'Oz' Cost Mere $60,000," *Port Arthur (TX) News*, January 1, 1939.

"Out Hollywood Way," *Motion Picture Daily*, vol. 43, no. 119, May 23, 1938.

"Out Hollywood Way," *Motion Picture Daily*, vol. 44, no. 68, October 6, 1938.

"Out Hollywood Way," *Motion Picture Daily*, vol. 44, no. 96, November 15, 1938.

"'Over the Rainbow' Staged," *Brooklyn (NY) Daily Eagle*, April 10, 1915.

"Owls Are Owls, Hollywood Finds," *Brooklyn (NY) Daily Eagle*, July 24, 1939.

"'Oz' Beats Toppers in Seven Key Cities," *Daily Variety*, vol. 24, no. 65, August 21, 1939.

"'Oz' Biz Above Normal in Key Spots," *Showmen's Trade Review*, vol. 31, no. 5, August 26, 1939.

"'Oz' Caravan Itinerary Routed in Ill., Wis.," *Boxoffice*, September 16, 1939.

"'Oz' Caravan Returns," *Motion Picture Daily*, vol. 46, no. 77, October 19, 1939.

"Oz Comes to Life in the Movies," *Publishers Weekly*, vol. CXXXVI, no. 3, July 15, 1939.

"Oz Enthusiast," *Ames (IA) Daily Tribune*, September 24, 1938.

"'Oz' Grosses Good $15,000 in Twin Cities," *Motion Picture Daily*, vol. 46, no. 46, September 6, 1939.

"'Oz' Is Cleveland Winner at $6,000," *Motion Picture Daily*, vol. 46, no. 46, September 6, 1939.

"'Oz' Mail Order Sale," *Daily Variety*, vol. 24, no. 52, August 5, 1939.

"'Oz' Opens at Carthay in Mid-August," *Daily Variety*, vol. 24, no. 28, July 8, 1939.

"'Oz' Opens Here (23) at Loew's and Chinese," *Daily Variety*, vol. 24, no. 48, August 1, 1939.

"'Oz' Opens to Big Crowd of Kids," *Daily Variety*, vol. 24, no. 62, August 17, 1939.

"'Oz' Pantomime Story Is Told," *Amarillo (TX) Globe-Times*, March 23, 1933.

"'Oz' Pens Opening History," *Film Daily*, vol. 76, no. 34, August 18, 1939.

"'Oz' Preem at Carthay About Aug. 10," *Daily Variety*, vol. 24, no. 45, July 28, 1939.

"'Oz' Premiere Set for Chinese Theatre (15)," *Daily Variety*, vol. 24, no. 51, August 4, 1939.

"Oz's Witch in Car 54," *Binghamton (NY) Press*, May 17, 1963.

"'Oz' Whizzes," *Hollywood Reporter*, vol. LIII, no. 20, August 21, 1939.

Padan, Wiley, "It's True!," *Estherville (IA) Daily News*, October 20, 1938.

Palms, June, and Carolyn Dawson, "Pocket o' Songs," *Photoplay*, vol. 22, no 2, January 1943.

"Pan and Fan Mail," *Independent Press-Telegram* (Long Beach, California), August 28, 1966.

Parsons, Louella O., "Disney May Do 'Alice in Wonderland,'" *Pittsburgh (PA) Post-Gazette*, February 23, 1933.

Parsons, Louella O., "Disney's 'Snow White' Inaugurates New Cycle of Fantasy Films: Studios Get Busy, 'Wizard of Oz' on Schedule," *San Antonio (TX) Light*, March 5, 1938.

Parsons, Louella O., "Wizard of Oz to Be Made in Color Film," *Fresno (CA) Bee*, October 1, 1933.

Parsons, Louella O., "Wizard of Oz Will be Made as Extravaganza in Colors," *San Antonio (TX) Light*, October 4, 1933.

Parsons, Louella O., Hollywood column, *San Antonio (TX) Light*, December 11, 1937.

Parsons, Louella O., Hollywood column, *Charleston (WV) Gazette*, January 7, 1938.

Parsons, Louella O., Hollywood column, *San Antonio (TX) Light*, January 12, 1938.

Parsons, Louella O., Hollywood column, *San Antonio (TX) Light*, March 2, 1938.

Parsons, Louella O., Hollywood column, *Charleston (WV) Gazette*, March 16, 1938

Parsons, Louella O., Hollywood column, *Fresno (CA) Bee*, May 29, 1938.

Parsons, Louella O., Hollywood column, *Syracuse (NY) Journal*, June 20, 1938.

Parsons, Louella O., Hollywood column, *San Antonio (TX) Light*, January16, 1939.

Parsons, Louella O., Hollywood column, *Charleston (WV) Gazette*, December 17, 1939.

Parsons, Louella O., Hollywood column, *Charleston (WV) Gazette*, February 27, 1940.

Parsons, Louella O., Hollywood column, *San Antonio (TX) Light*, March 1, 1940.

Parsons, Louella O., Hollywood column, *Sunday Times* (Cumberland, MD), July 25, 1948.

Parsons, Louella O., Hollywood column, *Sunday Times* (Cumberland, MD), December 12, 1948.

Patrick, Corbin, "Future Attractions to Keep Record in Jeopardy," *Indianapolis (IN) Star*, August 28, 1938.

Patrick, Corbin, "MGM Considers Plan to Star Laurel and Hardy in Film of 'Wizard of Oz,'" *Indianapolis (IN) Star*, September 27, 1933.

"Paul Harrison in Hollywood," *Hope (AR) Star*, November 29, 1938.

"Penney's Store Holds Wizard of Oz Party," *Oakland (CA) Tribune*, August 23, 1939.

Phair, George E., "Retakes," *Daily Variety*, vol. 24, no. 66, August 22, 1939.

"Pictures," *Variety*, vol. LXXVIII, no. 10, April 22, 1925.

"Pipes, Channels, Sounds: 'The Wizard of Oz,' Capitol's Feature, Filmed with Elaborate Network Erected for Sound Effects," *Brooklyn (NY) Eagle*, August 20, 1939.

"Pirouette on Lawn Pain for Bolger," *Pittsburgh (PA) Post-Gazette*, October 15, 1938.

"Police Hunt Dog Featured in Movie," *San Antonio (TX) Express*, February 1, 1940.

Polier, Rex, "Judy Garland's 'Wizard of Oz' Will Be Colorcast on Saturday," *Philadelphia Bulletin*, October 28, 1956.

Pooler, James S., "Witch Is a Bum to the Children," *Detroit (MI) Free Press*, September 13, 1939.

Porter, James, "Kansas City," *Hollywood Reporter*, vol. LIII, no. 23, August 24, 1939.

"Pre-release Reviews of Features," *Motion Picture News*, April 25, 1925.

"Preview—The Wizard of Oz," *Daily Variety*, vol. 24, no. 56, August 10, 1939.

"Prize Beauty in 'The New Wizard of Oz,'" *The Moving Picture World*, vol. 23, no. 7, February 13, 1915.

"Prod'r Top Caster at MGM but Director at Goldwyn," *Hollywood Reporter*, vol. XXXXVII, no. 47, September 30, 1938.

"Progress and Trends of Motion Picture Entertainment," *Reading (PA) Times*, April 4, 1935.

"Public Demanded The Wizard of Oz," *Bonham (TX) Daily Favorite*, August 12, 1939.

"Puppet Styles Moscow to Seattle," *Theatre Arts Monthly*, December 1934.

"Purely Personal," *Motion Picture Daily*, vol. 37, no. 20, January 24, 1935.

"Radio Whispers," *Radio Mirror*, July 1939.

"Rambling Reporter," *Hollywood Reporter*, vol. XXXXVIII, no. 20, October 27, 1938.

"Rambling Reporter," *Hollywood Reporter*, vol. XXXXVIII, no. 26, November 3, 1938.

"Rambling Reporter," *Hollywood Reporter*, vol. XXXXVIII, no. 42, November 22, 1938.

"Rambling Reporter," *Hollywood Reporter*, vol. LIII, no. 26, August 28, 1939.

Ranson, Jo, "Out of a Blue Sky," *Brooklyn (NY) Daily Eagle*, October 15, 1933.

Ranson, Jo, "Radio Dial-Log," *Brooklyn (NY) Daily Eagle*, October 25, 1933.

"Rapf Making Eight for Metro Lineup," *Boxoffice*, vol. 32, no. 14, February 26, 1938.

"Rare Birds' Songs Recorded for Film," *Democrat and Chronicle* (Rochester, New York), April 16, 1939.

"Ray Bolger Who Can't Afford It Lost Nine Pounds," *Manitowoc (WI) Herald-Times*, March 2, 1939.

Reed, Ted, "'Wizard of Oz' Opens at Loew's," *Harrisburg (PA) Telegraph*, August 19, 1939.

"Reel News," *Montana Butte Standard*, February 5, 1939.

Reid, James, "Who Said 'The Terrible Teens'" *Motion Picture*, vol. LIX, no. 4, May 1940.

"Response to Public Appreciation Doubles Technicolor Volume for 1939," *Hollywood Reporter*, vol. XLIX, no. 24, December 31, 1938.

"Return of 'Wizard of Oz' Brings Joy to Hearts of Film Goers," *Post-Standard* (Syracuse, NY), March 11, 1949.

Revell, Nellie, "Air Line News," *Variety*, vol. 114, no. 2, March 27, 1934.

Rhea, Janice, "Over the Rainbow," *Naugatuck (CT) Daily News*, August 1, 1942.

Rice, Charlie, "The Cowardly Lion Strikes Back," *Dallas (TX) Morning News*, March 24, 1963.

Robbins, Nelson, "Interviews—Interviewing," *Variety*, vol. LXXXXI, no. 11, January 27, 1926.

Robb, Stewart, "The Red Wizard of Oz," *New Masses*, October 4, 1938.

"Robert Gardner Says," *Hollywood Red Ink*, August 26, 1938.

Roberts Barton, Olive, "A Book a Day," *The Bee* (Danville, VA), August 17, 1938.

Roberts, Eleanor, "I Sent For Judy," Boston Herald (MA), March 15, 1970.

Roberts, Ned, "Dolls Come Back from Oz to Start Spring Cleaning," *Tampa Bay (FL) Times*, January 17, 1939.

Roberts, W. Aldolphe, "My Chat with Jackie," *Motion Picture*, vol. XXVIII, no. 12, January 1925.

"Robust Comedy Gone," *Brooklyn (NY) Daily Eagle*, July 30, 1939.

Rohauer, Raymond, "Mervyn LeRoy," *A Tribute to Mervyn LeRoy*. New York: The Gallery of Modern Art, December 23, 1966.

Ross, George, "Broadway," *Pittsburgh (PA) Press*, March 8, 1939.

Rosson, Harold, transcript of interviews conducted by Bill Gleason, January 6, 10, 14, 1971, February 5, 18, 1971, and April 24, 1971, Center for Advanced Film Studies, the American Film Institute.

"Round-Up of Neglected People," *Photoplay*, February 1940.

Runyon, Damon, "The Brighter Side," *Herald Star* (Steubenville, OH), August 24, 1939.

Russell, Norton, "What Mickey Rooney Means to Judy Garland," *Radio and Television Mirror*, December 1939.

"Sad Paradox," *Altoona (PA) Tribune*, September 6, 1939.

Saltmarsh, Max, "The Clouded Moon," *Albilene (TX) Reporter-News*, August 10, 1938.

Sampas, Charles G. "N.Y.-Hollywood," *Lowell (MA) Sun*, September 8, 1938.

Sampas, Charles G. "N.Y.-Hollywood," *Lowell (MA) Sun*, January 6, 1940.

Sarmento, William E., Editorial on *The Wizard of Oz, Lowell (MA) Sun*, clipping circa December 10, 1961.

"Scarecrow Dance Like Rattles of Skeleton," *Utica (NY) Observer-Dispatch*, September 25, 1938.

Scarfone, Jay, and William Stillman. *The Wizardry of Oz: The Artistry and Magic of the 1939 MGM Classic*. New York: Applause Cinema and Theatre Books, 2004.

Schallert, Edwin, "Benny Stars in New 'Artists and Models,'" *Los Angeles Times*, February 18, 1938.

Schallert, Edwin, "Bolger Scarecrow in Wizard of Oz," *Los Angeles Daily Mirror*, March 7, 1938.

Schallert, Edwin, "Fairytale of Oz Called Milestone in Fantasy," *Los Angeles Times*, August 16, 1939.

Schallert, Edwin, "Fantasy Again in Foreground," *Los Angeles Times*, February 15, 1925.

Schallert, Edwin, "Hollywood," *Democrat and Chronicle* (Rochester, NY), August 14, 1934.

Schallert, Edwin, "James Cagney Slated to Play Western Hero," *Los Angeles Times*, April 7, 1938.

Schecter, Scott. *Judy Garland: The Day-by-Day Chronicle of a Legend*. New York: Cooper Square Press, 2002.

Scheuer, Philip K., "Town Called Hollywood," *Los Angeles Times*, August 10, 1939.

Scheuer, Philip K., "Town Called Hollywood," *Los Angeles Times*, August 13, 1939.

"Schines Piqua Theatre—'The Wizard of Oz,'" *Piqua (OH) Daily Call*, September 18, 1939.

"Schubert Opens Season with 'The Tik-Tok Man of Oz,'" *St. Louis (MO) Times*, September 20, 1913.

Scott, Vernon, "Classic Films Number Two," *Lubbock (TX) Avalanche-Journal*, May 17, 1973.

Scott, Vernon, "Play It Again, Sam! A Look at This Week's Movies," *Windsor (Ontario, Canada) Star TV Times*, April 17, 1971.

"Screen and Radio," *Charleston (WV) Daily Mail*, April 6, 1939.

"The Screen Reporter," *Emporia (KS) Daily Gazette*, November 8, 1935.

Scribe, Phil M., "The Movie World," *Daily Notes* (Canonsburg, PA), November 24, 1933.

"Scorns Glory: He Likes California Life," *San Antonio (TX) Light*, August 7, 1938.

"Seattle Gives 'Wizard' Big $8,200 Lead," *Motion Picture Daily*, vol. 46, no. 46, September 6, 1939.

"Self-Supporting Zoo," *Winnipeg* (Manitoba, Canada) *Tribune*, December 17, 1938.

"Selig Activities," *Moving Picture World*, vol. 6, no. 1, January 8, 1910.

"Semon Finishes *Wizard of Oz*," *Exhibitor's Trade Review*, vol. 17, no. 5, December 27, 1924.

Sennwald, Andre, "'Kid Millions,' Mr. Goldwyn's New Screen Comedy, with Eddie Cantor, at the Rivoli," *New York Times*, November 12, 1934.

Sewell, Charles S., "Newest Reviews and Comment," *Moving Picture World*, April 25, 1925.

Shain, Sam, "Insider's Outlook," *Motion Picture Daily*, vol. 44, no. 127, December 30, 1938.

Sharpe, Howard, "The Private Life of a Talking Picture," *Photoplay*, vol. L, no. 1, July 1936.

Shaw, Len G., "'Wizard of Oz' Prodigal Piece," *Detroit (MI) Free Press*, August 25, 1939.

"Shirley Temple's Last Letter to Santa," *Photoplay*, vol. LIII, no. 1, January 1939.

"Showmen's Reviews: The Wizard of Oz," *Motion Picture Herald*, vol. 136, no. 7, August 12, 1939.

"Six Men Needed to Lift Midgets in Making of Oz," *Oregon Statesman* (Salem), December 31, 1939.

Skreen, C. J., "Yellow Brick Road Won't Be the Same," *Seattle Times*, March 5, 1970.

"Sky Rockets Recorded," *Charleston (WV) Daily Mail*, August 20, 1939.

Small, Frank, "Filming the World's Greatest Love Story," *Photoplay*, vol. L, no. 3, September 1936.

Smithson, E. J., "She Wants to Become an Actress!" *Hollywood*, vol. 26, no. 8, August 1937.

"Snapshots on the Lots," *Canberra* (Australia) *Times*, April 19, 1939.

"'Snow White' Success Spurs Others to Follow Suit; Para. Certain with Fleischer Prod.,"
    Hollywood Reporter, vol. XXXXIV, no. 9, February 19, 1938.

Soanes, Wood, "Curtain Calls," *Oakland (CA) Tribune*, September 9, 1924.

Soanes, Wood, "Curtain Calls," *Oakland (CA) Tribune*, December 5, 1933.

Soanes, Wood, "Curtain Calls," *Oakland (CA) Tribune*, July 13, 1934.

Soanes, Wood, "Curtain Calls," *Oakland (CA) Tribune*, January 6, 1939.

Soanes, Wood, "Curtain Calls," *Oakland (CA) Tribune*, August 3, 1939.

Soanes, Wood, "Curtain Calls," *Oakland (CA) Tribune*, August 18, 1939.

Soanes, Wood, "Curtain Calls," *Oakland (CA) Tribune*, November 29, 1948.

Soanes, Wood, "Curtain Calls: Fantasy Found Best in Cartoons," *Oakland (CA) Tribune*,
    September 26, 1939.

Soanes, Wood, "Wizard of Oz Magnificent Production," *Oakland (CA) Tribune*, August 18, 1939.

Soanes, Wood, "'Wizard of Oz' Returns with Old Charm," *Oakland (CA) Tribune*, August 12,
    1949.

"Sondergaard Is Empress," *Hollywood Reporter*, vol. XXXXVIII, no. 21, October 28, 1938.

"Songbird Caught in the Act," *Nevada State Journal*, April 2, 1938.

"Sonja Henie Will Appear at Arena," *Sandusky (OH) Register*, December 27, 1939.

Sorensen, Sterling, "Drama in Madison," *Capital Times* (Madison, WI), August 25, 1939.

"Sound Effects in the Movies: How It's Done," *Lowell (MA) Sun*, May 9, 1939.

Spear, Ivan, "Spearheads," *Boxoffice*, vol. 33, no. 25, November 12, 1938.

Spear, Ivan, "Spearheads," *Boxoffice*, vol. 34, no. 21, April 15, 1939.

"Special Toy Matinee Today," *Times Recorder* (Zanesville, OH), December 14, 1940.

Spencer, H. E., "Fiction a Poor Second," *Winnipeg Free Press*, March 15, 1939.

Spiro, J. D., "On the Lots," *Screen & Radio Weekly*, *Detroit (MI) Free Press*, February 12, 1939.

Spong, Dick, "Hometown Fan Fare," *Evening News* (Harrisburg, PA), March 15, 1939.

Spong, Dick, "Hometown Fan Fare," *Evening News* (Harrisburg, PA), August 12, 1939.

Spong, Dick, "Hometown Fan Fare," *Evening News* (Harrisburg, PA), August 14, 1939.

Sprague, Jeanne, "T'Ain't So!" *Screen Children*, vol. VII, no. 7, July 1938.

"'Stage Show on Ice' Here Feb. 28," *Lethbridge* (Alberta, Canada) *Herald*, February 24, 1940.

"'Stanley' Out Early for 'Wizard of Oz' Preem," *Daily Variety*, vol. 24, no. 60, August 15, 1939.

Starr, Eve, "'Wizard' Revivers Better Be Careful," *Oregon Statesman* (Salem), August 9, 1955.

"Stars at Showing of 'Oz': Witch Doesn't Scare Scarecrow, Tin Man," *San Diego Union*, February
    11, 1975.

"Stars Eat at Club in Weird Costume," *San Antonio (TX) Express*, January 27, 1939.

Start, Clarissa, "Comedians Improve with Age," *St. Louis (MO) Post-Dispatch*, March 25, 1941.

"Start Kid Series," *Film Daily*, vol. LV, no. 139, June 14, 1931.

"State More Winsome Than Warty, Rolla Clymer Tells Movie Makers," *Iola (KS) Register*,
    September 8, 1939.

St. C. Scotter, G., "To-Day," *Daily Gleaner* (Kingston, Jamaica), March 28, 1940.

Steen, Al, "Lippert Sees Diminishing Market for Small Films," *Motion Picture Daily*, vol. 74, no.
    57, September 21, 1953.

Stern, Harold, "Margaret Hamilton Quits Witch Roles," *Troy (NY) Record*, December 10, 1958.

Stillman, William, "Ken McLellan's Cartoon Dream," *Baum Bugle*, vol. 44, no. 3, Winter 2000.

Stillwell, Miriam, "The Story Behind Snow White's $10,000,000 Surprise Party," *Liberty*, April 9, 1938.

"Story of Oz to Be First Shown to Children," *Charleston (WV) Daily Mail*, September 22, 1935.

"Stromberg Gets Partners," *Western Carolinian* (Salisbury, North Carolina), November 15, 1946.

"Stromberg Names Metro Ace Directors, Writers," *Boxoffice*, December 17, 1938.

"Studio Notes," *Harrisburg (PA) Evening News*, February 20, 1939.

"Studio Size-Ups," *Film Bulletin*, vol. 5, no. 16, August 12, 1939.

Sullivan, Ed, "Hollywood," *Pittsburgh (PA) Press*, November 18, 1938.

Sullivan, Ed, "Hollywood," *Harrisburg (PA) Telegraph*, November 21, 1938.

Sullivan, Ed, "Hollywood," *Harrisburg (PA) Telegraph*, November 26, 1938.

Sullivan, Ed, "Hollywood," *Harrisburg (PA) Telegraph*, June 6, 1939.

Sullivan, Ed, "Hollywood," *Harrisburg (PA) Telegraph*, August 15, 1939.

Sullivan, Ed, "Hollywood," *Harrisburg (PA) Telegraph*, August 21, 1939.

Sullivan, Ed, "Hollywood," *Harrisburg (PA) Telegraph*, August 25, 1939.

Sullivan, Ed, "Hollywood," *Harrisburg (PA) Telegraph*, August 28, 1939

Sullivan, Ed, "Hollywood," *Pittsburgh (PA) Press*, October 13, 1939.

Sullivan, Ed, "The Face on the Cutting Room Floor," *Silver Screen*, vol. 8, no. 8, June 1938.

"Sure She'll Make Good on Screen, Child Says," *Pittsburgh (PA) Post-Gazette*, April 1, 1938.

"Swan Preaches Oz Story; Is Parable, View," *Capital Times* (Madison, WI), September 18, 1939.

Sweeney, Robert D., PFC, "On the Town," *Pacific Stars & Stripes*, December 30, 1954.

"Syracusan Writes Music for 'Oz' Film," *Syracuse (NY) Herald Journal*, August 15, 1939.

"Tale of Two Cities: Oz and Hollywood," *San Francisco Chronicle*, August 13, 1939.

"Talking It Over," *The Movies . . . and the people who make them*, vol. 1, no. 36, September 8, 1939.

"Taurog to Direct New Wizard of Oz," *Syracuse (NY) Herald*, August 21, 1938.

"Technicolor Sued Over 'Oz' Negative," *Variety*, vol. 114, no. 2, March 27, 1934.

Temple Black, Shirley, *Child Star*. New York: Warner Books, 1988.

"Ten Best Song Sellers Last Week," *Daily Variety*, vol. 24, no. 71, August 28, 1939.

Terrell, Dan S., "As I See the Movies," *Household*, April 1949.

"'Test Pilot' Suit Put Off to Fall," *Hollywood Reporter*, vol. XXXXVI, no. 50, August 5, 1938.

"The Best Bad Witch in the Whole World," *Paris (TX) News*, February 20, 1981.

"The Brighter Side," *Indiana (PA) Gazette*, April 26, 1946.

"The Children's Show," *Emporia (KS) Gazette*, May 19, 1917.

"The Hollywood Roundup," *Mount Carmel (PA) Item*, January 18, 1939.

"The Hollywood Roundup," *Amarillo (TX) Globe-Times*, August 17, 1939.

"The Tip-Off," *The Exhibitor*, vol. 22, no. 16, August 30, 1939.

"The Wizard of Oz," *Fox West Coast Bulletin*, August 12, 1939.

"The Wizard of Oz," *Picture Reports*, August 16, 1939.

"The Wizard of Oz," *Provo (UT) Evening Herald*, October 12, 1938.

"The Wizardry of The Wizard of Oz," *The Open Road for Boys*, vol. XXI, no. 10, October 1939.

"Third 'Nancy Drew,'" *Boxoffice*, October 8, 1938.

Thirer, Irene, "Judy Garland Grows Into One Size Smaller—and High Heels," *New York Post*, April 5, 1939.

Thomas, Bob, "Filmdom Celebrates Happy Yule Throughout Industry," *Long Beach (CA) Press-Telegram*, December 25, 1950.

Thomas, Bob, "Gene Kelly Seeks Movies for Children," *Winona (MN) Republican-Herald*, August 25, 1949.

Thomas, Bob, "Mervyn LeRoy Says Movie Previews Are Indispensable," *Kokomo (IN) Tribune*, February 11, 1955.

Thomas, Dan, "Hollywood Gossip," *Daily Times-News* (Burlington, NC), October 6, 1935.

Thomas, Dan, "Previewing the 1935 Movies," *Decatur (IL) Daily Review*, September 30, 1934.

"Thorpe Guns 'Wizard' with Garland and Bolger," *Hollywood Reporter*, vol. XXXXVIII, no. 4, October 8, 1938.

"Thorpe's Crew Returns from 'Finn' Locations," *Hollywood Reporter*, vol. XXXXVIII, no. 30, November 8, 1938.

"Thorpe Takes Over 'Oz' from Taurog," *Variety*, vol. 132, no. 1, September 14, 1938.

"3,000 Fans Greet Rooney, Garland in Washington," *Film Daily*, vol. 76, no. 28, August 10, 1939.

"Tiny Town," *Variety*, vol. 133, no. 1, December 14, 1938.

"To Begin Filming of 'Wizard of Oz,'" *Indianapolis (IN) News*, September 14, 1931.

"Toto's Kinfolks," *San Antonio (TX) Light*, August 31, 1939.

"Through the Studios: Previewing 1939's New Productions," *The Mail* (Adelaide, SA), February 11, 1939.

"Throws Dignity to the Winds to Get Laughs," *Carroll (IA) Daily Herald*, August 25, 1939.

"'Tik-Tok Man' Will Be Wound to Go North Sunday," *Los Angeles Express*, April 17, 1913.

Tildesley, Alice L., "How Kids Grow Up in Hollywood," *Oakland (CA) Tribune*, February 26, 1939.

Tidesley, Alice L., "Match Your Personality with Color," *Oakland (CA) Tribune*, January 8, 1939.

Torre, Marie, "Out of the Air," *Evening Review* (East Liverpool, OH), August 6, 1957.

"Toto Has Curious but Busy Film Record," *Port Arthur (TX) News*, September 24, 1939.

"Toto's 'Paw Prints' Autograph Prize," *Daily Times* (New Philadelphia, OH), October 14, 1939.

"Training Animals for the Pictures," *Nambour Chronicle and North Coast Advertiser* (Australia), June 16, 1939.

Trane, Harriet, "Tidbits by Trane," *Long Beach (CA) Independent*, August 17, 1939.

"Transcriptions," *Broadcasting*, July 15, 1939.

"Tuneful?" *Hollywood Reporter*, vol. XXXXVIII, no. 33, November 11, 1938.

Turner, Marjorie, "'Wizard of Oz' Charms Old and Young All Over Again," *Syracuse (NY) Herald-Journal*, March 11, 1949.

"26 'Wizard of Oz' Shorts Planned by Ray Smallwood," *Film Daily*, vol. LVI, no. 6, July 7, 1931.

"'20,000 Leagues' Back in Metro Prod. Lineup," *Variety*, vol. 130, no. 3, March 30, 1938.

Underhill, Duncan, "Bert Lahr: Hamlet of Burleycue," *Screenbook*, vol. 22, no. 1, August 1939.

"Unique Idea of 'Wizard of Oz' Kept It on Stage for a Sensational Run," *The Wizard of Oz* pressbook, 1939.

"Up-to-the-Minute Casting News," *Hollywood Reporter*, vol. XXXXX, no. 5, February 7, 1939.

"Ushers Named for Children's Movies," *Indianapolis (IN) News*, January 1, 1932.

Ussher, Bruno David, "Film Music and Its Makers," *Hollywood Spectator*, vol. 14, no. 4, May 27, 1939.

Vale, Virginia, "Star Dust," *Mowville (IA) Mail*, March 17, 1938.

Vale, Virginia, "Star Dust," *Mowville (IA) Mail*, August 18, 1939.

Vale, Virginia, "Star Dust," *Fredericksburg (IA) News*, September 7, 1939.

Vincent, Mal, "The Wizard Behind Oz," *Virginian-Pilot* (Norfolk), March 15, 1970.

"Visitor Leaves: Former Lucille Ryman Was Here for Month," *Decatur (IL) Herald*, November 9, 1938.

Wade, Jack, "We Cover the Studios," *Photoplay*, vol. LII, no. 4, April 1939.

Wagner, Leichester, "Hollywood Shots," *Nevada State Journal*, October 23, 1935.

Wales, Clarke, "Oz: Hollywood Discovers a Very Wonderful Land," *The Pioneer* (St. Paul, Minnesota), July 6, 1939.

Walker, Paul, "Judy Garland in Her Stocking Feet!" *Harrisburg (PA) Telegraph*, July 25, 1943.

Walker, Paul, "Reviews and Previews," *Harrisburg (PA) Telegraph*, July 25, 1939.

Walker, Paul, "Reviews and Previews," *Harrisburg (PA) Telegraph*, August 11, 1939.

Walker, Paul, "Reviews and Previews," *Harrisburg (PA) Telegraph*, August 14, 1939.

Walker, Paul, "Reviews and Previews," *Harrisburg (PA) Telegraph*, August 17, 1939.

Walker, Paul, "Reviews and Previews," *Harrisburg (PA) Telegraph*, August 23, 1939.

Wallace, Inez, "Billie Burke Lonely and Worried," *Cleveland (OH) Plain Dealer*, July 30, 1939.

"Walshe In 'Oz,'" *Hollywood Reporter*, vol. XXXXVII, no. 50, October 4, 1938.

"Walt Disney Buys Another 'Oz' Tale," *Berkshire (MA) Eagle*, December 20, 1956.

"Walter Winchell on Broadway," *Logansport (IN) Pharos-Tribune*, August 14, 1939.

"Walter Winchell on Broadway," *Logansport (IN) Pharos-Tribune*, August 21, 1939.

"Walter Winchell on Broadway," *Tucson (AZ) Daily Citizen*, August 10, 1942.

Walters, Gwenn, "Fantasy in Fashion," *Photoplay*, vol. 53, no. 8, August 1939.

Warren, Harry, transcript of interviews conducted by Irene Kahn Atkins, August 12 — November 29, 1972, Center for Advanced Film Studies, the American Film Institute.

"Watersmeet Lady Inspired Author of 'The Wizard of Oz,'" *Bessemer (MI) Herald*, September 1, 1939.

Watts, Stephen. *Behind the Screen: How Films Are Made*. London: Arthur Baker, Ltd., 1938.

"We Have Seen in Private: The Wizard of Oz," *Cine Radio Actualidad*, November 17, 1939.

"Wet Hero Results in Garland Film," *Democrat and Chronicle* (Rochester, NY), November 13, 1938.

White, Bob, "At the Theatres," *News-Palladium* (Benton Harbor, Michigan), August 21, 1939.

"Whiteman Airing 'Oz,'" *Daily Variety*, vol. 24, no. 50, August 3, 1939.

Whitley Fletcher, Adele, "How Deanna Durbin Lives," *Photoplay*, vol. LIV, no. 8, August 1940.

"Widow of Author of Wizard of Oz Takes Rest in Fargo," *Fargo (ND) Forum*, October 29, 1939.

Wilcox, Grace, "For Women Only," *Screen & Radio Weekly*, *Detroit (MI) Free Press*, December 11, 1938.

Wilcox, Grace, "For Women Only," *Screen & Radio Weekly*, *Detroit (MI) Free Press*, December 25, 1938.

Wilcox, Grace, "Hollywood Reporter, Personal . . . but Not Confidential," *Screen & Radio Weekly*, *Detroit (MI) Free Press*, September 3, 1939.

Wilkerson, W. R., "Tradeviews," *Hollywood Reporter*, vol. XXXXVIII, no. 20, October 27, 1938.

Wilk, Ralph, "A 'Little' from the Hollywood 'Lots,'" *Film Daily*, August 5, 1937.

Wilk, Ralph, "A 'Little' from the Hollywood 'Lots,'" *Film Daily*, August 13, 1937.

Wilk, Ralph, "A 'Little' from the Hollywood 'Lots,'" *Film Daily*, August 14, 1937.

Wilk, Ralph, "A 'Little' from the Hollywood 'Lots,'" *Film Daily*, June 14, 1938.

Wilk, Ralph, "A 'Little' from the Hollywood 'Lots,'" *Film Daily*, October 28, 1938.

Wilkinson, Lupton A., "Fame Is Fun for Judy," *Indianapolis (IN) Star*, October 8, 1939.

Williams, Scott, "Hello, Yellow Brick Road," *Journal Sentinel* (Milwaukee, WI), July 21, 2009.

Willson, Dixie, "The Wizardry of Oz," *Photoplay*, vol. 53, no. 8, August 1939.

"Will the Glory of Snow White Be Eclipsed by The Wizard of Oz?" *Cinemonde*, August 30, 1939.

Wilson, Earl, "It Happened Last Night," *Morning Herald* (Uniontown, PA), May 5, 1949.

Wilson Jr., Richard, *The Science Fiction Newsletter*, vol. 2, no. 9, July 30, 1938.

"Winninger in 'Wizard' Role," *Syracuse (NY) Herald*, August 16, 1938.

"With the Hollywood Reporter," *Middlesboro (KY) Daily News*, November 28, 1938.

"Wizard Falls Down," *The Mail* (Adelaide, SA), April 8, 1939.

"'Wizard' in Role After 30 Years," *Ogden (UT) Standard-Examiner*, August 10, 1938.

"'Wizard of Oz' as Mervyn LeRoy Maybe," *Variety*, vol. 130, no. 4, April 6, 1938.

"'Wizard of Oz' at Haven, Triumph for Mervyn LeRoy," *Olean (NY) Times-Herald*, August 28, 1939.

"Wizard of Oz Attraction at Ohio Theatre," *Lima (OH) News*, August 27, 1939.

"'Wizard of Oz' Author Broke," *Chicago Daily Tribune*, June 5, 1911.

"'Wizard of Oz' Blue Ribbon Award Winner for September," *Boxoffice*, vol. 35, no. 20, October 7, 1939.

"'Wizard of Oz' Caravan Off for St. Louis at Week-End," *Film Daily*, October 5, 1939.

"'Wizard of Oz' Coming to Rio," *Appleton (WI) Post-Crescent*, August 5, 1939.

"'The Wizard of Oz' Delightful Fantasy," *Film Bulletin*, vol. 5, no. 17, August 26, 1939.

"The Wizard of Oz," *The Exhibitor*, vol. 22, no. 13, August 9, 1939.

"The Wizard of Oz: Famed Adventure Loved by Everyone Is Worthy of Elaborate Campaign," *Showmen's Trade Review*, vol. 31, no. 5, August 26, 1939.

"'Wizard of Oz' Famed Fantasy of Syracusan, Makes Comeback to Thrill Millions of Children," *Syracuse (NY) Herald*, July 30, 1939.

"Wizard of Oz Folks Seen in Baum Fantasy," *Ogden (UT) Standard-Examiner*, September 4, 1938.

"The Wizard of Oz Has Hollywood Crazy," *Lima (OH) News*, October 30, 1938.

"'Wizard of Oz,' in Dazzling Technicolor, Is Vivid Family Entertainment, Nebraska," *Nebraska State Journal*, August 27, 1939.

"'Wizard of Oz' Is Full of Colorful Promotional Ideas," *Women's Wear Daily*, vol. 59, no. 34, August 18, 1939.

"'Wizard of Oz' Is Previewed at Fox," *San Bernardino (CA) County Sun*, June 5, 1939.

"'Wizard of Oz' Next at Loew's," *Post-Standard* (Syracuse, NY), March 9, 1949.

"'Wizard of Oz' Off," *Hollywood Reporter*, vol. XXI, no. 40, June 25, 1934.

"'Wizard of Oz' Operetta Written by Cousin of Local Musician," *Las Cruces (NM) Sun-News*, September 13, 1939.

"'Wizard of Oz' Phaeton and Ponies Tour City," *Mansfield (OH) News-Journal*, September 14, 1939.

"'Wizard of Oz' Resumes Today After Illness Lags," *Hollywood Reporter*, vol. XXXXX, no. 10, February 13, 1939.

"Wizard of Oz" Review, *Cinefilo*, September 15, 1939.

"'Wizard of Oz,' Selig's Big Easter Release," *Moving Picture World*, vol. 6, no. 10, March 12, 1910.

"'Wizard of Oz' Spectacular Musical for State," *Altoona (PA) Tribune*, August 18, 1939.

"Wizard of Oz Stunt," *Scranton (PA) Truth*, April 27, 1912.

"'Wizard of Oz' Will Be Single Billed for L.A. Run," *Daily Variety*, vol. 24, no. 58, August 12, 1939.

"Wizard Will Play in New Oz Theatre." *MGM Studio News*, April 1939.

Wolman, Martin, "Living Oz Dwarf Delights 2,000 Kids," *Wisconsin State Journal*, August 25, 1939.

"Woman Recalls Here Her Uncle Who Wrote 'Oz,'" *Minneapolis (MN) Journal*, September 3, 1939.

Woodbury, Mitchell, "'Oz' Actors Have Hard Time of It," *Pittsburgh (PA) Post-Gazette*, January 20, 1939.

Worswick, Mary, "An Artist as a Funny Play-Maker," *Leslie's Weekly*, January 5, 1905.

Young, Jack. *From the Files of a Hollywood Make-Up Artist*, unpublished manuscript, authors' collection, n.d.

"Youngsters from Three Churches Will Take Part in Operetta," *Syracuse (NY) Herald*, April 20, 1937.

"Ziegfeld Standards Used to Pick Girls," *Harrisburg (PA) Telegraph*, February 17, 1939.

Zunser, Jesse, "The Wizard of Oz," *Cue*, August 19, 1939.

Photo Credits

Page 3: L. Frank Baum (1856–1919) was an American author, actor, playwright, songwriter, and poet best remembered for his Oz book series, famously *The Wonderful Wizard of Oz* (1900). (Photographer unknown; authors' collection)

Page 10: The Tin Woodman, Scarecrow, and Cowardly Lion as rendered in 1904 by W. W. Denslow, illustrator of *The Wonderful Wizard of Oz*. (*Denslow's Scarecrow and the Tin-Man*, G. W. Dillingham Co, NY, 1904; authors' collection)

Page 17: The cast of *The Wizard of Oz* musical extravaganza (1902) from left to right: David Montgomery, Anna Laughlin, and Fred Stone. (Windeatt photo, Chicago, IL; authors' collection)

Page 29: *The Wizard of Oz* silent film (1925) starred, from left to right, Larry Semon, his fiancée Dorothy Dwan and Oliver "Babe" Hardy. (Chadwick Pictures production still, 1925, photographer unknown; authors' collection)

Page 36: Dorothy (Mary Ruth Boone) struggles in the clutches of the Evil Sorceress (Sissie Flynn) in the Meglin Kiddies film *The Land of Oz* (1931). (Meglin production still, photographer unknown; authors' collection)

Page 38: Dorothy (Nancy Kelly) welcomes the Scarecrow (Bill Adams) into the Honorable Order of Ozmites on the 1933–34 *The Wizard of Oz* radio program. (NBC Radio photograph, photographer unknown; authors' collection)

Page 46: Seattle's Cornish School of the Arts staged a marionette musical *Wizard of Oz* production that drew raves from critics and audiences, 1934–37. (Cornish School 1935 prospectus, Gateway Printing Co., Seattle, WA, photographer unknown; authors' collection)

Page 47: The musical play *Adventures in Oz* (1935) featured Ethel Barrymore Colt as Dorothy, with the Scarecrow (John Maroney) and the Cowardly Lion (John Neill). (Associated Press Photo, photographer unknown; authors' collection)

Page 52: Producer Samuel Goldwyn was inspired by Walt Disney's cartoons to acquire rights to *The Wizard of Oz* in 1933 for a Technicolor musical starring Eddie Cantor. (1930s publicity portrait, photographer unknown; authors' collection)

Page 57: After Fred Stone and daughter Paula performed a *Wizard of Oz* number at a 1936 Hollywood benefit, rumors circulated that the actor would reprise his Scarecrow role onscreen. (*Photoplay* photograph, McFadden Publications, Chicago, IL, 1936; authors' collection)

Page 65: MGM studio chief Louis B. Mayer, left, and his *Wizard of Oz* film producer, Mervyn LeRoy. (MGM publicity photograph, photographer unknown; authors' collection)

Page 79: Judy Garland (born Frances Gumm) was fifteen when assigned the role of Dorothy in February 1938. Her casting drew mixed reaction from Hollywood columnists and Oz fans alike. (MGM publicity portrait, photographer unknown; authors' collection)

Page 87: Terry the cairn terrier who portrayed Toto, shown front and center, was owned by Hollywood dog trainer Carl Spitz. Other prized motion picture canines from Spitz's kennel included, from left to right, Prince, Mr. Binkie, Musty, Buck, and Promise. (International Press Association photograph, November 23, 1940, photographer unknown; authors' collection)

Page 92 (left): Ray Bolger was originally cast as the Scarecrow in March 1938 but was demoted to the Tin Man before successfully lobbying a return to the Fred Stone strawman part. (MGM publicity portrait by Graybill; authors' collection)

Page 92 (right): MGM hoofer Buddy Ebsen was cast as the Scarecrow circa mid-April 1938, bumping Ray Bolger from the part. When Bolger insisted on being the Scarecrow, Ebsen became the Tin Man. (MGM publicity portrait by Clarence Sinclair Bull; authors' collection)

Page 95: Stage comedian Bert Lahr appears to channel his future Cowardly Lion alter ego in this 1934 publicity portrait for the film *No More West*. (*No More West* publicity portrait, photographer unknown; authors' collection)

Page 100: Gale Sondergaard poses in her glamorous black-sequined Wicked Witch of the West makeup and wardrobe, August 27, 1938. (MGM wardrobe test, photographer unknown; authors' collection)

Page 101: Actress Margaret Hamilton preferred comedic roles on film and stage but was to be revered as a villain for playing the Wicked Witch of the West. (Photographer unknown; authors' collection)

Page 108: After numerous contenders, veteran actor Frank Morgan aced his audition and was unanimously chosen to portray the Wizard, as well as his various counterparts. (MGM publicity portrait, photographer unknown; authors' collection)

Page 110: Actress and comedienne Billie Burke was selected to play Glinda the beautiful sorceress by Mervyn LeRoy, who said she was an "ideally friendly type" for the part. (MGM publicity portrait, photographer unknown; authors' collection)

Page 113: A 1920 newspaper triptych illustrates the transformation of simian impersonator Pat Walshe from man to beast. Walshe was cast as Nikko, the Wicked Witch's monkey familiar. (*Boston* [MA] *Post*, December 12, 1920; authors' collection)

Page 115: MGM contract player Mitchell Lewis was cast as the leader of the Winkie guard as well as a second, deleted role in the Emerald City. (MGM publicity portrait by Clarence Sinclair Bull; authors' collection)

Page 119 (top): The set design for *Our Gang Follies of 1938*'s nightclub dream sequence appears to have influenced Jack Martin Smith's vision of Munchkinland for MGM. (Image from *Our Gang Follies of 1938*/public domain)

Page 119 (bottom): (Munchkinland photograph courtesy of Heritage Auctions)

Page 121: Charley Becker, left, was cast as the Mayor of Munchkinland shortly after this photo was taken with Los Angeles deputy city marshal Don McDonald in late September 1938. (Acme Photo; authors' collection)

Page 124: This Lilliputian parade stopped traffic in November 1938 as the Munchkins report for work at the MGM Studios. (MGM publicity photograph, photographer unknown; authors' collection)

Page 125: MGM character actor Charley Grapewin was cast as Uncle Henry. Grapewin previously played in a road show production of *Oz* and gifted his script to Mervyn LeRoy. (MGM publicity portrait by Graybill; authors' collection)

Page 126: A January 3, 1939, makeup and wardrobe test for Sarah Padden as Aunt Em. Mervyn LeRoy selected Clara Blandick for the part as a nod to her role in his *Anthony Adverse*. (MGM makeup test by Rush; authors' collection)

Page 154: Farmhand Hickory's wind machine, though unseen on film, is dismissed as a "contraption" by Aunt Em. It is shown here for the first time, photographed February 21, 1939. (MGM keybook set still by George Hommel; authors' collection)

Page 157: This simplistic yet pivotal set was the transition from sepia-tone film stock to the Technicolor wonders of Munchkinland, just beyond the door, December 29, 1938. (MGM keybook set still by George Hommel; authors' collection)

Page 161: Exterior of the Emerald City's Wash & Brush Up Co., January 17, 1939, shows the sculpted fountain on right, little-seen on film. (MGM keybook set still by George Hommel; authors' collection)

Page 173: December 1938: On the Munchkinland set, makeup department head Jack Dawn (center) seeks approval from director Victor Fleming (far left) on a prototype design for Frank Morgan's Wizard (center right). (AMPAS/Margaret Herrick Library)

Page 175: Adrian, MGM's leading designer of wardrobe, reportedly relished the creative abandon offered by *The Wizard of Oz*, a favorite boyhood novel. (MGM publicity portrait, photographer unknown; authors' collection)

Page 184: In March 1938 MGM announced its latest child prodigy, singer-actress Janice Chambers, who substituted for Garland in *Wizard of Oz* tests. (Acme Photo; authors' collection)

Page 187: A preliminary sketch of Buddy Ebsen with a scarecrow mask overlay as rendered by MGM makeup artist William Tuttle. (AMPAS/Margaret Herrick Library)

Page 188: An August 27, 1938, wardrobe test shows Ray Bolger as the Scarecrow wearing the heavily quilted tunic and trousers previously worn by Buddy Ebsen. (MGM wardrobe test, photographer unknown; authors' collection)

Page 192: Frank Morgan tests his Professor Marvel makeup and wardrobe on the Tin Woodman set, November 17, 1938. (MGM wardrobe test, photographer unknown; authors' collection)

Page 195: Margaret Hamilton tests a version of her Wicked Witch makeup, October 8, 1938. A pageboy wig replaced this hairdress before reverting to the style shown here. (MGM makeup test, photographer unknown; authors' collection)

Page 197: The Witch's Winkie guards, thwarted by a falling chandelier, hold position for a reference still, December 3, 1938. (MGM keybook set still by George Hommel; authors' collection)

Page 203: By September 1938 Richard Thorpe replaced Norman Taurog as *Oz* director. Thorpe's reputation was that of an efficient, equipped, and expedient overseer. (MGM publicity portrait, photographer unknown; authors' collection)

Page 205: Ray Bolger's makeup by Norbert Miles is documented before on-set dress rehearsal, October 12, 1938. (MGM makeup test by Virgil Apger; Courtesy Kathi Miles)

Page 206: Under Richard Thorpe's direction, Dorothy (Judy Garland in a blonde wig) meets the Scarecrow (Ray Bolger) preceding his song and dance. While filming this scene, a malfunctioning light hailed sparks down over the actors. (MGM production still, photographer unknown; authors' collection)

Page 208: A production still taken in mid-October 1938 pictures, left to right, animal impersonator Pat Walshe, Judy Garland as a blonde, and character actress Margaret Hamilton as the Wicked Witch of the West. (MGM production still, photographer unknown; authors' collection)

Page 213: An October 14, 1938, reference still pictures the "Crossroads Land of Oz" set with Ray Bolger. Note the actual, withered cornstalks, no curbing, and cartooned cobblestones to simulate the Yellow Brick Road. (MGM keybook set still by Virgil Apger; authors' collection)

Page 214: A November 8, 1938, still of the "Crossroads Land of Oz" set pictures the revisions made under George Cukor prior to Victor Fleming's appointment as director. (MGM keybook set still by Virgil Apger; authors' collection)

Page 219: Director Victor Fleming, with daughter Sarah in 1937, was known for rescuing floundering film productions, as he did for *The Wizard of Oz* beginning in November 1938. (MGM publicity portrait, photographer unknown; authors' collection)

Page 223: Sheets of cardboard protect the Yellow Brick Road from scuffs and wear in between takes on the "Tin Man's House" set, November 17, 1938. (MGM keybook set still by Virgil Apger; authors' collection)

Page 227: Jack Haley reads from *The Wizard of Oz* to his adopted son Jimmy (in military school uniform), his two visiting nephews, and his son Jack Jr., seated next to Haley. (MGM publicity still, photographer unknown; authors' collection)

Page 232: The main cast of *The Wizard of Oz* at the poppy field's edge, December 9, 1938. (MGM publicity still, photographer unknown; authors' collection)

Page 237: Billed as "The Dancing Doll," diminutive Olga Nardone poses en pointe for an unidentified man on the Munchkinland set, December 21, 1938. (MGM publicity still, photographer unknown; authors' collection)

Page 240: On a filming break in December 1938, several female Munchkins pose with MGM brass including Victor Fleming, second from left, and Mervyn LeRoy, far right. (AMPAS/Margaret Herrick Library)

Page 249: Dorothy and her friends are captured for the film's climax on this "Tower and Battlements" set, December 6, 1938. (MGM keybook set still by George Hommel; authors' collection)

Page 253: The Wizard's runaway balloon is tethered before lift-off while Emerald City extras relax on break, January 24, 1939. (MGM keybook set still by George Hommel; authors' collection)

Page 259: A special-effects test of an uncredited actor as the disembodied Wizard's head was overseen by Technicolor cameraman Allen Davey. (MGM test clip, photographer unknown; authors' collection)

Page 261: The attack of the Winged Monkeys was filmed in early January 1939. Seen here are Haley, Bolger, Toto, and Lahr among extras and assistants. (AMPAS/Margaret Herrick Library)

Page 263: Victor Fleming indicates range of motion to one of the animated apple trees, circa November 9, 1938. (AMPAS/Margaret Herrick Library)

Page 272: Attired as Dorothy, Judy Garland poses for a Friday the 13th publicity still timed for newspaper publication on January 13, 1939. (Unknown newspaper clipping; authors' collection)

PHOTO CREDITS

Page 279: Film editor Blanche Sewell cut *The Wizard of Oz* after being selected by Mervyn LeRoy for her skill in handling "the emotion picture." (MGM publicity portrait, photographer unknown; authors' collection)

Page 285: Five Munchkin actors welcomed guests to the August 15, 1939, Hollywood premiere of *The Wizard of Oz* at Grauman's Chinese Theatre. (Courtesy Profiles in History)

Page 294: August 25, 1939: Mickey Rooney and Judy Garland kick off the national *Wizard of Oz* tour using the miniature coach and black Shetland ponies as featured in Munchkinland. (MGM publicity still, photographer unknown; authors' collection)

Page 00: Detail of a 1938 mechanical sketch of the Munchkinland carriage, as drafted by MGM artist Ted Rich, illustrates its floral-and-tendril design. (Courtesy Jennifer Manha) [This image wasn't called out in the manuscript]

Page 314: The night of February 29, 1940, seventeen-year-old Judy Garland beams with Mickey Rooney, who earlier that evening had presented her with a special juvenile Academy Award. (Press photograph by Hyman Fink; authors' collection)

Page 322: The April 1949 re-release of *The Wizard of Oz* at New York's Mayfair Theatre received nearly as much fanfare as the original 1939 opening. (MGM publicity still, photographer unknown; authors' collection)

Page 335: Promotional art for the 1960 television airing of *The Wizard of Oz* depicts the film's characters observed by the broadcast's hosts, actor Richard Boone and his son Peter. (CBS Television Network press photograph, artist unknown; authors' collection)

Page 341: Margaret Hamilton, Ray Bolger, and Jack Haley reunite for the 1970 telecast of *The Wizard of Oz*. (NBC-TV press photograph, photographer unknown; authors' collection)

Index

tk

Lightning Source UK Ltd.
Milton Keynes UK
UKHW032155201218
334255UK00012B/298/P